CONTENTS

CONTENTS

ABOUT
THIS BOOK

Fodor's Ratings

Everything in this guide is worth doing—we don't cover what isn't—but exceptional sights, hotels, and restaurants are recognized with additional accolades. **Fodor's** Choice ★ indicates our top recommendations; ★ highlights places we deem highly recommended. Care to nominate a new place? Visit Fodors.com/contact-us.

Trip Costs

We list prices wherever possible to help you budget well. Hotel and restaurant price categories from **$** to **$$$$** are noted alongside each recommendation. For hotels, we include the lowest cost of a standard double room in high season. For restaurants, we cite the average price of a main course at dinner or, if dinner isn't served, at lunch. For attractions, we always list adult admission fees; discounts are usually available for children, students, and senior citizens.

Hotels

Our local writers vet every hotel to recommend the best overnights in each price category, from budget to expensive. Unless otherwise specified, you can expect private bath, phone, and TV in your room. For expanded hotel reviews, facilities, and deals visit Fodors.com.

Restaurants

Unless we state otherwise, restaurants are open for lunch and dinner daily. We mention dress code only when there's a specific requirement and reservations only when they're essential or not accepted. To make restaurant reservations, visit Fodors.com.

Credit Cards

The hotels and restaurants in this guide typically accept credit cards. If not, we'll say so.

Listings

★ Fodor's Choice
★ Highly recommended
⊠ Physical address
✛ Directions or Map coordinates
🖅 Mailing address
☎ Telephone
🖷 Fax
⊕ On the Web
✆ E-mail
🖃 Admission fee
☉ Open/closed times
Ⓜ Metro stations
⊟ No credit cards

Hotels & Restaurants

🏨 Hotel
⇝ Number of rooms
⚲ Facilities
🍽 Meal plans
✕ Restaurant
🍴 Reservations
🎩 Dress code
🚭 Smoking

Outdoors

🏌 Golf
⛺ Camping

Other

☕ Family-friendly
⇨ See also
⊠ Branch address
☞ Take note

Cruise Primer

WORD OF MOUTH

"When you book online . . . you [will be given] the total [cost of the cruise] with taxes and fees. The cost (they tell you but you need to keep in mind) is normally around $10 per person in tips per day. You will set up an onboard account, and everything will be charged to that. Of course all meals are included. You can really spend as little or as much as you want. I went on one cruise and spent less than $200, and one more than $2,000. That depends on what you do outside of what is included."

—tmg

By Linda
Coffman

If you're considering a cruise but can't decide whether it's really for you, it's tempting to ask, "What's so special about a cruise vacation?" It's a good question. Until the age of the airplane, ocean travel was simply a means to get to your far-flung destination—often the only way. But even in the early decades of the 20th century, venerable ocean liners such as the *Normandie* offered the occasional round-trip cruise to an exotic locale.

Passengers on those earliest cruises didn't have a fun-in-the-sun mind-set as they sailed to faraway ports. They sailed to broaden their horizons and learn about ports of call that couldn't be reached by overland travel. Perhaps they booked a cruise to Panama to observe the construction of the canal or, like the *Normandie*'s passengers, were bound for Brazil and the daring excitement of Carnaval.

Regardless of *why* they were cruising, early cruisers steamed toward the unfamiliar with many fewer comforts than contemporary passengers enjoy. On the *Normandie*, air-conditioned comfort was available only in the ship's first-class dining room, though at least passengers could find relief from Rio's heat by taking a dip in one of the era's few outdoor swimming pools at sea. In those days, if an ocean liner had a permanent swimming pool, it was often indoors and deep in the hull.

Carnival Cruise Lines executives like to reminisce about the tiny "gyms" on their early ships, which were converted ocean liners, and then point to how far ship designs have evolved. I remember the old ships well. It was even difficult to find the casino on Carnival's first "Fun Ship," *Mardi Gras,* let alone locate the indoor swimming pool. That's hardly the case today. Designed for contemporary travelers and tastes, modern cruise ships carry passengers amid conveniences unheard of in the heyday of the North Atlantic ocean liner or even in the earliest vessels permanently dedicated to cruises. As more than 16 million passengers discovered when they went to sea in 2011, there's a lot to like on ships these days.

The allure of a modern sea cruise is its ability to appeal to a wide range of vacationers as a safe and convenient way to travel. Today's cruise ships are lively and luxurious floating resorts that offer something to satisfy the expectations of almost everyone. The first thing you'll find is that although cruise ships differ dramatically in the details and how they craft and deliver the cruise experience, most ships have the same basic features. And although the decisions and considerations in booking one cruise over another can be complex, the more you know about cruise travel in general, the better prepared you will be when it comes to making your choices.

BEFORE YOU GO

1

To expedite your preboarding paperwork, most cruise lines now allow you to register and do most everything on their websites. As long as you have your reservation number, you can provide the required immigration information, pre-reserve shore excursions, and even indicate any special requests from the comfort of your home. A handful of less "wired" cruise lines may still mail preboarding paperwork to you or your travel agent for completion after you make your final payment, and request that you return the forms by mail or fax. No matter how you submit them, be sure to make hard copies of any forms you fill out and bring them with you to the pier to smooth the embarkation process.

DOCUMENTS

It is every passenger's responsibility to have proper identification. If you arrive at the port without it, you may not be allowed to board, and the line will issue no fare refund. Most travel agents know the requirements and can guide you to the proper agency to obtain what you need if you don't have it.

Everyone must have proof of citizenship and identity to travel abroad. Effective June 1, 2009, travelers were required to present a passport or other approved document denoting citizenship and identity for all land *and* sea travel into the United States. Like most rules, there is a confusing exception—U.S. citizens traveling within the Caribbean on closed-loop cruises (cruises that begin and end in the same port) are still permitted to depart from or enter the United States with proof of identity, which includes a government-issued photo ID, such as a driver's license, along with proof of citizenship, such as a *certified* birth certificate with seal issued by the state where you were born. However, you may still be required to present a passport when you dock at a foreign port, depending on the islands or countries that your cruise ship is visiting. And if your cruise begins in one U.S. port and ends in a different port, you will be required to have a passport. Check with your cruise line to ensure you have the appropriate documents for the stops you'll be making on your cruise.

Even for cruises that begin and end in the same port, cruise lines strongly recommend that all passengers travel with a valid passport, and some may very well require them. Having a valid passport will also enable you to fly from the United States to meet your ship at the first port should you miss the scheduled embarkation, as well as allow you to leave the ship without significant delays and complications before the cruise ends if you must fly back to the United States due to an emergency.

Children under the age of 18, when they are not traveling with both parents, almost always require a letter of permission from the absent parent(s). Airlines, cruise lines, and immigration agents can deny minor children initial boarding or entry to foreign countries without proper proof of identification and citizenship *and* a notarized permission letter from absent or noncustodial parents. Your travel agent or cruise line can help with the wording of such a letter.

WHAT TO PACK

In terms of your wardrobe, cruise wear falls into three categories: casual, informal, and formal. Cruise documents should include information indicating how many evenings fall into each category. You will know when to wear what by reading your ship's daily newsletter—each evening's dress code will be prominently announced.

For the day, you'll need casual wear. For warm-weather cruises, you'll typically need swimwear, a cover-up, and sandals for pool and beach. Time spent ashore touring and shopping calls for shorts topped with T-shirts or polo shirts and comfy walking shoes. Conservative is a rule to live by in the Caribbean (most Caribbean islands are very socially conservative), and mix-and-match will save room in your suitcase. Forget denim, which is too hot, and concentrate on lighter fabrics that will breathe in the Caribbean heat. Although jeans are allowed in the dining rooms of most mainstream ships, at night casual generally means khaki-type slacks and nice polo or sport shirts for men. Ladies' outfits are sundresses, skirts and tops, or pants outfits. By sticking to two or three complementary colors and a few accessories, you can mix up tops and bottoms for a different look every night.

Informal dress—sometimes called "resort" or "smart" casual—is a little trickier. It applies only to evening wear, and can mean different things depending on the cruise line. Informal for women is a dressier dress or pants outfit; for men it almost always includes a sport coat and sometimes a tie. Check your documents carefully.

Formal night means dressing up, but these days even that is a relative notion. You will see women in everything from simple cocktail dresses to glittering formal gowns. A tuxedo (either all black or with white dinner jacket) or dark suit is required for gentlemen. If you have been a "mother of the bride" lately, chances are your outfit for the wedding is just perfect for formal night. For children, Sunday best is entirely appropriate.

Men can usually rent their formal attire from the cruise line, and if they do so, it will be waiting when they board. Be sure to make these arrangements in advance; your travel agent can get the details from the cruise line. But if you are renting a tux, buy your own studs: a surefire way to spot a rented tuxedo is by the inexpensive studs that come with it. Also, many men with a little "girth" consider a vest more comfortable than a cummerbund.

An absolute essential for women is a shawl or light sweater. Aggressive air-conditioning can make public rooms uncomfortable, particularly if you are sunburned from a day at the beach.

Put things you can't do without—such as prescription medication, spare eyeglasses, toiletries, a swimsuit, and change of clothes for the first day—in your carry-on. Most cruise ships provide soap, shampoo, and conditioner, so you probably won't need those.

And plan carefully. In fact, we'd strongly advise you to make a list so you don't forget anything.

ACCESSIBILITY ISSUES

As recently as the early 1990s, "accessibility" on a cruise ship meant little more than a few inside staterooms set aside for passengers with mobility issues. Most public restrooms and nearly all en suite bathrooms had a "step-over" threshold. Newer ships are more sensitive to the needs of passengers with disabilities, but many older ships still have physical barriers in both cabins and public rooms. And once you get off the ship—particularly in some Caribbean ports—your problems will be compounded.

All cruise lines offer a limited number of staterooms designed to be wheelchair- and scooter-accessible. Booking a newer vessel will generally assure more choices. On newer ships, public rooms are generally more accessible, and more facilities have been planned with wheelchair users in mind. Auxiliary aids, such as flashers for the hearing impaired and buzzers for visually impaired passengers, as well as lifts for swimming pools and hot tubs, are available upon request. However, more than the usual amount of preplanning is necessary for smooth sailing if you have special needs.

For example, when a ship is unable to dock—as is the case in Grand Cayman, for instance—passengers are taken ashore on tenders that are sometimes problematic even for the able-bodied to negotiate under adverse conditions. Some people with limited mobility may find it difficult to embark or disembark even when docked due to the steep angle of gangways during high or low tide at certain times of day. In some situations, crew members may offer assistance that involves carrying guests, but if the sea is choppy when tendering is a necessity, that might not be an option.

Passengers who require continuous oxygen or have service animals have further hurdles to overcome. You can bring both aboard a cruise ship, but your service animal may not be allowed to go ashore with you if the port has strict laws regarding animal quarantines.

INSURANCE

We believe that comprehensive trip insurance is especially valuable if you're booking a very expensive or complicated trip (particularly to an isolated region) or if you're booking far in advance. Who knows what could happen six months down the road? But whether or not you get insurance has more to do with how comfortable you are assuming all that risk yourself.

Comprehensive travel policies typically cover trip cancellation and interruption, letting you cancel or cut your trip short because of a personal emergency, illness, or, in some cases, acts of terrorism in your destination. Such policies also cover emergency evacuation and medical care. Some also cover you for trip delays because of bad weather or mechanical problems, as well as for lost or delayed baggage. Another type of coverage to look for is financial default—that is, when your trip is disrupted because a tour operator, airline, or cruise line goes out of business. Generally you must buy this when you book your trip or shortly thereafter, and it's only available to you if your operator isn't on a list of excluded companies.

If you're going abroad, consider buying medical-only coverage at the very least. Neither Medicare nor some private insurers cover medical expenses anywhere outside of the United States (including time aboard a cruise ship, even if it leaves from a U.S. port). Medical-only policies typically reimburse you for medical care (excluding that related to preexisting conditions) and hospitalization abroad, and provide for evacuation. You still have to pay the bills and await reimbursement from the insurer, though.

Expect comprehensive travel insurance policies to cost about 4% to 7% or 8% of the total price of your trip (it's more like 8%–12% if you're over age 70). A medical-only policy may or may not be cheaper than a comprehensive policy. Always read the fine print of your policy to make sure that you are covered for the risks that are of most concern to you. Compare several policies to make sure you're getting the best price and range of coverage available.

U.S. Travel Insurers Allianz Travel Insurance ☎ *800/284–8300*
⊕ *www.allianztravelinsurance.com.* **CSA Travel Protection** ☎ *800/711–1197*
⊕ *www.csatravelprotection.com.* **HTH Worldwide** ☎ *610/254–8700*
⊕ *www.hthworldwide.com.* **Travelex Insurance** ☎ *800/228–9792*
⊕ *www.travelex-insurance.com.* **Travel Guard International** ☎ *800/826–4919*
⊕ *www.travelguard.com.* **Travel Insured International** ☎ *800/243–3174*
⊕ *www.travelinsured.com.*

ARRIVING AND EMBARKING

Most cruise-ship passengers fly to the port of embarkation. If you book your cruise far enough in advance, you'll be given the opportunity to purchase an air-and-sea package, but it may or may not save you money on your flight. You can sometimes get a lower fare by booking your flight independently, so it's a good idea to check for the best fare available.

If you buy an air-and-sea package from your cruise line, a uniformed cruise-line agent will meet you (usually in the baggage claim area) to smooth your way from airport to pier. You will need to claim your own bags and give them to the transfer driver so they can be loaded on the bus. Upon arrival at the pier, luggage is automatically transferred to the ship for delivery to your cabin. The cruise line ground transfer system can also be available to passengers who book their own airfare. However, be sure to ask your travel agent how much it costs; you may find that a taxi or shuttle service is less expensive and more convenient.

In addition to the busiest embarkation ports such as Miami, Fort Lauderdale, and New York City, cruises now leave from less-familiar port cities all around the East and Gulf coasts. Galveston, Texas, and Port Canaveral, Florida, have become major home ports in recent years and are considered now to be among the nation's top 10 cruise ports. Many people prefer to drive to these ports if they are close enough to home; happily, secure parking is always available, either within the port itself or nearby.

BOARDING

Once the planning, packing, and anticipation are behind them, veteran cruise passengers sometimes view embarkation day as anticlimactic. However, for first-time cruise travelers, embarking on their first ship can be more than exhilarating—it can be downright intimidating. What exactly can you expect?

CHECK-IN

Once inside the cruise terminal, you'll see a check-in line. Actual boarding time is often scheduled for noon, but some cruise lines will begin processing early arrivals and then direct them to a "holding" area. During check-in you will be asked to produce your documents and any forms you were sent to complete ahead of time, plus proof of citizenship and a credit card (to cover onboard charges). You are issued a boarding card that functions as your shipboard charge card and often also doubles as your stateroom "key." At some point—usually before you enter the check-in area—you and your hand luggage will pass through a security procedure similar to those at airports.

Check-in lines can be long, particularly at peak times. If check-in starts at noon but continues to 4 pm, you can expect lines to trail off as the boarding deadline approaches. All passengers are anxious to get on board and begin their vacation, so if you arrive at one of the busy periods, keep in mind that this is not the time to get cranky if you have to wait.

Although the gangway is generally not removed until 30 minutes before sailing, U.S. government security regulations require cruise lines to submit certain passenger information to law enforcement authorities at least 60 minutes prior to departure. To meet that requirement, they must have the necessary information in their records at least 90 minutes before departure. If you arrive too late and your information is not in the system before the deadline, you run the risk of being denied boarding even if the ship hasn't sailed.

BOARDING THE SHIP

Once boarding begins, you will inevitably have your first experience with the ship's photographer and be asked to pose for an embarkation picture. It only takes a second, so smile. Later, you'll find those photos for purchase in the ship's photo center.

Procedures vary somewhat once you are greeted by staff members lined up just inside the ship's hull; however, you'll have to produce your boarding card for the security officer. At some point—either at the check-in desk or when boarding the ship for the first time—you will be photographed for security purposes; your image will display when your boarding card is "swiped" into a computer as you leave and reboard the ship in ports of call. Depending on the cruise line, you will be directed to your cabin, or a steward will relieve you of your carry-on luggage and accompany you. Stewards on high-end cruise lines not only show you the way, but hand you a glass of champagne as a welcome-aboard gesture. However, if you board early, don't be surprised if you are told cabins are not "ready" for occupancy—passageways to accommodations may even be roped off. In that case you can explore the ship, have lunch, or simply relax until an announcement is made that you can go to your cabin.

ON BOARD

Check out your cabin to make sure that everything is in order. Try the plumbing and set the air-conditioning to the temperature you prefer. Your cabin may feel warm while docked but will cool off when the ship is underway. You should find a copy of the ship's daily schedule in the cabin. Take a few moments to look it over—you will want to know what time the muster drill takes place (a placard on the back of your cabin door will indicate directions to your emergency station; the drill will happen before your ship leaves port), as well as meal hours and the schedule for various activities and entertainments.

Rented tuxedoes are either hanging in the closet or will be delivered sometime during the afternoon; bon voyage gifts sent by your friends or travel agent usually appear as well. Be patient if you are expecting deliveries, particularly on mega-ships. Cabin stewards participate in the ship's turnaround and are extremely busy, although yours will no doubt introduce himself at the first available opportunity. It will also be a while before your checked luggage arrives, so your initial order of business is usually the buffet, if you haven't already had lunch. Bring along the daily schedule to check over while you eat.

While making your way to the Lido buffet, you may see bar waiters offering trays of colorful and exotic drinks, often in souvenir glasses that you can keep. Beware—on most lines they are not complimentary! If you choose one, you will be asked to sign for it.

Do your plans for the cruise include booking shore excursions, dining in specialty restaurants, and indulging in spa treatments? The most popular tours sometimes sell out, restaurants fill up, and spas can be very busy during sea days, so your next stops should be the Shore Excursion Desk to book tours, the restaurant to secure reservations, and the spa to make appointments. Happily, some cruise lines allow you to complete your planning at home by booking some or all of those on their websites. If you have done so, your excursion tickets and dining and spa confirmations will be delivered to your stateroom.

Dining-room seating arrangements are another matter for consideration. Some people like to check the main dining room to determine where their table is located. If it is not to your liking, or if you requested a large table and find yourself assigned to a small one, you will want to see the head waiter. He or she will be stationed in a lounge with the seating charts handy to make changes. The daily schedule will indicate where and when to meet with him or her.

PAYING FOR THINGS ON BOARD

Let's step back a moment and take a look at what happened when you checked in at the pier. Because a cashless society prevails on cruise ships, an imprint was made of your credit card, or you had to place a cash deposit for use against your onboard charges. Then you were issued a charge card that usually doubles as your boarding card and stateroom "key." Most onboard expenditures are charged to your shipboard account with your signature as verification, with the possible exception of casino gaming—even so, you can often get "cash advances" against your account from the casino cashier.

An itemized bill is provided at the end of the voyage listing your purchases; some cruise lines make this information available online through a computer system accessed through your cabin's TV (Carnival, for instance, does this). In order to avoid surprises, it is a good idea to set aside your charge slips and request an interim printout of your bill from the purser to ensure accuracy. Should you change your mind about charging onboard purchases, you can always inform the purser and pay in cash or traveler's checks instead. If your cash deposit was more than you spent, you will receive a refund.

TIPPING

One of the most delicate—yet frequently debated—topics of conversation among cruise passengers involves the matter of tipping. Who do you tip? How much? What's "customary" and "recommended?" Should parents tip the full amount for children or is just half adequate? Why do you have to tip at all?

When transfers to and from your ship are a part of your air-and-sea program, gratuities are generally included for luggage handling. In that case, do not worry about the interim tipping. However, if you take a taxi to the pier and hand over your bags to a stevedore, be sure to tip him. Treat him with respect and pass along at least $5.

During your cruise, room-service waiters generally receive a cash tip of $1 to $3 per delivery. A 15% to 18% gratuity will automatically be added to each bar bill during the cruise. If you use salon and spa services, a similar percentage might be added to the bills there as well. If you dine in a specialty restaurant, you may be asked to provide a one-time gratuity for the service staff.

There will be a "Disembarkation Talk" on the last day of the cruise that explains tipping procedures. If you are expected to tip in cash, small white "tip" envelopes will appear in your stateroom that day. If you tip in cash, you usually give the tip envelope directly to each person on the last night of the cruise, but this practice is becoming increasingly rare. Most cruise lines now either automatically add gratuities to passengers' onboard charge accounts or offer the option. If that suits you, then do nothing further. However, you are certainly free to adjust the amounts up or down to more appropriate levels or ask that the charge be removed altogether if you prefer distributing cash gratuities.

Tips generally add up to about $10 to $25 per person per day. You tip the same amount for each person who shares the cabin, including children, unless otherwise indicated.

DINING

All food, all the time? Not quite, but it is possible to literally eat away the day and most of the night on a cruise. A popular cruise directors' joke is, "You came on as passengers, and you will be leaving as cargo." Although it is meant in fun, it does contain a ring of truth. Food—tasty and plentiful—is available 24 hours a day on most cruise ships, and the dining experience at sea has reached almost mythical proportions. Perhaps it has something to do with legendary midnight buffets, the absence of menu prices, or maybe it's the vast selection and availability.

RESTAURANTS

Every ship has at least one main restaurant and a Lido, or casual, buffet alternative. Increasingly important are specialty restaurants. Meals in the primary and buffet restaurants are included in the cruise fare, as are midday tea and snacks, late-night buffets, and most round-the-clock room service—an exception is Royal Caribbean, which charges a fee for delivery of late-night room service. Most mainstream cruise lines levy a surcharge for dining in alternative restaurants that may, or may not, also include a gratuity. With the exception of some connoisseur-wine-and-gourmet-food dining experiences, generally there is no additional charge on luxury cruise lines.

You may also find a pizzeria or a specialty coffee bar on your ship—increasingly popular favorites cropping up on ships old and new. Although pizza is complimentary, expect an additional charge for specialty coffees at the coffee bar and, quite likely, in the dining room as well. You will also likely be charged for sodas and drinks during meals other than iced tea, regular coffee, tap water, and fruit juice.

There is often a direct relationship between the cost of a cruise and the quality of its cuisine. The food is very sophisticated on some (mostly expensive) lines, among them Crystal, Cunard, Seabourn, SeaDream, Regent Seven Seas, and Silversea. In the more moderate price range, Oceania Cruises and Azamara Club Cruises have gained renown for their culinary stylings. The trend toward featuring specialty dishes and even entire menus designed by acclaimed chefs has spread throughout the cruise industry; however, on most mainstream cruise lines the food is the quality that you would find in any good hotel banquet—perfectly acceptable but certainly not great.

DINNER SEATINGS

If your cruise ship has traditional seatings for dinner, the one decision that may set the tone for your entire cruise is your dinner seating. Which is best? Early dinner seating is generally scheduled between 6 and 6:30 pm, while late seating can begin from 8:15 to 8:45 pm. So the "best" seating depends on you, your lifestyle, and your personal preference.

Families with young children and older passengers often choose an early seating. Early-seating diners are encouraged not to linger too long over dessert and coffee because the dining room has to be readied for late seating. Late seating is viewed by some passengers as more romantic and less rushed.

Cruise lines understand that strict schedules no longer satisfy the desires of all modern cruise passengers. Many cruise lines now include alternatives to the set schedules in the dining room, including casual dinner menus in their buffet facilities where more flexibility is allowed in dress and mealtimes. À la carte restaurants are showing up on more ships and offer yet another choice, though usually for an additional charge.

Open seating is primarily associated with more upscale lines; it allows passengers the flexibility to dine any time during restaurant hours and be seated with whomever they please.

Led by Norwegian Cruise Line and Princess Cruises, more contemporary and premium cruise lines, including Holland America Line, Celebrity Cruises, Royal Caribbean, and Carnival Cruise Lines, have introduced adaptations of open seating to offer variety and a more personalized experience for their passengers. Most cruise lines also offer casual evening meals in the Lido buffet, some featuring entrées similar to those served in the main dining room and with limited table service.

CHANGING TABLES

Cruise lines will never guarantee that you receive your preferred dinner seating, and table assignments are generally not confirmed until embarkation; however, every effort is made to satisfy all guests. Should there be a problem, see the maître d' for assistance. Changes after the first evening are generally discouraged, so if you want to change your seating or table, meet with dining-room staff and iron out problems on embarkation day. Check the daily program for time and location.

SPECIAL DIETS

Cruise lines make every possible attempt to ensure dining satisfaction. If you have special dietary considerations—such as low-salt, kosher, or food allergies—be sure to indicate them well ahead of time and check to be certain your needs are known by your waiter once on board. In addition to the usual menu items, "spa," vegetarian, low-calorie, low-carbohydrate, or low-fat selections, as well as children's menus are usually available. Requests for dishes not featured on the menu can often be granted if you ask in advance.

WINE

Wine typically costs about what you would expect to pay at a nice lounge or restaurant in a resort or a large U.S. city. Wine by the bottle is sometimes a more economical choice at dinner than ordering it by the glass. Any wine you don't finish will be kept for you and served the next night. Gifts of wine or champagne ordered from the cruise line (either by you, a friend, or your travel agent) can be taken to the dining room. Wine from any other source will incur a "corkage" fee of approximately $10 to $15 per bottle.

Drinking on Board

It's hard to avoid the ship's bars, since they are social centers, but alcoholic drinks are not usually included in your cruise fare, and bar bills can add up quickly. Drinks at the captain's welcome-aboard cocktail party and at cocktail parties held specifically for past cruisers are usually free. But if you pick up that boldly colored welcome-aboard cocktail as your ship pulls away from the dock, you may very well be asked to sign for it, and the cost will then be added to your shipboard account.

You should expect to pay about the same for a drink on board a cruise ship that you would pay in a bar at home: $5 to $6 for a domestic beer, $6 to $9 for a cocktail, $7 to $9 for a glass of wine, $1.25 to $2 for a soft drink. On virtually all ships, an automatic 15% gratuity will be added

to your tab. What most people don't consider is that specialty coffees are also added to your bar tab, so if you order a cappuccino—and on some ships that applies even if it's in the dining room after dinner—you'll see a charge of $4 to $6 on your bar bill.

To save money on your bar bill, you can follow a few simple strategies. In lounges, request the less expensive bar brands or the reduced-price drink-of-the-day. On some ships, discounted "beverage cards" for unlimited fountain soft drinks and/ or a set number of mixed drinks are available.

In international waters there are, technically, no laws against teenage drinking, but almost all ships now require passengers to be over 21 to purchase alcoholic beverages.

THE CAPTAIN'S TABLE

Legend has it that a nouveau-riche passenger's response to an invitation to dine with the captain during a round-the-world cruise was, "I didn't shell out all those bucks to eat with the help!" Although there are some cruise passengers who decline invitations to dine at the captain's table, there are far more who covet such an experience. You will know you have been included in that exclusive coterie when an embossed invitation arrives in your stateroom on the day of a formal dinner. RSVP as soon as possible—if you are unable to attend, someone else will be invited in your place.

Who is invited? If you are a frequent repeat cruiser, the occupants of an owner's suite, or if you hail from the captain's hometown or speak his native language, you may be considered. Honeymoon couples are sometimes selected at random, as are couples celebrating a golden wedding anniversary. Attractive, unattached female passengers often round out an uneven number of guests. Requests made by travel agents on behalf of their clients sometimes do the trick.

ENTERTAINMENT

It's hard to imagine, but in the early years of cruise travel, shipboard entertainment consisted of little more than poetry readings and recitals that exhibited the talents of fellow passengers. Those bygone days of sedate amusements in an intimate setting have been replaced by lavish showrooms where sequined and feathered showgirls strut their stuff on stage amid special effects not imagined in the past.

Seven-night Caribbean cruises usually include two original production shows. One of these might be a Las Vegas–style extravaganza and the other a best-of-Broadway show featuring old and new favorites from the Great White Way. Some ships even offer full Broadway productions and top Vegas entertainers. Other shows highlight the talents of individual singers, dancers, magicians, comedians, and even acrobats. Don't be surprised if you are plucked from the audience to take the brunt of a comedian's jokes or act as the magician's temporary assistant. Sit in the front row if appearing onstage appeals to you.

Whether it is relegated to a late-afternoon interlude between bingo and dinner or a featured evening highlight, the passenger talent show is often a "don't miss" production. From pure camp to stylishly slick, what passes for talent is sometimes surprising but seldom boring. Stand-up comedy is generally discouraged; however, passengers who want their performance skills to be considered should answer the call for auditions and plan to rehearse the show at least once.

Enrichment programs have become a popular pastime at sea. It may come as a surprise that port lecturers on many large contemporary cruise ships offer more information on shore tours and shopping than insight into the ports of call. If more cerebral presentations are important to you, consider a cruise on a line that features stimulating enrichment programs and seminars at sea. Speakers can include destination-oriented historians, popular authors, business leaders, radio or television personalities, and even movie stars.

LOUNGES AND NIGHTCLUBS

If you find the show-lounge stage a bit intimidating and want to perform in a more intimate venue, look for karaoke. Singing along in a lively piano bar is another shipboard favorite for would-be crooners.

Other lounges might feature easy-listening music, jazz, or combos for pre- and postdinner social dancing. Later in the evening, lounges pick up the pace with music from the 1950s and '60s; clubs aimed at a younger crowd usually have more contemporary dance music during the late-night hours.

CASINOS

A sure sign that your ship is in international waters is the opening of the casino. On most ships, lavish casinos pulsate with activity. The most notable exceptions are the family-oriented ships of Disney Cruise Line, which shun gaming in favor of more wholesome pastimes.

On ships that feature them, the rationale for locating casinos where most passengers must pass either through or alongside them is obvious—the unspoken allure of winning. In addition to slot machines in a variety of denominations, cruise-ship casinos might feature roulette, craps, and a variety of poker games—Caribbean Stud Poker, Let It Ride, Texas Hold 'Em, and blackjack, to name a few. Cruise lines strive to provide fair and professional gambling entertainment and supply gaming guides that set out the rules of play and betting limits for each game.

Casino hours vary based on the itinerary or location of the ship; most are required to close while in port, while others may be able to offer 24-hour slot machines and simply close table games. Every casino has a cashier, and you may be able to charge a cash advance to your onboard account, for a fee.

OTHER ENTERTAINMENT

Most vessels have a room for screening movies. On older ships and some newer ones, this is often a genuine cinema-style movie theater, while on other ships it may be just a multipurpose room. Over the course of a weeklong voyage a dozen films may be screened, each repeated several times. Theaters are also used for lectures, culinary demonstrations, religious services, and private meetings. The latest twist in video programming can be found on some Princess, Disney, Royal Caribbean, and Carnival ships—huge outdoor LED screens where movies, music video concerts, news channels, and even the ship's activities are broadcast for passengers lounging poolside.

With a few exceptions, cruise TVs have channels devoted to movies (continuously on some newer ships), shipboard lectures, news channels, and regular programs (thanks to satellite reception). Pay-per-view movies (for a charge) are available on some ships. Ships with in-cabin DVDs usually have a selection of movies available; sometimes there is a charge, but sometimes just a deposit is required.

Most medium and large ships have video arcades, and nearly all ships now have computer centers and, increasingly, Wi-Fi (either in public areas or throughout the ship).

SPORTS AND FITNESS

Onboard sports facilities might include a court for basketball, volleyball, tennis—or all three—a jogging track, or even an in-line skating track. Some ships are even offering innovative and unexpected features, such as rock-climbing walls, bungee trampolines, and surfing pools. You'll even be able to bowl on certain Norwegian Cruise Line ships. For the less adventurous, there's always table tennis and shuffleboard.

Naturally, you will find at least one swimming pool and possibly several. Cruise-ship pools are generally on the small side—more appropriate for cooling off than doing laps—and the majority contain filtered saltwater. But some are elaborate affairs with waterslides. Princess Grand–class ships have challenging, freshwater "swim against the current" pools for swimming enthusiasts who want to get their low-impact exercise while on board.

Golf is a perennial seagoing favorite of players who want to take their games to the next level and include the Caribbean's most beautiful and challenging courses on their scorecards. Shipboard programs can include clinics, use of full-motion golf cages, and even individual

Health and Safety at Sea

Safety begins with you, the passenger. Once settled into your cabin, locate life vests and review posted emergency instructions. Make sure vests are in good condition and learn to secure them properly. If you have a physical infirmity that may hamper a speedy exit from your cabin, make certain the ship's purser knows, so that in an emergency he or she can quickly dispatch a crew member to assist you. If you're traveling with children, be sure that child-size life jackets are placed in your cabin.

Before your ship leaves port, you'll be required to attend a mandatory lifeboat drill. Do so and listen carefully. If you're unsure about how to use your vest, now is the time to ask. Only in the most extreme circumstances will you need to abandon ship—but it has happened. The time you spend learning the procedure may serve you well in a mishap.

In actuality, the greatest danger facing cruise-ship passengers is fire. All cruise lines must meet international standards for fire safety, which require sprinkler systems, smoke detectors, and other safety features. Fires on cruise ships are not common, but they do happen, and these rules have made ships much safer. You can do your part by *not* using an iron in your cabin and taking care to properly extinguish smoking materials. Never throw a lit cigarette overboard—it could be blown back into an opening in the ship and start a fire.

All large ships have an infirmary to deal with minor medical emergencies, but these infirmaries are not suitable for dealing with major procedures. The ship's doctor should be able to treat you as well as any general practitioner or clinic ashore for minor problems. For really complicated medical conditions, such as a heart attack or appendicitis, the ship's medical team evacuates passengers to the nearest hospital ashore. While at sea, evacuation expenses can rise as fast as the helicopter that whisks the patient away. You'll need supplementary insurance to cover evacuation costs.

Two of the most prevalent diseases that spread through cruise-ship populations are influenza and noroviruses that cause intestinal and stomach upsets. Annual influenza vaccination is the primary method for preventing influenza and its complications. But to prevent all kinds of infections—including noroviruses—frequent hand-washing is also essential; take advantage of the dispensers of hand-sanitizer, and use it when entering any dining room. Or slip into the restroom to wash your hands with soap and hot water.

---

instruction from resident pros using state-of-the-art computer analysis. Once ashore, escorted excursions include everything needed for a satisfying round of play, including equipment and tips from the pro, and the ability to schedule tee times at exclusive courses.

FITNESS CENTERS

Cruise vacations can be hazardous to your waistline if you are not careful. Eating "out" for all meals and sampling different cuisines tend to pile on unaccustomed calories. But shipboard fitness centers have become ever more elaborate, offering state-of-the-art exercise machines, treadmills, and stair steppers, not to mention weights and weight machines. As a bonus, many fitness centers with floor-to-ceiling windows have the world's most inspiring sea views.

For guests who prefer a more social atmosphere as they burn off sinful chocolate desserts, there are specialized fitness classes for all levels of ability. High-impact, energetic aerobics are not for everyone, but any class that raises the heart rate can be toned down and tailored to individual capabilities. Stretching classes help you warm up for a light jog or brisk walk on deck, and there are even sit-for-fitness classes for mature passengers or those with delicate joints. Fees are usually charged for specialty classes, such as Pilates, spinning, and yoga. Personal trainers are usually on board to get you off on the right foot, also for a fee.

SPAS

With all the usual pampering and service in luxurious surroundings, simply being on a cruise can be a stress-reducing experience. Add to that the menu of spa and salon services at your fingertips and you have a recipe for total sensory pleasure. Spas have also become among the most popular of shipboard areas.

Some spa offerings sound good enough to eat. A Milk-and-Honey Hydrotherapy Bath, Coconut Rub and Milk Ritual Wrap or Float, and a Javanese Steam Wrap incorporating cinnamon, ginger, coffee, sea salt, and honey are just a few of the tempting items found on spa menus. Not quite as exotic sounding, other treatments and services are nonetheless therapeutic for the body and soul. Steiner Leisure is the largest spa and salon operator at sea (the company also operates the Mandara- and the Greenhouse-brand spas), with facilities on more than 100 cruise ships worldwide.

In addition to facials, manicures, pedicures, massages, and sensual body treatments, other hallmarks of Steiner Leisure are salon services and products for hair and skin. Founded in 1901 by Henry Steiner of London, a single salon prospered when Steiner's son joined the business in 1926 and was granted a Royal Warrant as hairdresser to Her Majesty Queen Mary in 1937. In 1956 Steiner won its first cruise-ship contract to operate the salon on board the ships of the Cunard Line. By the mid-1990s, Steiner Leisure began taking an active role in creating shipboard spas offering a wide variety of wellness therapies and beauty programs for both women and men.

SHIPBOARD SERVICES

COMMUNICATIONS

Just because you are out to sea does not mean you have to be out of touch. Ship-to-shore telephone calls can cost $2 to $15 a minute, so it makes more economic sense to use e-mail to remain in contact with your home or office. Most ships have basic computer systems, while some newer vessels offer more high-tech connectivity—even in-cabin

Crime on Ships

Crime aboard cruise ships has occasionally become headline news, thanks in large part to a few well-publicized cases. Most people never have any type of problem, but you should exercise the same precautions aboard ship that you would at home. Keep your valuables out of sight—on big ships virtually every cabin has a small safe. Don't carry too much cash ashore, use your credit card whenever possible, and keep your money in a secure place, such as a front pocket that's harder to pick. Single women traveling with friends should stick together, especially when returning to their cabins late at night. When assaults occur, it often comes to light that excessive drinking of alcohol was a factor. Be careful about befriending anyone, as you would anywhere, whether it's a fellow passenger or a member of the crew. Don't be paranoid, but do be prudent.

Your cruise is a wonderful opportunity to leave everyday responsibilities behind, but don't neglect to pack your common sense. After a few drinks it might seem like a good idea to sit on a railing or lean over the rail to get a better view of the ship's wake. Passengers have been known to fall. "Man overboard" is more likely to be the result of carelessness than criminal intent.

hookups or wireless connections for either your own laptop computer or one you can rent on board. Expect charges in the 75¢- to $1-per-minute range for the use of these Internet services. Ships usually offer some kind of package so that you get a reduced per-minute price if you pay a fee up front.

The ability to use your own mobile phone from the high seas is a relatively new alternative that is gaining popularity. It's usually cheaper than using a cabin phone if your ship offers the service, but it can still cost up to several dollars a minute. It's a rather ingenious concept, with the ship acting as a cell "tower" in international waters—you use your own cell phone and your own number when roaming at sea. If using your cell phone is essential, contact your mobile service carrier before leaving home to enable international roaming and dialing, and be sure to understand their roaming agreements to be certain that your carrier has one with your cruise line. When in port, depending on the agreements your mobile service provider has established, you may be able to connect to local networks. Rates for using the maritime service, as well as any roaming charges from Caribbean islands, are established by your mobile service carrier and are worth checking into before you leave home. They can be substantial (i.e., up to $2.50 or more per minute); text messages are cheaper but are usually charged at the higher international roaming rate of at least 50¢ per message and will be charged separately, even if you have a text-message plan. Most GSM tri-band phones from the United States will work in the Caribbean if your carrier has a roaming agreement.

LAUNDRY AND DRY CLEANING

Most cruise ships offer valet laundry and pressing (and some also offer dry-cleaning) service. Expenses can add up fast, especially for laundry, since charges are per item and the rates are similar to those charged in hotels. If doing laundry is important to you and you do not want to send it out to be done, many cruise ships have a self-service laundry room (which usually features an iron and ironing board in addition to washer and dryer). If you book one of the top-dollar suites, laundry service may be included for no additional cost. Upscale ships, such as those in the Regent Seven Seas Cruises, Silversea Cruises, Crystal Cruises, and Seabourn fleets, have complimentary self-service launderettes. On other cruise lines, such as Princess Cruises, Oceania Cruises, Carnival Cruise Lines, Disney Cruise Line, and Holland America Line (except Vista- and Signature-class ships), you can do your own laundry for about $3 or less per load. None of the vessels in the Norwegian Cruise Line, Royal Caribbean, or Celebrity Cruises fleets has self-service laundry facilities.

SHORE EXCURSION DESK

Manned by a knowledgeable staff, the Shore Excursion Desk can not only book ship-sponsored tours, but may also be the place to learn more about ports of call and garner information to tour independently. Although staff members and the focus of their positions vary widely, the least you can expect is basic information and port maps. On some ships the port lecturer may emphasize shopping and "recommended" merchants, with little to impart regarding sightseeing or the history and culture of ports. Happily, some shore-excursion staff members possess a wealth of information and share it without reservation.

DISEMBARKATION

All cruises come to an end eventually, and it hardly seems fair that you have to leave when it feels like your vacation has just begun, but leave you must. The disembarkation process actually begins the day before you arrive at your ship's home port. During that day your cabin steward delivers special luggage tags to your stateroom, along with customs forms and instructions. Some lines allow you to carry your luggage off the ship, and if you choose to do that, then you will not have to worry about placing your bags outside your cabin door the night before disembarkation; verify with your cruise line whether it's possible for you to do this, assuming you want to.

The night before you disembark, you'll need to set aside clothing to wear the next morning when you leave the ship. Many people dress in whatever casual outfits they wear for the final dinner on board, or change into travel clothes after dinner. Also, do not forget to put your passport or other proof of citizenship, airline tickets, and medications in your hand luggage.

If you are not carrying your luggage off-ship, then after you finish packing, attach your new luggage tags (they are color- or number-coded according to post-cruise transportation plans and flight schedules). Follow the instructions provided and place the locked luggage outside your stateroom door for pickup during the hours indicated.

A statement itemizing your onboard charges is delivered before you arise on disembarkation morning. Plan to get up early enough to check it over for accuracy, finish packing your personal belongings, and vacate your stateroom by the appointed hour. Any discrepancies in your onboard account should be taken care of before leaving the ship, usually at the purser's desk.

Room service is not available on most ships on the last day; however, breakfast is served in the main restaurant as well as the buffet. After breakfast there is not much to do but wait comfortably in a lounge or on deck for your tag color or number to be called; some lines now allow you to wait in your cabin. Disembarkation procedures can sometimes be drawn out by passengers who are unprepared. This is no time to abandon your patience or sense of humor. An announcement will be made when it is your turn to disembark. Have your cruise card in hand for security to scan you off the vessel. Also have your passport or other identification and completed customs form handy.

Remember that all passengers must meet with customs and immigration officials during disembarkation, usually in the terminal. Procedures vary and are outlined in your instructions. In some ports passengers must meet with the officials at a specified hour (usually very early) in an onboard lounge; in other ports, customs forms are collected in the terminal and passports/identification papers are examined there as well.

Once in the terminal, locate your luggage and proceed to your bus or taxi, or retrieve your vehicle from the parking lot.

CUSTOMS AND DUTIES

U.S. CUSTOMS

Before a ship docks, each individual or family must fill out a customs declaration. If your purchases total less than the limit for your destination, you will not need to itemize them. Be prepared to pay whatever duties are owed directly to the customs inspector, with cash or check. Be sure to keep receipts for all purchases; and you may be asked to show officials what you've bought.

After collecting your luggage in the terminal, you then stand in line to pass through the inspection point. This can take up to an hour.

ALLOWANCES

You're always allowed to bring goods of a certain value back home without having to pay any duty or import tax. There's also a limit on the amount of tobacco and liquor you can bring back duty-free, and some countries have separate limits for perfumes; for exact figures, check with your customs department. The values of so-called "duty-free" goods are included in these amounts. When you shop abroad—and in the Caribbean, this means all islands except for Puerto Rico, which is considered a part of the United States for customs purposes—save all your receipts, as customs inspectors may ask to see them as well as the items you purchased. If the total value of your goods is more than the duty-free limit, then you'll have to pay a tax (most often a flat percentage) on the value of everything beyond that limit.

Individuals entering the United States from the Caribbean are allowed to bring in $800 worth of duty-free goods for personal use ($1,600 from the U.S. Virgin Islands), including 1 liter of alcohol (2 liters if one was produced in the Caribbean and 5 liters from the USVI), one carton of cigarettes (or five if four were purchased in the U.S. Virgin Islands), and 100 non-Cuban cigars. Antiques and original artwork are also duty-free.

SENDING PACKAGES HOME

Although you probably won't want to spend your time looking for a post office, you can send packages home duty-free, with a limit of one parcel per addressee per day (except alcohol or tobacco products or perfume worth more than $5). You can mail up to $200 worth of goods for personal use; label the package "personal use" and attach a list of the contents and their retail value. If the package contains your used personal belongings, mark it "personal goods returned" to avoid paying duty on your laundry. You may also send up to $100 worth of goods as gifts, with the same limit of one parcel per addressee per day ($200 from the U.S. Virgin Islands); mark the package "unsolicited gift." Items you mailed do not affect your duty-free allowance on your return.

NONCITIZENS

Non–U.S. citizens who are returning home within hours of docking may be exempt from all U.S. Customs duties. Everything you bring into the United States must leave with you when you return home, though. When you reach your own country, you will have to pay duties there.

Cruising the Caribbean

WORD OF MOUTH

"We have spoken with many people who have cruised different lines, and they seem to prefer Royal Caribbean, Celebrity, Norwegian, and Princess for many different reasons."

—JanKF

By Linda
Coffman

More cruise ships ply the waters of the Caribbean than any other spot on Earth. Some are huge ships carrying more than 4,000 passengers; some are "midsize" ships welcoming about 1,500 cruisers; and others are comparatively small ships on which you'll find yourself with 300 or fewer other passengers. There are fancy ships and party ships, ships with sails, ships that pride themselves on the numbers of ports they visit, and ships that provide so much activity right on board that you hardly have time or inclination to go ashore. In peak season it's not uncommon for thousands of passengers to disembark from several ships into a small island port on the same day—a phenomenon not always enjoyed by locals. With such an abundance of cruise ships in this area, however, you can choose the ship and the itinerary that suit you best.

CHOOSING YOUR CRUISE

Some of the best "islands" in the Caribbean are the ones that float and move—they are called cruise ships. Just as Caribbean islands have distinct histories and cultures, cruise ships also have individual personalities. Determined by their size, the year they were built, and their style, on one hand, they can be bold, brassy, and exciting—totally unlike home, but a great place to visit. Big ships offer stability and a huge variety of activities and facilities. On the other hand, small ships feel intimate, like private clubs or, more appropriately, personal yachts. For every big-ship fan there is someone who would never set foot aboard a "floating resort." Examine your lifestyle—there's sure to be a cruise ship to match your expectations.

After giving some thought to your itinerary and where in the Caribbean you might wish to go, the ship you select is the most vital factor in your Caribbean cruise vacation, since it will not only determine which islands you will visit, but also how you will see them. Big ships visit major ports of call such as St. Thomas, St. Maarten/St. Martin, Nassau, and San Juan; when they call at smaller islands with shallower ports, passengers must disembark aboard shore tenders (small boats that ferry dozens of passengers to shore at a time). Or they may skip these smaller ports entirely. Small and midsize ships can visit smaller islands, such as St. Barths, St. Kitts, or Tortola, more easily; passengers are often able to disembark directly onto the pier without having to wait for tenders to bring them ashore.

ITINERARIES

You'll want to give some consideration to your ship's Caribbean itinerary when you are choosing your cruise. The length of the cruise will determine the variety and number of ports you visit, but so will the type of itinerary and the point of departure. **Round-trip cruises** start and end at the same point and usually explore ports close to one another; **one-way cruises** start at one point and end at another and range farther afield.

Almost all cruises in the Caribbean are round-trip cruises. On Caribbean itineraries you often have a choice of U.S. mainland departure points. Ships sailing out of San Juan can visit up to five ports in seven days, while cruises out of Florida can reach up to four ports in the same length of time. The Panama Canal can also be combined with a Caribbean cruise: the 50-mile (83-km) canal is a series of locks, which make up for the height difference between the Caribbean and the Pacific. Increasingly popular are partial transit cruises that enter the Panama Canal, anchor in Gatún Lake for a short time, and depart through the same set of locks.

EASTERN CARIBBEAN ITINERARIES

Eastern Caribbean itineraries consist of two or three days at sea as well as stops at some of the Caribbean's busiest cruise ports. A typical cruise will usually take in three or four ports of call, such as St. Thomas in the U.S. Virgin Islands, San Juan, or St. Maarten/St. Martin, along with a visit to the cruise line's "private" island for beach time. Every major cruise line has at least two of those popular islands on its itineraries. Some itineraries might also include others, such as Tortola, Dominica, Barbados, St. Kitts, or Martinique.

WESTERN CARIBBEAN ITINERARIES

Western Caribbean itineraries embarking from Galveston, Ft. Lauderdale, Miami, Port Canaveral, New Orleans, or Tampa might include Belize, Cozumel or the Costa Maya Cruise Port in Mexico, Key West, Grand Cayman, or Jamaica—all perfect for passengers who enjoy scuba diving, snorkeling, and exploring Mayan ruins. Ships often alternate itineraries in the Western Caribbean with itineraries in the Eastern Caribbean on a weekly basis, offering the ability to schedule a 14-night back-to-back cruise without repeating ports.

SOUTHERN CARIBBEAN ITINERARIES

Southern Caribbean cruises tend to be longer in duration, with more distant ports of call. They often originate in a port that is not on the U.S. mainland. Embarking in San Juan, for example, allows you to reach the lower Caribbean on a seven-day cruise with as many as four or five ports of call. Southern Caribbean itineraries might leave Puerto Rico for the Virgin Islands, Guadeloupe, Grenada, Curaçao, Barbados, Antigua, St. Lucia, Martinique, or Aruba. Smaller ships leave from embarkation ports as far south as Bridgetown, Barbados, and cruise through the Grenadines. Every major cruise line offers some Southern Caribbean itineraries, but these cruises aren't as popular as Western and Eastern Caribbean cruises.

OTHER ITINERARIES

In recent years shorter itineraries have grown in appeal to time-crunched and budget-constrained travelers. If you are planning your first cruise in the tropics, a short sailing to the Bahamas allows you to test your appetite for cruising before you take a chance on a longer and more expensive cruise. Embarking at Fort Lauderdale, Miami, Jacksonville, or Port Canaveral, you will cruise for three to five days, taking in at least one port of call (usually Nassau or Freeport in the Bahamas) and possibly a visit to a "private" island or Key West. Four- and five-night cruises may also include a day at sea. Cruises also depart from ports farther north on the east coast; you might depart from Charleston, Baltimore, or New York City and cruise to Bermuda or the Bahamas.

WHEN TO GO

Average year-round temperatures throughout the Caribbean are 78°F–85°F, with a low of 65°F and a high of 95°F; downtown shopping areas always seem to be unbearably hot. Low season runs from approximately mid-September through mid-April. Many travelers, especially families with school-age children, make reservations months in advance for the most expensive and most crowded summer months and holiday periods; however, with the many new cruise ships that have entered the market, you can often book fairly close to your departure date and still find room, although you may not get exactly the kind of cabin you would prefer. A summer cruise offers certain advantages: temperatures are virtually the same as in winter (cooler on average than in parts of the U.S. mainland), island flora is at its most dramatic, the water is smoother and clearer, and although there is always a breeze, winds are rarely strong enough to rock a ship. Some Caribbean tourist facilities close down in summer, however, and many ships move to Europe, Alaska, or the northeastern United States.

Hurricane season runs a full six months of the year—from June 1 through November 30. Although cruise ships stay well out of the way of these storms, hurricanes and tropical storms—their less-powerful relatives—can affect the weather throughout the Caribbean for days, and damage to ports can force last-minute itinerary changes.

CRUISE COSTS

The average daily price for Caribbean itineraries varies dramatically depending on several circumstances. The cost of a cruise on a luxury line such as Silversea or Seabourn may be three to four times the cost of a cruise on a mainstream line such as Carnival or even premium lines like Princess. When you sail will also affect your costs: published brochure rates are usually highest during the peak summer season and holidays. When snow blankets the ground and temperatures are in single digits, a Caribbean cruise can be a welcome respite and less expensive than land resorts, which often command top dollar in winter months.

CLOSE UP

Saving Money on Your Cruise Fare

You can save on your cruise fare in several ways. Obviously, you should shop around. Travel agent discounting of cruise prices has become a thing of the past, but one thing never changes—never, under any circumstances, pay brochure rate. You can do better, often as much as half off published fares. These are a few simple strategies you can follow:

■ Book early: Cruise lines discount their cruises if you book early, particularly during the annual "Wave" season between January and March.

■ Cruise during the off-season: If you take a cruise during the later months of hurricane season (especially October and November) or the period between Thanksgiving and Christmas, you'll often find specials.

■ Book late: Sometimes you can book a last-minute cruise at substantial savings if the ship hasn't filled all its cabins.

■ Choose accommodations with care: Cabins are usually standardized, and location determines the fare. Selecting a lower category can result in savings while giving up nothing in terms of cabin size and features.

■ Book a "guarantee": You won't be able to select your own cabin because the cruise line will assign you one in the category you book, but a "guarantee" fare can be substantially lower than a regular fare.

■ Cruise with friends and family: Book a minimum number of cabins, and your group can generally receive a special discounted fare.

■ Reveal your age and affiliations: Fare savings may be available for seniors and members of certain organizations, as well as cruise-line stockholders.

■ Cruise often: Frequent cruisers usually get discounts from their preferred cruise lines.

Solo travelers should be aware that single cabins have virtually disappeared from cruise ships, with the exception of Norwegian Cruise Line's newest ship Norwegian Epic. Taking a double cabin can cost twice the advertised per-person rates (which are based on double occupancy). Some cruise lines will find same-sex roommates for singles; each then pays the per-person, double-occupancy rate.

EXTRAS

In addition to the cost of your cruise, there are further expenses to consider, such as airfare to the port city. These days, virtually all cruise lines offer air add-ons, which are sometimes, but not always, less expensive than the lowest available airline fare. Shore excursions can also be a substantial expense; the best shore excursions are not cheap. But if you skimp too much on your excursion budget, you'll deprive yourself of an important part of the Caribbean cruising experience. Finally, there will be many extras added to your shipboard account during the cruise, including drinks (both alcoholic and nonalcoholic), activity fees (you pay to use that golf simulator), dining in specialty restaurants, spa services, and even cappuccino and espresso on most ships. These add-ons are no longer nominal fees, either; you pay top-dollar for most extras onboard mainstream ships, and the average post-cruise bill may be as much as 50% of the base cost of your cruise.

TIPPING

Tipping is another add-on. At the end of the cruise, it's customary to tip your room steward, dining-room waiter, and the person who buses your table. You should expect to pay an average of $10 to $15 per person per day in tips. Most major cruise lines are moving away from the traditional method of tipping the service staff in cash at the end of the cruise, instead adding the recommended amount per day to your onboard account to cover tips, which you may adjust upward or downward according to the level of service you receive. Bar bills generally include an automatic 15%–18% gratuity, so the one person you don't need to tip is your bartender. Some cruise lines have gratuities-included policies, though some passengers tip for any extra services received anyway. Each cruise line offers guidelines.

CRUISE LINES

Seated in an airplane after a week of enjoying an exceptionally nice cruise, I overheard the couple behind me discussing their "dreadful" cruise vacation. What a surprise when they mentioned the ship's name. It was the one I'd just spent a glorious week on. I never missed a meal; they hated the food. My cabin was comfortable and cheery, if not large; their identical accommodations resembled a "cave." One size definitely does not fit all in cruising. What's appealing to one passenger may be unacceptable to another. Ultimately, most cruise complaints arise from passengers whose expectations were not met. The couple I eavesdropped on were on the wrong cruise line and ship for them.

I enjoy cruises. Some have suited me more than others, but I've never sailed on a cruise that was completely without merit. Make no mistake about it: cruise lines have distinct personalities, but not all luxury or mainstream cruise lines are alike, although they will share many basic similarities. The cruise industry is a fluid one—that means that when new features are introduced, they may not be found on all ships, even those within the same cruise line. For instance, you won't find an ice-skating rink on any but the biggest Royal Caribbean ships. However, most cruise lines try to standardize the experience throughout their fleets, which is why you'll find a waterslide on every Carnival ship.

Just as trends and fashion evolve over time, cruise lines embrace the ebb and flow of change. To keep pace with today's lifestyles, some cruise lines strive to include something that will appeal to everyone on their ships. Others focus on narrower elements and are more traditional. Today's passengers have higher expectations, and they sail on ships that are far superior to their predecessors. And they often do so at a much lower comparable fare than in the past.

So which cruise line is best? Only you can determine which is best for you. You won't find ratings by Fodor's—either quality stars or value scores. Why? Think of those people seated behind me on the airplane. Ratings are personal and heavily weighted to the reviewer's opinion. Your responsibility is to select the right cruise for you—no one knows your expectations better than you do yourself. It's your time, money, and vacation that are at stake. No matter how knowledgeable your travel agent is, how sincere your friends are, or what any expert can tell you, you are the only one who really knows what you like. The short wait for a table might not bother you because you would prefer a casual atmosphere with open seating; however, some people want the security of a set time at an assigned table served by a waiter who gets to know their preferences. You know what you are willing to trade off in order to get what you want.

The following cruise-line profiles offer a general idea of what you can expect in terms of overall experience, quality, and service from each major cruise line that operates in the Caribbean and the Bahamas. You will want to compare the features of several cruise lines to determine which ones come closest to matching your needs. Then narrow them down further to a few that appeal most to you. Keep in mind that not all ships belonging to the cruise lines described in the following profiles are deployed in the Caribbean year-round; some head for Alaska and Europe during summer months; others call port cities on the Pacific coast their home for part of the year.

LUXURY CRUISE LINES

Comprising only 5% of the market, the exclusive luxury cruise lines, which include Crystal, Cunard, Regent Seven Seas, Seabourn, SeaDream, Silversea, and Windstar, offer high staff-to-guest ratios for personal service, superior cuisine in a single seating (except Crystal, with two assigned seatings and an open-seating option, and Cunard, with dual-class dining assignments), and a highly inclusive product with few onboard charges. These small and midsize ships offer much more space per passenger than you will find on the mainstream lines' vessels. Lines differ in what they emphasize, with some touting luxurious accommodations and entertainment and others focusing on exotic destinations and onboard enrichment.

If you consider travel a necessity rather than a luxury and frequent posh resorts, then you will appreciate the extra attention and the higher level of comfort that luxury cruise lines offer.

Itineraries on these ships often include the big casinos and most popular island beach resorts, but luxury ships also visit some of the less common Caribbean destinations. With a shallow draft and intimate size, the smaller luxury ships can visit such ports as Anguilla, St. Barths, Tobago, and Jost Van Dyke and Virgin Gorda in the British Virgin Islands.

MAINSTREAM CRUISE LINES

More than 85% of the Caribbean is covered by nearly a dozen mainstream cruise lines. They offer the advantage of something for everyone and nearly every available sports facility imaginable. Some ships even have ice-skating rinks, 18-hole miniature golf courses, bowling alleys, and rock-climbing walls.

Generally speaking, the mainstream lines have two basic ship sizes—large cruise ships and mega-ships—in their fleets. These cruise ships have plentiful outdoor deck space, and many have a wraparound outdoor promenade deck that allows you to stroll or jog the ship's perimeter. In the newest vessels, traditional meets trendy. You'll find atrium lobbies and expansive sun and sports decks, picture windows instead of port-holes, and cabins that open onto private verandas. For all their resort-style innovations, they still feature cruise-ship classics—afternoon tea, complimentary room service, and lavish pampering. The smallest ships carry 1,000 passengers or fewer, while the largest accommodate more than 3,000 passengers and are filled with diversions.

If you're into big, bold, brassy, and nonstop activity, these huge ships offer it all. The centerpiece of most mega-ships is a 3-, 5-, or even 11-story central atrium. However, these giant vessels are most readily distinguished by their profile: the boxy hull and superstructure rise as many as 14 stories and are capped by a huge sun- or sports deck with a jogging track and one or more swimming pools. Some mega-ships have a traditional wraparound promenade deck. Picture windows are stan-dard equipment, and cabins in the top categories have private veran-dahs. From their casinos and discos to their fitness centers, everything is bigger and more extravagant than on other ships. You may want to rethink a cruise aboard one of these ships if you want a little downtime, since you'll be joined by 1,500 to 5,400 fellow passengers.

OTHER CRUISE LINES

A few small cruise lines sail through the Caribbean and offer boutique to nearly bed-and-breakfast experiences. Notably, Windstar Cruises and Star Clippers appeal to passengers who eschew mainstream cruises. Most of these niche vessels accommodate 200 or fewer passengers, and their focus is on soft adventure. Cruising between nearby ports and anchor-ing out so passengers can swim and snorkel directly from the ship, their itineraries usually leave plenty of time for exploring and other activities on- or offshore. Many of these cruises schedule casual enrichment talks that often continue on decks, at meals, and during trips ashore.

AZAMARA CLUB CRUISES

"The adventuresome (yet pampered) soul has met its match" is the new slogan for this ultra-premium cruise line launched by parent company Royal Caribbean in 2007. The line comprises two ships, both built for now-defunct Renaissance Cruises and refitted for the deluxe-cruise crowd. Designed for exotic, destination-driven itineraries, Azamara offers a more intimate onboard experience, while allowing access to the more unusual ports of call experienced travelers want to visit. Since its launch, a number of amenities have been added to passengers' fares, with no charge for bottled water, specialty coffees and teas; shuttle bus service to/from port communities (where available); house wine served at lunches and dinners; and complimentary self-service laundry.

Enrichment programs, from culinary demonstrations to seminars by guest speakers and experts on a wide variety of topics, are some of the best on offer. The ships are designated resort casual, so there is no neces-sity to weigh down your luggage with formal attire—even though your butler is on hand to unpack for you if you have booked a suite. Evening entertainment leans toward sophisticated cabaret and jazz. Azamara ships are some of the most smoke-free at sea. Only a single small section in a forward area of the pool deck is designated for smokers. No other areas on the ships allow smoking, including cabins and balconies.

Your Shipmates. Azamara is designed to appeal to discerning travelers, primarily American couples of any age who appreciate a high level of service in an unstructured atmosphere. The ships are not family-oriented and do not have facilities or programs for children.

Food. Expect all the classic dinner favorites but with an upscale twist, such as gulf shrimp with cognac and garlic, or a filet mignon with black-truffle sauce. In addition to the open-seating main dining room, each Azamara ship offers two specialty restaurants: the Mediterranean-influenced Aqualina and the stylish steak-and-seafood restaurant Prime C. Specialty dining is complimentary for suite guests throughout the sailing (including Club World Owner's Suites, Club Ocean Suites, and Club Continent Suites). Guests in all other accommodations categories pay a $25 per person cover charge for specialty dining. Seating is on a space-available basis, and reservations are encouraged once on board. Daily in-cabin afternoon tea service and delivery of canapés are available to all passengers.

Fitness and Recreation. In addition to a well-equipped gym and an outdoor jogging track, Azamara's fitness program includes yoga at sunset, Pilates, and access to an onboard wellness consultant. Both ships offer a full menu of spa treatments, an outdoor spa relaxation lounge, and an aesthetics suite featuring acupuncture, laser hair removal, and micro-dermabrasion.

Service and Tipping. Gracious and polished service throughout the ships affords everyone an exclusive experience. Butler service is available for suite guests. Housekeeping and dining gratuities are included in the fare. A standard 18% gratuity is added to beverage charges and for spa services.

Contact **Azamara Club Cruises** ☎ 877/999–9553
⊕ www.azamaraclubcruises.com.

CARNIVAL CRUISE LINES

☾ The world's largest cruise line originated the "Fun Ship" concept in 1972 with the relaunch of an aging ocean liner that got stuck on a sandbar during its maiden voyage. Sporting red, white, and blue flared funnels, which are easily recognized from afar, new ships are continuously added to the fleet and rarely deviate from a successful pattern. Decor tends to be over the top, though an ongoing renovation plan is toning down the decor; each ship features themed public rooms and huge casinos, spas, and lavish entertainment in massive show lounges.

Cabins are spacious and comfortable, often larger than on other ships in this price category, and feature the "Carnival Comfort Bed" sleep system consisting of plush mattresses, luxury duvets, high-quality linens, and cushy pillows. Ship decor on many ships is undergoing a softening and modernizing while new features including a new pub, rum- and tequila-based pool bars, a Guy Fieri hamburger restaurant, and comedy brunch are being added to most ships.

Your Shipmates. Carnival's passengers are predominantly active Americans, mostly couples in their mid-30s to mid-50s. Many families enjoy Carnival cruises in the Caribbean year-round. Holidays and school vacation periods are very popular with families, and you'll see a lot of kids in summer. An estimated 670,000 children sailed on Carnival ships in 2011—a sixfold increase in the past decade.

Food. Carnival ships have both flexible dining options and casual alternative restaurants. While the tradition of two set mealtimes for dinner prevails on Carnival ships, the line's experiment with an open-seating concept—Your Time Dining—proved so successful that it has been implemented fleetwide. A specialty steakhouse restaurant on some ships requires a reservation and a $35 per person cover charge; other ships also have an Italian specialty restaurant with a $12 cover charge (complimentary for lunch).

Fitness and Recreation. Manned by staff members trained to keep passengers in shipshape form, Carnival's trademark spas and fitness centers are some of the largest and best equipped at sea. Spas and salons are operated by Steiner Leisure, and treatments include a variety of massages, body wraps, and facials; salons offer hair and nail services. Tooth whitening is a recent addition to the roster. Fitness centers have state-of-the-art cardio and strength-training equipment, a jogging track, and basic exercise classes at no charge. There's a fee for personal training, body-composition analysis, and specialized classes such as yoga and Pilates.

Service and Tipping. Service on Carnival ships is friendly but not polished. Stateroom attendants are not only recognized for their attention to cleanliness, but also for their expertise in creating towel animals that appear most nights during turn-down service. A gratuity of $11.50 per passenger, per day is automatically added to passenger accounts, and gratuities are distributed to stewards and waitstaff. Passengers may adjust the amount based on the level of service experienced. All beverage tabs at bars get an automatic 15% addition.

Contact **Carnival Cruise Lines** ☎ *305/599–2600 or 800/227–6482* ⊕ *www.carnival.com.*

CELEBRITY CRUISES

Founded in 1989, Celebrity has gained a reputation for fine food and professional service. The cruise line has built premium, sophisticated ships and developed signature amenities, including a specialty coffee shop, martini bar, large standard staterooms with generous storage, spas, and butler service for passengers booking the top suites. ConciergeClass makes certain premium ocean-view and balcony staterooms almost the equivalent of suites in terms of amenities and service.

Entertainment choices range from Broadway-style productions, captivating lounge shows, and lively discos to Monte Carlo–style casinos and specialty lounges. Multimillion-dollar art collections grace the entire fleet, which merged with Royal Caribbean International in 1997.

Your Shipmates. Celebrity caters to Americans, primarily couples from their mid-30s to mid-50s. During summer months and holiday periods you'll see many families with kids aboard. Each vessel has a dedicated playroom and offers planned activities for children and teens ages 3 to 17, plus Toddler Time for parents and their children under age 3. Some activities have additional fees; evening in-cabin babysitting can also be arranged for a fee.

Food. In early 2007 Celebrity announced plans to advance its already distinguished fleetwide culinary program to the next level. Each ship in the fleet has highly experienced teams headed by executive chefs and food and beverage managers, who have developed their skills in some of the world's finest restaurants and hotels. Although the tradition of two set mealtimes for dinner is still popular on Celebrity ships, the line has introduced an open-seating concept fleet-wide. Alternative restaurants offer fine dining in classic ocean-liner splendor, but most have a $40 per person supplement, much higher than on most cruise lines.

Fitness and Recreation. Celebrity's fitness centers and AquaSpa by Elemis are some of the most tranquil and nicely equipped at sea. State-of-the-art exercise equipment, a jogging track, and some fitness classes are available at no charge. Spa treatments include a variety of massages, body wraps, and facials. Each ship has an Acupuncture at Sea program administered by a specialist in Oriental medicine. Hair and nail services are offered in the salons.

Service and Tipping. Service on Celebrity ships is unobtrusive and polished. ConciergeClass adds an unexpected level of service and amenities that are usually reserved for passengers in top-category suites on other premium cruise lines. Gratuities, which may be adjusted, are automatically added to your onboard account on a daily basis in the following amounts: $11.50 per person per day for passengers in staterooms; $12 per person per day for passengers in ConciergeClass and AquaClass staterooms; and $15 per person per day for passengers in suites. An automatic gratuity of 15% is added to all beverage tabs.

Contact **Celebrity Cruises** ☎ *800/647–2251* ⊕ *www.celebritycruises.com.*

COSTA CRUISES

The Genoa-based Costa Crociere, parent company of Costa Cruises, had been in the shipping business for more than 100 years and in the passenger business for almost 50 years when Carnival Corporation gained sole ownership of the line in 2000, but the ships retain their original flavor. Costa's Italian-inspired vessels bring the Mediterranean vitality of *La Dolce Vita* to far-flung regions of the Caribbean. The ships are a combination of classic and modern design. A new vessel-building program has brought Costa ships into the 21st century with innovative, large-ship designs that reflect their Italian heritage and style without overlooking the amenities expected by modern cruisers.

Festive shipboard activities include games of boccie and a wacky toga party, yet there is also a nod to the traditional cruise-ship entertainment expected by North Americans. Supercharged social staffs work overtime to get everyone in the mood and encourage everyone to be a part of the action.

Your Shipmates. Passengers tend to be a little older than average—the average age is 54—and have an interest in all things Italian. Up to 80% of passengers are North Americans, and many of them are of Italian descent. You don't find a lot of first-time cruisers on Costa ships. Youth programs provide daily age-appropriate activities for children age 3 to 17. Group evening babysitting for youngsters ages 3 and up (children must be toilet trained) is available on request for a fee.

Food. Dining features regional Italian cuisines, a variety of pastas, chicken, beef, and seafood dishes, as well as authentic pizza. Costa dining is notable for its delicious, properly prepared pasta courses. Vegetarian and healthy diet choices are also offered. Alternative dining is by reservation only in the upscale supper clubs, which serve choice steaks and seafood from a Tuscan steakhouse menu as well as traditional Italian specialties. Costa chefs continue to celebrate the tradition of lavish late-night buffets during Caribbean cruises.

Fitness and Recreation. Costa places continuing emphasis on wellness and sybaritic pleasures. Spa treatments include a variety of massages, body wraps, and facials. Hair and nail services are available in the salons. State-of-the-art exercise equipment in the terraced gym, a jogging track, and basic fitness classes for all levels of ability are available.

Service and Tipping. Service in dining areas can be spotty and rushed, but is adequate—if not always overly friendly. Gratuities are added to onboard accounts in the following amounts: $11 per adult per day; 50% of that amount for teens between the ages of 14 and 17; and no charge for children under the age of 14. A 15% gratuity is automatically added to all beverage tabs.

Contact Costa Cruises ☏ *954/266–5600 or 800/462–6782* ⊕ *www.costacruises.com.*

CRYSTAL CRUISES

Crystal's midsize ships stand out for their modern design, amenities, and spaciousness. Built to deliver the first-rate service and amenities expected from a luxury line, including complimentary wines and premium spirits throughout the ships and open bar service in all lounges, these vessels nevertheless carry upward of 900 passengers—and have many big-ship facilities. Beginning with ship designs based on the principles of feng shui, no detail is too small to overlook to provide passengers with the best imaginable experience.

Crystal ships have long set standards for pampering—one reason these vessels often spend several days at sea rather than in port. To the typical litany of cruise-ship diversions, Crystal adds enrichment opportunities that include destination-oriented lectures and talks by scholars, political figures, and diplomats; hands-on classes in music and art; and deluxe theme cruises that emphasize such topics as food and wine or the fine arts. In 2012, Crystal became one of the last of the luxury lines to go all-inclusive

Your Shipmates. Affluent, well-traveled couples, from their late-30s to retirees, are typical. Although the cruises are adult-oriented, there are dedicated facilities for children from 3 to 17 that are staffed for some sailings, especially during holiday periods and the summer season; however, Crystal limits the number of children under 3 and does not allow infants less than 6 months of age.

Food. The food is a good enough reason to book a Crystal cruise. Dining in the main restaurants is an event starring Continental-inspired cuisine served by European-trained waiters. Off-menu requests are honored when possible, and special dietary considerations are handled with ease. Unlike most luxury lines, Crystal still offers two assigned dinner seatings in the main restaurant. Happily, a flexible option is now offered—with Open Dining by Reservation you may reserve a table in the dining room at the time of your choice each night of your cruise. Casual poolside dining from the grills is offered on some evenings in a relaxed, no-reservations-required option. A variety of hot and cold hors d'oeuvres ia served in bars and lounges every evening before dinner and again during the wee hours. Where service and the dishes really shine are in the specialty restaurants; each ship has Asian-inspired and Italian specialty restaurants, which are in high demand.

Fitness and Recreation. Large spas offer innovative treatments. Fitness centers feature a range of exercise and weight-training equipment and workout areas for aerobics classes, plus complimentary yoga and Pilates. Utilizing Le Monde Life Fitness bikes, Crystal ships offer "Tour de Spin," a complimentary indoor cycling program. In addition, golfers enjoy extensive shipboard facilities, including a driving-range practice cage and putting green.

Service and Tipping. Crystal's European-trained staff members provide gracious service in an unobtrusive manner. Penthouse accommodations include personal butler service. Effective in spring 2012, housekeeping and dining gratuities are included in the fare. A 15% gratuity is suggested for spa and beauty treatments.

Contact **Crystal Cruises** ☎ *310/785–9300 or 888/799–4625* ⊕ *www.crystalcruises.com.*

CUNARD LINE

One of the world's most distinguished names in ocean travel since 1840, Cunard Line has a history of deluxe transatlantic crossings and worldwide cruising that is legendary for comfortable accommodations, excellent cuisine, and personal service. Though the line is now owned by Carnival Corporation, its high-end ships retain a distinctly British sensibility. Cunard offers a short season of Caribbean cruises, which are highly prized by fans of the line.

Entertainment includes nightly production shows or cabaret-style performances and even plays. An authentic pub adds to the British ambience, while a wide variety of musical styles can be found for dancing and listening in other bars and lounges. Cunard's fine enrichment programs are presented by expert guest lecturers. You can preplan your activities prior to departure by consulting the syllabus of courses available online at Cunard Line's website.

Your Shipmates. Discerning, well-traveled British and American couples from their late-30s to retirees are drawn to Cunard's traditional style. The availability of spacious accommodations and complimentary self-service laundry facilities makes Cunard liners a good option for families, but the number of kids on board is usually fairly limited. Kid-friendly features include a dedicated play area for children 1 to 6. Separate programs are reserved for older children ages 7 to 12 and teens up to 17. Toddlers are supervised by English nannies, and complimentary group babysitting is available in the evenings.

Food. In the tradition of multiclass ocean liners, dining-room assignments are made according to the accommodation category booked, so you get the luxury you pay for. Passengers in Junior Suites are assigned to single-seating Princess Grill, while the posh Queen's Grill serves passengers booked in the most lavish suites. Some balcony accommodations receive single-seating Britannia Club dining assignments, all other passengers dine in one of two seatings in the dramatic Britannia Restaurant. Menus also include vegetarian and low-calorie selections. Specialty restaurants require reservations, and there is an additional charge.

Fitness and Recreation. Swimming pools, golf driving ranges, table tennis, paddle tennis, shuffleboard, and jogging tracks barely scratch the surface of onboard facilities dedicated to recreation. Fitness centers offer high-tech workout equipment, a separate weight room, and classes ranging from aerobics to healthy living workshops. The spas are top-notch, with a long menu of treatments and salon services for women and men.

Service and Tipping. Service is formal and sophisticated. Suggested gratuities of $13 per person per day (for Grill Restaurant accommodations) or $11 per person per day (all other accommodations) are automatically charged to shipboard accounts. A 15% gratuity is added to bar tabs. Direct gratuities for special service are allowed.

Contact **Cunard Line** ☎ *661/753–1000 or 800/728–6273* ⊕ *www.cunard.com.*

DISNEY CRUISE LINE

Disney Cruise Line launched its ships in 1998 and 1999, and expanded the fleet with a third ship in 2011; a fourth entered service in 2012. Dozens of the best ship designers, industry veterans, and Disney creative minds planned intensely for multiple years to produce these vessels, which make a positive impression on adults and children alike. Exteriors are reminiscent of the great ocean liners of the early 20th century, resplendent with two funnels and black hulls, but interiors are technologically up-to-the-minute and full of novel developments in dining, cabin, and entertainment facilities. Accommodations are especially family-friendly, and most have a split-bathroom configuration with a sink and bathtub in one section and a sink and toilet in the other.

Entertainment leans heavily on popular Disney themes and characters. Parents are actively involved in the audience with their children at shows, movies, "live" character meetings, deck parties, and dancing in the family nightclub. Teens have a supervised, no-adults-allowed club space. For adults, there are no-kids-allowed bars and lounges with live music, dancing, theme parties, and late-night comedy as well as daytime wine-tasting sessions, game shows, culinary-arts and home-entertaining demonstrations, and behind-the-scenes lectures.

Your Shipmates. The young and not so young all find Disney Cruises appealing. Multigenerational family groups are the core clientele for these ships. As expected, Disney ships have extensive, age-appropriate programs for children and teens. A nursery for infants as young as 3 months is available for an hourly fee, and the diapers you supply will be changed by attendants—a service not available on most cruise lines. You might be surprised at the number of honeymooners on board.

Food. Don't expect top chefs and gourmet food; the fare is all-American for the most part. Naturally, all restaurants have children's menus. In a novel twist on dining, passengers "rotate" between theme dining rooms, accompanied each night by their waitstaff. Palo, the adults-only Italian restaurant on each ship, requires reservations and has a cover charge. Similarly, adults on Disney Dream and Disney Fantasy can opt for specialty dining in Remy, Disney's first-ever premier dining restaurant serving French-inspired cuisine. Unlike on many cruise lines, fountain drinks at beverage stations and in dining rooms are complimentary.

Fitness and Recreation. Three swimming pools are designated for different groups: children, families, and adults. The salon and spa rival any afloat. Introduced on Disney ships are Spa Villas, indoor/outdoor treatment suites, each with a veranda with a hot tub and open-air shower. In addition to a nicely equipped fitness center and aerobics studio are a jogging track and basketball court.

Service and Tipping. Service is friendly, and particular importance is placed on treating children with the same courtesy extended to adults. Suggested gratuities are calculated on a per-person/per-cruise basis, and can be added to onboard accounts or offered in cash on the last night. For the dining-room server, assistant server, head server, and stateroom host/hostess, guidelines are $36 for three-night cruises, $48 for four-night cruises, and $84 for seven-night cruises. A 15% gratuity is added to bar service tabs.

Contact **Disney Cruise Line** ☎ *407/566–3500 or 888/325–2500* ⊕ *www.disneycruise.com.*

HOLLAND AMERICA LINE

Founded in 1873, Holland America Line (HAL) is one of the oldest names in cruising. Its cruises are classic, conservative affairs renowned for their grace and gentility. As its ships attract a more youthful clientele, Holland America has taken steps to shed its "old folks" image, now offering stops at a private island in the Bahamas, trendier cuisine, a culinary arts center, and an expanded children's program. Still, these are not party cruises, and Holland America has managed to preserve the refined and relaxing qualities that have always been its hallmark, even on sailings that cater more to younger passengers and families.

Luxury bedding, magnifying makeup mirrors, robes, fresh-fruit baskets, flat-screen TVs, and DVD players are found in all cabins. In addition, suites have duvets, fully stocked minibars, personalized stationery, and access to the exclusive Neptune Lounge. Explorations Café, powered by the *New York Times,* combines a coffee bar, computer center with Wi-Fi, and cozy library–reading room complete with tabletop versions of the *Times*' crossword puzzles.

Your Shipmates. No longer your grandparents' cruise line, today's Holland America also attracts families and discerning couples, mostly from their late 30s and up. Retirees are often still in the majority; however, during holidays and summer months you'll find more families with kids. Group activities are planned for children ages 3 to 7 and 8 to 12 in Club HAL. After Hours offers late-night activities from 10 pm until midnight for an hourly fee. Teens ages 13 to 17 have their own lounge with activities.

Food. You have your choice of two assigned seatings or open seating for evening meals in the formal dining room. In the reservations-required Pinnacle Grill alternative restaurant ($25 dinner; $10 lunch), fresh seafood and premium cuts of beef are used to prepare creative specialty dishes. On Signature-class ships, Tamarind offers Pan-Asian fare by reservation; there is a charge for dinner ($15), but lunch is complimentary. Delicious onboard traditions include afternoon tea, a Dutch Chocolate Extravaganza, and Holland America Line's signature bread pudding. Casual evening dining in the Lido restaurants offers a combination of buffet and waiter service. A portion of the Lido restaurant is transformed nightly into Canaletto, a complimentary casual Italian restaurant that requires reservations.

Fitness and Recreation. Well-equipped and fully staffed fitness facilities contain state-of-the-art exercise equipment; basic fitness classes are available at no charge, though you pay for personal training, yoga, and Pilates. You'll also find a jogging track, multiple swimming pools, and sports courts. Promenade decks encircle each ship and are popular for walking. The Greenhouse Spa offers a variety of treatments and salon services.

Service and Tipping. Professional, unobtrusive service by the Indonesian and Filipino staff is a fleetwide standard on Holland America Line. A standard gratuity of $12 per passenger per day (suite guests) or $11.50 per day (all other guests) is automatically added to shipboard accounts and is distributed to stewards and waitstaff. Room-service tips are offered in cash. An automatic 15% gratuity is added to bar-service tabs.

Contact **Holland America Line** ☎ *206/281–3535 or 800/577–1728* ⊕ *www.hollandamerica.com.*

MSC CRUISES

With several seasons of Caribbean sailing behind them, MSC Cruises has outgrown its newcomer status. More widely known as one of the world's largest cargo shipping companies, parent company Mediterranean Shipping Company has operated cruises with an eclectic fleet since the late 1980s, but expanded its cruising reach by introducing graceful, modern ships in the Caribbean.

While sailing Caribbean itineraries, MSC Cruises adopts activities that appeal to American passengers without abandoning those preferred by Europeans—prepare for announcements in several languages. In addition to trivia games, bingo, and cooking demonstrations, a popular option is Italian language classes. Nightly shows accentuate MSC Cruises' Mediterranean heritage—there might be an opera presentation in the main showroom and live music in the smaller lounges.

Your Shipmates. On Caribbean itineraries you will find most of your fellow passengers are American couples in the 35- to 55-year-old range and families. Children ages 3 to 17 are welcome to participate in age-appropriate youth programs; the Teenage Club is for youths 13 years and older.

Food. Dinner on MSC ships is centered around authentic Italian fare. Menus list Mediterranean regional specialties and classic favorites prepared from scratch. "Healthy Choice" and vegetarian items are offered as well as sugar-free desserts. In a nod to American tastes, chicken, sirloin steak, grilled salmon, and Caesar salad are always available in addition to the regular dinner menu. A daily highlight is the bread and pasta, freshly made on board, and authentic Italian pizza that is the best at sea. Midnight buffets are a retro food feature missing from most of today's cruises. Alternative restaurants are featured throughout the fleet, but vary by ship class. Coffee bars and ice-cream bars charge for specialty coffee drinks and frozen treats.

Fitness and Recreation. Up-to-date exercise equipment, a jogging track, and basic fitness classes for all levels are available. Spa treatments include a variety of massages, body wraps, and facials that can be scheduled à la carte or combined in packages to encompass an afternoon or the entire cruise.

Service and Tipping. Service can be inconsistent, but is more than acceptable—if not overly gracious. The mainly Italian staff are sometimes still befuddled by American habits and expectations. Customary gratuities are automatically charged to onboard accounts in the amount of $12 per person per day for adults and $6 for children. A 15% bar service charge is added to all bar purchases.

Contact MSC Cruises ☎ *800/666–9333* ⊕ *www.msccruisesusa.com.*

NORWEGIAN CRUISE LINE

Norwegian Cruise Line (NCL) was established in 1966, when one of Norway's oldest and most respected shipping companies, Oslo-based Klosters Rederi A/S, acquired the *Sunward* and repositioned the ship from Europe to the then-obscure Port of Miami. With the formation of a company called Norwegian Caribbean Lines, the cruise industry as we know it today was born. NCL launched an entirely new concept with its regularly scheduled cruises to the Caribbean on a single-class ship. No longer simply a means of transportation, the ship became a destination unto itself, offering guests an affordable alternative to land-based resorts.

Always a cruise-industry innovator, Norwegian Cruise Line's "Free-style" cruising introduced a wider variety of dining options in a casual, free-flowing atmosphere. Noted for top-quality, high-energy entertainment and emphasis on fitness facilities and programs, NCL combines action, activities, and a resort-casual atmosphere.

Your Shipmates. NCL's mostly American cruise passengers are active couples ranging from their mid-30s to mid-50s; some passengers may be in the over-55 age group. Many families enjoy cruising on NCL ships during summer months. Each NCL vessel offers the "Kid's Crew" program of supervised entertainment for young cruisers ages 2 to 17. For 13- to 17-year-olds there are clubs where they can hang out in adult-free zones.

Food. Main dining rooms serve what is traditionally deemed Continental fare, although it's about what you would expect at a really good hotel banquet. Where NCL stands above the ordinary is in their specialty restaurants, especially the French–Mediterranean Le Bistro (on all ships), the Pan-Asian restaurants, and steak houses (on the newer ships). In addition, you may find a Spanish tapas bar and an Italian trattoria. Most, but not all, specialty restaurants carry a cover charge and require reservations. An NCL staple, the late-night Chocoholic Buffet continues to be a favorite event.

Fitness and Recreation. Mandara Spa offers a long list of unusual and exotic spa treatments fleet-wide on NCL. State-of-the-art exercise equipment, jogging tracks, and basic fitness classes are available at no charge. There's a fee for personal training and specialized classes such as yoga and Pilates.

Service and Tipping. Although somewhat inconsistent, service is nonetheless congenial. A fixed service charge of $12 per person per day is added to shipboard accounts for passengers age 3 and up. An automatic 15% gratuity is added to bar tabs and 18% for spa services. Staff members are permitted to accept cash gratuities. Passengers in suites are asked to offer a cash gratuity to their concierge and butlers.

Contact **Norwegian Cruise Line** ☎ *305/436–4000 or 800/327-7030* ⊕ *www.ncl.com.*

OCEANIA CRUISES

This distinctive cruise line, founded by cruise-industry veterans with the know-how to satisfy inquisitive passengers with interesting ports of call and upscale touches for fares much lower than you would expect, is now owned by Prestige Cruise Holdings. Oceania uses mid-size "R-class" ships from the now-defunct Renaissance Cruises fleet, and launched a new ship class in winter 2011. Varied, destination-rich itineraries are an important characteristic of Oceania Cruises, and most Caribbean sailings are in the 10- to 12-night range. Before arrival in ports of call, lectures are presented on the historical background, culture, and traditions of the islands.

Intimate and cozy public spaces reflect the importance of socializing on Oceania ships. Evening entertainment leans toward light cabaret, solo artists, music for dancing, and conversation with fellow passengers; however, you'll find lively karaoke sessions as well. On sea days jazz or easy-listening melodies are played poolside.

Your Shipmates. Oceania Cruises appeal to singles and couples from their late-30s to well-traveled retirees who have the time for and prefer longer cruises. Most are attracted to the casually refined atmosphere, creative cuisine, and European service. Oceania Cruises are adult-oriented and not a good choice for most families; there are no dedicated children's facilities.

Food. Master chef Jacques Pépin designed the menus for Oceania, and the results are sure to please the most discriminating palate. Oceania simply serves some of the best food at sea, particularly impressive for a cruise line that charges far less than luxury rates. The main open-seating restaurant offers trendy French-Continental cuisine with an always-on-the-menu steak, seafood, or poultry choice and vegetarian option. Intimate specialty restaurants require reservations, but there is no additional charge.

Fitness and Recreation. Although small, the spa, salon, and well-equipped fitness center on Regatta-class ships are adequate for the number of passengers on board. There is a walking/jogging track circling the top of the ship. The Canyon Ranch SpaClub treatment menus list massages, body wraps, and facials. Forward of the locker rooms you will find a large therapy pool and quiet deck for relaxation and sunning on padded wooden steamer chaises.

Service and Tipping. Highly personalized service by a mostly European staff is crisp and efficient without being intrusive. Butlers are on hand to satisfy the needs of suite guests and will even assist with packing and unpacking upon request. A charge of $14.50 per person per day is added to onboard accounts, and an additional $6 per person per day is added for suite occupants with butler service. An 18% gratuity is automatically added to all beverage purchases and spa and salon services.

Contact **Oceania Cruises** ☎ *305/514–2300 or 800/531–5658* ⊕ *www.oceaniacruises.com.*

PRINCESS CRUISES

Rising from modest beginnings in 1965, when it began offering cruises to Mexico with a single ship, Princess has become one of the world's best-known cruise lines. Catapulted to stardom in 1977, when its flagship became the setting for *The Love Boat* television series, Princess introduced millions of viewers to the still-new concept of a seagoing vacation. Although the line does have some medium-size vessels, Princess more often follows the "bigger is better" trend. Its fleet sails to more destinations each year than any other major line.

All Princess ships feature the line's innovative "Personal Choice Cruising" program that gives passengers choice and flexibility in customizing their cruise experience—multiple dining locations, flexible entertainment, and affordable private balconies are all highlights. Enrichment programs feature guest lecturers and opportunities to learn new skills

Drinking and Gambling Ages

Many underage passengers have learned to their chagrin that the rules that apply on land are also adhered to at sea. On most mainstream cruise ships you must be 21 in order to imbibe alcoholic beverages. There are exceptions—for instance, on cruises departing from countries where the legal drinking age is typically lower than 21. By and large, if you haven't achieved the magic age of 21, your shipboard charge card will be coded as booze-free, and bartenders won't risk their jobs to sell you alcohol.

Gambling is a bit looser, and 18-year-olds can try their luck on cruise lines such as Carnival, Celebrity, Azamara, Silversea, Norwegian, and Royal Caribbean; most other cruise lines adhere to the age-21 minimum. Casinos are trickier to patrol than bars, though, and minors who look "old enough" may get away with dropping a few coins in an out-of-the-way slot machine before being spotted on a hidden security camera. If you hit a big jackpot, you may have a lot of explaining to do to your parents.

or crafts, but you'll still find staples such as bingo and art auctions. You can even earn PADI scuba-diving certification in just one week during select sailings.

Your Shipmates. Princess Cruises attract mostly American passengers ranging from their mid-30s to mid-50s. Longer cruises appeal to well-traveled retirees. Families can be found cruising together on the Princess fleet, particularly during summer months, when many children are on board. For young passengers ages 3 to 17, each Princess vessel (except Ocean and Pacific Princess) allows parents independent time ashore, and youth centers operate as usual during port days.

Food. Personal choices regarding where and what to eat abound, but unless you opt for traditional assigned seating, you might have a short wait for a table in one of the open-seating dining rooms. Menus are varied and extensive, and the results are good to excellent. A special menu is designed for children. Alternative restaurants are a staple throughout the fleet, but vary by ship class. Lido buffets on all ships are almost always open, and a pizzeria and grill offer casual daytime snack choices. The fleet's patisseries and ice-cream bars charge for specialty coffee, special pastries, and ice-cream treats. With balcony accommodations, you can enjoy a private Champagne Breakfast or Ultimate Balcony Dinner.

Fitness and Recreation. Spa and salon rituals include massages, body wraps, facials, and numerous hair and nail services, including treatments designed specifically for men, teens, and couples. Modern exercise equipment, a jogging track, and basic fitness classes are available at no charge. Grand-class ships have a resistance pool for lap swimming.

Service and Tipping. Professional service by an international staff is efficient and friendly. Princess suggests tipping $12 per person per day for passengers in suites and minisuites and $11.50 per person per day for all other passengers (including children). Gratuities are automatically added to onboard accounts; spa personnel are tipped at your discretion; 15% is added to bar bills.

Contact **Princess Cruises** ☎ 661/753–0000 or 800/774–6237 ⊕ *www.princess.com.*

REGENT SEVEN SEAS CRUISES

Regent Seven Seas Cruises sails an elegant fleet of vessels that offer a nearly all-inclusive cruise experience (including shore excursions) in sumptuous, contemporary surroundings. The line's spacious ocean-view staterooms have the industry's highest percentage of private balconies, and almost all drinks (except some premium brands) are now included.

Subtle improvements throughout the fleet have resulted in features such as computer service with Wi-Fi capability for your own laptop and cell phone access. New luxury bedding, Regent-branded bath amenities, flat-screen TVs, DVD players, and new clocks have been added to all cabins. Top suites also feature iPods and Bose speakers. Delightful ships feature exquisite service, generous staterooms with abundant amenities, a variety of dining options, and superior enrichment programs. Cruises are destination-focused, and most sailings host guest lecturers—historians, anthropologists, naturalists, and diplomats.

Your Shipmates. Regent Seven Seas Cruises are inviting to active, affluent, well-traveled couples ranging from their late 30s to retirees who enjoy the ships' elegance and destination-rich itineraries. Longer cruises attract passengers in the over-60 age group. Regent vessels are adult-oriented and do not have dedicated children's facilities; however, youth programs are offered on some sailings.

Food. Menus may appear to include the usual cruise-ship staples, but the results are some of the most outstanding meals at sea. Specialty dining varies within the fleet; when available, the sophisticated Signatures features the cuisine of Le Cordon Bleu of Paris; Prime 7 offers menus that rival the finest shoreside steak and seafood restaurants. In addition, Mediterranean-inspired bistro dinners are served in the daytime casual Lido buffet restaurants. Wines chosen to complement dinner menus are freely poured each evening.

Fitness and Recreation. Although gyms and exercise areas are well equipped, these are not large ships, so the facilities tend to be on the small side. Each ship has a jogging track, and the larger ones feature a variety of sports courts. The spas and salons are operated by the legendary Canyon Ranch SpaClub.

Service and Tipping. The efforts of a polished European staff go almost unnoticed, yet special requests are handled with ease. Butlers provide an additional layer of personal service to guests in the top-category suites. Gratuities are included in the fare, and none are expected. Passengers are allowed to donate to a crew welfare fund that benefits the ship's staff.

Contact **Regent Seven Seas Cruises** ☎ 954/776–6123 or 877/505–5370 ⊕ *www.rssc.com.*

ROYAL CARIBBEAN INTERNATIONAL

Big, bigger, biggest! More than a decade ago, Royal Caribbean launched the first of the modern mega-cruise ships for passengers who enjoy traditional cruising with a touch of daring and whimsy tossed in. These large-to-giant vessels are indoor–outdoor wonders, with every conceivable activity in a resortlike atmosphere, including atrium lobbies, shopping arcades, large spas, expansive sundecks, and rock-climbing walls. Several ships have such elaborate facilities as 18-hole miniature-golf courses, ice-skating rinks, and in-line skating tracks. Oasis-class ships, RCI's latest additions, and presently the world's largest cruise ships, even have surf parks and a zip-line at sea. Plush new bedding has been installed fleetwide.

The centerpiece of Royal Caribbean mega-ships is the multideck atrium, a hallmark that has been duplicated by many other cruise lines. The brilliance of this design is that all the major public rooms radiate from this central point, so you can learn your way around these huge ships within minutes of boarding. Ships in the Vision class are especially bright and airy, with sea views almost anywhere you happen to be. The main problem with RCI's otherwise well-conceived vessels is that there are often too many people on board, making embarkation, tendering, and disembarkation exasperating. However, Royal Caribbean is still one of the best-run and most popular cruise lines.

Your Shipmates. Royal Caribbean cruises have a broad appeal for active couples and singles, mostly in their 30s to 50s. Families are partial to the newer vessels that have larger staterooms, excellent kids' facilities, and seemingly endless choices of activities and dining options. Supervised age-appropriate activities are designed for children ages 3 through 17. For infants and toddlers 6 to 36 months of age, interactive playgroup sessions are planned; for teens, a separate area with a disco is an adult-free gathering spot. "Family-size" staterooms are available on most newer ships, but there are no self-service laundry facilities.

Food. Royal Caribbean offers the choice of an early or late dinner seating and an open-seating option that is available across the fleet. Windjammer Café and, on certain ships, the sunny Seaview Café or Park Café, are casual dining options. Each ship has a pizzeria, coffee bar, and ice-cream parlor, and Johnny Rockets 1950s-style diners (extra fee) can be found on most ships. Although Royal Caribbean doesn't place emphasis on celebrity chefs or specialty alternative restaurants, the line has introduced a more intimate dinner experience in the form of an Italian-specialty restaurant and a steak house on some ships. The Oasis-class ships feature two-dozen dining spots, ranging from a seafood café (*Oasis of the Seas*) or Mexican cantina (*Allure of the Seas*) and a cupcake bakery to more upscale specialty restaurants, many carrying extra charges.

Fitness and Recreation. Fabled for its range of top-of-the-line recreations, Royal Caribbean also delivers on the basics: most exercise classes, aimed at sweating off those extra calories, are included in the fare (although there's a fee for spinning, yoga, and Pilates classes, as well as personal training). Each ship has multiple swimming pools and a rock-climbing wall. Spas feature extensive treatment menus and full services for pampering adults and teens.

Service and Tipping. Service on Royal Caribbean ships is friendly but not consistent. Assigned meal seatings assure that most passengers get to know the waiters and their assistants, who in turn get to know the passengers' likes and dislikes; however, that can lead to a level of familiarity that some find uncomfortable. Tips can be prepaid when the cruise is booked, added onto shipboard accounts, or given in cash on the last night of the cruise. Suggested gratuities per passenger per day are: $5 for the cabin steward (or $7.25 for suite attendant); $3.75 for the waiter; $2.15 for the assistant waiter; and $0.75 for the head waiter. A 15% gratuity is automatically added to all bar tabs.

Contact **Royal Caribbean International** ☎ *305/539–6000 or 800/327–6700* ⊕ *www.royalcaribbean.com.*

SEABOURN CRUISE LINE

Ultraluxury pioneer Seabourn was founded on the principle that dedication to personal service in elegant surroundings would appeal to sophisticated, independent-minded passengers whose lifestyles demand the best. Its three nearly identical, all-suites ships received extensive makeovers in 2008, and were joined by newly launched larger vessels in 2009, 2010, and 2011. The "yachts" remain favorites with people who can take care of themselves but would rather do so aboard a luxury ship. Dining and evening socializing are generally more stimulating to Seabourn passengers than splashy song-and-dance reviews; however, proportionately scaled production and cabaret shows are presented in the main showroom and smaller lounge. The library stocks not only books but also movies.

You can expect complimentary wines and spirits, elegant amenities, and even the pleasure of minimassages while lounging poolside. Guest appearances by luminaries in the arts and world affairs highlight the enrichment program. Wine tasting, trivia contests, and other quiet pursuits might be scheduled, but most passengers prefer to simply do what pleases them.

Your Shipmates. Seabourn attracts mostly affluent, 50-plus and retired couples who are accustomed to evening formality. The ships are adult-oriented, with no children's programs or facilities, and are unable to accommodate children under 6 months (1 year for voyages of 15 days or longer).

Food. Exceptional cuisine is prepared to order and served in open-seating dining rooms. Creative menu offerings include foie gras, quail, and fresh seafood. Vegetarian dishes and offerings low in cholesterol, salt, and fat are prepared with the same care. Wines are chosen to complement each day's lunch and dinner menus, and caviar is always available. Evening dining alternatives include "Restaurant 2," which serves dinner nightly, and a second—even more laid-back—choice, the Grill on each ship serves sizzling steaks and seafood some nights on deck. Themed dining in The Colonnade, the casual daytime buffet restaurant, is available nightly on the trio of large ships. All require reservations but do not charge extra.

Past Passengers — An Exclusive Group

Your cruise is over—pat yourself on the back. Your plans and preparation for an out-of-the-ordinary trip have paid off, and you'll now have lasting memories of a great vacation. Before you even have a chance to fill your scrapbook, the cruise line wants you to consider doing it all over again. And why not? You're a seasoned sailor, so take advantage of your experience. To entice you back on a future cruise, you may find you're automatically a member of an exclusive club—Latitudes (Norwegian Cruise Line), Mariner Society (Holland America Line), Captain's Circle (Princess Cruises), Castaway Club (Disney Cruise Line), Venetian Society (Silversea Cruises), to name but a few. Members receive the cruise line's magazine for past passengers, exclusive offers, shipboard perks such as a repeaters' party hosted by the captain, and even members-only cruises.

Fitness and Recreation. Complimentary "massage moments" offered poolside are minipreviews of the soothing treatments available in the spa. A full array of cardio, strength, and weight-training equipment and basic fitness classes are available in the small gym, while some specialized fitness sessions are offered for a fee. The water-sports marina is popular with active passengers who want to jet-ski, windsurf, kayak, or swim in the integrated saltwater "pool" while anchored in calm waters.

Service and Tipping. Personal service and attention by the staff are the order of the day. Your preferences are noted and fulfilled without the necessity of reminders. Tipping is neither required nor expected.

Contact Seabourn Cruise Line ☎ *305/463–3000 or 800/929-9391* ⊕ *www.seabourn.com.*

SEADREAM YACHT CLUB

Launched in 1984 as Sea Goddess mega-yachts, these boutique ships have changed hands through the years, becoming SeaDream Yacht Club in 2002. Passengers enjoy an unstructured holiday at sea doing whatever pleases them, giving the diminutive vessels the feel of true private yachts with a select guest list. Other than a pianist in the tiny piano bar, a small casino, and movies in the main lounge, there is no roster of activities. The rocking late-night place to be is the Top of the Yacht Bar, where passengers gather to share the day's experiences and kick their shoes off to dance on the teak deck. The Captain hosts welcome-aboard and farewell cocktail receptions in the Main Salon each week. Otherwise, you are on your own to do as you please. A well-stocked library has books and movies for those who prefer quiet pursuits in the privacy of their staterooms.

Ports of call almost seem an intrusion on socializing amid the chic surroundings, although a picnic on a secluded beach adds the element of a private island paradise to each Caribbean cruise. While the ambience is sophisticated, all cruises are "yacht" casual, and you can leave your formal clothing at home. You can also leave your charge card in your pocket, as all beverages, including select wines and spirits, are complimentary.

Your Shipmates. SeaDream yachts appeal to energetic, affluent travelers of all ages, as well as groups. Passengers tend to be couples from 45-year-olds up to retirees. No children's facilities or organized activities are available, and these ships are not really suitable for passengers confined to wheelchairs. Although one stateroom on each vessel is designated "accessible," public facilities have thresholds, and the elevator doesn't reach the uppermost deck.

Food. Every meal is prepared to order using the freshest seafood and prime cuts of beef. Menus include vegetarian alternatives and Asian wellness cuisine for the health-conscious. Cheeses, petits fours, and chocolate truffles are offered with after-dinner coffee, and desserts are to die for. All meals are open seating, either in the main restaurant or, weather permitting, alfresco in the canopied Topsider Restaurant daily for breakfast, lunch, and special dinners. Wines are chosen to complement each luncheon and dinner menu.

Fitness and Recreation. Small gyms on each ship are equipped with treadmills, elliptical machines, recumbent bikes, and free weights. A personal trainer is available. SeaDream's unique Asian Spa facilities are also on the small side, yet offer a full menu of individualized gentle pampering treatments including massages, facials, and body wraps utilizing Eastern techniques. Mountain bikes are available for use ashore.

Service and Tipping. Personal service and attention to detail are amazing—you will be greeted by name within hours of boarding. Passenger preferences are shared among staff members who all work hard to assist one another. You seldom, if ever, have to repeat a request. Tipping is neither required nor expected.

Contact **SeaDream Yacht Club** ☎ 305/856–5622 or 800/707–4911 ⊕ www.seadreamyachtclub.com.

SILVERSEA CRUISES

Intimate ships, paired with exclusive amenities and unparalleled hospitality, are the hallmarks of Silversea luxury cruises. Personalization is a Silversea maxim. Ships offer more activities than other comparably sized luxury vessels, with guest lecturers on nearly every cruise. A multitiered show lounge is the setting for classical concerts, big-screen movies, and folkloric entertainers from ashore. All accommodations are spacious outside suites, most with private verandas. Silversea ships have large swimming pools in expansive Lidos. Silversea's third generation of ships introduced even more luxurious features when the 36,000-ton *Silver Spirit* launched late in 2009.

Although these ships schedule more activities than other comparably sized luxury vessels, you can either take part or opt instead for a good book and any number of quiet spots to read or snooze in the shade. Silversea is so all-inclusive that you'll find your room key/charge card is seldom used for anything but opening your suite door.

Your Shipmates. Silversea Cruises appeal to sophisticated, affluent couples who enjoy the country club–like atmosphere, exquisite cuisine, and polished service. You might see the occasional child, but children less than 6 months old are not permitted, and the cruise line limits the number of children under the age of 3 on board.

Food. Dishes from the galleys of Silversea's master chefs are complemented by those of La Collection du Monde, created by Silversea's culinary partner, the world-class chefs of Relais & Châteaux. Perhaps more compelling is the line's flair for originality. The pasta chef's daily special is a passenger favorite, as is the galley brunch, held just once each cruise, when the galley is transformed into a buffet restaurant. Special off-menu orders are prepared whenever possible. Nightly alternative-theme dinners in La Terrazza (by day, the buffet restaurant) feature regional specialties from the Mediterranean; an intimate dining experience aboard each vessel is Le Champagne—the Wine Restaurant, which is the only Relais & Châteaux restaurant at sea. *Silver Spirit* adds two additional dining options—Stars Supper Club, at no additional charge, and Asian-inspired Seishin Restaurant, for which there is a per-guest reservation fee.

Fitness and Recreation. The rather small gyms are well equipped with cardiovascular and weight-training equipment, and fitness classes are held in the mirror-lined, but somewhat confining, exercise room. South Pacific–inspired Mandara Spa offers numerous treatments, including exotic-sounding massages, facials, and body wraps.

Service and Tipping. Personalized service is exacting and hospitable, yet discreet; staff members strive for perfection and often achieve it. Personal preferences are remembered and satisfied. Tipping is neither required nor expected.

Contact Silversea Cruises ☏ *954/522–4477 or 800/722–9955* ⊕ *www.silversea.com.*

STAR CLIPPERS

In 1991 Star Clippers presented a new tall-ship alternative to sophisticated travelers looking for adventure at sea, but not on board a conventional cruise ship. Star Clippers vessels are the world's largest barkentine and full-rigged sailing ships—four- and five-masted sailing beauties filled with high-tech equipment as well as amenities more often found on private yachts. The ships rely on sail power while at sea unless conditions require the assistance of the engines. Minimum heeling, usually less than 6%, is achieved through judicious control of the sails.

Star Clippers are not cruise ships in the ordinary sense, with strict agendas and pages of activities. You can lounge on deck and simply soak in the nautical ambience or learn about navigational techniques from the captain. Cabins, which are very compact, do include such amenities as hair dryers, TVs, and telephones. Star Clippers ships also have swimming pools. Other features fall somewhere between those of a true sailing yacht and the high-tech Windstar ships. The differences are more than just in the level of luxury—Star Clippers are true sailing vessels. Prices, however, are a bit more affordable and often less than you would pay on a high-end cruise ship. Onboard accounts are charged in euros, even in the Caribbean.

Your Shipmates. Star Clippers cruises appeal to active, upscale American and European couples from their 30s on up who enjoy sailing, but in a casually sophisticated atmosphere with modern conveniences. Many sailings are split nearly equally between North American and European passengers. This is not a cruise line for the physically challenged; there are no elevators or ramps, nor are any staterooms or bathrooms wheelchair-accessible. Star Clippers ships are adult-oriented, and while children are allowed, there are no dedicated youth facilities.

Food. Not noted for gourmet fare, the international cuisine is what you would expect from a trendy shoreside bistro. Fresh fruits and fish are among the best choices from Star Clippers' galleys. In a nod to American tastes, dinner menus include an alternative steak selection. Lunch buffets are quite a spread of seafood, salads, and grilled items. Casual fare is offered for lunch or late-afternoon snacking on deck. Room service is only available to occupants of suites aboard *Royal Clipper.*

Fitness and Recreation. Formal exercise sessions take a backseat to water sports, although aerobics classes and swimming are featured on all ships. Only *Royal Clipper* has a marina platform that can be lowered in calm waters to access water sports and diving, however, the smaller ships replicate the experience by using launches. A gym/spa with an array of exercise equipment, free weights, spa treatments, and unisex hair services is found only on *Royal Clipper.*

Service and Tipping. Service is friendly and gracious, similar to what you would find in a boutique hotel or restaurant. Star Clippers recommends the following gratuities (always in euros): room steward, €3 per day; dining-room staff, €5 per day. Tips are pooled and shared; individual tipping is discouraged. A 15% gratuity is added to bar bills. Gratuities may be charged to your shipboard account.

Contact **Star Clippers** ☎ *305/442–0550 or 800/442–0551* ⊕ *www.starclippers.com.*

WINDSTAR CRUISES

Are they cruise ships with sails or sailing ships designed for cruises? In actuality they are masted sailing yachts, pioneers in the upscale sailing niche. Although the sails add speed, Windstar ships seldom depend on wind alone to sail. However, if you are fortunate and conditions are perfect, the total silence of pure sailing is a thrill. Although the ships' designs may be reminiscent of sailing vessels of yore, the amenities and shipboard service are among the best at sea.

In keeping with the line's exacting standards, all ocean-view staterooms and suites provide the comforts of home with sitting area, luxury linens and mattresses, DVD/CD player, Apple iPod nano and Bose Sound-Dock speakers, Wi-Fi, safe, minibar/refrigerator, international direct-dial phones, L'Occitane bath toiletries, hair dryer, plenty of closet space, and plush robes and slippers. An array of international newspapers, books, and games can be found in the library, and a wide selection of DVD titles and CDs is available for complimentary use. Life on board is unabashedly sybaritic, attracting a sophisticated, relatively young crowd who are happy to sacrifice bingo and pool games for the attractions of remote islands and water sports; even motorized water sports are included, and passengers pay extra only for scuba diving. Unfortunately, only basic beverages are included in the fare.

Your Shipmates. Windstar cruises appeal to upscale professional couples in their late 30s to 60s. These ships are especially popular with honeymooners. The ships were not designed for accessibility, and are not a good choice for the physically challenged. *Wind Surf*, for example, has only two elevators, and the smaller ships have none. There are no staterooms or bathrooms deemed "accessible," and gangways can be difficult to navigate, depending on the tide and angle of ascent. The unregimented atmosphere is adult-oriented; children are not encouraged, and there are no dedicated children's facilities.

Food. Windstar menus feature dishes with tropical accents, using fresh local ingredients whenever possible. In a nod to healthful dining, low-calorie and low-fat spa cuisine and vegetarian dishes are always available in the open-seating restaurants. A mid-cruise deck barbecue featuring grilled seafood and other favorites is offered on all cruises. Aboard *Wind Surf*, the specialty restaurant Degrees features themed dinners such as Italian, Indonesian, and Steak House at no additional charge, but reservations are required.

Fitness and Recreation. Windstar's massage and exercise facilities are quite small on *Wind Star* and *Wind Spirit*, as would be expected on ships that carry fewer than 150 passengers. However, on the larger *Wind Surf* the WindSpa and fitness areas are surprisingly large. An array of exercise equipment, free weights, and basic fitness classes are available in the gym and Nautilus room. A wide variety of massages, body wraps, and facial treatments are offered in the spa, while hair and nail services are available for women and men in the salon. Stern-mounted watersports marinas are popular with active passengers who want to kayak, windsurf, and water-ski.

Service and Tipping. Personal service is comprehensive, competent, and designed to create an elite and privileged atmosphere. Expect to be addressed by name within a short time of embarking. A service charge of $12 per person per day is automatically added to shipboard accounts. An automatic 15% gratuity is added to all bar tabs.

Contact **Windstar Cruises** ☎ *206/281–3535 or 800/258–7245*
⊕ *www.windstarcruises.com.*

Ports of Embarkation

WORD OF MOUTH

"If you depart from Florida, you may have more days at sea, so more days on the ship and fewer days visiting the islands . . . than if you depart from San Juan."

—Sassafrass

Miami is the world's cruise capital, and more cruise ships are based here year-round than anywhere else. Caribbean cruises depart for their itineraries from several ports on either of Florida's coasts, as well as from cities on the Gulf Coast and East Coast of the United States.

Generally, if your cruise is on an Eastern Caribbean itinerary, you'll likely depart from Miami, Fort Lauderdale, Jacksonville, or Port Canaveral; short three- and four-day cruises to the Bahamas also depart from these ports. Most cruises on Western Caribbean itineraries depart from Tampa, New Orleans, or Galveston, though some depart from Miami as well. Cruises from farther up the East Coast of the United States, including such ports as Baltimore, Maryland; Charleston, South Carolina; and even New York City, usually go to the Bahamas or sometimes Key West and often include a private-island stop or a stop elsewhere in Florida. Cruises to the Southern Caribbean might depart from Miami if they are 10 days or longer, but more likely they will depart from San Juan, Puerto Rico, or some other port deeper in the Caribbean.

Regardless of which port you depart from, air connections may prevent you from leaving home on the morning of your cruise or going home the day you return to port. Or you may wish to arrive early simply to give yourself a bit more peace of mind, or you may just want to spend more time in one of these interesting port cities. Many people choose to depart from New Orleans or Galveston just to have an excuse to spend a couple of days in the city before or after their cruise.

PORT ESSENTIALS

CAR RENTAL
Major Agencies Alamo ☎ 877/222-9075 ⊕ www.alamo.com. **Avis** ☎ 800/331-1212 U.S. reservations, 800/331-1084 international reservations ⊕ www.avis.com. **Budget** ☎ 800/527-0700 U.S. reservations, 800/472-3325 international reservations ⊕ www.budget.com. **Hertz** ☎ 800/654-3131 U.S. and Canada reservations, 800/654-3001 international reservations ⊕ www.hertz. com. **National Car Rental** ☎ 877/222-9058 ⊕ www.nationalcar.com.

SURCHARGES
To avoid a hefty refueling fee, fill the tank just before you turn in the car, but be aware that gas stations near rental outlets and airports may charge more than those farther away. This is a particular problem in Orlando, but it can be true in other Florida cities. If you plan to do a lot of driving (and if you can get a good price), it can sometimes be a better deal to buy a full tank of gas when you rent so you can return the car with an empty tank. However, it's never a good deal to pay the huge surcharge for not returning a tank full unless you simply have no other choice. Other surcharges may apply if you are under 25 or over 75, if you want to add an additional driver to the contract, or if you want to

drive over state borders or out of a specific radius from your point of rental. You'll also pay extra for child seats, which are compulsory for children under 5, and for a GPS navigation system or electronic toll pass. You can sometimes avoid the charge for insurance if you have your own, either from your own policy or from a credit card, but know what you are covered for, and read the fine print before making this decision.

DINING

Unless otherwise noted, the restaurants we recommend accept major credit cards and are open for both lunch and dinner. All prices in this guide are given in U.S. dollars, and the following price categories apply.

LODGING

Whether you are driving or flying into your port of embarkation, it is often more convenient to arrive the day before or to stay for a day after your cruise. For this reason we offer lodging suggestions for each port of embarkation.

The lodgings we list are convenient to the cruise port and the cream of the crop in each price category. We always list the facilities that are available, but we don't specify whether they cost extra; when pricing accommodations, always ask what's included. Properties are assigned price categories based on the range between their least expensive standard double room in high season (excluding holidays) and the most expensive. But if you find everything sold out or wish to find a more predictable place to stay, there are chain hotels at almost all ports of embarkation.

Assume that hotel rates do not include meals unless they are specified in the review.

BALTIMORE, MARYLAND

Evan Serpick and Roberta Sotonoff

Baltimore's charm lies in its neighborhoods. Although stellar downtown attractions such as the National Aquarium and Camden Yards draw torrents of tourists each year, much of the city's character can be found outside the Inner Harbor. Scores of Baltimore's trademark narrow redbrick row houses with white marble steps line the city's east and west sides. Some neighborhood streets are still made of cobblestone, and grand churches and museums and towering, glassy high-rises fill out the growing skyline. Now the city's blue-collar past mixes with present urban-professional revitalization. Industrial waterfront properties are giving way to high-end condos, and corner bars formerly dominated by National Bohemian beer—once made in the city—are adding microbrews to their beverage lists. And with more and more retail stores replacing old, run-down buildings and parking lots, Baltimore is one of the nation's up-and-coming cities.

ESSENTIALS

HOURS During the summer tourist season, most of Baltimore's stores and attractions usually open around 9 am and close around 9 pm.

INTERNET **Enoch Pratt Free Library.** Donated to the city of Baltimore in 1882 by its namesake, a wealthy merchant, the Enoch Pratt Free Library was one of the country's first free-circulation public libraries; it remains one of

Security

All cruise lines have instituted stricter security procedures in recent years; however, you may not even be aware of all the changes.

Some of the changes will be more obvious to you. For example, only visitors who have been authorized well in advance are allowed onboard. Proper identification (a government-issued photo ID) is required in all instances to board the ship, whether you are a visitor or passenger. Ship security personnel are stationed at all points of entry to the ship. All hand-carried items are searched by hand in every port (this applies to both crew and passengers).

Some of the changes are more behind the scenes. All luggage is scanned, whether you carry it aboard with you or not, and all packages and provisions brought onboard are scanned.

In addition, every ship has added professionally trained security officers and taken many other measures to ensure the safety of all passengers. Many cruise-line security personnel are former navy or marine officers with extensive maritime experience. Some cruise lines recruit shipboard security personnel from the ranks of former British Gurkha regiments. From Nepal, the Gurkhas are renowned as soldiers of the highest caliber.

the country's largest. The Pratt was remarkable for allowing any citizen to borrow books at a time when only the wealthy could afford to buy them. When the collection outgrew its original fortresslike rococo structure in 1933, Pratt's democratic ideals were incorporated into the new building's grand yet accessible design. Innovations such as a sidewalk-level entrance and department store–style exhibit windows set the standard for public libraries across the country. The building is still a treat to explore. A huge skylight illuminates the Central Hall's marble floors, gilded fixtures, mural panels depicting the history of printing and publishing, and oil portraits of the Lords Baltimore. The Children's Department, with a fishpond, puppet theater, and a large selection of books, is a real gem for little ones. An audio architecture tour of the museum is available at the circulation desk. ⊠ *400 Cathedral St., Mount Vernon* ☎ *410/396–5500* ⊕ *www.pratt.lib.md.us* ⊙ *June–Sept., Mon.– Wed. 10–8, Thurs. 10–5:30, Fri. and Sat. 10–5, Sun. 1–5; Oct.–May, Mon.–Wed. 11–7, Thurs. 10–5:30, Fri. and Sat. 10–5, Sun. 1–5.*

Visitor Information Baltimore Visitor Center ⊠ *401 Light St, Inner Harbor* ☎ *877/225–8466* ⊕ *www.baltimore.org.*

THE CRUISE PORT

Well marked and easily accessible by major highways, the South Locust Point Cruise Terminal is about a mile from center city. Several cruise lines offer seasonal cruises from the port; both *Carnival Pride* and *Enchantment of the Seas* are based here year-round. Ships dock near the main cruise building, which itself is little more than a hub for arrivals and departures. There are few facilities for passengers in the immediate port area, which is out of walking distance to Baltimore's attractions.

Exploring ▼

B&O Railroad
Museum **5**

Fort McHenry **1**

Maryland Science
Center **2**

National Aquarium
in Baltimore **4**

Oriole Park at
Camden Yards ...**6**

Port Discovery—
The Baltimore
Children's
Museum **3**

Restaurants ▼

Amicci's **7**

Attman's **6**

Bo Brooks **8**

Rusty Scupper ...**3**

Hotels ▼

Celie's
Waterfront B&B ..**5**

Hyatt Regency ...**3**

Marriott Baltimore
Waterfront **4**

Renaissance
Baltimore
Harborplace
Hotel **1**

During cruise season, taxis are the best transportation to the down-town area. They cost about $5 one-way and frequent the port. Taxis to Baltimore–Washington International Airport charge a flat rate of $35. Rental cars are generally not necessary; if you fly into Baltimore, you can see the majority of Baltimore by taxi. Guided tours of the city range from $20 to $60.

Information Port of Baltimore ⊠ *2001 E. McComas St.* ☎ *866/427–8963* ⊕ *www.cruisemaryland.com.*

Airports Baltimore–Washington International Airport (*BWI*). Baltimore–Washington International Airport ⊠ *Exit 2 off Baltimore-Washington Pkwy.* ☎ *410/859–7111* ⊕ *www.bwiairport.com.*

Airport Transfers Airport Taxis ☎ *410/859–1100* ⊕ *www.bwiairporttaxi.com.* **Arrow Taxicab** ☎ *410/358–9696.* **BWI Airport rail station** ☎ *410/672–6167* ⊕ *www.mtamaryland.com.* **BWI SuperShuttle** ☎ *800/258–3826* ⊕ *www.supershuttle.com.* **Carey Limousines** ☎ *410/880–0999, 888/880–0999* ⊕ *www.carey.com.* **Maryland Area Rail Commuter** (*MARC*) ☎ *800/325–7245, 410/539–5000* ⊕ *www.mtamaryland.com.* **Penn Station** ⊠ *1515 N. Charles St., Mount Vernon* ☎ *800/523–8720.* **Private Car/RMA Worldwide Chauffeured Transportation** ☎ *410/519–0000, 800/878–7743* ⊕ *www.rmalimo.com.*

PARKING

There's a secure parking lot next to the cruise terminal, where parking costs $15 per day. Drop off your luggage before parking.

EXPLORING BALTIMORE

☺ **B&O Railroad Museum.** The famous Baltimore & Ohio Railroad was
★ founded on the site that now houses this museum, which contains more than 120 full-size locomotives and a great collection of railroad memorabilia, from dining-car china and artwork to lanterns and signals. The 1884 roundhouse (240 feet in diameter and 120 feet high) adjoins one of the nation's first railroad stations. Train rides are available every day but Monday. The Iron Horse Café serves food and drinks. ⊠ *901 W. Pratt St., West Baltimore* ☎ *410/752–2490* ⊕ *www.borail.org* ⊠ *$14* ☉ *Mon.–Sat. 10–4, Sun. 11–4.*

Fort McHenry. This star-shaped brick fort is forever associated with Francis Scott Key and "The Star-Spangled Banner," which Key penned while watching the British bombardment of Baltimore during the War of 1812. Key had been detained onboard a truce ship, where he had been negotiating the release of one Dr. William Beanes, when the bombardment began; Key knew too much about the attack plan to be released. Through the next day and night, as the battle raged, Key strained to be sure, through the smoke and haze, that the flag still flew above Fort McHenry—indicating that Baltimore's defenders held firm. "By the dawn's early light" of September 14, 1814, he saw the 30- by 42-foot "Star-Spangled Banner" still aloft and was inspired to pen the words to a poem (set to the tune of an old English drinking song). The flag that flew above Fort McHenry that day had 15 stars and 15 stripes, and was hand-sewn for the fort. A visit to the fort includes a 15-minute history film, guided tour, and frequent living-history displays on summer weekends. To see how the formidable fortifications might have appeared to the bombarding British, catch a water taxi from the Inner Harbor to the fort instead of driving. ⊠ *E. Fort Ave., from Light St., take Key Hwy. for 1½ miles and follow signs, Locust Point* ☎ *410/962–4290* ⊕ *www.nps.gov/fomc* ⊠ *$7* ☉ *Memorial Day–Labor Day, daily 8–8; Labor Day–Memorial Day, daily 8–5.*

☺ **Maryland Science Center.** Originally known as the Maryland Academy of
★ Sciences, this 200-year-old scientific institution is one of the oldest in the United States. Now housed in a contemporary building, the three floors of exhibits on the Chesapeake Bay, Earth science, physics, the body, dinosaurs, and outer space are an invitation to engage, experiment, and explore. The center has a planetarium, a simulated archaeological dinosaur dig, an IMAX movie theater with a screen five stories high, and a playroom especially designed for young children. ⊠ *601 Light St., Inner Harbor* ☎ *410/685–5225* ⊕ *www.mdsci.org* ⊠ *$14.95* ☉ *Memorial Day–Labor Day, Thurs.–Sat. 10–8, Sun.–Wed. 10–6; Labor Day–Memorial Day, Tues.–Fri. 10–5, Sat. 10–6, Sun. 11–5.*

National Aquarium in Baltimore. The most-visited attraction in Maryland has more than 10,000 fish, sharks, dolphins, and amphibians dwelling in 2 million gallons of water. The Animal Planet Australia: Wild

Extremes exhibit mimics a river running through a gorge. It features lizards, crocodiles, turtles, bats, and a black-headed python, among other animals from Down Under. The aquarium also features reptiles, birds, plants, and mammals in its rain-forest environment, inside a glass pyramid 64 feet high. The rain-forest ecosystem harbors two-toed sloths in calabash trees, parrots in the palms, iguanas on the ground, and red-bellied piranhas in a pool (a sign next to it reads "do not put hands in pool"). Each day in the Marine Mammal Pavilion,

BALTIMORE BEST BETS

■ **Camden Yards.** Tour the stadium or, better yet, see an Orioles game if the team is playing while you're in town.

■ **Fort McHenry.** This historic fort is where Francis Scott Key saw the Stars and Stripes flying during the War of 1812.

■ **The National Aquarium.** This excellent museum is a great destination for families or adults.

Atlantic bottlenose dolphins are part of several entertaining presentations that highlight their agility and intelligence. The aquarium's famed shark tank and Atlantic coral reef exhibits are spectacular; you can wind through an enormous glass enclosure on a spiral ramp while hammerheads and brightly hued tropical fish glide by. Hands-on exhibits include such docile sea creatures as horseshoe crabs and starfish. Arrive early to ensure admission, which is by timed intervals; by noon, the wait is often two or three hours. ⊠ *Pier 3, Inner Harbor* ☎ *410/576–3800* ⊕ *www.aqua.org* ⊡ *$24.95* ☉ *Nov.–Feb., Sat.–Thurs. 10–5, Fri. 10–8; Mar.–June, Sept., and Oct., Sat.–Thurs. 9–5, Fri. 9–8; July–Aug. 19, daily 9–8; Aug. 20–31, Sat.–Thurs. 9–6, Fri. 9–8; visitors may tour for up to 1½ hrs after closing. Timed tickets may be required on weekends and holidays; purchase these early in the day.*

☉ **Oriole Park at Camden Yards.** Home of the Baltimore Orioles, Camden
★ Yards and the nearby area bustle on game days. Since it opened in 1992, this nostalgically designed baseball stadium has inspired other cities to emulate its neotraditional architecture and amenities. The Eutaw Street promenade, between the warehouse and the field, has a view of the stadium; look for the brass baseballs embedded in the sidewalk that mark where home runs have cleared the fence, or visit the Orioles Hall of Fame display and the monuments to retired Orioles. Daily 90-minute tours take you to nearly every section of the ballpark, from the massive, JumboTron scoreboard to the dugout to the state-of-the-art beer-delivery system. ⊠ *333 W. Camden St., Downtown* ☎ *410/685–9800 general information, 410/547–6234 tour times, 888/848–2473 tickets to Orioles home games* ⊕ *www.theorioles.com* ⊡ *Eutaw St. promenade free; tour $7* ☉ *Eutaw St. promenade daily 10–3, otherwise during games and tours; tours Mar.–Sept., Mon.–Sat. at 11, noon, 1, and 2; Oct., weekdays at 11:30 and 1:30, Sat. at 11, noon, 1, and 2, Sun. at 12:30, 1, 2, and 3; Nov., Mon.–Sat. at 11:30 and 1:30, Sun. at 12:30 and 2:30.*

☉ **Port Discovery—The Baltimore Children's Museum.** At this interactive museum, adults are encouraged to play every bit as much as children. A favorite attraction is the three-story KidWorks, a futuristic jungle gym on which the adventurous can climb, crawl, slide, and swing their way through stairs, slides, ropes, zip lines, and tunnels, and even cross a narrow footbridge three stories up. In Miss Perception's Mystery House, youngsters help solve a mystery surrounding the disappearance of the Baffeld family by sifting through clues; some are written or visual, and others are gleaned by touching and listening. Changing interactive exhibits allow for even more play. ⊠ *35 Market Pl., Inner Harbor* ☎ *410/727–8120* ⊕ *www.portdiscovery.com* ☜ *$12.95* ☉ *Memorial Day–Labor Day, Mon.–Sat. 10–5, Sun. noon–5; Labor Day–Memorial Day, Tues.–Fri. 9:30–4:30, Sat. 10–5, Sun. noon–5.*

SHOPPING

Baltimore isn't the biggest shopping town, but it does have some malls and good stores here and there. Hampden (the "p" is silent), a neighborhood west of Johns Hopkins University, has funky shops selling everything from housewares to housedresses along its main drag, 36th Street (better known as "The Avenue"). Some interesting shops can be found along Charles Street in Mount Vernon and along Thames Street in Fells Point. Federal Hill has a few fun shops, particularly for furnishings and vintage items.

Harborplace and the Gallery. At the Inner Harbor, the Pratt Street and Light Street pavilions of Harborplace and the Gallery contain almost 200 specialty shops that sell everything from business attire to children's toys. The Gallery has J. Crew, Banana Republic, and the Gap, among others. ⊠ *Baltimore* ☎ *410/332–4191.*

NIGHTLIFE

Fells Point, just east of the Inner Harbor; Federal Hill, due south; and Canton, due east, have hosts of bars, restaurants, and clubs that draw a rowdy, largely collegiate crowd. If you're seeking quieter surroundings, head for the upscale comforts of downtown or Mount Vernon clubs and watering holes.

BARS AND LOUNGES

The Brewer's Art. Part brewpub, part restaurant, and part lounge, this spot in a redone mansion feels young but urbane, with an ambitious menu, a clever wine list, and the Belgian-style beers it brews itself: try the potent, delicious Resurrection ale. The upstairs dining room serves seasonal dishes with high-quality, locally available ingredients to create European-style country fare that is both hearty and sophisticated. In the dungeonlike downstairs dining room and bar the menu and decor are more casual. Made with rosemary and garlic, the classic steak frites are a best bet. ⊠ *1106 N. Charles St., Mount Vernon* ☎ *410/547–6925* ⊕ *www.belgianbeer.com.*

Club Charles. With its stylized art deco surroundings, the funky Club Charles is a favorite hangout for an artsy crowd, moviegoers coming from the Charles Theater across the street, and, reputation has it, John Waters. ⊠ *1724 N. Charles St., Station North Arts District* ☎ *410/727–8815.*

Club Hippo. Club Hippo is Baltimore's longest-reigning gay bar. ⊠ *1 W. Eager St., Mount Vernon* ☏ *410/547–0069* ⊕ *www.clubhippo.com.*

Grand Central. A dance club, martini bar, and pub have all helped make Grand Central into a hip gay hot spot. ⊠ *1003 N. Charles St., Mount Vernon* ☏ *410/752–7133.*

Max's Taphouse. Beer lovers should visit Max's Taphouse, which has more than 70 brews on tap and about 300 more in bottles. ⊠ *737 S. Broadway, Fells Point* ☏ *410/675–6297* ⊕ *www.maxs.com.*

Red Maple. Red Maple is one of the city's most stylish spots for drinks and tapas. ⊠ *930 N. Charles St., Mount Vernon* ☏ *410/547–0149* ⊕ *www.930redmaple.com.*

13th Floor. At the top of the Belvedere Hotel, the 13th Floor offers a great view, a long martini list, and live dance music. ⊠ *1 E. Chase St., Mount Vernon* ☏ *410/347–0888.*

COMEDY CLUBS
The Comedy Factory. The Comedy Factory is the best local spot to see live standup. ⊠ *36 Light St., Inner Harbor* ☏ *410/752–4189.*

WHERE TO EAT

Baltimore loves crabs. Soft- or hardshell crabs, crab cakes, crab dip—the city's passion for clawed crustaceans seems to have no end. Flag down a Baltimore native and ask them where the best crab joint is, and you'll get a list of options. In addition to crabs and seafood, Baltimore's restaurant landscape also includes Italian, Afghan, Greek, American, tapas, and other cuisines. The city's dining choices may not compare with those of New York, or even Washington, but it does have some real standouts. Note that places generally stop serving by 10 pm, if not earlier.

$$ ✕ **Amicci's.** At this self-proclaimed "very casual eatery," you don't have
ITALIAN to spend a fortune to get a satisfying taste of Little Italy. Blue jean–clad diners and walls hung with movie posters make for a fun atmosphere. Service is friendly and usually speedy, and the food comes in large portions. Try the chicken Lorenzo: breaded chicken breast covered in a marsala wine sauce, red peppers, prosciutto, and provolone. Ⓢ *Average main: $16* ⊠ *231 S. High St., Little Italy* ☏ *410/528–1096* ⊕ *www.amiccis.com.*

$ ✕ **Attman's.** Open since 1915, this authentic New York–style deli near
DELI the Jewish Museum is the king of Baltimore's "Corned Beef Row." Of the three delis on the row, Attman's has the longest waits and steepest prices, but delivers the highest-quality dishes. Don't be put off by the long lines—they move fairly quickly, and the outstanding corned beef sandwiches are worth the wait, as are the pastrami, homemade chopped liver, and other oversize creations. Attman's closes at 6:30 pm daily. Ⓢ *Average main: $8* ⊠ *1019 Lombard St., Historic Jonestown* ☏ *410/563–2666* ⊕ *www.attmansdeli.com.*

$$$ ✕ **Bo Brooks.** Picking steamed crabs on Bo Brooks's waterfront deck as
SEAFOOD sailboats and tugs ply the harbor is a quintessential Baltimore pleasure. Locals spend hot summer days cracking into warm, spicy crabs and enjoying a refreshing pitcher of beer while a cool breeze blows in from the harbor. Brooks serves its famous crustaceans year-round, along with

a menu of Chesapeake seafood classics. Locals know to stick to the Maryland crab soup, crab dip, jumbo lump crab cakes, and fried oysters. $ *Average main: $23* ✉ *2701 Boston St., Canton* ☎ *410/558–0202* ⊕ *www.bobrooks.com.*

$$$ ✗ **Rusty Scupper.** A tourist favorite, the Rusty Scupper undoubtedly has
SEAFOOD   the best view along the waterfront; sunset here is magical, with the sun sinking slowly into the harbor as lights twinkle on the city's skyscrapers. The interior is decorated with light wood and windows from floor to ceiling; the house specialty is seafood, particularly the jumbo lump crab cake, but the menu also includes beef, chicken, and pasta. Reservations are essential on Friday and Saturday; service can be spotty. $ *Average main: $25* ✉ *402 Key Hwy., Inner Harbor* ☎ *410/727–3678* ⊕ *www. selectrestaurants.com/rusty/.*

WHERE TO STAY

When booking a hotel or bed-and-breakfast in Baltimore, focus on the Inner Harbor, where you're likely to spend a good deal of time. The downside to staying in hotels near downtown is the noise level, which can rise early in the morning and stay up late into the night—especially if there's a baseball or football game. For quieter options, head to neighborhoods like Fells Point and Canton.

For expanded reviews, facilities, and current deals, visit Fodors.com.

$$ 🏨 **Celie's Waterfront Bed & Breakfast.** Proprietors Nancy and Kevin Kupec
B&B/INN   oversee every detail of this small inn in the heart of Fells Point. **Pros:** intimate accommodations; situated next to an entertainment district. **Cons:** it can get noisy late at night. $ *Rooms from: $139* ✉ *1714 Thames St., Fells Point* ☎ *410/522–2323, 800/432–0184* ⊕ *www.celieswaterfront. com* ⇆ *7 rooms, 2 suites* ⦿ *Breakfast.*

$$$ 🏨 **Hyatt Regency.** This stretch of Light Street is practically a highway, but the unenclosed skyways allow ready pedestrian access to both Inner Harbor attractions and the convention center. **Pros:** the Inner Harbor is just a skywalk away. **Cons:** service can be slow and unhelpful. $ *Rooms from: $250* ✉ *300 Light St., Inner Harbor* ☎ *410/528–1234, 800/233– 1234* ⊕ *baltimore.hyatt.com* ⇆ *488 rooms, 26 suites.*

$$$ 🏨 **Marriott Baltimore Waterfront.** The city's tallest hotel and the only one directly on the Inner Harbor itself, this upscale 31-story Marriott has a neoclassical interior that uses multihue marbles, rich jewel-tone walls, and photographs of Baltimore architectural landmarks. **Pros:** nice amenities; great location and view. **Cons:** pricey compared to nearby hotels. $ *Rooms from: $239* ✉ *700 Aliceanna St., Inner Harbor East* ☎ *410/385–3000* ⊕ *www.marriotthotels.com/bwiwf* ⇆ *751 rooms.*

$$ 🏨 **Renaissance Baltimore Harborplace Hotel.** The most conveniently located of the Inner Harbor hotels—across the street from the shopping pavilions—the Renaissance Harborplace meets the needs of tourists, business travelers, and conventioneers. **Pros:** snappy service. **Cons:** some rooms are a bit threadbare. $ *Rooms from: $179* ✉ *202 E. Pratt St., Inner Harbor* ☎ *410/547–1200, 800/468–3571* ⊕ *www.renaissancehotels. com/bwish* ⇆ *562 rooms, 60 suites.*

CHARLESTON, SOUTH CAROLINA

Melissa
Bigner, Eileen
Robinson
Smith, Rob
Young

Charleston looks like a movie set, an 18th-century etching brought to life. The spires and steeples of more than 180 churches punctuate her low skyline, and tourists ride in horse-drawn carriages that pass grandiose, centuries-old mansions and gardens brimming with heirloom plants. Preserved through the poverty following the Civil War and natural disasters like fires, earthquakes, and hurricanes, much of Charleston's earliest public and private architecture still stands. And thanks to a rigorous preservation movement and strict Board of Architectural Review, the city's new structures blend with the old ones. If you're boarding your cruise ship here, it's worth coming a few days early to explore the historic downtown and to eat in one of the many superb restaurants. In late spring, plan in advance for the Spoleto U.S.A. Festival. For more than 30 memorable years, arts patrons have gathered to enjoy the international dance, opera, theater, and other performances at venues citywide. Piccolo Spoleto showcases local and regional concerts, dance, theater, and comedy shows.

ESSENTIALS

HOURS   Most shops are open from 9 or 10 am to at least 6 pm, but some are open later. A new city ordinance requires bars to close by 2 am.

INTERNET   While almost all hotels (and even B&Bs) offer some kind of Internet service, Internet cafés are rare in the Charleston historic district; however, many coffee shops, including all the local Starbucks, offer Wi-Fi.

Visitor Information Charleston Visitor Center ⊠ *375 Meeting St., Upper King* ☎ *843/853–8000, 800/868–8118* ⊕ *www.charlestoncvb.com* ⊠ *Free* ⊙ *Apr.– Oct., daily 8:30–5:30; Nov.–Mar., daily 8:30–5.*

THE CRUISE PORT

Cruise ships sailing from Charleston depart from the Union Pier Terminal, which is in Charleston's historic district. If you are driving, however, and need to leave your car for the duration of your cruise, take the East Bay Street exit off the new, majestic Ravenel Bridge on I–17 and follow the "Cruise Ship" signs. On ship embarkation days police officers will direct you to the ship terminal from the intersection of East Bay and Chapel streets. Cruise parking is located adjacent to Union Pier.

Information Port of Charleston ⊠ *Union Pier, 280 Concord St., Market area* ☎ *843/958–8298 for cruise information* ⊕ *www.port-of-charleston.com.*

AIRPORT TRANSFERS

Several cab companies service the airport, including the new Charleston Black Cab Company, which operates a fleet of genuine London cabs with uniformed drivers and costs about $10 more than calling a regular cab—about $50 to downtown. Airport Ground Transportation arranges shuttles, which cost $15 per person to the downtown area, $40 to $45 for a return trip to the airport. CARTA's bus No. 11, a public bus, now goes to the airport for a mere $1.25; it leaves downtown from the Meeting/Mary St. parking garage every 50 minutes, from 5:45 am until 11:09 pm.

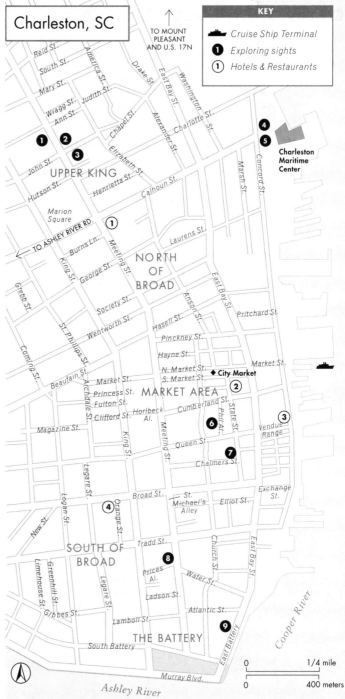

Charleston, SC

TO MOUNT
PLEASANT
AND U.S. 17N

KEY

🚢 Cruise Ship Terminal

1 Exploring sights

① Hotels & Restaurants

Charleston
Maritime
Center

UPPER KING

Marion
Square

TO ASHLEY RIVER RD.

NORTH
OF
BROAD

MARKET AREA

◆ City Market

SOUTH OF
BROAD

St.
Michael's
Alley

THE BATTERY

South Battery

Murray Blvd.

Ashley River

Cooper River

0   1/4 mile

0   400 meters

PARKING

Parking costs $17 per day ($119 per week) for regular vehicles, $40 per day ($280 per week) for RVs or other vehicles more than 20 feet in length. You pay in advance by cash, check, or credit card. A free shuttle bus takes you to the cruise-passenger terminal. Be sure to drop your large luggage off at Union Pier before you park your car; only carry-on size luggage is allowed on the shuttle bus, so if you have any bags larger than 22 inches by 14 inches, they will have to be checked before you park. Also, you'll need your cruise tickets to board the shuttle bus.

3

EXPLORING CHARLESTON

The heart of the city is on a peninsula, sometimes just called "downtown" by the nearly 60,000 residents who populate the area. Walking Charleston's peninsula is the best way to get to know the city. The main downtown historic district is roughly bounded by Lockwood Boulevard to the west, Calhoun Street to the north, the Cooper River to the east, and the Battery to the south. Nearly 2,000 historic homes and buildings occupy this fairly compact area divided into South of Broad (Street) and North of Broad. King Street, the main shopping street in town, cuts through Broad Street, and the most trafficked tourist area ends a few blocks south of the Crosstown, where U.S. 17 cuts across Upper King. If you don't wish to walk, there are bikes, pedicabs, and trolleys. Street parking is irksome, as meter readers are among the city's most efficient public servants. Parking garages, both privately and publicly owned, charge around $1.50 an hour.

Charleston Museum. While housed in a modern-day brick complex, this institution was founded in 1773 and is the country's oldest city museum. To the delight of fans of *Antiques Roadshow,* the collection is especially strong in South Carolina decorative arts, from silver to snuff boxes. Kids love the permanent Civil War exhibition, with plenty of Confederate uniforms, and have an interactive good old time on the second floor in galleries devoted to archaeology and natural history (don't miss the giant polar bear). Newer exhibits include "The Threads of War," which deals with the stripped-down fashions created during the Civil War shipping blockade (not exactly Scarlett's window drapes, but you get the picture). Combination tickets that give you admission to the Joseph Manigault House and the Heyward-Washington House are a bargain at $22. ⊠ *360 Meeting St., Upper King* ☎ *843/722–2996* ⊕ *www.charlestonmuseum.org* 🎫 *$10* ⊙ *Mon.–Sat. 9–5, Sun. 1–5.*

Charleston Visitor Center ⊠ *375 Meeting St., Upper King* ☎ *843/853–8000, 800/868–8118* ⊕ *www.charlestoncvb.com* 🎫 *Free* ⊙ *Apr.–Oct., daily 8:30–5:30; Nov.–Mar., daily 8:30–5.*

Edmondston-Alston House. Built in 1825 in late-Federal style, the house was transformed during the 1840s into the imposing Greek Revival structure you see today. Tours of the home—furnished with antiques, portraits, silver, and fine china—are informative. ⊠ *21 E. Battery, South of Broad* ☎ *843/722–7171* ⊕ *www.middletonplace.org* 🎫 *$10; $41 with combination ticket for Middleton Place* ⊙ *Tues.–Sat. 10–4:30, Sun. 1:30–4:30, Mon. 1–4:30.*

Fort Sumter National Monument. Set on a man-made island in Charleston's harbor, this is the hallowed spot where the Civil War began. On April 12, 1861, the first shot of the war was fired at the fort from Fort Johnson (now defunct) across the way. After a 34-hour battle, Union forces surrendered and Confederate troops occupied Sumter, which became a symbol of Southern resistance. The Confederacy managed to hold it, despite almost continual bombardment, from August 1863 to February of 1865. When it was finally evacuated, the fort was a heap of rubble. Today, the National Park Service oversees it, and rangers give interpretive talks and conduct guided tours. To reach the fort, you have to take a ferry; boats depart from Liberty Square Visitor Center, downtown, and from Patriot's Point in Mount Pleasant. There are six crossings daily between mid-March and mid-August. The schedule is abbreviated the rest of the year, so call ahead for details. For those using a GPS to find the boat departure points for Fort Sumter, remember to use the address for Patriots Point and Liberty Square, not the address for the fort itself. ✉ *1214 Middle St, Sullivan's Island* ☎ *843/577–0242, 843/883–3123* ⊕ *www.nps.gov/ fosu* ✍ *Fort free; ferry $17* ⊙ *Mid-Mar.–early Sept., daily 10–5:30; early Sept.–mid-Mar., daily 10–4 (11:30–4 Jan. and Feb.).*

> ### CHARLESTON BEST BETS
>
> ■ **Viewing Art.** The city is home to some 120 galleries, exhibiting art from Charleston, the South, and around the world. The Gibbes Museum of Art and a half-dozen other museums add to the cultural mix.
>
> ■ **The Battery.** The views from the point—both natural and man-made—are the loveliest in the city. Look west to see the harbor; to the east you'll find elegant Charleston mansions.
>
> ■ **Historic Homes.** Charleston's preserved, centuries-old, stately homes, including the Nathaniel Russell House, are highlights.

Fodor'sChoice ★ **Joseph Manigault House.** Considered by many to be the finest example of Federal-style architecture in the South, this 1803 home was built for a rich rice-planting family of Huguenot heritage. Having toured Europe as a gentleman architect, Gabriel Manigault returned to design this house for his brother Joseph as the city's first essay in neoclassicism. The house glows in red brick and is adorned with a two-story piazza balcony. Inside, marvels await: a fantastic "flying" staircase in the central hall; a gigantic Venetian window; elegant plasterwork and mantels; notable Charleston-made furniture; and a bevy of French, English, and American antiques, including some celebrated tricolor Wedgwood pieces. Outside, note the garden "folly." ✉ *350 Meeting St., Upper King* ☎ *843/722–2996* ⊕ *www. charlestonmuseum.org* ✍ *$10* ⊙ *Mon.–Sat. 10–5, Sun. 1–5.*

Fodor'sChoice ★ **Nathaniel Russell House.** One of the nation's finest examples of Adam-style architecture, the Nathaniel Russell House was built in 1808. Russell came to Charleston at age 27 from his native Bristol, Rhode Island, and became one of the city's leading merchants and Federalist fathers in post-Revolutionary times. The ornate interior is distinguished by its Romney portraits, lavish period furnishings, and the famous "free-flying" staircase that spirals up three stories with no visible support. The extensive formal garden is worth a leisurely stroll. ⊠ *51 Meeting St., South of Broad* ☎ *843/724–8481* ⊕ *www.historiccharleston.org* 🎫 *$10; $16 with admission to Aiken-Rhett House* ⊙ *Mon.–Sat. 10–5, Sun. 2–5.*

Fodor's Choice ★ **Old Slave Mart Museum.** This is likely the only building still in existence that was used for slave auctioning, a practice that ended in 1863. It is part of a complex called Ryan's Mart, which contains the slave jail, the kitchen, and the morgue. It is now a museum that recounts the history of Charleston's role in the slave trade, an unpleasant story but one that is vital to understand. Charleston once served as the center of commercial activity for the South's plantation economy, and slaves were the primary source of labor both within the city and on the surrounding plantations. After a recent renovation, galleries are now outfitted with some interactive exhibits, including push buttons that allow you to hear voices relating stories from the age of slavery. The museum is on one of the few remaining cobblestone streets in town. ⊠ *6 Chalmers St., Market area* ☎ *843/958–6467* ⊕ *www.charlestoncity.info* 🎫 *$7* ⊙ *Mon.–Sat. 9–5.*

Fodor's Choice ★ **St. Philip's (Episcopal) Church.** The namesake of Church Street, this graceful late-Georgian building is the second one to rise on its site: the congregation's first building burned down in 1835 and was rebuilt in 1838. During the Civil War, the steeple was a target for shelling; a shell that exploded in the churchyard during services one Sunday didn't deter the minister from finishing his sermon (afterward, the congregation gathered elsewhere for the duration of the war). Notable Charlestonians like John C. Calhoun are buried in the graveyard. ⊠ *146 Church St., Market area* ☎ *843/722–7734* ⊕ *www.stphilipschurchsc.org* ⊙ *Church weekdays 9–11 and 1–4; cemetery daily 9–4.*

☺ ★ **South Carolina Aquarium.** The 38,000-gallon Great Ocean Tank houses the tallest aquarium window in North America. Along with sharks, moray eels, and sea turtles, exhibits include more than 5,000 creatures, representing more than 350 species. You travel through the five major regions of the Southeast Appalachian Watershed: the Blue Ridge Mountains, the Piedmont, the Coastal Plain, the Coast, and the Atlantic Ocean. Like the ocean, the aquarium is in constant motion, always adding new exhibits and animals; the latest celebrity creature is an albino alligator. The 4-D theater combines 3-D imagery (with special effects like wind gusts and splashes of water), synchronized to favorite family films. ⊠ *100 Aquarium Wharf, Upper King* ☎ *843/720–1990, 800/722–6455* ⊕ *www.scaquarium.org* 🎫 *$24.95* ⊙ *Mar.–Aug., daily 9–5; Sept.–Feb., daily 9–4.*

SHOPPING

City Market. The Market area is a cluster of shops and restaurants centered around the City Market. Sweetgrass basket weavers work here, and you can buy the resulting wares, although these artisan-crafts have become expensive. There are T-shirts and souvenir stores here as well as upscale boutiques. In the covered, open-air market, vendors have stalls with everything from jewelry to dresses and purses. ⊠ *E. Bay and Market Sts., Market area.*

Fodor's Choice **King Street.** King Street is Charleston's main street and the major shop-
★ ping corridor downtown. The latest lines of demarcation dividing
the street into districts: Lower King (from Broad to Market streets)
is the Antiques District, as it is lined with high-end antiques dealers; Middle King (from Market to Calhoun streets) is now called the
Fashion District and is a mix of national chains like Banana Republic and Pottery Barn, alternative shops, and locally owned landmark
stores and boutiques; Upper King (from Calhoun to Spring streets)
has been dubbed the Design District. This up-and-coming area has
become known for its furniture and interior design stores selling home
fashion. Check out the events and stores. ⊠ *South Carolina* ⊕ *www.
kingstreetantiquedistrict.com, www.kingstreetfashiondistrict.com, and
www.kingstreetdesigndistrict.com.*

NIGHTLIFE

★ **Charleston Grill.** The elegant Charleston Grill has live jazz from 7 to 10
on Friday and 8 to 12 on Saturday. Shows range from the internationally acclaimed, Brazilian-influenced Quentin Baxter Ensemble to the
Bob Williams Duo, a father and son who play classical guitar and violin.
It draws a mature, upscale clientele, hotel guests, well-known locals,
and more recently an urbane thirtysomething crowd. ⊠ *Charleston
Place Hotel, 224 King St., Market area* ☎ *843/577–4522.*

Mercato. Mercato is a popular restaurant that has become almost as well
known for its roster of nightly entertainment Monday through Saturday from 6 to 10. Come early to get a seat at the long, elegant bar; it is
best to reserve one of the 12 downstairs tables for dinner, but they do
pipe the music into the second-floor dining room. ⊠ *102 N. Market St.,
Market area* ☎ *843/722–6393* ⊕ *www.mercatocharleston.com.*

Southend Brewery. Southend Brewery has a lively bar serving beer
brewed on the premises. Try the Carolina Blonde with the wood-oven
pizzas and the smokehouse barbecue. ⊠ *161 E. Bay St., Market area*
☎ *843/853–4677.*

Tommy Condon's. Listen to authentic Irish music Thursday through Saturday at rollicking Irish pub Tommy Condon's. On Wednesday and
Sunday a two-piece group plays Irish-influenced music and Americana.
Monday there is American music. Have some Irish nachos—cubed potatoes, cheddar cheese, jalapeños, tomatoes, and ranch dressing—with a
Guinness or Harp. ⊠ *15 Beaufain St., Market area* ☎ *843/577–3818*
⊕ *www.tommycondons.com.*

WHERE TO EAT

$ ✕ **Dixie Supply Bakery and Cafe.** It might be a lil' eatery buttressed by
SOUTHERN a Lil' Cricket convenience store, but don't be fooled by appearance.
Dixie Supply Bakery and Cafe belongs to an old Charlestonian family (and by old, we mean they arrived here in 1698 or so) that seeks
to honor its roots. Dixie dishes up Lowcountry and Southern classics:
shrimp and creamy stone-ground grits, fried chicken, and a mighty
fine tomato pie. Daily alternating blue-plate specials abound, including

fried green tomatoes, shrimp from nearby Wadmalaw Island, summer-squash-and-ricotta-cheese ravioli, and a steady assortment of locally plucked vegetables. $ *Average main: $6* ⊠ *62 State St., Market area* ☎ *843/722–5650* ⊕ *www.dixiecafecharleston.com.*

$ ✕ **Queen Street Grocery.** For crepes
AMERICAN and cold-pressed coffee, most folks turn to a venerable Charleston institution: Queen Street Grocery. Established in 1922, the corner

> **CHARLESTON CRUISE PACKAGES**
>
> For a listing of all hotel package discounts you can book along with your cruise, not to mention discounted tours (including the popular plantation tours), attractions, and shopping and dining coupons, visit ⊕ *www.charlestoncruisepackages.com.*

shop has endured several guises through the years: butchery, candy shop, and late-night convenience store. Though in 2008, Hank Weed and Mary Wutz returned the store to its roots as a neighborhood grocery store, sourcing much of the produce and other goods from local growers. It's a great preservation act, improved upon by QSG's newest offerings: sweet and savory crepes named for the islands surrounding Charleston. $ *Average main: $6* ⊠ *133 Queen St., Market area* ☎ *843/723–4121* ⊕ *www.qsg29401.com.*

WHERE TO STAY

While the city's best hotels and B&Bs are in the historic district, most of them do not have free parking. If you stay outside of downtown in a chain hotel, you will give up much in charm and convenience but pay significantly less, not to mention park for free. High-season rates are traditionally in effect from March through May and September through November.

For expanded reviews, facilities, and current deals, visit Fodors.com.

$$$ ⊞ **HarbourView Inn.** Ask for a room facing the harbor, and you can gaze out onto the kid-friendly fountain and 8 acres of Waterfront Park. **Pros:** Continental breakfast can be delivered to room; service is notable; only hotel on the harbor and Waterfront Park. **Cons:** rooms are off long, modern halls; rooms are not particularly spacious. $ *Rooms from: $239* ⊠ *2 Vendue Range, Market area* ☎ *843/853–8439, 888/853–8439* ⊕ *www.harbourviewcharleston.com* ⇱ *52 rooms* ⦿ *Breakfast.*

$$ ⊞ **Holiday Inn Historic District.** Thanks to its staff, this hotel has an outstanding track record for guest satisfaction. **Pros:** well-respected concierge Kevin McQuade offers excellent recommendations; self-parking in attached garage. **Cons:** 50% of rooms (along the back of hotel) have no view due to obstruction by other buildings; a long walk (about six blocks) to the Market. $ *Rooms from: $139* ⊠ *125 Calhoun St., Upper King* ☎ *843/805–7900, 877/805–7900* ⊕ *www.charlestonhotel.com* ⇱ *122 rooms, 4 suites* ⦿ *No meals.*

FORT LAUDERDALE, FLORIDA

Paul Rubio

In the 1960s Fort Lauderdale's beachfront was lined with T-shirt shops interspersed with quickie-food outlets, and downtown consisted of a lone office tower, some dilapidated government buildings, and motley other structures waiting to be razed. Today the beach is home to upscale shops and restaurants, while downtown has exploded with new office and luxury residential development. The entertainment and shopping areas—Las Olas Boulevard, Las Olas Riverfront, and Himmarshee Village—are thriving. And Port Everglades is giving Miami a run for its money in passenger cruising, with a dozen cruise-ship terminals, including the world's largest, hosting more than 20 cruise ships with some 3,000 departures annually. A captivating shoreline with wide ribbons of sand for beachcombing and sunbathing makes Fort Lauderdale and Broward County a major draw for visitors, and often tempts cruise-ship passengers to spend an extra day or two in the sun. Fort Lauderdale's 2-mile (3-km) stretch of unobstructed beachfront has been further enhanced with a sparkling promenade designed more for the pleasure of pedestrians than vehicles.

ESSENTIALS

HOURS   Many museums close on Monday.

INTERNET   If you have your own laptop, Broward County has created a fairly extensive Wi-Fi network with numerous hotspots in downtown Fort Lauderdale, providing free Internet access to anyone using suitably equipped laptops. There's also free Wi-Fi in the airport.

BOAT TOURS   A water taxi provides service along the intracoastal waterway in Fort Lauderdale between the 17th Street Causeway and Oakland Park Boulevard, and west into downtown along New River daily from 10 am until midnight. A day-pass costs $20.

Water Taxi. A great way to experience the multimillion-dollar homes, hotels, and seafood restaurants along Fort Lauderdale's waterways is via the public Water Taxi, which runs every 30 minutes beginning at 10 am and ending at midnight. An unlimited day pass serves as both a tour and a means of transportation between Fort Lauderdale's hotels and hot spots, though Water Taxi is most useful when viewed as a tour. It's possible to cruise all afternoon while taking in the waterfront sights. Captains and helpers indulge guests in fun factoids about Fort Lauderdale, white lies about the city's history, and bizarre tales about the celebrity homes along the Intracoastal. A day pass is $20. There are 12 pickup stations in Fort Lauderdale, and Water Taxi also connects Fort Lauderdale to Hollywood, where there are seven scheduled stops. ☎ 954/467–6677 ⊕ *www.watertaxi.com.*

Visitor Information Greater Fort Lauderdale Convention and Visitors Bureau ☎ 954/765–4466 ⊕ www.sunny.org.

THE CRUISE PORT

Port Everglades, Fort Lauderdale's cruise port (nowhere near the Everglades, but happily near the beach and less than 2 miles [3 km] from the airport), is among the world's largest, busiest ports. It's also the straightest, deepest port in the southeastern United States, meaning you'll be out to sea in no time flat once your ship sets sail. At a cost of $75 million, Cruise Terminal 18 has been tripled in size to accommodate Royal Caribbean's Oasis-class ships, the 5,400-passenger *Oasis of the Seas* and sister *Allure of the Seas*. The terminal's mega-size (240,000 square feet) accommodates both arriving and departing passengers and their luggage, simultaneously going through processing procedures. The port is south of downtown Fort Lauderdale, spread out over a huge area extending into Dania Beach, Hollywood, and a patch of unincorporated Broward County. A few words of caution: Schedule plenty of time to navigate the short distance from the airport, your hotel, or wherever else you might be staying, especially if you like to be among the first to embark for your sailing. Increased security (sometimes you'll be asked for a driver's license and/or other identification, and on occasion for boarding documentation upon entering the port, other times not) combined with increased traffic, larger parking facilities, construction projects, roadway improvements, and other obstacles mean the old days of popping over to Port Everglades and running up a gangplank in the blink of an eye are history.

If you are driving, there are two entrances to the port. One is from 17th Street, west of the 17th Street Causeway Bridge, turning south at the traffic light onto Eisenhower Boulevard. Or to get to the main entrance, take either State Road 84, running east–west, to the intersection of Federal Highway and cross into the port, or take I–595 east straight into the Port (I–595 becomes Eller Drive once inside the Port). I–595 runs east–west with connections to the Fort Lauderdale–Hollywood International Airport, U.S. 1 (Federal Highway), I–95, State Road 7 (U.S. 441), Florida's Turnpike, Sawgrass Expressway, and I–75.

Contact Port Everglades
✉ *1850 Eller Dr.* ☎ *954/523-3404*
⊕ *www.porteverglades.org.*

FORT LAUDERDALE BEST BETS
The Beach. With more than 20 miles of ocean shoreline, the scene at Greater Fort Lauderdale's best beaches, especially between Bahia Mar and Sunrise Boulevard, is not to be missed.
The Everglades. Take in the wild reaches in or near the Everglades with an airboat ride. Mosquitoes are friendly, so arm yourself accordingly.
Las Olas Boulevard and the Riverwalk. This is a great place to stroll before and after performances, dinner, libations, and other entertainment.

AIRPORT TRANSFERS

Fort Lauderdale–Hollywood International Airport is 4 miles (6 km) south of downtown and 2 miles (3 km [about 5 to 10 minutes]) from the docks. If you haven't arranged an airport transfer with your cruise line, you can take a taxi to the cruise-ship terminals. The ride in a metered taxi costs about $15 to $18, depending on your departure terminal. Taxi fares for up to four passengers, regulated by the county, are $4.50 for the first mile and $2.40 for each additional mile, 40¢ per minute for waiting time, plus a $2 surcharge for cabs departing from the airport. Yellow Cab is a major presence, and Go Airport Shuttle provides limousine or shared-ride service to and from Port Everglades to all parts of Broward County; fares to most Fort Lauderdale beach hotels are in the $25 to $30 range. Fort Lauderdale Shuttle offers one-way transportation from FLL Airport or surrounding hotels to Port Everglades Cruise Ships. For two people it's a total of $22, three people $25, and four people $32.

Contacts Go Airport Shuttle ☎ *954/561-8888, 800/244—8252*
⊕ *goairportshuttle.com.* **Fort Lauderdale Shuttle** ☎ *954/525-7796, 866/386-7433* ⊕ *fortlauderdaleshuttle.com.* **Yellow Cab** ☎ *954/777-7777*
⊕ *www.taxi9547777777.com.*

PARKING

Two covered parking facilities close to the terminals are Northport (expanded to 4,250 spaces) and Midport (for 2,000 vehicles). Use the Northport garage if your cruise leaves from Terminal 1, 2, or 4; use Midport if your cruise leaves from Terminal 19, 21, 22/24, 25, 26, 27, or 29. The Midport Surface Lot at Terminal 18 has 600 spaces. The cost is $15 per day for either garage or surface lot ($19 for oversize vehicles up to 20 feet). To save a few bucks on your parking tab, two separate companies, Park 'N Fly ($12 per day) and Park 'N Go ($12 per day) provide remote parking just outside Port Everglades, at the exit off I–595, with shuttles to all cruise terminals. Book ahead online for even deeper discounts.

Contacts Park 'N Fly ✉ *2200 N.E. 7th Ave., Dania Beach ✦ at the Port Everglades exit off I–595* ☎ *954/779–1776* ⊕ *www.pnf.com.* **Park 'N Go** ✉ *1101 Eller Dr. ✦ at the Port Everglades exit off I–595* ☎ *954/760–4525, 888/764–7275* ⊕ *www.bookparkngo.com.*

> **IT'S A GIRL**
>
> Even as far back as ancient times, mariners have traditionally referred to their ships as "she." To a seaman, a ship is as beautiful and comforting as his mother or sweetheart. You could say a good ship holds a special place in his heart.

3

EXPLORING FORT LAUDERDALE

Like its southeast Florida neighbors, Fort Lauderdale has been busily revitalizing for several years. In a state where gaudy tourist zones often stand aloof from workaday downtowns, Fort Lauderdale is unusual in that the city exhibits consistency at both ends of the 2-mile (3-km) Las Olas corridor. The sparkling look results from efforts to thoroughly improve both beachfront and downtown. Matching the downtown's innovative arts district, cafés, and boutiques is an equally inventive beach area with its own share of cafés and shops facing an undeveloped shoreline.

Ah-Tah-Thi-Ki Museum. A couple of miles from Billie Swamp Safari is Ah-Tah-Thi-Ki Museum, whose name means "a place to learn, a place to remember." This museum documents the traditions and culture of the Seminole Tribe of Florida through artifacts, exhibits, and reenactments of rituals and ceremonies. The 60-acre site includes a living-history Seminole village, nature trails, and a wheelchair-accessible boardwalk through a cypress swamp. Guided tours are available daily at 2:30. ✉ *34725 W. Boundary Rd., Western Suburbs and Beyond, Clewiston* ☎ *863/902–1113* ⊕ *www.ahtahthiki.com* 🎫 *$9* ⊗ *9–5*

Billie Swamp Safari. At the Billie Swamp Safari, experience the majesty of the Everglades firsthand. Daily tours of wildlife-filled wetlands and hammocks yield sightings of deer, water buffalo, raccoons, wild hogs, hawks, eagles, and alligators. Animal and reptile shows entertain audiences. Ecotours are conducted aboard motorized swamp buggies, and airboat rides are available, too. The on-site Swamp Water Café serves gator nuggets, frogs' legs, catfish, and Indian fry bread with honey. ✉ *Big Cypress Seminole Indian Reservation, 30000 Gator Tail Trail, Western Suburbs and Beyond, Clewiston* ☎ *863/983–6101, 800/949–6101* ⊕ *www.swampsafari.com* 🎫 *Swamp Safari Day Package (ecotour, shows, exhibits, and airboat ride) $49.95* ⊗ *Daily 9–6*

★ **Bonnet House Museum & Gardens.** A 35-acre oasis in the heart of the beach area, this subtropical estate on the National Register of Historic Places stands as a tribute to the history of Old South Florida. This charming home, built in the 1920s, was the winter residence of the late Frederic and Evelyn Bartlett, artists whose personal touches and small surprises are evident throughout. If you're interested in architecture, artwork, or the natural environment, this place is worth a visit. After admiring the fabulous gardens, be on the lookout for playful monkeys swinging from trees. ✉ *900 N. Birch Rd., Along the beach* ☎ *954/563–5393* ⊕ *www.bonnethouse.org* 🗐 *$20 for house tours, $10 for grounds only* 🕙 *Tues.–Sat. 10–4, Sun. 11–4.*

☾ **Butterfly World.** As many as 80 butterfly species from South and Central
★ America, the Philippines, Malaysia, Taiwan, and other Asian nations are typically found within the serene 3-acre site inside Tradewinds Park in the northwest reaches of Broward County. A screened aviary called North American Butterflies is reserved for native species. The Tropical Rain Forest Aviary is a 30-foot-high construction, with observation decks, waterfalls, ponds, and tunnels filled with thousands of colorful butterflies. There are lots of birds, too; and kids love going in the lorikeet aviary, where the colorful birds land on every limb! ✉ *3600 W. Sample Rd., Western Suburbs and Beyond, Coconut Creek* ☎ *954/977–4400* ⊕ *www.butterflyworld.com* 🗐 *$24.95* 🕙 *Mon.–Sat. 9–5, Sun. 11–5.*

☾ **Museum of Discovery & Science/AutoNation IMAX Theater.** With more than
Fodor'sChoice 200 interactive exhibits, the aim here is to entertain children—*and*
★ adults—with the wonders of science and the wonders of Florida. In 2012, the museum doubled in size, meaning twice the fun! Exhibits include the Ecodiscovery Center with an Everglades Airboat Adventure ride, resident otters, and an interactive Florida storm center. Florida Ecoscapes has a living coral reef, plus sharks, rays, and eels. Runways to Rockets offers stimulating trips to Mars and the moon while nine different cockpit simulators let you try out your pilot skills. The AutoNation IMAX theater, part of the complex, shows films, some in 3-D, on an 80-foot by 60-foot screen with 15,000 watts of digital surround sound broadcast from 42 speakers. ✉ *401 S.W. 2nd St., Downtown and Las Olas* ☎ *954/467–6637 museum, 954/463–4629 IMAX* ⊕ *www.mods. org* 🗐 *Museum $13, $18 with one IMAX show (not including full-length feature films)* 🕙 *Mon.–Sat. 10–5, Sun. noon–6.*

Riverwalk. Lovely views prevail on this paved promenade on the New River's north bank. On the first Sunday of every month a free jazz festival attracts visitors as does an organic farmers' market each Saturday from 9 to 1. From west to east, the Riverwalk begins at the residential New River Sound, passes through the Arts and Science District, then the historic center of Fort Lauderdale, and wraps around the New River until it meets with Las Olas Boulevard's shopping district. ✉ *Fort Lauderdale.*

BEACHES

Fort Lauderdale's **beachfront** offers the best of all possible worlds, with easy access not only to a wide band of beige sand but also to restaurants and shops. For 2 miles (3 km) heading north, beginning at the Bahia Mar yacht basin, along Route A1A you'll have clear views, typically across rows of colorful beach umbrellas, of the sea, and of ships passing into and out of nearby Port Everglades. If you're on the beach, gaze back on an exceptionally graceful promenade.

Pedestrians rank above vehicles in Fort Lauderdale. Broad walkways line both sides of the beach road, and traffic has been trimmed to two gently curving northbound lanes, where in-line skaters skim past slow-moving cars. On the beach side, a low masonry wall doubles as an extended bench, separating sand from the promenade. At night the wall is accented with ribbons of fiber-optic color, quite pretty when working, although outages are frequent. The most crowded portion of beach is between Las Olas and Sunrise boulevards. Tackier aspects of this onetime strip— famous for the springtime madness spawned by the film *Where the Boys Are*—are now but a fading memory, with the possible exception of the icon Elbo Room, an ever-popular bar at the corner of Las Olas and A1A.

North of the redesigned beachfront are another 2 miles (3 km) of open and natural coastal landscape. Much of the way parallels the **Hugh Taylor Birch State Recreation Area,** preserving a patch of primeval Florida.

SHOPPING

Las Olas Boulevard. Las Olas Boulevard is the heart and soul of Fort Lauderdale. Not only are the city's best boutiques, top restaurants, and art galleries found along this beautifully landscaped street, but Las Olas links Fort Lauderdale's growing downtown with its superlative beaches. Though you'll find a Cheesecake Factory on the boulevard, the thoroughfare tends to shun chains and welcomes one-of-a-kind clothing boutiques, chocolatiers, and ethnic eateries. Window shopping allowed. ⊠ *East Las Olas Boulevard, Downtown and Las Olas* ⊕ *www.lasolasboulevard.com.*

Las Olas Riverfront. Largely unoccupied, Las Olas Riverfront is a shopping and entertainment complex in downtown, along the city's serene riverfront. A movie theater remains, as do a few budget eateries and nightclubs. The complex's popularity quickly waned in the late 1990s and news of its demolition has been circulating for a decade. ⊠ *300 SW 1 Ave., Downtown and Las Olas.*

The Gallery at Beach Place. Just north of Las Olas Boulevard on Route A1A, this shopping gallery is attached to the mammoth Marriot Beach Place time share building. Spaces are occupied by touristy shops that sell everything from sarongs to alligator heads, chain restaurants like Hooter's, bars serving frozen drinks, and a super-sized CVS pharmacy, which sells everything you need for the beach. ■ **TIP→** **Beach Place has covered parking, and usually has plenty of spaces, but you can pinch pennies by using a nearby municipal lot that's metered.** ⊠ *17 S. Fort Lauderdale Beach Blvd., Along the beach* ⊕ *www.galleryatbeachplace.com.*

Galleria Fort Lauderdale. Fort Lauderdale's most upscale mall is just west of the Intracoastal Waterway. The split-level emporium entices with Neiman Marcus, Dillard's, Macy's, an Apple Store plus 150 specialty shops for anything from cookware to exquisite jewelry. Upgrades in 2010 included marble floors and fine dining options. Chow down at Capital Grille, Truluck's, Blue Martini, P.F. Chang's, or Seasons 52, or head for the food court, which will defy expectations with its international food-market feel. Galleria is open 10–9 Monday through Saturday, noon–5:30 Sunday. ⊠ *2414 E. Sunrise Blvd., Intracoastal and Inland* ☎ *954/564–1015* ⊕ *www.galleriamall-fl.com.*

NIGHTLIFE

O Lounge. This lounge and two adjacent establishments, **Yolo** and **Vibe**, on Las Olas and under the same ownership, cater to Fort Lauderdale's sexy yuppies, business men, desperate housewives, and hungry cougars letting loose during happy hour and on the weekends. Crowds alternate between Yolo's outdoor fire pit, O Lounge's chilled atmosphere and lounge music, and Vibe's more intense beats. Expect flashy cars in the driveway and a bit of plastic surgery. ⊠ *333 E. Las Olas Blvd., Downtown and Las Olas* ☎ *954/523–1000* ⊕ *www.yolorestaurant.com.*

Tarpon Bend. This casual restaurant transforms into a jovial resto-bar in the early evening, ideal for enjoying a few beers, mojitos, and some great bar food. It's consistently busy, day, night, and late night with both young professionals and families. ⊠ *200 S.W. 2nd St.* ☎ *954/523–3233* ⊕ *www.tarponbend.com.*

WHERE TO EAT

$$
SEAFOOD

✕ **Southport Raw Bar.** You can't go wrong at this unpretentious spot where the motto, on bumper stickers for miles around, proclaims, "eat fish, live longer, eat oysters, love longer, eat clams, last longer." Raw or steamed clams, raw oysters, and peel-and-eat shrimp are market priced. Sides range from Bimini bread to key lime pie, with conch fritters, beer-battered onion rings, and corn on the cob in between. Order wine by the bottle or glass, and beer by the pitcher, bottle, or can. Eat outside overlooking a canal, or inside at booths, tables, or in the front or back bars. Limited parking is free, and a grocery-store parking lot is across the street. ⑤ *Average main: $18* ⊠ *1536 Cordova Rd., Intracoastal and Inland* ☎ *954/525–2526* ⊕ *www.southportrawbar.com.*

$$$$
STEAKHOUSE

✕ **Steak 954.** It's not just the steaks that impress at Stephen Starr's super-star restaurant. The lobster and crab-coconut ceviche and the red snapper tiradito are divine; the butter-poached Maine lobster is perfection; and the raw bar showcases only the best and freshest seafood on the market. Located on the first floor of the swanky W Fort Lauderdale, Steak 954 offers spectacular views of the ocean for those choosing outdoor seating; or a sexy, sophisticated ambience for those choosing to dine in the main dining room, with bright tropical colors balanced with dark woods and an enormous jellyfish tank spanning the width of the restaurant. Sunday brunch is very popular, so arrive early for the best views. ⑤ *Average main: $35* ⊠ *W Fort Lauderdale, 401 N. Fort Lauderdale Beach Blvd., Along the beach* ☎ *954/414–8333* ⊕ *www.steak954.com.*

WHERE TO STAY

Fort Lauderdale has a growing and varied roster of lodging options, from beachfront luxury suites to intimate B&Bs to chain hotels along the Intracoastal Waterway. If you want to be on the beach, be sure to mention this when booking your room, since many hotels advertise "waterfront" accommodations that are actually on inland waterways, not the beach.

For expanded reviews, facilities, and current deals, visit Fodors.com.

$$$ ⬜ **Hyatt Regency Pier Sixty-Six Resort & Spa.** Don't let the '70s exterior of
RESORT the iconic 17-story tower fool you; this lovely 22-acre resort teems with
★ contemporary interior-design sophistication (after a successful $40 mil-
lion renovation of guest rooms and public spaces), and remains one of
Florida's few hotels where a rental car isn't necessary. **Pros:** great views;
plenty of activities; free shuttle to beach; easy Water Taxi access. **Cons:**
tower rooms are far less stylish than Lanai rooms; totally retro rotat-
ing rooftop restaurant is open to non-guests only for Sunday brunch.
⑤ *Rooms from: $159* ✉ *2301 S.E. 17th St. Causeway, Intracoastal and
Inland* ☎ *954/525–6666* ⊕ *www.pier66.com* ⇝ *384 rooms and suites*
⦿ *No meals.*

$$$ ⬜ **Pelican Grand Beach Resort.** Smack on Fort Lauderdale beach, this
RESORT yellow spired, Key West style property maintains its heritage of Old
🜄 Florida seaside charm with rooms adorned in florals, pastels, and
wicker; an old-fashioned emporium; and a small circulating lazy-river
pool that allows kids to float 'round and 'round. **Pros:** free popcorn in
the Postcard Lounge, directly on the beach, full-service on the beach.
Cons: high tide can swallow most of beach area, decor appeals to older
generations. ⑤ *Rooms from: $224* ✉ *2000 N. Atlantic Blvd., Along
the beach* ☎ *954/568–9431, 800/525–6232* ⊕ *www.pelicanbeach.com*
⇝ *135 rooms (some condominiums)* ⦿ *No meals.*

GALVESTON, TEXAS

Updated by
Kristin Finan

A thin strip of an island in the Gulf of Mexico, Galveston is big sister
Houston's beach playground—a year-round coastal destination just 50
miles away. Many of the first public buildings in Texas, including a post
office, bank, and hotel, were built here, but most were destroyed in the
Great Storm of 1900. Those that endured have been well preserved,
and the Victorian character of the Historic Downtown Strand shopping
district and the neighborhood surrounding Broadway is still evident. On
the Galveston Bay side of the island (northeast), quaint shops and cafés
in old buildings are near the Seaport Museum, harbor-front eateries,
and the cruise-ship terminal. On the Gulf of Mexico side (southwest),
resorts and restaurants line coastal Seawall Boulevard. The 17-foot-
high seawall abuts a long ribbon of sand and provides a place for roll-
erblading, bicycling, and going on the occasional surrey ride. The city
was badly damaged from flooding during Hurricane Ike in 2008, but
businesses are now up and running, with few remnants of the storm.

Galveston is a port of embarkation for cruises on Western Caribbean
itineraries. It's an especially popular port of embarkation for people
living in the southeastern states who don't wish to fly to their cruise.
Carnival and Royal Caribbean have ships based in Galveston, offering four-, five-, and seven-day cruises along the Mexican coast and to
Jamaica, Grand Cayman, Belize, Bahamas, Key West and Honduras,
plus a 14-night cruise to the Azores and Spain. Princess Cruises and
Disney Cruise Lines will set sail from Galveston in 2012.

ESSENTIALS

HOURS   Shops in the historic district are usually open until at least 7. During peak season some stay open later; the rest of the time they close at 6. This is also the city's nightlife district, and is hopping until late.

INTERNET   The best place to check your email is at your hotel. Most of the hotels in Galveston offer some kind of Internet service, though usually for a fee. If you have a laptop, the city has a relatively extensive network of free Wi-Fi zones, including several spots on the Strand.

Visitor Information Galveston Visitors Center ⊠ *Ashton Villa, 2328 Broadway* ☎ *888/425–4753* ⊕ *www.galveston.com.*

THE CRUISE PORT

The relatively sheltered waters of Galveston Bay are home to the Texas Cruise Ship Terminal. It's only 30 minutes to open water from here. Driving south from Houston on I–45, you cross a long causeway before reaching the island. Take the first exit, Harborside Drive, left after you've crossed the causeway onto Galveston Island. Follow that for a few miles to the port. Turn left on 22nd Street (also called Kempner Street); there is a security checkpoint before you continue down a driveway. The drop-off point is set up much like an airport terminal, with pull-through lanes and curbside check-in.

Port Contacts Port of Galveston ⊠ *Harborside Dr. and 22nd St.* ☎ *409/765–9321* ⊕ *www.portofgalveston.com.*

AIRPORT TRANSFERS

The closest airports are in Houston, 50 miles from Galveston. Houston has two major airports: Hobby Airport, 9 miles (15 km) southeast of downtown, and George Bush Intercontinental, 15 miles (24 km) northeast of the city. Traffic into Galveston can be delayed because of ongoing construction.

Unless you have arranged airport transfers through your cruise line, you'll have to make arrangements to navigate the miles between the Houston airport at which you land and the cruise-ship terminal in Galveston. Galveston Limousine Service provides scheduled transportation (return reservations required) between either airport and Galveston hotels or the cruise-ship terminal. Hobby is a shorter ride (1 hour, $45 one-way, $80 round-trip), but Intercontinental (2 hours, $55 one-way, $100 round-trip) is served by more airlines, including international carriers. Taking a taxi allows you to set your own schedule, but can cost twice as much (it's also important to note that there aren't always enough taxis to handle the demands of disembarking passengers, so you might have to wait after you leave your ship). Negotiate the price before you get in.

Contacts Galveston Limousine Service ☎ *800/640–4826* ⊕ *www.galvestonlimousineservice.com.*

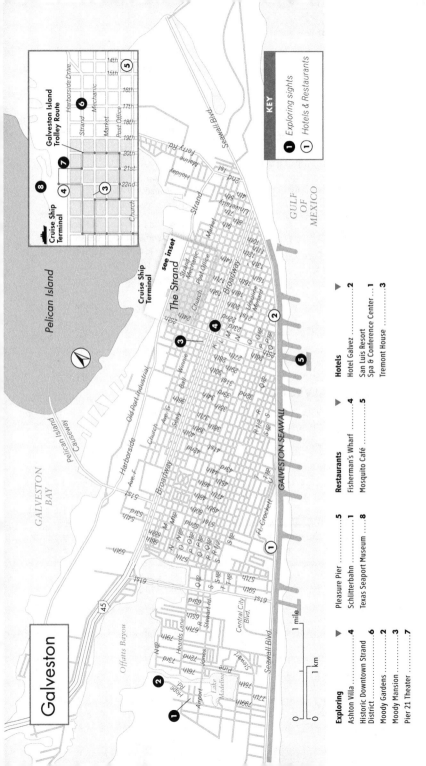

Galveston

Pelican Island

GALVESTON BAY

GULF OF MEXICO

Offatts Bayou

Pelican Island Causeway

Cruise Ship Terminal

see inset

The Strand

GALVESTON SEAWALL

Galveston Island Trolley Route

Cruise Ship Terminal

KEY

➊ Exploring sights

① Hotels & Restaurants

Exploring

Ashton Villa **4**
Historic Downtown Strand
District **6**
Moody Gardens **2**
Moody Mansion **3**
Pier 21 Theater **7**

▶ Pleasure Pier **5**
Schlitterbahn **1**
Texas Seaport Museum .. **8**

▶ **Restaurants**
Fisherman's Wharf **4**
Mosquito Café **5**

Hotels
Hotel Galvez **2**
San Luis Resort
Spa & Conference Center ... **1**
Tremont House **3**

0 ___ 1 km
0 ___ 1 mile

PARKING

Parking is coordinated by the Port Authority. After you drop off your checked luggage and passengers at the terminal, you receive a color-coded parking pass from the attendant, with directions to a parking lot for your cruise departure. The lots are approximately ½ mile (1 km) from the terminal. Check-in, parking, and boarding are generally allowed four hours prior to departure. A shuttle bus (carry-on luggage only) runs back and forth between the lots and the terminal every 7 to 12 minutes on cruise arrival and departure days (be sure to drop off your luggage *before* you park the car). The lot is closed other days. Port Authority security checks the well-lighted, fenced-in lots every two hours; there is also a limited amount of covered parking. Parking for a 5-day cruise is $50, 7-day is $70 ($80 covered). Cash, traveler's checks, and credit cards (Visa and MasterCard only) are accepted for payment.

> **GALVESTON BEST BETS**
>
> ■ **Historic Homes.** The island has some lovely historic homes to explore, particularly during early May, when the Historic Homes Tour lets you into many that aren't usually open to the public.
>
> ■ **Moody Gardens.** There are enough activities at this park to keep any kid happy.
>
> ■ **The Historic Downtown Strand District.** Galveston's historic district is a great place to stroll, shop, and eat.

EXPLORING GALVESTON

Ashton Villa. Ashton Villa, a formal Italianate villa, was built in 1859 of brick. Look for the curtains that shielded the more modest Victorian guests from the naked cupids painted on one wall. It's now home to the Galveston Island Visitor Information Center; group tours can be arranged. ⊠ *2328 Broadway* ☎ *409/762–3933.*

Historic Downtown Strand District. This shopping area is defined by the architecture of its 19th- and early-20th-century buildings, many of which survived the storm of 1900 and are on the National Register of Historic Places. When Galveston was still a powerful port city—before the Houston Ship Channel was dug, diverting most boat traffic inland—this stretch, formerly the site of stores, offices, and warehouses, was known as the Wall Street of the South. As you stroll up the Strand, you'll pass dozens of shops and cafés. ⊠ *Between Strand and Postoffice St., 25th and 19th Sts.* ⊕ *www.thestrand.com.*

Ⓒ **Moody Gardens.** Moody Gardens is a multifaceted entertainment and educational complex inside pastel-colored glass pyramids. Attractions include the 13-story **Aquarium Pyramid,** showcasing marine life from four oceans in tanks and touch pools; **Rainforest Pyramid,** a 40,000-square-foot tropical habitat for exotic flora and fauna; **Discovery Pyramid,** a joint venture with NASA featuring more than 40 interactive exhibits; and two **IMAX theaters,** one of which has a space adventure ride. Outside, **Palm Beach** has white-sand beach, landscaped grounds, man-made lagoons, a kid-size waterslide and games, and beach chairs. ⊠ *1 Hope Blvd.* ☎ *800/582–4673* ⊕ *www.moodygardens.com* 💳 *$8.95–$15.95 per venue, $44.95 day pass or $49.94 two-day pass* ☉ *Memorial Day–Labor Day, daily 10–9; Labor Day–Memorial Day, weekdays 10–6, weekends 10–8.*

Moody Mansion. Moody Mansion, the residence of generations of one of Texas's most powerful families, was completed in 1895. Tour its interiors of exotic woods and gilded trim filled with family heirlooms and personal effects. ⊠ *2618 Broadway* ☎ *409/762–7668* ⊕ *www. moodymansion.org* 💳 *$8* ☉ *Daily 10–3; tours offered hourly.*

Pier 21 Theater. At this Harborside Drive theater, watch the Great Storm of 1900 come back to life in a multimedia presentation that includes video clips of archival drawings, still photos, and narrated accounts from survivors' diaries. Also playing is a film about the exploits of pirate Jean Lafitte, who used the island as a base. ⊠ *Pier 21, Harborside Dr. and 21st St.* ☎ *409/763–8808* ⊕ *www.galveston.com/pier21theatre* 💳 *Great Storm $5, Pirate Island $4* ☉ *Sun.–Thurs. 11–6, Fri. and Sat. 11–8.*

Pleasure Pier. Owned by the ubiquitous Landry's Inc., this amusement park and entertainment district built on a historic pier over the Gulf of Mexico has a little something for everyone. Like thrills? Look danger in the face on the Iron Shark roller coaster, which reaches speeds of 52 miles an hour and includes a 100-foot vertical lift. Into games? Try your luck along the midway. Feeling hungry? Texas's first Bubba Gump Shrimp Co. is among your options. The attractions here can be expensive and parking can be difficult, but overall it offers an enjoyable time for visitors to Galveston. Hours vary quite a bit seasonally, but the park is open year-round with restricted hours and days from fall through spring. ⊠ *2501 Seawall Blvd.* ☎ *855/789–7437* ⊕ *www.pleasurepier.com* 💳 *$21.99 all-day pass; individual rides begin at $4 each* ☉ *June–Labor Day, daily 10–12; off-season hours vary so call or check the website.*

Schlitterbahn. The entire family will have a fun time at this water park, located on the bay side of the island. Schlitterbahn features speed slides, lazy river rides, uphill water coasters, a wave pool (with surfing), and water playgrounds for the little ones. There's even a heated indoor water park for chilly winter months. During summer, less expensive afternoon-only rates are in effect, and ticket prices drop in the off-season. Actually closing times do vary by the season, so outside of the busiest months of June through August, verify closing times on the park's website, or call for exact hours. ⊠ *2026 Lockheed St.* ☎ *409/770–9283* ⊕ *www.schlitterbahn.com* 💳 *$42.99* ☉ *Mid-May–late Aug., daily 10–8; Mar.–mid-May and Oct.–Dec., weekends 10–5.*

Texas Seaport Museum. Aboard the restored 1877 tall ship *Elissa*, detailed interpretive signs provide information about the shipping trade in the 1800s, including the routes and cargoes this ship carried into Galveston. Inside the museum building is a replica of the historic wharf and a one-of-a-kind computer database containing the names of more than 133,000 immigrants who entered the United States through Galveston after 1837. ⊠ *Pier 21, Number 8* ☎ *409/763–1877* ⊕ *www. galvestonhistory.org/Texas_Seaport_Museum.asp* 💳 *$8* ☉ *Weather permitting 9–5 weekdays and 8–6 weekends.*

BEACHES

Galveston Island State Park. Galveston Island State Park, on the western, unpopulated end of the island, is a 2,000-acre natural beach habitat ideal for birding, walking, and renewing your spirit. It's open daily from 8 am to 10 pm. ✉ *3 Mile Rd., 10 miles (16 km) southwest on Seawall Blvd.* ☎ *409/737–1222* ⊕ *www.galvestonislandstatepark.org* ▣ *$3.*

Seawall. The Seawall on the Gulf-side waterfront attracts runners, cyclists, and rollerbladers. Just below it is a long, free beach near many big hotels and resorts. ✉ *Seawall Blvd., from 61st St. to 25th St.*

Stewart Beach Park. Stewart Beach Park has a bathhouse, amusement park, bumper boats, miniature-golf course, and a water coaster in addition to saltwater and sand. It's open weekdays 9 to 5, weekends 8 to 6 from March through May; weekdays 8 to 6 and weekends 8 to 7 from June through September; and weekends 9 to 5 during the first two weekends of October. ✉ *6th St. and Seawall Blvd.* ☎ *409/765–5023* ▣ *$5 per vehicle.*

SHOPPING

The Emporium at Eibands. More than 50 antiques dealers are represented at The Emporium at Eibands, an upscale showroom filled with custom upholstery, bedding and draperies, antique furniture, and interesting architectural finds. ✉ *2201 Postoffice St.* ☎ *409/750–9536.*

Head to Footsies. Head to Footsies offers footwear for men and women along with trendy women's accessories and fashions from sportswear to eveningwear. ✉ *2211 Strand St.* ☎ *409/762–2727.*

Old Strand Emporium. Old Strand Emporium is a charming deli and grocery reminiscent of an old-fashioned ice-cream parlor and sandwich shop, with candy bins, packaged nuts, and more. ✉ *2112 Strand* ☎ *409/515–0715.*

Strand. The Strand is the best place to shop in Galveston. Old storefronts are filled with gift shops, antiques stores, and one-of-a-kind boutiques. ✉ *Bounded by Strand and Postoffice Streets (running east–west) and 25th and 19th streets (running north–south)* ⊕ *www.thestrand.com.*

NIGHTLIFE

For a relaxing evening, choose any of the harborside restaurant–bars on piers 21 and 22 to sip a glass of wine or a frozen Hurricane as you watch the boats go by.

The Grand 1894 Opera House. The Grand 1894 Opera House stages musicals and hosts concerts year-round. It's worth visiting for the ornate architecture alone. Sarah Bernhardt and Anna Pavlova both performed on this storied stage. ✉ *2020 Postoffice St.* ☎ *409/765–1894, 800/821–1894* ⊕ *www.thegrand.com.*

WHERE TO EAT

$$$ ✕**Fisherman's Wharf.** Even though
SEAFOOD Landry's has taken over this harbor-
side institution, locals keep coming
here for the reliably fresh seafood
and reasonable prices. Dine indoors
or watch the boat traffic (and wait-
ing cruise ships) from the patio.
Start with a cold combo, like boiled
shrimp and grilled rare tuna. For
entrées, the fried fish, shrimp, and
oysters are hard to beat. $ *Average
main: $24* ✉ *Pier 22, 2200 Harbor-
side Dr.* ☎ *409/765–5708* ⊕ *www.
fishermanswharfgalveston.com.*

BOARDING PASSES

Modern ID cards and scanning
equipment record passenger com-
ings and goings on the majority
of cruise ships these days. With a
swipe through a machine (it looks
much like a credit-card swipe at
the supermarket), security person-
nel know who is on board the
vessel at all times. On almost all
ships passengers' pictures are
recorded digitally at check-in.

$ ✕**Mosquito Café.** This popular eat-
AMERICAN ery in Galveston's historic East End serves fresh, contemporary food—
including some vegetarian dishes—in a hip, high-ceilinged dining room
and on an outdoor patio. Wake up to a fluffy egg frittata or a home-
made scone topped with whipped cream, or try a large gourmet salad
for lunch. The grilled snapper with Parmesan grits is a hit in the eve-
ning. $ *Average main: $10* ✉ *628 14th St.* ☎ *409/763–1010* ⊕ *www.
mosquitocafe.com* ☾ *Closed Mon. No dinner Sun.*

WHERE TO STAY

For expanded reviews, facilities, and current deals, visit Fodors.com.

$$$$ ⌂ **Hotel Galvez, a Wyndham Grand Hotel.** This renovated six-story Span-
HOTEL ish colonial hotel, built in 1911, was once called "Queen of the Gulf."
Pros: directly on beach, incredible pool area, beautiful grounds; recently
renovated rooms. **Cons:** rooms can be small (especially the bath-
rooms) $ *Rooms from: $269* ✉ *2024 Seawall Blvd.* ☎ *409/765–7721*
⎙ *409/765–5780* ⊕ *www.wyndham.com* ⤺ *231 rooms* ⦿ *No meals.*

$$$$ ⌂ **San Luis Resort, Spa & Conference Center.** A long marble staircase along-
RESORT side a slender fountain with sculpted dolphins welcomes you to the
beachfront elegance of this resort. **Pros:** great Gulf views, nice pool
area. **Cons:** public parking (non-valet) is not convenient. $ *Rooms
from: $329* ✉ *5222 Seawall Blvd.* ☎ *409/744–1500, 800/445–0090*
⎙ *409/744–8452* ⊕ *www.sanluisresort.com* ⤺ *244 rooms* ⦿ *No meals.*

$$ ⌂ **Tremont House, a Wyndham Grand Hotel.** A four-story atrium lobby,
HOTEL with ironwork balconies and full-size palm trees, showcases an 1872
hand-carved rosewood bar in what was once a busy dry-goods warehouse. **Pros:** beautiful, historic environment, great location; free Wi-Fi.
Cons: not a fun scene for young single travelers. $ *Rooms from: $139*
✉ *2300 Ship's Mechanic Row* ☎ *409/763–0300* ⎙ *409/763–1539*
⊕ *www.wyndham.com* ⤺ *119 rooms* ⦿ *No meals.*

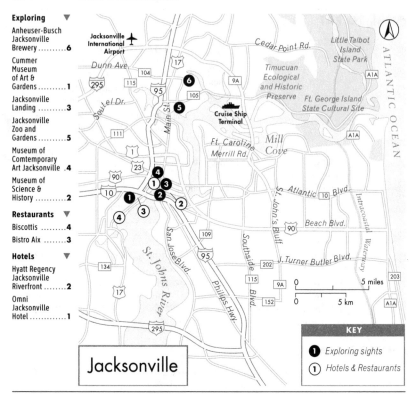

Jacksonville

KEY

1 Exploring sights

① Hotels & Restaurants

JACKSONVILLE, FLORIDA

Sharon
Hoffmann

One of Florida's oldest cities and at 758 square miles (1,926 square km) the largest city in the continental United States in terms of land area, Jacksonville is underrated, and makes a worthwhile vacation spot for an extra day or two before or after your cruise. It offers appealing downtown riverside areas, handsome residential neighborhoods, the region's only skyscrapers, a thriving arts scene, and, for football fans, the NFL Jaguars and the NCAA Gator Bowl. Remnants of the Old South flavor the city, especially in the Riverside/Avondale historic district, where moss-draped oak trees frame prairie-style bungalows and Tudor Revival mansions, and palm trees, Spanish bayonet, and azaleas populate Jacksonville's landscape. Northeast of the city, Amelia Island and Fernandina Beach offer some of the nicest coastline in Florida.

ESSENTIALS

HOURS Many museums close on Monday.

INTERNET Most people access the Internet in their hotel, and most hotels offer some kind of Internet access, often Wi-Fi.

Visitor Information Visit Jacksonville ✉ 208 N. Laura St., Suite 102, Downtown ☎ 904/798–9111, 800/733–2668 ⊕ www.visitjacksonville.com.

THE CRUISE PORT

Limited in the sizes of ships it can berth, JAXPORT currently serves as home port to the *Carnival Fascination*, which departs weekly on four- and five-night cruises to Key West and the Bahamas during the fall and winter cruising seasons, with occasional week-long sailings to Grand Turk, Half Moon Cay, and Nassau. The facility is fairly sparse, consisting basically of some vending machines and restrooms, but the embarkation staff receives high marks. The terminal itself is a temporary structure; a permanent cruise terminal has been under consideration for some time, but its fate is uncertain at this writing.

> ### JACKSONVILLE BEST BETS
>
> ■ **Budweiser Brewery Tour.** Behind the scenes on the making of one of the country's most popular beers.
>
> ■ **Jacksonville Zoo.** One of the best midsize zoos you'll visit.
>
> ■ **Museum of Contemporary Art Jacksonville.** Though small, this excellent museum is an unexpected treat in northeast Florida.

JAXPORT is about 15 minutes from Jacksonville International Airport. Take I–95 South to S.R. 9-A East. Follow 9-A to Heckscher Drive (S.R. 105) west until you reach August Drive. Head south on August Drive, and follow the signs to the cruise terminal.

Port Contacts Jacksonville Port Authority ✉ *9810 August Dr.* ☎ *904/357–3006* ⊕ *www.jaxport.com.*

AIRPORT TRANSFERS

The transfer from Jacksonville airport takes about 15 minutes and costs $30 for up to three passengers by taxi, not including tip.

Yellow Cab–Jacksonville ☎ *904/355–8294.*

PARKING

There is a fenced and guarded parking lot next to the cruise terminal, within walking distance. Parking costs $15 per day for regular vehicles, $25 for RVs. You must pay in advance by cash or major credit card.

EXPLORING JACKSONVILLE

Because Jacksonville was settled along both sides of the twisting St. Johns River, a number of attractions are on or near a riverbank. Both sides of the river, which is spanned by myriad bridges, have downtown areas and waterfront complexes of shops, restaurants, parks, and museums; some attractions can be reached by water taxi or the Skyway Express monorail system—scenic alternatives to driving back and forth across the bridges—but a car is generally necessary.

Anheuser-Busch Jacksonville Brewery Tour. Guided tours give a behind-the-scenes look at how barley, malt, rice, hops, and water form the King of Beers. Or you can hightail it through the self-guided tour and head straight to the free beer tastings (if you're 21 years or older, that is). ✉ *111 Busch Dr.* ☎ *904/696–8373* ⊕ *www.budweisertours.com* ✉ *Free* ☉ *Mon.–Sat. 10–4; guided tours, call for availability.*

Cummer Museum of Art & Gardens. The Wark Collection of early-18th-century Meissen porcelain is just one reason to visit this former riverfront estate, which includes 13 permanent galleries with more than 5,500 items spanning more than 8,000 years, and 3 acres of riverfront gardens reflecting northeast Florida's blooming seasons and indigenous varieties. Art Connections allows kids to experience art through hands-on, interactive exhibits. The Thomas H. Jacobsen Gallery of American Art focuses on works by American artists, including Max Weber, N.C. Wyeth, and Paul Manship. ⊠ *829 Riverside Ave., Riverside* ☎ *904/356–6857* ⊕ *www.cummer.org* ⌦ *$10, free Tues. 4–9* ⊙ *Tues. 10–9, Wed.–Fri. 10–4, Sat. 10–5, Sun. noon–5.*

Jacksonville Landing. During the week, this riverfront market caters to locals and tourists alike, with specialty shops, full-service restaurants—including a sushi bar, Italian bistro, and a steak house—and an internationally flavored food court. The Landing hosts more than 250 weekend events each year, ranging from the good clean fun of the Lighted Boat Parade and Christmas Tree Lighting to the just plain obnoxious Florida/Georgia game after-party, as well as live music (usually of the local cover-band variety) in the courtyard. ⊠ *2 W. Independent Dr., Downtown* ☎ *904/353–1188* ⊕ *www.jacksonvillelanding. com* ⌦ *Free* ⊙ *Mon.–Thurs. 10–8, Fri.–Sat. 10–9, Sun. noon–5:30; restaurant hrs vary.*

⟳
Fodor'sChoice
★
Jacksonville Zoo and Gardens. What's new at the zoo? Plenty. Not only has it seen the births of a rare Amur leopard and a greater kudu calf, but it has Tuxedo Park, a controlled environment for a group of Magellanic penguins. Among the other highlights are rare waterfowl and the Serona Overlook, which showcases some of the world's most venomous snakes. The Florida Wetlands is a 2½-acre area with black bears, bald eagles, white-tailed deer, and other animals native to Florida. The African Veldt has alligators, elephants, and white rhinos, among other species of African birds and mammals. The Range of the Jaguar, winner of the Association of Zoos and Aquarium's Exhibit of the Year, includes 4 acres of exotic big cats as well as 20 other species of animals. Play Park contains a splash park, forest play area, maze, and discovery building; Stingray Bay has a 17,000-gallon pool where visitors can pet and feed the mysterious creatures; and Butterfly Hollow is a flower-filled "fairy world" open seasonally. Parking is free. ⊠ *370 Zoo Pkwy., off Heckscher Dr. E* ☎ *904/757–4463* ⊕ *www. jaxzoo.org* ⌦ *$14.95* ⊙ *Daily 9–5; extended hrs summer weekends and holidays.*

Fodor'sChoice
★
Museum of Contemporary Art Jacksonville. In this loftlike downtown building, the former headquarters of the Western Union Telegraph Company, a permanent collection of 20th-century art shares space with traveling exhibitions. The museum encompasses five galleries and ArtExplorium, a highly interactive educational exhibit for kids, as well as a funky gift shop and Café Nola, open for lunch on weekdays and for dinner on Thursday. MOCA Jacksonville also hosts film series and workshops throughout the year, and packs a big art-wallop into a relatively small 14,000 square feet. Sunday is free for families; a once-a-month Art Walk is free to all. ⊠ *Hemming Plaza, 333 N. Laura St.* ☎ *904/366–6911*

⊕ *www.mocajacksonville.org* ✉ *$8* ⊙ *Tues., Wed., Fri., and Sat. 10–4, Thurs. 10–8, Sun. noon–4; Art Walk 1st Wed. of month 5–9.*

☾ **Museum of Science & History.** MOSH, once known in Jacksonville as "the children's museum," is for all ages these days, especially with the

installation of the Konica Minolta Super MediaGlobe II. Translation? It's the next generation of planetarium, one that can project shows of all kinds on the dome—from blockbuster movies to live NASA feeds to the 3-D laser shows that accompany the ever-popular, weekend Cosmic Concerts. The resolution here is significantly sharper than that of the most hi-def TV currently on the market, so whether you're a kid "flying" on a snowflake or an adult falling into darkness during *Black Holes: The Other Side of Infinity*, the experience is awesome.

MOSH also has a wide variety of interactive exhibits like the JEA Science Theatre, where you can participate in live experiments related to electricity and electrical safety; the Florida Naturalist's Center, where you can explore northeast Florida wildlife; and the Universe of Science, where you'll learn about properties of physical science through hands-on demonstrations. ✉ *1025 Museum Circle* ☎ *904/396–6674* ⊕ *www.themosh.org* ✉ *Museum $10, museum and planetarium $15, Cosmic Concerts $5; Fri. $5 all admissions* ⊙ *Mon.–Thurs. 10–5, Fri. 10–8, Sat. 10–6, Sun. 1–5.*

SHOPPING

Five Points. This small but funky shopping district less than a mile southwest of downtown has new and vintage-clothing boutiques, shoe stores, and antiques shops. It also has a handful of eateries and bars, not to mention some of the city's most colorful characters. ✉ *Intersection of Park, Margaret, and Lomax Sts., Riverside.*

San Marco Square. Dozens of interesting apparel, home, and jewelry stores and restaurants are in 1920s Mediterranean revival–style buildings. ✉ *San Marco and Atlantic Blvds., San Marco* ⊕ *www.mysanmarco.com.*

The Shoppes of Avondale. The highlights here include upscale clothing and accessories boutiques, art galleries, home-furnishings shops, a chocolatier, and trendy restaurants. ✉ *St. Johns Ave., between Talbot Ave. and Dancy St., Avondale* ⊕ *www.shoppesofavondale.com.*

WHERE TO EAT

JAXPORT's location on Jacksonville's Westside means there aren't too many nearby restaurants. But by taking a 10- to 15-minute drive south, you'll find a wealth of restaurants for all tastes and price categories.

$$ ✕ **Biscottis.** The local artwork on the redbrick walls is a mild distraction
AMERICAN from the jovial yuppies, soccer moms, and metrosexuals—all of whom are among the crowd jockeying for tables in this midsize restaurant. Elbows almost touch, but no one seems to mind. The menu offers the

unexpected: wild mushroom ravioli with a broth of corn, leek, and dried apricot; or curry-grilled swordfish with cucumber-fig bordelaise sauce. Be sure to sample from Biscottis's decadent desserts (courtesy of "b the bakery"). Brunch, a local favorite, is served until 3 on weekends. ⑤ *Average main: $20* ✉ *3556 St. Johns Ave.* ☎ *904/387–2060* ⊕ *www. biscottis.net* ⌣ *Reservations not accepted.*

$$$ ✕ **Bistro Aix.** When a Jacksonville restaurant can make Angelinos feel
ECLECTIC   like they haven't left home, that's saying a lot. With its slick black-leather booths, 1940s brickwork, velvet drapes, and intricate marbled globes, Bistro Aix (pronounced "X") is just that place. Regulars can't get enough of the creamy onion soup, crispy calamari, and house-made potato chips with warm blue-cheese appetizers or entrées like oak-fired fish Aixoise, grilled salmon, and filet mignon. Aix's resident pastry chef ensures no sweet tooth leaves unsatisfied. For the most part, waitstaff are knowledgeable and pleasant, though some patrons find their demeanor snooty, except, of course, the ones from L.A. Call for preferred seating. ⑤ *Average main: $21* ✉ *1440 San Marco Blvd., San Marco* ☎ *904/398–1949* ⊕ *www.bistrox.com* ⌣ *Reservations essential* ☾ *No lunch weekends.*

WHERE TO STAY

Hotels near the cruise terminals are few and far between, so most cruisers needing a room make the drive to Downtown (15 minutes) or to the Southbank or Riverside (20 minutes).

For expanded reviews, facilities, and current deals, visit Fodors.com.

$$$ 🏨 **Hyatt Regency Jacksonville Riverfront.** It doesn't get much more conve-
HOTEL   nient than this 19-story, downtown, waterfront hotel within walking distance of Jacksonville Landing, Florida Theatre, Times-Union Center, corporate office towers, and the county courthouse. **Pros:** riverfront location; rooftop pool and gym; free Wi-Fi in public areas; 24-hour business center; hypoallergenic rooms available. **Cons:** not all rooms are riverfront; slow valet service; no minibars; fee for in-room Wi-Fi. ⑤ *Rooms from: $179* ✉ *225 E. Coastline Dr., Downtown* ☎ *904/588–1234* ⊕ *www.jacksonville.hyatt.com* ⮑ *963 rooms, 21 suites.*

$$ 🏨 **Omni Jacksonville Hotel.** Jacksonville's most luxurious and glamor-
HOTEL   ous hotel underwent a multimillion-dollar update in 2011—right
☾   down to new flat-screen HD TVs in its chic, spacious guest rooms—
★   with more renovations slated for 2012. **Pros:** four-diamond on-site restaurant; downtown location; large rooms; rooftop pool; great kids' offerings. **Cons:** congested valet area; restaurant pricey; can be chaotic when there's a show at the Times-Union Center across the street. ⑤ *Rooms from: $129* ✉ *245 Water St.* ☎ *904/355–6664, 800/843–6664* ⊕ *www.omnijacksonville.com* ⮑ *354 rooms, 4 2-bed-room suites* ⎪⎧⎪ *No meals.*

MIAMI, FLORIDA

Paul Rubio

Miami is the busiest of Florida's very busy cruise ports. Because there's so much going on here, you might want to schedule an extra day or two before and/or after your cruise to explore North America's most Latin city. Downtown is a convenient place to stay if you are meeting up with a cruise ship, but South Beach is still the crown jewel of Miami. Miami Beach, particularly the Art Deco District in South Beach—the square-mile section between 6th and 23rd streets—is the heart of Miami's vibrant nightlife and restaurant scene. But you may also want to explore beyond the beach, including the Little Havana, Coral Gables, and Coconut Grove sections of the city.

ESSENTIALS

HOURS   Most of the area's attractions are open every day.

INTERNET   Most people choose to go online at their hotel.

Visitor Information Greater Miami Convention & Visitors Bureau
⊠ *701 Brickell Ave., Suite 2700, Miami* ☎ *305/539–3000, 800/933–8448 in U.S.*
⊕ *www.miamiandbeaches.com.* **Miami Beach Visitors Center** ⊠ *1901 Convention Center Dr., Hall C, Miami Beach* ☎ *786/276-2763, 305/673-7400 Miami Beach Tourist Hotline* ⊕ *www.miamibeachguest.com.*

THE CRUISE PORT

The Port of Miami, in downtown Miami near Bayside Marketplace and the MacArthur Causeway, justifiably bills itself as the Cruise Capital of the World. Home to eight cruise lines and the largest year-round cruise fleet in the world, the port accommodates more than 3 million passengers a year for sailings from three to 14 days and sometimes longer duration. Air-conditioned terminals include the newer terminals D and E, with dramatic public art installations reflecting sun-drenched waters off the Florida coastline and the Everglades ecosystems. There's duty-free shopping and limousine service. You can get taxis at all the terminals, and car-rental agencies offer shuttles to off-site lots.

If you are driving, take I–95 north or south to I–395. Follow the directional signs to the Biscayne Boulevard exit. When you get to Biscayne Boulevard, make a right. Go to 5th Street, which becomes Port Boulevard (look for the American Airlines Arena); then make a left and go over the Port Bridge. Follow the directional signs to your terminal.

Contacts Port of Miami ⊠ *1015 North American Way, Miami* ☎ *305/347–4800*
⊕ *www.miamidade.gov/portofmiami.*

AIRPORT TRANSFERS

If you have not arranged an airport transfer through your cruise line, you have a couple of options for getting to the cruise port. The first is a taxi, and fares are regulated by the county, with a flat fare of $24 from Miami International Airport (MIA). This fare is per trip, not per passenger, and includes tolls and $1 airport surcharge but not a tip. SuperShuttle vans transport passengers between MIA and local hotels, as well as the Port of Miami. At MIA the vans pick up at the ground level of each concourse (look for clerks with yellow shirts, who will flag

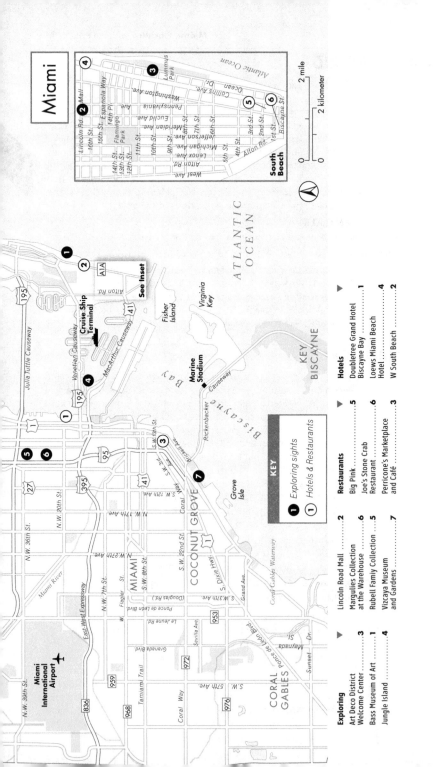

Miami

South Beach

Lincoln Rd Mall • 2
16th St
15th St Espanola Way
14th Pl
14th St
Flamingo Park
11th St
10th St
9th St
8th St
7th St
6th St
5th St
4th St
3rd St
2nd St
1st St

West Ave
Alton Rd
Lenox Ave
Michigan Ave
Jefferson Ave
Meridian Ave
Euclid Ave
Pennsylvania Ave
Washington Ave
Collins Ave
Ocean Dr
Lummus Park
Biscayne St

14th St
13th St
12th St

Atlantic Ocean

0   2 mile
0   2 kilometer

Miami International Airport

N.W. 39th St.
N.W. 36th St.
N.W. 20th St.
N.W. 17th Ave.
N.W. 27th Ave.
N.W. 7th Ave.
Miami River
W. Flagler St.
East-West Expressway

Julia Tuttle Causeway
Venetian Causeway
MacArthur Causeway
Alton Rd.
See Inset
Cruise Ship Terminal

195
41

MIAMI
S.W. 8th St.
Coral Way
S.W. 3rd Ave.
Brickell Ave.
Ponce de Leon Blvd. (Douglas Rd.)
Le Jeune Rd.
S.W. 37th Ave.

953

CORAL GABLES
Granada Blvd
Seville Ave.
Grand Ave.
S.W. 22nd St.
S. Dixie Hwy.
Coral Gables Waterway
Ponce de Leon Blvd.
Maynada St.
Sunset Dr.
Coral Way
S.W. 57th Ave.
Tamiami Trail

959
968
972
976

COCONUT GROVE
S.W. 12th Ave.
Grove Isle
Rickenbacker Causeway

Marine Stadium

ATLANTIC OCEAN

Biscayne Bay

Fisher Island
Virginia Key
KEY BISCAYNE
Causeway

195
95
395
27
836

KEY

🔺 Exploring sights

① Hotels & Restaurants

▶ **Exploring**

Art Deco District Welcome Center **3**

Bass Museum of Art **1**

Jungle Island **4**

Lincoln Road Mall **2**

Margulies Collection at the Warehouse **6**

Rubell Famiy Collection **5**

Vizcaya Museum and Gardens **7**

▶ **Restaurants**

Big Pink **5**

Joe's Stone Crab Restaurant **6**

Perricone's Marketplace and Café **3**

▶ **Hotels**

Doubletree Grand Hotel Biscayne Bay **1**

Loews Miami Beach Hotel **4**

W South Beach **2**

one down). SuperShuttle service from MIA is available on demand; for the return it's best to make reservations 24 hours in advance. The cost from MIA to the cruise port is $15 per person, or $50 if you want the entire van to yourselves.

Information Super Shuttle. This 24-hour service runs air-conditioned vans between MIA and the Homestead-Florida City area; pickup is outside baggage claim and costs around $55 per person depending on your destination. For the return to MIA, reserve 24 hours in advance and know your pickup zip code for a price quote. ⊠ *Florida City* ☎ *305/871–2000* ⊕ *www.supershuttle.com.*

PARKING
Street-level lots are right in front of each of the cruise terminals. In 2010 the $15-million Parking Garage D (with 873 spaces on four levels) opened near two recently constructed terminals serving Carnival Cruise Lines. Altogether the port's three parking garages (each with an open-air top floor) accommodate 5,871 vehicles, with 56 spaces designated for handicapped guests and another half-dozen or so for passengers with infants. The cost for all, payable in advance, is $20 per day ($40 for RVs) and $7 for short-term parking of less than 4 hours for drop-off/pick-up. You can pay with cash or a credit card, although only with American Express, MasterCard, or Visa. There is no valet parking, but a shuttle for cruise passengers (one is wheelchair-accessible) can pick you up at the parking garage/lot, take you to the appropriate terminal, and return you to your vehicle after your cruise.

> **MIAMI BEST BETS**
>
> ■ **South Beach.** Take a 10- to 15-minute cab to South Beach for great people-watching, an Art Deco tour, or a bit of sun.
>
> ■ **Bayside Marketplace.** If you want to stay close to the port, grab some outdoor drinks and eclectic eats at touristy Bayside Marketplace.
>
> ■ **Bill Baggs Cape Florida State Park.** Unleash your outdoor enthusiasm at Key Biscayne's Bill Baggs Cape Florida State Park.
>
> ■ **Vizcaya Museum.** One of south Florida's largest historic homes is one of the city's best museums.

EXPLORING MIAMI

In the 1950s Miami was best known for alligator wrestlers and you-pick strawberry fields or citrus groves. Well, things have changed. Miami on the mainland is South Florida's commercial hub, while its sultry sister Miami Beach (America's Riviera) encompasses 17 islands in Biscayne Bay. Seducing winter refugees with its sunshine, beaches, palms, and nightlife, this is what most people envision when planning a trip to what they think of as Miami. If you want to do any exploring, you'll have to drive.

Art Deco District Welcome Center. Run by the Miami Design Preservation League, the center provides information about the buildings in the district. An improved gift shop sells 1930s–50s art deco memorabilia, posters, and books on Miami's history. Several tours—covering Lincoln Road, Española Way, North Beach, and the entire Art Deco

District, among others—start here. You can choose from a self-guided iPod audio tour or join one of the regular morning walking tours at 10:30 am, every day except Thursday when the tour takes place at 6:30 pm. Arrive at the center 15 minutes beforehand. All of the options provide detailed histories of the art deco hotels as well as an

> **CAUTION**
>
> Airline carry-on restrictions are being updated continuously. Check with your airline before packing, and be aware that large purses will sometimes be counted as a carry-on item!

introduction to the art deco, Mediterranean revival, and Miami Modern (MiMo) styles found within the Miami Beach Architectural Historic District. Don't miss the special boat tours during Art Deco Weekend, in early January. *(⇨ For a map of the Art Deco District and info on some of the sites there, see the "A Stroll Down Deco Lane" in-focus feature.)* ✉ *1001 Ocean Dr., at Ocean Dr., South Beach, Miami Beach* ☎ *305/672–2014* ⊕ *www.mdpl.org* 💬 *Tours $20* ☉ *Daily 9:30–7.*

Bass Museum of Art. Special exhibitions join a diverse collection of European art at this museum whose original building is constructed of keystone and has unique Maya-inspired carvings. An expansion designed by Japanese architect Arata Isozaki houses another wing and an outdoor sculpture garden. Works on permanent display include *The Holy Family,* a painting by Peter Paul Rubens; *The Tournament,* one of several 16th-century Flemish tapestries; and works by Albrecht Dürer and Henri de Toulouse-Lautrec. Docent tours are by appointment but free with entry. ✉ *2100 Collins Ave., South Beach, Miami Beach* ☎ *305/673–7530* ⊕ *www.bassmuseum.org* 💬 *$8* ☉ *Wed.–Sun. noon–5.*

⟳ **Jungle Island.** Originally located deep in south Miami and known as Parrot Jungle, South Florida's original tourist attraction opened in 1936 and moved closer to Miami Beach in 2003. Located on Watson Island, a small stretch of land off I–395 between Downtown Miami and South Beach, Jungle Island is far more than a park where cockatoos ride tricycles; this interactive zoological park is home to just about every unusual and endangered species you would want to see, including a rare albino alligator, a liger (lion and tiger mix), and myriad exotic birds. The most intriguing offerings are the VIP animal tours, including the Lemur Experience ($45 for 45 minutes), in which the highly social primates make themselves at home on your lap or shoulders. Jungle Island offers complimentary shuttle service to most Downtown Miami and South Beach hotels. ✉ *1111 Parrot Jungle Trail, off MacArthur Causeway (I–395), Downtown, Miami* ☎ *305/400–7000* ⊕ *www.jungleisland.com* 💬 *$32.95, plus $8 parking* ☉ *Weekdays 10–5, weekends 10–6.*

⟳ **Lincoln Road Mall.** This open-air pedestrian mall flaunts some of Miami's best people-watching. The eclectic interiors of myriad fabulous restaurants, colorful boutiques, art galleries, lounges, and cafés are often upstaged by the bustling outdoor scene. It's here among the prolific alfresco dining enclaves that you can pass the hours easily beholding the beautiful people. Indeed, outdoor restaurant and café seating take center stage along this wide pedestrian road adorned with towering date palms, linear pools, and colorful broken-tile mosaics. Some of the shops

Fodor'sChoice
★

on Lincoln Road are owner-operated boutiques carrying a smart variety of clothing, furnishings, jewelry, and decorative elements. You'll also find typical upscale chain stores—French Connection, Banana Republic, and so on. Lincoln Road is fun, lively, and friendly for people—old, young, gay, and straight—and their dogs.

Two landmarks worth checking out at the eastern end of Lincoln Road are the massive 1940s keystone building at 420 Lincoln Road, which has a 1945 Leo Birchanky mural in the lobby, and the 1921 Mission-style Miami Beach Community Church, at Drexel Avenue. The Lincoln Theatre (No. 541–545), at Pennsylvania Avenue, is a classical four-story art deco gem with friezes. At Euclid Avenue there's a monument to Morris Lapidus, the brains behind Lincoln Road Mall, who in his 90s watched the renaissance of his whimsical South Beach creation. At Lenox Avenue, a black-and-white art deco movie house with a Mediterranean barrel-tile roof is now the Colony Theater (1040 Lincoln Rd.), where live theater and experimental films are presented. ⊠ *Lincoln Rd., between Washington Ave. and Alton Rd., South Beach, Miami Beach* ⊕ *www.lincolnroad.org.*

Margulies Collection at the Warehouse. Make sure a visit includes a stop at the Margulies Collection at the Warehouse. Martin Margulies's collection of vintage and contemporary photography, videos, and installation art in a 45,000-square-foot space makes for eye-popping viewing. Admission proceeds go to a local homeless shelter for women and children. ⊠ *591 N.W. 27th St., between N.W. 5th and 6th Aves., Wynwood, Miami* ☎ *305/576–1051* ⊕ *www.margulieswarehouse.com* ⊡ *$10* ⊗ *Nov.–Apr., Wed.–Sat. 11–4.*

Rubell Family Collection. Fans of edgy art will appreciate the Rubell Family Collection. Mera and Don Rubell have accumulated work by artists from the 1970s to the present, including Jeff Koons, Cindy Sherman, Damien Hirst, and Keith Haring. ⊠ *95 N.W. 29th St., between N. Miami and N.W. 1st Aves., Wynwood, Miami* ☎ *305/573–6090* ⊕ *www.rfc.museum* ⊡ *$10* ⊗ *Dec.–July, Tues.–Sat. 10–6.*

Fodor's Choice ★ **Vizcaya Museum and Gardens.** Of the 10,000 people living in Miami between 1912 and 1916, about 1,000 of them were gainfully employed by Chicago industrialist James Deering to build this European-inspired residence. Once comprising 180 acres, this National Historic Landmark now occupies a 30-acre tract that includes a rockland hammock (native forest) and more than 10 acres of formal gardens with fountains overlooking Biscayne Bay. The house, open to the public, contains 70 rooms, 34 of which are filled with paintings, sculpture, antique furniture, and other fine and decorative arts. The collection spans 2,000 years and represents the Renaissance, baroque, rococo, and neoclassical periods. The 90-minute self-guided Discover Vizcaya Audio Tour is available in multiple languages for an additional $5. Guided tours are also available in English, Wednesday through Monday at 11:30, 12:30, 1:30, and 2:30. Moonlight tours, offered on evenings that are nearest the full moon, provide a magical look at the gardens; call for reservations. ⊠ *3251 S. Miami Ave., Coconut Grove, Miami* ☎ *305/250–9133* ⊕ *www.vizcayamuseum.org* ⊡ *$15* ⊗ *Wed.–Mon. 9:30–4:30.*

BEACHES

Fodor's Choice ★ **Bill Baggs Cape Florida State Park.** Thanks to inviting beaches, sunsets, and a tranquil lighthouse, this park at Key Biscayne's southern tip is worth the drive. In fact, the 1-mile stretch of pure beachfront has been named several times in Dr. Beach's revered America's Top 10 Beaches list. It has 18 picnic pavilions available as daily rentals, two cafés that serve light lunches (Lighthouse Café, overlooking the Atlantic Ocean, and the Boater's Grill, on Biscayne Bay), and plenty of space to enjoy the umbrella and chair rentals. A stroll or ride along walking and bicycle paths provides wonderful views of Miami's dramatic skyline. From the southern end of the park you can see a handful of houses rising over the bay on wooden stilts, the remnants of Stiltsville, built in the 1940s and now protected by the Stiltsville Trust. The nonprofit group was established in 2003 to preserve the structures, because they showcase the park's rich history. Bill Baggs has bicycle rentals, a playground, fishing piers, and guided tours of the **Cape Florida Lighthouse,** South Florida's oldest structure. The lighthouse was erected in 1845 to replace an earlier one damaged in an 1836 Seminole attack, in which the keeper's helper was killed. Free tours are offered at the restored cottage and lighthouse at 10 am and 1 pm Thursday to Monday. Be there a half hour beforehand. **Amenities:** food and drink, lifeguards, parking, showers, toilets. **Best for:** solitude, sunsets, walking. ✉ *1200 S. Crandon Blvd., Key Biscayne* ☎ *305/361–5811* ⊕ *www.floridastateparks.org/capeflorida* 💵 *$8 per vehicle; $2 per person on bicycle, bus, motorcycle, or foot* ⊙ *Daily 8–dusk.*

Fodor's Choice ★ **South Beach.** A 10-block stretch of white sandy beach hugging the turquoise waters along Ocean Drive—from 5th to 15th streets—is one of the most popular in America, known for drawing unabashedly modelesque sunbathers and posers. With the influx of new luxe hotels and hotspots from 16th to 25th streets, the South Beach stand-and-pose scene is now bigger than ever. The beaches crowd quickly on the weekends with a blend of European tourists, young hipsters, and sun-drenched locals offering Latin flavor. Separating the sand from the traffic of Ocean Drive is palm-fringed **Lummus Park,** with its volleyball nets and chickee huts (huts made of palmetto thatch over a cypress frame) for shade. The beach at **12th Street** is popular with gays, in a section often marked with rainbow flags. Locals hang out on 3rd Street beach, in an area called **SoFi** (South of Fifth) where they watch fit Brazilians play foot volley, a variation of volleyball that uses everything but the hands. Because much of South Beach leans toward skimpy sunning—women are often in G-strings and casually topless—many families prefer the tamer sections of Mid- and North Beach. Metered parking spots next to the ocean are a rare find. Instead, opt for a public garage a few blocks away and enjoy the people-watching as you walk to find your perfect spot on the sand. **Amenities:** food and drink; lifeguards; parking (fee); showers; toilets. **Best for:** partiers; sunrise; swimming; walking. ✉ *Ocean Dr., from 5th to 15th Sts., then Collins Ave. to 25th St., South Beach, Miami Beach* ☎ *305/673–7714.*

SHOPPING

In Greater Miami you're never more than 15 minutes from a major commercial area that serves as both a shopping and entertainment venue for tourists and locals. The shopping is great on a two-block stretch of **Collins Avenue** between 6th and 8th streets. The busy **Lincoln Road Mall** is just a few blocks from the beach and convention center, making it popular with locals and tourists. There's an energy here, especially on weekends, when the pedestrian mall is filled with locals. Creative merchandise, galleries, and a Sunday-morning antiques market can be found among the art galleries and cool cafés. An 18-screen movie theater anchors the west end of the street.

> **PACK IT, POST IT**
>
> Pack a pad of Post-It notes when you take a cruise. They come in handy when you need to leave messages for your cabin steward, family, and shipboard friends.

NIGHTLIFE

Miami's pulse pounds with nonstop nightlife that reflects the area's potent cultural mix. On sultry, humid nights with the huge full moon rising out of the ocean and fragrant night-blooming jasmine intoxicating the senses, who can resist Cuban salsa, Jamaican reggae, and Dominican merengue, with some disco and hip-hop thrown in for good measure? When this place throws a party, hips shake, fingers snap, bodies touch. It's no wonder many clubs are still rocking at 5 am.

WHERE TO EAT

At many of the hottest spots you'll need a reservation to avoid a long wait for a table. And when you get your check, note whether a gratuity is included; most restaurants add 15% (ostensibly for the convenience of—and protection from—Latin-American and European tourists who are used to this practice in their homelands and would not normally tip), but you can reduce or supplement it depending on your opinion of the service. One of Greater Miami's most popular pursuits is bar-hopping. Bars range from intimate enclaves to showy see-and-be-seen lounges to loud, raucous frat parties. There's a New York–style flair to some of the newer lounges, which are increasingly catering to the Manhattan party crowd who escape to South Beach for long weekends. If you're looking for a relatively non-frenetic evening, your best bet is one of the chic hotel bars on Collins Avenue.

$$ ✕ **Big Pink.** The decor in this innovative, superpopular diner may remind
AMERICAN you of a roller-skating rink—everything is pink Lucite, stainless steel, and campy (think sports lockers as decorative touches)—and the menu is 3 feet tall, complete with a table of contents. Food is solidly all-American, with dozens of tasty sandwiches, pizzas, turkey or beef burgers, and side dishes, each and every one composed with gourmet flair. Big Pink also makes a great spot for brunch. ⑤ *Average main: $14* ✉ *157 Collins Ave., South Beach, Miami Beach* ☎ *305/532–4700* ⊕ *www. mylesrestaurantgroup.com.*

$$$$ ✕ **Joe's Stone Crab Restaurant.** In South Beach's decidedly new-money
SEAFOOD scene, the stately Joe's Stone Crab is an old-school testament to good
Fodor's Choice food and good service. South Beach's most storied restaurant started
★ as a turn-of-the-century eating house when Joseph Weiss discovered
succulent stone crabs off the Florida coast. Almost a century later, the
restaurant stretches a city block and serves 2,000 dinners a day to local
politicians and moneyed patriarchs. Stone crabs, served with legendary
mustard sauce, crispy hash browns, and creamed spinach, remain the
staple. Though stone-crab season runs from October 15 to May 15,
Joe's remains open year-round (albeit with a limited schedule) serving
other phenomenal seafood dishes. Finish your meal with tart key lime
pie, baked fresh daily. ■ TIP➔ **Joe's famously refuses reservations, and
weekend waits can be three hours long—yes, you read that correctly—so
come early or order from Joe's Take Away next door.** ⑤ *Average main: $42*
✉ *11 Washington Ave., South Beach, Miami Beach* ☎ *305/673–0365,
305/673–4611 for takeout* ⊕ *www.joesstonecrab.com* ⌚ *Reservations
not accepted* ⊘ *No lunch Sun. and Mon. and mid-May–mid-Oct.*

$$ ✕ **Perricone's Marketplace and Café.** Brickell Avenue south of the Miami
ITALIAN River is burgeoning with Italian restaurants, and this lunch place for
Fodor's Choice local bigwigs is the biggest and most popular among them. It's housed
★ partially outdoors and partially indoors in an 1880s Vermont barn. Reci-
pes were handed down from generation to generation, and the cooking
is simple and good. Buy your wine from the on-premises deli, and enjoy
it (for a small corking fee) with homemade minestrone; a generous anti-
pasto; linguine with a sauté of jumbo shrimp, scallops, and calamari;
or gnocchi with four cheeses. The homemade tiramisu and cannoli are
top-notch. ⑤ *Average main: $22* ✉ *Mary Brickell Village, 15 S.E. 10th
St., Downtown, Miami* ☎ *305/374–9449* ⊕ *www.perricones.com.*

WHERE TO STAY

Staying in downtown Miami will put you close to the cruise terminals,
but there is little to do at night. South Beach is the center of the action
in Miami Beach, but it's fairly distant from the port. Staying in Miami
Beach, but north of South Beach's Art Deco District, will put you on
the beach but nominally closer to the port.

For expanded reviews, facilities, and current deals, visit Fodors.com.

$ ▦ **Doubletree Grand Hotel Biscayne Bay.** Near the Port of Miami at the
HOTEL north end of downtown, this waterfront hotel offers relatively basic,
spacious rooms and convenient access to and from the cruise ships and
downtown, making it a good crash pad for budget-conscious cruise
passengers. **Pros:** marina; proximity to port. **Cons:** still need a cab to
get around; dark lobby and neighboring arcade of shops; worn rooms.
⑤ *Rooms from: $171* ✉ *1717 N. Bayshore Dr., Downtown, Miami*
☎ *305/372–0313, 800/222–8733* ⊕ *www.doubletree.com* ⟋ *152
rooms, 56 suites* ⦿ *No meals.*

$$$ ▦ **Loews Miami Beach Hotel.** Loews Miami Beach, a two-tower 800-
HOTEL room megahotel with top-tier amenities, a massive spa, a great pool,
and direct beachfront access, is good for families, businesspeople,
groups, and pet-lovers. **Pros:** top-notch amenities including a beautiful

oceanfront pool and immense spa; pets welcome. **Cons:** intimacy is lost due to its large size. $\boxed{S}$ *Rooms from: $399* ✉ *1601 Collins Ave., South Beach, Miami Beach* ☎ *305/604–1601, 800/235–6397* ⊕ *www. loewshotels.com/miamibeach* ⬎ *733 rooms, 57 suites* ⦿| *No meals.*

$$$$
HOTEL
Fodor's Choice
★
❑ **W South Beach.** Fun, fresh, and funky, this W is also the flagship for the brand's evolution towards young sophistication, which means less club music in the lobby, more lighting, and more attention to the $40 million art collection lining the lobby's expansive walls. **Pros:** pool scene; masterful design; ocean-view balconies in each room. **Cons:** not a classic art deco building; hit-or-miss service. $\boxed{S}$ *Rooms from: $431* ✉ *2201 Collins Ave., South Beach, Miami Beach* ☎ *305/938–3000* ⊕ *www.whotels.com/southbeach* ⬎ *334 rooms* ⦿| *No meals.*

NEW ORLEANS, LOUISIANA

The spiritual and cultural heart of New Orleans is the French Quarter, where the city was settled by the French in 1718. You could easily spend several days visiting museums, shops, and eateries in this area, but you can get a small sense of the place quickly. If you have time, the rest of the city's neighborhoods, radiating out from this focal point, also make for rewarding rambling. The mansion-lined streets of the Garden District and Uptown, the aboveground cemeteries that dot the city, and the open air along Lake Pontchartrain provide a nice balance to the commercialization of the Quarter. Despite its sprawling size, New Orleans has a small-town vibe, perhaps due to locals' shared cultural habits and history.

ESSENTIALS

HOURS Shops in the French Quarter tend to be open late, but stores in most of the malls close by 9. Restaurants tend to be open late as well.

INTERNET **French Quarter Postal Emporium.** French Quarter Postal Emporium offers Internet service and is also a mailing center. ✉ *1000 Bourbon St.* ☎ *504/525–6651* ⊕ *www.frenchquarterpostal.com.*

Visitor Information New Orleans Convention & Visitors Bureau ☎ *800/672–6124, 504/566–5011* ⊕ *www.neworleanscvb.com.* **New Orleans Multicultural Tourism Network** ⊕ *www.soulofneworleans.com.*

THE CRUISE PORT

The Julia Street Cruise Terminal is at the end of Julia Street on the Mississippi River; the Erato Street Terminal is just to the north. Both terminals are behind the Ernest M. Morial Convention Center. You can walk to the French Quarter from here in about 10 minutes; it's a short taxi ride to the Quarter or nearby hotels. Carnival and Norwegian base ships here at least part of the year.

If you are driving, you'll probably approach New Orleans on I–10. Take the Business 90 West/Westbank exit, locally known as Pontchartrain Expressway, and proceed to the Tchoupitoulas Street/South Peters Street exit. Continue to Convention Center Boulevard, where you will take a right turn. Continue to Henderson Street, where you will turn left,

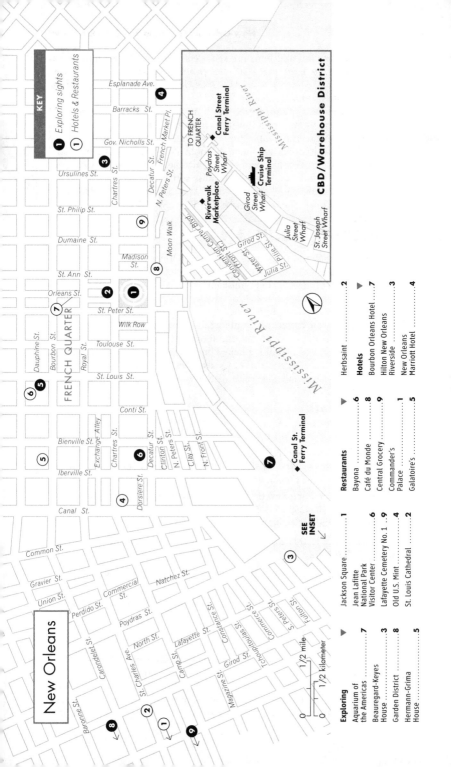

New Orleans

KEY

● Exploring sights

① Hotels & Restaurants

CBD/Warehouse District

Mississippi River

TO FRENCH QUARTER

◆ Canal Street Ferry Terminal

Poydras Street Wharf

Cruise Ship Terminal

Girod Street Wharf

Riverwalk Marketplace

Julia Street Wharf

St. Joseph Street Wharf

Convention Center Blvd

Front St.

Girod St.

Water St.

Julia St.

Tchoupitoulas St.

Moon Walk

French Market Pl.

Esplanade Ave.

Barracks St.

Gov. Nicholls St.

Ursulines St.

St. Philip St.

Dumaine St.

St. Ann St.

Orleans St.

St. Peter St.

Wilk Row

Toulouse St.

St. Louis St.

Conti St.

Bienville St.

Iberville St.

Canal St.

Decatur St.

N. Peters St.

Chartres St.

Chartres St.

Royal St.

Bourbon St.

Dauphine St.

FRENCH QUARTER

Madison St.

Exchange Alley

Clinton St.

N. Peters St.

Clay St.

N. Front St.

Dorsiere St.

SEE INSET

Mississippi River

◆ Canal St. Ferry Terminal

Common St.

Gravier St.

Union St.

Perdido St.

Poydras St.

Natchez St.

Commercial St.

Lafayette St.

North St.

Camp St.

Girod St.

Commerce St.

Fulton St.

St. Peters St.

Constance St.

Magazine St.

Tchoupitoulas St.

St. Charles Ave.

Carondelet St.

Baronne St.

0   1/2 mile

0   1/2 kilometer

and then continue to Port of New Orleans Place. Take a left on Port of New Orleans Place to Julia Street Terminals 1 and 2, or take a right to get to the Robin Street Wharf.

Port Contacts Port of New Orleans ✉ *Port of New Orleans Pl., at foot of Julia St.* ☎ *504/522–2551* ⊕ *www.portno.com.*

AIRPORT TRANSFERS

Shuttle-bus service to and from the airport and the cruise port is available through Airport Shuttle New Orleans. Buses leave regularly from the ground level near the baggage claim. Return trips to the airport need to be booked in advance. The cost one-way is $20 per person, and the trip takes about 45 minutes.

> ## NEW ORLEANS BEST BETS
>
> ■ **Aquarium of the Americas.** Especially good for families is this fantastic aquarium near the city's convention center.
>
> ■ **Eating Well.** A highlight in New Orleans is dining. If you ever wanted to splurge on a great restaurant meal, this is the place to do it. At the very least, have a beignet at Café du Mond.
>
> ■ **Hermann-Grima House.** This is one of the best-preserved historic homes in the French Quarter.

A cab ride to or from the airport from uptown or downtown New Orleans costs $25 for the first two passengers and $12 for each additional passenger; there's a fuel surcharge of $1 per trip (not per passenger). At the airport, pick-up is on the lower level, outside the baggage claim area. There may be an additional charge for extra baggage.

Contacts Airport Shuttle New Orleans ☎ *504/522–3500, 866/596–2699* ⊕ *www.airportshuttleneworleans.com.*

PARKING

If you are spending some time in the city before or after your cruise, finding a parking space is fairly easy in most of the city, except for the French Quarter, where meter maids are plentiful and tow trucks eager. If in doubt about a space, pass it up and pay to use a parking lot. Avoid parking spaces at corners and curbs: less than 15 feet between your car and the corner will result in a ticket. Watch for temporary "No Parking" signs, which pop up along parade routes and film shoots. Long-term and overnight parking are extremely expensive at hotels and garages. Parking for the duration of your cruise is available for $16 per night and is on Erato Street; if you want, SeaCaps will take your bags directly to the ship so you just have to deal with your hand luggage. RVs can park in a lot on Poydras Street next to Terminal 2 at the Julia Street dock for $32 per night.

EXPLORING NEW ORLEANS

The **French Quarter,** the oldest part of the city, lives up to all you've heard: it's alive with the sights, sounds, odors, and experiences of a major entertainment hub. At some point, ignore your better judgment and take a stroll down **Bourbon Street,** past the bars, restaurants, music clubs, and novelty shops that have given this strip its reputation as the playground of the South. Be sure to find time to stop at Café du Monde for chicory-laced coffee and beignets. With its beautifully landscaped gardens surrounding elegant antebellum homes, the **Garden District** is mostly residential, but most home-owners do not mind your enjoying the sights from outside the cast-iron fences surrounding their magnificent properties.

🕙 **Aquarium of the Americas.** Power failures during Katrina resulted in the
Fodor'sChoice major loss of the aquarium's collection of more than 7,000 aquatic crea-
★ tures. In a dramatic gesture of solidarity, aquariums around the country joined together with the Aquarium of the Americas in an effort to repopulate its stock. The museum, now fully reopened, has four major exhibit areas—the Amazon Rain Forest, the Caribbean Reef, the Mississippi River, and the Gulf Coast—all of which have fish and animals native to that environment. A special treat is the Seahorse Gallery, which showcases seemingly endless varieties of these beautiful creatures. The aquarium's spectacular design allows you to feel part of the watery worlds by providing close-up encounters with the inhabitants. A gift shop and café are on the premises.

Woldenberg Riverfront Park, which surrounds the aquarium, is a tranquil spot with a view of the Mississippi. ■**TIP➔ You can combine tickets for the aquarium and Audubon Insectarium** ($33), the aquarium and **Entergy IMAX Theater** ($28), or all three ($40), but the best deal is the "Audubon Experience": aquarium, IMAX, Insectarium, and **Audubon Zoo** for $35 (tickets are good for 45 days). ✉ *1 Canal St., French Quarter* ☎ *504/581–4629, 800/774–7394* ⊕ *www.auduboninstitute. org* ✑ *$21* ☉ *Tues.–Sun. 10–5.*

Beauregard-Keyes House. This stately 19th-century mansion with period furnishings was the temporary home of Confederate general P.G.T. Beauregard. The house and grounds had severely deteriorated by the 1940s, when the well-known novelist Frances Parkinson Keyes moved in and helped restore it. Her studio at the back of the large courtyard remains intact, complete with family photos, original manuscripts, and her doll, fan, and teapot collections. Keyes wrote 40 novels in this studio, all in longhand, among them the local favorite, *Dinner at Antoine's.* The house suffered some roof damage during Katrina, resulting in water stains along the dining room ceiling. Undaunted, the staff has reopened the site and continues its normal tour schedule. If you do not have time to tour the house, take a peek through the gates at the beautiful walled garden at the corner of Chartres and Ursulines streets. Landscaped in the same sun pattern as Jackson Square, the garden is in bloom throughout the year. ✉ *1113 Chartres St., French Quarter* ☎ *504/523–7257* ⊕ *www.bkhouse.org* ✑ *$10* ☉ *Mon.–Sat. 10–3, tours on the hr.*

Garden District. The Garden District is divided into two sections by Jackson Avenue. Upriver from Jackson is the wealthy **Upper Garden District,** where the homes are meticulously kept. Below Jackson, the **Lower Garden District** is considerably rougher. Though the homes here are often just as structurally beautiful, most of them lack the recent restorations of those of the Upper Garden District. The streets are also less well patrolled; wander cautiously. **Magazine Street,** lined with antiques shops and coffeehouses (ritzier along the Upper Garden District, hipper along the Lower Garden District), serves as a southern border to the Garden District, and St. Charles Avenue forms the northern border.

Hermann-Grima House. One of the largest and best-preserved examples of American architecture in the Quarter, this Georgian-style house has the only restored private stable and the only working 1830s Creole kitchen in the Quarter. American architect William Brand built the house in 1831. The house fortunately sustained only minor damage during Katrina and is open for visits and tours. Cooking demonstrations on the open hearth are held here all day Tuesdsay and Thursday from October through May. You'll want to check the gift shop, which has many local crafts and books. ⊠ *820 St. Louis St., French Quarter* ☎ *504/525–5661* ⊕ *www.hgghh.org* ✉ *$12, combination ticket with Gallier House $20* ⊙ *Mon., Tues., Thurs., and Fri. 10–2, Sat. noon–3; tours on the hr.*

☜ **Jackson Square.** Surrounded by historic buildings and plenty of the city's atmospheric street life, the heart of the French Quarter is this beautifully landscaped park. Among the notable buildings around the square are **St. Louis Cathedral** and **Faulkner House.** Two Spanish colonial–style buildings, the **Cabildo** and the **Presbytère,** flank the cathedral. The handsome rows of brick apartments on each side of the square are the **Pontalba Buildings.** The park is landscaped in a sun pattern, with walkways set like rays streaming out from the center, a popular garden design in the royal court of King Louis XIV, the Sun King. In the daytime, dozens of artists hang their paintings on the park fence and set up outdoor studios where they work on canvases or offer to draw portraits of passersby. These artists are easy to engage in conversation and are knowledgeable about many aspects of the Quarter and New Orleans. Musicians, mimes, tarot-card readers, and magicians perform on the flagstone pedestrian mall surrounding the square, many of them day and night.

Originally called the Place d'Armes, the square was founded in 1718 as a military parade ground. It was also the site of public executions carried out in various styles, including burning at the stake, beheading, breaking on the wheel, and hanging. A **statue of Andrew Jackson,** victorious leader of the Battle of New Orleans in the War of 1812, commands the center of the square; the park was renamed for him in the 1850s. The words carved in the base on the cathedral side of the statue—"The Union must and shall be preserved"—are a lasting reminder of the Federal troops who occupied New Orleans during the Civil War and who inscribed them. ⊠ *French Quarter* ⊙ *Park daily 8 am–dusk; flagstone paths on park's periphery open 24 hrs.*

Jean Lafitte National Park Visitor Center. This center has free visual and sound exhibits on the customs of various communities throughout the state, as well as information-rich daily riverfront tours called "history strolls." The one-hour daily tour leaves at 9:30 am; tickets are handed out one per person (you must be present to get a ticket), beginning at 9 am, for that day's tour only. Arrive at least 15 minutes before tour time to be sure of a spot. The office also supervises and provides information on Jean Lafitte National Park Barataria Unit, a nature preserve (complete with alligators) across the river from New Orleans, and the Chalmette Battlefield, where the Battle of New Orleans was fought in the War of 1812. Each year in January, near the anniversary of the battle, a reenactment is staged at the Chalmette site. You'll need a car to visit the preserve or the battlefield. ✉ *419 Decatur St., French Quarter* ☎ *504/589–2636* ⊕ *www.nps.gov/jela* ☼ *Daily 9–5.*

Fodor's Choice ★ **Lafayette Cemetery No. 1.** Built in 1833, Lafayette Cemetery No. 1 was the first planned cemetery in the city, and remains a testament to the city's history. The cemetery was built during a time when the area was seeing a large influx of Italian, German, Irish, and American immigrants from the North. Many who fought or played a role in the Civil War have plots here, indicated by plaques and headstones that detail the site of their death. Several of the tombs also reflect the toll the yellow-fever epidemic took on the city during the 19th century, which affected mostly children and newcomers to the city; 2,000 yellow-fever victims were buried here in 1852. Movies such as *Interview with the Vampire* and *Easy Rider* have used this walled cemetery for its eerie beauty. Open to the public every day except Sunday, the cemetery is a short walk from the streetcar and a beautiful spot to learn about New Orleans's history. ✉ *1400 block of Washington Ave., Upper Garden District* ☼ *Weekdays 7–2:30, Sat. 7–noon; Save Our Cemeteries tours Jan. and Feb., Mon., Wed., Fri., and Sat. at 10:30; Mar.–Dec., Mon.–Sat. at 10:30.*

Old U.S. Mint. Minting began in 1838 in this ambitious Ionic structure, a project of President Andrew Jackson. The New Orleans mint was to provide currency for the South and the West, which it did until Louisiana seceded from the Union in 1861. Both the short-lived Republic of Louisiana and the Confederacy minted coins here. When Confederate supplies ran out, the building served as a barracks, then a prison, for Confederate soldiers; the production of U.S. coins recommenced only in 1879. It stopped again, for good, in 1909. After years of neglect, the federal government handed the Old Mint over to Louisiana in 1966; the state now uses the quarters to exhibit collections of the Louisiana State Museum. At the Barracks Street entrance, notice the one remaining sample of the mint's old walls—it'll give you an idea of the building's deterioration before its restoration. Hurricane Katrina ripped away a large section of the copper roof, and for months, the twisted metal remained on the ground here, one of the most dramatic reminders of the storm in the French Quarter. After years of repairs, the museum reopened to the public in October 2007.

The principal exhibit here is the **New Orleans Jazz Collection,** a brief but evocative tour through the history of traditional New Orleans jazz. The collection has been closed since Katrina, but work continues toward a grand reopening. In the meantime, the second floor houses smaller exhibits on the history of jazz that include some of the hightlights of the collection, such as Louis Armstrong's first cornet. The third floor of the building is now a performance space for the Jazz National Historic Park, offering free performances throughout the week. Check in with the helpful Park Ranger office on the first floor for performance details.

The **Louisiana Historical Center,** which holds the French and Spanish Louisiana archives, is open free to researchers by appointment. At the foot of Esplanade Avenue, notice the memorial to the French rebels against early Spanish rule, the first instance of a New World rebellion against a European power. The rebel leaders were executed on this spot and give nearby Frenchmen Street its name. ⊠ *400 Esplanade Ave., French Quarter* ☎ *504/568–6993* ☱ *Free* ☉ *Tues.–Sun. 10–5.*

St. Louis Cathedral. The oldest active cathedral in the United States, this iconic church and basilica at the heart of the Old City is named for the 13th-century French king who led two crusades. The current building, which replaced two structures destroyed by fire, dates from 1794 (although it was remodeled and enlarged in 1851). The austere interior is brightened by murals covering the ceiling and stained-glass windows along the first floor. Pope John Paul II held a prayer service for clergy here during his New Orleans visit in 1987; to honor the occasion, the pedestrian mall in front of the cathedral was renamed Place Jean Paul Deux. Of special interest is his portrait in a Jackson Square setting, which hangs on the cathedral inner side wall. Pick up a brochure ($1) for a self-guided tour; books about the cathedral are available in the gift shop. Docents often give free tours.

■ TIP→ **Nearly every evening in December brings a free concert at the cathedral, in addition to the free concert series throughout the year.**

The statue of the Sacred Heart of Jesus dominates St. Anthony's Garden, which extends behind cathedral-basilica to Royal Street. The garden is also the site of a monument to 30 members of a French ship who died in a yellow-fever epidemic in 1857. The garden has been redesigned by famed French landscape architect Louis Benech, who also redesigned the Tuileries gardens in Paris, and impressively restored in 2011. ⊠ *615 Père Antoine Alley, French Quarter* ☎ *504/525–9585* ⊕ *www.stlouiscathedral.org* ☱ *Free* ☉ *Dailiy 7–5.*

> ### CALLING CARDS
>
> Print cards with your name, address, phone number, and email address to share with new friends. Stiff, business card–style paper can be purchased at nearly any office supply store, and you can make the cards on your computer at home. Having your cards handy sure beats hunting for pens and scribbling on scraps of paper to swap addresses.

SHOPPING

The fun of shopping in New Orleans is in the regional items available throughout the city, in the smallest shops or the biggest department stores. You can take home some of the flavor of the city: its pralines (pecan candies), seafood (packaged to go), Louisiana red beans and rice, coffee (pure or with chicory), and creole and Cajun spices (cayenne pepper, chili, and garlic). There are even packaged mixes of such local favorites as jambalaya, gumbo, beignets, and the sweet red local cocktail called the Hurricane. Cookbooks also share the secrets of preparing distinctive New Orleans dishes. The French Quarter is well known for its fine antiques shops, located mainly on Royal and Chartres streets. The main shopping areas in the city are the French Quarter, with narrow, picturesque streets lined with specialty, gift, fashion, and antiques shops and art galleries; the Central Business District (CBD), populated mostly with jewelry, specialty, and department stores; the Warehouse

District, best known for contemporary arts galleries and cultural museums; Magazine Street, home to antiques shops, art galleries, home-furnishing stores, dining venues, fashion boutiques, and specialty shops; and the Riverbend/Maple Street area, filled with clothing stores and some specialty shops.

Jax Brewery. A historic building that once was a factory for Jax beer now holds an upscale mall filled with local shops and a few national chain stores, such as Chico's, along with a food court and balcony overlooking the Mississippi River. Shops carry souvenirs, clothing, books, and more, with an emphasis on New Orleans–themed items. The mall is open daily, and during summer days serves as an air-conditioned refuge. ⊠ *600 Decatur St., French Quarter* ☎ *504/566–7245* ⊕ *www.jacksonbrewery.com.*

Riverwalk Marketplace. Built in what was once the International Pavilion for the 1984 World's Fair, the Riverwalk Marketplace offers a few national chain stores, such as the Gap, Chico's, and Ann Taylor Loft, as well as shops filled with souvenirs, jewelry, shoes, and merchandise with local themes. There's a food court, a Café du Monde, and a balcony overlooking the Mississippi River that provides a picturesque place to take a break from shopping. Appropriately placed next to the food court is the Southern Food and Beverage Museum, which explores the food and culture of local cuisine. Outside the mall is Spanish Plaza, the scene of frequent outdoor concerts and special events. ⊠ *1 Poydras St., Warehouse District* ☎ *504/522–1555* ⊕ *www.riverwalkmarketplace.com.*

NIGHTLIFE

No American city places such a premium on pleasure as New Orleans. From swank hotel lounges to sweaty dance clubs, refined jazz clubs and raucous Bourbon Street bars, this city is serious about frivolity. And famous for it. Partying is more than an occasional indulgence in this city—it's a lifestyle. Bars tend to open in the early afternoon and stay open into the morning hours; live music, though, follows a more restrained schedule. Some jazz spots and clubs in the French Quarter stage evening sets around 6 or 9 pm; at a few clubs, such as the Palm Court, the bands actually finish by 11 pm. But this is the exception: for the most part, gigs begin between 10 and 11 pm, and locals rarely emerge for an evening out before 10. Keep in mind that the lack of legal closing time means that shows advertised for 11 may not start until after midnight.

Harrah's New Orleans. The only land-based casino in the New Orleans area, Harrah's contains 115,000 square feet of gaming space divided into five areas, each with a New Orleans theme: Jazz Court, Court of Good Fortune, Smugglers Court, Mardi Gras Court, and Court of the Mansion. There are also 100 table games, 2,100-plus slots, and live entertainment at Masquerade, which includes an ice bar, lounge, video tower, and dancing show. Check the website for seasonal productions, including music, theater, and comedy. Dining and libation choices include the extensive Harrah's buffet, Cafés on Canal food court, Besh Steak House, Bamboo Court, Gordon Biersch, Grand Isle, and Ruth's

Chris Steak House. The last three are part of Harrah's newly developed Fulton Street Mall, a pedestrian promenade that attracts casual strollers, club goers, and diners. ⊠ *8 Canal St., CBD* ☎ *504/533–6000, 800/427–7247* ⊕ *www.harrahs.com* ⊗ *Daily 24 hrs.*

Mulate's. Across the street from the Convention Center, this large restaurant seats 400, and the dance floor quickly fills with couples twirling and two-stepping to authentic Cajun bands from the countryside. Regulars love to drag first-timers to the floor for impromptu lessons. The home-style Cajun cuisine is quite good, and the bands play until 10:30 or 11 pm. ⊠ *201 Julia St., Warehouse District* ☎ *504/522–1492.*

Pat O'Brien's. Sure, it's touristy, but there are reasons Pat O's has been a must-stop on the New Orleans cocktail trail for so long. For one thing, there's plenty of room to spread out, from the elegant side bar and piano bar that flank the carriageway entrance to the lush (and in winter, heated) patio. Friendly staff, an easy camaraderie among patrons, and a signature drink—the pink, fruity, and extremely potent Hurricane, which comes with a souvenir glass—make this French Quarter stalwart a pleasant afternoon diversion. Expect a line on weekend nights, and remember to return your glass to get back the deposit if you don't want to keep it. ⊠ *718 St. Peter St., French Quarter* ☎ *504/525–4823.*

Fodor's Choice **Preservation Hall.** The jazz tradition that flowered in the 1920s is
★ enshrined in this cultural landmark by a cadre of distinguished New Orleans musicians, most of whom were schooled by an ever-dwindling group of elder statesmen. There is limited seating on benches—many patrons end up squatting on the floor or standing in back—and no beverages are served or allowed. Nonetheless, the legions of satisfied customers regard an evening here as an essential New Orleans experience. Cover charge is $10, but can run a bit higher for special appearances. Call ahead for performance times; sometimes the show ends before you even begin pre-partying. ⊠ *726 St. Peter St., French Quarter* ☎ *504/522–2841, 504/523–8939* ⊕ *www.preservationhall.com.*

Fodor's Choice **The Spotted Cat.** Jazz, old time, and swing bands perform nightly at this
★ rustic club right in the thick of the Frenchmen Street action. Weekends feature afternoon sets as well. Drinks cost a little more at this cash-only destination, but there's never a cover charge and the entertainment is great—from the the popular bands to the cadres of young, rock-step swing dancers. ⊠ *623 Frenchmen St., Faubourg Marigny* ☎ *504/943–3887* ⊕ *spottedcatmusicclub.com.*

★ **Tipitina's.** A bust of legendary New Orleans pianist Professor Longhair, or "Fess," greets visitors at the door of this Uptown landmark, which takes its name from one of his most popular songs. As the concert posters pinned to the walls attest, Tip's hosts a wide variety of touring bands and local acts. The long-running Sunday-afternoon Cajun dance still packs the floor. The Tipitina's Foundation has an office and workshop upstairs, where local musicians affected by Hurricane Katrina can network, gain access to resources, and search for gigs. Although the neighborhood's not especially dangerous, it's probably most convenient to take a cab to this slightly out-of-the-way location. ⊠ *501 Napoleon Ave., Uptown* ☎ *504/895–8477.*

SIGHTSEEING TOURS

Several local tour companies give two- to four-hour city tours by bus that include the French Quarter, the Garden District, uptown New Orleans, and the lakefront. Prices range from $25 to $125 per person, depending on the kind of experience. Both Gray Line and New Orleans Tours offer a longer tour that combines a two-hour city tour by bus with a two-hour steamboat ride on the Mississippi River. Gray Line and Tours by Isabelle both offer tours of Hurricane Katrina devastation as well.

Tour Contacts New Orleans Tours ☎ *504/592–1991* ⊕ *www.notours.com.*

WHERE TO EAT

$$$
SOUTHWESTERN
Fodor's Choice
★

✕ **Bayona.** "New World" is the label Louisiana native Susan Spicer applies to her cooking style, and resulting delicious dishes include the goat cheese crouton with mushrooms, one of the Bayona's specialties, or the Caribbean pumpkin soup with coconut. A legendary favorite at lunch is the sandwich of smoked duck, cashew peanut butter, and pepper jelly. ■ **TIP→ A three-course small-plates lunch is available on Saturday for $25.** The imaginative dishes on the constantly changing menu are served in an early-19th-century Creole cottage that glows with flower arrangements, elegant photographs, and trompe l'oeil murals suggesting Mediterranean landscapes. Don't skip the sweets, like a maple-semolina cake with golden-raisin compote and pomegranate sauce. ⑤ *Average main: $28* ⊠ *430 Dauphine St., French Quarter* ☎ *504/525–4455* ⊕ *www.bayona.com* ☾ *Closed Sun. No lunch Mon. and Tues.*

$
CAFÉ
☟
Fodor's Choice
★

✕ **Café du Monde.** No trip to New Orleans is complete without a cup of chicory-laced café au lait and some of the addictive, sugar-dusted beignets at this venerable Creole institution. The tables under the green-and-white-striped awning, with views of Jackson Square, are jammed at every hour with locals and tourists. ■ **TIP→ If there's a line for table service, head around back to the takeout window and get your coffee and beignets to go. You can enjoy them overlooking the river right next door, or in Jackson Square.** The most magical time to go is just before dawn, before the bustle starts, when you can hear the birds in the crepe myrtles across the way. The New Orleans–area satellite locations (Riverwalk Marketplace in the CBD, Lakeside Shopping Center in Metairie, Esplanade Mall in Kenner, Oakwood Mall in Gretna, and Veterans Boulevard in Metairie) lack the character of the original. ⑤ *Average main: $3* ⊠ *800 Decatur St., French Quarter* ☎ *504/525–4544* ⊕ *www. cafedumonde.com* ▭ *No credit cards.*

$
DELI
☟
Fodor's Choice
★

✕ **Central Grocery.** This old-fashioned Italian grocery store makes authentic muffulettas, one of the gastronomic gifts of the city's Italian immigrants. Good enough to challenge the po'boy as the champion local sandwich, a muffuletta is made by filling round loaves of seeded bread with ham, salami, provolone, Emmentaler cheese, and a salad of marinated olives; there is a version without meat for vegetarians. The sandwiches, about 10 inches in diameter, are sold in wholes and halves. ■ **TIP→ The muffulettas are huge! Unless you're starving, you'll do fine with a half.** You can eat at one of the counters or get your muffuletta to go and dine on a bench on Jackson Square or the Moon Walk along the

Mississippi riverfront. The Grocery closes at 5 pm. ⑤ *Average main: $8* ✉ *923 Decatur St., French Quarter* ☎ *504/523–1620* ⊘ *Closed Sun. and Mon. No dinner.*

$$$$
CREOLE
✕ **Commander's Palace.** No restaurant captures New Orleans's gastronomic heritage and celebratory spirit as well as this one, long considered the grande dame of New Orleans fine dining. Recent renovations added new life, especially upstairs, where the Garden Room's glass walls have marvelous views of

> **GET MUGGED**
>
> Take along an insulated mug with a lid that you can fill at the beverage station in the buffet area. Your drinks will stay hot or cold, and you won't have to worry about spills. Most bartenders will fill the mug with ice and water or a soft drink. With a straw, your ice will not melt instantly while you lounge at the pool.

the giant oak trees on the patio below. The menu's classics include a spicy and meaty turtle soup; shrimp and tasso Henican (shrimp stuffed with ham, with pickled okra); a wonderful griddle-seared Gulf fish; and poached oysters in absinthe cream sauce under a pastry dome. Among the addictive desserts is the bread-pudding soufflé: it's too good not to try, but it might ruin you for other bread puddings. The weekend brunch is a not-to-be-missed New Orleans tradition. Jackets are preferred at dinner. ⑤ *Average main: $39* ✉ *1403 Washington Ave., Garden District* ☎ *504/899–8221* ⊕ *www.commanderspalace.com* ⌂ *Reservations essential.*

$$$
CREOLE
Fodor's Choice
★
✕ **Galatoire's.** With many of its recipes dating to 1905, Galatoire's epitomizes the old-style French-Creole bistro. Fried oysters and bacon en brochette are worth every calorie, and the brick-red rémoulade sauce sets a high standard. Other winners include veal chops with optional Béarnaise sauce, and seafood-stuffed eggplant. Downstairs in the white-tableclothed, narrow dining room, lit with gleaming brass chandeliers, is where boisterious regulars congregate and make for excellent entertainment; you can only reserve a table in the renovated upstairs rooms. Friday lunch starts early and continues well into the evening. Shorts and T-shirts are never allowed; a jacket is required for dinner and all day Sunday. ⑤ *Average main: $27* ✉ *209 Bourbon St., French Quarter* ☎ *504/525–2021* ⊕ *www.galatoires.com* ⊘ *Closed Mon.*

$$$
SOUTHERN
Fodor's Choice
★
✕ **Herbsaint.** Chef Donald Link (also of Cochon and Cochon Butcher) turns out food that sparkles with robust flavors and top-grade ingredients at this casually upscale restaurant. Small plates and starters such as a daily gumbo, charcuterie, and house-made pastas are mainstays. Don't overlook the rich and flavorful Louisiana shrimp and grits with tasso and okra. Also irresistible are the lamb neck with mushroom farro, and the muscovy duck-leg confit with dirty rice and citrus gastrique. For dessert, banana brown-butter tart will ensure return trips. The plates provide most of the color in the lighthearted, often noisy, rooms. The wine list is expertly compiled and reasonably priced. ⑤ *Average main: $27* ✉ *701 St. Charles Ave., Warehouse District* ☎ *504/524–4114* ⊕ *www.herbsaint.com* ⌂ *Reservations essential* ⊘ *Closed Sun. No lunch Sat.*

WHERE TO STAY

You can stay in a large hotel near the cruise-ship terminal or in more intimate places in the French Quarter. Hotel rates in New Orleans tend to be on the high end, though deals abound.

For expanded reviews, facilities, and current deals, visit Fodors.com.

$$ 🖼 **Bourbon Orleans Hotel.** In the center of the French Quarter, this hotel
HOTEL   also has lots of attractions inside as well. **Pros:** meticulous renovation done in 2011, with upgraded bedding and furnishings; free Wi-Fi and gym; beautiful courtyard and pool. **Cons:** lobby level is often crowded and noisy due to curious passersby; hotel is steps from loud, 24-hour Bourbon Street bars; no breakfast. **TripAdvisor:** "royal treatment," "a class in itself," "great staff." ⑤ *Rooms from: $169* ✉ *717 Orleans Ave., French Quarter* ☏ *504/523–2222* ⊕ *www.bourbonorleans.com* ⇗ *218 rooms, 28 suites* ❘◉❘ *No meals.*

$$$$ 🖼 **Hilton New Orleans Riverside.** The sprawling multilevel Hilton complex
HOTEL   sits right on the Mississippi, with superb views. **Pros:** well-maintained
☾   facilities; hotel runs like a well-oiled machine; great security. **Cons:** the city's biggest hotel; typical chain service and surroundings; groups can overwhelm lobby. ⑤ *Rooms from: $279* ✉ *2 Poydras St., CBD* ☏ *504/561–0500, 800/445–8667* ⊕ *www.hilton.com* ⇗ *1,600 rooms, 60 suites* ❘◉❘ *No meals.*

$$$ 🖼 **New Orleans Marriott Hotel.** This skyscraper hotel has a fabulous view
HOTEL   of the Quarter, the CBD, and the river; it's an easy walk from the Canal Place mall, the Riverwalk, and the Convention Center. **Pros:** excellent chef-driven restaurant; good location; stunning city and river views. **Cons:** typical chain hotel; inconsistent service; lacks charm; daily charge for Wi-Fi and phone calls. ⑤ *Rooms from: $264* ✉ *555 Canal St., French Quarter* ☏ *504/581–1000, 800/228–9290* ⊕ *www. neworleansmarriott.com* ⇗ *1,274 rooms, 55 suites* ❘◉❘ *No meals.*

NEW YORK, NEW YORK

A few cruise lines now base Caribbean-bound ships in New York City year-round; other ships do seasonal cruises to New England and Bermuda or trans-Atlantic crossings. If you're coming to the city from outside the immediate area, you can easily arrive the day before and do a bit of sightseeing and perhaps take in a Broadway show. The cruise port in Manhattan is fairly close to Times Square and Midtown hotels and theaters. But the New York City region now has three major cruise ports. You can also leave from Cape Liberty Terminal in Bayonne, New Jersey, on both Celebrity and Royal Caribbean ships. There's also a cruise terminal in Red Hook, Brooklyn, and this terminal serves Princess ships as well as Cunard's *Queen Mary 2.*

ESSENTIALS

HOURS   They say that New York never sleeps, and that's particularly true around Times Square, where some stores are open until 11 pm or later even during the week. But most stores outside of the immediate Times Square area are open from 9 or 10 until 6 or 7. Many museums close on Monday.

INTERNET Internet service is offered by most New York hotels, and there are independent Internet cafés all over town. You might even see cheap Internet service in pizzerias and delis. Starbucks offers wireless service for free, or you can use the free outdoor Wi-Fi network in Bryant Park (6th Avenue, between 42nd and 41st streets).

> **CAUTION**
>
> Items confiscated by airport security will not be returned to you. If you are uncertain whether something will pass the security test, pack it in your checked luggage.

3

Visitor Information **NYC & Company Convention & Visitors Bureau** ⌧ *810 7th Ave., between W. 52nd and W. 53rd Sts., 3rd fl., Midtown West* ☎ *212/484–1200* ⊕ *www.nycgo.com.* **Times Square Information Center** ⌧ *1560 Broadway, between 46th and 47th Sts., Midtown West* ☎ *212/768–1560* ⊕ *www.timessquarenyc.org* Ⓜ *N, Q, R, S, 1, 2, 3, 7 to 42nd St./Times Square.*

THE CRUISE PORT

The New York Passenger Ship Terminal is on the far west side of Manhattan, five very long blocks from the Times Square area, between 48th and 52nd streets; the vehicle entrance is at 55th Street. Traffic can be backed up in the area on days that cruise ships arrive and depart, so allow yourself enough time to check in and go through security. There are no nearby subway stops, though city buses do cross Midtown at 50th and 42nd streets. If you don't have too much luggage, it is usually faster and more convenient to have a taxi drop you off at the intersection of 50th Street and the West Side Highway, directly across the street from the entrance to the lower level of the terminal; then you can walk right in and take the escalator or elevator up to the embarkation level.

Cape Liberty Terminal in Bayonne is off Route 440. From the New Jersey Turnpike, take Exit 14A, then follow the signs for 440 South, and make a left turn into the Cape Liberty Terminal area (on Port Terminal Boulevard). If you are coming from Long Island, you cross Staten Island, and after crossing the Bayonne Bridge take 440 North, making a right into the terminal area. If you are coming from Manhattan, you can also reach the terminal by public transit. Take the New Jersey Transit light-rail line from the PATH trains in Hoboken; get off at the Bayonne stop, and from there you can take a taxi to the terminal (about 2 miles [3 km] away); there may be a free shuttle bus on cruise sailing dates, but confirm that with your cruise line.

The Brooklyn cruise terminal at Pier 12 in Red Hook, which opened in April 2006, is not convenient to public transportation, so you should plan to take a taxi, drive, or take the bus transfers offered by the cruise lines (the cost for this is about $45 per person from either LaGuardia or JFK). There is a secure, 500-car outdoor parking lot on-site. To reach the terminal from LaGuardia Airport, take I–278 W (the Brooklyn-Queens Expressway), Exit 26, Hamilton Avenue; the terminal entrance is actually off Browne Street. From JFK, take I–278 E (again, the Brooklyn-Queens Expressway), and then the same exit. If

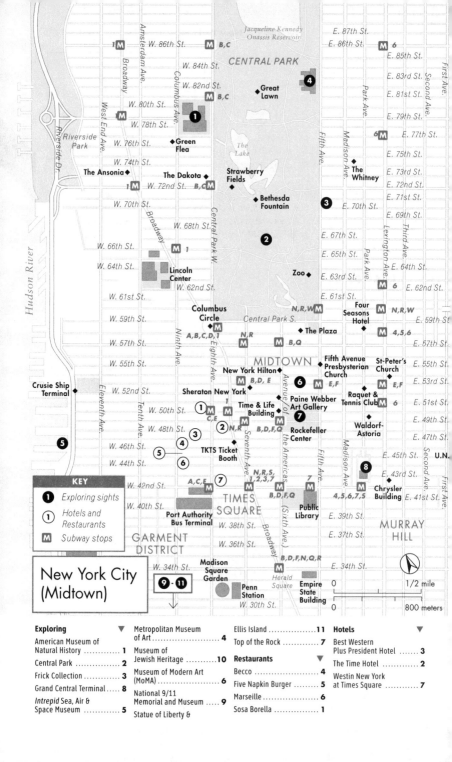

New York City
(Midtown)

you arrive early, there's not much in the neighborhood, but there are a few neighborhood delis and restaurants about 15 minutes away on foot; the area is a safe place to walk around during daylight hours, though it's very industrial and unattractive. Red Hook is the home of ships from the Carnival, Princess, and Cunard cruise lines.

Information Cape Liberty Terminal ✉ *14 Port Terminal Blvd., Bayonne, New Jersey* ☎ *201/823–3737* ⊕ *www. cruiseliberty.com.* **New York Passenger Ship Terminal** ✉ *711 12th Ave., vehicle entry at 55th St., Midtown West, New York, New York* ☎ *212/246–5450* ⊕ *www.nycruiseterminal.com* ✉ *Pier 12, Bldg. 112, Red Hook, Brooklyn, New York* ☎ *718/858–3450.*

NEW YORK BEST BETS

■ **An Art Museum.** Take your pick: the Met, MOMA, or the Frick, but museum-going is a true highlight of New York.

■ **A Broadway Show.** The theater experience in New York is better than almost anywhere else in the world.

■ **Statue of Liberty.** Just the sight of Lady Liberty will melt the coldest heart, though the highlight of the trip is actually the Ellis Island museum, not the statue itself.

AIRPORT TRANSFERS

A cab to or from JFK to the passenger-ship terminal in **Manhattan** will cost $45 (a flat fare) plus toll and tip; expect to pay at least $35 on the meter if you are coming from LaGuardia and at least $50 or $60 (not including tolls of about $10 and the tip) from Newark in a regular taxi (from Newark airport, it's usually more cost-effective to call for a car service to pick you up; these services have a flat fare of about $48, not including the tolls and tip).

From Newark Airport it's approximately $30 to **Cape Liberty,** $80 from JFK (plus tolls and tip, so count on at least $110 and be aware that taxis are not obligated to take this route from JFK), and $90 from LaGuardia (plus tolls and tip; count on paying more than $110). Royal Caribbean offers bus service from several Mid-Atlantic and Northeast cities on sailing dates, but confirm that with the cruise line.

If your cruise is leaving from **Red Hook,** the taxi fare will be much cheaper if you fly into either La Guardia (about $30) or JFK (about $40); you'll pay at least $80 from Newark Airport (not including tolls and tip). Cruise lines provide bus transfers from all three of the area's airports, but it may be cheaper to take a taxi if you are traveling with more than one other person. Note that all these taxi fares do not include tolls and tips. From Newark, the tolls to Brooklyn can be substantial, adding almost $20 to the fare.

PARKING

You can park at the New York Passenger Ship Terminal for a staggering $30 a day; the fee is payable in advance in cash or traveler's checks (no credit cards).

Parking at Cape Liberty Terminal in Bayonne is $19 per day, payable in cash, traveler's checks, and major credit cards.

Parking at Red Hook, Brooklyn, costs $23 for the first 24 hours and then $20 per day.

TOP ATTRACTIONS

There's no way to do justice to even the most popular tourist stops in New York. Below is information about several top attractions. If you have only a day in the city, choose one or two attractions and buy a Metro card to facilitate easy transfers between the subway and bus (put on as much money as you think you'll use in a day but no less than $4.50). There's a moving series of panels about the World Trade Center at the so-called "Ground Zero" site across from the Millennium Hotel (take the 1 train to Cortlandt Street or the E to World Trade Center); there's another series of memorial panels underneath at the World Trade Center PATH station, which is accessible from the main, streetside memorial area. Times Square is approximately 20 minutes by foot from the cruise terminal; just walk straight out of the gate and east along 48th Street.

Fodor's Choice
★ **American Museum of Natural History.** With 45 exhibition halls and more than 32 million artifacts and specimens, the world's largest and most important museum of natural history can easily occupy you for half a day. The dioramas might seem dated, but are fun. The dinosaur exhibits are probably the highlight. Attached to the museum is the **Rose Center for Earth and Space,** with various exhibits and housing the **Hayden Planetarium** and an **IMAX Theater.** ⊠ *Central Park West at W. 79 St., Upper West Side* ☎ *212/769–5100* ⊕ *www.amnh.org* ☜ *$19 suggested donation, includes admission to Rose Center for Earth and Space* ☉ *Daily 10–5:45* Ⓜ *B, C to 81st St./Museum of Natural History.*

☾ **Central Park.** Without Central Park's 843 acres of meandering paths,
Fodor's Choice tranquil lakes, ponds, and open meadows, New Yorkers might be a lot
★ less sane. You can drop by the zoo (near 64th Street, on the east side) or the famous Bethesda Fountain (mid-park, at around 72nd Street), but the main draw is just to wander the lanes. Central Park has one of the lowest crime rates in the city. Still, use common sense and stay within sight of other park visitors, and don't go into the park after dark. Directions, park maps, and events calendars can be obtained from volunteers at two 5th Avenue **information booths,** at East 60th Street and East 72nd Street. ☎ *212/794–6564 Dairy visitor center, 646/310–6600 Central Park Conservancy* ⊕ *www.centralparknyc.org* Ⓜ *A, D, or 1 to Columbus Circle; N, Q, R to 5th Ave.–59th St.*

Fodor's Choice
★ **Frick Collection.** Coke-and-steel baron Henry Clay Frick (1849–1919) amassed this superb art collection far from the soot and smoke of Pittsburgh, where he made his fortune. The mansion was designed by Thomas Hastings and built in 1913–14. It opened in 1935, but still resembles a gracious private home, albeit one with bona fide masterpieces in almost every room. This is the best small museum in town by a mile. An audio guide is included with admission. Children under 10 are not admitted, and those age 10–16 with adult only. ⊠ *1 E. 70th St., at 5th Ave., Upper East Side* ☎ *212/288–0700* ⊕ *www.frick.org* ☜ *$18* ☉ *Tues.–Sat. 10–6, Sun. 11–5* Ⓜ *6 to 68th St./Hunter College.*

Fodor's Choice
★ **Grand Central Terminal.** Grand Central is not only the world's largest (76 acres) and the nation's busiest (500,000 commuters and subway riders use it daily) railway station, but also one of the world's greatest

public spaces ("justly famous," as critic Tony Hiss noted, "as a cross-roads, a noble building . . . and an ingenious piece of engineering"). A massive four-year renovation completed in October 1998 restored the 1913 landmark to its original splendor—and then some. There's a nice audio tour for rent for $5 per adult. The **Municipal Art Society** (☎ 212/935–3960 ⊕ www.mas.org) leads architectural tours of the terminal that begin here every Wednesdays from 12:30 to 2. Reservations are not required, and a $10 donation is suggested. Meet at the information booth, Main Concourse. Grand Central also has the city's largest Apple store. ✉ *Main entrance, E. 42nd St. at Park Ave., Midtown East* ☎ 212/935–3960 ⊕ *www. grandcentralterminal.com* Ⓜ *4, 5, 6, 7, S to 42nd St./Grand Central.*

> **CAUTION**
>
> If you still use film, do not pack it in checked luggage, since the newest airport screening equipment will ruin it. Put it in your carry-on instead.

Intrepid Sea, Air & Space Museum. Formerly the USS *Intrepid*, this 900-foot aircraft carrier is serving out its retirement as the centerpiece of Manhattan's only floating museum. An A-12 Blackbird spy plane, lunar landing modules, helicopters, seaplanes, and two dozen other aircraft are on deck. Docked alongside, and also part of the museum, are the *Growler*, a strategic-missile submarine; the *Edson*, a Vietnam-era destroyer; and several other battle-scarred naval veterans. Children can explore the ships' skinny hallways and winding staircases, as well as manipulate countless knobs, buttons, and wheels. New in 2012 is the *Enterprise*, one of the U.S. space program's original shuttles (though this particular shuttle never flew in space). This museum is within easy walking distance of the main cruise piers in Manhattan. Ticket prices are $2 cheaper if purchased online in advance. ✉ *Pier 86, W 46th St. and 12th Ave., Midtown West* ☎ 212/245–0072, 877/957–7447 ⊕ *www.intrepidmuseum.org* ✆ *$24 ($30 with space shuttle)* ☉ *Apr.– Oct., Mon.–Fri. 10–5, Sat.–Sun. 10–6; Nov.–Mar., Tues.–Sun. 10–5; last admission 1 hr before closing* Ⓜ *A, C, E to 42nd St.; M42 bus to pier.*

Fodor'sChoice ★ **The Metropolitan Museum of Art.** If Manhattan held no other museum than the colossal Metropolitan Museum of Art, you could still occupy yourself for days roaming its labyrinthine corridors. The Metropolitan Museum has more than 2 million works of art representing 5,000 years of history, so it's a good idea to plan ahead; looking at everything here could take a week. ✉ *1000 5th Ave., at 82nd St., Upper East Side* ☎ 212/535–7710 ⊕ *www.metmuseum.org* ✆ *$25 suggested donation; $7 for audio guide* ☉ *Tues.–Thurs. and Sun. 9:30–5:30, Fri. and Sat. 9:30–9* Ⓜ *4, 5, 6 to 86th St.*

Museum of Jewish Heritage—A Living Memorial to the Holocaust. In a granite hexagon rising 85 feet above Robert F. Wagner Jr. Park at the southern end of Battery Park City, this museum pays tribute to the 6 million Jews who perished in the Holocaust. It's one of the best such museums in the country. ✉ *36 Battery Pl., Battery Park City, Financial District* ☎ 646/437–4202 ⊕ *www.mjhnyc.org* ✆ *$12, free Wed. 4–10* ☉ *Thurs. and Sun.–Tues. 10–5:45, Wed. 10–8, Fri. and eve of Jewish holidays 10–3* Ⓜ *4, 5 to Bowling Green.*

Fodor'sChoice   **The Museum of Modern Art (MoMA).**
★ The masterpieces—Monet's *Water Lilies*, Picasso's *Les Demoiselles d'Avignon*, Van Gogh's *Starry Night*—are still here, but for now the main draw at MoMA is, well, MoMA. A "modernist dream world" is how critics described the museum after its $425 million

> **CAUTION**
>
> Store any irreplaceable valuables in the ship purser's safe rather than the one in your cabin. Some insurance policies will not cover the loss of items left in your cabin.

face-lift. Unfortunately, the museum was an instant success, which means lines are sometimes down the block. For the shortest wait, get here before the museum opens; you can avoid some of the crowding by entering through the 54th Street side. Be prepared for sticker shock when you buy your ticket. ⊠ *11 W. 53rd St., between 5th and 6th Aves., Midtown East* ☎ *212/708–9400* ⊕ *www.moma.org* 🖃 *$25* ⊙ *Sat.–Mon., Wed., and Thurs. 10:30–5:30, Fri. 10:30–8. Closed Tues.* Ⓜ *E, M to 5th Ave./53rd St.; B, D, F, M to 47th–50th Sts./ Rockefeller Center.*

National 9/11 Memorial and Museum. This somber work, designed by Michael Arad and Peter Walker, reflects none of the setbacks and complications to the building process that have arisen in the years since that tragedy. Central to the memorial and museum are recessed, 30-foot waterfalls that sit on the footprint where the Twin Towers once stood. Every minute, some 60,000 gallons of water cascades down the sides and then down into smaller square holes in the center of the pools. The pools are each nearly an acre in size, and they are said to be the largest manmade waterfalls in North America. Until the construction going on throughout the rest of the World Trade Center site is finished, a visit to the memorial requires dealing with strict security, including a trip through airport-like scanners. No large bags are allowed, there's no bag storage, and no public restrooms, either. ■ **TIP→** It's best to book a free, timed ticket online before your visit, but at low-traffic times stand-by tickets may also be available, both at the site and from the Preview Site (90 Vesey Street) and the Visitor Center (90 West Street). ⊠ *Entry at northeast corner of Albany and Greenwich Sts., Financial District* ☎ *212/266–5211 for reservation help* ⊕ *www.911memorial.org* 🖃 *Free (with timed ticket obtained in advance)* ⊙ *Memorial: early Mar.–early Oct., daily 10–8; early Oct.–early Mar., daily 10–6 (daily 10–8 for wks around Thanksgiving and Christmas; last entry an hr before closing); Visitor center: early Mar.–early Oct., daily 10–8:30; early Oct.–early Mar., daily 10–7 (daily 10–8:30 for wks around Thanksgiving and Christmas)* Ⓜ *1, N, or R to Rector St.; 2, 3, 4, 5, A, C, J, Z to Fulton St.–Broadway-Nassau; E to World Trade Center/Church St.*

Statue of Liberty and Ellis Island. Though you must endure a long wait and onerous security, it's worth the trouble to see one of the iconic images of New York. But the truth is that a trip to the statue is time-consuming and laborious; Ellis Island is a much better investment of your time, especially if you have only a day or two in New York. The narrow, double-helix stairs leading to the statue's crown closed after 9/11, but access reopened on July 4, 2009. The statue itself is closed at this writing but was expected to reopen in Fall 2012; when it is open, access to the crown is strictly limited, and tickets must be booked months in advance; otherwise, it's possible to view the museum in the pedestal, but even those tickets often sell out. Much more interesting—and well worth exploring—is the Ellis Island museum, which traces the story of immigration in New York City with moving exhibits throughout the restored processing building. Go early if you want to see everything, and allow plenty of time for security and lines. The ferry stops first at the statue and then continues to Ellis Island. ⊠ *Liberty Island, Suite 210, New York Harbor* ☎ *212/363–3200, 877/523–9849 ticket reservations* ⊕ *www.statueofliberty.org* ⊠ *Free but ferry $13 round-trip (includes Ellis Island), $21 with audio guide, crown tickets $3* ☉ *Daily 9:30–5; last ferry at 3:30, extended hrs in summer.*

Fodor's Choice **Top of the Rock.** Rockefeller Center's multifloor observation deck, first
★ opened in 1933, and closed in the early 1980s, reopened in 2005. Though overpriced, the experience is infinitely better than that at the Empire State Building, where interminable lines spoil most of the fun. Arrive just before sunset for the best views (which include the Empire State Building). ⊠ *Entrance on 50th St., between 5th and 6th Aves., 30 Rockefeller Plaza, Midtown West* ☎ *212/698–2000, 212/698–2000* ⊕ *www.topoftherocknyc.com* ⊠ *$25 adult; children under 6 not admitted* ☉ *Daily 8–midnight; last elevator at 11 pm* Ⓜ *B, D, F, M to 47th– 50th Sts./Rockefeller Center.*

SHOPPING

You can find almost any major store from virtually any designer or chain in Manhattan. High-end designers tend to be along **Madison Avenue,** between 55th and 86th streets. Some are along **57th Street,** between Madison and 7th avenues. **Fifth Avenue,** starting at Saks Fifth Avenue (at 50th Street) and going up to 59th Street, is a hodgepodge of high-end stores and more accessible options, including the high-end department store Bergdorf-Goodman, at 58th Street. More interesting and individual stores can be found in **SoHo** (between Houston and Canal, West Broadway and Lafayette), and the **East Village** (between 14th Street and Houston, Broadway and Avenue A). **Chinatown** is chock-full of designer knockoffs, crowded streets, and dim sum palaces; though frenetic during the day, it's a fun stop. The newest group of stores in Manhattan is at the **Time-Warner Center,** at Columbus Circle (at 8th Avenue and 59th Street); the high-rise mall has upscale stores and some of the city's best-reviewed and most expensive new restaurants.

BROADWAY SHOWS

Scoring tickets to Broadway shows is fairly easy except for the very top draws. For the most part, the top ticket price for Broadway musicals is now around $140; the best seats for Broadway plays can run as high as $130.

Telecharge ☎ *212/239–6200* ⊕ *www.telecharge.com.*

Ticketmaster ☎ *212/307–4100* ⊕ *www.ticketmaster.com.*

TKTS. For tickets at 25% to 50% off the usual price, head to TKTS. The kiosks accept cash and traveler's checks—no credit cards. ⊠ *Duffy Sq., W. 47th St. and Broadway, Midtown West, New York* Ⓜ *N, R, W to 49th St.; 1, 9 to 50th St.*

WHERE TO EAT

The restaurants we recommend below are all in Midtown West, near Broadway theaters and hotels. Make reservations at all but the most casual places or face a numbing wait.

$$
ITALIAN
✕**Becco.** An ingenious concept makes Becco a prime Restaurant Row choice for time-constrained theatergoers. There are two pricing scenarios: one includes an all-you-can-eat selection of antipasti and three pastas served hot out of pans that waiters circulate around the dining room; the other adds a generous entrée to the mix. The pasta selection changes daily, but often includes gnocchi, fresh ravioli, and fettuccine in a cream sauce. The entrées include braised veal shank, grilled double-cut pork chop, and rack of lamb, among other selections. $ *Average main: $23* ⊠ *355 W. 46th St., between 8th and 9th Aves., Midtown West* ☎ *212/397–7597* ⊕ *www.becco-nyc.com* Ⓜ *A, C, E to 42nd St.*

$
AMERICAN
✕**Five Napkin Burger.** This perennially packed Hell's Kitchen burger place/brasserie has been a magnet for burger lovers since day one. Bottles of Maker's Mark line the sleek, alluringly lighted bar in the back, a collection of antique butcher's scales hangs on a tile wall near the kitchen, and meat hooks dangle from the ceiling between the light fixtures. Though there are many menu distractions—deep-fried pickles, warm artichoke dip, to name a few—the main attractions are the juicy burgers, like the original 10-ounce chuck with a tangle of onions, Gruyère cheese, and rosemary aioli. There's a patty variety for everyone, including a ground lamb *kofta* and an onion ring–topped ahi tuna burger. For dessert, have an über-thick black-and-white malted milkshake. $ *Average main: $16* ⊠ *630 9th Ave., at 45th St, Midtown West* ☎ *212/757–2277* ⊕ *www.5napkinburger.com* Ⓜ *A, C, E to 42nd St./8th Ave.*

$$
MEDITERRANEAN
✕**Marseille.** With great food and a convenient location near several Broadway theaters, Marseille is perpetually packed. The Mediterranean creations are continually impressive, including the bouillabaisse, the signature dish of the region for which the restaurant is named—a mélange of mussels, shrimp, and white fish in a fragrant broth, topped with a garlicky crouton and served with rouille on the side. Leave room for the spongy beignets with chocolate and raspberry dipping sauces. $ *Average main: $22* ⊠ *630 9th Ave., at W. 44th St., Midtown West* ☎ *212/333–2323* ⊕ *www.marseillenyc.com* ⌖ *Reservations essential* Ⓜ *A, C, E to 42nd St./Port Authority Bus Terminal.*

$$
ITALIAN
✕**Sosa Borella.** This is one of the Theater District's top spots for reliable food at a reasonable cost. The bi-level, casual Argentinian-Italian eatery is an inviting and friendly space where diners choose from a wide range of options. The lunch menu features staples like warm

sandwiches and entrée-size salads, whereas the dinner menu is slightly gussied up with meat, fish, and pasta dishes (the rich agnolotti with lamb Bolognese sauce, topped with a wedge of grilled pecorino cheese, is a must-try). The freshly baked bread served at the beginning of the meal with pesto dipping sauce is a nice touch as you wait for your meal. The service can be slow at times, so leave yourself plenty of time before the show. ⑤ *Average main: $25* ✉ *832 8th Ave., between 50th and 51st Sts., Midtown West* ☎ *212/262–8282* ⊕ *www.sosaborella. com* Ⓜ *C, E, 1 to 50th St.*

WHERE TO STAY

There are no real bargains in the Manhattan hotel world, and you'll find it difficult to get a decent room for under $250 during much of the year. However, occasional weekend deals can be found. All the hotels we recommend for cruise passengers are on the West Side, in relatively easy proximity to the cruise ship terminal.

For expanded reviews, facilities, and current deals, visit Fodors.com.

$ 🏨 **Best Western Plus President Hotel.** After a $15 million renovation that
HOTEL transformed it from a ho-hum Best Western, the President is the only politically themed hotel in the city, starting with the purple color scheme, a combination of Republican red and Democratic blue. **Pros:** sleek rooms for the price; convenient location; unique theme. **Cons:** cramped lobby; dark bathrooms; poor views. ⑤ *Rooms from: $249* ✉ *234 W. 48th St., between 8th Ave. and Broadway, Times Square* ☎ *212/246–8800, 800/828–4667* ⊕ *www.thepresidenthotel.com* ⇌ *334 rooms* ⦿ *No meals* Ⓜ *C, E to 50th St.*

$ 🏨 **The Time Hotel.** One of the neighborhood's first boutique hotels, this
HOTEL spot half a block from the din of Times Square tempers trendiness with a touch of humor. **Pros:** acclaimed and popular Serafina restaurant downstairs; surprisingly quiet for Times Square location; good turndown service. **Cons:** decor makes the rooms a little dated; service is inconsistent; water pressure is lacking. ⑤ *Rooms from: $275* ✉ *224 W. 49th St., between Broadway and 8th Ave., Midtown West* ☎ *212/246–5252, 877/846–3692* ⊕ *www.thetimeny.com* ⇌ *164 rooms, 29 suites* ⦿ *No meals* Ⓜ *1, C, E to 50th St.*

$$ 🏨 **Westin New York at Times Square.** This giant Midtown hotel has every-
HOTEL thing you'd expect, at fairly reasonable prices, though without much style. **Pros:** busy Times Square location; big rooms; great gym. **Cons:** busy Times Square location; small bathroom sinks; some rooms need to be refreshed. ⑤ *Rooms from: $319* ✉ *270 W. 43rd St., at 8th Ave., Midtown West* ☎ *212/201–2700, 866/837–4183* ⊕ *www.westinny. com* ⇌ *863 rooms, 29 suites* ⦿ *No meals* Ⓜ *A, C, E to 42nd St./ Times Sq.*

NORFOLK, VIRGINIA

Ramona Settle Founded in 1680, Norfolk is no newcomer to the cruise business. One famous passenger, Thomas Jefferson, arrived here in November 1789 after a two-month crossing of the Atlantic. More than 200 years later, this historic seaport welcomes more than 300,000 cruise passengers annually. Situated at the heart of nautical Hampton Roads, Norfolk is home to the largest naval base in the world and is also a major commercial port.

ESSENTIALS

HOURS Most stores are open weekdays from 10 to 9. Some museums close on Monday and/or Tuesday.

INTERNET Most of the hotels offer free Wi-Fi service if you have your own laptop. If not, you may be able to find an Internet café, but the local Norfolk Public Library has free Internet access, so why pay?

Norfolk Public Library ⊠ *235 E. Plume St.* ☎ *757/664–7323* ⊕ *www.npl. lib.va.us.*

Visitor Information Norfolk Convention and Visitors Bureau ⊠ *232 E. Main St.* ☎ *757/664–6620, 800/368–3097* ⊕ *www.visitnorfolktoday.com.*

THE CRUISE PORT

The new Half Moone Cruise and Celebration Center, as Norfolk calls its cruise terminal, is in the center of the attractive, downtown waterfront. It's within walking distance of numerous attractions and amenities. From I–264, take the City Hall exit (Exit 10). At the light, turn right on St. Paul's Boulevard, and follow the signs to the Cedar Grove parking lot.

Information Half Moone Cruise and Celebration Center ⊠ *1 Waterside Dr.* ⊕ *www.cruisenorfolk.org.*

AIRPORT TRANSFERS

Norfolk International Airport (ORF) is 9 miles (15 km) and 20 minutes away from the cruise terminal. One-way, shared shuttle costs range from $7.50 to $22 per person, and a taxi costs about $18 to $25.

Contacts Norfolk Airport Shuttle Service ☎ *866/823–4626* ⊕ *www. jamesrivertrans.com.* **Norfolk International Airport** (*ORF*) ⊠ *2200 Norview Ave.* ☎ *757/857–3351* ⊕ *norfolkairport.com.*

PARKING

Cedar Grove Parking is the designated facility for cruise passengers. The parking fee ($15 daily) is paid upon entering the lot; Visa, MasterCard, American Express, cash, and traveler's checks are accepted. Less than 1 miles (1½ km) from I–264, this lot is located on Monticello Avenue between Virginia Beach Boulevard and Princess Anne Road in Downtown Norfolk. Shuttles run regularly to the cruise terminal.

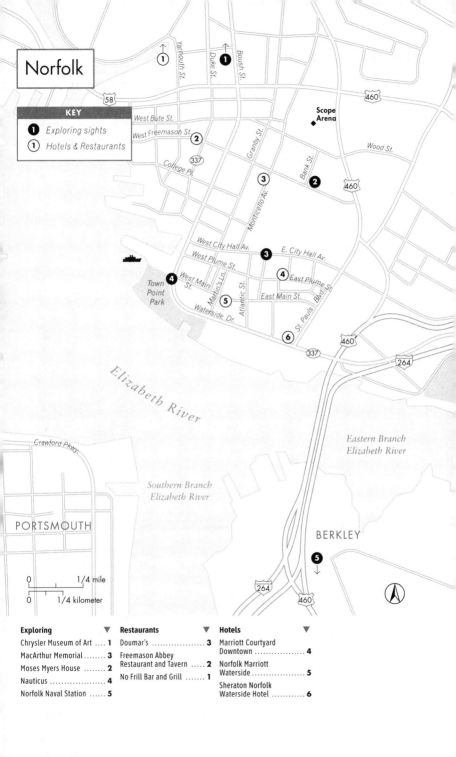

Norfolk

KEY

❶ *Exploring sights*
① *Hotels & Restaurants*

Yarmouth St.
Duke St.
Boush St.

Scope Arena

West Bute St.
West Freemason St.
Granby St.
Wood St.
Bank St.
College Pl.
Monticello Av.
West City Hall Av.
E. City Hall Av.
West Plume St.
West Main St.
Martin's Ln.
Atlantic St.
East Plume St.
East Main St.
St. Pauls Blvd.
Waterside Dr.

Town Point Park

Elizabeth River

Crawford Pkwy.

Southern Branch Elizabeth River

Eastern Branch Elizabeth River

PORTSMOUTH

BERKLEY

| 0 | 1/4 mile |
| 0 | 1/4 kilometer |

EXPLORING NORFOLK

History meets high-tech in this waterfront city. From 18th-century historic homes and a major art museum to 20th-century battleships and nuclear-powered aircraft carriers, Norfolk has many interesting sites to explore, several of them free and most within walking distance of the cruise terminal.

★ **Chrysler Museum of Art.** By any standard, the Chrysler Museum of Art downtown qualifies as one of America's major art museums. The permanent collection includes works by Rubens, Gainsborough, Renoir, Picasso, Cézanne, Matisse, Warhol, and Pollock, a list that suggests the breadth available here.

> **NORFOLK BEST BETS**
>
> ■ **Chrysler Museum of Art.** Though far from New York, Chicago, or Los Angeles, this is one of the major art museums in the United States.
>
> ■ **Nauticus.** The National Maritime Center is one of the region's most popular attractions, and especially good for families.
>
> ■ **Norfolk Naval Station.** This giant naval base, the home of the Atlantic Fleet, is an impressive site in itself.

Classical and pre-Columbian civilizations are also represented. The decorative-arts collection includes exquisite English porcelain and art nouveau furnishings. The Chrysler is home to one of the most important glass collections in America, which includes glass objects from the 6th century BC to the present, with particularly strong holdings in Tiffany, French art glass, and English cameo, as well as artifacts from ancient Rome and the Near and Far East. ⊠ *245 W. Olney Rd.* ☎ *757/664–6200* ⊕ *www.chrysler.org* ✉ *Free* ☉ *Wed. 10–9, Thurs.–Sat. 10–5, Sun. 12–5.*

MacArthur Memorial. The MacArthur Memorial is the burial place of one of America's most distinguished military officers. General Douglas MacArthur (1880–1964) agreed to this navy town as the site for his monument because it was his mother's birthplace. In the rotunda of the old City Hall, converted according to MacArthur's design, is the mausoleum; 11 adjoining galleries house mementos of MacArthur's career, including his signature corncob pipe and the Japanese instruments of surrender that concluded World War II. However, this is a monument not only to General MacArthur but to all those who served in wars from the Civil to the Korean War. Its Historical Center holds 2½ million documents and more than 100,000 photographs, and assists scholars, students, and researchers from around the world. The general's staff car is on display in the gift shop, where a 24-minute biography is shown. ⊠ *Bank St. and City Hall Ave.* ☎ *757/441–2965* ⊕ *www.macarthurmemorial.org* ✉ *Free (donations accepted)* ☉ *Mon.–Sat. 10–5, Sun. 11–5.*

Moses Myers House. The Federal redbrick Moses Myers House, built by its namesake between 1792 and 1796, is exceptional, and not just for its elegance. The furnishings, 70% of them original, include family portraits by Gilbert Stuart and Thomas Sully. A transplanted New Yorker as well as Norfolk's first Jewish resident, Myers made his fortune in Norfolk in shipping, then served as a diplomat and a customhouse officer. His grandson married James Madison's grandniece; his great-grandson served as mayor; and the family kept the house for five generations. ⊠ *323 E. Free Mason St.* ☎ *757/333–1086* ⊕ *www.chrysler. org/houses.asp* ⊵ *Free* ☉ *Fri.–Sun. noon–5.*

☺ **Nauticus.** A popular attraction on Norfolk's redeveloped downtown
★ waterfront, Nauticus is a maritime science museum featuring hand-on exhibits, interactive theaters, and high-definition films that celebrate the local connection to the seaport. Visitors can touch a shark, learn about weather and underwater archaeology, and explore the mysteries of the Elizabeth River. A NOAA Environmental Resource Center is an invaluable stop for education materials. Temporary exhibits in both the Changing Gallery and Forecastle Gallery keep things fresh. The Hampton Roads Naval Museum on the second floor and the battleship *Wisconsin* adjacent to the building are also popular attractions operated by the U.S. Navy, and are included in the Nauticus admission. ⊠ *1 Waterside Dr.* ☎ *757/664–1000* ⊕ *www.nauticus.org* ⊵ *$11.95* ☉ *Daily 10–5.*

Norfolk Naval Station. On the northern edge of the city, the Norfolk Naval Station is an impressive sight, home to more than 100 ships of the Atlantic Fleet. The base was built on the site of the Jamestown Exposition of 1907; many of the original buildings survive and are still in use. Several large aircraft carriers, built at nearby Newport News, call Norfolk home port and can be seen from miles away, especially at the bridge-tunnel end of the base. You may see two, each with a crew of up to 6,300, beside slightly smaller amphibious carriers that discharge marines in both helicopters and amphibious assault craft. The submarine piers, floating dry docks, supply center, and air station are all worth seeing. The *Victory Rover* and *Carrie B.* provide boat tours from downtown Norfolk to the naval station, and Hampton Roads Transit operates tour trolleys most of the year, departing from the naval-base tour office. Visitor access is by tour only, and photo ID is required to enter the base. ⊠ *9079 Hampton Blvd.* ☎ *757/444–7955* ⊕ *www.navstanorva.navy.mil/tour* ⊵ *Tour $7.50 (cash only and there is no ATM on premises)* ☉ *Tours: Jan. 1–Mar. 15, Tues.–Sun. at 1:30; Mar. 16–May 17, every ½ hr 11–2; May 18–Aug. 30, every 30 mins 10–2; Aug. 31–Nov. 1, hourly 11–2; Nov. 2–Dec. 31, Tues.–Sun. at 1:30.*

SHOPPING

If you forget to pack something for your cruise, you'll find stores galore within walking distance of the cruise terminal at the handsome MacArthur Center Mall.

d'Art Center. You can meet painters, sculptors, glassworkers, jewelers, photographers, and other artists at work in their studios at the d'Art Center ; the art is for sale. ⊠ *Selden Arcade, 208 E. Main St.* ☎ *757/625–4211* ⊕ *www.d-artcenter.org.*

Ghent. An eclectic mix of chic shops, including antiques stores, bars, and eateries, lines the streets of Ghent, a turn-of-the-20th-century neighborhood that runs from the Elizabeth River to York Street, to West Olney Road and Llewellyn Avenue. The intersection of Colley Avenue and 21st Street is the hub.

Palace Shops. In Ghent the upscale clothing and shoe boutiques at the Palace Shops are a good place to search out some finery. ⊠ *21st St. and Llewellyn Ave.*

> **BEACH AND BUY**
>
> A nylon tote bag that folds compactly into its own pocket can be used as a beach bag during your cruise and as an extra carry-on for your return home.

WHERE TO EAT

In addition to hotel restaurants, downtown Norfolk has many fine-dining restaurants as well as casual eateries in Waterside Festival Marketplace, where there's a versatile food court, and in the MacArthur Center Mall, including Johnny Rockets and Kincaid's—good food values for the price.

$ ✕ **Doumar's.** After he introduced the world to its first ice-cream cone at

BARBECUE the 1904 World's Fair in St. Louis, Abe Doumar founded this drive-in institution in 1934. It's still operated by his family. Waitresses carry to your car the specialties of the house: barbecue, limeade, and ice cream in waffle cones made according to an original recipe. For breakfast, try the Egg-O-Doumar, a bargain at $2.70. The Food Network's "Diners, Drive-Ins, and Dives" featured Doumar's twice in 2008. Ⓢ *Average main: $3* ⊠ *20th St. and Monticello Ave.* ☎ *757/627–4163* ⊕ *www. doumars.com* ☉ *Closed Sun.*

$$ ✕ **Freemason Abbey Restaurant and Tavern.** This former church near the

AMERICAN historic business district has been drawing customers for a long time, and not without reason. It has 40-foot-high cathedral ceilings and large windows, making for an airy, and dramatic, dining experience. You can sit upstairs, in the large choir loft, or in the main part of the church downstairs. Beside the bar just inside the entrance is an informal sort of "diner" area, but with the whole menu to choose from. Regular appetizers include artichoke dip and Santa Fe shrimp. There's a dinner special every weeknight, such as lobster, prime rib, and wild game (wild boar or alligator, for example). Ⓢ *Average main: $15* ⊠ *209 W. Freemason St.* ☎ *757/622–3966* ⊕ *www.freemasonabbey.com.*

$$ ✕ **No Frill Bar and Grill.** This expansive café is in an antique building in

CAFÉ the heart of Ghent. Beneath a tin ceiling and exposed ductwork, a cen-

★ tral bar is surrounded by several dining spaces with cream-and-mustard walls and wooden tables. Signature items include the ribs; the Funky Chicken Sandwich, a grilled chicken breast with bacon, tomato, melted Swiss cheese, and Parmesan pepper dressing on rye; and the Spotswood Salad of baby spinach, Granny Smith apples, and blue cheese. Ⓢ *Average main: $13* ⊠ *806 Spotswood Ave., at Colley Ave.* ☎ *757/627–4262* ⊕ *www.nofrillgrill.com.*

WHERE TO STAY

There are hotels within walking distance of the cruise port, or if you have a car, there are numerous chain motels on the outskirts of town where you can save a little money.

For expanded reviews, facilities, and current deals, visit Fodors.com.

$$ ⓣ **Marriott Courtyard Downtown.** Built in 2005, this eight-story hotel is near everything visitors want to see and where business travelers need to be. **Pros:** convenient downtown location. **Cons:** the hotel has a smoke-free policy. ⑤ *Rooms from: $139* ⊠ *520 Plume St.* ☎ *757/963–6000, 800/321–2211* ☐ *757/963–6001* ⊕ *www.marriott.com* ↩ *137 rooms, 3 suites.*

$$$ ⓣ **Norfolk Marriott Waterside.** Located in the redeveloped downtown area, this hotel is connected to the Waterside Festival Marketplace shopping area by a ramp and it's close to Town Point Park, site of many festivals. **Pros:** great central location; two blocks from the Waterside Festival Marketplace. **Cons:** parking is pricey, and a walk with luggage. ⑤ *Rooms from: $209* ⊠ *235 E. Main St.* ☎ *757/627–4200, 800/228–9290* ☐ *757/628–6452* ⊕ *www.marriott.com* ↩ *396 rooms, 8 suites.*

$$$ ⓣ **Sheraton Norfolk Waterside Hotel.** Modern is the word for this hotel's furnishings, from the bright, spacious lobby to the ample rooms and large suites. **Pros:** the only hotel that is truly on the waterfront; nice touches such as snacks and cold water served all day; restaurant has a terrific view of Portsmouth. **Cons:** parking—for Norfolk—is pricey; overcrowded rooms may be hard to maneuver for some. ⑤ *Rooms from: $195* ⊠ *777 Waterside Dr.* ☎ *757/622–6664* ☐ *757/625–8271* ⊕ *www.sheraton.com* ↩ *426 rooms, 20 suites.*

PORT CANAVERAL, FLORIDA

Steve Master   This once-bustling commercial fishing area is still home to a small shrimping fleet, charter boats, and party fishing boats, but its main business these days is as a cruise-ship port. Cocoa Beach itself isn't the spiffiest place around, but what *is* becoming quite clean and neat is the north end of the port, where the Carnival, Disney, and Royal Caribbean cruise lines set sail, as well as Sun Cruz and Sterling casino boats. Port Canaveral is now Florida's second-busiest cruise port. Because of Port Canaveral's proximity to Orlando theme parks (about an hour away), many cruisers combine a short cruise with a stay in the area. The port is also convenient to popular Space Coast attractions such as the Kennedy Space Center and United States Astronaut Hall of Fame in Titusville.

ESSENTIALS

HOURS Most of the area's attractions are open every day.

INTERNET Most people choose to go online at their hotel.

Visitor Information Space Coast Office of Tourism ⊠ *430 Brevard Ave., Suite 150, Cocoa* ☎ *877/572–3224, 321/433–4470* ⊕ *www.space-coast.com.*

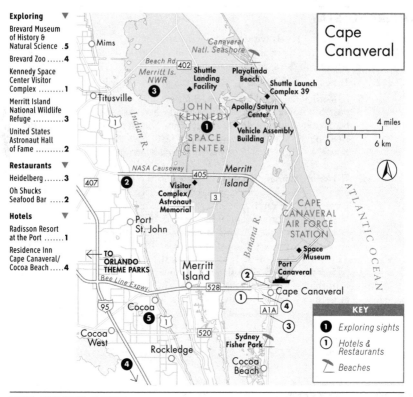

THE CRUISE PORT

Port Canaveral sees more than 4.6 million passengers passing through its terminals annually. The port expects its business to grow, predicting for instance that it will soon host twice the number of one-day ship visits it did in 2009, for a total of 126.

The port has six cruise terminals and is home to ships from Carnival Cruise Lines, Disney Cruise Line, and Royal Caribbean International. Other cruise lines, such as Holland America and Norwegian Cruise Line, operate seasonally. The port serves as the embarkation point for three-, four-, and seven-day cruises to the Bahamas, Key West, Mexico, Jamaica, and the Virgin Islands.

In Brevard County, Port Canaveral is on State Road (S.R.) 528, also known as the Beeline Expressway, which runs straight to Orlando, which has the nearest airport. To drive to Port Canaveral from there, take the north exit out of the airport, staying to the right, to S.R. 528 (Beeline Expressway) East. Take S.R. 528 directly to Port Canaveral; it's about a 45-minute drive.

Port Contacts Canaveral Port Authority ⊠ *445 Challenger Rd., Suite 301, Cape Canaveral* ☎ *321/783–7831, 888/767–8226* ⊕ *www.portcanaveral.org.*

AIRPORT TRANSFERS

If you are flying into the area, the Orlando airport is 45 minutes away from the docks. If you have not arranged airport transfers with your cruise line, you will need to make your own arrangements. Taxis are expensive, but many companies offer shared minivan and bus shuttles to Port Canaveral. They are all listed on the Canaveral Port Authority Web site. Some shuttles charge for the entire van, which is a good deal for groups but not for individuals or couples; some will charge a per-person rate. Expect to pay at least $38 per person round-trip, and check the Internet for coupons and special offers.

> ### PORT CANAVERAL BEST BETS
>
> ■ **Kennedy Space Center.** Kennedy Space Center in Titusville is the region's biggest attraction.
>
> ■ **Merritt Island.** If you want to get out and commune with nature, this is the place, especially for bird-watchers.
>
> ■ **Orlando Theme Parks.** With Orlando just an hour away, many cruisers combine a theme-park visit with their cruise.

You will need to make a reservation in advance regardless of which service you use. Some cruisers who want to do some exploring before the cruise rent a car at the airport and drop it off at the port, which houses several major rental-car agencies.

Contacts AAA Cruise Line Connection ☎ 407/908–5566 ⊕ www.aaasuperride.com. **Busy Traveler Transport Service** ☎ 321/453–5278, 800/496–7433 ⊕ www.abusytraveler.com.

PARKING

Outdoor gated lots and a six-story parking garage are near the terminals and cost $120 per week for vehicles up to 20 feet in length and $208 per week for vehicles over 20 feet, which must be paid in advance, either in cash, traveler's checks, or by major credit card (MasterCard and Visa only).

EXPLORING THE CAPE CANAVERAL AREA

With the Kennedy Space Center just 20 minutes away, there is plenty to do in and around Cape Canaveral, though many folks opt to travel the extra hour into Orlando to visit the popular theme parks.

Brevard Museum of History & Natural Science. This is the place to come to see what the lay of the local land looked like in other eras. Hands-on activities draw children, who especially migrate toward the Imagination Center, where they can act out history or reenact a space shuttle flight. Not to be missed is the Windover Archaeological Exhibit of 7,000-year-old artifacts indigenous to the region. In 1984, a shallow pond revealed the burial ground of more than 200 American Indians who lived in the area about 7,000 years ago. Preserved in the muck were bones and, to the archeologists' surprise, the brains of these ancient people. Nature lovers appreciate the museum's butterfly garden and the nature center with 22 acres of trails encompassing three distinct ecosystems—sand pine hills, lake lands, and marshlands. ⊠ 2201 Michigan Ave., Cocoa ☎ 321/632–1830 ⊕ www.brevardmuseum.org ⊡ $6 ☉ Thurs.–Sat. 10–4.

☼ **Brevard Zoo.** At the only Association of Zoo and Aquariums–accredited
Fodor's Choice zoo built by a community, you can stroll along the shaded boardwalks
★ and get a close-up look at rhinos, giraffes, cheetahs, alligators, crocodiles, giant anteaters, marmosets, jaguars, eagles, river otters, kanga-
roos, exotic birds, and kookaburras. Alligator, crocodile, and river-otter
feedings are held on alternate afternoons—and no, the alligators do not
dine on the otters. Stop by Paws-On, an interactive learning playground
with a petting zone, wildlife detective training academy, and the Indian
River Play Lagoon. Hand-feed a giraffe in Expedition Africa or a lorikeet in the Australian Free Flight Aviary, and step up to the Wetlands
Outpost, an elevated pavilion that's a gateway to 22 acres of wetlands
through which you can paddle kayaks and keep an eye open for the
4,000 species of wildlife that live in these waters and woods. Adventurers seeking a chimp's-eye view can zipline through the zoo on Treetop
Trek. ⊠ *8225 N. Wickham Rd., Melbourne* ☎ *321/254-9453* ⊕ *www.
brevardzoo.org* ⌧ *$14.50; $19 including train and giraffe and lorikeet
food; Treetop Trek $15–$48* ⊗ *Daily 9:30–5, last admission 4:15.*

☼ **Kennedy Space Center Visitor Complex.** This must-see attraction, just
Fodor's Choice southeast of Titusville, is one of Central Florida's most popular sights.
★ Located on a 140,000-acre island 45 minutes outside Orlando, Kennedy
Space Center is NASA's launch headquarters. The Visitor Complex gives
guests a unique opportunity to learn about—and experience—the past,
present, and future of America's space program.

Interactive programs make for the best experiences here, but if you want
a low-key overview of the facility (and if the weather is foul) take the bus
tour, included with admission. Buses depart every 15 minutes, and you
can get on and off any bus whenever you like. Stops include the Launch
Complex 39 Observation Gantry, which has an unparalleled view of
the launchpads and Apollo/Saturn V Center, with a don't-miss presentation at the Firing Room Theatre, where the launch of America's first
lunar mission, 1968's *Apollo VIII*, is re-created with a ground-shaking,
window-rattling liftoff. The Apollo/Saturn V center also features one
of three remaining Saturn V moon rockets. Astronaut Encounter Theater has two daily programs where retired NASA astronauts share their
adventures in space travel and show a short film. The most moving
exhibit is the Astronaut Memorial, a 70,400-pound black-granite tribute to astronauts who lost their lives in the name of space exploration.

More befitting Walt Disney World or Universal Studios (complete with
the health warnings), the Shuttle Launch Experience is the center's most
spectacular attraction. Designed by a team of astronauts, NASA experts,
and renowned attraction engineers, the 44,000-square-foot structure uses
a sophisticated motion-based platform, special-effects seats, and high-
fidelity visual and audio components to simulate the sensations experienced in an actual space-shuttle launch, including MaxQ, Solid Rocker
Booster separation, main engine cutoff, and External Tank separation.
The journey culminates with a breathtaking view of Earth from space.

The only back-to-back twin IMAX theater in the world is in the complex, too. Several add-on tours and activities are available as well if
you have extra time. ⊠ *Rte. 405, Kennedy Space Center, Titusville*

☎ 877/313–2610 ⊕ *www.kennedyspacecenter.com* ✉ *$43, includes bus tour, IMAX space movies, Visitor Complex shows and exhibits, and Astronaut Hall of Fame* ☉ *Space Center opens daily at noon, closing times vary by season, last regular tour 3 hrs before closing; closed certain launch dates.*

Fodor'sChoice **Merritt Island National Wildlife Refuge.** Owned by the National Aero-
★ nautics and Space Administration (NASA), this 140,000-acre refuge, which adjoins the Canaveral National Seashore, acts as a buffer around Kennedy Space Center while protecting 1,000 species of plants and 500 species of wildlife, including 15 considered federally threatened or endangered. It's an immense area dotted by brackish estuaries and marshes and patches of land consisting of coastal dunes, scrub oaks, pine forests and flatwoods, and palm and oak hammocks. You can borrow field guides and binoculars at the visitor center (5 miles east of U.S. 1 in Titusville on State Road 402) to track down falcons, ospreys, eagles, turkeys, doves, cuckoos, owls, and woodpeckers, as well as loggerhead turtles, alligators, and otters. A 20-minute video about refuge wildlife and accessibility—only 10,000 acres are developed—can help orient you.

You might take a self-guided tour along the 7-mile Black Point Wildlife Drive. On the Oak Hammock Foot Trail you can see wintering migratory waterfowl and learn about the plants of a hammock community. If you exit the north end of the refuge, look for the Manatee Observation Area just north of the Haulover Canal (maps are at the visitor center). They usually show up in spring and fall. There are also fishing camps, fishing boat ramps, and six hiking trails scattered throughout the area. Most of the refuge is closed 24 hours prior to a launch. ⊠ *Rte. 402, across Titusville Causeway, Titusville* ☎ *321/861–0667, 321/861–0669 visitor center* ⊕ *www.fws.gov/merrittisland* ✉ *Free* ☉ *Daily sunrise–sunset; visitor center weekdays 8–4:30, Sat. 9–5 and Sun. 9–5 (Nov.–Mar.).*

United States Astronaut Hall of Fame. The original *Mercury 7* team and the later *Gemini, Apollo, Skylab,* and shuttle astronauts contributed to make the hall of fame the world's premium archive of astronauts' personal stories. Authentic memorabilia and equipment from their collections tell the story of human space exploration. You can watch videotapes of historic moments in the space program and see one-of-a-kind items like Wally Schirra's relatively archaic *Sigma 7* Mercury space capsule, Gus Grissom's space suit (colored silver only because NASA thought silver looked more "spacey"), and a flag that made it to the moon. The exhibit First on the Moon focuses on crew selection for *Apollo 11* and the Soviet Union's role in the space race. Don't miss Simulation Station, a hands-on discovery center with interactive exhibits that help you learn about space travel. One of the more challenging activities is a space-shuttle simulator that lets you try your hand at landing the craft—and afterward replays a side view of your rolling and pitching descent. ⊠ *6225 Vectorspace Blvd., Titusville* ☎ *877/313–2610* ⊕ *www.kennedyspacecenter.com* ✉ *$20* ☉ *Opens daily at noon, closing times vary by season (call for details).*

ORLANDO THEME PARKS

🕑 **SeaWorld Orlando.** In the world's largest marine adventure park, every attraction is devoted to demonstrating the ways that humans can protect the mammals, birds, fish, and reptiles that live in the ocean and its tributaries. The presentations are gentle reminders of our responsibility to safeguard the environment, and you'll find that SeaWorld's use of humor plays a major role in this education. The park is small enough that, armed with a map that lists show times, you can plan a chronological approach that flows easily from one attraction to the next. Near the intersection of I–4 and the Beeline Expressway; take I–4 to Exit 71 or 72 and follow signs. ✉ *7007 Sea Harbor Dr., International Drive Area, Orlando* ☎ *888/800–5447* ⊕ *www.seaworld.com* 🖃 *$81.99 for a 1-day ticket ($10 cheaper if bought online in advance)* ⊙ *Daily 9–6 or 7, until as late as 10 summer and holidays; educational programs daily, some beginning as early as 6:30 am.*

🕑 **Universal Orlando.** The resort consists of **Universal Studios** (the original movie theme park), **Islands of Adventure** (the second theme park, which includes The Wizarding World of Harry Potter), and **CityWalk** (the dining-shopping-nightclub complex). Although it's bordered by residential neighborhoods and thickly trafficked International Drive, Universal Orlando is surprisingly expansive yet intimate and accessible, with two massive parking complexes, easy walks to all attractions, and a motor launch that cruises to the hotels. Universal Orlando emphasizes "two parks, two days, one great adventure," but you may find the presentation, creativity, and cutting-edge technology bring you back for more. ✉ *1000 Universal Studios Plaza, Orlando* ☎ *407/363–8000* ⊕ *www.universalorlando.com* 🖃 *1-day, 1-park ticket $88* ⊙ *Usually daily 9–7, but hrs vary seasonally; CityWalk restaurants and bars have individual open hrs.*

🕑 **Walt Disney World.** Walt Disney World is a huge complex of theme parks and attractions, each of which is worth a visit. Parks include the **Magic Kingdom,** a family favorite and the original here; **Epcot,** Disney's international, educational park; **Disney Hollywood Studios,** a movie-oriented theme park; and **Disney's Animal Kingdom,** which is much more than a zoo. Beyond these, there are water parks, elaborate minigolf courses, a sports center, resorts, restaurants, and nightlife. If you have only one day, you'll have to concentrate on a single park; Disney–MGM Studios or Animal Kingdom are easiest to do in a day, but arrive early and expect to stay until park closing, which might be as early as 5 pm for Animal Kingdom or as late as 11 pm during busy seasons at the Magic Kingdom. The most direct route to the Disney Parks from Port Canaveral is S.R. 528 (the Beeline Expressway) to I–4; when you get through Orlando, follow the signs to Disney and expect traffic. ✉ *Lake Buena Vista* ☎ *407/824–4321* ⊕ *disneyworld.disney. go.com* 🖃 *1-day, 1-park pass $99* ⊙ *Most parks open by 9 am; closing hrs vary, but usually 5 pm for Animal Kingdom and 6–11 pm for other parks, depending on season.*

BEACHES

Playalinda Beach. The southern access for the Canaveral National Seashore, remote Playalinda Beach has pristine sands and is the longest stretch of undeveloped coast on Florida's Atlantic seaboard. Hundreds of giant sea turtles come ashore here from May through August to lay their eggs. Fourteen parking lots anchor the beach at 1-mile intervals. From Interstate 95, take Exit 249 and head east. Bring bug repellent in case of horseflies, and note that you may see some unauthorized clothing-optional activity. **Amenities:** lifeguards (May 30–September 1); parking (fee); toilets. **Best for:** solitude; swimming; walking. ⊠ *Northern end of Rte. 402/Beach Rd., Titusville* ☎ *321/867–4077* ⊕ *www.nps.gov/cana* ✇ *$5 per vehicle for national seashore.*

> **WRITE EASY**
>
> Preaddress a page of stick-on labels before you leave home; use them for postcards to the folks back home and you will not have to carry along a bulky address book.

SHOPPING

Cocoa Beach Surf Company. The world's largest surf complex has three floors of boards, apparel, sunglasses, and anything else a surfer, wannabe-surfer, or souvenir-seeker could need. Also on-site are a 5,600-gallon fish and shark tank and the Shark Pit Bar & Grill. Here you can also rent surfboards, bodyboards, and wet suits, as well as umbrellas, chairs, and bikes. And staffers teach grommets (dudes) and gidgets (chicks)—from kids to seniors—how to surf. There are group, semiprivate, and private lessons available in one-, two-, and three-hour sessions. Prices range from $40 (for a one-hour group lesson) to $120 (three-hour private). All gear is provided. ⊠ *4001 N. Atlantic Ave., Cocoa Beach* ☎ *321/799–9930.*

Fodor'sChoice ★ **Ron Jon Surf Shop.** It's impossible to miss Ron Jon: it takes up nearly two blocks along Route A1A and has a giant surfboard and an art-deco facade painted orange, blue, yellow, and turquoise. What started in 1963 as a small T-shirt and bathing-suit shop has evolved into a 52,000-square-foot superstore that's open every day 'round the clock. The shop rents water-sports gear as well as chairs and umbrellas, and it sells every kind of beachwear, surf wax, plus the requisite T-shirts and flip-flops. ⊠ *4151 N. Atlantic Ave., Rte. A1A, Cocoa Beach* ☎ *321/799–8820* ⊕ *www.ronjonsurfshop.com.*

WHERE TO EAT

The Cove at Port Canaveral has several restaurants if you are looking for a place to eat right at the port.

$$$

GERMAN

✗ **Heidelberg.** As the name suggests, the cuisine here is definitely German, from the sauerbraten served with potato dumplings and red cabbage to the beef Stroganoff and spaetzle to the classically prepared Wiener schnitzel. All the soups and desserts are homemade; try the Viennese-style apple strudel and the rum-zapped almond-cream tortes.

Elegant interior touches include crisp linens and fresh flowers. There's live music Friday and Saturday evenings. You can also dine inside the jazz club, Heidi's, next door. ⑤*Average main: $28* ✉*7 N. Orlando Ave., opposite City Hall, Cocoa Beach* ☎*321/783–6806* ⊕*www.heidisjazzclub.com* ⊘*Closed Mon.*

> ### EXTRA BATTERIES
>
> Even if you don't think you'll need them, bring along extra camera batteries and change them before you think the old ones are dead.

$ ✕**Oh Shucks Seafood Bar.** At the only open-air seafood bar on the beach,
SEAFOOD   at the entrance of the Cocoa Beach Pier, the main item is oysters, served on the half shell. You can also grab a burger here, crab legs by the pound, or Oh Shucks's most popular item, coconut beer shrimp. Some diners complain that the prices don't jibe with the ultracasual atmosphere (e.g., plastic chairs), but they're also paying for the "ex-Pierience." During high season, there's live entertainment on Wednesday, Friday, Saturday, and Sunday. ⑤*Average main: $12* ✉*401 Meade Ave., Cocoa Beach Pier, Cocoa Beach* ☎*321/783–7549.*

WHERE TO STAY

Many local hotels offer cruise packages that include one night's lodging, parking for the duration of your cruise, and transportation to the cruise port.

For expanded reviews, facilities, and current deals, visit Fodors.com.

$$ 📷 **Radisson Resort at the Port.** For cruise-ship passengers who can't wait
HOTEL   to get under way, this splashy resort, done up in pink and turquoise, already feels like the Caribbean. **Pros:** cruise-ship convenience; pool area; free shuttle. **Cons:** rooms around the pool can be noisy; loud air-conditioning in some rooms; no complimentary breakfast. ⑤*Rooms from: $130* ✉*8701 Astronaut Blvd., Cape Canaveral* ☎*321/784–0000, 888/201–1718* ⊕*www.radisson.com/capecanaveralfl* ↩*284 rooms, 72 suites* ❐*No meals.*

$$$ 📷 **Residence Inn Cape Canaveral/Cocoa Beach.** Billing itself as the closest
HOTEL   all-suites hotel to the Kennedy Space Center, this four-story Residence Inn, painted cheery yellow, is also convenient to other area attractions such as Port Canaveral, the Cocoa Beach Pier, the Brevard Zoo, and Cocoa Village, and is only an hour from the Magic Kingdom. **Pros:** helpful staff; free breakfast buffet; pet-friendly. **Cons:** less than picturesque views; street noise in some rooms. ⑤*Rooms from: $179* ✉*8959 Astronaut Blvd., Cape Canaveral* ☎*321/323–1100, 800/331–3131* ⊕*www.marriott.com* ↩*150 suites* ❐*Breakfast.*

SAN JUAN, PUERTO RICO

Heather
Rodino

In addition to being a major port of call, San Juan is also a common port of embarkation for cruises on Southern Caribbean itineraries.

For information on dining, shopping, nightlife, and sightseeing see ⇨ *San Juan, Puerto Rico in Chapter 4.*

THE CRUISE PORT

Most cruise ships dock within a couple of blocks of Old San Juan. The Paseo de la Princesa, a tree-lined promenade beneath the city wall, is a nice place for a stroll—you can admire the local crafts and stop at the refreshment kiosks. A tourist information center is close to the cruise terminal area. Major sights in Old San Juan are mere blocks from the piers, but be aware that the streets are narrow and steeply inclined in places. Even if you have only a few hours before your cruise, you'll have time to do a little sightseeing. A few ships dock across the bay; if yours does, you'll need to take a taxi everywhere.

AIRPORT TRANSFERS

The ride from the Luis Muñoz Marín International Airport, east of downtown San Juan, to the docks in Old San Juan takes about 20 minutes, depending on traffic. The white "Taxi Turistico" cabs, marked by a logo on the door, have a fixed rate of $19 to the cruise-ship piers; there is a $1 charge for each piece of luggage. Other taxi companies charge by the mile, which can cost a little more. Be sure the driver starts the meter, or agree on a fare beforehand.

Visitor Information Puerto Rico Tourism Company ✉ *Rafael Hernández Airport, Hwy. 2, Km 148.7, Aguadilla* ☎ *787/890–3315* ⊕ *www.seepuertorico.com.*

WHERE TO STAY

If you are planning to spend one night in San Juan before your cruise departs, you'll probably find it easier to stay in Old San Juan, where the cruise-ship terminals are. But if you want to spend a few extra days in the city, there are other possibilities near good beaches a bit farther out. We make some nightlife suggestions in the San Juan port of call section (*see* ⇨ *San Juan in Chapter 4*).

For expanded reviews, facilities, and current deals, visit Fodors.com.

$$
B&B/INN

The Gallery Inn. Nothing like this rambling, eclectic inn exists anywhere else in San Juan—or Puerto Rico, for that matter. **Pros:** one-of-a-kind lodging; ocean views; wonderful classical music concerts. **Cons:** no elevator; several narrow, winding staircases; an uphill walk from rest of Old San Juan; no sign out front; sometimes raucous pet macaws and cockatoos. ⑤ *Rooms from: $185* ✉ *204–206 Calle Norzagaray, Old San Juan* ☎ *787/722–1808* ⊕ *www.thegalleryinn.com* ⌂ *20 rooms, 5 suites* ⑩ *Breakfast.*

$$$
HOTEL
Fodor's Choice
★

Hotel El Convento. Carmelite nuns once inhabited this 350-year-old convent, but there's no longer anything austere about it. **Pros:** lovely building; atmosphere to spare; plenty of nearby dining options. **Cons:** near some noisy bars; small pool and small bathrooms. ⑤ *Rooms from:*

$260 ✉ 100 Calle Cristo, Old San Juan ☎ 787/723–9020 🌐 www.elconvento.com ⇆ 63 rooms, 5 suites 🍴 No meals.

$$$ HOTEL **Sheraton Old San Juan Hotel & Casino.** This hotel's triangular shape subtly echoes the cruise ships docked nearby. **Pros:** harbor views; near many dining options; good array of room types. **Cons:** motel feel to guest rooms; noise from casino overwhelms lobby and restaurants; Wi-Fi in public areas only. *$ Rooms from: $259 ✉ 100 Calle Brumbaugh, Old San Juan ☎ 787/721–5100, 866/376–7577 🌐 www.sheratonoldsanjuan.com ⇆ 200 rooms, 40 suites 🍴 No meals.*

TAMPA, FLORIDA

Kate Bradshaw

Although glitzy Miami seems to hold the trendiness trump card and Orlando is the place your kids want to visit annually until they hit middle school, the Tampa Bay area has that elusive quality that many attribute to the "real Florida." The state's second-largest metro area is less fast-lane than its biggest (Miami), or even Orlando, but its strengths are just as varied, from broad cultural diversity to a sun-worshipping beach culture. Florida's third-busiest airport, a vibrant business community, world-class beaches, and superior hotels and resorts—many of them historic—make this an excellent place to spend a week or a lifetime. Several ships are based here year-round and seasonally, most doing Western Caribbean itineraries.

ESSENTIALS

HOURS Some museums are closed on Monday.

INTERNET Most people choose to access the Internet through their hotels. Starbucks has free Wi-Fi.

Visitor Information Tampa Bay & Company *✉ 401 E. Jackson St., Suite 2100 ☎ 800/448–2672, 813/223–1111 🌐 www.visittampabay.com.* **Ybor City Chamber Visitor Bureau** *✉ 1600 E. 8th Ave., Suite B104 ☎ 813/241–8838 🌐 www.ybor.org.*

THE CRUISE PORT

Tampa is the largest shipping port in the state of Florida, and it's becoming ever more important to the cruise industry, now with three passenger terminals. In Tampa's downtown area, the port is linked to nearby Ybor City and the rest of the Tampa Bay Area by the TECO streetcar line.

To reach the port by car, take I–4 West to Exit 1 (Ybor City), and go south on 21st Street. To get to terminals 2 and 6, turn right on Adamo Drive (Highway 60), then left on Channelside Drive.

Contacts Tampa Port Authority *✉ 1101 Channelside Dr. ☎ 813/905–7678, 800/741–2297 🌐 www.tampaport.com.*

AIRPORT TRANSFERS

Both Bay Shuttle and SuperShuttle provide shared van service to and from the airport and the cruise terminal. Expect to pay about $13 to $14 per person.

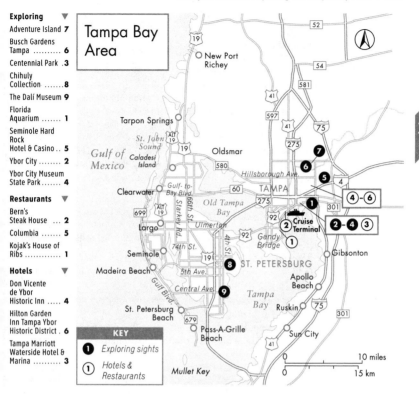

KEY

❶ Exploring sights

① Hotels &
Restaurants

Information Blue One Transportation ☎ 813/282–7351
⊕ www.blueonetransportation.com. **SuperShuttle** ☎ 727/572–1111,
800/282–6817 ⊕ www.supershuttle.com.

PARKING

Parking is available at the port directly across from the terminals. For
Terminal 2 (Carnival Cruise Lines), parking is in a garage across the
street. For Terminal 3 (Royal Caribbean and Norwegian Cruise Line),
parking is also in a garage across the street. For Terminal 6 (Holland
America Line), parking is outdoors in a guarded, enclosed lot. The cost
is $15 a day, payable by credit card (MasterCard or Visa) or in cash.

EXPLORING THE TAMPA BAY AREA

Florida's west-coast crown jewel as well as its business and commercial hub, Tampa has high-rises and heavy traffic. Amid the bustle is
the region's greatest concentration of restaurants, nightlife, stores, and
cultural events.

 ↻ **Adventure Island.** From spring until fall, rides named Splash Attack, Gulf
Scream, and Key West Rapids promise heat relief at Busch Gardens'
water park. Tampa's most popular "wet" park features waterslides
and artificial wave pools, along with tranquil "beaches" in a 30-acre

package. One of the attraction's headliners, Riptide, challenges you to race three other riders on a sliding mat through twisting tubes and hairpin turns. Planners of this park also took the younger kids into account, with offerings such as Fabian's Funport, which has a scaled-down pool and interactive water gym. Along with a volleyball complex and a rambling river, there are cafés, snack bars, picnic and sunbathing areas, changing rooms, and, the newest addition, private cabanas. ✉ *4500 Bougainvillea Ave., less than 1 mile north of Busch Gardens, Central Tampa* ☎ *813/987–5660, 888/800–5447* ⊕ *www.adventureisland.com* ✆ *$44.95; parking $12* ☉ *Mid-Mar.–late Oct., daily 10–5.*

☾ **Busch Gardens Tampa.** Drawing some
Fodor's Choice   4½ million visitors each year, Busch
★   Gardens Tampa is a major theme park, with seven popular roller coasters being the biggest lure. But this is also a world-class zoo, with more than 2,000 animals, and a live entertainment venue that provides a full day (or more) of fun for the whole family. If you want to beat the crowds, start in the back of the park and work your way around clockwise. The 335-acre adventure park's habitats offer views of some of the world's most endangered and exotic animals. For the best animal sightings, go to their habitats early, when it's cooler. Catering to the shorter set, the Sesame Street Safari of Fun is a 5-acre kids' playground with Sesame-themed rides, shows, and water adventures. The Air Grover Rollercoaster takes kids (and parents) on minidives and twisty turns over the Sahara, while Rosita's Djembe Fly-Away (a swing ride) and Elmo's Safari Go-Round (carousel) get them swinging and screeching. If you're looking to cool off, your best bets are Oscar's Swamp Stomp, Zoe-Patra & the Hippos of the Nile (a flume ride), or Bert & Ernie's Water Hole—complete with bubblers, geysers, water jets, and dumping buckets. Character lunches are available (but you might want to wait until after your rides). ✉ *3000 E. Busch Blvd., 8 miles northeast of downtown Tampa and 2 miles east of I–275 Exit 50, Central Tampa* ☎ *813/987–5000, 888/800–5447* ⊕ *www.buschgardens. com* ✆ *$77.99; parking $13* ☉ *Daily 10–6.*

Centennial Park. You can step back into the past at Centennial Park, which re-creates a period streetscape and hosts a farmer's market called the "Fresh Market" every Saturday. ✉ *8th Ave. and 19th St., Ybor City.*

Fodor's Choice   **Chihuly Collection.** For the uninitiated, those passing this collection's
★   polished exterior may think it's a gallery like any other. Yet what's contained inside is an experience akin to *Alice in Wonderland*. This, the first permanent collection of world-renowned glass sculptor Dale

---

TAMPA BEST BETS

■ **Busch Gardens.** The area's best theme park is a good family destination.

■ **Florida Aquarium.** The aquarium is next to the cruise port, so you can just walk, making it a good option even if you have a couple of hours to kill before boarding (they'll even store your luggage if you want to visit after disembarking).

■ **The Dalí Museum.** One of the finest and most interesting museums in the United States.

■ **Ybor City.** For nightlife and restaurants, this historic district is Tampa's hot spot.

Chihuly's work, has such impossibly vibrant, larger-than-life pieces as "Float Boat" and "Ruby Red Icicle." You can tour the museum independently or with one of its volunteer docents (no added cost; tours are given hourly on the half-hour during the week). Each display is perfectly lit, which adds to the drama of Chihuly's designs. After passing under a hallway with a semi-transparent ceiling through which a brilliant array of smaller glass pieces shine, you'll wind up at the breathtaking finale, "Mille Fiore" ("Thousand Flowers"), a spectacular, whimsical glass montage mimicking a wildflower patch, critters and all. Check out the gift shop at the end if you'd like to take some of the magic home with you. A combination ticket gets you a glimpse into Morean Arts Center's off-site glass-blowing studio, where you can watch resident artisans create a unique glass piece before your eyes. ⊠ *400 Beach Dr., Downtown, St. Petersburg* 🕾 *727/822–7872* ⊕ *www.moreanartscenter.com.* 🎫 *$15* ⏱ *Mon.–Wed. and Fri.–Sat. 10–6, Thurs. 10–8, Sun. 12–6.*

Fodor's Choice **The Dalí Museum.** Inside and out, the waterfront Dalí Museum, which
★ opened on 1/11/11 (Dali is said to have been into numerology), is almost as remarkable as the Spanish surrealist's work. The state-of-the-art building has a surreal geodesic-like glass structure called the Dalí Enigma, as well as an outdoor labyrinth and a DNA-inspired spiral staircase leading up to the collection. All this, before you've even seen the collection, which is one of the most comprehensive of its kind—courtesy of Ohio magnate A. Reynolds Morse, a friend of Dalí's.

Here, you can scope out his early impressionistic works and see how the painter evolved into the visionary he's now seen to be. The mind-expanding paintings in this downtown headliner include *Eggs on a Plate Without a Plate, The Hallucinogenic Toreador,* and more than 90 other oils. You'll also discover more than 2,000 additional works including watercolors, drawings, sculptures, photographs, and objets d'art. Free hour-long tours are led by well-informed docents. ⊠ *1 Dali Blvd., St. Petersburg* 🕾 *727/823–3767* ⊕ *www.thedali.org* 🎫 *$21* ⏱ *Mon.–Wed. and Fri.–Sat. 10–5:30, Thurs. 10–8, Sun. noon–5:30.*

⟳ **Florida Aquarium.** Although eels, sharks, and stingrays are the head-
★ liners, the Florida Aquarium is much more than a giant fishbowl. This architectural landmark features an 83-foot-high, multitier, glass dome; 250,000 square feet of air-conditioned exhibit space; and more than 20,000 aquatic plants and animals representing species native to Florida and the rest of the world—from black-tip sharks to leafy sea dragons.

Floor-to-ceiling interactive displays, behind-the-scenes tours, and in-water adventures allow kids to really get hands-on—and even get their feet wet. Adventurous types (certified divers age 15 and up) can dive with mild-mannered sharks and sea turtles, participate in shark-feeding programs (age 12 and up), or shallow-water swim with reef fish such as eels and grouper (age 6 and up).

However, you don't have to get wet to have an interactive experience: the Ocean Commotion exhibit offers virtual dolphins and whales and multimedia displays and presentations, and even allows kids to upload video to become part of the exhibit. The Coral Reef Gallery is a

500,000-gallon tank with viewing windows, an awesome 43-foot-wide panoramic opening, and a walk-through tunnel that gives the illusion of venturing into underwater depths. There you see a thicket of elkhorn coral teeming with tropical fish, and a dark cave reveals sea life you would normally see only on night dives.

If you have two hours, try the Wild Dolphin Adventure Cruise, which takes up to 130 passengers onto Tampa Bay in a 72-foot catamaran for an up-close look at bottlenose dolphins and other wildlife. The outdoor Explore a Shore exhibit, which gives younger kids a chance to release some energy, is an aquatic playground with a waterslide, water-jet sprays, and a climbable replica pirate ship. Last but not least, two black-footed South African penguins make daily appearances in the Coral Reef Gallery. For an extra cost, you can get an up-close look at the daily lives of these penguins during the half-hour-long Penguins: Backstage Pass demonstration. ⊠ *701 Channelside Dr., Downtown* 🕿 *813/273–4000* ⊕ *www.flaquarium.org* 🖾 *Aquarium $19.95; Adventure Cruise $21.95; Aquarium/Adventure Cruise combo $35.95; Penguins: Backstage Pass $30; Dive with the Sharks $175; Swim with the Fishes $75; parking $6* ☉ *Daily 9:30–5.*

Seminole Hard Rock Hotel & Casino. In addition to playing one of the hundreds of Vegas-style slot machines, gamers can get their kicks at the casino's poker tables and video-gaming machines. The lounge serves drinks 24 hours a day. Hard Rock Cafe, of course, has live music, dinner, and nightlife. There is a heavy smell of cigarette smoke here, as with most casinos. ⊠ *5223 N. Orient Rd., off I–4 at N. Orient Rd. exit, East Tampa* 🕿 *813/627–7625, 866/502–7529* ⊕ *www.seminolehardrock. com* 🖾 *Free* ☉ *Daily 24 hrs.*

Fodor's Choice ★ **Ybor City.** Tampa's lively Latin quarter is one of only a few National Historic Landmark districts in Florida. Bordered by I–4 to the north, 22nd Street to the east, Adamo Drive to the south, and Nebraska Avenue to the West, it has antique-brick streets and wrought-iron balconies. Cubans brought their cigar-making industry to Ybor (pronounced *ee*-bore) City in 1886, and the smell of cigars—hand-rolled by Cuban immigrants—still wafts through the heart of this east Tampa area, along with the strong aroma of roasting coffee. These days the neighborhood is one of Tampa's hot spots, if at times a rowdy one, as empty cigar factories and historic social clubs have been transformed into trendy boutiques, art galleries, restaurants, and nightclubs. ⊠ *Ybor City.*

Ybor City Museum State Park. This park provides a look at the history of the cigar industry. Admission includes a tour of La Casita, one of the shotgun houses occupied by cigar workers and their families in the late 1890s. ⊠ *1818 E. 9th Ave., between Nuccio Pkwy. and 22nd St. from 7th to 9th aves., Ybor City* 🕿 *813/247–6323* ⊕ *www.ybormuseum.org* 🖾 *$4* ☉ *Daily 9–5; walking tours Sat. 10:30.*

BEACHES

☼ **Fort De Soto Park.** Spread over five small islands, 1,136-acre Fort De Soto Park lies at the mouth of Tampa Bay. It has 7 miles of waterfront (much of it beach), two fishing piers, a 4-mile hiking and skating trail, picnic-and-camping grounds, and a historic fort that kids of any age can explore. The fort for which it's named was built on the southern end of Mullet Key to protect sea lanes in the gulf during the Spanish-American War. Roam the fort or wander the beaches of any of the islands within the park. Kayaks and beach cruisers are available for rental. ⊠ *3500 Pinellas Bayway St., Tierra Verde* ☏ *727/582–2267* ⊕ *www.pinellascounty.org/park/05_ft_desoto.htm* ⊡ *$5* ⊙ *Beaches, daily sunrise–sunset; fishing and boat ramp, 24 hrs.*

☼ **Pass-a-Grille Beach.** At the southern tip of St. Pete Beach (past the Don

Fodor'sChoice ★ Cesar), this is the epitome of Old Florida. One of the most popular beaches in the area, it skirts the west end of charming, historic Pass-a-Grille, a neighborhood that draws tourists and locals alike with its stylish yet low-key mom-and-pop motels and restaurants. On weekends, check out the Art Mart, an open-air market off the boulevard between 9th and 10th avenues that showcases the work of local artisans. **Best for:** families, windsurfing, sunsets. **Amenities:** toilets, showers, food and drink, parking. ⊠ *1000 Pass-a-Grille Way, St. Pete Beach.*

SHOPPING

Centro Ybor. Ybor City's destination within a destination is this dining-and-entertainment palace. It has shops, trendy bars and restaurants, and a 20-screen movie theater. ⊠ *1600 E. 8th Ave., Ybor City.*

Channelside Bay Plaza. An anchor of downtown Tampa's Channelside district, this complex has movie theaters, shops, restaurants, and clubs. Its numerous watering holes also allow it to double as a key Tampa nightlife destination. ⊠ *615 Channelside Dr., Downtown.*

International Plaza. If you want to grab something at Neiman Marcus or Nordstrom, this is the place. You'll also find Betsey Johnson, J.Crew, L'Occitane, Louis Vuitton, Tiffany & Co., and many other upscale shops. Stick around after hours, when watering holes in the mall's courtyard become a high-end club scene. ⊠ *2223 N. West Shore Blvd., Airport Area, Tampa* ⊕ *www.shopinternationalplaza.com.*

Old Hyde Park Village. It's a typical upscale shopping district in a quiet, shaded neighborhood near the water. Williams-Sonoma and Brooks Brothers are mixed in with bistros and sidewalk cafés. ⊠ *Swann Ave., near Bayshore Blvd., Hyde Park.*

NIGHTLIFE

Although there are more boarded storefronts than in the past, the biggest concentration of nightclubs, as well as the widest variety, is found along 7th Avenue in Ybor City. It becomes a little like Bourbon Street in New Orleans on weekend evenings.

Centro Cantina. There are lots of draws here: a balcony overlooking the crowds on Seventh Avenue, live music Thursday through Sunday nights, a large selection of margaritas, and more than 30 brands of tequila. Food is served until 2 am. ⊠ *1600 E. 8th Ave., Ybor City* ☎ *813/241–8588.*

Hub. Considered something of a dive—but a lovable one—by a loyal and young local following that ranges from esteemed jurists to nose-ring-wearing night owls, the Hub is known for strong drinks and a jukebox that goes well beyond the usual. ⊠ *719 N. Franklin St., Downtown* ☎ *813/229–1553.*

WHERE TO EAT

$$$$
STEAKHOUSE
Fodor'sChoice
★

✕ **Bern's Steak House.** With the air of an exclusive club, this is one of Florida's finest steak houses. Rich mahogany paneling and ornate chandeliers define the legendary Bern's, where the chef ages his own beef, grows his own organic vegetables, and roasts his own coffee. There's also a Cave Du Fromage, housing a discriminating selection of artisanal cheeses from around the world. Cuts of topmost beef are sold by weight and thickness. There's a 60-ounce strip steak that's big enough to feed your pride (of lions), but for most appetites the veal loin chop or 8-ounce chateaubriand is more than enough. The wine list includes approximately 7,000 selections (with 1,000 dessert wines). After dinner, tour the kitchen and wine cellar before having dessert upstairs in a cozy booth. The dessert room is a hit. For a real jolt, try the Turkish coffee with an order of Mississippi mud pie. Casual business attire is recommended. ⑤ *Average main: $32* ⊠ *1208 S. Howard Ave., Hyde Park* ☎ *813/251–2421* ⊕ *www.bernssteakhouse.com* ⌕ *Reservations essential Jacket and tie.*

$$
SPANISH
Fodor'sChoice
★

✕ **Columbia.** Make a date for some of the best Latin cuisine in Tampa. A fixture since 1905, this magnificent structure with an old-world air and spacious dining rooms takes up an entire city block and seems to feed the entire city—locals as well as visitors—throughout the week, but especially on weekends. The paella, bursting with seafood, chicken, and pork, is arguably the best in Florida, and the 1905 salad—with ham, olives, cheese, and garlic—is legendary. The menu has Cuban classics such as *boliche criollo* (tender eye of round stuffed with chorizo sausage), *ropa vieja* (shredded beef with onions, peppers, and tomatoes), and *arroz con pollo* (chicken with yellow rice). Don't miss the flamenco dancing show every night but Sunday. This place is also known for its sangria. If you can, walk around the building and check out the elaborate, antique decor along every inch of the interior. ⑤ *Average main: $19* ⊠ *2117 E. 7th Ave., Ybor City* ☎ *813/248–4961* ⊕ *www.columbiarestaurant.com.*

$$
SOUTHERN

✕ **Kojak's House of Ribs.** Few barbecue joints can boast the staying power of this family-owned and -operated pit stop. Located along a shaded stretch in South Tampa, it debuted in 1978 and has since earned a following of sticky-fingered regulars who have turned it into one of the most popular barbecue stops in central Florida. It's located in a 1927 house complete with veranda, pillars supporting the overhanging roof, and brick steps. Day and night, three indoor dining rooms and an outdoor dining porch have a steady stream of hungry patrons digging into tender pork spareribs that are dry-rubbed and tanned overnight before visiting the smoker for a couple of hours. Then they're bathed in the sauce of your choice. Kojak's also has a nice selection of sandwiches, including sloppy chicken and country-style sausage. This is definitely not the kind of place you'd want to bring a vegan. $ *Average main: $14* ⊠ *2808 Gandy Blvd., South Tampa* ☎ *813/837–3774* ⊕ *www. kojaksbbq.net* ☉ *Closed Mon.*

WHERE TO STAY

If you want to be close to the cruise-ship terminal, then you'll have to stay in Tampa, but if you want to spend more time in the area and perhaps stay on the beach, St. Petersburg and the beaches are close by.

For expanded reviews, facilities, and current deals, visit Fodors.com.

$$$
B&B/INN
★
Don Vicente de Ybor Historic Inn. Built as a home in 1895 by town founder Don Vicente de Ybor, this inn shows that the working-class cigar city had an elegant side, too. **Pros:** elegant rooms; rich in history; walking distance to nightlife. **Cons:** rowdy neighborhood on weekend nights. $ *Rooms from: $175* ⊠ *1915 Republica de Cuba, Ybor City* ☎ *813/241–4545, 866/206–4545* ⊕ *donvicenteinn.com* ⇌ *13 rooms, 3 suites* ¶◎¶ *Breakfast.*

$$$
HOTEL
★
Hilton Garden Inn Tampa Ybor Historic District. Although its modern architecture makes it seem out of place in this historic district, this chain hotel's location across from Centro Ybor is a plus. **Pros:** good location for business travelers; reasonable rates. **Cons:** chain-hotel feel; far from downtown. $ *Rooms from: $179* ⊠ *1700 E. 9th Ave., Ybor City* ☎ *813/769–9267* ⊕ *www.hiltongardeninn.com* ⇌ *84 rooms, 11 suites* ¶◎¶ *No meals.*

$$$$
HOTEL
Tampa Marriott Waterside Hotel & Marina. Across from the Tampa Convention Center, this downtown hotel was built for conventioneers but is also convenient to tourist spots such as the Florida Aquarium and the Channelside and Hyde Park shopping districts. **Pros:** great downtown location; near shopping. **Cons:** gridlock during rush hour; streets tough to maneuver; area sketchy after dark. $ *Rooms from: $290* ⊠ *700 S. Florida Ave., Downtown* ☎ *888/268–1616* ⊕ *www.marriott.com* ⇌ *683 rooms, 36 suites* ¶◎¶ *No meals.*

Ports of Call

WORD OF MOUTH

"The islands on [the Southern Caribbean] route are very nice IMHO. Also it's easy to do excursions with a local guide. There will be plenty of them on the dock as you exit the ship. The prices are usually reasonable too."

—jacketwatch

Nowhere in the world are conditions better suited to cruising than in the Caribbean Sea. Tiny island nations, within easy sailing distance of one another, form a chain of tropical enchantment that curves from Cuba in the north all the way down to the coast of Venezuela. There's far more to life here than sand and coconuts, however. The islands are vastly different, with a variety of cultures, topographies, and languages represented. Colonialism has left its mark, and the presence of the Spanish, French, Dutch, Danish, and British is still felt. Slavery, too, has left its cultural legacy, blending African overtones into the colonial/Indian amalgam. The one constant, however, is the weather. Despite the islands' southerly latitude, the climate is surprisingly gentle, due in large part to the cooling influence of the trade winds.

The Caribbean is made up of the Greater Antilles and the Lesser Antilles. The former consist of those islands closest to the United States: Cuba, Jamaica, Hispaniola (Haiti and the Dominican Republic), and Puerto Rico. (The Cayman Islands lie south of Cuba.) The Lesser Antilles, including the Virgin, Windward, and Leeward islands and others, are greater in number but smaller in size, and constitute the southern half of the Caribbean chain.

GOING ASHORE

Traveling by cruise ship presents an opportunity to visit many places in a short time. The flip side is that your stay in each port of call will be brief. For this reason cruise lines offer shore excursions, which maximize passengers' time. There are a number of advantages to shore excursions arranged by your ship: in some destinations, transportation may be unreliable, and a ship-packaged tour is the best way to see distant sights. Also, you don't have to worry about missing the ship. The disadvantage of a shore excursion is the cost—you usually pay more for the convenience of having the ship do the legwork for you, but it's not always a lot more. Of course, you can always book a tour independently, hire a taxi, or use foot power to explore on your own. For each port of call included in this guide we've provided some suggestions for the best ship-sponsored excursions—in terms of both quality of experience and price—as well as some suggestions for what to do if you want to explore on your own.

ARRIVING IN PORT

When your ship arrives in a port, it will tie up alongside a dock or anchor out in a harbor. If the ship is docked, passengers walk down the gangway to go ashore. Docking makes it easy to move between the shore and the ship.

TENDERING

If your ship anchors in the harbor, you will have to take a small boat—called a launch or tender—to get ashore. Tendering is a nuisance; however, participants in shore excursions are given priority. Passengers wishing to disembark independently may be required to gather in a public room, get sequenced tendering passes, and wait until their numbers are called. The ride to shore may take as long as 20 minutes. If you don't like waiting, plan to go ashore an hour or so after the ship drops its anchor. On a very large ship, the wait for a tender can be quite long and frustrating.

Because tenders can be difficult to board, passengers with mobility problems may not be able to visit certain ports. The larger ships are more likely to use tenders. It is usually possible to learn before booking a cruise whether the ship will dock or anchor at its ports of call.

Before anyone is allowed to walk down the gangway or board a tender, the ship must be cleared for landing. Immigration and customs officials board the vessel to examine the ship's manifest or possibly passports and sort through red tape. It may be more than an hour before you're allowed ashore. You will be issued a boarding pass, which you'll need to get back on board.

RETURNING TO THE SHIP

Cruise lines are strict about sailing times, which are posted at the gangway and elsewhere and announced in the daily schedule of activities. Be sure to be back on board (not on the dock waiting to get a tender back to the ship) at least an hour before the announced sailing time or you may be stranded. If you are on a shore excursion that was sold by the cruise line, however, the captain will wait for your group before casting off. That is one reason many passengers prefer ship-packaged tours.

If you're not on one of the ship's tours and the ship sails without you, immediately contact the cruise line's port representative, whose phone number is often listed on the daily schedule of activities. You may be able to hitch a ride on a pilot boat, although that is unlikely. Passengers who miss the boat must pay their own way to the next port.

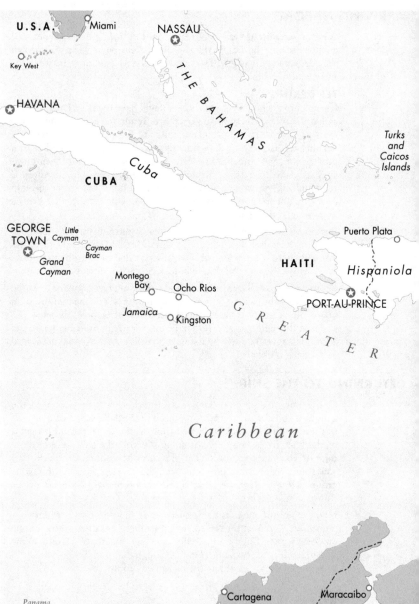

Caribbean

4

ATLANTIC OCEAN

DOMINICAN
REPUBLIC

☆ SANTO
DOMINGO

LEEWARD ISLANDS

St. John   Tortola
St. Thomas   Virgin Gorda
                        Anguilla
☆   St. Barthélemy
SAN JUAN   St. Maarten/   Saba   Barbuda
St.   St. Martin
Puerto   Croix   St. Eustatius
Rico   St. Kitts   Antigua
                    Nevis
                 Montserrat   Marie
                                Galante
                 Guadeloupe

ANTILLES

Dominica

Martinique
Fort-de-France

Sea

WINDWARD

St. Lucia

Barbados

St. Vincent

Bequia   Bridgetown
The
Grenadines
Carriacou
St. George's

WILLEMSTAD

Aruba   Islas Los   Grenada
      Bonaire   Roques
☆ Curaçao   Tobago

LESSER ANTILLES

Port of Spain   Trinidad

La Guaira

☆
CARACAS

VENEZUELA

0   200 miles
0   300 km

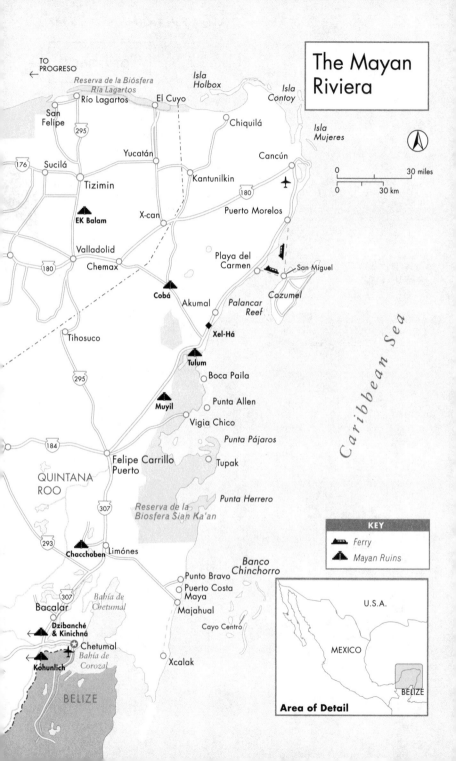

CARIBBEAN ESSENTIALS

CURRENCY

The U.S. dollar is the official currency on Puerto Rico, the U.S. Virgin Islands, the Turks and Caicos, Bonaire, and the British Virgin Islands. On Grand Cayman you will usually have a choice of Cayman or U.S. dollars when you take money out of an ATM, and you may even be able to get change in U.S. dollars. In Cozumel, Calica, Costa Maya, and Progreso, the Mexican peso is the official currency. The euro is used in a handful of French islands (St. Barth, St. Martin, Martinique, Guadeloupe). In most Caribbean ports U.S. paper currency (not coins) is accepted readily. When you pay in dollars you'll almost always get change in local currency, so it's best to carry bills in small denominations. If you need local currency (say, for a trip to one of the French islands that uses the euro), change money at a local bank or use an ATM for the best rate. Most major credit cards are accepted all over the Caribbean, except at local market stalls and small establishments.

KEEPING IN TOUCH

Internet cafés are now fairly common on many islands, and you'll sometimes find Internet cafés in the cruise-ship terminal itself—or perhaps in an attached or nearby shopping center. If you want to call home, most cruise-ship terminal facilities have phones that accept credit cards or local phone cards (local phone cards are almost always the cheapest option). And on most islands GSM multi-band mobile phones will work, though roaming charges may be steep (some plans include Puerto Rico and the U.S. Virgin Islands in their nationwide calling regions).

WHERE TO EAT

Cuisine on the Caribbean's islands is as varied as the islands themselves. The region's history as a colonial battleground and ethnic melting pot creates plenty of variety and adds lots of unusual tropical fruit and spices. In fact, the one quality that defines most Caribbean cooking is its spiciness, acquired from nutmeg, mace, allspice, peppers, saffron, and many other seasonings grown in the islands. Dress is generally casual, although throughout the islands beachwear is inappropriate most anywhere except on the beach. Unless otherwise noted, prices are given in U.S. dollars.

SHORE EXCURSIONS

Typical excursions include an island or town bus tour, a visit to a beach or rum factory, a boat trip, a snorkeling or diving trip, and charter fishing. In recent years, however, shore excursions have gotten more adventurous, with mild river-rafting, parasailing, jet-skiing, hiking, and biking added to the mix. It's often easier to take a ship-arranged excursion, but it's almost never the cheapest option.

If you prefer to break away from the pack, find a knowledgeable taxi driver or tour operator—they're usually within a stone's throw of the pier—or wander around on your own. A group of four to six people will usually find this option more economical and practical than will a single person or a couple.

Renting a car is also a good option on many islands—again, the more people, the better the deal. But get a good island map before you set off, and be sure to find out how long it will take you to get around.

Conditions are ideal for water sports of all kinds—scuba diving, snorkeling, windsurfing, sailing, waterskiing, and fishing excursions abound. Your shore-excursion director can usually arrange these activities for you if the ship offers no formal excursion.

> **BUYING LIQUOR AND PERFUME**
>
> If you buy duty-free liquor or perfume while in a Caribbean port, don't forget that you may not bring it aboard your flight home. You will have to put it in your checked bags. Many liquor stores will pack your bottles in bubble wrap and pack them in a good cardboard box. Take advantage of this service.

PRIVATE ISLANDS

Linda Coffman

When evaluating the "best" Caribbean ports of call, many repeat cruise passengers often add the cruise lines' own private islands to their lists of preferred destinations.

The cruise lines established "private" islands to provide a beach break on an island (or part of one) reserved for their exclusive use. While most passengers don't select an itinerary based solely upon calling at a private island, they usually consider them a highlight of their cruise vacation. The very least you can expect of your private island is lush foliage and a wide swath of beach surrounded by azure water. Facilities vary, but a beach barbecue, water-sports equipment rental, lounge chairs, hammocks, and restrooms are standard. Youth counselors come ashore to conduct sand-castle building competitions and lead junior pirates on swashbuckling island treasure hunts.

The use of strollers and wheelchairs equipped with all-terrain wheels may be offered on a complimentary first-come, first-served basis. However, with the exception of some participation sports on the beach, plan to pay for most water toys and activities. Costs associated with private-island fun and recreation can range from $8 for use of a snorkel vest (you may use your own snorkel equipment; however, in the event a floatation vest is required for safety, you must rent one) to $30 for rental of an entire snorkeling outfit for the day (mask, fins, snorkel vest, a mesh bag, fish identification card, and fish food). You can often take a banana-boat ride for $16 to $19 (15-minute ride), sail a small boat or catamaran for $30 to $50 (one hour), paddle a kayak for $18 to $38 (half-hour to hour-and-a-half), ride Jet Skis for $59 to $99 (45 minutes to one hour), parasail for a hefty $79 to $84 (10 minutes or less), or fly through the treetops on a zip line for $89. Floating mats are a relative bargain at $6 to $12 for all-day lounging in the water. You might also find open-air massage cabanas with pricing comparable to the spa charges onboard.

There is generally no charge for food or basic beverages such as those served onboard ship. While soft drinks and tropical cocktails can usually be charged to your shipboard account, you might want to bring a small amount of cash ashore for souvenir shopping, which is usually possible from vendors set up on or near the beach. You will also want to bring beach towels ashore and return them to the ship at the end of the day, because, as Princess Cruises reminds passengers, "Although the locals may offer to do this for you, unfortunately we seldom see the towels again!"

Even if you do nothing more than lie in a shaded hammock and sip fruity tropical concoctions, the day can be one of the most fun and relaxing of your entire cruise.

ISLANDS BY CRUISE LINE

4

Carnival Cruise Lines is currently the only major cruise line without an extensive private island experience available to the entire fleet. However, select Carnival itineraries include calls at Half Moon Cay, Holland America Line's private paradise, where "Fun Ship" passengers can use all the facilities and participate in organized activities. Similarly, certain Regent Seven Seas cruises include beach days at Cayo Levantado, located off the Samaná Peninsula on the northeast coast of the Dominican Republic.

Although they do not stop at "private islands" in the strictest sense, the smaller ships of Seabourn and SeaDream offer passengers a day ashore on secluded private beaches where they can enjoy lavish barbecues and take a break from swimming and snorkeling to indulge in champagne and caviar served in the surf.

COSTA CRUISES

An unspoiled island paradise, Costa's **Catalina Island** is just off the coast of the Dominican Republic. Passengers can participate in Costa's "Beach Olympics," schedule a seaside massage, or just kick back on a chaise longue or a complimentary water float. Water-toy rentals, banana-boat rides, and sailing tours are available from independent concessionaires. Local vendors set up souvenir shops offering crafts and T-shirts. The ship provides the food for a lunch barbecue and tropical beverages at the beach bar.

Activities: Snorkeling, sailing, jet-skiing, waterskiing, hiking, volleyball, organized games, massages, shopping.

DISNEY CRUISE LINE

Disney's **Castaway Cay** has a dock, so passengers simply step ashore (rather than tendering, as is required to reach most cruise lines' private islands). Like everything associated with Disney, the line's private island is almost too good to be true. Located in the Abacos, a chain in the Bahamas, only 10% of Castaway Cay is developed, leaving plenty of unspoiled area to explore in Robinson Crusoe fashion. Trams are provided to reach separate beaches designated for children, teens, families, and adults, and areas where Disney offers age-specific activities and extensive, well-planned children's activities. Biking and hiking are so popular that two nature trails—one of them with an observation tower—are mapped out. Passengers can swim to a water platform complete with two slides or cool off in a 2,400-square-foot water-play area equipped with water jets and a splash pad. A 1,200-square-foot soft wet deck area provides freshwater fun for children with an array of pop jets, geysers, and bubblers. There is no charge for the water-play facilities. Excursions range from as passive as a glass-bottom-boat tour to the soaring excitement of parasailing. An interactive experience with stingrays is educational and safe—the gentle creatures' barbs are blunted for safety. In addition to barbecue fare served in two buffet areas with covered seating and several beverage stations, beach games, island-style music, and a shaded game pavilion, there are shops, massage cabanas by the sea, and even a post office. Popular with couples as well as families, 20 private rental cabanas provide the luxury of a deluxe beach retreat with an option to add the personalized service of a cabana host. Teens have their own private retreat just steps from the beach.

Activities: Snorkeling, kayaking, parasailing, sailing, jet-skiing, paddleboats, water cycles, banana boat rides, fishing, bicycles, basketball, billiards, hiking, Ping-Pong, shuffleboard, soccer, volleyball, organized games, massages, shopping.

HOLLAND AMERICA LINE
Little San Salvador, one of the Bahamian out-islands, was renamed **Half Moon Cay** by Holland America Line to honor Henry Hudson's ship (depicted on the cruise line's logo) as well as to reflect the beach's crescent shape. Even after development, the island is still so unspoiled that it has been named a Wild Bird Preserve by the Bahamian National Trust. Passengers, who are welcomed ashore at a West Indies Village complete with shops and straw market, find Half Moon Cay easily accessible—all facilities are connected by hard-surfaced and packed-sand pathways and meet and exceed ADA requirements. An accessible tram also connects the welcome center with the food pavilion and bars; wheelchairs with balloon tires are available. In addition to the beach area for lazing in the sun or in the shade of a rented clamshell, the island has a post office, Bahamian-style chapel, a lagoon where you can interact with stingrays, and the Captain Morgan on the Rocks Island Bar in a "beached" pirate ship. For family fun, you'll find a beachfront water park with waterslides and fanciful sea creatures tethered to the sandy bottom of the shallow water. Massage services are available, as are fitness activities. Air-conditioned cabanas can be rented for the day, with or without the services of your own butler.

Activities: Scuba diving, snorkeling, windsurfing, kayaking, parasailing, sailing, jet-skiing, Aqua Bikes, fishing, bicycles, basketball, hiking, horseback riding, shuffleboard, volleyball, massages, shopping.

NORWEGIAN CRUISE LINE
Only 120 miles east of Fort Lauderdale in the Berry Island chain of the Bahamas, much of **Great Stirrup Cay** looks as it did when it was acquired by Norwegian Cruise Line in 1977, with bougainvillea, sea grape, and coconut palms as abundant as the colorful tropical fish that inhabit the reef. The first uninhabited island purchased to offer cruise-ship passengers a private beach day, Great Stirrup Cay's white-sand beaches are fringed by coral and ideal for swimming and snorkeling. Permanent

facilities have been added to and improved in the intervening years and a seawall was erected to reduce beach erosion and preserve the environment. A straw market, water-sports centers, bars, volleyball courts, beachside massage stations, a food pavilion, and a 40-feet high and 175-feet long Hippo inflatable waterslide round out the facilities. Sand wheelchairs are available on the island, but the only paved pathway is along the seawall. Extensive island improvements began in 2010 with the excavation of a new entrance channel for tenders and construction of tender docking facilities and a welcome pavilion that is now the site for landings. As a result, the beachfront has been expanded significantly to alleviate crowding. Private beachfront cabanas, two dining facilities, a kid's play area, wave runners, a floating Aqua Park with a variety of water toys, kayak tours through man-made rivers within the island, an ecocruise, and a stingray encounter experience have been added.

Activities: Snorkeling, kayaking, parasailing, sailing, paddleboats, Ping-Pong, hiking, volleyball, organized games, massages, shopping.

PRINCESS CRUISES

Princess Cays is a 40-acre haven on the southern tip of Eleuthera Island in the Bahamas. Not quite an uninhabited island, it nevertheless offers a wide ribbon of beach, long enough for passengers to splash in the surf, relax in a hammock, or limbo to the beat of local music and never feel crowded. In a similar fashion to booking shore excursions, snorkeling equipment, sea boards, floats, kayaks, paddle wheelers, banana boat rides, aqua chairs, beach clamshells, and bungalows can be prereserved on Princess Cruises' website. All other equipment and activities must be booked onboard. Nestled in a picturesque palm grove, private bungalows with air-conditioning and ceiling fans and a deck for lounging can be rented for parties of up to six. The Sanctuary at Princess Cays, complete with bungalows for parties of four, is an adults-only haven. A pirate-theme play area for children is supervised. In addition to three tropical bars and the area where a Bahamian barbecue is served, permanent facilities include small shops that sell island crafts and trinkets, but if you head around the back and through the fence, independent vendors sell similar goods for lower prices.

Activities: Snorkeling, kayaking, banana boat rides, sailing, paddleboats, Aqua Bikes, windsurfing, surf fishing, deep sea fishing, hiking, organized games, shopping.

ROYAL CARIBBEAN, CELEBRITY CRUISES, AND AZAMARA CLUB CRUISES

Royal Caribbean, Azamara Club Cruises, and Celebrity Cruises passengers have twice as many opportunities to visit a private island. The lines share two, and many Caribbean itineraries include one or the other.

Coco Cay is a 140-acre island in the Berry Island chain between Nassau and Freeport. Originally known as Little Stirrup Cay, it's within view of Great Stirrup Cay (NCL's private island) and the snorkeling is just as good, especially around a sunken airplane and a replica of Blackbeard's flagship, *Queen Anne's Revenge*. In addition to activities and games ashore, Coco Cay has one of the largest Aqua Parks in the Caribbean, where children and adults alike can jump on an in-water trampoline or climb a floating sand castle before they dig into a beach barbecue or explore a nature trail. Attractions also include an inflatable 40-foot waterslide (fun for adults and kids alike) and a Power Wheels track, where youngsters age 3 to 8 can take a miniature car for a spin at a sedate 3 mph. Rounding out the facilities are a Bahamian marketplace, several beach bars, and numerous hammocks for relaxation in the sun or shade.

Activities: Scuba diving, snorkeling, jet-skiing, kayaking, parasailing, hiking, volleyball, organized games, shopping.

Labadee is a 260-acre peninsula approximately 6 miles (10 km) from Cap Haitien on the secluded north coast of Haiti (the port of call is sometimes called "Hispaniola"). Passengers can step ashore on the dock, from which water taxis and five different walking paths, trails, and avenues lead to many areas throughout the peninsula, including the Labadee Town Square and Dragon's Plaza, where a welcome center and central tram station are located. In addition to swimming, water sports, an Aqua Park with floating trampolines and waterslides, and nature trails to explore, bonuses on Labadee are an authentic folkloric show presented by island performers and a market featuring work of local artists and crafters, where you might find an interesting painting or unique wood carving. More adventurous activities include an Alpine Coaster, a thrilling roller coaster experience, and one of the most exciting—and at 2,600 feet in length the longest—zip-line experiences in the Caribbean, which takes place 500 feet above the beaches of Labadee, where riders can reach speeds of 40 to 50 mph over the water. Due to the proximity of Labadee to mainland Haiti, in the past it has occasionally been necessary to cancel calls there due to political unrest. In that event, an alternate port is usually scheduled. The Barefoot Beach Club & Cabanas is reserved for top suite guests and those who rent one of the 20 cabanas, which can accomodate 4–5 guests. Only the nine Palm Cabanas are wheelchair-accessible, but even they have two steps to climb.

Activities: Snorkeling, jet-skiing, kayaking, parasailing, hiking, volley-ball, organized games, shopping.

ANTIGUA (ST. JOHN'S)

Jordan Simon

Some say Antigua has so many beaches that you could visit a different one every day for a year. Most have snow-white sand, and many are backed by lavish resorts that offer sailing, diving, windsurfing, and snorkeling. The largest of the British Leeward Islands, Antigua was the headquarters from which Lord Horatio Nelson (then a mere captain) made his forays against the French and pirates in the late 18th century. You may wish to explore English Harbour and its carefully restored Nelson's Dockyard, as well as tour old forts, historic churches, and tiny villages. Appealing aspects of the island's interior include a small tropical rain forest ideal for hiking and ziplining, ancient Native American archaeological digs, and restored sugar mills. Due to time constraints, it's best to make trips this far from port with an experienced tour operator, but you can easily take a taxi to any number of fine beaches on your own and escape from the hordes descending from the ship.

Antigua

KEY
Beaches
Dive Sites

ESSENTIALS

CURRENCY Eastern Caribbean (EC) dollar (EC$2.67 to US$1). U.S. dollars are generally accepted, but change is given in EC.

INTERNET There are some small Internet cafés in St. John's and English Harbour; ask at the tourist information booth at the cruise-ship pier.

TELEPHONES GSM tri-band mobile phones from the United States and United Kingdom usually work on Antigua; you can also rent one from LIME (formerly Cable & Wireless) or APUA (Antigua Public Utilities Authority). Basic rental costs range between EC$25 and EC$50 per day. You can use the LIME Phone Card (available in $5, $10, and $20 denominations in most hotels and post offices) for local and long-distance calls.

COMING ASHORE

Though some ships dock at the deepwater harbor in downtown St. John's, most use Heritage Quay, a multimillion-dollar complex with shops, condominiums, a casino, and a food court. Most St. John's attractions are an easy walk from Heritage Quay; the older part of the city is eight blocks away. A tourist information booth is in the main docking building.

If you intend to explore beyond St. John's, consider hiring a taxi driver–guide. Taxis meet every cruise ship. They're unmetered; fares are fixed, and drivers are required to carry a rate card. Agree on the fare before setting off (make sure you know whether the price quoted is one-way or round-trip), and plan to tip drivers 10%. Some cabbies may take you from St. John's to English Harbour and wait for a "reasonable" amount of time (about a half hour) while you look around, for about $50; you can usually arrange an island tour for around $25 per hour. Renting your own car isn't usually practical, since you must purchase a $20 temporary driving permit in addition to the car-rental fee, which is usually about $50 per day in the high season.

BEST BETS FOR CRUISERS

■ **Dickenson Bay Beach.** One of Antigua's best beaches.

■ **Ecotourism.** Explore the island's forested interior on foot or surrounding coves by kayak.

■ **Jolly Harbour.** A cheap day pass at the Jolly Harbour Resort is a great day at the beach.

■ **Nelson's Dockyard.** This is one of the Caribbean's best historic sights, with many stores, restaurants, and bars.

■ **St. John's.** There's excellent duty-free shopping, especially in Heritage Quay and Redcliffe Quay.

EXPLORING ANTIGUA

Falmouth. This town sits on a lovely bay backed by former sugar plantations and sugar mills. The most important historic site here is St. Paul's Church, which was rebuilt on the site of a church once used by troops during the Horatio Nelson period. ⊠ *Antigua.*

Ft. George. East of Liberta—one of the first settlements founded by freed slaves—on Monk's Hill, this fort was built from 1689 to 1720. Among the ruins are the sites for 32 cannons, water cisterns, the base of the old flagstaff, and some of the original buildings. ⊠ *Antigua.*

Fodor's Choice ★ **Nelson's Dockyard.** Antigua's most famous attraction is the world's only Georgian-era dockyard still in use, a treasure trove for history buffs and nautical nuts alike. In 1671 the governor of the Leeward Islands wrote to the Council for Foreign Plantations in London, pointing out the advantages of this landlocked harbor. By 1704 English Harbour was in regular use as a garrisoned station.

In 1784, 26-year-old Horatio Nelson sailed in on the HMS *Boreas* to serve as captain and second-in-command of the Leeward Island Station. Under him was the captain of the HMS *Pegasus,* Prince William Henry, duke of Clarence, who was later crowned King William IV. The prince acted as best man when Nelson married Fannie Nisbet on Nevis in 1787.

When the Royal Navy abandoned the station at English Harbour in 1889, it fell into a state of decay, though adventuresome yachties still lived there in near-primitive conditions. The Society of the Friends of English Harbour began restoring it in 1951; it reopened with great fanfare as Nelson's Dockyard on November 14, 1961. Within the compound are crafts shops, restaurants, and two splendidly restored 18th-century hotels, the Admiral's Inn and the Copper & Lumber Store Hotel, worth peeking into. Water taxis will ferry you between points for EC$5. The Dockyard National Park also includes serene nature trails accessing beaches, rock pools, and crumbling plantation ruins and hilltop forts.

The **Dockyard Museum,** in the original Naval Officer's House, presents ship models, mock-ups of English Harbour, displays on the people who worked there and typical ships that docked, silver regatta trophies, maps, prints, antique navigational instruments, and Nelson's very own telescope and tea caddy. ⊠ *English Harbour* ☎ *268/481–5027 for Dock-yard Museum, 268/481–5028 for National Parks Authority* ⊕ *www.nationalparksantigua.com* ☑ *$2 suggested donation* ☉ *Daily 9–5.*

St. John's. Antigua's capital, with some 45,000 inhabitants (approximately half the island's population), lies at sea level at the inland end of a sheltered northwestern bay. Although it has seen better days, a couple of notable historic sights and some good waterfront shopping areas make it worth a visit. At the far south end of town, where Market Street forks into Valley and All Saints roads, haggling goes on every Friday and Saturday, when locals jam the **Public Market** to buy and sell fruits, vegetables, fish, and spices. Ask before you aim a camera; your subject may expect a tip. This is old-time Caribbean shopping, a jambalaya of sights, sounds, and smells. ⊠ *Antigua.*

Anglican Cathedral of St. John the Divine. At the south gate of the Anglican Cathedral of St. John the Divine are figures of St. John the Baptist and St. John the Divine, said to have been taken from one of Napoléon's ships and brought to Antigua. The original church was built in 1681, replaced by a stone building in 1745, and destroyed by an earthquake in 1843. The present neo-baroque building dates from 1845; the parishioners had the interior completely encased in pitch pine, hoping to forestall future earthquake damage. Tombstones bear eerily eloquent testament to the colonial days. ⊠ *Between Long and Newgate Sts., St. John's* ☎ *268/461–0082.*

Heritage Quay. Shopaholics head directly for Heritage Quay, an ugly multimillion-dollar complex. The two-story buildings contain stores that sell duty-free goods, sportswear, down-island imports (paintings, T-shirts, straw baskets), and local crafts. There are also restaurants, a bandstand, and a casino. Cruise-ship passengers disembark here from the 500-foot-long pier. Expect heavy shilling. ⊠ *High and Thames Sts.*

Museum of Antigua and Barbuda. Signs at the Museum of Antigua and Barbuda say "Please touch," encouraging you to explore Antigua's past. The museum occupies the former courthouse, which dates from 1750. The superlative museum gift shop carries such unusual items as calabash purses, seed earrings, warri boards (warri being an African game brought over to the Caribbean), and lignum vitae pipes, as well as historic maps and local books (including engrossing, detailed monographs on varied subjects by the late Desmond Nicholson, a longtime resident). ⊠ *Long and Market Sts., St. John's* ☎ *268/462–1469* ⊕ *www.antiguamuseum.org* ☑ *$3; children under 12 free* ☉ *Mon.–Fri. 8:30–4, Sat. 10–2, closed Sun.*

Redcliffe Quay. Redcliffe Quay, at the water's edge just south of Heritage Quay, is the most appealing part of St. John's. Attractively restored (and superbly re-created) buildings in a riot of cotton-candy colors house shops, restaurants, and boutiques and are linked by court-yards and landscaped walkways. ✉ *St. John's.*

Shirley Heights. This bluff affords a spectacular view of English Harbour. The heights are named for Sir Thomas Shirley, the governor who fortified the harbor in 1787. At the top is Shirley Heights Lookout, a restaurant built into the remnants of the 18th-century fortifications. Most notable for its boisterous Sunday barbecues that continue into the night with live music and dancing, it serves dependable burgers, pumpkin soup, grilled meats, and rum punches. ✉ *Antigua.*

Dows Hill Interpretation Centre. Not far from Shirley Heights is the Dows Hill Interpretation Centre, where observation platforms provide still more sensational vistas of the English Harbour area. A multime-dia sound-and-light presentation on island history and culture, spot-lighting lifelike figures and colorful tableaux accompanied by running commentary and music, results in a cheery, if bland, portrait of Anti-guan life from Amerindian times to the present. ✉ *Antigua* ☎ *268/460–1379 for National Parks Authority* ⊕ *www.nationalparksantigua.com* ☒ *EC$15* ☉ *Daily 9–5.*

☼ **Stingray City Antigua**. Stingray City Antigua is a carefully reproduced "natural" environment nicknamed by staffers the "retirement home," though the 30-plus stingrays, ranging from infants to seniors, are frisky. You can stroke, feed, even hold the striking gliders ("they're like puppy dogs," one guide swears), as well as snorkel in deeper, protected waters. The tour guides do a marvelous job of explaining the animals' habits, from feeding to breeding, and their preda-tors (including man). ✉ *Seaton's Village* ☎ *268/562–7297* ⊕ *www.stingraycityantigua.com.*

SHOPPING

Redcliffe Quay, on the waterfront at the south edge of St. John's, is by far the most appealing shopping area. Several restaurants and more than 30 boutiques, many with one-of-a-kind wares, are set around landscaped courtyards shaded by colorful trees. **Heritage Quay**, in St. John's, has 35 shops—including many that are duty-free—that cater to the cruise-ship crowd, which docks almost at its doorstep. Outlets here include Benetton, the Body Shop, Sunglass Hut, Dolce & Gabbana, and Oshkosh B'Gosh. There are also shops along **St. John's, St. Mary's, High,** and **Long streets**. The tangerine-and-lilac-hue four-story **Vendor's Mall** at the intersection of Redcliffe and Thames streets gathers the pushy, pesky vendors that once clogged the narrow streets. It's jammed with stalls; air-conditioned indoor shops sell some higher-price, if not higher-quality, merchandise. On the west coast the Mediterranean-style, arcaded **Jolly Harbour Marina** holds some interesting galleries and shops, as do the marinas and Main Road snaking around English and Fal-mouth Harbours.

★ **Goldsmitty.** Hans Smit is the Goldsmitty, an expert goldsmith who turns gold, black coral, and precious and semiprecious stones into one-of-a-kind works of art. ⊠ *Redcliffe Quay, St. John's* ☎ *268/462–4601* ⊕ *www.goldsmitty.com.*

Isis. Island and international bric-a-brac, such as antique jewelry, hand-carved walking sticks, and glazed pottery, are available at Isis. ⊠ *Redcliffe Quay, St. John's* ☎ *268/462–4602.*

★ **Noreen Phillips.** Glitzy appliquéd and beaded evening wear—inspired by the colors of the sea and sunset—in sensuous fabrics ranging from chiffon and silk to Italian lace and Indian brocade are created at Noreen Phillips. ⊠ *Redcliffe Quay, St. John's* ☎ *268/462–3127.*

ACTIVITIES

ADVENTURE TOURS

★ **Adventure Antigua.** The enthusiastic Eli Fuller, who is knowledgeable not only about the ecosystem and geography of Antigua but also about its history and politics (his grandfather was the American consul), runs Adventure Antigua. His thorough seven-hour excursion (Eli dubs it "re-creating my childhood explorations") includes stops at Guiana Island (for lunch and guided snorkeling), Pelican Island, Bird Island, and Hell's Gate. The company also offers a fun, shorter "Xtreme amusement park ride" variation on a racing boat catering to adrenaline junkies who "feel the need for speed" that also visits Stingray City, as well as a more sedate Antigua Classic Yacht sail-and-snorkel experience that explains the rich West Indian history of boatbuilding. ⊠ *Antigua* ☎ *268/727–3261, 268/726–6355* ⊕ *www.adventureantigua.com.*

Antigua Rainforest Canopy Tours. Play Tarzan and Jane at Antigua Rainforest Canopy Tours. You should be in fairly good condition for the ropes challenges, which require upper-body strength and stamina; there are height and weight restrictions. But anyone (vertigo or acrophobia sufferers, beware) can navigate the intentionally rickety "Indiana Jones–inspired" suspension bridges, then fly (in secure harnesses) over a rain-forest-filled valley from one towering turpentine tree to the next on lines with names like "Screamer" and "Leap of Faith." Admission varies slightly, but is usually $85. It's open Monday–Saturday from 8 to 6, with two scheduled tours at 9 and 11 (other times by appointment). ⊠ *Fig Dr., Wallings* ☎ *268/562–6363* ⊕ *www. antiguarainforest.com.*

DIVING

Antigua is an unsung diving destination, with plentiful undersea sights to explore, from coral canyons to sea caves. Barbuda alone features roughly 200 wrecks on its treacherous reefs. The most accessible wreck is the 1890s bark *Andes*, not far out in Deep Bay, off Five Islands Peninsula. Among the favorite sites are **Green Island, Cades Reef,** and **Bird Island** (a national park). Memorable sightings include turtles, stingrays, and barracuda darting amid basalt walls, hulking boulders, and stray 17th-century anchors and cannon. One advantage is accessibility in many spots for shore divers and snorkelers. Double-tank dives run about $90.

Dockyard Divers. Owned by British ex-merchant seaman Captain A.G. "Tony" Fincham, Dockyard Divers is one of the island's most established outfits and offers diving and snorkeling trips, PADI courses, and dive packages with accommodations. They're geared to seasoned divers, but staff work patiently with novices. Tony is a wonderful source of information on the island; ask him about the "Fincham's Follies" musical extravaganza he produces for charity. ⊠ *Nelson's Dockyard, English Harbour* ☎ *268/460–1178* ⊕ *www.dockyard-divers.com.*

> **CAUTION**
>
> Do not bother packing beach towels. They will be provided for your use by the cruise ship and will be given out when you go ashore.

KAYAKING

★ **"Paddles" Kayak Eco Adventure.** "Paddles" Kayak Eco Adventure takes you on a 3½-hour tour of serene mangroves and inlets with informative narrative about the fragile ecosystem of the swamp and reefs and the rich diversity of flora and fauna. The tour ends with a hike to sunken caves and snorkeling in the North Sound Marine Park, capped by a rum punch at the fun Creole-style clubhouse. Experienced guides double as kayaking and snorkeling instructors, making this an excellent opportunity for novices. Conrad and Jennie's brainchild is one of Antigua's better bargains. ⊠ *Seaton's Village* ☎ *268/463–1944* ⊕ *www.antiguapaddles.com.*

BEACHES

Dickenson Bay. Along a lengthy stretch of powder-soft white sand and exceptionally calm water you can find small and large hotels, water sports, concessions, and beachfront restaurants. There's decent snorkeling at either point. ⊠ *2 miles (3 km) northeast of St. John's, along main coast road.*

Johnson's Point/Crabbe Hill. This series of connected, deserted beaches on the southwest coast looks out toward Montserrat, Guadeloupe, and St. Kitts. Notable beach bar–restaurants include OJ's, Gibson's, and Turner's. The water is generally placid, though not good for snorkeling. ⊠ *3 miles (5 km) south of Jolly Harbour complex, on main west-coast road.*

Pigeon Point. Near Falmouth Harbour lie two fine white-sand beaches. The leeward side is calmer, the windward side is rockier, and there are sensational views and snorkeling around the point. Several restaurants and bars are nearby, though Bumpkin's (and its potent banana coladas) satisfies most on-site needs. ⊠ *Off main south-coast road, southwest of Falmouth.*

WHERE TO EAT

$$ ✕ **Big Banana—Pizzas in Paradise.** This tiny, often crowded spot is tucked
PIZZA   into one side of a restored 18th-century rum warehouse with broad plank floors, wood-beam ceiling, and stone archways. Cool, Benetton-style photos of locals and musicians jamming adorn the brick walls.

Big Banana serves some of the island's best pizza—try the lobster or the seafood variety—as well as such tasty specials as conch salad, fresh fruit crushes, classic pastas, and sub sandwiches bursting at the seams. There's live entertainment some nights, and a large-screen TV for sports fans. $ *Average main: $16* ⊠ *Redcliffe Quay, St. John's* ☎ *268/480–6985* ⊕ *www.bigbanana-antigua.com* ⊗ *Closed Sun.*

$$$$

ECLECTIC

★

✕**Coconut Grove.** Coconut palms grow through the roof of this open-air thatched restaurant, flickering candlelight illuminates colorful local murals, waves lap the white sand, and the warm waitstaff provides just the right level of service. Jean-François Bellanger's superbly presented dishes fuse French culinary preparations with island ingredients. The kitchen can be uneven, the wine list is unimaginative and overpriced (save for the occasional $31 specials), and the buzzing happy-hour bar crowd lingering well into dinnertime can detract from the otherwise romantic atmosphere. Nonetheless, Coconut Grove straddles the line between casual beachfront boîte and elegant eatery with aplomb. $ *Average main: $30* ⊠ *Siboney Beach Club, Dickenson Bay* ☎ *268/462–1538* ⊕ *www.coconutgroveantigua.net* ⚓ *Reservations essential.*

ARUBA (ORANJESTAD)

Vernon
O'Reilly
Ramesar

Few islands can boast the overt dedication to tourism and the quality of service that Aruba offers. The arid landscape is full of attractions to keep visitors occupied, and the island offers some of the most dazzling beaches in the Caribbean. Casinos and novelty nightclubs abound in Oranjestad, giving the capital an almost Las Vegas appeal. To keep tourists coming back year after year, the island boasts a tremendous variety of restaurants ranging from upscale French eateries to toes-in-the-sand casual dining. Aruba may not be an unexplored paradise, but hundreds of thousands of tourists make it a point to beat a path here every year. Because it's not a very large island, cruise-ship visitors can expect to see a large part of the island on their day ashore. Or they can simply see several of the beautiful beaches. Whether you're planning to be active or to simply relax, this is an ideal cruise port.

ESSENTIALS

CURRENCY The Aruban florin (AFl 1.79 to US$1). The florin is pegged to the U.S. dollar, and Arubans accept U.S. dollars readily, so you need only acquire local currency for pocket change. Note that the Netherlands Antilles florin used on Curaçao is not accepted on Aruba.

TELEPHONE When making calls to anywhere in Aruba, simply dial the seven-digit number. AT&T customers can dial 800–8000 from special phones at the cruise dock and in the airport's arrival and departure halls. Otherwise dial 121 to contact the international operator to place an international call.

COMING ASHORE

The Port of Oranjestad is a busy place and is generally full of eager tourists looking for souvenirs or a bite to eat. The port can accommodate up to five ships at a time (and frequently does). The Renaissance

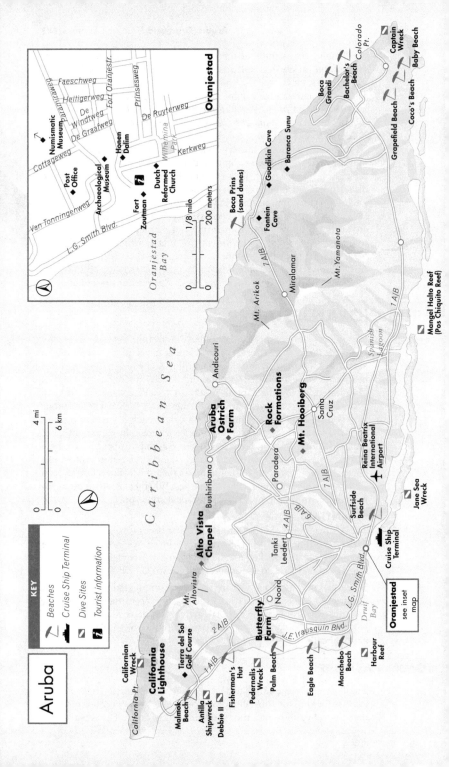

Aruba

KEY

⟍ Beaches
🚢 Cruise Ship Terminal
◢ Dive Sites
ℹ Tourist Information

Caribbean Sea

California Point Wreck
Californian Wreck
California Lighthouse
Malmok Beach
Antilla Shipwreck
Debbie II
Fisherman's Hut
Tierra del Sol Golf Course
Mt. Altovista
Pedernalis Wreck
Palm Beach
Alto Vista Chapel
Noord
Butterfly Farm
J.E. Irausquin Blvd.
Eagle Beach
Manchebo Beach
Harbour Reef
Druif Bay
2 A/B
1 A/B
Bushiribana
Aruba Ostrich Farm
Rock Formations
Paradera
Mt. Hooiberg
Tanki Leendert
4 A/B
6 A/B
Andicouri
Santa Cruz
Surfside Beach
7 A/B
Reina Beatrix International Airport
Cruise Ship Terminal
L.G. Smith Blvd.
Oranjestad see inset map
Jane Sea Wreck
Spanish Lagoon
Mangel Halto Reef (Pos Chiquito Reef)
1 A/B
Miralamar
Mt. Yamanota
Mt. Arikok
7 A/B
Boca Prins (sand dunes)
Fontein Cave
Guadikin Cave
Baranca Sunu
Boca Grandi
Bachelor's Beach
Grapefield Beach
Coco's Beach
Captain Wreck
Baby Beach
Colorado Pt.

0   4 mi
0   6 km

Oranjestad

Faeschweg
Heitigerweg
De Windtweg
De Graafweg
Cottageweg
Van Tonningenweg
L.G. Smith Blvd.
Caraïbaniaweg
Fort Oranjestr.
Prinsesweg
De Ruyterweg
Kerkweg
Wilhelmina Park
Numismatic Museum
Post Office
Archeological Museum
Fort Zoutman
Honen Dalim
Dutch Reformed Church
Oranjestad
Oranjestad Bay

0   200 meters
0   1/8 mile

Marketplace is right on the port, as are a number of souvenir shops and some decent and inexpensive restaurants. The main shopping areas of Oranjestad are all within 10 minutes' walk of the port.

Taxis can be flagged down on the street that runs alongside the port (look for license plates with a "TX"

tag). Rates are fixed (i.e., there are no meters; the rates are set by the government and displayed on a chart), though you and the driver should agree on the fare before your ride begins. Rides to Eagle Beach run about $10; to Palm Beach, about $11. If you want to rent a car, you can do so for a reasonable price; driving is on the right, just as in the United States, and it's pretty easy to get around, though a four-wheel-drive vehicle does help in reaching some of the more out-of-the-way places.

EXPLORING ARUBA

Alto Vista Chapel. Alone near the island's northwest corner sits this scenic little chapel. The wind whistles through the simple mustard-color walls, eerie boulders, and looming cacti. Along the side of the road back to civilization are miniature crosses with depictions of the stations of the cross and hand-lettered signs with "Pray for us Sinners" and other heartfelt evocations of faith. ✛ *To get here, follow the rough, winding dirt road that loops around the island's northern tip, or, from the hotel strip, take Palm Beach Road through three intersections and watch for the asphalt road to the left just past the Alto Vista Rum Shop.* ✉ *Oranjestad.*

★ **Aruba Ostrich Farm.** Everything you ever wanted to know about the world's largest living birds can be found at this farm. A large *palapa* (palm-thatched roof) houses a gift shop and restaurant that draws large bus tours, and tours of the farm are available every half hour. This operation is virtually identical to the facility in Curaçao; it's owned by the same company. ✉ *Makividiri Rd., Paradera* ☎ *297/585–9630* ⊕ *www.arubaostrichfarm.com* ⌧ *$12* ☉ *Daily 9–4.*

☖ **Butterfly Farm.** Hundreds of butterflies from around the world flutter about this spectacular garden. Guided 30- to 45-minute tours (included in the price of admission) provide an entertaining look into the life cycle of these insects, from egg to caterpillar to chrysalis to butterfly. After your initial visit, you can return as often as you like for free during your vacation. ✉ *J.E. Irausquin Blvd., Palm Beach* ☎ *297/586–3656* ⊕ *www. thebutterflyfarm.com* ⌧ *$15* ☉ *Daily 9–4:30; last tour at 4.*

California Lighthouse. The lighthouse, built by a French architect in 1910, stands at the island's far northern end. Although you can't go inside, you can climb the hill to the lighthouse base for some great views. It's surrounded by huge boulders and sand dunes; in this stark landscape you might feel as though you've just landed on the moon. ✉ *Oranjestad.*

Mt. Hooiberg. Named for its shape (*hooiberg* means "haystack" in Dutch), this 541-foot peak lies inland just past the airport. If you have the energy, you can climb the 562 steps to the top for an impressive view of Oranjestad (and Venezuela on clear days). ⊠ *Oranjestad.*

Oranjestad. Aruba's charming capital is best explored on foot. L.G. Smith Boulevard, the palm-lined thoroughfare in the center of town, runs between pastel-painted buildings, old and new, of typical Dutch design. You'll find many malls with boutiques and shops here. ⊠ *Aruba.*

Archaeological Museum of Aruba. This small museum has two rooms chock-full of fascinating artifacts from the indigenous Arawak people, including farm and domestic utensils dating back hundreds of years. ⊠ *J.E. Irausquin Blvd. 2A, Oranjestad* ☎ *297/582–8979* 🖃 *Free* ☉ *Tues.–Sun. 10–5.*

Ft. Zoutman. One of the island's oldest edifices, Aruba's historic fort was built in 1796 and played an important role in skirmishes between British and Curaçao troops in 1803. The Willem III Tower, named for the Dutch monarch of that time, was added in 1868 to serve as a lighthouse. Over time the fort has been a government office building, a police station, and a prison; now its historical museum displays Aruban artifacts in an 18th-century house. ⊠ *Zoutmanstraat, Oranjestad* ☎ *297/582–6099* 🖃 *Free* ☉ *Weekdays 8–noon and 1–4.*

Numismatic Museum. This museum displays more than 40,000 historic coins and paper money from around the world. A few pieces were salvaged from shipwrecks in the region. Some of the coins circulated during the Roman Empire, the Byzantine Empire, and the ancient Chinese dynasties; the oldest dates from the 3rd century BC. The museum had its start as the private collection of an Aruban who dug up some old coins in his garden. It's now run by his granddaughter. ⊠ *Weststraat, Oranjestad* ☎ *297/582–8831* 🖃 *$5* ☉ *Weekdays 9–4, Saturday 8–noon.*

Rock Formations. The massive boulders at Ayo and Casibari are a mystery, as they don't match the island's geological makeup. You can climb to the top for fine views of the arid countryside. On the way you'll doubtless pass Aruba whiptail lizards—the males are cobalt blue, and the females are blue-gray with light-blue dots. The main path to Casibari has steps and handrails, and you must move through tunnels and along narrow steps and ledges to reach the top. At Ayo you can find ancient pictographs in a small cave (the entrance has iron bars to protect the drawings from vandalism). You may also encounter boulder climbers,

---

ARUBA BEST BETS

■ **Oranjestad.** Aruba's capital is pretty and easy to explore on foot, and it's impossible to get lost.

■ **Eagle Beach.** One of the most beautiful beaches in the Caribbean, with miles of white sand.

■ **Nightlife.** If your ship stays in port late, take advantage of the island's great bar scene and its many casinos.

■ **Snorkeling.** Though you can't dive here, you can snorkel to get a glimpse of what's under the sea.

■ **Windsurfing.** Constant wind allows this adrenaline sport to thrive in Aruba.

who are increasingly drawn to Ayo's smooth surfaces. Access to Casibari is via Tanki Highway 4A; you can reach Ayo via Route 6A. Watch carefully for the turnoff signs near the center of the island on the way to the windward side.

SHOPPING

Caya G.F. Betico Croes. Aruba's chief shopping street, Caya G.F. Betico Croes is lined with several shops advertising "duty-free prices" (again, these are not truly duty-free), boutiques, and jewelry stores noted for the aggressiveness of their vendors on cruise-ship days. ⊠ *Aruba.*

Paseo Herencia. It's all about style at this shopping center, which is just minutes away from the high-rise hotel area. The great bell tower, the nightly dancing-waters shows, and the selection of restaurants pull in shoppers. Offerings include Cuban cigars, the fine leather goods of Mario Hernández, Italian denim goods at Moda & Stile, perfumes, cosmetics, and lots of souvenir shops. ⊠ *L.G. Smith Blvd., Palm Beach* ☎ *297/586–6533.*

Port of Call Marketplace. Stores here sell fine jewelry, perfumes, low-priced liquor, batiks, crystal, leather goods, and fashionable clothing. ⊠ *L.G. Smith Blvd. 17, Oranjestad, Aruba.*

Renaissance Marketplace. Five minutes from the cruise-ship terminal, the Renaissance Marketplace, also known as Seaport Mall, has more than 120 stores selling merchandise to meet every taste and budget; the Seaport Casino is also here. ⊠ *L.G. Smith Blvd. 82, Oranjestad.*

Royal Plaza Mall. Across from the cruise-ship terminal, the Royal Plaza Mall has cafés, a post office (open weekdays 8 to 3:30), and such stores as Nautica, Benetton, Tommy Hilfiger, and Gandelman Jewelers. There's also a cybercafé for those who want to send email and get their caffeine all in one stop. ⊠ *L.G. Smith Blvd. 94, Oranjestad.*

ACTIVITIES

BIKING

Pedal pushing is a great way to get around the island; the climate is perfect, and the trade winds help to keep you cool.

Melchor Cycle Rental. ATVs and bikes. ⊠ *Bubali 106B, Noord* ☎ *297/ 587–1787.*

Rancho Notorious. Exciting mountain-biking tours are available here. The 2½-hour tour to the Alto Vista Chapel and the California Lighthouse are $50 ($75 with bike rental). ⊠ *Boroncana, Noord* ☎ *297/586–0508* ⊕ *www.ranchonotorious.com.*

DIVING AND SNORKELING

With visibility of up to 90 feet, the waters around Aruba are excellent for snorkeling and diving. Advanced and novice divers alike will find plenty to occupy their time, as many of the most popular sites—including some interesting shipwrecks—are found in shallow waters ranging from 30 to 60 feet.

★ **De Palm Watersports.** This is one of the best choices for your undersea experience; the options go beyond basic diving. You can don a helmet and walk along the ocean floor near De Palm Island, home of huge blue parrot fish. You can even do Snuba—which is like scuba diving but without the heavy air tanks—a four-hour snuba adventure costs $133. ⊠ *L.G. Smith Blvd. 142, Oranjestad* ☎ *297/582–4400, 800/766–6016* ⊕ *www.depalm.com.*

GOLF

★ **Tierra del Sol.** This stunning course is on the northwest coast near the California Lighthouse. Designed by Robert Trent Jones Jr., this 18-hole championship course combines Aruba's native beauty—cacti and rock formations—with the lush greens of the world's best courses. The green fees vary depending on the time of day (from December to March it is $159 in the morning, $129 for early afternoon, and $100 from 3 pm). The fee includes a golf cart equipped with a communications system that allows you to order drinks for your return to the clubhouse. Half-day golf clinics, a bargain at $45, are available Monday, Tuesday, and Thursday. The pro shop is one of the Caribbean's most elegant, with an extremely attentive staff. ⊠ *Malmokweg* ☎ *297/586–0978.*

KAYAKING

Kayaking is a popular sport on Aruba, especially along the south coast, where the waters are calm. It's a great way to explore the coastline.

BEACHES

The beaches on Aruba are beautiful, clean, and easily reached from the cruise-ship terminal in Oranjestad.

Fodor's Choice   **Eagle Beach.** On the southwestern coast, across the highway from what ★   is quickly becoming known as Time-Share Lane, is one of the Caribbean's—if not the world's—best beaches. With all the resorts here, this mile-plus-long beach is always hopping. The white sand is literally dazzling, and sunglasses are essential. Many of the hotels have facilities on or near the beach, and refreshments are never far away. **Amenities:** food and drink; toilets. **Best for:** swimming; walking; sunset. ⊠ *J.E. Irausquin Blvd., north of Manchebo Beach.*

Manchebo Beach (*Punta Brabo*). Impressively wide, the white sand shoreline in front of the Manchebo Beach Resort is where officials turn a blind eye to the occasional topless sunbather. This beach merges with Druif Beach, and most locals use the name Manchebo to refer to both. **Amenities:** food and drink; toilets. **Best for:** swimming. ⊠ *J.E. Irausquin Blvd., at Manchebo Beach Resort.*

Palm Beach. This stretch runs from the Westin Aruba Resort, Spa & Casino to the Marriott's Aruba Ocean Club. It's the center of Aruban tourism, offering good swimming, sailing, and other water sports. In some spots you might find a variety of shells that are great to collect, but not as much fun to step on barefoot—bring sandals. **Amenities:** food and drink; toilets; water sports. **Best for:** swimming; walking. ⊠ *J.E. Irausquin Blvd., between Westin Aruba Resort, Spa & Casino and Marriott's Aruba Ocean Club.*

WHERE TO EAT

$$$
CUBAN
★
✕**Cuba's Cookin'.** Nightly entertainment, great authentic Cuban food, and a lively crowd are the draws here. The empanadas are excellent, as is the chicken stuffed with plantains. Don't leave without trying the roast pork, which is pretty close to perfection. The signature dish is the *ropa vieja*, a sautéed flank steak served with a rich sauce (the name literally translates as "old clothes"). Service can be a bit spotty at times, depending on how busy it gets. There's often live music. $ *Average main: $24* ✉ *Renaissance Marketplace, L.G. Smith Blvd. 82, Oranjestad* ☎ *297/588–0627* ⊕ *www.cubascookin.com.*

$$
CARIBBEAN
✕**Gostoso.** Locals adore the magical mixture of Portuguese, Aruban, and international dishes on offer at this consistently excellent establishment. The decor walks a fine line between kitschy and cozy, but the atmosphere is relaxed and informal and outdoor seating is available. The *bacalhau* vinaigrette (dressed salted cod) is a delightful Portuguese appetizer and pairs nicely with most of the Aruban dishes on the menu. Meat lovers are sure to enjoy the Venezuelan mixed grill, which includes a 14-ounce steak and chorizo accompanied by local sides like fried plantain. $ *Average main: $24* ✉ *Caya Ing Roland H. Lacle 12, Oranjestad* ☎ *297/588–0053* ⊕ *www.gostosoaruba.com* ⟨ *Reservations essential* ⊙ *Closed Mon.*

BARBADOS (BRIDGETOWN)

Jane E. Zarem

Barbadians (Bajans) are a warm, friendly, and hospitable people, who are genuinely proud of their country and culture. Although tourism is the island's number one industry, the island has a sophisticated business community and stable government, so life here doesn't skip a beat after passengers return to the ship. Barbados is the most "British" island in the Caribbean. Afternoon tea is a ritual, and cricket is the national sport. The atmosphere, though, is hardly stuffy. This is still the Caribbean, after all. Beaches along the island's south and west coasts are picture-perfect, and all are available to cruise passengers. On the rugged east coast, the Atlantic Ocean attracts world-class surfers. The northeast is dominated by rolling hills and valleys, while the interior of the island is covered by acres of sugarcane and dotted with small villages. Historic plantations, a stalactite-studded cave, a wildlife preserve, rum distilleries, and tropical gardens are among the island's attractions. Bridgetown is the capital city, and its downtown shops and historic sites are a short walk or taxi ride from the pier.

ESSENTIALS

CURRENCY
The Barbados dollar (BDS$) is pegged to the U.S. dollar at the rate of BDS$1.99 to US$1. U.S. dollars (but not coins) are accepted universally across the island, but change is given in Barbados currency.

INTERNET
You'll find Internet cafés in and around Bridgetown and at St. Lawrence Gap on the south coast. Rates range from $2 for 15 minutes to $8 or $9 per hour.

TELEPHONE
Your cell phone should work in Barbados, although roaming charges can be costly. Alternatively, you can purchase phone cards at the

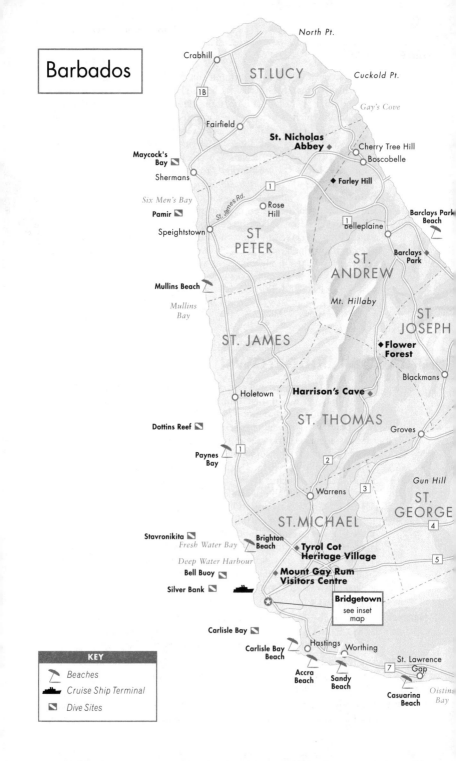

Barbados

North Pt.

Crabhill

ST. LUCY

Cuckold Pt.

1B

Gay's Cove

Fairfield

St. Nicholas Abbey ◆

Cherry Tree Hill

Boscobelle

Maycock's Bay 🤿

◆ Farley Hill

Shermans

1

Six Men's Bay

St. James Rd.

Rose Hill

Belleplaine

1

Barclays Park Beach 🏖

Pamir 🤿

Speightstown

ST PETER

ST. ANDREW

Barclays Park ◆

Mullins Beach 🏖

Mt. Hillaby

ST. JOSEPH

Mullins Bay

◆ Flower Forest

ST. JAMES

Blackmans

Holetown

Harrison's Cave ◆

Dottins Reef 🤿

ST. THOMAS

Groves

Paynes Bay 🏖

1

2

Gun Hill

Warrens

3

ST. GEORGE

ST. MICHAEL

Stavronikita 🤿

4

Fresh Water Bay

Brighton Beach ◆

Tyrol Cot Heritage Village ◆

Deep Water Harbour

Bell Buoy 🤿

Mount Gay Rum Visitors Centre ◆

5

Silver Bank 🤿

Bridgetown see inset map

Carlisle Bay 🤿

Carlisle Bay Beach 🏖

Hastings

Worthing

St. Lawrence Gap

Accra Beach 🏖

Sandy Beach 🏖

7

Oistins Bay

Casuarina Beach 🏖

KEY

🏖 Beaches

🚢 Cruise Ship Terminal

🤿 Dive Sites

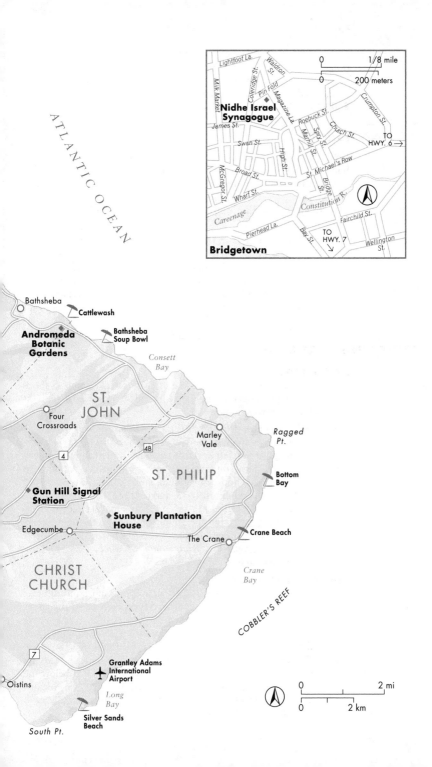

Bridgetown

Nidhe Israel Synagogue

ATLANTIC OCEAN

Lightfoot La.
Milk Market
Coleridge St.
Waldron St.
Pin Fold
Magazine La.
James St.
Roebuck St.
Crumpton St.
Swan St.
Marhill St.
Spry St.
Church St.
TO HWY. 6 →
High St.
Broad St.
McGregor St.
St. Michael's Row
Wharf St.
Bridge St.
Constitution R.
Fairchild St.
Careenage
Pierhead La.
Bay St.
TO HWY. 7
Wellington St.

0   1/8 mile
0   200 meters

Bathsheba
Cattlewash
Andromeda Botanic Gardens
Bathsheba Soup Bowl
Consett Bay
Four Crossroads
ST. JOHN
Marley Vale
Ragged Pt.
4
4B
ST. PHILIP
Bottom Bay
Gun Hill Signal Station
Sunbury Plantation House
Edgecumbe
Crane Beach
The Crane
Crane Bay
CHRIST CHURCH
COBBLER'S REEF
7
Grantley Adams International Airport
Oistins
Long Bay
Silver Sands Beach
South Pt.

0   2 mi
0   2 km

cruise-ship terminal. Direct-dialing to the United States, Canada, and other countries is efficient and reasonable. Some toll-free numbers cannot be accessed in Barbados. To charge your overseas call on a major credit card or U.S. calling card without incurring a surcharge, dial 800/225–5872 (800/CALL-USA) from any phone.

COMING ASHORE

Up to eight ships at a time can dock at Bridgetown's Deep Water Harbour, on the northwest side of Carlisle Bay near Bridgetown. The cruise-ship terminal has duty-free shops, handicraft vendors, a post office, a telephone station, a tourist information desk, and a taxi stand. To get downtown, follow the shoreline to the Careenage. It's a 15-minute walk or a $4 taxi ride.

Taxis await ships at the pier. Drivers accept U.S. dollars and appreciate a 10% tip. Taxis are unmetered and operate at an hourly rate of $35 to $40 per carload (up to three passengers). Most drivers will cheerfully narrate an island tour. You can rent a car with a valid driver's license, but rates are steep—$60 to $85 per day during the high season—and some agencies require a two-day rental at that time. Note, too, that driving is on the left, British-style.

EXPLORING BARBADOS

BRIDGETOWN

This bustling capital city is a major duty-free port with a compact shopping area. The principal thoroughfare is Broad Street, which leads west from National Heroes Square.

Nidhe Israel Synagogue. Providing for the spiritual needs of one of the oldest Jewish congregations in the Western Hemisphere, this synagogue was formed by Jews who left Brazil in the 1620s and introduced sugarcane to Barbados. The adjoining cemetery has tombstones dating from the 1630s. The original house of worship, built in 1654, was destroyed in an 1831 hurricane, rebuilt in 1833, and restored with the assistance of the Barbados National Trust in 1987. Friday-night services are held during the winter months, but the building is open to the public year-round. Shorts are not acceptable during services but may be worn at other times. ⊠ *Synagogue La., Bridgetown, St. Michael* ☎ *246/436–6869* 🖼 *Donation requested* ☽ *Weekdays 9–4.*

CENTRAL AND WEST

☾ **Gun Hill Signal Station.** The 360-degree view from Gun Hill, 700 feet **Fodor's Choice** above sea level, gave this location strategic importance to the 18th- ★ century British army. Using lanterns and semaphore, soldiers based here could communicate with their counterparts at the Garrison on the south coast and at Grenade Hill in the north. Time moved slowly in 1868, and Captain Henry Wilkinson whiled away his off-duty hours by carving a huge lion from a single rock—which is on the hillside just below the tower. Come for a short history lesson but mainly for the view; it's so gorgeous, military invalids were once sent here to convalesce. ⊠ *Gun Hill, St. George* ☎ *246/429–1358* 🖼 *$5* ☽ *Weekdays 9–5.*

☺ **Harrison's Cave.** This limestone cav-
Fodor's Choice ern, complete with stalactites, sta-
★ lagmites, subterranean streams, and a 40-foot waterfall, is a rare find in the Caribbean—and one of Barbados's most popular attractions. Tours include a nine-minute video presentation and a 40-minute underground journey through the cavern via electric tram. The visitor center has interactive displays, life-size models and sculptures, a souvenir shop, restaurant facilities, and elevator access to the tram for people with disabilities. Tours fill up fast, so make a reservation. ⊠ *Hwy. 2, Welchman Hall, St. Thomas* ☎ *246/417–3700* ⊕ *www. harrisonscave.com* 🎫 *$30* ⊙ *Daily 8:30–4:30 (last tour 3:45).*

★ **Mount Gay Rum Visitors Centre.** On this popular tour, you learn the colorful story behind the world's oldest rum—made in Barbados since 1703. Although the distillery is in the far north, in St. Lucy Parish, tour guides explain the rum-making procedure. Equipment, both historic and modern, is on display, and rows and rows of barrels are stored in this location. The 45-minute tour runs hourly (last tour begins at 3:30 weekdays; 2:30 on Saturday) and concludes with a tasting and an opportunity to buy bottles of rum and gift items—and even have lunch or cocktails, depending on the time of day. ⊠ *Spring Garden Hwy., Brandons, St. Michael* ☎ *246/425–8757* ⊕ *www.mountgayrum.com* 🎫 *$7, $50 with lunch; $35 with cocktails* ⊙ *Weekdays 9–5.*

NORTH AND EAST

Fodor's Choice **Andromeda Botanic Gardens.** More than 600 beautiful and unusual plant
★ specimens from around the world are cultivated in 6 acres of gardens nestled among streams, ponds, and rocky outcroppings overlooking the sea above the Bathsheba coastline. The gardens were created in 1954 with flowering plants collected by the late horticulturist Iris Bannochie. They're now administered by the Barbados National Trust. The Hibiscus Café serves snacks and drinks. ⊠ *Bathsheba, St. Joseph* ☎ *246/433–9384* 🎫 *$10* ⊙ *Daily 9–5.*

Fodor's Choice **St. Nicholas Abbey.** The island's oldest great house (circa 1650) was
★ named after the original British owner's hometown, St. Nicholas Parish near Bristol, and Bath Abbey nearby. Its stone-and-wood architecture makes it one of only three original Jacobean-style houses still standing in the Western Hemisphere. It has Dutch gables, finials of coral stone, and beautiful grounds that include an old sugar mill. The first floor, fully furnished with period furniture and portraits of family members, is open to the public. Fascinating home movies, shot by a previous owner's father, record Bajan life in the 1930s. Behind the greathouse is

4

a rum distillery with a 19th-century steam press. Visitors can purchase artisanal plantation rum produced nearby (the Abbey's production will become fully aged about 2018) and enjoy light refreshments at the terrace café. ⊠ *Cherry Tree Hill, St. Peter* ☎ *246/422–5357* ⊕ *www.stnicholasabbey.com* ⊠ *$17.50* ⊗ *Sun.–Fri. 10–3:30.*

> ### TIME TIP
>
> If you don't want to rely on shipboard wake-up calls, be sure to bring your own travel alarm clock; most staterooms do not have clocks.

SOUTH

Fodor's Choice ★ **Sunbury Plantation House and Museum.** Lovingly rebuilt after a 1995 fire destroyed everything but the thick flint-and-stone walls, Sunbury offers an elegant glimpse of the 18th and 19th centuries on a Barbadian sugar estate. Period furniture, old prints, and a collection of horse-drawn carriages lend an air of authenticity. A buffet luncheon is served daily in the courtyard for $31 per person. A five-course candlelight dinner is served ($100 per person, reservations required) two nights a week at the 200-year-old mahogany dining table in the Sunbury dining room. ⊠ *Off Hwy. 5, Six Cross Roads, St. Philip* ☎ *246/423–6270* ⊕ *www.barbadosgreathouse.com* ⊠ *$7.50* ⊗ *Daily 9–4:30.*

Tyrol Cot Heritage Village. This coral-stone cottage just south of Bridgetown was constructed in 1854 and is preserved as an example of period architecture. In 1929, it became the home of Sir Grantley Adams, the first premier of Barbados and the namesake of its international airport. Part of the Barbados National Trust, the cottage is filled with antiques and memorabilia that belonged to the late Sir Grantley and Lady Adams. It's also the centerpiece of an outdoor "living museum," where artisans and craftsmen have their workshops in a cluster of traditional chattel houses. Workshops are open, crafts are for sale, and refreshments are available at the "rum shop" primarily during the winter season and when cruise ships are in port. ⊠ *Rte. 2, Codrington Hill, St. Michael* ☎ *246/424–2074* ⊠ *$5.75* ⊗ *Weekdays 9–5.*

SHOPPING

Duty-free shopping is found in Bridgetown's Broad Street stores and their branches in Holetown and at the cruise-ship terminal. Stores are generally open weekdays 8:30–4:30, Saturday 8:30–1. ■ **TIP→ To purchase items duty-free, you must show your passport and cabin key card.**

Best of Barbados. Best of Barbados was the brainchild of architect Jimmy Walker as a place to showcase the works of his artist wife. Now with five locations, the shops offer products that range from Jill Walker's frameable prints, housewares, and textiles to arts and crafts in both "native" style and modern designs. Everything is made or designed on Barbados. ⊠ *Quayside Centre, Main Rd., Rockley, Christ Church* ☎ *246/435–6820* ⊕ *www.best-of-barbados.com.*

Fodor's Choice ★ **Earthworks Pottery.** Earthworks is a family-owned and -operated pottery workshop, where you can purchase anything from a dish or knickknack to a complete dinner service or one-of-a-kind art piece. You can find the characteristically blue or green pottery—and, more recently, peach and brown hues—decorating hotel rooms and for sale in gift shops throughout the island; but the biggest selection (including some "seconds") is at Earthworks, where you also can watch the potters at work. ✉ *Edgehill Heights, St. Thomas* ☎ *246/425–0223* ⊕ *www.earthworkspottery.com* ⊗ *Closed Sun.*

★ **Pelican Craft Centre.** Pelican is made up of a cluster of workshops halfway between the cruise-ship terminal and downtown Bridgetown where craftspeople create and sell locally made leather goods, batik, basketry, carvings, jewelry, glass art, paintings, pottery, and other items. It's open weekdays 9 to 5 and Saturday 9 to 2; things here are most active when cruise ships are in port. ✉ *Princess Alice Hwy., Bridgetown, St. Michael* ☎ *246/427–5350.*

ACTIVITIES

FISHING

Billfisher II. *Billfisher II*, a 40-foot Pacemaker, accommodates up to six passengers with three fishing chairs and five rods. Captain Winston ("The Colonel") White has been fishing these waters since 1975. His full-day charters include a full lunch and guaranteed fish (or a 25% refund); all trips include drinks and transportation to and from the boat. ✉ *Bridge House Wharf, The Careenage, Bridgetown, St. Michael* ☎ *246/431–0741.*

Blue Jay & Blue Marlin. *Blue Jay* is a spacious, fully equipped, 45-foot Sport Fisherman; *Blue Marlin* is a 36-foot Sport Fisherman. Each has a crew that knows the water's denizens—blue marlin, sailfish, barracuda, and kingfish. Most fishing is done by trolling. Drinks, snacks, bait, tackle, and transfers are provided. ✉ *Fishing Charters Barbados, Inc., 50 Ridge Ave., Durants, Christ Church* ☎ *246/234–1688* ⊕ *www.bluemarlinbarbados.com.*

GOLF

Barbados Golf Club. Barbados Golf Club, the first public golf course on Barbados, is an 18-hole championship course (6,805 yards, par 72) redesigned in 2000 by golf course architect Ron Kirby. Green fees with a cart are $125 for 18 holes; $80 for 9 holes. Unlimited three-day and seven-day golf passes are available. Several hotels offer preferential tee-time reservations and reduced rates. Club and shoe rentals are available. ✉ *Hwy. 7, Durants, Christ Church* ☎ *246/428–8463* ⊕ *www.barbadosgolfclub.com.*

Fodor's Choice ★ **Country Club at Sandy Lane.** At the prestigious Country Club at Sandy Lane, golfers can play on the Old Nine or on either of two 18-hole championship courses: the Tom Fazio–designed Country Club Course or the spectacular Green Monkey Course, reserved for hotel guests and club members only. Golfers have complimentary use of the club's driving range. The Country Club Restaurant and Bar, which overlooks the 18th hole, is open to the public. Green fees in high season are $155 for 9 holes ($135 for hotel guests) or $240 for 18 holes ($205 for hotel guests). Golf carts, caddies, or trolleys are available for hire, as are clubs and shoes. Carts are equipped with GPS, which alerts you to upcoming traps and hazards, provides tips on how to play the hole, and allows you to order refreshments! ⊠ *Sandy Lane, Hwy. 1, Paynes Bay, St. James* ☎ *246/444–2500* ⊕ *www.sandylane.com/golf.*

BEACHES

All beaches on Barbados are open to cruise-ship passengers. The west coast has the stunning coves and white-sand beaches dear to the hearts of postcard publishers, plus calm, clear water for snorkeling and swimming. Waterskiing and parasailing are also available on most beaches along the south and west coasts. Windsurfing is best on the south coast.

Accra Beach. This popular beach, also known as Rockley Beach, is next to the Accra Beach Hotel. You'll find gentle surf and a lifeguard, plenty of nearby restaurants for refreshments, a children's playground, and beach stalls for renting chairs and equipment for snorkeling and other water sports. Parking is available at an on-site lot. ⊠ *Hwy. 7, Rockley, Christ Church.*

Brighton Beach. Calm as a lake, this is where you can find locals taking a quick dip on hot days. Just north of Bridgetown, Brighton Beach is also home to the Cockspur Beach Club. ⊠ *Spring Garden Hwy., Brighton, St. Michael.*

Fodor's Choice ★ **Mullins Beach.** This lovely beach just south of Speightstown is a perfect place to spend the day. The water is safe for swimming and snorkeling, there's easy parking on the main road, and Mullins Restaurant serves snacks, meals, and drinks—and rents chairs and umbrellas. ⊠ *Hwy. 1, Mullins Bay, St. Peter.*

Paynes Bay Beach. The stretch of beach just south of Sandy Lane is lined with luxury hotels. It's a very pretty area, with plenty of beach to go around and good snorkeling. Public access is available at several locations along Highway 1, though parking is limited. ⊠ *Hwy. 1, Paynes Bay, St. James.*

Pebbles Beach. On the southern side of Carlisle Bay, adjacent to the Hilton Barbados just south of Bridgetown, this broad half circle of white sand is one of the island's best beaches—but it can become crowded on weekends and holidays. Park at Harbour Lights or at the Boatyard Bar and Bayshore Complex, both on Bay Street, where you can also rent umbrellas and beach chairs and buy refreshments. ⊠ *Off Bay St., south of Bridgetown, Needham's Point, St. Michael.*

WHERE TO EAT

$$$
CARIBBEAN
Fodor's Choice ★
✕ The Atlantis. For decades, an alfresco lunch on the Atlantis deck overlooking the ocean has been a favorite of visitors touring the east coast and Bajans alike. Totally renovated and reopened in 2009 by the owners of Little Good Harbour and the Fishpot on the west coast, the revived restaurant effectively combines the atmosphere and good food that have always been the draw with an up-to-date, rather elegant dining room and a top-notch menu that focuses on local produce, seafood, and meats. The Bajan buffet lunch on Wednesday and Sunday

is particularly popular; it's also well used for special occasions for local folks. At dinner, entreés include fresh fish, lobster (sometimes), roasted black-belly lamb or free-range chicken, fricassee of rabbit, and more. Or choose more traditional pepper pot, saltfish, or chicken stew with peas and rice, cou-cou, yam pie, or breadfruit mash, all of which are available at the Bajan buffet. Rotis and cutters (sandwiches) are always available, along with pasta specials, salads, soups, and fried flying fish. $ *Average main: $30* ⊠ *Tent Bay, St. Joseph* ☎ *246/433–9445* ⊕ *www.atlantishotelbarbados.com* ⌖ *Reservations essential* ⊘ *No dinner Sun.*

$$$ ✕ **Waterfront Café.** This friendly bistro alongside the Careenage is the
CARIBBEAN perfect place to enjoy a drink, snack, or meal—and to people-watch. Locals and tourists alike gather for all-day alfresco dining on sandwiches, salads, fish, pasta, pepper-pot stew, and tasty Bajan snacks such as buljol, fish cakes, or plantation pork (plantains stuffed with spicy minced pork). The panfried flying-fish sandwich is especially popular. In the evening you can gaze through the arched windows while savoring nouvelle Caribbean cuisine, enjoying cool trade winds, and listening to live jazz. There's a special Caribbean buffet and steel-pan music on Tuesday night from 7 to 9. $ *Average main: $25* ⊠ *The Careenage, Bridgetown, St. Michael* ☎ *246/427–0093* ⊕ *www.waterfrontcafe.com.* *bb* ⊘ *Closed Sun.*

BELIZE CITY, BELIZE

Lan Sluder   Belize probably has the greatest variety of flora and fauna of any country of its size in the world. Here you'll often find more iguanas or howler monkeys than humans. A few miles off the mainland is the Belize Barrier Reef, a great wall of coral stretching the entire 200-mile (333-km) length of the coast. Over 200 cayes (pronounced keys) dot the reef like punctuation marks, and three coral atolls lie farther out to sea. All are superb for diving and snorkeling. Many, like Ambergris Caye (pronounced *Am*-bur-griss Key) and Caye Caulker, are cheery resort islands with ample bars and restaurants, easily reachable on day trips from Belize City. The main choice you'll have to make is whether to stay in Belize City for a little stroll and shopping, and perhaps a dram at one of the Fort George hotels or restaurants, or alternatively to head out by boat, rental car, taxi, or tour on a more active adventure.

ESSENTIALS

CURRENCY   Since U.S. currency is universally accepted, there's no need to acquire the Belize dollar (BZ$2 to US$1).

FLIGHTS   Especially if you are going to Ambergris Caye, you may prefer to fly, or you can water-taxi over and fly back to maximize your time. There are hourly flights on two airlines. The flight to Caulker takes about 10 minutes and that to San Pedro about 25 minutes. The cost is about BZ$250 round-trip to either island. Be sure you fly out of Belize City's Municipal, not out of the international airport north of the city.

Maya Island Airways ☎ *223/1140, 223/0734* ⊕ *www.mayaregional.com.*

Tropic Air ☎ 226/2012, 800/422–3435 in U.S. or Canada ⊕ www.
tropicair.com.

INTERNET **Click & Sip Internet Café** ⊠ Fort St., in Tourism Village ☎ 223/1305.

TELEPHONE Calling locally or internationally is easy, but rates are high; around
BZ$1.50 a minute for calls to the United States. To call the United
States, dial 001 or 10–10–199 plus the area code and number. Pay
phones, which are located in the Fort Street Tourism Village where you
are tendered, and elsewhere downtown, accept only prepaid Belize Telecommunications Ltd. (BTL) phone cards, available in shops in denominations from $5 to $50. Special "USA Connect" prepaid cards, for
sale at some stores in Belize City, in denominations of $5 to $20, claim
discounts of as much as 57% for calls to the United States only. Your
U.S.-based GSM phone will probably work on Belize's GSM 1900 system, but you will pay a high surcharge to use it abroad. Foreign calling cards are generally blocked in Belize. Call 113 for local directory
assistance, and 115 for an operator.

Visitor Information Belize Tourism Board ⊠ 64 Regent St. ☎ 227/2420
⊕ www.travelbelize.org.

COMING ASHORE

Because Belize City's harbor is shallow, passengers are tendered in. If you're going the independent route, try to get in line early for the tenders, as it sometimes takes 90 minutes or more for all the passengers to be brought ashore. You arrive at the Fort Street Tourism Village complex. It has a collection of gift shops, restaurants, and tour operators nicely situated along the harbor. Bathrooms are spick-and-span, too. At this writing, construction is sputtering on a much-delayed $50-million cruise terminal south of the city center; when it will finally open is anyone's guess.

Taxis, tour guides, and car-rental desks are readily available. Cabs cost BZ$7–BZ$10 for one person between any two points in the city, plus BZ$1 for each additional person. Taxi fares at night are slightly higher. Outside the city, and from downtown to the suburbs, you're charged by the distance you travel. Hourly rates are negotiable, but expect to pay around $30, or $150 for the day. Drivers are required to display a Taxi Federation rate card. There's no need to tip cab drivers. You can also rent a car at the Tourism Village, but rates can be high (at least $75 per day), and gas is also expensive. Green directional signs point you to nearby destinations such as the Belize Zoo. The Wet Lizard, next to the Tourism Village, also organizes tours for cruise-ship passengers.

EXPLORING BELIZE

Many Belize hands will tell you that the best way to see Belize City is through a rearview window. But, with an open mind to its peculiarities, and with a little caution (the city has a crime problem, but the tourist police keep a close watch on cruise-ship passengers), you may decide Belize City has a raffish, atmospheric charm rarely found in other Caribbean ports of call. You might even see the ghost of Graham Greene, who visited Belize in 1978 as a guest of General Torrijos.

BELIZE CITY

A 5- to 10-minute stroll from the colorful Fort Street Tourism Village brings you into the other worlds of Belize City. On the north side of Haulover Creek is the colonial-style Fort George, where large old homes, stately but sometimes down at the heels, take the breezes off the sea and share their space with hotels and restaurants. On the south side is bustling Albert Street, the main commercial thoroughfare. But don't stroll too far since parts of Belize City are unsafe. During the daylight hours, as long as you stay within the main commercial district and the Fort George area—and ignore the street hustlers—you should have no problem.

★ **Fort George Lighthouse and Bliss Memorial.** Towering over the entrance to Belize Harbor, the lighthouse stands guard on the tip of Fort George Point. It was designed and funded by the country's greatest benefactor, Baron Bliss. The English nobleman never actually set foot on the Belizean mainland, but in his will he bequeathed most of his fortune to the people of Belize, and the date of his death, March 9, is celebrated as a national holiday. He is buried here, in a small, low mausoleum perched on the seawall, up a short run of limestone stairs. The lighthouse is for photo ops only—you can't enter it. ⊠ *Marine Parade, near Radisson Fort George Hotel, Fort George.*

★ **House of Culture.** Formerly called Government House, the city's finest colonial structure is said to have a design inspired by the illustrious British architect Sir Christopher Wren. Built in 1814, it was once the residence of the governor-general, the queen's representative in Belize. Following Hurricane Hattie in 1961, the governor and the rest of the government moved to Belmopan, and the house became a venue for social functions and a guesthouse for visiting VIPs. (Queen Elizabeth stayed here in 1985, Prince Philip in 1988.) Now it's open to the public. You can peruse its archival records, art, silver, glassware, and furniture collections, or mingle with the tropical birds that frequent the gardens. Although there's a gated parking area, this is not available for visitors—you'll need to park on Regent Street. ⊠ *Regent St. at Southern Fore-shore, opposite St. John's Cathedral, Commercial District* ☎ *227/3050* 🖃 *BZ$10* ☉ *Weekdays 9–4.*

★ **Museum of Belize.** This small but interesting museum was a Belize City jail from the 1850s to 1993. Displays on Belize history and culture include ancient Mayan artifacts, eclectic memorabilia, colorful Belize postage stamps, and an actual jail cell. Exhibitions change frequently. ⊠ *Ga-bourel La., Belize Central Bank Compound, Fort George* ☎ *223/4524* ⊕ *www.nichbelize.org* 🖃 *BZ$20* ☉ *Mon.–Thurs. 8–5; Fri. 8–4:30.*

St. John's Cathedral. On Albert Street's south end is the oldest Anglican church in Central America and the only one outside England where kings were crowned. From 1815 to 1845, four kings of the Mosquito Coast (a British protectorate along the coast of Honduras and Nicaragua) were crowned here. The cathedral, built of brick brought to British Honduras as ballast on English ships, is thought to be the oldest building in Belize, other than Mayan structures. Its foundation stone was laid in 1812. Inside, it has whitewashed walls and mahogany pews. The roof is constructed of local sapodilla wood, with mahogany beams. ⊠ *Albert St. at Regent St., Opposite the House of Culture, Commercial District* ☎ *227/3029* ☉ *Daily 9–6, with Sunday services at 7 am, 9:30 am, and 6 pm.*

INLAND FROM BELIZE CITY

☾
⚒
★
Altun Ha. If you've never experienced an ancient Mayan city, make a trip to Altun Ha, which is a modern translation in Mayan of the name "Rockstone Pond," a nearby village. It's not Belize's most dramatic site—Caracol and Lamanai vie for that award—but it's one of the most accessible and most thoroughly excavated. The first inhabitants settled before 300 BC, and their descendants finally abandoned the site after AD 1000. At its height during the Classic period the city was home to 10,000 people. Tours from Belize City, Orange Walk, and Crooked Tree also are options. Altun Ha is a regular stop on cruise ship excursions. Several tour operators in San Pedro and Caye Caulker also offer day trips to Altun Ha, often combined with lunch at the nearby Maruba Resort Jungle Spa. Most of these tours are by boat, landing at Bomba Village. From here, a van makes the short ride to Altun Ha. ⊹ *From*

Belize City, take Northern Hwy. north to Mile 18.9. Turn right (east) on Old Northern Hwy., which is only partly paved, and go 10½ miles (17 km) to signed entrance road to Altun Ha on left. Follow this paved road 2 miles (3 km) to visitor center. ☎ *822/2106 Belize Institute of Archeology* 🎫 *BZ$20* 🕐 *Daily 9–5.*

BELIZE CITY BEST BETS

■ **Belize Zoo.** Though small, this collection of native Belize wildlife is excellent.

■ **Cave Tubing.** If you are not claustrophobic, this is an unforgettable excursion.

■ **Diving.** Belize is becoming known as one of the world's best dive destinations. For the certified, this is a must.

■ **Snorkeling in Hol Chan.** The water is teeming with fish, and you don't need to be certified to enjoy the underwater world here.

🔄 Fodor's Choice ★ **Belize Zoo.** One of the smallest, but arguably one of the best, zoos in the Americas, the Belize Zoo packs a lot into 29 acres. Containing more than 125 native species, the zoo has self-guided tours through several Belizean ecosystems—rain forest, lagoons, and riverine forest. Along with the spotted jaguar (the zoo's rare black jaguar died of natural causes in late 2008), you'll see the country's four other wild cats: the puma, margay, ocelot, and jaguarundi. Perhaps the zoo's most famous resident is April, a Baird's tapir that is more than a quarter-century old. The zoo owes its existence to the dedication and drive of one gutsy woman, Sharon Matola. An American who came to Belize as part of a film crew, Matola stayed on to care for some of the semi-tame animals used in the production. She opened the zoo in 1983, and in 1991 it moved to its present location. ✉ *Mile 29, Western Hwy.* ☎ *220/8004* ⊕ *www.belizezoo.org* 🎫 *BZ$20 adults, BZ$10 children* 🕐 *Daily 8–5.*

🔄 **Community Baboon Sanctuary.** One of Belize's most fascinating wildlife conservation projects is the Community Baboon Sanctuary, which is actually a haven for black howler monkeys. Spanning a 20-mile (32-km) stretch of the Belize River, the reserve was established in 1985 by a group of local farmers. The howler monkey—an agile bundle of black fur with a disturbing roar—was then zealously hunted throughout Central America and was facing extinction. Today the sanctuary is home to nearly 1,000 black howler monkeys, as well as numerous species of birds and mammals. Exploring the Community Baboon Sanctuary is easy, thanks to about 3 miles (5 km) of trails that start near a small museum and visitor center. The admission fee includes a 45-minute guided nature tour during which you definitely will see howlers. ✉ *Community Baboon Sanctuary, 31 miles (50 km) northwest of Belize City, Bermudian Village* ☎ *220/2181* ⊕ *www.howlermonkeys.org* 🎫 *BZ$14 (includes monkey spotting tour)* 🕐 *Daily 8–5.*

★ **Crooked Tree Wildlife Sanctuary.** Crooked Tree Wildlife Sanctuary is one of Belize's top birding spots. The 16,400-acre sanctuary includes more than 3,000 acres of lagoons, swamp, and marsh, surrounding what is essentially an inland island. Traveling by canoe, you're likely to see iguanas, crocodiles, coatis, and turtles. The sanctuary's most prestigious visitors, however, are the jabiru storks, which usually visit between November and May. With a wingspan up to 12 feet, the jabiru is the largest flying bird in the Americas. For birders the best time to come is in the dry season, roughly from February to late May, when lowered water levels cause birds to group together to find water and food, making them easy to spot. Birding is good year-round, however, and the area is more scenic when the lagoons are full. ⊠ *Turn west off Northern Hwy. at Mile 30.8, then drive 2 miles (3 km)* ☎ *223/4987 for Belize Audubon Society* ⊕ *www.belizeaudubon.org/ parks/ctws.htm* ⊠ *BZ$8.*

Hummingbird Highway. Hands down, Hummingbird Highway is the most scenic roadway in Belize. The Hummingbird, a paved two-lane road, runs 54½ miles (91 km) from the junction of the Western Highway at Belmopan to Dangriga. Technically, only the first 32 miles (53 km) is the Hummingbird—the rest is the Stann Creek District Highway, but most people ignore that distinction. As measured from Belmopan at the junction of the Western Highway—the road has a few mileposts running from Dangriga north, but we'll ignore them—the Hummingbird first winds through limestone hill country, passing St. Herman's Cave (Mile 12.2) and the inland Blue Hole (13.1). It then starts rising steeply, with the Maya Mountains on the west or right side, past Five Blue Lake (23). The views, of green mountains studded with cohune palms and tropical hardwoods, are incredible. At the Hummingbird Gap (Mile 26, elevation near 1,000 feet, with mountains nearby over 3,000 feet), you're at the crest of the highway and now begin to drop down toward the Caribbean Sea. At Middlesex village (32), technically the road becomes the Stann Creek District Highway. Now you're in citrus country, with groves of grapefruit and Valencia oranges. At Mile 48.7 you pass the turn-off to the Southern Highway and at Mile 54.5 you enter Dangriga, with the sea just ahead. ⊠ *Belmopan to Dangriga, Hummingbird Hwy., Belmopan.*

☙ **St. Herman's Blue Hole National Park.** Less than a half hour south of Belmopan, the 575-acre St. Herman's Blue Hole National Park has a natural turquoise pool surrounded by mosses and lush vegetation, wonderful for a cool dip. The "inland Blue Hole" is actually part of an underground river system. On the other side of the hill is St. Herman's Cave, once inhabited by the Maya. To explore St. Herman's cave beyond the first 300 yards or so, you must be accompanied by a guide (available at the park), and no more than five people can enter the cave at one time. With a guide, you also can explore part of another cave system here, the Crystal Cave (sometimes called the Crystalline Cave), which stretches for miles; the additional cost is BZ$20 per person for a two-hour guided tour. The main park visitor center is 12½ miles (20½ km) from Belmopan. St. Herman's Blue Hole National Park is managed by the Belize Audubon Society. ⊠ *Mile 42.5, Hummingbird Hwy., Belmopan* ☎ *223/5004 Belize Audubon Society* ⊠ *BZ$10* ☉ *Daily 8–4:30.*

THE CAYES

Ambergris Caye. Ambergris is the queen of the cayes. With a population of around 9,000, the island's only town, San Pedro, remains a small, friendly, and prosperous village. It has one of the highest literacy rates in the country and an admirable level of awareness about the fragility of the reef. The large number of substantial private houses being built on the edges of town is proof of how much tourism has enriched San Pedro. A water taxi from the Marine Terminal takes about 75 minutes and costs BZ$20 each way. You can also fly.

Fodor's Choice

★

Hol Chan Marine Reserve. The reef's focal point for diving and snorkeling near Ambergris Caye is the Hol Chan Marine Reserve (Maya for "little channel"), 4 miles (6 km) southeast of San Pedro at the southern tip of Ambergris. It's a 20-minute boat ride from San Pedro. Hol Chan is a break in the reef about 100 feet wide and 20 feet–35 feet deep, through which tremendous volumes of water pass with the tides. The 3-square-mile (8-square-km) park has a miniature Blue Hole, a 12-foot-deep cave whose entrance often attracts the fairy basslet, an iridescent purple-and-yellow fish frequently seen here. The reserve is also home to a large moray eel population.

Because fishing is off-limits here, divers can see abundant marine life, including spotted eagle rays. There are throngs of squirrelfish, butterfly fish, parrotfish, and queen angelfish, as well as Nassau groupers, barracuda, and large shoals of yellowtail snappers. Altogether, more than 160 species of fish have been identified in the marine reserve, along with 40 species of coral, and five kinds of sponges. Hawksbill, loggerhead, and green turtles have also been found here, along with spotted and common dolphins, several species of sharks, and West Indian manatees. ⊠ *Off southern tip of Ambergris Caye* ☎ *526/2247 Hol Chan office in San Pedro* ⊕ *www.holchanbelize.org.*

Caye Caulker. On Caye Caulker, where the one village is home to around 2,000 people, brightly painted houses on stilts line the coral-sand streets. Although the island is being developed more each year, flowers still outnumber cars 10 to 1 (golf carts, bicycles, and bare feet are the preferred means of transportation). The living is easy, as you might guess from all the *no shirt, no shoes, no problem* signs at the bars. This is the kind of place where most of the listings in the telephone directory give addresses like "near football field." A water taxi from the Marine Terminal costs about BZ$20 each way and takes about 45 minutes.

SHOPPING

Belize does not have the crafts tradition of its neighbors, Guatemala and Mexico, and imported goods are expensive due to high duties, but hand-carved items of ziricote or other local woods make good souvenirs. Near the Swing Bridge at Market Square is the **Commercial Center,** which has some food and craft vendors on the first floor and a restaurant and shops on the second. The **Fort Street Tourism Village,** where the ship tenders come in, is a collection of bright and clean gift shops selling T-shirts and Belizean and Guatemalan crafts. Beside the Tourism Village is an informal **Street Vendor Market,** with funkier goods and performances by a "Brukdown" band or a group of Garifuna drummers.

Belizean Handicraft Market Place. Belizean Handicraft Market Place (formerly National Handicraft Center) has Belizean souvenir items, including hand-carved figurines, handmade furniture, pottery, and woven baskets. The prices are about as good as you'll find anywhere in Belize, and the sales clerks are friendly. It faces the small Memorial Park, which commemorates the Battle of St. George's Caye and is just a short stroll from the harbor front, the Tourism Village, and many of the hotels in the Fort George area, including the Radisson, Chateau Caribbean, and The Great House. ⊠ *2 S. Park St., in Fort George area across from Memorial Park* ☎ *223/3627.*

ACTIVITIES

CANOPY TOURS

You may feel a little like Tarzan as you dangle 80 feet above the jungle floor, suspended by a harness, moving from one treetop platform to another.

Jaguar Paw/Chukka Caribbean. Jaguar Paw, formerly a jungle lodge and now a tour operation and part of the Chukka Caribbean tours empire, off Mile 37 of the Western Highway, has eight zip line platforms set 100 to 250 feet apart. At the last platform you have to rappel to the ground. There's a 240-pound weight limit. Zip line tours often are combined with cave tubing in the Caves Branch River. The cost is around BZ$120–BZ$180, depending on the tour and whether lunch and transportation are included. ☎ *223/4438* ⊕ *www.chukkacaribbean.com.*

CAVE TUBING

Very popular with cruise passengers are river-tubing trips that go through a cave, where you'll turn off your headlamp for a minute of absolute darkness, but these are not for the claustrophobic or those afraid of the dark.

Cave-Tubing in Belize ☎ *605/1575* ⊕ *www.cave-tubing.com.*

DIVING AND SNORKELING

Most companies on Ambergris Caye offer morning and afternoon single-tank dives; snorkel trips begin mid-morning or early afternoon. Dive and snorkeling trips that originate in Caye Caulker are a bit cheaper.

Amigos del Mar. Amigos del Mar, established in 1991, is perhaps the island's most consistently recommended dive operation. The PADI facility offers a range of local dives as well as trips to Turneffe Atoll and Lighthouse Reef in a fast 48-foot dive boat. Amigos charges BZ$150 per person for a local two-tank dive, not including equipment rental, and BZ$500 for a 12-hour trip to the Blue Hole, including park fee and lunch but not equipment rental. ⊠ *On water off Barrier Reef Dr., near Mayan Princess Hotel, Ambergris Caye* ☎ *226/2706* ⊕ *www.amigosdive.com.*

Raggamuffin Tours. Go out for a snorkel on a sailboat with Raggamuffin Tours, which goes to Hol Chan for BZ$100, including the park entrance fee, lunch, and cocktails. ⊠ *Front St., Caye Caulker* ☎ *226/0348* ⊕ *www.raggamuffintours.com.*

INDEPENDENT TOURS

Several Belize City–based tour guides and operators offer custom trips for ship passengers; companies will usually meet you at the Fort Street Tourism Village.

Belize Trips ☎ *223/0376, 561/210–7015 U.S. number* ✉ *info@belize-trips.com* ⊕ *www.belize-trips.com.*

Ecological Tours & Services ✉ *Tourism Village, Fort St.* ☎ *223/4874* ⊕ *www.ecotoursbelize.com.*

BEACHES

Although the barrier reef limits the wave action and brings seagrass to the shore floor, the wide sandy beaches of Ambergris Caye are among the best in Belize. All beaches in Belize are public. **Mar de Tumbo,** 1½ miles (3 km) south of town near the Tropica Hotel, is the best beach on the south end of the island. **North Ambergris,** accessible by water taxi from San Pedro or by golf cart over the bridge to the north, has miles of narrow beaches and fewer people. **Ramon's Village's beach,** across from the airstrip, is the best in the town area. The beaches on Caulker are not as good as those on Ambergris. Along the front side of the island is a narrow strip of sand, but the water is shallow and swimming conditions are poor. The **Split,** on the north end of the village (turn to your right from the main public pier), is the best place on Caye Caulker for swimming.

WHERE TO EAT

$
LATIN AMERICAN

✕ Nerie's. Always packed with locals, Nerie's is the vox populi of dining in Belize City. The many traditional dishes on the menu include fry jacks for breakfast and cow-foot soup for lunch. At dinner stew chicken with rice and beans and a soft drink will set you back only BZ$11. ✉ *Queen and Daly Sts., Commercial District* ☎ *223/4028* ▬ *No credit cards* ✉ *Douglas Jones St., Commercial District* ☎ *224/5199* ▬ *No credit cards.*

$$
AMERICAN
Fodor's Choice
★

✕ Riverside Tavern. Owned and managed by the Bowen (Belikin beer) family, Riverside Tavern opened in 2006 and immediately became one of the city's most popular restaurants. The huge signature hamburgers are arguably the best in Belize. (The 6-ounce burger is BZ$16.) The Riverside has added new steak and prime rib dishes, from cattle from the Bowen farm at Gallon Jug. Sit inside in air-conditioned comfort, at tables set around a huge bar, or on the outside covered patio overlooking Haulover Creek. This is one of the few restaurants in Belize with a dress code—shorts aren't allowed at night. The fenced, guarded parking lot right in front of the restaurant makes it easy and safe to park for free. **$** *Average main: BZ$24* ✉ *2 Mapp St., off Freetown Rd., Commercial District* ☎ *223/5640.*

BERMUDA

Sirkka Huish

Basking in the Atlantic, 508 miles (817 km) due east of Cape Hatteras, North Carolina, restrained and polite Bermuda is a departure from other sunny, beach-strewn isles. You won't find laid-back locals wandering around barefoot proffering piña coladas. Bermuda is somewhat formal, and despite the gorgeous weather, residents wearing stockings and heels or jackets, ties, Bermuda shorts, and knee socks are a common sight, whether on the street by day or in restaurants at night. On Bermuda's 22 square miles (57 square km) you will discover that pastel cottages, quaint shops, and manicured gardens betray a more staid, suburban way of life. A self-governing British colony since 1968, Bermuda has maintained some of its English character even as it is increasingly influenced by American culture. Most cruise ships make seven-night loops from U.S. embarkation ports, with four nights at sea and three tied up in port. Increasingly popular are round-trip itineraries originating in northeastern embarkation ports that include a single day or overnight port call in Bermuda before continuing south to the Bahamas or the Caribbean.

ESSENTIALS

CURRENCY   The Bermuda dollar (B$) is on par with the U.S. dollar. You can use American money anywhere, but change is often given in Bermudian currency. ATMs are common.

INTERNET   Expect to pay as much as $10 per hour to check your email on Bermuda. **Logic Communications** ☎ 441/296–9600.

TELEPHONE   To make a local call, simply dial the seven-digit number. You can find specially marked AT&T USADirect phones at the airport, the cruise-ship dock in Hamilton, and King's Square and Ordnance Island in St. George's. You can also make international calls with a calling card from the main post office. You can make prepaid international calls from the Cable & Wireless Office, which also has international fax services, Monday through Friday from 9 to 4:45.

COMING ASHORE

Three Bermuda harbors serve cruise ships: Hamilton (the capital), St. George's, and King's Wharf at the Royal Naval Dockyard.

In Hamilton, cruise ships tie up right on the city's main street, Front Street. A Visitors Service Bureau is next to the ferry terminal, also on Front Street and nearby; maps and brochures are displayed in the cruise terminal itself.

St. George's actually has two piers that accommodate cruise ships. One is on Ordnance Island, which is in the heart of the city; another pier is nearby at Penno's Wharf. A Visitors Service Bureau is at the World Heritage Centre, 19 Penno's Wharf.

King's Wharf, in the Royal Naval Dockyard at the westernmost end of the island, is the most isolated of the three cruise-ship berthing areas, and it is where the largest vessels dock. But it is well connected to the rest of the island by taxi, bus, and ferry. A Visitors Service Bureau is adjacent to bus stops and the ferry pier.

Taxis are the fastest and easiest way to get around the island, but they are also quite expensive. Four-seater taxis charge $6.40 for the first mile and $2 for each subsequent mile. For a personalized taxi tour of the island, the minimum duration is three hours, at $40 per hour for one to four people and $55 an hour for five or six, excluding tip. If you can round up a group of people, this is often cheaper than an island tour offered by your ship. Tip drivers 15%. Rental cars are prohibited, but the island has a good bus and ferry system. You can also rent scooters, but this can be dangerous for the unitiated and is not recommended.

EXPLORING BERMUDA

HAMILTON

Bermuda's capital since 1815, the city of Hamilton is a small, bustling harbor town. It's the economic and social center of Bermuda, with busy streets lined with shops and offices. International influences, from both business and tourism, have brought a degree of sophistication unusual in so small a city. There are several museums and galleries to explore, but the favorite pastimes are shopping in Hamilton's numerous boutiques and dining in its many upscale restaurants.

☾ **Bermuda Underwater Exploration Institute (BUEI).** The 40,000-square-foot
★ Ocean Discovery Centre showcases local contributions to oceanographic research and undersea discovery. Guests can ogle the world-class shell collection amassed by resident Jack Lightbourne (three of the 1,000 species were identified by and named for Lightbourne himself); or visit a gallery honoring native-born archaeologist Teddy Tucker to see booty retrieved from Bermudian shipwrecks. The types of gizmos that made such discoveries possible are also displayed: including a replica of the bathysphere William Beebe and Otis Barton used in their record-smashing 1934 dive. ⊠ *40 Crow Lane, off E. Broadway, Hamilton* ☎ *441/292–7219* ⊕ *www.buei.org* ⊠ *$12.50* ⊙ *Weekdays 9–5, weekends 10–5; last admission at 4.*

★ **City Hall & Arts Centre.** Set back from the street behind a fountain and pond, City Hall contains Hamilton's administrative offices as well as two art galleries and a performance hall. Instead of a clock, its tower is topped with a bronze wind vane—a prudent choice in a land where the weather is as important as the time. The building itself was designed in 1960 by Bermudian architect Wilfred Onions, a champion of balanced simplicity. Massive cedar doors open onto an impressive lobby notable for its beautiful chandeliers and portraits of mayors past and present. To the left is City Hall Theatre, a major venue for concerts, plays, and dance performances. To the right are the civic offices, where you can find souvenirs such as pens, T-shirts, and paperweights showing the Corporation of Hamilton's logo. A handsome cedar staircase leads upstairs to two upper-floor art galleries. (An elevator gets you there, too.) ⊠ *17 Church St., Hamilton* ☎ *441/292–1234* ⊙ *City Hall weekdays 9–5; National Gallery and Society of the Arts weekdays 10–4, Sat. 10–2.*

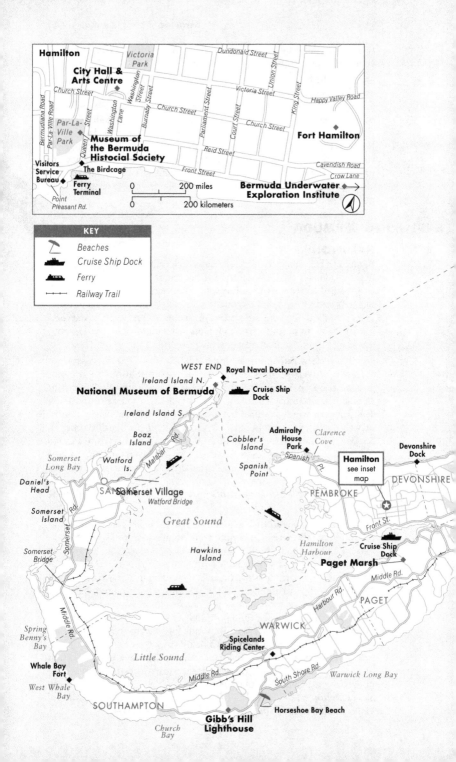

Hamilton

City Hall & Arts Centre

Victoria Park

Dundonald Street

Union Street

King Street

Church Street

Victoria Street

Happy Valley Road

Bermudiana Road

Par-La-Ville Road

Washington Street

Burnaby Street

Washington Lane

Church Street

Church Street

Parliament Street

Court Street

King Street

Par-La-Ville Park

Museum of the Bermuda Histoical Society

Queen Street

Reid Street

Fort Hamilton

Cavendish Road

Visitors Service Bureau

The Birdcage

Front Street

Crow Lane

Ferry Terminal

Point Pleasant Rd.

Bermuda Underwater Exploration Institute

| 0 | | 200 miles |
| 0 | | 200 kilometers |

KEY

	Beaches
	Cruise Ship Dock
	Ferry
	Railway Trail

WEST END

Royal Naval Dockyard

Ireland Island N.

National Museum of Bermuda

Cruise Ship Dock

Ireland Island S.

Boaz Island

Cobbler's Island

Admiralty House Park

Clarence Cove

Devonshire Dock

Somerset Long Bay

Watford Is.

Malabar Rd.

Spanish Point

Spanish Pt.

Hamilton see inset map

DEVONSHIRE

Daniel's Head

SAN...

Somerset Village

Watford Bridge

PEMBROKE

Somerset Island

Great Sound

Front St.

Somerset Bridge

Hawkins Island

Hamilton Harbour

Cruise Ship Dock

Paget Marsh

Somerset Rd.

Middle Rd.

Spring Benny's Bay

Little Sound

PAGET

Harbour Rd.

Middle Rd.

WARWICK

Whale Bay Fort

Spicelands Riding Center

South Shore Rd.

Warwick Long Bay

West Whale Bay

Middle Rd.

Middle Rd.

South Shore Rd.

SOUTHAMPTON

Horseshoe Bay Beach

Church Bay

Gibb's Hill Lighthouse

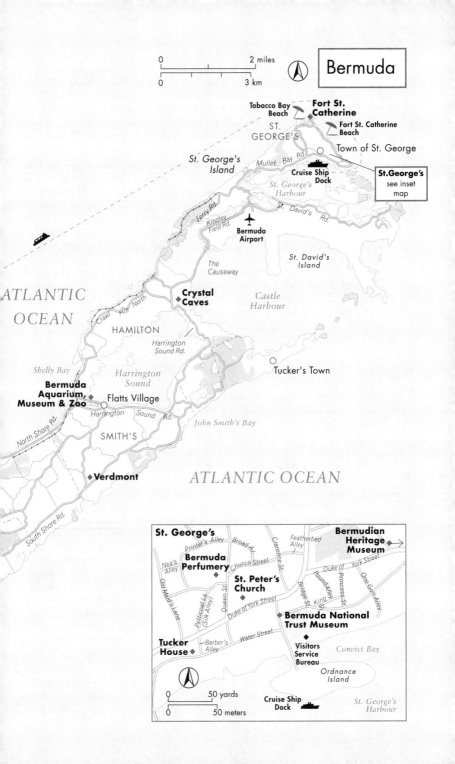

☾ **Fort Hamilton.** This imposing moat-ringed fortress has underground pas-
★ sageways that were cut through solid rock by Royal Engineers in the
1860s. Built to defend the West End's Royal Naval Dockyard from
land attacks, it was outdated even before its completion, but remains a
fine example of a polygonal Victorian fort. Even if you're not a big fan
of military history, the hilltop site's stellar views and stunning gardens
make the trip worthwhile. ⊠ *Happy Valley Rd., Hamilton* ☎ *441/292–
1234* ⌨ *Free* ⊙ *Daily 8–sunset.*

Museum of the Bermuda Historical Society/Bermuda National Library. This
Georgian house was once owned by Postmaster William Bennet Perot
and his family. The library was established in 1839, and its reference
section has virtually every book ever written about Bermuda, as well as
a microfilm collection of Bermudian newspapers dating back to 1784.
To the left of the library entrance is the Historical Society's museum.
The collection is eclectic, chronicling the island's past through interesting—and in some cases downright quirky—artifacts. Check out the
portraits of Sir George Somers and his wife, painted around 1605, and
of William Perot and his wife that hang in the entrance hall. The newest
exhibit is a selection of portraits of prominent Bermudians painted in
the 1970s. ⊠ *13 Queen St., opposite Reid St., Hamilton* ☎ *441/295–
2905 library, 441/295–2487 museum* ⊕ *www.bnl.bm* ⌨ *Library free;
museum donations accepted* ⊙ *Library Mon.–Thurs. 8:30–7, Fri. 10–5,
Sat. 9–5, Sun. 1–5; closed Sun. and at 6 Mon.–Thurs. in July and Aug.;
museum weekdays 10–2, closes at 1 in winter* ☞ *Tours by appointment.*

ST. GEORGE'S

The settlement of Bermuda began in what is now the town of St. George
nearly 400 years ago, when the *Sea Venture* was shipwrecked on Bermuda's treacherous reefs on its way to the colony of Jamestown, Virginia. No trip to Bermuda is complete without a visit to this historic
town and UNESCO World Heritage Site.

Bermuda National Trust Museum at the Globe Hotel. Erected as a governor's
mansion around 1700, this building became a hotbed of activity during the American Civil War. From here, Confederate Major Norman
Walker coordinated the surreptitious flow of guns, ammunition, and
war supplies from England, through Union blockades, into American
ports. It saw service as the Globe Hotel during the mid-19th century
and became a National Trust property in 1951. A short video, *Bermuda, Centre of the Atlantic,* recounts the history of Bermuda, and a
memorabilia-filled exhibit entitled "Rogues & Runners: Bermuda and
the American Civil War" describes St. George's when it was a port
for Confederate blockade runners. ■TIP→ This is where you will also
find the St. George's Visitor Information Centre. ⊠ *32 Duke of York St.,
St. George's* ☎ *441/297–1423* ⊕ *www.bnt.bm* ⌨ *$5; $10 combination
ticket includes admission to Tucker House and Verdmont* ⊙ *Apr.–Oct.,
Mon.–Sat. 10–4; Nov.–Mar., Mon., Wed., and Sat., 10–4.*

★ **Bermuda Perfumery & Gardens.** In 2005 this perfumery moved from
Bailey's Bay in Smith's Parish, where it had been based since 1928,
to historic Stewart Hall. Although the location changed, the techniques it uses did not: the perfumery still manufactures and bottles

all its island-inspired scents on-site using more than 3,000 essential oils extracted from frangipani, jasmine, oleander, and passionflower. Guides are available to explain the entire process, and there's a small museum that outlines the company's history. ⊠ *Stewart Hall, 5 Queen St., St. George's* ☏ *441/293–0627* ⊕ *www. lilibermuda.com* ☞ *Free* ⊙ *Mon.– Sat. 9–5.*

♻ **Ordnance Island.** Ordnance Island, directly across from King's Square, is dominated by a splendid bronze statue of Sir George Somers, commander of the *Sea Venture.* Somers looks surprised that he made it safely to shore—and you may be surprised that he ever chose to set sail again when you spy the nearby *Deliverance II.* It's a full-scale replica of one of two ships—the other was the *Patience*—built under Somers's supervision to carry survivors from the 1609 wreck onward to Jamestown. But considering her size (just 57 feet from bow to stern) *Deliverance II* hardly seems ocean-worthy by modern standards. ⊠ *Across from King's Sq., St. George's.*

BERMUDA BEST BETS

■ **Gibbs Hill Lighthouse.** Make the climb to the top, where the reward is an expansive view of the inlets and harbors.

■ **National Museum of Bermuda.** Absorb Bermuda's nautical and military history in this Royal Navy Dockyard museum.

■ **St. George's.** Attend the pierside show hosted by the town crier, where gossips and nagging wives are drenched in a dunking stool.

Fodor's Choice ★ **St. Peter's Church.** Because parts of this whitewashed stone church date back to 1620, it holds the distinction of being the oldest continuously operating Anglican church in the Western Hemisphere. It was not, however, the first house of worship to stand on this site. It replaced a 1612 structure made of wooden posts and palmetto leaves that was destroyed in a storm. The present church was extended in 1713 (the oldest part is the area around the triple-tier pulpit), with the tower and wings being added in the 19th century. ⊠ *33 Duke of York St., St. George's* ☏ *441/297–2459* ⊕ *www.stpeters.bm* ☞ *Donations appreciated* ⊙ *Mon.–Sat. 10–4, Sun. service at 11:15.*

Tucker House. Tucker House was built in the 1750s for a merchant who stored his wares in the cellar (a space that now holds an archaeological exhibit). But it's been associated with the Tucker family ever since Henry Tucker, president of the Governor's Council and a key participant in the Bermuda Gunpowder Plot, purchased it in 1775. His descendents lived here until 1809, and much of the fine silver and heirloom furniture was donated by them. The kitchen, however, is dedicated to another notable—Joseph Haine Rainey—who is thought to have operated a barber's shop in it during the Civil War. (Barber's Alley, around the corner, is also named in his honor.) As a freed slave from South Carolina, Rainey fled to Bermuda at the outbreak of the war. Afterward he returned to the United States and, in 1870, became the first black man to be elected to the House of Representatives. A short flight of stairs leads down to the kitchen, originally a separate building, and to an enclosed kitchen garden. ⊠ *5 Water St., St. George's* ☏ *441/297–0545* ⊕ *www. bnt.bm* ☞ *$5; $10 combination ticket includes admission to National*

Trust Museum in Globe Hotel and Verdmont ⊙ May–Oct., Mon.–Fri. 10–2; Nov.–Apr., Wed.–Fri. 10–2.

ELSEWHERE ON THE ISLAND

Fodor's Choice ★

Bermuda Aquarium, Museum & Zoo. The BAMZ, established in 1926, has always been a pleasant diversion. But following an ambitious decade-long expansion program, it rates as one of Bermuda's premier attractions. In the aquarium the big draw is the North Rock Exhibit, a 140,000-gallon tank that gives you a diver's-eye view of the area's living coral reefs and the colorful marine life it sustains. ⊠ *40 N. Shore Rd., Flatts Village, Hamilton Parish* ☎ *441/293–2727* ⊕ *www.bamz. org* ⊡ *$10* ⊙ *Daily 9–5, last admission at 4; North Rock dive talk at 1:10 daily and seal feeding at 1:30 and 4 daily.*

Fodor's Choice ★

Crystal Caves. Bermuda's limestone caves have been attracting attention since the island was first settled. After being closed to the public for decades, it reopened in 2001. Set aside 30 minutes to see one cave; 75 minutes if you plan to take in both. ⊠ *8 Crystal Caves Rd., off Wilkinson Ave., Bailey's Bay, Hamilton Parish* ☎ *441/293–0640* ⊕ *www.bermudacaves.com* ⊡ *One cave $20; combination ticket $27* ⊙ *Daily 9:30–4:30; last combination tour at 4.*

★

Fort St. Catherine. This restored hilltop fort is arguably the most formidable looking one on the island. Surrounded by a dry moat and accessed by a drawbridge, it has enough tunnels, towers, redoubts, and ramparts to satisfy even the most avid military historian—or adrenaline-fueled child. The original fort was built around 1614 by Bermuda's first governor, Richard Moore, but it was remodeled and enlarged at least five times. In fact, work continued on it until late in the 19th century. ⊠ *15 Coot Pond Rd., St. George's Parish* ☎ *441/297–1920* ⊡ *$7* ⊙ *Weekdays 10–4.*

★

Gibb's Hill Lighthouse. This cast-iron lighthouse soars above Southampton Parish. Designed in London and opened in 1846, the tower stands 117 feet high and 362 feet above the sea. The light was originally produced by a concentrated burner of four large, circular wicks. The haul up the 185 spiral stairs is an arduous one—particularly if you dislike heights or tight spaces. But en route to the top you can stop to catch your breath on eight landings, where photographs and drawings of the lighthouse help divert attention from your aching appendages. ⊠ *68 St. Anne's Rd., Southampton Parish* ☎ *441/238–8069* ⊕ *www.bermudalighthouse.com* ⊡ *$2.50* ⊙ *Daily 9:30–4:30. Closed mid-Jan.–mid-Feb.*

Fodor's Choice ★

National Museum of Bermuda. The Maritime Museum, ensconced in Bermuda's largest fort, displays its collections in a series of old munitions warehouses that surround the parade grounds and Keep Pond. Insulated from the rest of the Dockyard by a moat and massive stone ramparts, it is entered by way of a drawbridge. Built as both home and headquarters for the Dockyard commissioner, the house later served as a barracks during World War I and was used for military intelligence during World War II. Today, after an award-winning restoration, it contains exhibits on Bermuda's social and military history. A must-see is the Hall of History, a mural of Bermuda's history covering 1,000 square feet. It took local artist Graham Foster more than 3½ years to paint. ⊠ *Old Royal Naval Dockyard, Dockyard* ☎ *441/234–1418* ⊕ *www.bmm.bm* ☒ *$10* ⊙ *Daily 9:30–4.*

Paget Marsh. Take a walk on the wild side at Paget Marsh: a 25-acre tract of land that's remained virtually untouched since presettlement times. These unspoiled habitats can be explored via a boardwalk that features interpretive signs describing the endemic flora and fauna. When listening to the cries of the native and migratory birds that frequent this natural wetland, you can quickly forget that bustling Hamilton is just minutes away. ⊠ *Lovers La., Paget Parish* ☎ *441/236–6483* ⊕ *www. bnt.bm* ☒ *Free* ⊙ *Daily sunrise–sunset.*

Ⓒ **Verdmont House Museum.** Even if you think you've had your fill of old houses, Verdmont deserves a look. The National Trust property, which opened as a museum in 1956, is notable for its Georgian architecture. Yet what really sets this place apart is its pristine condition. Though used as a residence until the mid-20th century, virtually no structural changes were made to Verdmont since it was erected around 1710. Former owners never even added electricity or plumbing (so the "powder room" was strictly used for powdering wigs). ⊠ *6 Verdmont La., off Collector's Hill, Smith's Parish* ☎ *441/236–7369* ⊕ *www.bnt.bm* ☒ *$5; $10 combination ticket with Bermuda National Trust Museum in Globe Hotel and Tucker House* ⊙ *May–Oct., Tues.–Thurs. and Sat. 10–4; Nov.–Apr., Wed. and Sat. 10–4.*

SHOPPING

Hamilton has the greatest concentration of shops in Bermuda, and Front Street is its pièce de résistance. Lined with small, pastel-color buildings, this most fashionable of Bermuda's streets houses sedate department stores and snazzy boutiques, with several small arcades and shopping alleys leading off it. A smart canopy shades the entrance to the 55 Front Street Group, which houses Crisson Jewelers. Modern Butterfield Place has galleries and boutiques selling, among other things, Louis Vuitton leather goods. The Emporium, a renovated building with an atrium, has a range of shops, from antiques to souvenirs.

St. George's Water Street, Duke of York Street, Hunters Wharf, Penno's Wharf, and Somers Wharf are the sites of numerous renovated buildings that house branches of Front Street stores, as well as artisans' studios. Historic King's Square offers little more than a couple of T-shirt and souvenir shops.

In the West End, **Somerset Village** has a few shops, but they hardly merit a special shopping trip. However, the **Clocktower Mall**, in a historic building at the Royal Naval Dockyard, has a few more shopping opportunities, including branches of Front Street shops and specialty boutiques. The Dockyard is also home to the Craft Market, the Bermuda Arts Centre, and Bermuda Clayworks.

ACTIVITIES

BICYCLING

The best and sometimes only way to explore Bermuda's nooks and crannies—its little hidden coves and 18th-century tribe roads—is by bicycle or motor scooter. A popular option for biking in Bermuda is the **Railway Trail**, a dedicated cycle path blissfully free of cars. Running intermittently the length of the old Bermuda Railway (old "Rattle 'n' Shake"), this trail is scenic and restricted to pedestrian and bicycle traffic. You can ask the staff at any bike-rental shop for advice on where to access the trail.

Eve Cycle. With three convenient locations around the island, Eve's has moved its head office to Dockyard, just a few yards from the cruise terminal. It's about the only bike shop to still rent out adult mountain bikes, as well as motor scooters, including your mandatory helmet. The staff readily supplies advice on where to ride, and you'll have to pay an extra $20 for third-party insurance. Other branches are in St. George's and Paget, and if these are a bit of a walk from your accommodation, a shuttle service is offered. ⊠ *10 Dockyard Terr., Dockyard* ☎ *441/236–6247* ⊕ *www.evecycles.com.*

GOLF

Golf courses make up nearly 17% of the island's 21.6 square mi. The scenery on the courses is usually spectacular, with flowering trees and shrubs decked out in multicolor blossoms against a backdrop of brilliant blue sea and sky. The layouts are remarkably challenging, thanks to capricious ocean breezes, daunting natural terrain, and the clever work of world-class golf architects.

Fairmont Southampton Golf Club. Spreading across the hillside below the high-rise Fairmont Southampton, this executive golf course is known for its steep terrain, giving players who opt to walk (for sunset tee times only) an excellent workout. ⊠ *Fairmont Southampton Resort, 101 South Rd., Southampton Parish* ☎ *441/239–6952* ⊕ *www.fairmont.com/Southampton* ⚑ *Green fees $84 before 2:30 pm with cart mandatory, $65 after 2:30 pm with cart or $45 walking. Pull-cart rental $7.50. Shoe rentals $10. Titleist club rentals $35. Lessons $50 a half hour, $100 per hour* ⚐ *18 holes. 2,684 yards. Par 54. Rating: 53.7.*

★ **Mid Ocean Club.** The elite Mid Ocean Club is a 1921 Charles Blair Macdonald design revamped in 1953 by Robert Trent Jones Sr. *Golf Digest* ranked it 45th in the top 50 courses outside the United States. ⊠ *1 Mid Ocean Dr., off S. Shore Rd., Tucker's Town* ☎ *441/293–1215* ⊕ *www.themidoceanclubbermuda.com* ⚑ *Green fees $250 ($100 when playing with a member). Non-members must be sponsored by a club member (your hotelier can arrange this); non-member starting times available Mon., Wed., and Fri. except holidays. Caddies $55 for double or $65 for single per bag (tip not included). Cart rental $30 per person. Shoe rentals $6. Club rentals $45. Lessons $55 a half hour, $100 per hour* ⚐ *18 holes. 6,548 yards. Par 71. Rating: blue tees, 73.0; white tees, 71.3; red tees, 75.0.*

SNORKELING

Snorkeling cruises are generally offered from April through September. Smaller boats, which limit capacity to 10 to 16 passengers, offer more personal attention and focus more on the beautiful snorkeling areas themselves. Guides on such tours often relate interesting historical and ecological information about the island. Some larger boats take up to 40 passengers.

Jessie James Cruises. Half-day trips aboard the 31-foot glass-bottomed boat *Pisces*, which holds up to 17 people, cost $65, $45 for children (ages 8–10). The boat takes you to three different sites, including at least two shipwrecks. ⊠ *11 Clarence St., St. George's* ☎ *441/236–4804* ⊕ *www.jessiejames.bm.*

BEACHES

☾ **Elbow Beach.** Swimming and bodysurfing are great at this beach, which
★ is bordered by the prime strand of sand reserved for guests of the Elbow Beach Hotel on the left, and the ultra-exclusive Coral Beach Club beach area on the right. It's a pleasant setting for a late-evening stroll, with the lights from nearby hotels dancing on the water, but the romance dissipates in daylight, when the beach is noisy and crowded. Protective coral reefs make the waters the safest on the island, and a good choice for families. A lunch wagon sometimes sells fast food and cold drinks during the day, and Mickey's Beach Bar (part of the Elbow Beach Hotel) is open for lunch and dinner, though it may be difficult to get a table. **Pros:** beautiful stretch of beach; safest waters on the island, snorkel rental shop. **Cons:** busy; parking fills up quickly; need to watch out for stray footballs and volleyballs. ⊠ *Off South Rd., Paget Parish* Ⓜ *Bus 2 or 7 from Hamilton.*

☾ **Horseshoe Bay.** When locals say they're going to "the beach," they're
Fodor'sChoice generally referring to Horseshoe Bay, the island's most popular. With
★ clear water, a 0.3-mile crescent of pink sand, a vibrant social scene, and the uncluttered backdrop of South Shore Park, Horseshoe Bay has everything you could ask of a Bermudian beach. **Pros:** adjoining beach is perfect for small children; snack bar with outdoor seating. **Cons:** the bus stop is a long walk up a huge hill; gets very crowded; busiest beach on the island. ⊠ *Off South Rd., Southampton Parish* ☎ *441/238–2651* Ⓜ *Bus 7 from Hamilton.*

Tobacco Bay. The most popular beach near St. George's—about 15 minutes northwest of the town on foot—this small north-shore strand is huddled in a coral cove. Its beach house has a snack bar, equipment rentals, toilets, showers, changing rooms, and ample parking. It's a 10-minute hike from the bus stop in the town of St. George's, or you can flag down a St. George's Minibus Service van and ask for a lift ($2 per person). In high season the beach is busy, especially midweek, when the cruise ships are docked. **Pros:** beautiful rock formations in the water; great snorkeling. **Cons:** so popular it becomes overcrowded; no bus stops nearby. ⊠ *Coot Pond Rd., St. George's Parish* ☎ *441/297–2756* Ⓜ *Bus 10 or 11 from Hamilton.*

WHERE TO EAT

$
BRITISH

✕ **Docksider.** Locals come to mingle at this sprawling Front Street sports bar. It's generally more popular as a drinking venue, as it can get quite overcrowded and rowdy. But if you want to catch the game on the big screen with everyone else, an all-day menu of standard pub fare is available, as well as local fish. Go for the English beef pie, fish-and-chips, or a fish sandwich, and sip your dessert—a Dark 'n Stormy—out on the porch as you watch Bermuda stroll by. Or if you can't make up your mind, you can always rely on the hearty full English breakfast to fill you up. Food is served until 10 pm. The pub has a good jukebox and there's often a DJ or a band on summer weekends. ⑤ *Average main: $15* ⊠ *121 Front St., Hamilton* ☎ *441/296–3333* ⊕ *www.dockies.com.*

$
CARIBBEAN

✕ **Spring Garden Restaurant & Bar.** If you've never had Barbadian or, as Barbados natives like to call it, "Bajan" food, come sit under the indoor palm tree and try panfried flying fish—a delicacy in Barbados. Another good choice is the broiled mahimahi served in creole sauce, with peas and rice. During lobster season, an additional menu appears, featuring steamed, broiled, or curried lobster ($38.50 for the complete dinner). For dessert, try coconut cream pie or raspberry-mango cheesecake. Or eat with the locals at the Friday lunchtime bargain buffet; help yourself to as many starters, mains, and desserts you can eat for $22. ⑤ *Average main: $18* ⊠ *19 Washington La., off Reid St., Hamilton* ☎ *441/295–7416* ⊙ *Closed Sun.*

BONAIRE (KRALENDIJK)

Vernon
O'Reilly
Ramesar

Starkly beautiful Bonaire is the consummate desert island. Surrounded by pristine waters, it is a haven for divers and snorkelers, who flock here from around the world to take advantage of the excellent visibility, easily accessed reefs, and bountiful marine life. Bonaire is the most rustic of the three ABC islands, and despite its dependence on tourism it manages to maintain its identity and simple way of life. There are many good restaurants, most of which are within walking distance of the port. Most of the island's 14,000-some inhabitants live in and around Kralendijk, which must certainly qualify as one of the cutest and most compact capitals in the Caribbean. The best shopping is to be found along the very short stretch of road that constitutes "downtown." Bonaire's beaches tend to be small and rocky, but there is a nice stretch of sandy beach at Lac Bay. It is entirely possible to see almost all of the sights and sounds of the island in one day by taking one of the island tours on offer.

ESSENTIALS

CURRENCY
As of January 2011 the U.S. dollar became the official currency, replacing the NAf guilder, and the island has several ATMs, particularly in Kralendijk.

INTERNET
Bonaire Access ⊠ *Harbourside Mall, Kralendijk* ☎ *599/717–6040.*

TELEPHONE
You can make international calls from from the Telbo central phone company office (next to the tourism office in Kralendijk), which is

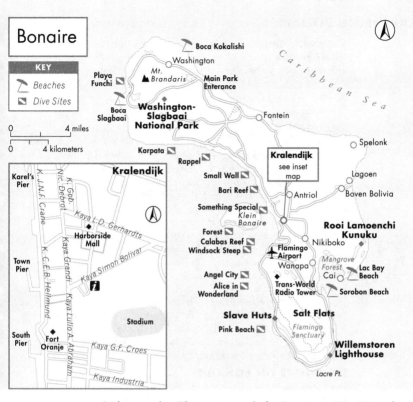

open 24 hours a day. The country code for Bonaire is 599; 717 is the exchange for every four-digit telephone number on the island. When making interisland calls, dial 717 plus the local four-digit number.

COMING ASHORE

One of the great benefits of Bonaire to cruise passengers is that the port is right in downtown Kralendijk. Ships usually tender passengers ashore. A four-minute walk takes you to most of the best shopping and restaurants on the island.

Bonaire lives for tourism; upon the arrival of a cruise ship, the locals are ready, and an impromptu crafts market springs up in the park across from the port entrance. Taxis wait right at the port and operate on fixed government rates. All the sights of Kralendijk are within easy walking distance, and a taxi ride to one of the larger resorts on the island will run between $11 and $15. A half-day island tour by taxi costs about $25 per hour for up to two passengers and will allow you to see most of the major sights. Fares increase by 50% between midnight and 6 am.

EXPLORING BONAIRE

Two routes, north and south from Kralendijk, the island's small capital, are possible on the 24-mile-long (39-km-long) island; either route will take from a few hours to a full day, depending on whether you stop to snorkel, swim, dive, or lounge. Those pressed for time will find that it's easy to explore the entire island in a day if stops are kept to a minimum.

KRALENDIJK

Bonaire's small, tidy capital city (population 3,000) is five minutes from the airport. The main drag, J. A. Abraham Boulevard, turns into **Kaya Grandi** in the center of town. Along it are most of the island's major stores, boutiques, and restaurants. Across Kaya Grandi, opposite the Littman jewelry store, is Kaya L. D. Gerharts, with several small supermarkets, a handful of snack shops, and some of the better restaurants. Walk down the narrow waterfront avenue called Kaya C.E.B. Hellmund, which leads straight to the **North and South piers.** In the center of town, the Harbourside Mall has chic boutiques. Along this route is **Ft. Oranje,** with its cannons. From December through April, cruise ships dock in the harbor once or twice a week. The diminutive ocher-and-white structure that looks like a tiny Greek temple is the **fish market;** local anglers no longer bring their catches here (they sell out of their homes these days), but you can find plenty of fresh produce brought over from Colombia and Venezuela. Pick up the brochure *"Walking and Shopping in Kralendijk"* from the tourist office to get a map and full listing of all the monuments and sights in the town.

ELSEWHERE ON BONAIRE

☾ **Rooi Lamoenchi Kunuku.** Owner Ellen Herrera restored her family's home-
★ stead north of Lac Bay, in the Bonairean *kadushi* (cactus) wilderness, to educate tourists and residents about the history and tradition of authentic kunuku living and show unspoiled terrain in two daily tours. You must make an appointment in advance and expect to spend a couple of hours. ⊠ *Kaya Suiza 23, Playa Baribe* ☎ *599/717–8489* ⌨ *$21* ☉ *By appointment only.*

Salt Flats. You can't miss the salt flats—voluptuous white drifts that look like mountains of snow. Harvested once a year, the "ponds" are owned by Cargill, Inc., which has reactivated the 19th-century salt industry with great success (one reason for that success is that the ocean on this part of the island is higher than the land—which makes irrigation a snap). Keep a lookout for the three 30-foot obelisks—white, blue, and red—that were used to guide the trade boats coming to pick up the salt. Look also in the distance across the pans to the abandoned solar salt-works that's now a designated **flamingo sanctuary.** With the naked eye you might be able to make out a pink-orange haze just on the horizon; with binoculars you will see a sea of bobbing pink bodies. The sanctuary is completely protected, and no entrance is allowed (flamingos are extremely sensitive to disturbances of any kind).

☾ **Slave Huts.** The salt industry's gritty history is revealed in Rode Pan, the site of two groups of tiny slave huts. The white grouping is on the right side of the road, opposite the salt flats; the second grouping, called the red slave huts (though they appear yellow), stretches across the road toward the island's southern tip. During the 19th century, slaves working the salt pans by day crawled into these huts to rest. Each Friday afternoon they walked seven hours to Rincon to weekend with their families, returning each Sunday. Only very small people will be able to enter, but walk around and poke your head in for a look.

⟲ **Washington–Slagbaai National Park.** Once a plantation producing divi-divi trees (the pods were used for tanning animal skins), aloe (used for medicinal lotions), charcoal, and goats, the park is now a model of conservation. It's easy to tour the 13,500-acre tropical desert terrain on the dirt roads. As befits a wilderness sanctuary, the well-marked, rugged routes force you to drive slowly enough to appreciate the animal life and the terrain. (Think twice about coming here if it has rained recently—the mud you may encounter will be more than inconvenient.) If you're planning to hike, bring a picnic lunch, camera, sunscreen, and plenty of water. There are two routes: the long one (22 miles [35½ km]) is marked by yellow arrows, the short one (15 miles [24 km]) by green arrows. Goats and donkeys may dart across the road, and if you keep your eyes peeled, you may catch sight of large iguanas camouflaged in the shrubbery. A useful guide to the park is available at the entrance for about $6. To get here, take the secondary road north from the town of Rincon. The Nature Fee for swimming and snorkeling also grants you free admission to this park—simply present proof of payment and some form of photo ID. ☎ *599/717–8444* ⊕ *www.washingtonparkbonaire. org* ✉ *Free with payment of scuba diving Nature Fee ($25) or $15 without* ⊙ *Daily 8–5; you must enter before 3.*

Willemstoren Lighthouse. Bonaire's first lighthouse was built in 1837 and is now automated (but closed to visitors). Take some time to explore the beach and notice how the waves, driven by the trade winds, play a crashing symphony against the rocks. Locals stop here to collect pieces of driftwood in spectacular shapes and to build fanciful pyramids from objects that have washed ashore.

SHOPPING

Although it is a relatively small town, Kralendijk offers a good range of high-end items like watches and jewelry at attractive prices. There are a number of souvenir shops offering T-shirts and trinkets lining the main street of Kaya Grandi.

> **BONAIRE BEST BETS**
>
> ■ **Diving.** Bonaire is one of the world's top diving destinations. Shore diving is especially good.
>
> ■ **Snorkeling.** With reefs close to shore, snorkeling is good right off the beach.
>
> ■ **Flamingo spotting.** These shy, graceful birds are one of Bonaire's scenic delights.
>
> ■ **Kralendijk.** The accessible town has a nice assortment of restaurants and stores.
>
> ■ **Washington–Slagbaai National Park.** Bonaire's best land-based sight is this well-preserved national park.

4

★ **Atlantis.** This shop carries a large range of precious and semiprecious gems; the tanzanite collection is especially beautiful. You will also find Sector, Raymond Weil, and Citizen watches, among others, all at great savings. Since gold jewelry is sold by weight here, it's an especially good buy. ⊠ *Kaya Grandi 32B* ☏ *599/717–7730.*

JanArt Gallery. On the outskirts of town, JanArt Gallery sells unique paintings, prints, and art supplies; artist Janice Huckaby also hosts art classes. ⊠ *Kaya Gloria 7* ☏ *599/717–5246.*

Littman's. Owner Steven Littman handpicks many of the items available in this upscale jewelry and gift shop during his regular trips to Europe. Look for Rolex, Omega, Cartier, and Tag Heuer watches; fine gold jewelry; antique coins; nautical sculptures; resort clothing; and accessories. ⊠ *Kaya Grandi 33* ☏ *599/717–8160.*

Yenny's Art. Whatever you do, make a point of visiting Yenny's Art. Roam around her house, which is a replica of a traditional Bonaire town complete with her handmade life-size dolls and the skeletons of all her dead pets. Lots of fun (and sometimes kitschy) souvenirs made out of driftwood, clay, and shells are all handmade by Jenny. ⊠ *Kaya Betico Croes 6, near post office* ☏ *599/717–5004.*

ACTIVITIES

BICYCLING

Bonaire is generally flat, so bicycles are an easy way to get around. Because of the heat it's essential to carry water if you're planning to cycle for any distance, and especially if your plans involve exploring the deserted interior. There are more than 180 miles (290 km) of unpaved routes (as well as the many paved roads) on the island.

Cycle Bonaire. Cycle Bonaire rents mountain bikes and gear (trail maps, water bottles, helmets, locks, and repair and first-aid kits) for $25 a day or $100 for six days; half-day and full-day guided excursions start at $65, not including bike rental. ⊠ *Kaya Gobernador N. Debrot 77A* ☏ *599/717–2229.*

DIVING AND SNORKELING

Diving and snorkeling are almost a religion on Bonaire, and are by far the most popular activities for cruise passengers. Bonaire has some of the best reef diving this side of Australia's Great Barrier Reef. It takes only 5 to 25 minutes to reach many sites, the current is usually mild, and although some reefs have sudden, steep drops, most begin just offshore and slope gently downward at a 45-degree angle. General visibility runs 60 to 100 feet, except during surges in October and November. You can see several varieties of coral: knobby-brain, giant-brain, elkhorn, staghorn, mountainous star, gorgonian, and black.

☾ ★ **Larry's Shore & Wild Side Diving.** Run by a former army combat diver, Larry's Shore & Wild Side Diving offers a variety of appealing options ranging from the leisurely to downright scary. This company has become an extremely popular choice, so try to book as early as possible. ☏ *599/790–9156* ⊕ *www.larryswildsidediving.com.*

Mushi Mushi. The *Mushi Mushi* is a catamaran offering a variety of two- and three-hour cruises starting at $50 per person. It departs from the Bonaire Nautico Marina in downtown Kralendijk (opposite the restaurant It Rains Fishes). ☎ *599/790–5399.*

BEACHES

Don't expect long stretches of glorious powdery sand. Bonaire's beaches are small, and though the water is blue (several shades of it, in fact), the sand isn't always white. Bonaire's National Parks Foundation requires all non-divers to pay a $10 annual Nature Fee in order to enter the water anywhere around the island (divers pay $25). The fee can be paid at most dive shops.

Klein Bonaire. Just a water-taxi hop across from Kralendijk, this little island offers picture-perfect white-sand beaches. The area is protected, so absolutely no development has been allowed. Make sure to pack everything before heading to the island, including water and an umbrella to hide under, because there are no refreshment stands or changing facilities, and there's almost no shade to be found. Boats leave from the Town Pier, across from the City Café, and the round-trip water-taxi ride costs roughly $20 per person.

Lac Bay Beach. Known for its festive music on Sunday nights, this open bay area with pink-tinted sand is equally dazzling by day. It's a bumpy drive (10 to 15 minutes on a dirt road) to get here, but you'll be glad when you arrive. It's a good spot for diving, snorkeling, and kayaking (as long as you bring your own), and there are public restrooms and a restaurant for your convenience. ⊠ *Off Kaminda Sorobon, Lac Cai.*

Windsock Beach (*aka Mangrove Beach*). Near the airport (just off E.E.G. Boulevard), this pretty little spot looks out toward the north side of the island and has about 200 yards of white sand along a rocky shoreline. It's a popular dive site, and swimming conditions are good. ⊠ *Off E.E.G. Blvd., near Flamingo Airport.*

WHERE TO EAT

$$
EUROPEAN
★

✕ **Appetite.** This delightful establishment is an oasis of chic. The historic house offers cozy private rooms and a large courtyard, which always seems to be buzzing. The menu encourages diners to forget the main course and order a series of starters, but such items as stewed veal cheek with crispy sweetbreads are worth the splurge. The restaurant is just a few steps away from the Tourism Corporation Bonaire office. ⑤ *Average main: $25* ⊠ *Kaya Grandi 12* ☎ *599/717–3595* ⊙ *Closed Sun.*

$$
ECLECTIC
Fodor's Choice
★

✕ **City Café/City Restaurant.** This busy waterfront eatery is also one of the most reliable nightspots on the island, so it's always hopping day or night. Breakfast, lunch, and dinner are served daily at reasonable prices. Seafood is always featured, as are a variety of sandwiches and salads. The pita sandwich platters are a good lunchtime choice for the budget challenged. Weekends, there's always live entertainment and dancing. This is the place to people-watch on Bonaire, as it seems everyone ends up at City Café eventually. ⑤ *Average main: $19* ⊠ *Hotel Rochaline, Kaya Grandi 7* ☎ *599/717–8286* ⊕ *www.citybonaire.com.*

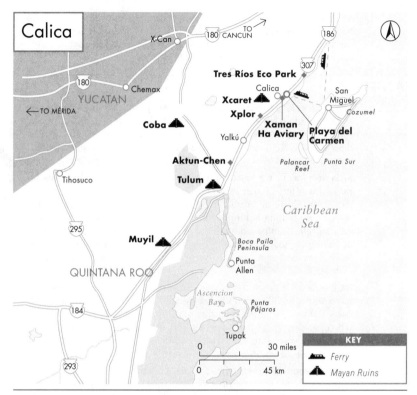

Calica

TO CANCUN

X-Can

Tres Ríos Eco Park

Chemax

YUCATAN

← TO MÉRIDA

Calica

Xcaret

Xplor

San Miguel

Cozumel

Coba

Yalkú

Xaman Ha Aviary

Playa del Carmen

Aktun-Chen

Palancar Reef

Punta Sur

Tihosuco

Tulum

Caribbean Sea

Muyil

Boca Paila Peninsula

QUINTANA ROO

Punta Allen

Ascencion Bay

Punta Pájaros

Tupak

KEY	
🚢	*Ferry*
🔺	*Mayan Ruins*

0 ——————— 30 miles
0 ——————— 45 km

CALICA (PLAYA DEL CARMEN), MEXICO

Valerie
Hamilton

Just minutes away from Calica, Playa del Carmen has become one of Latin America's fastest-growing communities, with a pace almost as hectic as Cancún's. Hotels, restaurants, and shops multiply here faster than you can say "Kukulcán." Some are branches of Cancún establishments whose owners have taken up permanent residence in Playa, while others are owned by American and European expats (predominately Italians) who came here years ago. It makes for a varied, international community. Avenida 5, the first street in town parallel to the beach, is a long pedestrian walkway with shops, cafés, and street performers; small hotels and stores stretch north from this avenue. Avenida Juárez, running east–west from the highway to the beach, is the main commercial zone for the Riviera Maya corridor. Here locals visit the food shops, pharmacies, hardware stores, and banks that line the curbs. People traveling the coast by car usually stop here to stock up on supplies—its banks, grocery stores, and gas stations are the last ones until Tulum.

ESSENTIALS

CURRENCY   The Mexican peso (MX$12.05 to US$1). U.S. dollars and credit cards are widely accepted in the area, from the port to Playa del Carmen, but it's best to have pesos—and small bills—when you visit ruins, where cashiers often run out of change. There is no advantage to paying in dollars, but there may be an advantage to paying in cash.

INTERNET Playa del Carmen offers free Wi-Fi in all public parks and along Calle 4 between avenues 15 and 10. There are also several Internet cafés on Avenida 5 in Playa del Carmen. The Casa Tucan hotel also has free Wi-Fi in its restaurant, making it a popular spot for cruise passengers.

Casa Tucan ⊠ *Calle 4 between Avs. 10 and 15, Playa del Carmen* ☎ *984/873–0283* ⊕ *www.casatucan.de.*

TELEPHONE Most pay phones accept prepaid Ladatel cards, sold in 30-, 50-, or 100-peso denominations. To use the card, insert it in the pay phone's slot, dial 001 (for calls to the United States) or 01 (for calls within Mexico), followed by the area code and number. Credit is deleted from the card as you use it, and the balance is displayed on the small screen on the phone.

> ### CALICA BEST BETS
>
> ■ **A Day at Xcaret.** Particularly for families, this ecological theme park is a great way to spend the day.
>
> ■ **Beaches.** The beaches in the Riviera Maya are stellar.
>
> ■ **Diving.** From Playa del Carmen it's only a short hop to some of the Yucatán's best dive sites.
>
> ■ **Shopping.** Playa del Carmen's Avenida 5 can easily keep you occupied for your day in port if you are a shopaholic.

COMING ASHORE

The port at Calica, about 3 miles south of the town of Playa del Carmen (between Playa del Carmen and Xcarat), is small. Sometimes ships actually dock, and other times passengers are tendered to shore. There is a makeshift market at the port, where locals sell crafts. Beyond that, there is not much to do, and you'll need to head into Playa del Carmen proper to find restaurants and even tour operators. If you really want to shop, skip the vendors at the port and head to Playa del Carmen's Avenida 5, where you can easily spend an afternoon browsing shops and enjoying restaurants.

Taxis and tour buses are available at the port to take you to Playa del Carmen and other destinations, but lines often form as passengers wait for taxis, so plan accordingly if you really want to pack a lot of activity into your day. Your taxi will have you in Playa del Carmen or in Xcaret in under 10 minutes, but you'll pay a whopping $10 for the short trip.

EXPLORING CALICA

Aktun-Chen. Aktun-Chen is Mayan for "the cave with cenotes inside," and these amazing underground caves, estimated to be about 5 million years old, are the area's largest. You walk through the underground passages, past stalactites and stalagmites, until you reach the cenote with its various shades of deep green. There's also a canopy tour and one cenote where you can swim. This is a top family attraction, and one

Fodor's Choice
★

that's not as crowded or touristy as Xplor, Xel-Há, or Xcaret. ⊠ *Carretera 307, Km 107* ☎ *984/109–2061* ⊕ *www.aktunchen.com* ✉ *$26 cave tour, $38 canopy tour, $21 cenote tour; children 6 and under free* ⊙ *Mon.–Sat. 9–5.*

⛰️ **Muyil.** This photogenic archaeological site just 9 miles (15 km) down the 307 from Tulúm, at the northern end of the Sian Ka'an biosphere reserve, is underrated. Once known as Chunyaxché, it's now called by its ancient name, Muyil (pronounced moo-*hill*). It dates from the late preclassic era, when it was connected by road to the sea and served as a port between Cobá and the Mayan centers in Belize and Guatemala. A 15-foot-wide *sacbé*, built during the postclassic period, extended from the city to the mangrove swamp and was still in use when the Spaniards arrived. The most notable site at Muyil today is the remains of the 56-foot **Castillo**—one of the tallest on the Quintana Roo coast—at the center of a large acropolis. The ruins stand near the edge of a deep-blue lagoon and are surrounded by almost impenetrable jungle—so be sure to bring insect repellent. You can drive down a dirt road on the side of the ruins to swim or fish in the lagoon. The bird-watching is also exceptional here; come at dawn, before the site officially opens (there's no gate) to make the most of it. ⊠ *Carretera 307, 9 miles (15 km) south of Tulúm, Sian Ka'an* ⊕ *muyil. smv.org* ✉ *$3* ⊙ *Daily 8–5.*

PLAYA DEL CARMEN

Once upon a time, Playa del Carmen was a fishing village with a ravishing deserted beach. The villagers fished and raised coconut palms to produce copra, and the only foreigners who ventured here were beach bums and travelers catching ferries to Cozumel. That was a long time ago, however. These days the beach is far from deserted, although it is still delightful, with its alabaster-white sand and turquoise-blue waters. In fact Playa has become one of Latin America's fastest-growing communities, with a population of more than 135,000 and a pace almost as hectic as Cancún's. The ferry pier, where the hourly boats arrive from and depart for Cozumel, is another busy part of town. The streets leading from the dock have shops, restaurants, cafés, a hotel, and food stands. If you take a stroll north from the pier along the beach, you'll find the serious sun worshippers. On the pier's south side is the sprawling Playacar complex. The development is a labyrinth of residences and all-inclusive resorts bordered by an 18-hole championship golf course. ⛿ *3 miles (5 km) north of Calica.*

Xaman Ha Aviary. The excellent 32-acre Xaman Ha Aviary, in the middle of the Playacar development, is home to more than 30 species of native birds. Bring insect repellent. It's open daily 9 to 5, and admission is $22. ⊠ *Paseo Xaman-Ha, Playacar* ☎ *984/873–0330* ⊕ *www. aviarioxamanha.com.*

⛰️ **Tulum.** Tulúm is one of the few Mayan cities known to have been inhabited when the conquistadores arrived in 1518. In the 16th century it was a trade center, a safe harbor for trade goods from rival Mayan factions who considered the city neutral territory. Although you can see the ruins thoroughly in two hours, you might want to allow extra time

Fodor's Choice ★

for a swim or a stroll on the beach. The largest and most-photographed structure, the **Castillo** (Castle), looms at the edge of a 40-foot limestone cliff just past the Temple of the Frescoes. Atop it, at the end of a broad stairway, is a temple with stucco ornamentation on the outside and traces of fine frescoes inside the two chambers. A few small altars sit atop a hill at the north side of the cove, with a good view of the Castillo and the sea. ⊠ *Carretera 307, Km 133, Tulum* ☎ *983/837–2411* *$5 entrance, $3 parking, $4 video fee, $1.50 shuttle from parking to ruins* ⊙ *Daily 8–5.*

Xcaret. Among the most popular attractions are the Paradise River raft tour that takes you on a winding, watery journey through the jungle; the Butterfly Pavilion, where thousands of butterflies float dreamily through a botanical garden while New Age music plays in the background; and an ocean-fed aquarium where you can see local sea life drifting through coral heads and sea fans. The entrance fee covers only access to the grounds and the exhibits; all other activities and equipment—from sea treks and dolphin tours to lockers and swim gear—are extra. The $99 Plus Pass includes park entrance, lockers, snorkel equipment, food, and drinks. You can buy tickets from any travel agency or major hotel along the coast. ⊠ *Carretera 307, Km 282, Xcaret* ☎ *800/292–2738, 888/XCARET1 in US* ⊕ *www.xcaret. com* *$69 Basic Pass; $99 Plus Pass* ⊙ *Daily 8:30 am–9:30 pm in winter; open until 10:30 pm in summer.*

Xplor. Designed for thrill-seekers, this 125-acre park features underground rafting in stalactite-studded water caves and cenotes. Swim in a stalactite river, ride in an amphibian vehicle, or soar across the park on 13 of the longest zip-lines in Mexico. The price includes all food, drink, and equipment. ⊠ *Carretera 307, Km 282* ☎ *984/147– 6560, 888/XCARET1 in U.S.* ⊕ *www.xplor.travel* *$99* ⊙ *Mon.– Sat. 8:30–5.*

SHOPPING

Playa del Carmen's Avenida 5 between calles 4 and 10 is the best place to shop along the coast. Boutiques sell folk art and textiles from around Mexico, and clothing stores carry lots of sarongs and beachwear made from Indonesian batiks. A shopping area called Calle Corazon, between calles 12 and 14, has a pedestrian street, art galleries, restaurants, and boutiques.

Hacienda Tequila. Hacienda Tequila sells 480 different types of tequila and kitschy Mexican crafts and souvenirs. Free tastings are available, and there's an exhibit that walks you through the world of agave booze. ⊠ *Av. 5 and Calle 14, Playa del Carmen, Playa del Carmen* ☎ *984/803–0821.*

La Hierbabuena Artesanía. At La Hierbabuena Artesanía, owner Melinda Burns offers a collection of fine Mexican clothing and crafts. ⊠ *Av. 5 between Calles 8 and 10, Playa del Carmen* ☎ *984/873–1741.*

ACTIVITIES

DIVING

Abyss. The PADI- and SSI-affiliated Abyss offers introductory courses and dive trips ($50 for one tank, $70 for two tanks). They also run dives in Tulum, as Cenote Dive Center. ⊠ *Av. 1 between Calles 10 and 12, Playa del Carmen* ☎ *984/873–2164* ⊕ *www.abyssdiveshop.com.*

Tank-Ha Dive Center. Playa's original dive outfit, Tank-Ha Dive Center has PADI-certified teachers and runs diving and snorkeling trips to the reefs and caverns. A one-tank dive costs $45; for a two-tank trip it's $65. Dive packages are also available, as well as trips to Cozumel. ⊠ *Calle 10 between Avs. 5 and 10, Playa del Carmen, Playa del Carmen* ☎ *984/873–0302* ⊕ *www.tankha.com.*

GOLF

Casa Club de Golf. Playa del Carmen's golf course is an 18-hole, par-72 championship course designed by Robert von Hagge. The green fee is $180; there's also a special twilight fee of $120. Information is available from the Casa Club de Golf. ⊠ *Playa del Carmen* ☎ *984/873–0624, 998/881–6088.*

WHERE TO EAT

$$ ✕ **Babe's Noodles & Bar.** Photos and paintings of old Hollywood pinup
THAI   models share decor space with a large stone Buddha at this Swedish-
★   owned Thai restaurant, known for its fresh and interesting fare cooked to order. Try the spring rolls with peanut sauce, or the Korean sesame noodles, made with chicken or pork, veggies, chile, and sesame and peanut cream, and wash it all down with a refreshing lemonade, blended with ice and mint. If the original, dark and funky place is full, head to their second location on Avenida 5 between Calles 28 and 30. $ *Average main: $10* ⊠ *Calle 10 between Avs. 5 and 10, Playa del Carmen* ☎ *984/130–1006* ⊕ *www.babesnoodlesandbar.com* $ *Average main: $10* ⊠ *Av. 5 between Calles 28 and 30, Playa del Carmen* ☎ *984/745–1668.*

$ ✕ **Hot.** This cheap streetside breakfast café opens at 7 am, and it's one of
CAFÉ   the first places you can get breakfast before early-morning sightseeing. Known for Mexican egg dishes like the chile-and-cheese omelet, which will get your day off to a spicy start, Hot also serves more pedestrian packaged muffins and pastry. Salads and sandwiches are available at lunch. $ *Average main: $5* ⊠ *Calle 14 Norte, between Avs. 5 and 10, Playa del Carmen* ☎ *984/879–4520* ⊕ *www.hotbakingcompany.com* ⊟ *No credit cards.*

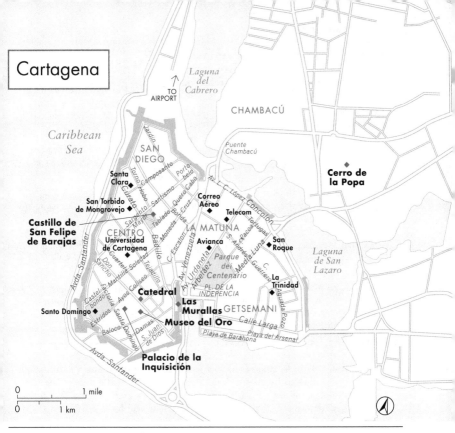

Cartagena

TO AIRPORT

Laguna del Cabrero

CHAMBACÚ

Caribbean Sea

SAN DIEGO

Puente Chambacú

Cerro de la Popa

Santa Clara

San Torbido de Mongrovejo

Castillo de San Felipe de Barajas

CENTRO

Universidad de Cartagena

Avda. Santander

Jardín

Torno Hoto

Camposanto

Portebelo

Salgado

Santismo

Tablada

Quero Cabo

Moneda

Honda

Cruz

C. Escalon

Badillo

C. Venezuela

Av. Urdaneta

Arbelaez

Correo Aéreo

Telecom

LA MATUNA

Av. L. C. López

Concolon

S. Andrés

Tortugas

San Roque

Medio Luna

C. Guerrero

Avianca

Parque del Centenario

PL. DE LA INDEPENCIA

La Trinidad

Laguna de San Lazaro

Santo Domingo

Catedral

Don Sancho

Castel

Victoria

Cuartel

Matritilla

Soledad

Taullillo

pondo

Estribos

Santa Domingo

Ayos

Coliseo

Damas

S. Juan de Dios

Balcco

GETSEMANI

Las Murallas

Museo del Oro

Calle Larga

Playa de Barahona

Playa del Arsenal

Aguada Pozo

Palacio de la Inquisición

Avda. Santander

0 — 1 mile
0 — 1 km

CARTAGENA, COLOMBIA

Marlise Kast

Ever wondered what the "Spanish Main" refers to? This is it. Colombia's Caribbean coast invokes ghosts of conquistadors, pirates, and missionaries journeying to the New World in search of wealth, whether material or spiritual. Anchoring this shore is the magnificent colonial city of Cartagena—officially *Cartagena de Indias* (Cartagena of the Indies)—founded in 1533. Gold and silver passed through here en route to Spain, making the city an obvious target for pirates, hence the construction of Cartagena's trademark walls and fortresses. Outside the *Ciudad Amurallada* (walled city) lie less historic beaches and water excursions. If Colombia conjures up images of drug lords and paramilitary guerillas, think again; security is quite visible (without being oppressive) here in the country's top tourist destination. Take the same precautions you would visiting any city of one million people, and you should have a grand time.

ESSENTIALS

CURRENCY The Colombian peso (COP 1,821 to US$1). In Colombia, peso prices are denoted with the "$" sign, too. If they carry a lot of zeros, they likely are not dollar prices, but always ask. ATMs are ubiquitous around town.

INTERNET   Upon arrival or before departure, you can check your email at the bank of computers in the Terminal de Cruceros.

SAFETY   Security is tighter in Cartagena than elsewhere in Colombia, so you certainly can navigate the city on your own. (Knowing some Spanish helps.) However, the scarcity of English speakers and English signage at the city's tourist attractions and the persistence of vendors, street touts, and the periodic con artist mean that many cruise passengers opt for the reassurance of an organized shore excursion. If you set out on your own, under no circumstances should you deal with anyone who approaches you on the street offering to change money; rip-offs are guaranteed.

TELEPHONE   The Terminal de Cruceros has ample phones for your use. Local numbers in Cartagena have seven digits. For international calls, dial 009 followed by country and area codes and local number. The U.S. mobile carrier AT&T offers roaming options in this region of Colombia for calls back to the United States; if you have a tri-band GSM phone it should work.

CARTAGENA BEST BETS

■ **Cruise the Harbor.** A boat trip around the city's inner bay allows to you appreciate the city's formidable walls and fortresses.

■ **Islas del Rosario.** The beaches of nearby Islas del Rosario are an hour away by boat.

■ **Ride a Coche.** Take the quintessential horse-and-buggy ride through the streets.

■ **Walk Las Murallas.** Walking the city's massive stone walls is a favorite tourist pastime.

■ **Visit Palacio de la Inquisición.** Cartagena's most-visited sight is this historic—and creepy—center for the Spanish Inquisition.

COMING ASHORE

Cruise ships dock at the modern Terminal de Cruceros (cruise terminal) on Isla de Manga, an island connected by a bridge to the historic city center, about 2 miles (3 km) northwest of the docks. You'll find telephones, Internet cafés, and a duty-free shop in the terminal.

A small army of taxis waits in front of the terminal. Expect to pay 15,000 pesos for the 10-minute drive to the walled city; the same fare will get you to the nearby beaches at Bocagrande. Drivers are all too happy to take you on your own do-it-yourself guided tour. Most charge around 18,000 pesos for an hour of waiting time. There's little need to rent a car here. Cartagena, at least the area of tourist interest, is so compact, and walking the labyrinth of cobblestone streets in the Old City is far more enjoyable than driving.

EXPLORING CARTAGENA

Nothing says Cartagena quite like a ride in a horse-drawn carriage, or *coche,* as it is known locally. Drivers are a wealth of information about Cartagena, and many do speak English. The downside for you is that most rides begin near dusk—it's a far cooler time of the day, after all—and your need to be back on ship may not coincide with that schedule. Do check. You can pick up carriages at many places, including the Plaza de los Coches, near the Puerta del Reloj in the walled city, or the Hotel Caribe in Bocagrande. Expect to pay around $200 (in U.S. dollars) for a two-hour tour, or around $60 for a half-hour (this kind of excursion is best when the cost is split among a group).

Castillo de San Felipe de Barajas. Designed by Antonio de Arévalo in 1639, the Fort of St. Philip's steep-angled brick and concrete battlements were arranged so that if part of the castle were conquered the rest could still be defended. A maze of tunnels, minimally lit today to allow for spooky exploration, still connects vital points of the fort. Notice the near-perfect acoustics in the tunnels here: Occupants could hear the footsteps of the approaching enemy. The climb is strenuous, but you'll be rewarded with some of the best views in Cartagena. You can walk here from the walled city in about 30 minutes. A taxi ride—expect to pay about 10,000 pesos one way—is the easier option. ⊠ *Av. Pedro de Heredia at Carrera 17* ☏ *575/666–4790* ☒ *18,000 pesos* ☉ *Daily 8–6.*

Catedral Metropolitana. Any Latin American city centers on its cathedral and main square. Plaza de Bolívar—a statue of South American liberator Simón Bolívar stands watch over the square—is a shady place from which to admire Cartagena's 16th-century cathedral. (It's officially the "Catedral Basílica Metropolitana de Santa Catalina de Alejandria.") Construction lasted from 1577 to 1612. British pirates attacked and pillaged the site about halfway through the process, a fate that befell many buildings in Cartagena in those early days. The colorful bell tower and dome date from the early 20th century. Inside is a massive gilded altar. ⊠ *Plaza de Bolívar* ☏ *575/664–5308* ⊕ *www.arquicartagenadeindias.org.*

Fodor's Choice **Cerro de la Popa.** For spectacular views of Cartagena, ascend this hill
★ around sunset. Because of its strategic location, the 17th-century monastery here intermittently served as a fortress during the colonial era. It now houses a museum and a chapel dedicated to the Virgen de la Candelaria, Cartagena's patron saint. Taxis charge around 8,000 pesos one way to bring you here—have them wait—and the sight can be included on one of Cartagena's popular chiva (horsedrawn carriage) tours. ⚠ **Under no circumstances should you walk between the city center and the hill; occasional muggings of tourists have been reported along the route.** ⊠ *2 miles (3 km) southeast of Ciudad Amurallada* ☏ *575/666–2331* ☒ *8,000 pesos* ☉ *Daily 8:30–5.*

Las Murallas. Cartagena survived only because of its walls, and its *murallas* remain today the city's most distinctive feature. Repeated sacking by pirates and foreign invaders convinced the Spaniards of the need to enclose the region's most important port. Construction began in 1600 and finished in 1796. The Puerta del Reloj is the principal gate to the innermost sector of the walled city. Its four-sided clock tower was a relatively late addition (1888) and has become the symbol of the city. Walking along the thick walls is still today one of Cartagena's time honored pastimes, especially late in the afternoon when you can watch the setting sun redden the Caribbean. ✉ *Area bounded by Bahía de las Ánimas, Laguna de San Lázaro, and Caribbean Sea.*

Museo del Oro y Arqueología. The Gold and Archaeological Museum, an institution funded and operated by Colombia's Central Bank, displays an assortment of artifacts culled from the Sinús, an indigenous group that lived in this region 2,000 years ago. ✉ *Carrera 4 No. 33–26* ☎ *575/660–0778* 🎫 *Free* ☉ *Tues.–Fri. 10–1 and 3–7, Sat. 10–1 and 2–5, Sun. 11–4.*

Fodor'sChoice
★
Palacio de la Inquisición. Arguably Cartagena's most visited tourist site documents the darkest period in the city's history. A baroque limestone doorway marks the entrance to the 1770 Palace of the Inquisition, the headquarters of the repressive arbiters of political and spiritual orthodoxy who once exercised jurisdiction over Colombia, Ecuador, and Venezuela. Although the museum displays benign colonial and pre-Columbian artifacts, everyone congregates on the ground floor to "Eeewww!" over the implements of torture—racks and thumbscrews, to name but two. We recommend you hire an English-speaking guide since many of the displays need explainations and all signs are in Spanish. ✉ *Carrera 4 No. 33–26* ☎ *575/665–4229* 🎫 *14,000 pesos* ☉ *Mon.–Sat. 9–6, Sun. 10–4.*

SHOPPING

Think "Juan Valdez" if you're looking for something to take the folks back home. Small bags of fine Colombian coffee, the country's signature souvenir, are available in most tourist-oriented shops. Colombia also means emeralds, and you'll find plenty in the jewelry shops on or near Calle Pantaleón, beside the cathedral. Don't forget the duty-free shop in the Terminal de Cruceros for those last-minute purchases.

Las Bóvedas, a series of arched storerooms in the Ciudad Amurallada's northern corner now houses about two-dozen shops with the best selection of local and national crafts. If you're looking for emeralds, visit the jewelry shops on or near Calle Pantaleón, beside the cathedral.

ACTIVITIES

DIVING
Coral reefs line the coast south of Cartagena, although warm-water currents have begun to erode them in recent years. There is still good diving to be had in the Islas del Rosario, an archipelago of 27 coral islands about 21 miles (35 km) southwest of the city.

Buzos de Barú. Buzos de Barú at the Hotel Caribe organizes snorkeling trips to the Islas del Rosario, scuba diving at underwater-wreck sites, and dive instruction. ✉ *Hotel Caribe, Local 9, Bocagrande* ☎ *575/665–7675* ⊕ *www.buzosdebaru.com.*

BEACHES

For white sand and palm trees, your best bet is **Playa Blanca,** about 15 minutes away by boat. Many people opt for a visit to the **Islas del Rosario,** a verdant archipelago surrounded by aquamarine waters and coral reefs. Tour boats leave from the Muelle de los Pegasos, the pier flanked by statues of two flying horses that is just outside the city walls. Plenty of men with boats will also offer to take you on the one-hour journey. A final option is **Bocagrande,** the resort area on a 3-mile-long (5-km-long) peninsula south of the walled city. High-rise hotels and condos front the gray-sand beach. It gets quite crowded and is very lively, but Bocagrande is probably not the Caribbean beach of which you've always dreamed.

WHERE TO EAT

$$ × **Café San Pedro.** Although it serves Colombian fare, this restaurant's ECLECTIC eclectic menu also includes dishes from Thailand, Italy, and Japan. You can also drop by to have a drink and to watch the activity on the plaza from one of the outdoor tables. $ *Average main: $22,000* ⊠ *Plaza San Pedro, Claver 30–11* ☏ *575/664–5121* ☯ *Closed Sun.*

$$ × **Paco's.** Heavy beams, rough terra-cotta walls, wooden benches, and LATIN AMERICAN tunes from an aging Cuban band are the hallmarks of this downtown eatery. Drop by for a drink and some tapas, or try the more substantial *langostinos a la sifú* (lobsters fried in batter). You can sit in the dining room or outside on the Plaza Santo Domingo. $ *Average main: $25,000* ⊠ *Plaza Santo Domingo, Calle 35 No. 3–02* ☏ *575/660–1638.*

COLÓN, PANAMA

David Duden-hoefer and Jeffrey Van Fleet

When you consider the decades it took to build the canal, not to mention the lives lost and government failures and triumphs involved during its construction, it comes as no surprise that the Panama Canal is often called the Eighth Wonder of the Modern World. Best described as an aquatic bridge, the Panama Canal connects the Caribbean Sea with the Pacific Ocean by raising ships up and over Central America, through artificially created Gatún Lake, the highest point at 85 feet above sea level, and then lowering them back to sea level by using a series of locks, or water steps. A masterful engineering feat, three pairs of locks—Gatún, Pedro Miguel, and Miraflores—utilize gravity to fill and drain as ships pass through chambers 1,000 feet long by 110 feet wide that are "locked" by doors weighing 80 tons apiece, yet actually float into position. Most cruise ships pass through the canal seasonally, when repositioning from one coast to the other; however, partial transits have become an increasingly popular "destination" on regularly scheduled 10- and 11-night Caribbean itineraries. These loop cruises enter the canal from the Caribbean Sea and sail into Gatún Lake, where they remain for a few hours as passengers are tendered ashore for excursions. Ships then pass back through the locks, returning to the Caribbean and stopping at either Cristobal Pier or Colón 2000 Pier to retrieve passengers at the conclusion of their tours.

A day transiting the canal's Gatún Locks begins before dawn as your passenger ship passes through *Bahia Limon* and lines up with dozens of other vessels to await its turn to enter. Before your ship can proceed, two pilots and a narrator will board. The sight of a massive cruise ship

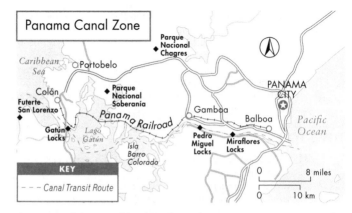

being raised dozens of feet into the air by water is so mesmerizing that passengers eagerly crowd all forward decks at the first lock. If you don't find a good viewing spot, head for the rear decks, where there is usually more room and the view is just as intriguing. If you remain aboard, as many passengers do, you'll find plenty of room up front later in the day as your ship retraces its path down to the sea. Due to the tight scheduling of the day's activities—it takes at least 90 minutes for a ship to pass through Gatún Locks—passengers who wish to go ashore early in the day are advised to sign up for one of the many available shore excursions.

ESSENTIALS

CURRENCY   The U.S. dollar, called the balboa, is the currency in Panama; the country does mint its own coins.

INTERNET   There's an Internet café at the Colón 2000 Pier.

TELEPHONE   You'll find telephones inside Colón's cruise terminal where you can purchase phone cards, a handy and inexpensive way to make calls.

COMING ASHORE

Colón, Panama's second-largest city, has little to offer of historic interest, and is simply a jumping-off point to the rain forest and a wide variety of organized tours. Infrequent cruise itineraries may include a day docked in Colón, rather than a partial canal transit. However, no matter how much time your ship spends in Colón, it is usually easier (and recommended) to take an organized shore excursion. If you don't want to go on a ship-sponsored shore excursion, taxi drivers also await ship arrivals, and some can be acceptable private guides for $100 to $120 per day if you just want to explore Portabelo or San Lorenzo. However, as in any foreign port, before setting out with any unofficial car and driver, you should set a firm price and agree upon an itinerary as well as look over the vehicle carefully. It's also possible to rent a car from either Budget or Hertz, both of which have desks at the Colón 2000 terminal.

Although entry time into the canal is always approximate, passenger ships have priority, and most pass through Gatún Locks early in the morning. Passengers booked on shore excursions begin the tendering process soon after the ship sets anchor, which can be as early as 8:30 am. Alternatives to excursions offered by your cruise ship are available from independent tour operators that can be arranged in advance through websites or travel agents. You will likely be informed that Panamanian regulations restrict passengers going ashore in Gatún Lake to only those who have booked the cruise line's excursions; however, anyone who has a shore-excursion reservation with a local company should be able to leave the vessel. Before making independent tour arrangements, confirm with your cruise line that you will be allowed to go ashore after presenting your private tour confirmation to the shore-excursion staff on board the ship.

> ## COLÓN BEST BETS
>
> ■ **Explore an Embera Village.** You'll travel by dugout canoe through Chagres National Park.
>
> ■ **Kayak on Gatún Lake.** You can paddle among the many islands and mangrove forests.
>
> ■ **Panama Railway.** Take a train trip to Panama City for a quick sightseeing tour (you can come back by taxi to save some time).
>
> ■ **Portobelo.** Visit historic Panamanian forts.
>
> ■ **Rain Forest Aerial Tram.** Travel to Gamboa Rainforest Resort and see the rain forest canopy from above.

Upon completion of either full or partial canal transits, cruise ships generally dock at either Cristobal Pier or Colón 2000 Pier late in the afternoon, where they may remain for several hours. Passengers who remained on board throughout the canal passage have the opportunity to go ashore, and land tours end at the terminals, where passengers rejoin the ship. A second terminal opened in 2008 and became the homeport for Royal Caribbean's *Enchantment of the Seas*, with the Panamanian government aggressively courting other cruise companies to set up shop here as well. All of Colón is considered a high-crime area, and pickpockets have been known to strike even in the seemingly secure areas of the cruise-ship terminals. If you go ashore, you are well advised to leave jewelry and other valuables aboard ship and carry only the cash you need.

EXPLORING THE PANAMA CANAL ZONE

The provincial capital of **Colón,** beside the canal's Atlantic entrance, has clearly seen better days, as the architecture of its older buildings attests. Its predominantly Afro-Caribbean population has long had a vibrant musical scene, and in the late 19th and early 20th centuries Colón was a relatively prosperous town. But it spent the second half of the 20th century in steady decay, and things have only gotten worse in the 21st century. For the most part, the city is a giant slum, with unemployment at 30% to 40% and crime on the rise. ⚠ **Travelers who explore Colón on foot are simply asking to be mugged,** and the route between the train station and the bus terminal is especially notorious; do all your traveling in a taxi or rental car. If you do the Panama Railway trip on your own without a tour company, take one of the shuttle vans or hire a taxi to the train station.

Esclusas de Gatún (*Gatún Locks*). Seven miles (12 km) south of Colón are the Esclusas de Gatún, a triple-lock complex that's nearly a mile long and raises and lowers ships the 85 feet between sea level and Gatún Lake. There's a small viewing platform at the locks and a simple visitor center that's nothing compared to the center at Miraflores Locks. However, the sheer magnitude of the Gatún Locks—they are the canal's largest—is impressive, especially when packed with ships. You have to cross the locks on a swinging bridge to get to San Lorenzo and the **Represa Gatún** (Gatún Dam), which holds the water in Gatún Lake. At 1½ miles long, it was the largest dam in the world when it was built, a title it held for several decades. Get there by taking the first left after crossing the locks. ⊠ *7 miles (12 km) south of Colón* ▦ *Free* ☉ *Daily 8–4.*

Fuerte San Lorenzo (*San Lorenzo Fort*). Perched on a cliff overlooking the mouth of the Chagres River are the ruins of the ancient Spanish Fuerte San Lorenzo, destroyed by pirate Henry Morgan in 1671 and rebuilt shortly after, then bombarded a century later. The Spaniards built Fort San Lorenzo in 1595 in an effort to protect the South American gold they were shipping down the Chagres River. The fortress's commanding position and abundant cannons weren't enough of a deterrent for Morgan, whose men managed to shoot flaming arrows into the fort, causing a fire that set off stored gunpowder and forced the Spanish troops to surrender. Morgan then led his men up the river and across the isthmus to sack Panamá Viejo. In the 1980s UNESCO restored the fort to its current condition, which is pretty sparse—it hardly compares to the extensive colonial ruins of Portobelo. Nevertheless, the setting is gorgeous, and the view from that promontory of the blue-green Caribbean, the coast, and the vast jungle behind it is breathtaking. ⚠ **Be careful walking around the edge outside the fort; there are some treacherous precipices, and guardrails are almost nonexistent. One visitor did have a fatal fall several years ago.** ⊠ *14 miles (23 km) northwest of Gatún Locks* ▦ *Free* ☉ *Daily 8–4.*

LAGO GATÚN (*GATÚN LAKE*)

Covering about 163 square miles, an area about the size of the island nation Barbados, Gatún Lake extends northwest from Parque Nacional Soberanía to the locks of Gatún, just south of Colón. The lake was created when the U.S. government dammed the Chagres River, between 1907 and 1913, so that boats could cross the isthmus at 85 feet above sea level. By creating the lake, the United States saved decades of digging that a sea-level canal would have required. When it was completed, Gatún Lake was the largest man-made lake in the world. The canal route winds through its northern half, past several forest-covered islands (the largest is Barro Colorado, one of the world's first biological reserves). The lake itself is home to crocodiles, manatees, and peacock bass, a species introduced from South America and popular with fishermen. Fishing charters for bass, snook, and tarpon are out of Gamboa.

PORTOBELO

★ Portobelo is an odd mix of colonial fortresses, clear waters, lushly forested hills, and an ugly little town of cement-block houses crowded amid the ancient walls. It holds some of Panama's most interesting colonial ruins, with rusty cannons still lying in wait for an enemy assault, and is a UNESCO World Heritage Site, together with San Lorenzo.

Iglesia de San Felipe. One block east of the Real Aduana is the Iglesia de San Felipe, a large white church dating from 1814 that's home to the country's most venerated religious figure: the **Cristo Negro** (Black Christ). According to legend, that statue of a dark-skinned Jesus carrying a cross arrived in Portobelo in the 17th century on a Spanish ship bound for Cartagena, Colombia. Each time the ship tried to leave, it encountered storms and had to return to port, convincing the captain to leave the statue in Portobelo. Each year the Cristo Negro is clothed in a new purple robe, donated by somebody who's earned the honor. Many of the robes that have been created for the statue over the past century are on display in the Museo del Cristo Negro (Black Christ Museum) in the Iglesia de San Juan, a smaller, 17th-century church next to the Iglesia de San Felipe. ⊠ *Calle Principal, Portobelo* ☎ *$1* ⊘ *Weekdays 8–4, weekends 8:30–3.*

Parque Nacional Portobelo (*Portobelo National Park*). The forested hills that rise up behind the bay are part of Parque Nacional Portobelo, a vast marine and rain-forest reserve contiguous with Chagres National Park. Though several towns lie within the park, and much of its lowlands were deforested years ago, its inaccessible mountains are covered with dense forest that holds plenty of flora and fauna. Extending from offshore coral reefs up to the cloud forest atop 3,212-foot Cerro Brujo, the park comprises an array of ecosystems and is rich in biodiversity. The coastal area is home to everything from ospreys to sea turtles, and the mountains shelter spider monkeys, brocket deer, harpy eagles, and an array of other endangered wildlife. There is no proper park entrance, but you can explore patches of its forested coast and mangrove estuaries on boat trips from Portobelo, when you might see birds such as the ringed kingfisher and fasciated tiger heron.

Portobelo's largest and most impressive fort is **Fuerte San Jerónimo,** at the end of the bay, which is surrounded by the "modern" town. It was built in the 1600s but was destroyed by English Admiral Edward Vernon and rebuilt to its current state in 1758. Its large interior courtyard was once a parade ground, but it's now the venue for all annual celebrations involving congo dancers, including New Year's, Carnaval, the Festival de Diablos y Congos (shortly after Carnaval), and the town's patron saint's day (March 20).

Fuerte San Fernando, one of three Spanish forts you can visit at Portobelo, is surrounded by forest and is a good place to see birds. It lies directly across the bay from Batería Santiago, on the left as you drive toward town. Look for a large structure with cannons pointed at the entrance to the bay. The youngest of Portobelo's forts, **Batería Santiago** was built in the 1860s, after Vernon's fateful attack. The thick walls are coral, which was cut from the platform reefs that line the coast.

Coral was more abundant and easier to cut than the igneous rock found inland, so the Spanish used it for most construction in Portobelo. ■ TIP➔ Local boatmen who are usually sitting near the dock next to Batería Santiago can take you across the bay to explore Fuerte San Fernando for **$3**. They also offer transportation to several local beaches, as well as a trip into the estuary at the end of the bay. ⊠ *Surrounding Portobelo, Portobelo* ☎ *448–2165, 442–8348* ⌑ *Free* ☉ *24 hrs.*

Real Aduana (*Royal Customs House*). Near the entrance to Fuerte San Jerónimo is the Real Aduana, where servants of the Spanish crown made sure that the king and queen got their cut from every ingot that rolled through town. Built in 1630, the Real Aduana was damaged during pirate attacks and then destroyed by an earthquake in 1882, only to be rebuilt in 1998. It is an interesting example of colonial architecture—note the carved coral columns on the ground floor—and it houses a simple museum with some old coins, cannonballs, and displays on Panamanian folklore. ⊠ *Calle de la Aduana, Portobelo* ⌑ *$1* ☉ *Tues.–Sat. 9–4, weekends 8:30–3.*

SHOPPING

Both Cristobal Pier and Colón 2000 Pier have large shopping malls, where you will find Internet access, telephones, refreshments, and duty-free souvenir shops in relatively secure environments. Stores in both locations feature local crafts such as baskets, wood carvings, and toys, as well as liquor, jewelry, and the ubiquitous souvenir T-shirts. In addition to shops and cafés, Cristobal Pier features an open-air arts and craft market; Colón 2000 Pier has a well-stocked supermarket. Portobelo has a wide-ranging artisan market next to Iglesia de San Felipe.

The most unique locally made souvenirs are colorful appliquéd *molas,* the whimsical textile artwork created by native Kuna women, who come from the San Blas Islands; they are likely to be hand stitching new designs while they sell the ones they just completed. If you take an excursion to Portobelo, the prices may be better there where several Kuna women are usually selling their molas in the artisan market next to the church.

WHERE TO EAT

$$
SEAFOOD
✕ **Restaurante Los Cañones.** This rambling restaurant with tables among palm trees and Caribbean views is one of Panama's most attractive lunch spots. The food and service fall a little short of the setting, but not so far that you'd want to scratch it from your list. In good weather, dine at tables edging the sea surrounded by dark boulders and lush foliage. The other option is the open-air restaurant, decorated with shells, buoys, and driftwood, with a decent view of the bay and forested hills. House specialties include *pescado entero* (whole fried red snapper), *langosta al ajillo* (lobster scampi), and *centolla al jengibre* (king crab in a ginger sauce). ⑤ *Average main: $12* ⊠ *1 mile (2 km) before Portobelo on left* ☎ *448–2980* ▭ *No credit cards* ☉ *Closes at 7 pm.*

COSTA MAYA, MEXICO

Valerie
Hamilton

Puerto Costa Maya is an anomaly. Unlike other tourist attractions in the area (the island of Cozumel being the primary Yucatán cruise port), this port of call near Mahahual has been created exclusively for cruise-ship passengers. The port added a second berth in July 2008. This latest addition known as "New Mahahual" is comprised of theme restaurants like Hard Rock Cafe and Señor Frog's, as well as boutique shops and chain stores such as Lapis Jewelry.

At first glance, the port complex itself may seem to be little more than an outdoor mall. The docking pier (which can accommodate three ships at once) leads to a 70,000-square-foot bazaar-type compound where shops selling local crafts—jewelry, pottery, woven straw hats and bags, and embroidered dresses—are interspersed with duty-free stores and souvenir shops. There are two alfresco restaurants, which serve seafood, American-friendly Mexican dishes like tacos and quesadillas, and cocktails at shaded tables. An outdoor amphitheater stages eight daily performances of traditional music and dance.

The strip of beach edging the complex has been outfitted with colorful lounge chairs and *hamacas* (hammocks), and may tempt you to linger and sunbathe. If you want to have a truly authentic Mexican experience, though, you'll take advantage of the day tours offered to outlying areas. These give you a chance to see some of the really spectacular sights in this part of Mexico, many of which are rarely visited. This is one port where the shore excursion is the point, and there are no options except to purchase what your ship offers. You can preview what excursions may be offered on the Puerto Costa Maya's own website.

Among the best tours are those that let you explore the gorgeous (and usually deserted) Mayan ruin sites of Kohunlich, Dzibanché, and Chacchoben. The ancient pyramids and temples at these sites, surrounded by jungle that's protected them for centuries, are still dazzling to behold. Since the sites are some distance from the port complex—and require some road travel in one of the port's air-conditioned vans—these tours are all-day affairs. One of the most popular activities with cruise passengers is the three-hour ATV excursion along jungle roads and the Mahahual coastline. Although an adventure,

---

COSTA MAYA BEST BETS

- **Chacchoben.** This archaeological site is near the Belize border.

- **Kohunlich.** This ruined city is best known for its great temples with sculpted masks.

- **Mahahual.** This small fishing village (pronounced *Ma-ha-wal*) near the cruise pier has plenty of fine sand and glassy waters for a cushy afternoon in the sun.

- **Snorkeling at Banco Chinchorro.** Excellent catamaran snorkeling trips go here.

- **Xcalak.** This national reserve offers excellent saltwater fly-fishing and deserted beaches.

4

the ATVs tend to be a nuisance to residents and business owners, not to mention wildlife.

Prior to a devastating 2007 hurricane, there was no real reason to go into the small, nearby fishing village of Mahahual (pronounced ma-ha-*wal*). Though there are still about 300 residents, post-hurricane renovations have put the village on the map; it now has its own pier as well as a smattering of hotels, restaurants, and shops. Be sure to venture beyond "New Mahahual," which lacks the charm of the nearby beachfront area. Its cement boardwalk along the beach has made Mahahual an ideal spot for a sunset stroll. The crystal-clear waters and unspoiled beaches are delightful for snorkeling, diving, and fishing.

ESSENTIALS

CURRENCY   The Mexican peso. U.S. dollars and credit cards are accepted by everyone at the port. There is no advantage to paying in dollars, but there may be an advantage to paying in cash.

INFORMATION   **Puerto Costa Maya** ⊕ *www.puertocostamaya.com.*

TELEPHONE   In most parts of the country, pay phones (predominantly operated by Telmex) accept only prepaid cards (*tarjetas Lada*), sold in 30-, 50-, 100-, or 200-peso denominations at newsstands, pharmacies, minimarkets, or grocery stores. Coin-only pay phones are few and far between.

WHERE TO EAT

$ ✗ **100% Agave.** Fernando's beloved palapa shack is a Mahahual institution, with a friendly, homey atmosphere that's made the restaurant a sort of ersatz visitor bureau. The affordable menu features Mexican and Yucatecan specialties with a generous splash of gringo—great food that's an even better bang for your buck. Should you be in the market for a margarita, don't be shy—this is the place for expert guidance on all things agave, as suggested by the name, and the man-size tequila bottle out front. ⑤ *Average main: $5* ⊠ *Calle Huachinango, 2nd road parallel to the Malecon, Mahahual* ▭ *No credit cards.*

MEXICAN
★

$ ✗ **Nacional Beach Club.** Many travelers stumble on this colorful beach club and end up staying past sunset. For just $10, you get a beach chair, umbrella, and access to the pool, shower, and changing facilities. Margaritas can be delivered to you beachside or you can escape the heat by grabbing a bite in the enclosed patio. By day you can munch on tacos, enchiladas, and sandwiches and by night enjoy the delicious smoked fish or grilled shrimp. The $2 Coronas and free Wi-Fi make this a popular spot to while away the day. There are also three bungalows for rent if you feel like staying the night. ⑤ *Average main: $8* ⊠ *Av. Mahahual, Mahahual* ☎ *983/110–5354 cell, 983/834–5719* ⊕ *www. nacionalbeachclub.com* ▭ *No credit cards.*

MEXICAN
★

COZUMEL, MEXICO

Valerie
Hamilton

Cozumel, with its sun-drenched ivory beaches fringed with coral reefs, fulfills the tourist's vision of a tropical Caribbean island. It's a heady mix of the natural and the commercial. Despite a mini-construction boom in the island's sole city, San Miguel, there are still wild pockets scattered throughout the island where flora and fauna flourish. Smaller than Cancún, Cozumel surpasses its fancier neighbor in many ways. It has more history and ruins, superior diving and snorkeling, more authentic cuisine, and a greater diversity of handicrafts at better prices. The numerous coral reefs, particularly the world-renowned Palancar Reef, attract divers from around the world. On a busy cruise-ship day the island can seem completely overrun, but it's still possible to get away, and some good Mayan sights are within reach on long (and expensive) shore excursions.

ESSENTIALS

CURRENCY The Mexican peso. U.S. dollars and credit cards are widely accepted in the area, from the port to Playa del Carmen, but it's best to have pesos—and small bills—when you visit ruins where cashiers often run out of change. There is no advantage to paying in dollars, but there may be an advantage to paying in cash.

INTERNET **Coffeenet** ⊠ *Av. Rafael E. Melgar at Calle 11* ☎ *987/872–6394* ⊕ *coffeenet.freeservers.com.*

TELEPHONE In most parts of the country, pay phones (predominantly operated by Telmex) accept only prepaid cards (*tarjetas Lada*), sold in 30-, 50-, 100-, or 200-peso denominations at newsstands, pharmacies, minimarkets, or grocery stores. Coin-only pay phones are few and far between. Most people use their own cell phones.

COMING ASHORE

As many as six ships call at Cozumel on a busy day, tendering passengers to the downtown pier in the center of San Miguel or docking at the two international piers 4 miles (6 km) away. From the downtown pier you can walk into town or catch the ferry to Playa del Carmen. Taxi tours are also available. A four-hour island tour (4 people maximum), including the ruins and other sights, costs about $70 to $100, but negotiate the price before you get in the cab. The international pier is close to many beaches, but you'll need a taxi to get into town. There's rarely a wait for a taxi, but prices are high, and drivers are often aggressive, asking double or triple the reasonable fare. When in doubt, ask to see the rate card required of all taxi drivers. Expect to pay $10 for the ride into San Miguel from the pier. Tipping is not necessary.

Passenger ferries to Playa del Carmen leave Cozumel's main pier approximately every other hour from 5 am to 10 pm. They also leave Playa del Carmen's dock about every other hour on the hour, from 6 am to 11 pm (but note that service sometimes varies according to demand). The trip takes 45 minutes. Verify the times: bad weather and changing schedules can prompt cancellations.

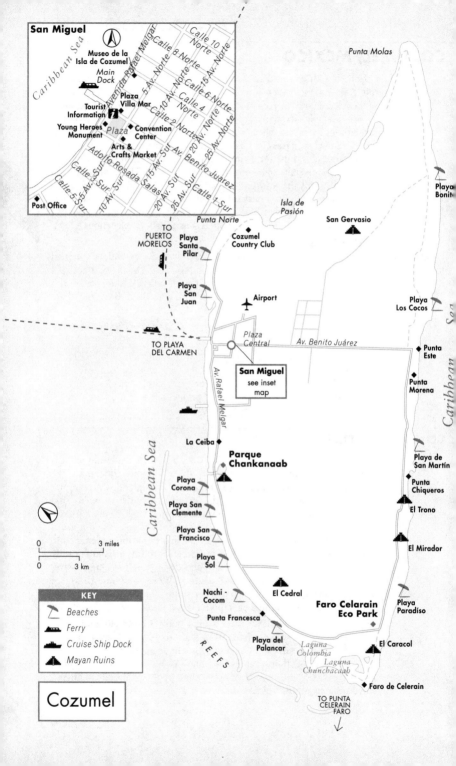

EXPLORING COZUMEL

San Miguel is not tiny, but you can easily explore the waterfront and plaza area on foot. The main attractions are the small eateries and shops that line the streets and the main square, where the locals congregate in the evening.

> **SHIP SALES**
>
> If you find prices on board too much to bear, shop the ship's boutiques on the last day of your cruise, when they are likely to run special sales.

El Cedral. Spanish explorers discovered this site, once the hub of Mayan life on Cozumel, in 1518. Later it became the island's first official city, founded in 1847. Today it's a farming community with small, well-tended houses and gardens. Conquistadores tore down much of the Mayan temple, and the U.S. Army Corps of Engineers destroyed the rest to make way for the island's first airport during World War II. So there's little in the way of actual ruins apart from one small stone arch, but if you're in the market for souvenirs, vendors around the main plaza display embroidered blouses and hammocks. ⊠ *Turn at Km 17.5 off Carretera Sur or Av. Rafael E. Melgar, then drive 2 miles (3 km) inland to site* ⊡ *Free* ☉ *Daily dawn–dusk.*

Faro Celarain Eco Park. This 247-acre national preserve at Cozumel's southernmost tip is a protected habitat for numerous birds and animals, including crocodiles, flamingos, egrets, and herons. At the park's (and the island's) southernmost point stands the **Faro de Celarain,** a lighthouse that's now a museum of navigation. Climb the 134 steps to the top for the best view on the island. Spot crocodiles and birds from observation towers near **Laguna Colombia** or **Laguna Chunchacaab,** or visit the ancient Mayan lighthouse **El Caracol,** designed to whistle when the wind blows in a certain direction. Beaches here are wide and deserted, and there's great snorkeling offshore. Snorkeling equipment is available for rent, as are kayaks, and there are restrooms at the museum and by the beach. Leave your car at the Faro and take park shuttles or rental bikes to the beach. Without a rental car, expect to pay about $40 for a round-trip taxi ride from San Miguel. ⊠ *Southernmost point of Carretera Sur and coastal road* ⊡ *$14* ☉ *Daily 8–4.*

Parque Chankanaab. The National Park of Chankanaab, translated as "small sea," consists of a saltwater lagoon, an archaeological park, and a botanical garden, with reproductions of a Mayan village and Olmec, Toltec, Aztec, and Mayan stone carvings scattered throughout.

You can swim, scuba dive, or snorkel at the beach. There's plenty to see beneath the surface: underwater caverns, a sunken ship, crusty old cannons and anchors, and a sculpture of la Virgen del Mar (Virgin of the Sea), all populated by parrotfish and sergeant majors galore. To preserve the ecosystem, park rules forbid touching the reef or feeding the fish. You'll also find dive shops, restaurants, gift shops, a snack stand, and dressing rooms with lockers and showers right on the sand. ⊠ *Carretera Sur, Km 9* ☎ *987/872–9760* ⊕ *www.cozumelparks.com* ⊡ *$21* ☉ *Daily 8–4.*

ⵌ **San Gervasio.** Surrounded by a forest, these temples make up Cozumel's largest remaining Mayan and Toltec site. San Gervasio was the island's capital and ceremonial center, dedicated to the fertility goddess Ixchel. The classic- and postclassic-style buildings and temples were continuously occupied from AD 300 to 1500. Typical architectural features include limestone plazas and arches atop stepped platforms, as well as stelae and bas-reliefs. Be sure to see the temple "Las Manitas," with red handprints all over its altar. Plaques in Mayan, Spanish, and English clearly describe each structure. ⊠ *From San Miguel, take cross-island road (follow signs to airport) east to San Gervasio access road; turn left and follow road 4½ miles (7 km)* ☎ *987/871–4431* ⊠ *$8* ☉ *Daily 8–4.*

> ## COZUMEL BEST BETS
>
> ■ **Diving and Snorkeling.** Excellent reefs close to shore make either diving or snorkeling a must-do activity.
>
> ■ **Mayan Ruins.** Some of the most famous and dazzling ruins are reachable from Cozumel, and if you have never seen a Mayan pyramid, this is your chance.
>
> ■ **People-watching.** You can spend hours just sitting in the main plaza (or at a sidewalk café) watching island life pass by.

★ **San Miguel.** San Miguel is Cozumel's only town. The waterfront has been taken over by large shops selling jewelry, imported rugs, leather boots, and souvenirs to cruise-ship passengers, but the northern end of the *malecón*, past Calle 10 Norte, is a pleasant area lined with sculptures of Mayan gods and goddesses that draws more locals than tourists. The town feels more traditional as you head inland to the pedestrian streets around the plaza, where family-owned restaurants and shops cater to locals and savvy travelers. There are plenty of benches for watching the action. Facing the square is an artisan's market, a good stop for souvenirs. ⊠ *Cozumel.*

Museo de la Isla de Cozumel. Filling two floors of a former hotel, Cozumel's island museum has displays on natural history—the island's origins, endangered species, topography, and coral-reef ecology—as well as human history during the pre-Columbian and colonial periods. The photos of the island's transformation over the 20th and 21st centuries are especially fascinating, as is the exhibit of a typical Mayan home. Guided tours are available. ⊠ *Av. Rafael E. Melgar, between Calles 4 and 6 Norte* ☎ *987/872–1475* ⊠ *$4* ☉ *Daily 9–5, Sun closes at 4.*

SHOPPING

Cozumel's main souvenir-shopping area is downtown along Avenida Rafael E. Melgar and on some side streets around the plaza. There are also clusters of shops at **Plaza del Sol** (east side of the main plaza) and **Vista del Mar** (⊠ *Av. Rafael E. Melgar 45*). As a general rule, the newer, trendier shops line the waterfront, and the better craft shops can be found around Avenida 5a. Malls at the cruise-ship piers aim to please passengers seeking jewelry, perfume, sportswear, and low-end souvenirs at high-end prices.

Most downtown shops accept U.S. dollars; many goods are priced in dollars. To get better prices, pay with cash—some shops tack a hefty surcharge on credit-card purchases. Shops, restaurants, and streets are always crowded between 10 am and 2 pm, but get calmer in the evening. Traditionally, stores are open from 9 to 1 (except Sunday) and 5 to 9, but those nearest the pier tend to stay open all day, particularly during high season. Most shops are closed Sunday morning.

ACTIVITIES

DIVING AND SNORKELING

Cozumel is famous for its reefs. In addition to Chankanaab Nature Park, a great dive site is La Ceiba Reef, in the waters off La Ceiba and Sol Caribe hotels. Here lies the wreckage of a sunken airplane blown up for a Mexican disaster movie. Cozumel has plenty of dive shops to choose from.

Aqua Safari. One of the island's oldest and most professional shops, Aqua Safari provides beginning and advanced PADI certification and daily introductory scuba courses. Owner Bill Horn has long been involved in efforts to protect the reefs and stays on top of local environmental issues. ⊠ *Av. Rafael E. Melgar 429, between Calles 5 and 7 Sur* ☎ *987/872–0101.*

Blue Angel. Blue Angel offers combo dive and snorkel trips so families who don't all scuba can still have fun together. Along with dive trips to local reefs, they offer PADI courses. ⊠ *Carretera Sur Km 2.2* ☎ *987/872–1631, 866/779–9986.*

Eagle Ray Divers. Eagle Ray Divers offers snorkeling trips and dive instruction. (The three-reef snorkel trip lets nondivers explore beyond the shore.) As befits their name, the company keeps track of the eagle rays that appear off Cozumel from December to February and runs trips for advanced divers to walls where the rays congregate. Beginners can also see rays around some of the reefs. ⊠ *La Caleta Marina near the Presidente InterContinental hotel* ☎ *987/872–5735, 866/465–1616 in U.S.* ⊕ *www.eagleraydivers.com.*

FISHING

You can charter high-speed fishing boats for about $420 per half-day or $600 per day (with a maximum of six people). Your hotel can help arrange daily charters—some offer special deals, with boats leaving from their own docks.

Albatros Deep Sea Fishing. Albatros Deep Sea Fishing offers full-day trips that include boat and crew, tackle and bait, and lunch (quesadillas or your own fresh catch) with beer and soda starting at $575 for up to six people. ⊠ *Cozumel* ☎ *987/872–7904, 630/938–7603* ⊕ *www. albatroscharters.com.*

3 Hermanos. This oufit specializes in deep-sea and fly-fishing trips, with rates for a half-day deep-sea fishing trip starting at $350. (A full day runs $450.) They also offer scuba-diving trips, and their boats are available for group charters—a great way to snorkel and cruise at your own pace—for $400 for up to six passengers. ⊠ *Marina, Puerto*

Abrigo ☎*987/107–0655 mobile, 651/755–4897 in U.S.* ⊕*www.cozumelfishing.com.*

BEACHES

Cozumel's beaches vary from sandy treeless stretches to isolated coves to rocky shores. Most of the development is on the leeward (western) side. Beach clubs have sprung up on the southwest coast; admission, however, is usually free, as long as you buy food and drinks. Clubs offer typical tourist fare: souvenir shops, *palapa* (thatch-roofed) restaurants, kayaks, and cold beer. A cab ride from San Miguel to most clubs costs about $15 each way. Reaching beaches on the windward (eastern) side is more difficult, but the solitude is worth it.

★ **Playa Palancar.** South of the resorts, down a rutted and potholed road and way off the beaten path lies the serene Playa Palancar. The on-site dive shop can outfit you for trips to the famous Palancar Reef just off-shore. There's also a water-sports center, a bar-café, and a long beach with hammocks hanging under coconut palms. **Amenities:** food and drink, showers, restrooms, parking lot. **Best for:** snorkeling, swimming. ⊠ *Carretera Sur* 🖾 *Free.*

Playa San Francisco. Playa San Francisco was one of the first beach clubs on the coast. The inviting 3-mile (5-km) stretch of sandy beach, which extends along Carretera Sur south of Parque Chankanaab at about Km 14, is among the longest and finest on Cozumel. In lieu of a fee, there's a $10 minimum purchase of food or drinks for adults. **Amenities:** chaise longues, food concessions, lockers, parking lot, showers. **Best for:** banana-boat rides, boat diving, families, parasailing. ⊠ *Carretera Costera Sur, Km 14.*

Punta Chiqueros. Punta Chiqueros, a half moon-shaped cove sheltered by an offshore reef, is the first popular swimming area as you drive north on the coastal road. (It's about 8 miles [12 km] north of Faro Celarain Park.) Part of a longer beach that some locals call Playa Bonita, it has fine sand, clear water, and moderate waves. This is a great place to swim, watch the sunset, and eat fresh fish at the restaurant, also called Playa Bonita. **Amenities:** food concession, parking on road. **Best for:** families, sunbathing, swimming ⊠ *Cozumel.*

WHERE TO EAT

$$ ✕ **Guido's.** Chef Yvonne Villiger works wonders with fresh fish—if the
ITALIAN wahoo with capers and black olives is on the menu, don't miss it. But
★ Guido's is best known for its pizzas baked in a wood-burning oven, which makes sections of the indoor dining room rather warm. Enjoy a pitcher of sangria in the pleasant, roomy courtyard instead. ⑤ *Average main: $15* ⊠ *Av. Rafael E. Melgar 23, between Calles 6 and 8 Norte* ☎ *987/872–0946, 987/869–2589* ⊗ *No lunch Sun.*

$$$ ✕ **Pancho's Backyard.** Marimbas play beside a bubbling fountain in
MEXICAN the charming courtyard behind one of Cozumel's best folk-art shops.
★ Though Pancho's is always busy, the waitstaff is patient and helpful. Cruise-ship passengers seeking a taste of Mexico pack the place at

lunch; dinner is a bit more serene. The American-style, English menu is geared toward tourists, but regional ingredients like smoky chipotle chile make even the standard steak stand out. Other stars: the cilantro cream soup and shrimp flambéed with tequila. Pancho's is one of only two Cozumel restaurants to have earned a special "H" rating for hygienic standards and staff training. $ *Average main: $15* ⊠ *Av. Rafael Melgar, between Calles 8 and 10 Norte* ☏ *987/872–2141* ⊕ *www. panchosbackyard.com* ⊗ *No lunch Sun.*

CURAÇAO (WILLEMSTAD)

Vernon O'Reilly-Ramesar

Try to be on deck as your ship sails into Curaçao. The tiny Queen Emma floating bridge swings aside to allow ships to pass through the narrow channel. Pastel gingerbread buildings on shore look like dollhouses, especially from a large cruise ship. Although the gabled roofs and red tiles show a Dutch influence, the gleeful colors of the facades are peculiar to Curaçao. It's said that an early governor of the island suffered from migraines that were aggravated by the color white, so all the houses were painted in hues from magenta to mauve. Thirty-five miles (56 km) north of Venezuela and 42 miles (68 km) east of Aruba, Curaçao is, at 38 miles (61 km) long and 3 to 7.5 miles (5 to 12 km) wide, the largest of the Netherlands Antilles. Although always sunny, it's never stiflingly hot here because of the constant trade winds. Water sports attract enthusiasts from all over the world, and the reef diving is excellent.

ESSENTIALS

CURRENCY The NAf guilder (NAf 1.79 to US$1). U.S. currency is accepted almost everywhere on the island, and ATMs are plentiful. The currency is expected to be changed to the Caribbean guilder in 2012 (this currency will also be used by St. Martin).

INTERNET **Café Internet** ⊠ *Handelskade 3B, Punda, Willemstad* ☏ *5999/465–5088.* **Wireless Internet Café** ⊠ *Hanchi Snoa 4, Punda, Willemstad* ☏ *5999/ 461–0590.*

TELEPHONE The telephone system is reliable. To place a local call, dial the seven-digit number. A local call costs NAf 0.50 from a pay phone. Direct-dial access is also available at the AT&T calling center at the cruise-ship terminal and at the megapier in Otrobanda. From other public phones, use phones marked "lenso"; many more of these have been added around the island in recent years. You can also call direct from the air-conditioned Digicel center using a prepaid phone card (open 8 am to 5:30 pm, Monday through Saturday; the center also offers Internet access).

COMING ASHORE

Ships dock at the terminal just beyond the Queen Emma Bridge, which leads to the floating market, cafés, and the shopping district. The walk to downtown takes less than 10 minutes. Easy-to-read maps are posted dockside and in the shopping area. The terminal has a duty-free shop, telephones, and a taxi stand.

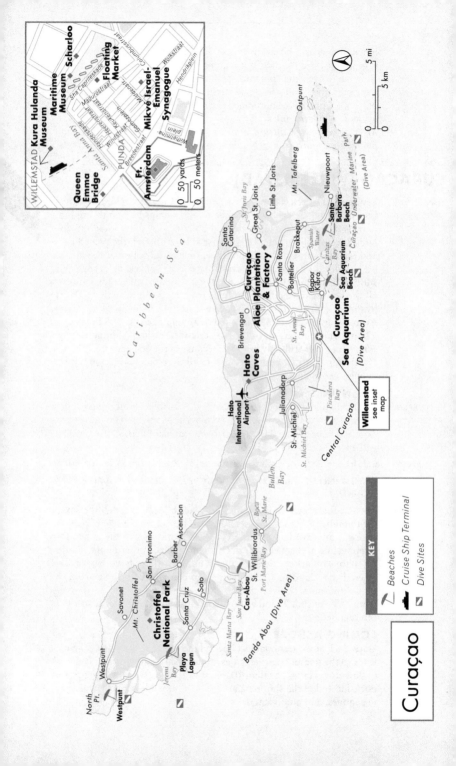

Curaçao

WILLEMSTAD

Kura Hulanda Museum
Maritime Museum
Scharloo
Floating Market
Mikvé Israel-Emanuel Synagogue
Sha Caprileskade
Columbusstraat
Madurostraat
Keukenstraat
Gomezplein
Wolkstraat
Hendrikplein
Windstraat
Breedestraat
Handelskade
Heerenstraat
Wilhelmina-plein
PUNDA
Ft. Amsterdam
Queen Emma Bridge
Santa Anna Bay

0   50 yards
0   50 meters

Caribbean Sea

North Pt.
Westpunt
Savonet
Mt. Christoffel
San Hyronimo
Barber
Ascencion
Santa Cruz
Soto
San Juan Bay
St. Willibrordus
St. Marie
Boca
St. Michiel Bay
Bullen Bay
Brievengat
Julianadorp
St. Michiel

Christoffel National Park
Playa Lagun
Jeremi Bay
Santa Marta Bay
Port Marie Bay
Cas-Abou
Banda Abou (Dive Area)
Piscadera Bay
Central Curaçao

Hato International Airport
Hato Caves

Santa Catarina
St. Joris Bay
Great St. Joris
Little St. Joris
Santa Rosa
Curaçao Aloe Plantation & Factory
Bottelier
Mt. Tafelberg
Nieuwpoort
Ostpunt
Santa Barbara Beach
Curaçao Underwater Marine Park (Dive Area)
Brakeput
Spanish Water
Caribas Bay
Bapor Kibra
Sea Aquarium Beach
Curaçao Sea Aquarium (Dive Area)
St. Anna Bay

Willemstad
see inset map

KEY

Beaches
Cruise Ship Terminal
Dive Sites

0   5 mi
0   5 km

Taxis, which meet every ship, have meters, although rates are still fixed from point to point of your journey. The government-approved rates, which do not include waiting time, can be found in a brochure called "Taxi Tariff Guide," available at the cruise-ship terminal and at the tourist board. Rates are for up to four passengers. There's a 25% surcharge after 11 pm. It's easy to see the sights on Curaçao without going on an organized shore excursion. Downtown can be done on foot, and a taxi for up to four people will cost about $45 an hour. Taxi fares to places in and around the city range from $8 to $20. Car rentals are available but are not cheap (about $40 per day, plus $10 compulsory insurance).

> **CURAÇAO BEST BETS**
>
> ■ **Diving.** After Bonaire, Curaçao has probably the best diving in the region.
>
> ■ **Punda.** Willemstad's chic and beautiful shopping area is a joy to explore on foot.
>
> ■ **Curaçao Sea Aquarium.** Explore the wonders of the ocean without getting wet.
>
> ■ **Floating Market.** This unique market is a fun destination, even though it's mostly fruits and vegetables.
>
> ■ **Kurá Hulanda Museum.** This is the island's best historical museum.

EXPLORING CURAÇAO

WILLEMSTAD

Willemstad is small and navigable on foot. You needn't spend more than two or three hours wandering around here, although the narrow alleys and various architectural styles are enchanting. English, Spanish, and Dutch are widely spoken. Narrow Santa Anna Bay divides the city into two sides: Punda, where you'll find the main shopping district, and Otrabanda (literally, the "other side"), where the cruise ships dock. Punda is crammed with shops, restaurants, monuments, and markets. Otrabanda has narrow, winding streets full of colonial homes notable for their gables and Dutch-influenced designs.

You can cross from Otrabanda to Punda in one of three ways: walk over the Queen Emma Bridge; ride the free ferry, which runs when the bridge swings open to let seagoing vessels pass; or take a cab across the Juliana Bridge (about $9). On the Punda side of the city, Handelskade is where you'll find Willemstad's most famous sights—the colorful colonial buildings that line the waterfront. The original red roof tiles came from Europe on trade ships as ballast.

★ **Floating Market.** Each morning dozens of Venezuelan schooners laden with tropical fruits and vegetables arrive at this bustling market on the Punda side of the city. Mangoes, papayas, and exotic vegetables vie for space with freshly caught fish and herbs and spices. The buying is best at 6:30 am—too early for many people on vacation—but there's plenty of action throughout the afternoon. Any produce bought here should be thoroughly washed or peeled before being eaten. ✉ *Sha Caprileskade, Punda, Willemstad.*

Ft. Amsterdam. Step through the archway of this fort and enter another century. The entire structure dates from the 1700s, when it was the center of the city and the island's most important fortification. Now it houses the governor's residence, a church (which has a small museum), and government offices. Outside the entrance, a series of majestic gnarled *wayaka* trees are fancifully carved with human forms—the work of local artist Mac Alberto. ⊠ *Foot of Queen Emma Bridge, Punda, Willemstad* ☎ *5999/461–1139* ⌨ *Fort free, church museum $2* ⊙ *Weekdays 9:30–1, Sun. service at 10.*

Fodor's Choice **Kurá Hulanda Museum.** This fascinating anthropological museum reveals ★ the island's diverse roots. Housed in a restored 18th-century village, the museum is built around a former mercantile square (Kurá Hulanda means "Holland courtyard"), where the Dutch once sold slaves. An exhibit on the transatlantic slave trade includes a gut-wrenching replica of a slave-ship hold. Other sections feature relics from West African empires, examples of pre-Columbian gold, and Antillean art. The complex is the brainchild of Dutch philanthropist Jacob Gelt Dekker, and the museum grew from his personal collection of artifacts. ⊠ *Klipstraat 9, Otrobanda, Willemstad* ☎ *5999/434–7765* ⊕ *www.kurahulanda. com* ⌨ *$9* ⊙ *Thurs.–Sat. 10–5.*

Maritime Museum. The museum—designed to resemble the interior of a ship—gives you a sense of Curaçao's maritime history, using model ships, historic maps, nautical charts, navigational equipment, and audiovisual displays. Topics explored in the exhibits include the development of Willemstad as a trading city, Curaçao's role as a contraband hub, the remains of *De Alphen* (a Dutch marine freighter that exploded and sank in St. Anna Bay in 1778 and was excavated in 1984), the slave trade, the development of steam navigation, and the role of the Dutch navy on the island. The museum also offers a two-hour guided tour (Wednesday and Saturday, 2 pm) on its "water bus" through Curaçao's harbor—a route familiar to traders, smugglers, and pirates. The museum is wheelchair accessible. ⊠ *Van der Brandhofstraat 7, Scharloo, Willemstad* ☎ *5999/465–2327* ⊕ *www.curacaomaritime.com* ⌨ *Museum $6, museum and harbor tour $15* ⊙ *Tues.–Sat. 9–4.*

★ **Mikvé Israel-Emanuel Synagogue.** The temple, the oldest in continuous use in the Western Hemisphere, is one of Curaçao's most important sights and draws thousands of visitors a year. The synagogue was dedicated in 1732 by the Jewish community, which had already grown from the original 12 families who came from Amsterdam in 1651. They were later joined by Jews from Portugal and Spain fleeing persecution from the Inquisition. White sand covers the synagogue floor for two symbolic reasons: a remembrance of the 40 years Jews spent wandering the desert, and a re-creation of the sand used by secret Jews, or *conversos,* to muffle sounds from their houses of worship during the Inquisition. English and Hebrew services are held Friday at 6:30 pm and Saturday at 10 am. Men who attend should wear a jacket and tie. Yarmulkes are provided to men for services and tours. ⊠ *Hanchi Snoa 29, Punda, Willemstad* ☎ *5999/461–1067* ⊕ *www.snoa.com* ⌨ *$6; donations also accepted* ⊙ *Weekdays 9–4:30.*

Queen Emma Bridge. Affectionately called the Swinging Old Lady by the locals, this bridge connects the two sides of Willemstad—Punda and Otrobanda—across the Santa Anna Bay. The bridge swings open at least 30 times a day to allow passage of ships to and from the sea. The original bridge, built in 1888, was the brainchild of the American consul Leonard Burlington Smith, who made a mint off the tolls he charged for using it: 2¢ per person for those wearing shoes, free to those crossing barefoot. Today it's free to everyone. The bridge was dismantled and completely repaired and restored in 2005. ⊠ *Willemstad.*

Scharloo. The Wilhelmina Drawbridge connects Punda with the once-flourishing district of Scharloo, where the early Jewish merchants built stately homes. The architecture along Scharlooweg (much of it from the 17th century) is magnificent, and, happily, many of the colonial mansions that had become dilapidated have been meticulously renovated. The area closest to Kleine Werf is a red-light district and fairly run-down, but the rest is well worth a visit. ⊠ *Willemstad.*

ELSEWHERE ON THE ISLAND

★ **Christoffel National Park.** The 1,239-foot Mt. Christoffel, Curaçao's highest peak, is at the center of this 4,450-acre garden and wildlife preserve. The exhilarating climb up—a challenge to anyone who hasn't grown up scaling the Alps—takes about two hours for a reasonably fit person. On a clear day, the panoramic view from the peak stretches to the mountain ranges of Venezuela.

Throughout the park are eight hiking trails and a 20-mile (32-km) network of driving trails (use heavy-treaded tires if you wish to explore the unpaved stretches). All these routes traverse hilly fields full of prickly pear cacti, divi-divi trees, bushy-haired palms, and exotic flowers. Guided nature walks, horseback rides, and jeep tours can be arranged through the main park office. If you're going without a guide, first study the *Excursion Guide to Christoffel Park,* sold at the visitor center. It outlines the various routes and identifies the indigenous flora and fauna. Start out early, as by 10 am the park starts to feel like a sauna.

Watch for goats and small animals that might cross your path, and consider yourself lucky if you see any of the elusive white-tailed deer. Horseback tours are conducted from Rancho Alfin, which is in the park. Reservations are required. Additionally, most island sports outfitters offer some kind of activity in the park, such as kayaking, specialized hiking tours, and drive-through tours *(⇨ Sports and Activities, below).* ⊠ *Savonet* ☎ *5999/864–0363 for information and tour reservations, 5999/462–6262 for jeep tours, 5999/864–0535 for horseback tours* ⊡ *$10* ⊙ *Mon.–Sat. 8–4, Sun. 6–3; last admission 90 min before closing.*

Curaçao Aloe Plantation & Factory. Drop in for a fascinating tour that takes you through the various stages of production of aloe vera, renowned for its healing powers. You'll get a look at everything from the fields to the final products. At the gift shop, you can buy CurAloe products, including homemade goodies like soap, pure aloe gel, and pure aloe juice, as well as sunscreen and other skin-care products. The plantation is on the way to the Ostrich Farm and run by the same owner. Tours begin throughout the day. ⊠ *Weg Naar Groot St. Joris z/n, Groot St. Joris* ☎ *5999/767–5577* ⊕ *www. aloecuracao.com* 🎫 *$7* ⊙ *Mon.– Sat. 9–4; last tour at 3.*

🐢★ **Curaçao Sea Aquarium.** You don't have to get your feet wet to see the island's underwater treasures. The aquarium has about 40 saltwater tanks filled with more than 400 varieties of marine life. A restaurant, a snack bar, two photo centers, and souvenir shops are on-site.

⊠ *Seaquarium Beach, Bapor Kibra z/n* ☎ *5999/461–6666* ⊕ *www.curacao-sea-aquarium.com* 🎫 *Aquarium $19; Dolphin Academy $89–$169* ⊙ *Aquarium daily 8:30–5:30, Dolphin Academy daily 8:30–4:30.*

★ **Hato Caves.** Stalactites and stalagmites form striking shapes in these 200,000-year-old caves. Hidden lighting adds to the dramatic effect. Indians who used the caves for shelter left petroglyphs about 1,500 years ago. More recently, slaves who escaped from nearby plantations used the caves as a hideaway. Hour-long guided tours wind down to the pools in various chambers. Keep in mind that there are 49 steps to climb up to the entrance and the occasional bat might not be to everyone's taste. To reach the caves, head northwest toward the airport, take a right onto Gosieweg, follow the loop right onto Schottegatweg, take another right onto Jan Norduynweg and a final right onto Rooseveltweg, and follow signs. ⊠ *Rooseveltweg z/n, Hato* ☎ *5999/868–0379* 🎫 *$8* ⊙ *Daily 10–4.*

SHOPPING

From Dutch classics like embroidered linens, delft earthenware, cheeses, and clogs to local artwork and handicrafts, shopping in Curaçao can turn up some fun finds. But don't expect major bargains on watches, jewelry, or electronics; Willemstad is not a duty-free port (the few establishments that claim to be "duty-free" are simply absorbing the cost of some or all of the tax rather than passing it on to consumers); however, if you come prepared with some comparison prices, you might still dig up some good deals. Hours are usually Monday through Saturday, from 8 to noon and 2 to 6. Most shops are within the six-block area of Willemstad described above. The main shopping streets are Heerenstraat, Breedestraat, and Madurostraat.

Boolchand's. Head here for electronics, jewelry, Swarovski crystal, Swiss watches, cameras, and more, sold behind a facade of red-and-white checkered tiles. ⊠ *Heerenstraat 4B, Punda, Willemstad* ☎ *5999/461–6233.*

Cigar Emporium. A sweet aroma permeates Cigar Emporium, where you can find the largest selection of Cuban cigars on the island, including H. Upmann, Romeo y Julieta, and Montecristo. Visit the climate-controlled cedar cigar room. However, remember that Cuban cigars cannot be taken back to the United States legally. ⊠ *Gomezplein, Punda, Willemstad* ☎ *5999/465–3955.*

New Amsterdam. Hand-embroidered tablecloths, napkins, and pillowcases, as well as blue delft, are available at New Amsterdam. ⊠ *Gomezplein 14, Punda, Willemstad* ☎ *5999/461–2437.*

ACTIVITIES

BIKING

Wanna Bike Curaçao. So you wanna bike Curaçao? Wanna Bike Curaçao has the fix: kick into gear and head out for a guided mountain-bike tour through the Caracas Bay peninsula and the salt ponds at the Jan Thiel Lagoon. Although you should be fit to take on the challenge, mountain-bike experience is not required. Tour prices vary, depending on skill level and duration, and cover the bike, helmet, water, refreshments, park entrance fee, and guide—but don't forget to bring a camera. ⊠ *Jan Thiel Beach z/n, Jan Thiel, Willemstad* ☎ *5999/527–3720* ⊕ *www.wannabike.com.*

DIVING AND SNORKELING

☾ ★ **Ocean Encounters.** Ocean Encounters is the largest dive operator on the island. Its operations cover the popular east-coast dive sites, including the *Superior Producer* wreck, where barracudas hang out, and a tugboat wreck. West-end hot spots—including the renowned Mushroom Forest and Watamula dive sites—are accessible from the company's outlet at Westpunt. Ocean Encounters offers a vast menu of scheduled shore and boat dives and packages, as well as certified PADI instruction. In July, the dive center sponsors a kids' sea camp in conjunction with the Sea Aquarium. ⊠ *Lions Dive & Beach Resort, Seaquarium Beach, Bapor Kibra z/n* ☎ *5999/461–8131* ⊕ *www.oceanencounters.com.*

BEACHES

☾ **Cas Abao.** This white-sand gem has the brightest blue water in Curaçao, a treat for swimmers, snorkelers, and sunbathers alike. You can take respite beneath the hut-shaded snack bar. The restrooms and showers are immaculate. You can rent beach chairs, paddleboats, and snorkeling and diving gear. The entry fee is $3, and the beach is open from 8 to 6. Turn off Westpunt Highway at the junction onto Weg Naar Santa Cruz; follow until the turnoff for Cas Abao, and then drive along the winding country road for about 10 minutes to the beach. ⊠ *West of St. Willibrordus, about 3 miles (5 km) off Weg Naar Santa Cruz.*

☾ **Playa Knip.** Two protected coves offer crystal-clear turquoise waters. Big (Groot) Knip is an expanse of alluring white sand, perfect for swimming and snorkeling. You can rent beach chairs and hang out under the *palapas* (thatch-roof shelters) or cool off with ice cream at the snack bar. There are restrooms here but no showers. It's particularly crowded on Sunday and school holidays. Just up the road, also in a protected cove, Little (Kleine) Knip is a charmer, too, with picnic tables and palapas. Steer clear of the poisonous manchineel trees. There's no fee for these beaches. ⊠ *Just east of Westpunt, Banda Abou.*

○ **Seaquarium Beach.** This 1,600-foot stretch of sandy beach is divided into separate sections, each uniquely defined by a seaside resort or restaurant as its central draw. By day, no matter where you choose to enter the palm-shaded beach, you can find lounge chairs in the sand, thatched shelters, and restrooms. The sections at Mambo and Kontiki beaches also have showers. The island's largest water-sports center (Ocean Encounters at Lions Dive) caters to nearby hotel guests and walk-ins. Mambo Beach is always a hot spot and quite a scene on weekends, especially during the much-touted Sunday-night fiesta that's become a fixture of the island's nightlife. The ubiquitous beach mattress is also the preferred method of seating for the Tuesday-night movies at Mambo Beach (check the *K-Pasa* guide for listings—typically B-films or old classics—and reserve your spot with a shirt or a towel). At Kontiki Beach, you can find a spa, a hair braider, and a restaurant that serves refreshing piña colada ice cream. Unless you're a guest of a resort on the beach, the entrance fee to any section is $3 until 5 pm, then free. After 11 pm, you must be 18 or older to access the beach. ⊠ *About 1 mile (1½ km) east of downtown Willemstad, Bapor Kibra z/n.*

WHERE TO EAT

$ ✕ **Awa di Playa.** Formerly a fisherman's hangout, this ramshackle shed-
CAFÉ   like structure located on an ocean inlet gives way to an equally ramshackle interior and some of the best local lunches anywhere on the island. There's no menu—the waiter will tell you what's available, and you can watch it being cooked in the tiny kitchen. The presentation isn't fancy, and the occasional fly makes an appearance, but the food is honest and delicious. ⑤ *Average main: $8* ⊠ *Behind Hook's Hut and Hilton, Piscadera Bay, Willemstad* ☎ *5999/462–6939* ▭ *No credit cards* ⊗ *No dinner.*

$$ ✕ **Gouverneur de Rouville Restaurant & Café.** Dine on the veranda of a
ECLECTIC   restored 19th-century Dutch mansion overlooking the Santa Anna Bay
★   and the resplendent Punda skyline. Though often busy and popular with tourists, the ambience makes it worth a visit. Intriguing soup options include Cuban banana soup and Curaçao-style fish soup. *Keshi yena* (seasoned meat wrapped in cheese and then baked) and spareribs are among the savory entrées. After dinner, you can stick around for live music at the bar, which stays open until 1 am. The restaurant is also popular for lunch and attracts crowds when cruise ships dock. Reserve ahead if you would like a balcony table. ⑤ *Average main: $24* ⊠ *De Rouvilleweg 9, Otrobanda, Willemstad* ☎ *5999/462–5999* ⊕ *www.de-gouverneur.com.*

DOMINICA (ROSEAU)

Roberta
Sotonoff

In the center of the Caribbean archipelago, wedged between the two French islands of Guadeloupe, to the north, and Martinique, to the south, Dominica is a wild place. So unyielding is the terrain that colonists surrendered efforts at colonization, and the last survivors of the Caribbean's original people, the Carib Indians, have made her rugged northeast their home. Dominica—just 29 miles (47 km) long and 16 miles (26 km) wide—is an English-speaking island, though family and place names are a mélange of French, English, and Carib. The capital is Roseau (pronounced rose-*oh*). If you've had enough of casinos, crowds, and swim-up bars and want to take leave of everyday life—to hike, bike, trek, and spot birds and butterflies in the rain forest; explore waterfalls; discover a boiling lake; kayak, dive, snorkel, or sail in marine reserves; or go out in search of the many resident whale and dolphin species—this is the place to do it.

4

ESSENTIALS

CURRENCY The Eastern Caribbean dollar (EC$2.70 to US$1). U.S. currency is readily accepted, but you will get change in EC dollars. Most major credit cards are accepted, as are traveler's checks.

INTERNET **Cyber Land Internet Café** ⊠ *6 King George St., Roseau* ☎ *767/449–9000* ⊕ *cybercafes.com* ⊗ *8 am–10 pm* ⊠ *Woodstone Shopping Mall, Roseau* ⊠ *Grandby St., Portsmouth.*

COMING ASHORE

In Roseau most ships dock along the bay front. Across the street from the pier, in the old post office, is a visitor information center. Taxis, minibuses, and tour operators are available at the berths. If you do decide to tour with one of them, choose one who is certified, and be explicit when discussing where you will go and how much you will pay—don't be afraid to ask questions. The drivers usually quote a fixed fare, which is regulated by the Division of Tourism and the Transportation Board, and also offer their services for tours anywhere on the island beginning at $25 to $30 an hour for up to four people; a four- to five-hour island tour for up to four people will cost approximately $200. You can rent a car in Roseau for about $45–$50, not including insurance and a mandatory EC$30 (US$12) driving permit, but it can be difficult to find things, so you might do better on a guided tour here.

EXPLORING DOMINICA

Most of Dominica's roads are narrow and winding, so you'll need a few hours to take in the sights. Be adventurous, whether you prefer sightseeing or hiking—you'll be amply rewarded.

☼ ★ **Carib Indian Territory.** In 1903, after centuries of conflict, the Caribbean's first settlers, the Kalinago (more popularly known as the Caribs), were granted approximately 3,700 acres of land on the island's northeast coast. Here a hardened lava formation, **L'Escalier Tête Chien** (Snake's Staircase), runs down into the Atlantic. The name is derived from a snake whose head resembles that of a dog. The ocean alongside

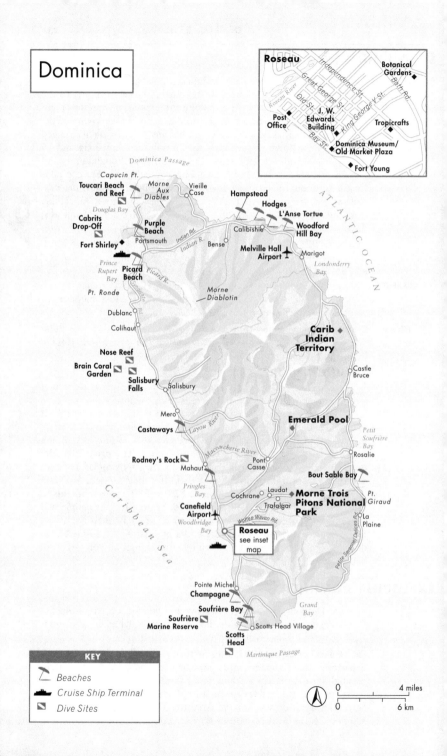

Dominica

Roseau

Botanical Gardens

Independence St.
Great George St.
King George V St.
Bath Rd.

Roseau River
Old St.

Post Office

J. W. Edwards Building

Tropicrafts

Bay St.

Dominica Museum / Old Market Plaza

Fort Young

Dominica Passage

Capucin Pt.

Toucari Beach and Reef

Morne Aux Diables

Vieille Case

Hampstead

Hodges

L'Anse Tortue

Woodford Hill Bay

Douglas Bay

Cabrits Drop-Off

Purple Beach

Portsmouth

Indian Rd.

Calibishie

Bense

Indian R.

Melville Hall Airport

Marigot

Fort Shirley

Londonderry Bay

Prince Rupert Bay

Picard Beach

Picard R.

Pt. Ronde

Morne Diablotin

Dublanc

Colihaut

ATLANTIC OCEAN

Carib Indian Territory

Castle Bruce

Nose Reef

Brain Coral Garden

Salisbury Falls

Salisbury

Mero

Layou River

Emerald Pool

Petit Soufrière Bay

Castaways

Macoucherie River

Rosalie

Rodney's Rock

Mahaut

Pont Casse

Bout Sable Bay

Pringles Bay

Cochrane

Laudat

Trafalgar

Morne Trois Pitons National Park

Pt. Giraud

Canefield Airport

Wotten Waven Rd.

La Plaine

Woodbridge Bay

Roseau
see inset map

Caribbean Sea

Pointe Michel

Champagne

Soufrière Bay

Soufrière Marine Reserve

Scotts Head Village

Grand Bay

Scotts Head

Martinique Passage

Petite Savanne Delices Rd.

KEY

Beaches

Cruise Ship Terminal

Dive Sites

0   4 miles
0   6 km

Carib Territory is particularly fierce. The shore is full of countless coves and inlets. According to Carib legend, every night the nearby Londonderry Islets transform into grand canoes to take the spirits of the dead out to sea.

A chief administers the Carib Territory on which about 3,000 natives reside. The reservation's Catholic church in Salybia has a canoe as its altar, which was designed by Dr. Lennox Honychurch, a local historian, author, and artist.

Kalinago Barana Autê. You might catch canoe builders at work at Kalinago Barana Autê, the Carib Territory's place to learn about Kalinago customs, history, and culture. A guided, 45-minute tour explores the village, stopping along the way to see some traditional dances and to learn about plants, dugout canoes, basket weaving, and cassava bread making. The path offers wonderful viewpoints of the Atlantic and a chance to glimpse Isukulati Falls. ⊠ *Crayfish River, Carib Territory* ☏ *767/445–7979* ⊕ *www.kalinagobaranaaute.com* 🏷 *Basic package is about $10* ☉ *Daily 9–5.*

☺ **Emerald Pool.** Quite possibly the most visited nature attraction on the island, this emerald-green pool fed by a 50-foot waterfall is an easy trip to make. To reach this spot in the vast Morne Trois Pitons National Park, you follow a trail that starts at the side of the road near the reception center (it's an easy 20-minute walk). Along the way, there are lookout points with views of the windward (Atlantic) coast and the forested interior. If you don't want a crowd, check whether there are cruise ships in port before going out, as this spot is popular with cruise-ship tour groups. ⊠ *Dominica.*

★ **Morne Trois Pitons National Park.** A UNESCO World Heritage Site, this 17,000-acre swath of lush, mountainous land in the south-central interior (covering 9% of Dominica) is the island's crown jewel. Named after one of the highest (4,600 feet) mountains on the island, it contains the island's famous "boiling lake," majestic waterfalls, and cool mountain lakes. There are four types of vegetation zones here. Ferns grow 30 feet tall, wild orchids sprout from trees, sunlight leaks through green canopies, and a gentle mist rises over the jungle floor. A system of trails has been developed in the park, and the Division of Forestry and Wildlife works hard to maintain them—with no help from the excessive rainfall and the profusion of vegetation that seems to grow right before your eyes. Access to the park is possible from most points, though the easiest approaches are via the small mountaintop villages of Laudat (pronounced lau-*dah*) and Cochrane.

On your way to Boiling Lake you pass through the **Valley of Desolation,** a sight that definitely lives up to its name. Harsh sulfuric fumes have destroyed virtually all the vegetation in what must once have been a lush forested area. Small hot and cold streams with water of various colors—black, purple, red, orange—web the valley. Stay on the trail to avoid breaking through the crust that covers the hot lava. During this hike you'll pass rivers where you can refresh yourself with a dip (a particular treat is a soak in a hot-water stream on the way back). At the beginning of the Valley of Desolation trail is the **TiTou Gorge,** where you can swim in the pool or relax in the hot-water springs along one side. If you're a strong swimmer, you can head up the gorge to a cave (it's about a five-minute swim) that has a magnificent waterfall; a crack in the cave about 50 feet above permits a stream of sunlight to penetrate the cavern.

Also in the national park are some of the island's most spectacular waterfalls. The 45-minute hike to **Sari Sari Falls**, accessible through the east-coast village of La Plaine, can be hair-raising. But the sight of water cascading some 150 feet into a large pool is awesome. So large are these falls that you feel the spray from hundreds of yards away. Just beyond the village of Trafalgar and up a short hill is the reception facility, where you can purchase passes to the national park and find guides to take you on a rain-forest trek to the twin **Trafalgar Falls**; the 125-foot-high waterfall is called the Father, and the wider, 95-foot-high one, the Mother. ⊠ *Dominica.*

> ## DOMINICA BEST BETS
>
> ■ **Kalinago Barana Autê.** This reserve is a great place to learn about the fierce Caribs.
>
> ■ **Rain-Forest Trips.** Hiking in Dominica's rain forest is the best way to experience its natural beauty.
>
> ■ **Snorkeling in Champagne.** A bubbling volcanic vent makes you feel as if you are snorkeling in champagne.
>
> ■ **Whale-Watching.** November through February offers the best whale-watching in the Caribbean.
>
> ■ **Indian River.** A rowboat ride on the river is relaxing and peaceful.

Boiling Lake. The undisputed highlight of the park is the Boiling Lake. Reputedly one of the world's largest such lakes, it's a cauldron of gurgling gray-blue water, 70 yards wide and of unknown depth, with water temperatures from 180°F to 197°F. Although generally believed to be a volcanic crater, the lake is actually a flooded fumarole—a crack through which gases escape from the molten lava below. As many visitors discovered in late 2004, the "lake" can sometimes dry up, though it fills again within a few months and, shortly after that, once more starts to boil. It has returned to its pre-2004 levels. The two- to four-hour (one way) hike up to the lake is challenging (on a very rainy day, be prepared to slip and slide the whole way up and back). You'll need attire appropriate for a strenuous hike, and a guide is a must. Most guided trips start early (no later than 8:30 am) for this all-day, 7-mile (11-km) round-trip trek. ⊠ *Dominica.*

Roseau. Although it's one of the smallest capitals in the Caribbean, Roseau has the highest concentration of inhabitants of any town in the eastern Caribbean. Caribbean vernacular architecture and a bustling marketplace transport visitors back in time. Although you can walk the entire town in about an hour, you'll get a much better feel for the place on a leisurely stroll.

For some years now, the Society for Historical Architectural Preservation and Enhancement (SHAPE) has organized programs and projects to preserve the city's architectural heritage. Several interesting buildings have already been restored. **Lilac House,** on Kennedy Avenue, has three types of gingerbread fretwork, latticed veranda railings, and heavy hurricane shutters. The **J.W. Edwards Building,** at the corner of Old and King George V streets, has a stone base and a wooden second-floor gallery. The **Old Market Plaza** is the center of Roseau's historic district, which was laid out by the French on a radial plan rather than a grid, so streets such as Hanover, King George V, and Old radiate from this area. South of the marketplace is the Fort Young Hotel,

> **BIBS**
>
> With limited and expensive laundry facilities on ships, you may not want to spend your free time cleaning up after your child. It's convenient to bring along a pack of disposable bibs for mealtimes to keep baby's clothing cleaner and stain-free, avoiding messy garments after meals and a lot of laundry time on board the ship.

built as a British fort in the 18th century; the nearby statehouse, public library, and Anglican cathedral are also worth a visit. New developments at the bay front on Dame M.E. Charles Boulevard have brightened up the waterfront. ⊠ *Southwest side of the island, Roseau.*

Botanical Gardens. The 40-acre Botanical Gardens, founded in 1891 as an annex of London's Kew Gardens, is a great place to relax, stroll, or watch a cricket match. In addition to the extensive collection of tropical plants and trees, there's also a parrot aviary. At the Forestry Division office, which is also on the garden grounds, you can find numerous publications on the island's flora, fauna, and national parks. The forestry officers are particularly knowledgeable on these subjects and can also recommend good hiking guides. ⊠ *Valley Rd.* ☎ *767/266–3811, 767/266–3812* ⊕ *www.da-academy.org/dagardens. html* 🔊 *Free* ☉ *Daily 6 am–7 pm.*

Dominica Museum. The old post office now houses the Dominica Museum. This labor of love by local writer and historian Dr. Lennox Honychurch contains furnishings, documents, prints, and maps that date back hundreds of years; you can also find an entire Carib hut as well as Carib canoes, baskets, and other artifacts. ⊠ *Dame M.E. Charles Blvd., opposite cruise-ship berth* ☎ *767/448–2401* 🔊 *$3* ☉ *Weekdays 9–4, Sat. 9–2; closed Sun. except when a cruise ship is in port.*

SHOPPING

Dominicans produce distinctive handicrafts, with various communities specializing in their specific products. The crafts of the Carib Indians include traditional baskets made of dyed *larouma* reeds and waterproofed with tightly woven *balizier* leaves. These are sold in the Carib Indian Territory and Kalinago Barana Autê as well as in Roseau's shops. Vertivert straw rugs, screw-pine tableware, *fwije* (the trunk of the forest tree fern), and wood carvings are just some examples. Also notable are local herbs, spices, condiments, and herb teas.

One of the easiest places to pick up a souvenir is the Old Market Plaza, just behind the Dominica Museum, in Roseau. Slaves were once sold here, but today handcrafted jewelry, T-shirts, spices, souvenirs, batik, and lacquered and woven bamboo boxes and trays are available from a group of vendors in open-air booths set up on the cobblestones. These are usually busiest when there's a cruise ship berthed across the street. On these days you can also find a vast number of vendors along the bay front.

Baroon International. Baroon International sells unusual jewelry from Asia, the United States, and other Caribbean islands. It also features pieces that are assembled in the store, as well as personal accessories, souvenirs, and special gifts. ⊠ *Kennedy Ave. at Old St., Roseau* ☎ *767/449–2888.*

Kalinago Barana Autê. Kalinago Barana Autê sells handicrafts including carvings, pottery, and lovely handwoven baskets, which you can watch the women weave. ⊠ *Salybia, Carib Territory* ☎ *767/445–7979* ⊕ *www. kalinagobaranaaute.com* ☽ *Daily 9–5.*

ACTIVITIES

ADVENTURE PARKS

☾ **Rainforest Adventures Dominica.** Rainforest Adventures Dominica gives you a bird's-eye view of a pristine forest aboard an open, eight-person gondola. For 90 minutes to two hours, you slowly skim the treetop canopy while a guide provides scientific information about the flora and fauna. At the top there is an optional walking tour that is worth the steps. The cost is $64. A zipline has recently been added (tram & zip US$99 or trail and zip US$50). Transportation and lunch are extra. This is a popular attraction for cruise-ship passengers, so try to reserve ahead. ⊠ *Laudat* ☎ *767/448–8775, 767/440–3266, 866/759–8726 in U.S.* ⊕ *www.rfat.com.*

☾ **Wacky Rollers.** Wacky Rollers will make you feel as if you are training for the marines as you swing on a Tarzan-style rope and grab onto a vertical rope ladder, rappel across zip lines, and traverse suspended log bridges, a net bridge, and four monkey bridges (rope loops). It costs $65 for the adult course and should take from 1½ to 3½ hours to conquer the 28 "games." There is also an abbreviated kids' course for $25 (kids 10 and under). Wacky Rollers also organizes adventure tours around the island plus kayak and tubing trips. Although the office is in Roseau, the park itself is in Hillsborough Estate, about 20 to 25 minutes north of Roseau. ⊠ *Front St., Roseau* ☎ *767/440–4386* ⊕ *www.wackyrollers.com.*

DIVING AND WHALE-WATCHING

Fodor's Choice Dominica has been voted one of the top 10 dive destinations in the
★ world by *Skin Diver* and *Rodale's Scuba Diving* magazines—and has won many other awards for its underwater sites. They are truly memorable. There are numerous highlights all along the west coast of the island, but the best are those in the southwest—within and around **Soufrière/Scotts Head Marine Reserve.** There is a $2 fee per person to dive, snorkel, or kayak in the reserve. The conditions for underwater photography, particularly macrophotography, are unparalleled. Rates start at about $55 for a single-tank dive and about $90 for a two-tank dive or from about $75 for a resort course with one open-water dive. All scuba-

diving operators also offer snorkeling. Equipment rents for $10 to $25 a day; trips with gear range from $15 to $35. A 10% tax is not included.

Anchorage Dive & Whale Watch Center. The Anchorage Dive & Whale Watch Center has two dive boats that can take you out day or night. It also offers PADI instruction (all skill levels), snorkeling and whale-watching trips, and shore diving. It has many of the same trips as Dive Dominica. ✉ *Anchorage Hotel, Castle Comfort* ☎ *767/448–2638* ⊕ *www.anchoragehotel.dm.*

Dive Dominica. Dive Dominica, one of the island's dive pioneers, conducts NAUI, PADI, and SSI courses as well as Nitrox certification courses. With four boats, it offers diving, snorkeling, and whale-watching trips and packages including accommodation at the Castle Comfort Lodge. Its trips are similar to Anchorage's. ✉ *Castle Comfort Lodge, Castle Comfort* ☎ *767/448–2188, 646/502–6800 in U.S.* ⊕ *www. divedominica.com.*

HIKING

★ Dominica's majestic mountains, clear rivers, and lush vegetation conspire to create adventurous hiking trails. The island is crisscrossed by ancient footpaths of the Arawak and Carib Indians and the Nègres Maroons, escaped slaves who established camps in the mountains. Existing trails range from easygoing to arduous. To make the most of your excursion, you'll need sturdy hiking boots, insect repellent, a change of clothes (kept dry), and a guide. Hikes and tours run $25 to $80 per person, depending on destinations and duration. A poncho or light raincoat is recommended. Some of the natural attractions within the island's national parks require visitors to purchase a site pass. These are sold for varying numbers of visits. A single-entry site pass costs $5, and a week pass $12.

Bertrand Jno Baptiste. Local bird and forestry expert Bertrand Jno Baptiste leads hikes up Morne Diablotin and along the Syndicate Nature Trail; if he's not available, ask him to recommend another guide. ✉ *Dominica* ☎ *767/245–4768.*

Discover Dominica Authority. Hiking guides can be arranged through the Discover Dominica Authority. ✉ *Kennedy Ave., 1st Floor Financial Centre, Roseau* ☎ *767/448–2045* ⊕ *www.discoverdominica.com.*

BEACHES

☼ **Champagne.** On the west coast, just south of the village of Pointe Michel, this stony beach is hailed as one of the best spots for swimming, snorkeling, and diving but not for sunning. It gets its name from volcanic vents that constantly puff steam into the sea, which makes you feel as if you are swimming in warm champagne. A boardwalk leads to the beach from Soufrière/Scotts Head Marine Reserve. ✉ *1 mile (1½ km) south of Pointe Michel, Soufrière.*

WHERE TO EAT

$ ✕ **Cocorico.** It's hard to miss the umbrella-shaded chairs and tables at
ECLECTIC   this Parisian-style café on a prominent bay-front corner in Roseau.
☾   Breakfast crepes, croissants, baguette sandwiches, and piping-hot café
★   au lait are available beginning at 8:30 am. Throughout the day you can
relax indoors or out and enjoy any of the extensive menu selections
with the perfect glass of wine, and you can even surf the Internet on
its computers. In the cellar downstairs, the Cocorico wine store has a
reasonably priced selection from more than eight countries plus a wide
assortment of pâtés and cheeses, crepes, sausages, cigars, French bread,
and chocolates. ⑤ *Average main: US$10* ✉ *Bay Front at Kennedy Ave.,
Roseau* ☎ *767/449–8686* ⊕ *www.natureisle.com/cocorico/* ⊘ *Closed
Sun. unless ship is in port, then 10–4.*

$ ✕ **Pearl's Cuisine.** In a Creole town house in central Roseau, chef Pearl,
CARIBBEAN   with her robust and infectious character, prepares some of the island's
best local cuisine, such as callaloo soup, fresh fish, and rabbit. Her menu
changes daily, but she offers such local delicacies as *sousse* (pickled pigs'
feet), blood pudding, and rotis. When sitting down, ask for a table on
the open-air gallery that overlooks Roseau and prepare for an abundant portion, but make sure you leave space for dessert. If you're on
the go, enjoy a quick meal from the daily, varied menu in the ground-
floor snack bar. You're spoiled for choice when it comes to the fresh
fruit juices. ⑤ *Average main: US$12* ✉ *50 King George V St., Roseau*
☎ *767/448–8707* ⊘ *Closed Sun. No dinner.*

FALMOUTH, JAMAICA

Catherine
MacGillivray

Midway between Ocho Rios and Montego Bay, Falmouth, which was
founded in 1769, prospered from Jamaica's status as the world's leading sugar producer. With more than 80 sugar estates nearby, the town
was meticulously mapped out in the colonial tradition, with streets
named after British royalty and heroes. The richness of the town's
historic Georgian structures, many of which are still occupied and
maintained, is reflected in its heritage. The city has long been heralded
for its forward-thinking hygiene policies (the first piped water supply
system in the Western Hemisphere—established here in 1799—continues to be a source of pride) and progressive politics (Falmouth was
the birthplace of Jamaica's abolitionist movement in the early 19th
century). The site of many slave revolts, Falmouth's residents turned
scores of the town's buildings into safe houses for escaped slaves until
the practice of slavery was outlawed in Jamaica in 1838. While Falmouth is seeing a revival with the opening of a purpose-built cruise
port in 2011, buildings that may seem unimpressive as they undergo
restoration are still rich in history. In 1996 the Jamaican government
declared Falmouth a National Monument.

ESSENTIALS

CURRENCY   The Jamaican dollar (J$84 to US$1). Currency-exchange booths are
located in the pier area as well as just outside the entrance gate on Seaboard Street; however, the U.S. dollar is accepted virtually everywhere,

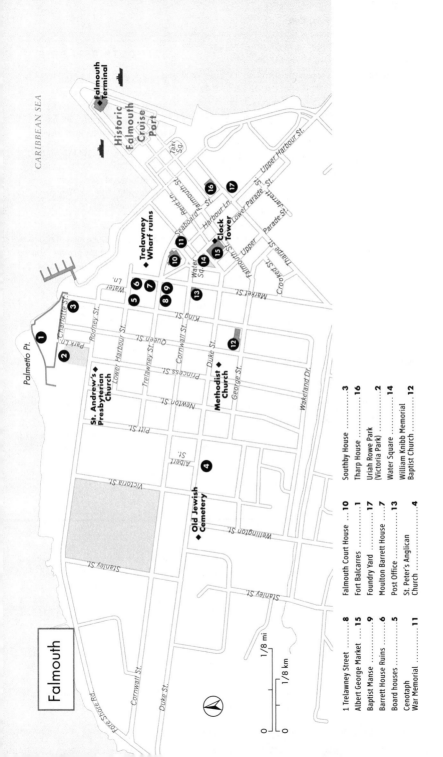

Falmouth

CARIBBEAN SEA

Palmetto Pt.

Falmouth Terminal

Historic Falmouth Cruise Port

Taxi Sq.

Trelawney Wharf ruins

Clock Tower

St. Andrew's Presbyterian Church

Methodist Church

Old Jewish Cemetery

Cenotaph War Memorial **11**

1 Trelawney Street **8**
Albert George Market ... **15**
Baptist Manse **9**
Barrett House Ruins **6**
Board houses **5**

Falmouth Court House ... **10**
Fort Balcarres **1**
Foundry Yard **17**
Moulton Barrett House ... **7**
Post Office **13**
St. Peter's Anglican Church **4**

Southby House **3**
Tharp House **16**
Uriah Rowe Park (Victoria Park) **2**
Water Square **14**
William Knibb Memorial Baptist Church **12**

1/8 mi
1/8 km
0

though change may be made in Jamaican dollars.

INTERNET The entire Falmouth Cruise Port is a Wi-Fi hot spot accessible for a fee by passengers with personal computers. Numerous cafés and bars outside the port area also offer Internet service for a nominal fee.

TELEPHONE Public telephones are located in the communications center at the Falmouth Cruise Terminal. Travelers also find public phones in the post office at the corner of Cornwall and Market streets. Some U.S. phone companies won't permit credit-card calls to be placed from Jamaica because they've been victims of fraud, so collect calls are often the top option. GSM cell phones equipped with tri-band or world-roaming service will find coverage throughout the Falmouth area.

FALMOUTH BEST BETS

■ **Good Hope Plantation.** The expansive view of the plantation grounds and surrounding countryside from the front garden includes the Martha Brae River.

■ **Historic Falmouth Walking Tour.** Absorb Falmouth's Colonial-era history and discover the town's landmarks and Georgian architectural treasures.

■ **Tharp House.** Located within the Falmouth Cruise Port, the town home of sugar planter John Tharp is one of Falmouth's most historic building. Once a tax collector's office, it is now expected to become a maritime museum.

COMING ASHORE

Cruise ships, including the world's largest, are able to dock at the Falmouth Cruise Port's two berths. A Visitors Information facility is in the pier area. The town is right outside the port gates, and places of interest are easily within walking distance. Currency-exchange booths are in the pier area as well as just outside the entrance gate on Seaboard Street. Further, the cruise-port area has Wi-Fi service (paid) for passengers with laptops. The Falmouth tourist trolley offers a half-hour tour of the town with regular departures from the Port Transportation Center. Tickets and trolley schedules are available in the trolley kiosk at the Taxi Shelter building.

For travel out of town, buses and taxis are available. Bus fare to the beach is $20 round-trip, and taxis are priced by the hour at $35 for up to four people for either a guided tour or transportation to a specific destination. Falmouth's location, almost equidistant to both Montego Bay and Ocho Rios, makes most tours offered at those ports available from Falmouth as well. In truth, though, it's often difficult to book activities privately in Jamaica, so this is one place in the Caribbean where it's usually to your advantage to take a shore excursion offered by your ship. Many of the most popular and adventurous tours are operated by Chukka Caribbean and can only be booked by cruise passengers directly with the cruise lines, as space is pre-sold to ships for their arrival dates. Coaches for pre-booked tours pick up passengers inside the Cruise Port, but authorized independent tour operators are also available there to arrange tours on the spot. Car rental isn't recommended in Jamaica because of the narrow roads and aggressive drivers.

EXPLORING FALMOUTH

Falmouth's streets, which were laid out in a grid plan in the mid-1700s, are easily explored on your own. However, even with a map, finding your way around can be confusing due to a lack of street signs. Should you become disoriented or require directions, look for a member of the Falmouth Tourism Courtesy Corps wearing official white shirts and hats. They are on hand to assist visitors and can help with finding a taxi outside the cruise port.

Points of interest include the Falmouth Courthouse and the adjacent Cenotaph War Memorial; Water Square, where Falmouth residents got running water before New York City; Barrett House Ruins, the remains of the town home of planter William Barrett, who owned much of the land upon which the town is built; and Fort Balcarres, built to guard Falmouth Harbor. Other sights include fine examples of Falmouth's Georgian-era architecture, based on classic Greek and Roman designs and adapted to local conditions to create a unique island style. Georgian buildings are recognizable by their double-hung sash windows, keystones, columns, symmetry of facade, and full-length verandas. Constructed of a native limestone over brick and remarkably preserved, most structures are still in use as either private residences or commercial buildings.

WHAT TO SEE OUTSIDE OF FALMOUTH

Good Hope Plantation. Located 20 minutes from Falmouth, the Good Hope estate was the basis of one of the largest sugar fortunes made in 19th-century Jamaica and contains a rare inventory of restored historic buildings. The Great House was built in 1755 by Thomas Williams for his bride Elizabeth, who died shortly after their marriage and was buried beneath the ground-floor entryway. Subsequently purchased by John Tharp, who also acquired all the adjoining plantations, Good Hope eventually grew to 9,000 acres in its heyday. On today's 2,000-acre estate, with views overlooking the Queen of Spain Valley, the Martha Brae River, and the Cockpit Mountains, all rooms in the Great House are furnished with 18th- and 19th-century Jamaican antiques and, until recently, served as a tourist guest house. Visitors can choose from a variety of activities, including a carriage ride through the grounds, river-tubing on the Martha Brae River, zip-lining through the canopy over the river, ATV exploring, or a more sedate tour of the Great House itself, with or without lunch on the garden patio. Tours are operated by Chukka Caribbean and cannot be purchased independently. So only cruise passengers are able to visit. ⊠ *1 Trelawny St., Falmouth* ☎ *876/469–3444* ⊕ *www.goodhopejamaica.com* ⊠ *Cost of activities varies* ☉ *Daily during cruise ship docking hours.*

SHOPPING

Coming ashore, you will find more than five-dozen shops along the Cruise Port's pedestrian thoroughfares housing well-known international and established Jamaican merchants. Also in the port is a covered open-air craft market, where some 40 vendors offer their wares and items such as T-shirts, caps, and local seasonings. In town, souvenir vendors set up on Seaboard Street near the Courthouse. Water Square is the location of the Albert George Shopping and Historical Center, where artisans offer local craftwork that showcases the history and culture of the area. The upscale Shops at Rose Hall are within fairly easy reach by taxi between Falmouth and Montego Bay.

ACTIVITIES

Most adventure activities offered to cruise-ship passengers in Montego Bay and Ocho Rios, including water sports, trips to nearby beaches, golf, river-rafting, and sightseeing, are also available to cruise passengers in Falmouth. See both Montego Bay and Ocho Rios for more information.

Falmouth Heritage Walks. This leisurely paced walk takes you through Falmouth's commercial and residential streets while your guide shares the little-known history of the town and what made it a rich and significant port in the late 18th and early 19th centuries. Your guide will also explain how the movement to abolish slavery was essentially founded in Falmouth when you visit the former home and grave of the famous abolitionist William Knibb. The full tour takes about 2 hours 15 minutes. ⊠ *Falmouth* ☎ *876/407–2245* ⊕ *www.falmouthheritagewalks. com* ✉ *$25* ⊗ *Times vary throughout the day when ships are in port.*

BEACHES

Doctor's Cave Beach, in the heart of Montego Bay, is easily accessible by private taxi from the cruise port for $20 per person round-trip. The beach itself also has an admission fee.

WHERE TO EAT

$

JAMAICAN

✕ **Club Nazz and Restaurant.** Conveniently located on Market Street just 100 yards west of Falmouth's major landmark, Water Square, the restaurant is housed in a restored and brightly painted Georgian-style building that once served as the town's temporary courthouse. Open seven days a week, locals and visitors alike dig into Jamaican cuisine, such as curried goat, jerk chicken or pork, and rice and peas. For the less adventurous, there are burgers and fries. The full-service bar offers cold Red Stripe beer, soft drinks, and almost any rum drink you can think of. Sadly, most cruise ships set sail before the evening nightclub scene gets underway with performances by a wide cross-section of musicians. ⑤ *Average main: US$12* ⊠ *23 Market St., Falmouth* ▭ *No credit cards.*

FREEPORT-LUCAYA, BAHAMAS

Ramona Settle Grand Bahama Island, the fourth-largest island in the Bahamas, lies only 52 miles (84 km) off Palm Beach, Florida. In 1492, when Columbus first set foot in the Bahamas, Grand Bahama was already populated. Skulls found in caves attest to the existence of the peaceable Lucayans, who were constantly fleeing the more bellicose Caribs. But it was not until the 1950s, when the harvesting of Caribbean yellow pine trees (now protected by Bahamian environmental law) was the island's major industry, that American financier Wallace Groves envisioned Grand Bahama's grandiose future as a tax-free port for the shipment of goods to the United States. It was in that era that the city of Freeport and later Lucaya evolved. They are separated by a 4-mile (6-km) stretch of East Sunrise Highway, although few can tell you where one community ends and the other begins. Most of Grand Bahama's commercial activity is concentrated in Freeport, the Bahamas' second-largest city. Lucaya, with its sprawling shopping complex and water-sports reputation, stepped up to the role of island tourism capital. Resorts, beaches, a casino, and golf courses make both cities popular with visitors.

4

ESSENTIALS

CURRENCY The Bahamian dollar, which trades one-to-one with the U.S. dollar, is universally accepted. There's no need to acquire any Bahamian currency.

INTERNET Port Lucaya Marina has free Wi-Fi service if you have your own laptop.

TELEPHONE Calling locally or internationally is easy in the Bahamas. To place a local call, dial the seven-digit phone number. To call the United States, dial 1 plus the area code. Pay phones cost 25¢ per call; Bahamian and U.S. quarters are accepted, as are BATELCO phone cards. To place a call using a calling card, use your long-distance carrier's access code or dial 0 for the operator. But beware of using the dedicated long-distance public telephones, which are quite costly. Although most U.S. cell phones work in the Bahamas, the roaming coast can be very high, so check with your provider in advance.

COMING ASHORE

Cruise-ship passengers arrive at Lucayan Harbour, which has a clever Bahamian-style look, extensive cruise-passenger terminal facilities, and an entertainment-shopping village. The harbor lies about 10 minutes west of Freeport. Taxis and limos meet all cruise ships. Two passengers are charged $20 and $27 for trips to Freeport and Lucaya, respectively. Fare to Xanadu Beach is $21; it's $30 to Taïno Beach. The price per person drops $5 for larger groups. It's customary to tip taxi drivers 15%. A three-hour sightseeing tour of the Freeport-Lucaya area costs $25 to $35. Four-hour East or West End trips cost about $40. At this writing, an additional two-berth cruise-ship port in William's Town is undergoing the approval process, but no opening date is set yet.

Grand Bahama's flat terrain and straight, well-paved roads make for good scooter riding. Rentals run $35 a day (about $15 an hour). Helmets are required and provided. Look for small rental stands in parking lots and along the road in Freeport and Lucaya and at the larger resorts.

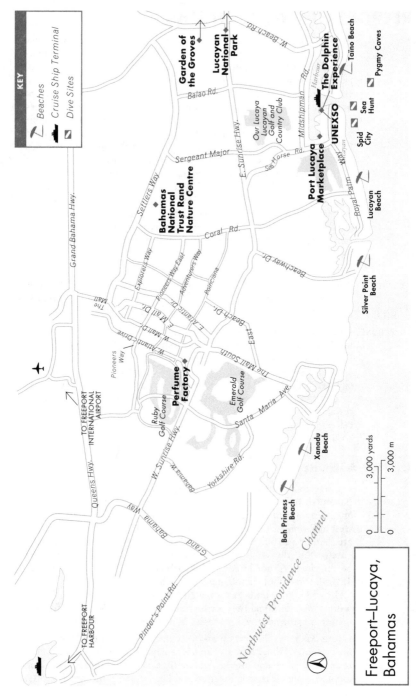

KEY

↗ Beaches

⛴ Cruise Ship Terminal

◨ Dive Sites

Freeport–Lucaya, Bahamas

Garden of the Groves

Lucayan National Park

W. Beach Rd.

Balao Rd.

The Dolphin Experience

Taino Beach

Pygmy Caves

Harbour

Our Lucaya Lucaya Golf and Country Club

Midshipman Rd.

UNEXSO

Sea Hunt

Sergeant Major

E. Sunrise Hwy.

Sea Horse Rd.

Port Lucaya Marketplace

Spid City

Settlers Way

Bahamas National Trust Rand Nature Centre

Coral Rd.

Royal Palm Way

Lucayan Beach

Explorers Way

Pioneers Way East

Adventurers Way

Poinciana

Beachway Dr.

Silver Point Beach

The Mall

Pioneers Way

E. Atlantic Dr.

E. Mall Dr.

Beach Rd.

E. Beach Dr.

Grand Bahama Hwy.

W. Atlantic Drive

W. Mall Dr.

The Mall South

Perfume Factory

Ruby Golf Course

Emerald Golf Course

Santa Maria Ave.

W. Sunrise Hwy.

Bahamia W.

Yorkshire Rd.

Grand Bahama Way

Queens Hwy.

TO FREEPORT INTERNATIONAL AIRPORT

Pinder's Point Rd.

TO FREEPORT HARBOUR

Bah Princess Beach

Xanadu Beach

Northwest Providence Channel

0   3,000 yards

0   3,000 m

It's usually cheaper to rent a car than to hire a taxi. Automobiles, jeeps, and vans can be rented at the Grand Bahama International Airport. Some agencies provide free pickup and delivery service to the cruise-ship port and Freeport and Lucaya, but prices are still not cheap; cars begin at $65 per day.

EXPLORING FREEPORT-LUCAYA

Grand Bahama is the only planned island in the Bahamas. Its towns, villages, and sights are well laid out but far apart. Downtown Freeport and Lucaya are both best appreciated on foot. Buses and taxis can transport you the 4-mile (6-km) distance between the two. In Freeport shopping is the main attraction. Bolstered by the Our Lucaya Resort complex, Lucaya has its beautiful beach and water-sports scene, plus more shopping and a big, beautiful new casino. Outside of town, isolated fishing villages, beaches, natural attractions, and the once-rowdy town of West End make it worthwhile to hire a tour or rent a car. The island stretches 96 miles (154 km) from one end to the other.

FREEPORT

★ **Bahamas National Trust Rand Nature Centre.** On 100 acres just minutes from downtown Freeport, a half mile of self-guided botanical trails shows off 130 types of native plants, including many orchid species. The center is the island's birding hot spot, where you might spy a red-tailed hawk or a Cuban emerald hummingbird. Visit the caged one-eyed Bahama parrot the center has adopted, and a Bahama boa, a species that inhabits most Bahamian islands, but not Grand Bahama. On Tuesday and Thursday free (with admission) guided tours depart at 10:30 am. The visitor center hosts changing local art exhibits. ⊠ *E. Settlers Way, Freeport* ☎ *242/352–5438* 🖻 *$5* ⊗ *Weekdays 9–4; guided nature walk by advance reservation.*

Perfume Factory. Behind the now nearly defunct International Bazaar, the quiet and elegant Perfume Factory occupies a replica 19th-century Bahamian mansion—the kind built by Loyalists who settled in the Bahamas after the American Revolution. The interior resembles a tasteful drawing room. This is the home of Fragrance of the Bahamas, a company that produces perfumes, colognes, and lotions using the scents of jasmine, cinnamon, gardenia, spice, and ginger. Take a free five-minute tour of the mixology laboratory and get a free sample. For $30 an ounce, you can blend your own perfume using any of the 35 scents ($15 for 1½ ounces of blend-it-yourself body lotion). Sniff mixtures until they hit the right combination, then bottle, name, and take home the personalized potion. ⊠ *Behind International Bazaar, W. Sunrise Hwy. and Mall Dr., on access road, Freeport* ☎ *242/352–9391* ⊕ *www.perfumefactory.com* 🖻 *Free* ⊗ *Weekdays 9:30–5, Sat. 11–3.*

LUCAYA

Lucaya, on Grand Bahama's southern coast and just east of Freeport, was developed as the island's resort center. These days it's booming with the megaresort complex called the Our Lucaya Resort, a fine sandy beach, championship golf courses, a casino, a first-class dive operation, and Port Lucaya's shopping and marina facilities. Most cruise ships offer excursions that include a day at Our Lucaya.

The Dolphin Experience. Encounter Atlantic bottlenose dolphins in Sanctuary Bay at one of the world's first and largest dolphin facilities, about 2 miles east of Port Lucaya. A ferry takes you from Port Lucaya to the bay to observe and photograph the animals. If you don't mind getting wet, you can sit on a partially submerged dock or stand waist deep in the water and one of these friendly creatures will swim up to you. You can also engage in one of two swim-with-the-dolphins programs, but participants must be 55 inches or taller. The Dolphin Experience began in 1987, when it trained five dolphins to interact with people. Later, the animals learned to head out to sea and swim with scuba divers on the open reef. A two-hour dive program is available. You can buy tickets for the Dolphin Experience at UNEXSO in Port Lucaya, but be sure to make reservations as early as possible. ✉ *Port Lucaya, Lucaya* ☎ *242/373–1244, 800/992–3483* ⊕ *www.unexso.com* 🖾 *2-hr interaction program $82, 2-hr swim program $169, dolphin dive $219, open-ocean experience $199* ☉ *Daily 8–5.*

> **FREEPORT-LUCAYA BEST BETS**
>
> ■ **Diving with UNEXSO.** Simply one of the world's most respected diving facilities.
>
> ■ **The Dolphin Experience.** Choose your level of involvement.
>
> ■ **East End.** Venture beyond the city to the quiet fishing settlements east of Freeport.
>
> ■ **Lucayan National Park.** Explore caves, hike to the beach, or kayak its mangrove tidal creek.
>
> ■ **Shopping.** Duty-free shopping in the Port Lucaya Marketplace is still good; be sure to haggle if you shop at the straw markets.

Fodor's Choice ★ **Underwater Explorers Society (UNEXSO).** One of the world's most respected diving facilities, UNEXSO welcomes more than 50,000 individuals each year and trains hundreds of them in scuba diving. Facilities include a 17-foot-deep training pool with windows that look out on the harbor, changing rooms and showers, docks, equipment rental, an outdoor café, and an air-tank filling station. Daily dive excursions range from one-day discovery courses and dives to specialty shark, dolphin, and cave diving. ✉ *On wharf at Port Lucaya Marketplace, Lucaya* ☎ *242/373–1244, 800/992–3483* ⊕ *www.unexso.com* 🖾 *One-tank reef dives $59, Discover Scuba course $109, night dives $79, dolphin dives $219, shark dives $99* ☉ *Daily 8–5.*

BEYOND FREEPORT-LUCAYA

Grand Bahama Island narrows at picturesque West End, once Grand Bahama's capital and still home to descendants of the island's first settlers. Seaside villages, with concrete-block houses painted in bright blue and pastel yellow, fill in the landscape between Freeport and West End. The East End is Grand Bahama's "back-to-nature" side. The road east from Lucaya is long, flat, and mostly straight. It cuts through a vast pine forest to reach McLean's Town, the end of the road.

Garden of the Groves. This vibrant 12-acre garden, featuring a trademark chapel and waterfalls, is filled with native Bahamian flora, butterflies, and birds. Interpretative signage identifies plant and animal species. First opened in 1973, the park was renovated and reopened in 2008;

additions include a labyrinth modeled after the one at France's Chartres Cathedral, colorful shops and galleries, a playground, and a multideck outdoor café. Explore on your own or take a guided tour at 10 or 2 (except Sunday). ⊠ *Midshipman Rd. and Churchill Dr., Eastern Grand Bahama* ☎ *242/374-7778* ⊕ *www.thegardenofthegroves.com* 🖃 *$15* ☉ *Daily 9–5; guided tours at 10 and 2 Mon.–Sat.*

HANGERS
Folding or inflatable travel hangers are useful if you need to dry out hand laundry or a bathing suit in your cabin. The ones in your cabin's closet may not be removable.

Lucayan National Park. In this extraordinary 40-acre seaside land preserve, trails and elevated walkways wind through a natural forest of wild tamarind and gumbo-limbo trees, past an observation platform, a mangrove swamp, sheltered pools, and one of the largest explored underwater cave systems in the world (more than 6 miles long).

You can enter the caves at two access points; one is closed in June and July, the bat-nursing season. Twenty miles east of Lucaya, the park contains examples of the island's five ecosystems: beach, hardwood forest, mangroves, rocky coppice, and pine forest. Across the road from the caves, two trails form a loop. Creek Trail's boardwalk showcases impressive interpretive signage, and crosses a mangrove-clotted tidal creek to Gold Rock Beach, a narrow, lightly visited strand of white sand edged by some of the island's highest dunes and jewel-tone sea. ⊠ *Grand Bahama Hwy.* ☎ *242/352–5438* ⊕ *www.bnt.bs/parks_lucayan.php* 🖃 *$3* ☉ *Daily 8:30–4:30.*

SHOPPING

In the stores, shops, and boutiques on Grand Bahama you can find duty-free goods costing up to 40% less than what you might pay back home. At the numerous perfume shops fragrances are often sold at a sweet-smelling 25% below U.S. prices. Be sure to limit your haggling to the straw markets.

★ **Port Lucaya Marketplace.** Lucaya's capacious and lively shopping complex—a dozen low-rise, pastel-painted colonial buildings whose style was influenced by traditional island homes—is on the waterfront 4 miles east of Freeport and across the street from a massive resort complex. The shopping center, whose walkways are lined with hibiscus, bougainvillea, and croton, has about 100 well-kept establishments, among them waterfront restaurants and bars, and shops that sell clothes, crystal and china, watches, jewelry, perfumes, and local arts and crafts. The marketplace's centerpiece is **Count Basie Square,** where live bands often perform Rake 'n' Scrape and gospel in the gazebo bandstand. Lively outdoor watering holes line the square, which is also *the* place to celebrate the holidays: a tree-lighting ceremony takes place in the festively decorated spot and fireworks highlight the New Year's Eve party. ⊠ *Sea Horse Rd., Lucaya* ☎ *242/373–8446* ⊕ *www.portlucayamarketplace. com* ☉ *Daily 10–6.*

ACTIVITIES

FISHING

Private boat charters for up to four people cost $300 and up for a half-day and $350 and up for a full day. Bahamian law limits the catching of game fish to six each of dolphinfish, kingfish, tuna, or wahoo per vessel.

Reef Tours Ltd. This company offers deep-sea fishing for four to six people on custom boats. Equipment and bait are provided free. All vessels are licensed, inspected, and insured. Trips run from 8:30 to 12:15 and from 1 to 4:45, weather permitting ($130 per angler, $60 per spectator). Full-day trips are also available, as are bottom-fishing excursions, glass-bottom boat tours, snorkeling trips, and sailing–snorkeling cruises. Reservations are essential. ⊠ *Port Lucaya Marketplace* ☎ *242/373–5880* ⊕ *www.bahamasvacationguide.com/reeftours.*

GOLF

Fodor's Choice ★ **Our Lucaya Beach and Golf Resort Lucayan Course.** This golf course, designed by Dick Wilson, is a dramatic 6,824-yard, par-72, 18-hole course featuring a balanced six straight holes, six classic left-turning doglegs, and six right-turning holes. The 18th hole has a double lake, towering limestone structure, and a clubhouse nearby. Its state-of-the-art instruction facilities include a practice putting green with bunker and chipping areas, covered teaching bays, and a teaching seminar area. A shared electric cart is included in green fees. Ask about special "twilight" fees that are as low as $55 for 9 holes. ⊠ *Our Lucaya Beach and Golf Resort, Lucaya* ☎ *242/373–2002, 866/870–7148* ⊕ *www.ourlucaya. com/golf/the-lucayan-course* ⌨ *Resort guests $120, nonguests $130.*

Ruby Golf Course. This course reopened in 2008 with renovated landscaping but basically the same 18-hole, par-72 Jim Fazio design—a lot of sand traps and challenges on holes 7, 9, 10, and 18—especially playing from the blue tees. Hole 10 requires a tee shot onto a dogleg right fairway around a pond. There's a small restaurant-bar and pro shop at the 18th hole. ⊠ *West Sunrise Hwy. and Wentworth Ave., Freeport* ☎ *242/352–1851* ⌨ *$65–$90.*

BEACHES

Some 60 miles of magnificent, pristine stretches of sand extend between Freeport-Lucaya and the island's eastern end. Most are used only by people who live in adjacent settlements. The beaches have no public facilities, so beachgoers often headquarter at one of the local beach bars, which provide free transportation. **Lucayan Beach** is readily accessible from the town's main drag and is always lively and lovely. **Taïno Beach,** near Freeport, is fun for families, water-sports enthusiasts, and partyers. Near Freeport, **Xanadu Beach** provides a mile of white sand. Gold Rock Beach is about 45 minutes from the cruise port, but it's one of the most widely photographed beaches in the Bahamas; at low time, unique sandbars and ridges form.

WHERE TO EAT

$ **⤬ Billy Joe's on the Beach.** Eating fresh conch salad and drinking Kalik
BAHAMIAN beer with your toes in the sand: it doesn't get any better or more Baha-
★ mian. Billy Joe was such a fixture on the beach, selling his freshly made-
on-the-spot (watch it being prepared!) conch salad, cracked conch, and
grilled conch (minced and cooked with tomatoes, onions, and bell peppers in an aluminum packet on the barbecue), that when Our Lucaya
opened, the owners allowed him to stay on the property. This is where
resort guests go "slumming" without having to travel farther than the
edge of the resort's beach. Fried lobster, cheeseburgers, and cracked
conch are other specialties. $ *Average main: $11* ⊠ *Lucaya Beach,
Lucaya* ☎ *242/373–1333* ▭ *No credit cards.*

$$ **⤬ Pier One.** Blown down in the 2004 hurricanes, Pier One is back with
SEAFOOD a sturdier building decorated with the old trademark nautical para-
phernalia. Diners have their choice of picnic tables around the balcony
or inside the spacious dining and bar area. Popular with cruise-ship
passengers because of its location at the port entrance, the restaurant
also hosts shark feedings nightly at 7, 8, and 9. To go with this activity,
order specialties such as smoked shark, shark fritters, blackened lemon
shark fillet, or shark curry with bananas. The extensive menus also
offer mussels, panfried mahi, grouper Cordon Bleu, lobster and mush-
rooms with cream, chicken curry, fettuccini with seafood, and steaks.
$ *Average main: $25* ⊠ *Freeport Harbour* ☎ *242/352–6674* ⊕ *www.
pieronebahamas.com* ⤝ *Reservations essential.*

GRAND CAYMAN, CAYMAN ISLANDS

Jordan Simon   The largest and most populous of the Cayman Islands, Grand Cay-
man is also one of the most popular cruise destinations in the Western
Caribbean, largely because it doesn't suffer from the ailments afflicting
many larger ports: panhandlers, hasslers, and crime. Instead, the Cay-
man economy is a study in stability, and the environment is healthy
and prosperous. Though the island is rather featureless, Grand Cay-
man is a diver's paradise, with pristine waters and a colorful variety
of marine life. Compared with other Caribbean ports, there are fewer
things to see on land here; instead, the island's most impressive sights
are underwater. Snorkeling, diving, and glass-bottom-boat and sub-
marine rides top every ship's shore-excursion list, and can also be
arranged at major aquatic shops if you don't go on a ship-sponsored
excursion. Grand Cayman is also famous for the nearly 600 offshore
banks in George Town; not surprisingly, the standard of living is high,
and nothing is cheap.

ESSENTIALS

CURRENCY   The Cayman Island dollar (CI$1 to US$1.25). The U.S. dollar is
accepted everywhere, and ATMs often dispense cash in both curren-
cies, though you may receive change in Cayman dollars. Prices are
often quoted in Cayman dollars, so make sure you know which cur-
rency you're dealing with so you don't end up paying 25% more than
you expected.

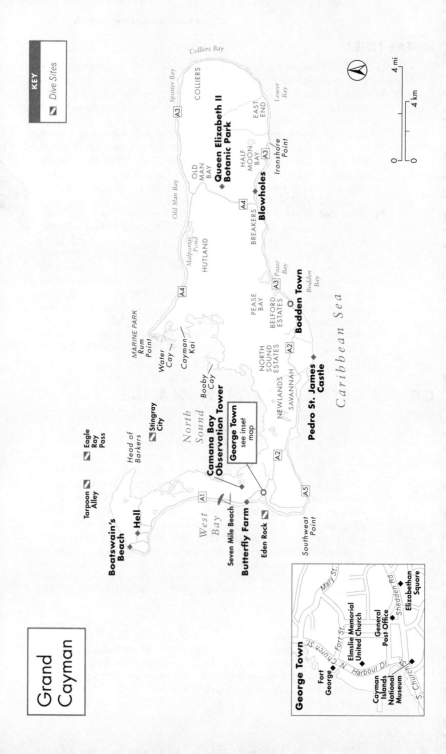

Grand Cayman

KEY

◢ *Dive Sites*

Colliers Bay

Spotter Bay

A3

COLLIERS

Lower Bay

EAST END

Queen Elizabeth II Botanic Park

HALF MOON BAY

A3

Ironshore Point

OLD MAN BAY

Blowholes

A4

BREAKERS

Old Man Bay

Malportas Pond

HUTLAND

A4

MARINE PARK
Rum Point

PEASE BAY

Pease Bay

A3

Bodden Town

Bodden Bay

Water Cay

Cayman Kai

BELFORD ESTATES

Booby Cay

North Sound

NORTH SOUND ESTATES

A2

NEWLANDS

SAVANNAH

Pedro St. James Castle

Caribbean Sea

Head of Barkers

◢ **Stingray City**

Camana Bay Observation Tower

George Town
see inset map

A2

◢ **Tarpoon Alley**

◢ **Eagle Ray Pass**

Boatswain's Beach

Hell

West Bay

A1

Seven Mile Beach

Butterfly Farm

◢ **Eden Rock**

A5

Southweat Point

0   4 km

0   4 mi

George Town

Mary St.

Fort St.

N. Church St.

Elmslie Memorial United Church

General Post Office

Shedden Rd.

Elizabethan Square

Fort George

N. Harbour Dr.

Cayman Islands National Museum

S. Church St.

TELEPHONE To dial the United States, dial 1 followed by the area code and telephone number. To place a credit-card call, dial 800/744–7777; credit-card and calling-card calls can be made from any public phone.

COMING ASHORE

Ships anchor in George Town Harbour and tender passengers onto Harbour Drive, the center of the shopping district. If you just want to walk around town and shop or visit Seven Mile Beach, you're probably better off on your own, but the Stingray Sandbar snorkeling trip is a highlight of many Caribbean vacations and fills up quickly on cruise-ship days, so it's often better to order that excursion from your ship, even though it will be more crowded and expensive than if you took an independent trip.

A tourist information booth is on the pier, and taxis queue for disembarking passengers. Taxi fares are determined by an elaborate structure set by the government, and although rates may seem high, cabbies rarely try to rip off tourists. Ask to see the chart if you want to check a quoted fare. Taxi drivers won't usually do hourly rates for small-group tours; you must arrange a sightseeing tour with a company. Car rentals range in price from $40 to $95 per day (plus a $7.50 driving permit), so they are a good option if you want to do some independent exploring. You can easily see the entire island and have time to stop at a beach in a single day. ⚠ **Driving in the Cayman Islands is on the left (as in the United Kingdom), though the steering wheel will be on the left (as in the United States).**

EXPLORING GRAND CAYMAN

GEORGE TOWN

Begin exploring the capital by strolling along the waterfront Harbour Drive to **Elmslie Memorial United Church,** named after the first Presbyterian missionary to serve in Cayman. Its vaulted ceiling, wooden arches, and sedate nave reflect the religious nature of island residents. In front of the court building, in the center of town, names of influential Caymanians are inscribed on the **Wall of History,** which commemorates the islands' quincentennial in 2003. Across the street is the **Cayman Islands Legislative Assembly Building,** next door to the **1919 Peace Memorial Building.** In the middle of the financial district is the **General Post Office,** built in 1939. Let the kids pet the big blue iguana statues.

⥁ **Cayman Islands National Museum.** Built in 1833, the historically significant
Fodor'sChoice clapboard home of the national museum has had several different incar-
★ nations over the years, serving as courthouse, jail, post office, and dance hall. It features an ongoing archaeological excavation of the Old Gaol and excellent 3-D bathymetric displays, murals, dioramas, and videos that illustrate local geology, flora and fauna, and island history. The first floor focuses on natural history, including a microcosm of Cayman ecosystems, from beaches to dry woodlands and swamps, and offers such interactive elements as a simulated sub. Upstairs, the cultural exhibit

features renovated murals, video history reenactments, and 3-D back panels in display cases holding thousands of artifacts ranging from a 14-foot catboat with animatronic captain to old coins and rare documents painting a portrait of daily life and past industries such as shipbuilding and turtling, stressing Caymanians' resilience when they had little contact with the outside world. There are also temporary exhibits focusing on aspects of Caymanian culture, a local art collection, and interactive displays for kids. ☒ *Harbour Dr., George Town* ☎ *345/949–8368* ⊕ *www.museum. ky* ▨ *$8* ☉ *Weekdays 9–5, Sat. 9–1.*

ELSEWHERE ON THE ISLAND

☾ **Blowholes.** When the easterly trade winds blow hard, crashing waves force water into caverns and send impressive geysers shooting up as much as 20 feet through the ironshore. The blowholes were partially filled during Hurricane Ivan in 2004, so the water must be rough to recapture their former elemental drama. ☒ *Frank Sound Rd., roughly 10 miles (16 km) east of Bodden Town, near East End.*

☾ **Boatswain's Beach.** Cayman's premier attraction, the Turtle Farm,
Fodor's Choice has been rebranded and transformed into a marine theme park. The
★ expanded complex now has several souvenir shops and restaurants. Still, the turtles remain a central attraction, and you can tour ponds in the original research–breeding facility with thousands in various stages of growth, some up to 600 pounds and more than 70 years old. Turtles can be picked up from the tanks, a real treat for children and adults as the little creatures flap their fins and splash the water. Four areas—three aquatic and one dry—cover 23 acres; different-color bracelets determine access (the steep full-pass admission includes snorkeling gear). The park helps promote conservation, encouraging interaction (a tidal pool houses invertebrates such as starfish and crabs) and observation. Audio tours are available with different focuses, from butterflies to bush medicine. The last stop is the living museum, **Cayman Street**, complete with facades duplicating different types of vernacular architecture; an herb and fruit garden; porch-side artisans, musicians, and storytellers; model catboats; live cooking on an old-fashioned caboose (outside kitchen) oven; and interactive craft demonstrations from painting mahogany to thatch weaving. ☒ *825 Northwest Point Rd., Box 812, West Bay* ☎ *345/949–3894* ⊕ *www.boatswainsbeach.ky* ▨ *Comprehensive ticket $45; Turtle Farm only, $30* ☉ *Daily 8:30–4:30.*

GRAND CAYMAN BEST BETS

■ **Diving.** If you're a diver, you'll find several good sites close to shore.

■ **Queen Elizabeth II Botanic Garden.** A beautiful garden has native plants and rare blue iguanas.

■ **Seven Mile Beach.** One of the Caribbean's best beaches is a short ride from the cruise pier.

■ **Shopping.** George Town has a wide range of shops near the cruise-ship pier.

■ **Stingray City.** This is one of the most fun adventures the Caribbean has to offer.

Bodden Town. In the island's original south-shore capital you can find an old cemetery on the shore side of the road. Graves with A-frame structures are said to contain the remains of pirates. There are also the ruins of a fort and a wall erected by slaves in the 19th century. The National Trust runs tours of the restored 1840s Mission House. A curio shop serves as the entrance to what's called the Pirate's Caves ($8), partially underground natural formations that are more hokey (decked out with fake treasure chests and mannequins in pirate garb, with an outdoor petting zoo) than spooky. ⊠ *Grand Cayman.*

🕐 **Camana Bay Observation Tower.** This 75-foot structure provides striking
★ 360-degree panoramas of otherwise flat Grand Cayman, sweeping from George Town and Seven Mile Beach to the North Sound. The double-helix staircase is impressive in its own right. Running alongside the steps (though an elevator is also available), a floor-to-ceiling mosaic replicates the look and feel of a dive from seabed to surface. Constructed of countless tiles in 114 different colors, it's one of the world's largest marine-themed mosaic installations. Benches and lookout points encourage you to take your time and take in the views as you ascend. Afterward you can enjoy 500-acre Camana Bay's gardens, waterfront boardwalk, and pedestrian paths lined with shops and restaurants, or frequent live entertainment. ⊠ *Extending between Seven Mile Beach and North Sound, 2 miles (3 km) north of George Town, Camana Bay* ☎ *345/640–3500* ⊕ *www.camanabay.com* ☎ *Free* ☼ *Sunrise–10 pm.*

Hell. Quite literally the tourist trap from Hell, this attraction does offer free admission, fun photo ops, and sublime surrealism. Its name refers to the quarter-acre of menacing shards of charred brimstone thrusting up like vengeful spirits (actually blackened and "sculpted" by acid-secreting algae and fungi over millennia). The attractions are the small post office and a gift shop where you can get cards and letters postmarked from Hell, not to mention wonderfully silly postcards titled "When Hell Freezes Over" (depicting bathing beauties on the beach), "The Devil Made Me Do It" bumper stickers, Scotch bonnet–based Hell sauce, and "The coolest shop in Hell" T-shirts. ⊠ *Hell Rd., West Bay* ☎ *345/949–3358* ☎ *Free* ☼ *Daily 9–6.*

Fodor'sChoice **Pedro St. James Castle.** Built in 1780, the greathouse is Cayman's oldest
★ stone structure and the only remaining late-18th-century residence on the island. In its capacity as courthouse and jail, it was the birthplace of Caymanian democracy, where in December 1831 the first elected parliament was organized and in 1835 the Slavery Abolition Act signed. The structure still has original or historically accurate replicas of sweeping verandas, mahogany floors, rough-hewn wide-beam ceilings, outside louvers, stone and oxblood- or mustard-color lime-wash-painted walls, brass fixtures, and Georgian furnishings (from tea caddies to canopy beds to commodes). Paying obsessive attention to detail, the curators even fill glasses with faux wine. The mini-museum also includes a hodgepodge of displays from slave emancipation to old stamps. The buildings are surrounded by 8 acres of natural parks and woodlands. You can stroll through landscaping of native Caymanian flora and experience one of the most spectacular views on the island from atop the dramatic Great Pedro Bluff. First watch the impressive multimedia theater show, complete with

smoking pots, misting rains, and two film screens where the story of Pedro's Castle is presented on the hour. The poignant Hurricane Ivan Memorial outside uses text, images, and symbols to represent important aspects of that horrific 2004 natural disaster. ✉ *Pedro Castle Rd., Box 305, Savannah* ☎ *345/947–3329* ⊕ *www.pedrostjames.ky* 🔳 *$10* ☉ *Daily 9–5.*

STROLLERS

Parents should bring along an umbrella stroller for walks around the ship as well as the ports of call; people often underestimate how big ships are. It also comes in handy at the airport. Wheel baby right to the departure gate—the stroller is gate checked and will be waiting for you when you arrive at your port of embarkation.

Fodor's Choice ★ **Queen Elizabeth II Botanic Park.** This 65-acre wilderness preserve showcases a wide range of indigenous and nonindigenous tropical vegetation, approximately 2,000 species in total. Splendid sections include numerous water features from limpid lily ponds to cascades; a Heritage Garden with a traditional cottage and "caboose" (outside kitchen) that includes crops that might have been planted on Cayman a century ago; and a Floral Colour Garden arranged by color, the walkway wandering through sections of pink, red, orange, yellow, white, blue, mauve, lavender, and purple. A 2-acre lake and adjacent wetlands includes three islets that provide a habitat and breeding ground for native birds just as showy as the floral displays: green herons, black-necked stilts, American coots, blue-winged teal, cattle egrets, and rare West Indian whistling ducks. The nearly mile-long Woodland Trail encompasses every Cayman ecosystem from wetland to cactus thicket, buttonwood swamp to lofty woodland with imposing mahogany trees. You'll encounter birds, lizards, turtles, agoutis, and more, but the park's star residents are the protected endemic blue iguanas, found only in Grand Cayman. The world's most endangered iguana, they're the focus of the National Trust's Blue Iguana Recovery Program, a captive breeding and reintroduction facility. This section of the park is usually closed to the general public, though released "blue dragons" hang out in the vicinity. The Trust conducts 90-minute behind-the-scenes safaris Monday–Saturday at 11 am for $30. ✉ *367 Botanic Rd.* ☎ *345/947–9462* ⊕ *www.botanic-park.ky* 🔳 *$10* ☉ *Apr.–Sept., daily 9–6:30; Oct.–Mar., daily 9–5:30; last admission 1 hr before closing.*

SHOPPING

★ **Cathy Church's Underwater Photo Centre and Gallery.** Come see a collection of the acclaimed underwater shutterbug's spectacular color and limited-edition black-and-white underwater photos. Have Cathy autograph her latest coffee-table book and regale you with anecdotes of her globe-trotting adventures. The store also carries the latest marine camera equipment, and she'll schedule private underwater photography instruction as well on her own dive boat outfitted with special graphics-oriented computers to critique your work. She also does wedding photography, both above and underwater. ✉ *S. Church St., George Town* ☎ *345/949–7415* ⊕ *www.cathychurch.com.*

★ **Guy Harvey's Gallery and Shoppe.** This is where world-renowned marine biologist, conservationist, and artist Guy Harvey showcases his aquatic-inspired action-packed art in nearly every conceivable medium, branded tableware, and sportswear (even logo soccer balls and Zippos). The soaring, two-story 4,000-square-foot space is almost more theme park than store, with monitors playing his sportfishing videos, wood floors inlaid with tile duplicating rippling water, dangling catboats "attacked" by lifelike shark models, and life-size murals honoring such classics as Hemingway's *Old Man and the Sea.* Original paintings, sculpture, and drawings are expensive, but there's something (tile art, prints, lithographs, and photos) in most price ranges. ⊠ *49 S. Church St., George Town* ☎ *345/943–4891.*

★ **Kirk Freeport Plaza.** This downtown shopping center, home to the Kirk Freeport flagship department store, is ground zero for couture; it's also known for its boutiques selling fine watches and jewelry, china, crystal, leather, perfumes, and cosmetics, from Baccarat to Bulgari, Raymond Weil to Waterford and Wedgwood (the last two share their own autonomous boutique). Just keep walking—there's plenty of eye-catching, mind-boggling consumerism in all directions: Boucheron, Cartier (with its own mini-boutique), Chanel, Clinique, Christian Dior, Clarins, Estée Lauder, Fendi, Guerlain, Lancôme, Yves Saint Laurent, Issey Miyake, Jean Paul Gaultier, Nina Ricci, Rolex, Roberto Coin, Rosenthal and Royal Doulton china, and more. ⊠ *Cardinal Ave., George Town.*

Landmark. Stores in the Landmark sell perfumes, treasure coins, and upscale beachwear; Breezes by the Bay restaurant is upstairs. ⊠ *Harbour Dr., George Town.*

Tortuga Rum Company. This company bakes, then vacuum-seals, more than 10,000 of its world-famous rum cakes daily, adhering to the original "secret" century-old recipe. There are eight flavors, from banana to Blue Mountain coffee. The 12-year-old rum, blended from private stock though actually distilled in Guyana, is a connoisseur's delight for after-dinner sipping. You can buy a fresh rum cake at the airport on the way home at the same prices as at the factory store. ⊠ *N. Sound Rd., Industrial Park, George Town* ☎ *345/949–7701* ⊕ *www. tortugarumcakes.com.*

ACTIVITIES

DIVING AND SNORKELING

Pristine water (visibility often exceeding 100 feet [30 meters]), breathtaking coral formations, and plentiful and exotic marine life mark the **Great Wall**—a world-renowned dive site just off the north side of Grand Cayman. A must-see for adventurous souls is **Stingray City** in the North Sound, noted as the best 12-foot (3½-meter) dive in the world, where dozens of stingrays congregate, tame enough to suction squid from your outstretched palm. Nondivers gravitate to **Stingray Sandbar,** a shallower part of the North Sound, which has become a popular snorkeling spot; it is also a hangout for the stingrays. If someone tells you that the minnows are in at **Eden Rock,** drop everything and dive here (on South Church Street, south of George Town). The schools swarm around you as you glide through the grottoes, forming quivering curtains of liquid silver as shafts of sunlight pierce the sandy bottom.

🕐 **DiveTech.** DiveTech has opportu-
Fodor's Choice nities for shore diving at its two
★ north-coast locations, which provide loads of interesting creatures, a mini-wall, and the North Wall. With quick access to West Bay, the boats are quite comfortable. Technical training (a specialty of owner Nancy Easterbrook) is unparalleled, and the company offers good, personable service as well as the latest gadgetry such as underwater DPV scooters. ✉ *Cobalt Coast Resort & Suites, 18-A Sea Fan Dr., West Bay* ☎ *345/946–5658, 888/946–5656* ⊕ *www.divetech.com.*

🕐 **Red Sail Sports.** Red Sail Sports offers daily trips from most of the major hotels. Dives are often run as guided tours, a perfect option for beginners. If you're experienced and your air lasts a long time, consult the boat captain to see if he requires that you come up with the group (determined by the first person who runs low on air). There is a full range of kids' dive options for ages 5 to 15, including SASY and Bubblemakers. The company also operates Stingray City tours, dinner and sunset sails, and just about every major water sport from Wave Runners to windsurfing. ✉ *Grand Cayman* ☎ *345/949–8745, 345/623–5965, 877/506–6368* ⊕ *www.redsailcayman.com.*

FISHING

Cayman waters are abundant with blue and white marlin, yellowfin tuna, sailfish, dolphinfish, bonefish, and wahoo. Two-dozen boats are available for charter.

★ **Sea Star Charters.** Sea Star Charters, aka Clinton's Watersports, is run by Clinton Ebanks, a fine and very friendly Caymanian who will do whatever it takes to make sure that you have a wonderful time on his two 27- and 28-foot cabin cruisers (and from the 35-foot trimaran used primarily for snorkeling cruises), enjoying light-tackle, bone-, and bottom-fishing. He's a good choice for beginners and offers a nice cultural experience as well as sailing charters and snorkeling with complimentary transportation and equipment. Only cash and traveler's checks are accepted. ✉ *Grand Cayman* ☎ *345/949–1016, 345/916–5234.*

HIKING

★ **Mastic Trail.** The National Trust's internationally significant Mastic Trail, used in the 1800s as the only direct path to and from the North Side, is a rugged 2-mile (3-km) slash through 776 dense acres of woodlands, black mangrove swamps, savannah, agricultural remnants, and ancient rock formations. It embraces more than 700 species, including Cayman's largest remaining contiguous ancient forest (one of the heavily deforested Caribbean's last examples). A comfortable walk depends on weather—winter is better because it's drier, though flowering plants such as the banana orchid set the trail ablaze in summer. Call the National Trust to determine suitability and to book a guide for $30; tours are run daily from 9 to 5 by appointment only, regularly on Wednesday at 9 am (sometimes earlier in summer). Or walk on the wild side with a $5 guidebook that provides information on the ecosystems you traverse, the endemic wildlife you might encounter, seasonal changes, poisonous plants to avoid, and folkloric uses of various flora. The trip takes about three hours. ⊠ *Frank Sound Rd., entrance by fire station at botanic park, Breakers, East End* ☏ *345/749–1121, 345/749–1124 for guide reservations* ⊕ *www.nationaltrust.org.ky.*

BEACHES

Fodor'sChoice ★ **Seven Mile Beach.** Grand Cayman's west coast is dominated by the famous Seven Mile Beach—actually a 6½-mile-long (10-km-long) expanse of powdery white sand overseeing lapis water stippled with a rainbow of parasails and kayaks. The width of the beach varies with the season; toward the south end it narrows and disappears altogether south of the Marriott, leaving only rock and ironshore. It starts to broaden into its normal silky softness anywhere between Tarquyn Manor and the Reef Grill at Royal Palms. Free of litter and pesky peddlers, it's an unspoiled (though often crowded) environment. Most of the island's resorts, restaurants, and shopping centers sit along this strip. At the public beach toward the north end you can find chairs for rent ($10 for the day, including a beverage), a playground, water toys aplenty, two beach bars, restrooms, and showers. The best snorkeling is at either end, by the Marriott and Treasure Island or off the northern section called Cemetery Reef Beach. ⊠ *West Bay Rd., Seven Mile Beach.*

WHERE TO EAT

$$
CARIBBEAN ✕ **Breezes by the Bay.** There isn't a bad seat in the house at this nonstop feel-good fiesta festooned with tiny paper lanterns, Christmas lights, ship murals, model boats, and Mardi Gras beads (you're "lei'd" upon entering). Wraparound balconies take in a dazzling panorama from South Sound to Seven Mile Beach. It's a joyous nonstop happy hour all day every day, especially at Countdown to Sunset. Signs promise "the good kind of hurricanes," referring to the 23-ounce signature "category 15" cocktails with fresh garnishes; rum aficionados will find 48 varieties (flights available). Equally fresh food at bargain prices, including homemade baked goods and ice creams, isn't an afterthought. Chunky, velvety conch chowder served in a bread bowl or near-definitive conch fritters are meals in themselves. Hefty sandwiches are slathered with yummy jerk mayo or garlicky aioli. Signature standouts include meltingly moist whole fish escoveitch, curry chicken, popcorn shrimp, jerk-glazed pork chops, and any pie from the new pizza station. ⑤ *Average main: $19* ⊠ *Harbor Dr., George Town* ☏ *345/943–8439* ⊕ *www.breezesbythebay.com.*

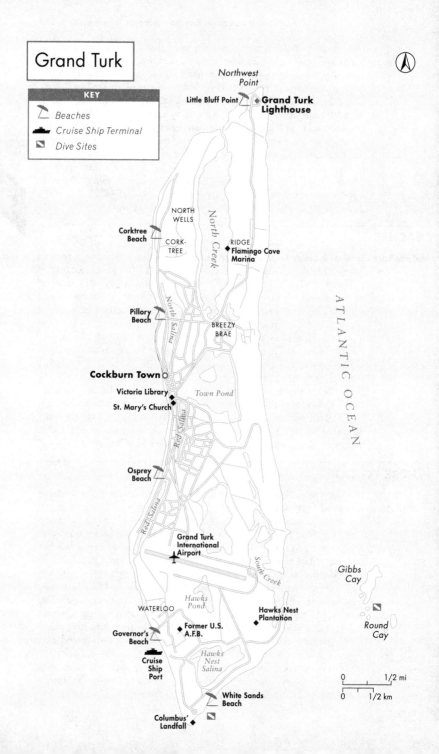

$$
CARIBBEAN
✕ **Sunshine Grill.** This cheerful, cherished locals' secret serves haute comfort food at bargain-basement prices. Even the chattel-style poolside building, painted a delectable lemon with lime shutters, whets the appetite. Sunshine ranks high in the island's greatest burger debate, while the jerk chicken egg rolls and fabulous fish and Cuban chicken tacos elevate pub grub to an art form. Wash it down with one of the many signature libations, like the Painkiller. Take advantage of affordably priced nightly dinner specials such as Thai chili salmon, red snapper amandine, and Cuban pork loin with *sofrito* (a dip of cilantro, garlic, onions, tomatoes, and oregano). $ *Average main: $17* ⊠ *Sunshine Suites, West Bay Rd., Seven Mile Beach* ☎ *345/949–3000.*

GRAND TURK, TURKS AND CAICOS ISLANDS

4

Ramona Settle

Just 7 miles (11 km) long and a little over 1 mile (1½ km) wide, Grand Turk, the political capital of the Turks and Caicos Islands, has been a longtime favorite destination for divers eager to explore the 7,000-foot-deep pristine coral walls that drop down only 300 yards out to sea. On shore, the tiny, quiet island is home to white-sand beaches, the National Museum, and a small population of wild horses and donkeys, which leisurely meander past the white-walled courtyards, pretty churches, and bougainvillea-covered colonial inns on their daily commute into town. The main settlement on the island is tranquil Cockburn Town, and that's where most of the small hotels, not to mention Pillory Beach, can be found. Although it has the second-largest number of inhabitants of all the Turks and Caicos Island, Grand Turk's permanent population has still not reached 4,000.

ESSENTIALS

CURRENCY
The U.S. dollar. You'll find branches of Scotiabank and FirstCaribbean on Grand Turk, with ATMs; all of these are in tiny Cockburn Town.

INTERNET
There's no Internet café at the cruise center, but if you have a laptop, you might take it to the restaurant at the Osprey Beach Hotel, where you can take advantage of the hotel's free Wi-Fi.

TELEPHONE
To make local calls, dial the seven-digit number. To make calls from the Turks and Caicos, dial 0, then 1, the area code, and the number. All telephone service is provided by LIME (formerly Cable & Wireless), and your U.S. cell phone may work on Grand Turk. Calling cards are available, or you can make a call using AT&T's USADirect by dialing 800/872–2881 to charge the call to your credit card or an AT&T prepaid calling card.

COMING ASHORE

Cruise ships dock at the southern end of the island, near the former U.S. Air Force base south of the airport. The purpose-built, $40 million cruise center is about 3 miles (5 km) from tranquil Cockburn Town, Pillory Beach, and the Ridge, and far from most of the western shore dive sites. The center has many facilities, including shopping, a large, freeform pool, car-rental booths, and even a dock from which many sea-bound excursions depart. Governor's Beach is adjacent to the cruise-ship complex and one of the island's best beaches, but others are right in and around Cockburn Town.

If you want to come into Cockburn Town, it's reachable by taxi. Taxi rates are per person and by "zone"; you'll find a rate card outside the cruise terminal. You can also rent a car to explore the island on your own terms and schedule.

Grand Turk Cruise Terminal. Grand Turk Cruise Terminal has a website that shows all the cruise schedules, lists all the shops at the terminal, and completely outlines options for excursions and transportation. A bonus is the live webcam so you can check the actual weather at any given moment. ⊠ *South Base, Grand Turk Cruise Terminal* ☎ *649/946–1040* ⊕ *www.grandturkcc.com.*

Grace Bay Car Rentals. Grace Bay Car Rentals has an office at the port, so you can see the sights on your own time. Remember, driving is on the left. ⊠ *Providenciales* ☎ *649/231–8500* ⊕ *www.gracebaycarrentals.com.*

EXPLORING GRAND TURK

Pristine beaches with vistas of turquoise waters, small local settlements, historic ruins, and native flora and fauna are among the sights on Grand Turk. Fewer than 4,000 people live on this 7½-square-mile (19-square-km) island, and it's hard to get lost, as there aren't many roads.

COCKBURN TOWN

The buildings in the colony's capital and seat of government reflect a 19th-century Bermudian style. Narrow streets are lined with low stone walls and old street lamps, which are now powered by electricity. The once-vital *salinas* (natural salt pans, where the sea leaves a film of salt) have been restored, and covered benches along the sluices offer shady spots for observing wading birds, including flamingos that frequent the shallows. Be sure to pick up a copy of the tourist board's *Heritage Walk* guide to discover Grand Turk's rich architecture.

Her Majesty's Prison. This prison was built in the 19th century to house runaway slaves and slaves who survived the wreck of the *Trouvadore* in 1841. After the slaves were granted freedom, the prison housed criminals and even modern-day drug runners until it closed in the 1990s. The last hanging here was in 1960. Now you can see the cells, solitary-confinement area, and exercise patio. The prison is open only when there is a cruise ship at the port. ⊠ *Pond St., Cockburn Town.*

☾ ★ **Turks and Caicos National Museum.** In one of the oldest stone buildings on the islands, the national museum houses the Molasses Reef wreck, the earliest shipwreck—dating to the early 1500s—discovered in the Americas. The natural-history exhibits include artifacts left by Taíno, African, North American, Bermudian, French, and Latin American settlers. The museum has a 3-D coral reef exhibit, a walk-in Lucayan cave with wooden artifacts, and a gallery dedicated to Grand Turk's little-known involvement in the Space Race (John Glenn made landfall here after being the first American to orbit the Earth). An interactive children's gallery keeps knee-high visitors "edutained." The museum also claims that Grand Turk was where Columbus first landed in the New World. The most original display is a collection of messages in bottles that have washed ashore from all over the world. ⊠ *Duke St., Cockburn Town* ☏ *649/946–2160* ⊕ *www.tcmuseum.org* 🏷 *$5* ⊙ *Mon., Tues., Thurs., and Fri. 9–4, Wed. 9–5, Sat. 9–1.*

WATER
Tap water on your ship is perfectly safe to drink; purchasing bottled water is only necessary if you prefer the taste.

ELSEWHERE ON THE ISLAND

Grand Turk Lighthouse. More than 150 years old, the lighthouse, built in the United Kingdom and transported piece by piece to the island, used to protect ships in danger of wrecking on the northern reefs. Use this panoramic landmark as a starting point for a breezy cliff-top walk by following the donkey trails to the deserted eastern beach. ⊠ *Lighthouse Rd., North Ridge.*

SHOPPING

There's not much to buy in Grand Turk, and shopping isn't a major activity here. However, there is a duty-free mall right at the cruise-ship center, where you'll find the usual array of upscale shops, including Ron Jon's Surf Shop, the largest Margaritaville in the world, and Piranha Joe's. There are also shops in Cockburn Town itself.

ACTIVITIES

Most of the activities offered to cruise-ship passengers can be booked only on your ship. These include a horseback ride and swim, dune-buggy safaris, and 4x4 safaris.

BICYCLING

Oasis Divers. The island's mostly flat terrain isn't very taxing, and most roads have hard surfaces. Take water with you: there are few places to stop for refreshments. Most hotels have bicycles available, but you can also rent them for $10 to $15 a day from Oasis Divers. They now offer fun Segway tours. ⊠ *Duke St., Cockburn Town* ☏ *649/946–1128* ☏ *800/892–3995* ⊕ *www.oasisdivers.com.*

DIVING AND SNORKELING

★ In these waters you can find undersea cathedrals, coral gardens, and countless tunnels, but note that you must carry and present a valid certificate card before you'll be allowed to dive. As its name suggests, the **Black Forest** offers staggering black-coral formations as well as the occasional black-tip shark. In the **Library** you can study fish galore, including large numbers of yellowtail snapper. At the Columbus Passage separating South Caicos from Grand Turk, each side of a 22-mile-wide (35-km-wide) channel drops more than 7,000 feet. From January through March thousands of Atlantic humpback whales swim through en route to their winter breeding grounds. **Gibb's Cay,** a small cay a couple of miles off Grand Turk, where you can swim with stingrays, makes for a great excursion.

Blue Water Divers. Blue Water Divers has been in operation on Grand Turk since 1983 and is the only PADI Gold Palm five-star dive center on the island. Owner Mitch will undoubtedly put some of your underwater adventures to music in the evenings when he plays at the Osprey Beach Hotel or Salt Raker Inn. ⊠ *Duke St., Cockburn Town* 🕿 *649/946–2432* ⊕ *www.grandturkscuba.com.*

Oasis Divers. Oasis Divers specializes in complete gear handling and pampering treatment. It also supplies Nitrox and rebreathers. ⊠ *Duke St., Cockburn Town* 🕿 *649/946–1128* ⊕ *www.oasisdivers.com.*

BEACHES

Grand Turk is spoiled for choices when it comes to beach options: sunset strolls along miles of deserted beaches, picnics in secluded coves, beachcombing on the coralline sands, snorkeling around shallow coral heads close to shore, and admiring the impossibly turquoise-blue waters.

Governor's Beach. A beautiful crescent of powder-soft sand and shallow, calm turquoise waters front the official British governor's residence, called Waterloo, framed by tall casuarina trees that provide plenty of natural shade. To have it all to yourself, go on a day when cruise ships are not in port. On days when ships are in port, the beach is lined with lounge chairs. ⊠ *Grand Turk.*

Pillory Beach. With sparkling neon turquoise water, this is the prettiest beach on Grand Turk; it also has great off-the-beach snorkeling. ⊠ *Grand Turk.*

WHERE TO EAT

$

AMERICAN

✕ **Jack's Shack.** For a more local feel, walk 500 meters down the beach from the cruise terminal and you'll find Jack's Shack. This beach bar gets lively with volleyball, and offers chair rentals and tropical drinks. Casual food such as burgers and hot dogs satisfy your hunger. Print a coupon from the website for a free shot of T&C's local rum, Bamberra. ⑤ *Average main: $17* ⊠ *500 meters north of cruise terminal, Grand Turk Cruise Port Terminal* 🕿 *649/232–0099* ⊗ *Closed anytime a ship is not in port* ☞ *Open when ship is at port.*

$$

AMERICAN

✕ **Jimmy Buffet's Margaritaville.** The only chain restaurant (so far) in all of the Turks and Caicos is the place to partake in cruise activities even when you're not on a cruise ship. One of the largest Margaritavilles in the world is at the Grand Turk Cruise Terminal and open to all comers (both cruisers and anyone else on the island) when a cruise ship is parked at the dock. Tables are scattered around a large winding pool; there's even a DJ and a FlowRider (a wave pool where you can surf on land—for a fee). You can enjoy 52 flavors of margaritas or the restaurant's own beer, Landshark, while you eat casual bar food such as wings, quesadillas, and burgers. The food is good, the people-watching is great. ⑤ *Average main: $17* ⊠ *Grand Turk Cruise Terminal* 🕿 *649/946–1880* ⊕ *www.margaritavillecaribbean.com* ⊗ *Closed when no cruise ship is at pier.*

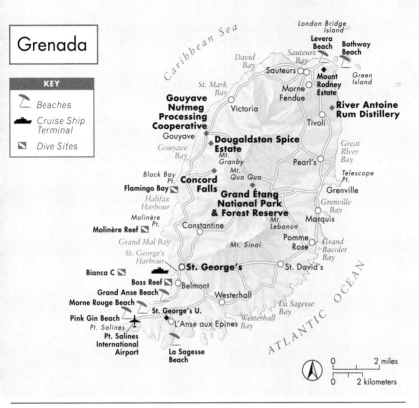

Grenada

KEY

⚠️ Beaches

🚢 Cruise Ship Terminal

◣ Dive Sites

Caribbean Sea

London Bridge Island

Levera Beach

Bathway Beach

David Bay

Sauteurs Bay

Sauteurs

Mount Rodney Estate

Green Island

St. Mark Bay

Morne Fendue

Gouyave Nutmeg Processing Cooperative

Victoria

River Antoine Rum Distillery

Tivoli

Gouyave

Gouyave Bay

Dougaldston Spice Estate

Mt. Granby

Pearl's

Great River Bay

Black Bay Pt.

Concord Falls

Mt. Qua Qua

Telescope Pt.

Flamingo Bay ◣

Grenville

Halifax Harbour

Grand Étang National Park & Forest Reserve

Grenville Bay

Molinère Pt.

Constantine

Mt. Lebanon

Marquis

Molinère Reef ◣

Grand Mal Bay

Mt. Sinai

Pomme Rose

Grand Bacolet Bay

St. George's Harbour

Bianca C ◣

St. George's

St. David's

Boss Reef ◣

Belmont

Grand Anse Beach ⚠️

Westerhall

Morne Rouge Beach ⚠️

La Sagesse Bay

Pink Gin Beach ⚠️

St. George's U.

L'Anse aux Epines

Westerhall Bay

Pt. Salines

Pt. Salines International Airport

La Sagesse Beach

ATLANTIC OCEAN

0   2 miles

0   2 kilometers

GRENADA (ST. GEORGE'S)

Jane E. Zarem   Nutmeg, cinnamon, cloves, cocoa . . . those heady aromas fill the air in Grenada (pronounced gruh-*nay*-da). Only 21 miles (33½ km) long and 12 miles (19½ km) wide, the Isle of Spice is a tropical gem of lush rain forests, white-sand beaches, secluded coves, exotic flowers, and enough locally grown spices to fill anyone's kitchen cabinet. St. George's is one of the most picturesque capital cities in the Caribbean, St. George's Harbour is one of the most picturesque harbors, and Grenada's Grand Anse Beach is one of the region's finest beaches. The island has friendly, hospitable people and enough good shopping, restaurants, historic sites, and natural wonders to make it a popular port of call. About one-third of Grenada's visitors arrive by cruise ship, and that number continues to grow each year.

ESSENTIALS

CURRENCY   Eastern Caribbean (E.C.) dollar (EC$2.67 to US$1). U.S. dollars (but not coins) are generally accepted, but change is given in E.C. currency.

TELEPHONE   Prepaid phone cards, which can be used in special card phones throughout the Caribbean for local or international calls, are sold in various denominations at shops, attractions, transportation centers, and other convenient outlets. For international calls using a major credit card, dial 111; to place a collect call or use a calling card, dial 800/225–5872 from any telephone. Pay phones are available at the Cruise Ship Terminal welcome center, the LIME office on the Carenage in St. George's, shopping centers, and other convenient locations.

COMING ASHORE

The Cruise Ship Terminal near Market Square, on the north side of St. George's, accommodates two large ships; up to four can anchor in the outer harbor. A full range of passenger facilities is available at the terminal, which opens directly into the Esplanade Mall and the minibus terminus; it is also a block from Market Square. You can easily tour the capital on foot, but be prepared to climb up and down steep hills. If you don't want to walk up and down through town, you can find a taxi ($3 or $4 each way) or a water taxi right at the terminal to take you around to the Carenage ($4 each way) or to Grand Anse Beach ($8 each way). To explore areas beyond St. George's, hiring a taxi or arranging a guided tour is more sensible than renting a car. Taxis are plentiful, and fixed rates to popular island destinations are posted at the terminal's welcome center.

A taxi ride from the terminal to Grand Anse Beach will cost $15, but water taxis are a less expensive and more picturesque way to get there; the one-way fare is about $8 per person, depending on the number of passengers. Minibuses are the least expensive way to travel between St. George's and Grand Anse; pay EC$1.50 (55¢), but hold on to your hat. They're crowded with local people getting from here to there and often make quick stops and take turns at quite a clip. Still, it's an inexpensive, fun, and safe way to travel around the island. If you want to rent a car and explore on your own, be prepared to pay $12 for a temporary driving permit (this is arranged by the car-rental agency) and about $55 to $75 for a day's car rental.

EXPLORING GRENADA

★ **Concord Falls.** About 8 miles (13 km) north of St. George's, a turnoff from the West Coast Road leads to Concord Falls—actually three separate waterfalls. The first is at the end of the road; when the currents aren't too strong, you can take a dip under the cascade. Reaching the two other waterfalls requires an hour's hike into the forest reserve. The third and most spectacular waterfall, at Fountainbleu, thunders 65 feet over huge boulders and creates a small pool. It's smart to hire a guide for that trek. The path is clear, but slippery boulders toward the end can be treacherous without assistance. ⊠ *Off West Coast Rd., Concord, St. John* ⌨ *Changing room $2* ⊗ *Daily 9–5.*

⟳ **Dougaldston Spice Estate.** Just south of Gouyave, this historic plantation, now primarily a museum, still grows and processes spices the old-fashioned way. You can see cocoa, nutmeg, mace, cloves, and other spices laid out on giant racks to dry in the sun. A worker will be glad to explain the process (and will appreciate a small donation). You can buy spices for about $4 a bag. ⊠ *Gouyave, St. John* ⌨ *Free* ⊗ *Weekdays 9–4.*

🍃 **Gouyave Nutmeg Processing Coop-**
★ **erative.** Touring the nutmeg-processing co-op, in the center of the west-coast fishing village of Gouyave (pronounced *gwahv*), is a fragrant, fascinating way to spend half an hour. You can learn all about nutmeg and its uses, see the nutmegs laid out in bins, and watch the workers sort them by hand and pack them into burlap bags for shipping worldwide. The three-story plant turned out 3 million pounds of Grenada's most famous export each year before Hurricane Ivan's devastating effect on the crop in 2004, when most of the nutmeg trees were destroyed. Locals estimate that it will still be several more years before the nutmeg industry returns to pre-hurricane levels. ⊠ *Gouyave, St. John* ☎ *473/444–8337* 🖅 *$1* ⊙ *Weekdays 10–1 and 2–4.*

> ### GRENADA BEST BETS
>
> ■ **The Beach.** Grand Anse Beach is one of the Caribbean's most beautiful.
>
> ■ **Diving and Snorkeling.** Explore dozens of fish-filled sites off Grenada's southwest coast.
>
> ■ **Market Square.** Market Square is a bustling produce and spice market.
>
> ■ **Nutmeg.** Don't miss a visit to a nutmeg cooperative (and get a pocketful to take home).
>
> ■ **Waterfalls.** Concord Falls, just south of Gouyave, and Annandale Falls are among the island's most spectacular.

4

🍃 **Grand Étang National Park & Forest Reserve.** Deep in the mountainous inte-
★ rior of Grenada is a bird sanctuary and forest reserve with miles of hiking trails, lookouts, and fishing streams. **Grand Étang Lake** is a 36-acre expanse of cobalt-blue water that fills the crater of an extinct volcano 1,740 feet above sea level. Although legend has it the lake is bottomless, maximum soundings are recorded at 18 feet. The informative **Grand Étang Forest Center** has displays on the local wildlife and vegetation. A forest manager is on hand to answer questions. A small snack bar and souvenir stands are nearby. ⊠ *Main interior road, between Grenville and St. George's, St. Andrew* ☎ *473/440–6160* 🖅 *$1* ⊙ *Daily 8:30–4.*

River Antoine Rum Distillery. At this rustic operation (pronounced River An-*twyne*), kept open primarily as a museum, a limited quantity of Rivers rum is produced by the same methods used since the distillery opened in 1785. The process begins with the crushing of sugarcane from adjacent fields. The result is a potent overproof rum, sold only in Grenada, that will knock your socks off. (A less strong version is also available.) ⊠ *River Antoine Estate, St. Patrick* ☎ *473/442–7109* 🖅 *$2* ⊙ *Guided tours daily 9–4.*

St. George's. Grenada's capital is a bustling West Indian city, much of which remains unchanged from colonial days. Narrow streets lined with shops wind up, down, and across steep hills. Brick warehouses cling to the waterfront, and pastel-painted homes rise from the waterfront and disappear into steep green hills.

Picturesque **St. George's Harbour,** a submerged volcanic crater, is, arguably, the prettiest harbor in the Caribbean. Schooners, ferries, and tour boats tie up along the seawall or at the small dinghy dock.

The **Carenage** (pronounced car-a-*nahzh*), which surrounds horseshoe-shaped St. George's Harbour, is the capital's center. Warehouses, shops, and restaurants line the waterfront. The *Christ of the Deep* statue that sits on the pedestrian plaza at the center of the Carenage was presented to Grenada by Costa Cruise Line in remembrance of its ship, *Bianca C,* which burned and sank in the harbor in 1961 and is now a favorite dive site.

An engineering feat for its time, the 340-foot-long **Sendall Tunnel** was built in 1895 and named for an early governor. It separates the harbor side of St. George's from the Esplanade on the bay side of town, where you can find the markets (produce, meat, and fish), the Cruise Ship Terminal, the Esplanade Mall, and the public bus station. ⊠ *St. George.*

Grenada National Museum. The Grenada National Museum, a block from the Carenage, is built on the foundation of a French army barracks and prison that was originally built in 1704. The small museum has exhibitions of news items, photos, and proclamations relating to the 1983 intervention, along with the childhood bathtub of Empress Joséphine (who was born on Martinique), and other memorabilia. ⊠ *Young and Monckton Sts., St. George's* ☎ *473/440–3725* 🖃 *$1* ☉ *Weekdays 9–4:30, Sat. 10–1.*

Ft. George. Ft. George is high on the hill at the entrance to St. George's Harbour. It's Grenada's oldest fort—built by the French in 1705 to protect the harbor. No shots were ever fired here until October 1983, when Prime Minister Maurice Bishop and some of his followers were assassinated in the courtyard. The fort now houses police headquarters but is open to the public daily. The 360-degree view of the capital city, St. George's Harbour, and the open sea is spectacular. ⊠ *Church St., St. George's* 🖃 *$2.*

Market Square. Don't miss St. George's Market Square, a block from the Cruise Ship Terminal. It's open every weekday morning but really comes alive on Saturday from 8 to noon. Vendors sell baskets, spices, brooms, clothing, knickknacks, coconut water, and heaps of fresh produce. Historically, Market Square is where parades begin and political rallies take place. ⊠ *Granby St., St. George's.*

Ft. Frederick. Overlooking the city of St. George's and the inland side of the harbor, historic Ft. Frederick provides a panoramic view of about one-fourth of Grenada. The fort was started by the French and completed in 1791 by the British; it was also the headquarters of the People's Revolutionary Government before and during the 1983 coup. Today you can get a bird's-eye view of much of Grenada from here. ⊠ *Richmond Hill.*

SHOPPING

Grenada's best souvenirs or gifts for friends back home are spice baskets filled with cinnamon, nutmeg, mace, bay leaves, cloves, turmeric, and ginger. You can buy them for as little as $4 in practically every shop, at the open-air produce market at **Market Square** in St. George's, at the vendor stalls near the pier, and at the **Vendor's Craft and Spice Market** on Grand Anse Beach. Vendors also sell handmade fabric dolls, coral jewelry, seashells, and hats and baskets handwoven from green palm fronds. Bargaining is not appropriate in the shops, and it isn't customary with vendors—although most will offer you "a good price."

★ **Art Fabrik.** At Art Fabrik, you'll find batik fabric created by hand by as many as 45 home workers. It's sold either by the yard or as dresses, shirts, shorts, hats, and scarves. An area of the boutique is dedicated to demonstrating the batik process. ⊠ *Young St., St. George's, St. George* ☎ *473/440–0568* ⊕ *www.artfabrikgrenada.com.*

Tikal. Regional artwork, jewelry, batik items, and fashions are the specialties at Tikal. ⊠ *Young St., St. George's* ☎ *473/440–2310.*

> ### ID CASES
>
> You can keep track of your boarding pass, shipboard charge/key card, and picture ID when you go ashore by slipping them into a bi-fold business-card carrying case. Cases with a sueded finish are less likely to fall out of your pocket. With security as tight as it is these days, you don't want to lose your ID.

ACTIVITIES

DIVING AND SNORKELING

You can see hundreds of varieties of fish and some 40 species of coral at more than a dozen sites off Grenada's southwest coast—only 15 to 20 minutes by boat—and another couple of dozen sites around Carriacou's reefs and neighboring islets. Depths vary from 20 to 120 feet, and visibility varies from 30 to 100 feet.

A spectacular dive is *Bianca C,* a 600-foot cruise ship that caught fire in 1961, sank to 100 feet, and is now encrusted with coral and serves as a habitat for giant turtles, spotted eagle rays, barracuda, and jacks. **Boss Reef** extends 5 miles (8 km) from St. George's Harbour to Point Salines, with a depth ranging from 20 to 90 feet. **Flamingo Bay** has a wall that drops to 90 feet and is teeming with fish, sponges, sea horses, sea fans, and coral. **Molinère Reef** slopes from about 20 feet below the surface to a wall that drops to 65 feet. It's a good dive for beginners, and advanced divers can continue farther out to view the wreck of the *Buccaneer,* a 42-foot sloop.

Aquanauts Grenada. Every morning Aquanauts Grenada heads out on two-tank dive trips, accommodating no more than eight divers, to both the Caribbean and Atlantic sides of Grenada. Also available: guided snorkel trips; beach snorkeling; and special activities, courses, and equipment for children. ⊠ *Spice Island Beach Resort, Grand Anse Beach, Grand Anse, St. George* ☎ *473/444–1126, 850/303–0330 in U.S.* ⊕ *www.aquanautsgrenada.com.*

EcoDive. This company offers two dive trips daily, both drift and wreck dives, as well as weekly trips to dive Isle de Rhonde. EcoDive also runs Grenada's marine-conservation and education center, which conducts coral-reef monitoring. ⊠ *Coyaba Beach Resort, Grand Anse Beach, Grand Anse, St. George* ☎ *473/444–7777* ⊕ *www.ecodiveandtrek.com.*

4

FISHING

Deep-sea fishing around Grenada is excellent, with marlin, sailfish, yellowfin tuna, and dolphin fish topping the list of good catches. You can arrange sportfishing trips that accommodate up to five people starting at $475 for a half day and $700 for a full day.

True Blue Sportfishing. British-born Captain Gary Clifford, who has been fishing since the age of 6, has run True Blue Sportfishing since 1998. He offers big-game charters on the 31-foot *Yes Aye*. It has an enclosed cabin, a fighting chair, and professional tackle. Refreshments and courtesy transport are included. ⊠ *True Blue Bay Marina, True Blue, St. George* ☎ *473/444–2048* ⊕ *www.yesaye.com.*

BEACHES

Bathway Beach. This broad strip of sand on Grenada's far northern shore has a natural reef that protects swimmers from the rough Atlantic surf. There are changing rooms at the Levera National Park headquarters. **Amenities:** parking (no fee); toilets. **Best for:** solitude; swimming; walking. ⊠ *Levera National Park, Levera, St. Patrick.*

Fodor'sChoice
★

Grand Anse Beach. In the southwest is Grenada's loveliest and most popular beach: a gleaming 2-mile (3-km) semicircle of white sand lapped by clear, gentle surf. Sea grape trees and coconut palms provide shady escapes from the sun. Brilliant rainbows frequently spill into the sea from the high green mountains that frame St. George's Harbour to the north. The Grand Anse Craft & Spice Market and a water taxi dock are at the midpoint of the beach. The public entrance is through Camerhogne Park, where there are restrooms and changing facilities. **Amenities:** food and drink; parking (no fee); toilets; water sports. **Best for:** swimming; walking. ⊠ *3 miles (5 km) south of St. George's, Grand Anse, St. George.*

WHERE TO EAT

Restaurants add an 8% government tax to your bill and usually add a 10% service charge; if not, tip 10% to 15% for a job well done.

$$
CARIBBEAN
🕒
★

✕**Belmont Estate.** Luncheon is served! If you're visiting the northern reaches of Grenada, plan to stop at Belmont Estate, a 400-year-old working nutmeg and cocoa plantation. Settle into the breezy open-air dining room, which overlooks enormous trays of nutmeg, cocoa, and mace drying in the sunshine. A waiter will offer some refreshing local juice and a choice of callaloo or pumpkin soup. Then head to the buffet and help yourself to salad, rice, stewed chicken, beef curry, stewed fish, and vegetables. Dessert may be homemade ice cream, ginger cake, or another delicious confection. Afterward, feel free to take a tour of the museum, cocoa fermentary, sugarcane garden, and old cemetery. Farm animals (and a couple of monkeys) roam the property, and there's often folk music and dancing on the lawn. ⑤ *Average main: $18* ⊠ *Belmont, St. Patrick* ☎ *473/442–9524* ⊕ *www.belmontestate.net* ⊘ *Closed Sat. No dinner.*

$$
CARIBBEAN

✕**The Nutmeg.** West Indian specialties, fresh seafood, great hamburgers, and a waterfront view make The Nutmeg a favorite with locals and visitors alike. It's upstairs on the Carenage (above the Sea Change

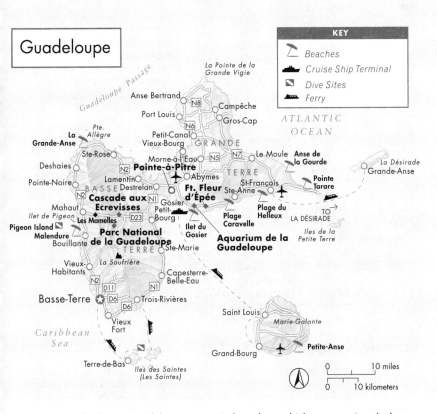

Guadeloupe

KEY

- Beaches
- Cruise Ship Terminal
- Dive Sites
- Ferry

La Pointe de la Grande Vigie

Guadeloupe Passage

Anse Bertrand

Port Louis

Campêche

Gros-Cap

ATLANTIC OCEAN

Pte. Allègre

Petit-Canal

La Grande-Anse

Vieux-Bourg

GRANDE

Ste-Rose

Morne-à-l'Eau

Le Moule

Anse de la Gourde

La Désirade Grande-Anse

Deshaies

Pointe-à-Pitre

TERRE

Pointe-Noire

Lamentin

Abymes

St-François

Pointe Tarare

Destrelan

Ft. Fleur d'Épée

Ste-Anne

BASSE

Cascade aux Ecrevisses

Mahaut

Petit-Bourg

Gosier

Plage du Helleux

TO LA DÉSIRADE

Îlet de Pigeon

Les Mamelles

Plage Caravelle

Pigeon Island

Îlet du Gosier

Îles de la Petite Terre

Malendure

Parc National de la Guadeloupe

Aquarium de la Guadeloupe

Bouillante

Ste-Marie

TERRE

Vieux-Habitants

La Soufrière

Capesterre-Belle-Eau

Basse-Terre

Trois-Rivières

Caribbean Sea

Saint Louis

Marie-Galante

Vieux Fort

Grand-Bourg

Petite-Anse

Terre-de-Bas

Îles des Saintes (Les Saintes)

0   10 miles

0   10 kilometers

bookstore), with large, open windows from which you can view the harbor activity as you eat. Try the callaloo soup, curried lambi, fresh seafood, or a steak—or just stop by for a roti and a rum punch. $ *Average main: $18* ✉ *The Carenage, St. George's, St. George* ☎ *473/435–9525.*

GUADELOUPE (POINTE-À-PITRE)

Eileen Robinson Smith

On a map, Guadeloupe looks like a giant butterfly resting on the sea between Antigua and Dominica. Its two wings—Basse-Terre and Grande-Terre—are the two largest islands in the 659-square-mile (1,706-square-km) Guadeloupe archipelago. The Rivière Salée, a 4-mile (6-km) channel between the Caribbean and the Atlantic, forms the "spine" of the butterfly. A drawbridge near Pointe-à-Pitre, the main city, connects the two islands. Gorgeous scenery awaits, as Guadeloupe is one of the most physically attractive islands in the Caribbean. If you're seeking a resort atmosphere, casinos, and nearly white sandy beaches, your target is Grande-Terre. On the other hand, Basse-Terre's Parc National de la Guadeloupe, laced with trails and washed by waterfalls and rivers, is a 74,100-acre haven for hikers, nature lovers, and anyone brave enough to peer into the steaming crater of an active volcano. The tropical beauty suggests the mythical Garden of Eden.

ESSENTIALS

CURRENCY The euro. Some of the larger liquor and jewelry stores may accept dollars, but don't count on that. You cannot cash traveler's checks or dollars at the bank, only at a bureau de change, so ATMs are your best bet if you need euros; facing the tourist office, there is one just to the right at the bank.

INTERNET Pointe-à-Pitre has several Internet cafés (there is one right at the new cruise pier); the tourist office can point you in the direction of several more in the immediate vicinity.

TELEPHONE To call the United States from Guadeloupe, dial 001, the area code, and the local number. For calls within Guadeloupe, you now have to put 0590 before the six-digit number. You'll need to purchase a *télécarte* at the post office or at tobacco and grocery shops in order to use the phone booths.

> ## GUADELOUPE BEST BETS
>
> ■ **Beaches.** The southern coast of Grand-Terre has stretches of soft, nearly white sand.
>
> ■ **Diving.** Jacques Cousteau called the reef off Pigeon Island one of the world's top dive sites.
>
> ■ **Hiking.** The Parc National de la Guadeloupe is one of the Caribbean's most spectacular scenic destinations.
>
> ■ **Shopping.** Though Point-à-Pitre itself can be frenetic, it does have a good choice of French goods.

COMING ASHORE

Ships now dock at the new cruise terminal at Pier 5/6, which houses an Internet café, a duty-free shop, and the colorful Karuland Village, where cruisers can browse and buy spices, pareos, and souvenirs or just sit and listen to the local music while having coconut ice cream. In downtown Pointe-à-Pitre, it is about a five-minute walk from the shopping district. Passengers are greeted by local musicians and hostesses, usually dressed in the traditional madras costumes—and often dispensing samplings of local rum and creole specialties. These multilingual staffers operate the information booth and can pair you up with an English-speaking taxi driver for a customized island tour. To get to the main tourist office, walk along the quay to the Place de la Victoire; it is a large white Victorian building with wraparound veranda.

Taxis are metered and expensive; during rush hour, they can be *very* expensive. Renting a car is a good way to see Guadeloupe, but it is expensive and best booked in advance. Be aware that traffic around Pointe-à-Pitre can be dreadful during rush hour, so allow plenty of time to drop off your car rental and get back to the ship. There are many rental agencies at the airport, but that is a €35 taxi ride from the city at least.

EXPLORING GUADELOUPE

Aquarium de la Guadeloupe. Unique in the Antilles, this aquarium in the marina near Pointe-à-Pitre is a good place to spend an hour. The well-planned facility has an assortment of tropical fish, crabs, lobsters, moray eels, coffer fish, and some live coral. It's also a fascinating turtle rescue center, and the shark tank is spectacular. ⊠ *Pl. Créole off rte. N4, Pointe-à-Pitre, Grande-Terre* ☎ *0590/90–92–38* ⊕ *www. aquariumdelaguadeloupe.com* ⊠ *€10.50* ☯ *Daily 9–7.*

Ft. Fleur d'Épée. The main attraction in Bas-du-Fort is this 18th-century fortress, which hunkers down on a hillside behind a deep moat. It was the scene of hard-fought battles between the French and the English in 1794. You can explore its well-preserved dungeons and battlements and take in a sweeping view of Iles des Saintes and Marie-Galante. ⊠ *Bas-du-Fort, Grande-Terre* ☎ *0590/90–94–61* ⊠ *Free* ☯ *Mon.–Sun. 9–5.*

★ **Parc National de la Guadeloupe.** This 74,100-acre park has been recognized by UNESCO as a Biosphere Reserve. Before going, pick up a *Guide to the National Park* from the tourist office; it rates the hiking trails according to difficulty, and most are quite difficult indeed. Most mountain trails are in the southern half. The park is bisected by the route de la Traversée, a 16-mile (26-km) paved road lined with masses of tree ferns, shrubs, flowers, tall trees, and green plantains. It's the ideal point of entry. Wear rubber-soled shoes and take along a swimsuit, a sweater, and perhaps food for a picnic. Try to get an early start to stay ahead of the hordes of cruise-ship passengers making a day of it. Check on the weather; if Basse-Terre has had a lot of rain, give it up. In the past, after intense rainfall, rockslides have closed the road for months. ⊠ *Administrative Headquarters, rte. de la Traversée, St-Claude, Basse-Terre* ☎ *0590/80–86–00* ⊕ *www.guadeloupe-parcnational.com* ⊠ *Free* ☯ *Weekdays 8–5:30.*

Cascade aux Ecrevisses. Within the Parc National de la Guadeloupe, Crayfish Falls is one of the island's loveliest (and most popular) spots. There's a marked trail (walk carefully—the rocks can be slippery) leading to this splendid waterfall, which dashes down into the Corossol River—a good place for a dip. Come early, though; otherwise you definitely won't have it to yourself. ⊠ *St-Claude, Basse-Terre* ⊕ *www. guadeloupe-parcnational.com.*

Pointe-à-Pitre. Although not the capital, this is the island's largest city, a commercial and industrial hub in the southwest of Grande-Terre. The Isles of Guadeloupe have 450,000 inhabitants, 99.6% of whom live in the cities. Pointe-à-Pitre is bustling, noisy, and hot—a place of honking horns and traffic jams and cars on sidewalks for want of a parking place. By day its pulse is fast, but at night, when its streets are almost deserted, you don't want to be there.

The Centre St-John Perse has transformed old warehouses into a cruise-terminal complex that consists of the spartan Hotel St-John, restaurants, shops, and the port authority headquarters. An impressive terminal serves the ferries that depart for Iles des Saintes, Marie-Galante, Dominica, Martinique, and St. Lucia.

The heart of the old city is Place de la Victoire; surrounded by wooden buildings with balconies and shutters (including the tourism office) and by sidewalk cafés, it was named in honor of Victor Hugues's 1794 victory over the British. During the French Revolution, Hugues ordered the guillotine set up here so that the public could witness the bloody end of 300 recalcitrant royalists.

Even more colorful is the bustling marketplace, between rues St-John Perse, Frébault, Schoelcher, and Peynier. It's a cacophonous place, where housewives bargain for spices, herbs (and herbal remedies), and a bright assortment of papayas, breadfruits, christophenes, and tomatoes. ⊠ *Pointe-à-Pitre, Grande-Terre.*

Cathédrale de St-Pierre et St-Paul. For fans of French ecclesiastical architecture, there's the imposing Cathédrale de St-Pierre et St-Paul, built in 1807. Although battered by hurricanes, it has fine stained-glass windows and Creole-style balconies and is reinforced with pillars and ribs that look like leftovers from the Eiffel Tower. ⊠ *Rue Alexandre Isaac at rue de l'Eglise, Grande-Terre.*

Musée St-John Perse. Anyone with an interest in French literature and culture (not your average sightseer) won't want to miss the Musée St-John Perse, which is dedicated to Guadeloupe's most famous son and one of the giants of world literature, Alexis Léger, better known as St-John Perse, winner of the Nobel Prize for literature in 1960. Some of his finest poems are inspired by the history and landscape—particularly the sea—of his beloved Guadeloupe. The museum contains a collection of his poetry and some of his personal belongings. Before you go, look for his birthplace at 54 rue Achille René-Boisneuf. ⊠ *Rue Achille René-Boisneuf, Pointe-à-Pitre, Grande-Terre* ☎ *0590/90–01–92* ✑ *€3* ☺ *Mon.–Fri. 9–5, Sat. 8:30–12:30.*

Musée Schoelcher. Musée Schoelcher celebrates Victor Schoelcher, a high-minded abolitionist from Alsace who fought against slavery in the French West Indies in the 19th century. The museum contains many of his personal effects, and exhibits trace his life and work. ⊠ *24 rue Peynier, Grande-Terre* ☎ *0590/82–08–04* ✑ *€3* ☺ *Weekdays 9–5.*

SHOPPING

For serious shopping in Pointe-à-Pitre, browse the boutiques and stores along rue Schoelcher, rue Frébault, and rue Noizières. The multicolored market square and stalls of La Darse are filled mostly with vegetables, fruits, delicious homemade rum liqueurs, and housewares. The air is filled with the fragrance of spices, and they have lovely gift baskets of spices and vanilla lined with madras fabric.

Dody. Across from the market, Dody is the place to go if you want white eyelet (blouses, skirts, dresses, even bustiers). The shop has a high-quality designer line, but you will pay €100 to €300 for a single piece. There's lots of madras, too, which is especially cute in children's clothing. ⊠ *31 rue Frébault, Pointe-à-Pitre, Grande-Terre* ☎ *0590/82–18–59.*

Vendôme. Guadeloupe's exclusive purveyor of Stendhal and Germaine Monteil cosmetics is Vendôme. ⊠ *8–10 rue Frébault, Pointe-à-Pitre, Grande-Terre* ☎ *0590/83–42–84.*

ACTIVITIES

DIVING

The main diving area at the **Cousteau Underwater Park,** just off Basse-Terre near Pigeon Island, offers routine dives to 60 feet. The numerous glass-bottom boats and other crafts make the site feel like a marine parking lot; however, the underwater sights are spectacular. Guides and instructors are certified under the French CMAS (some also have PADI, but none have NAUI). Most operators offer two-hour dives three times per day for about €45 to €50 per dive; three-dive packages are €120 to €145. Hotels and dive operators usually rent snorkeling gear.

⏰ **Les Heures Saines.** Les Heures Saines is the premier operator for dives in the Cousteau Underwater Park. Trips to Les Saintes offer one or two dives for average and advanced divers, with plenty of time for lunch and sightseeing. Wreck, night, and Nitrox diving are also available. The instructors, many of them English speakers, are excellent with children. The company also offers winter whale- and dolphin-watching trips with marine biologists as guides. These tours, aboard a 60-foot catamaran, cost €55 (less for children). ✉ *Le Rocher de Malendure, Plage de Malendure, Bouillante, Basse-Terre* ☎ *0590/98–86–63* ⊕ *www. heures-saines.gp.*

HIKING

Fodor's Choice ★ With hundreds of trails and countless rivers and waterfalls, the **Parc National de la Guadeloupe** on Basse-Terre is the main draw for hikers. Some of the trails should be attempted only with an experienced guide. All tend to be muddy, so wear a good pair of boots. Know that even the young and fit can find these outings arduous; the unfit may find them painful.

Vert Intense. Vert Intense organizes fascinating hikes in the national park and to the volcano. You move from steaming hot springs to an icy waterfall in the same hike. Guides are patient and safety-conscious, and can bring you to heights that you never thought you could reach, including the top of Le Soufrière. The volcano hike costs only €30 but must be booked four days in advance. A mixed-adventure package spanning three days costs €225. The two-day bivouac and other adventures can be extreme sport, so before you decide to play Indiana Jones, know what is expected. The French-speaking guides, who also know some English and Spanish, can take you to other tropical forests and rivers, where the sport of canyoning can still be practiced. If you are just one or two people, the company can team you up with a group. ✉ *Rte. de la Soufrière, Mourne Houel, Basse-Terre* ☎ *0590/99–34–73, 0690/55–40–47* ⊕ *www.vert-intense.com.*

BEACHES

Plage de la Grande-Anse. One of Guadeloupe's widest beaches has soft beige sand sheltered by palms. To the west it's a round verdant mountain. It has a large parking area and some food stands, but no other facilities. The beach can be overrun on Sunday, not to mention littered.

Right after the parking lot, you can see signage for the creole restaurant Le Karacoli; if you have lunch there (it's not inexpensive), you can *sieste* on the chaise longues. ⊠ *Rte. N6, north of Deshaies, Deshaies, Basse-Terre.*

Plage Caravelle. Just southwest of Ste-Anne is one of Grande-Terre's longest and prettiest stretches of sand, the occasional dilapidated shack notwithstanding. Protected by reefs, it's also a fine snorkeling spot. Club Med occupies one end of this beach, and nonguests can enjoy its beach and water sports, as well as lunch and drinks, by buying a day pass. You can also have lunch on the terrace of La Toubana Hotel & Spa, then descend the stairs to the beach or enjoy lunch at its beach restaurant, wildly popular on Sunday. ⊠ *Rte. N4, southwest of Ste-Anne, Ste-Anne, Grande-Terre.*

Plage de Malendure. Across from Pigeon Island and the Jacques Cousteau Underwater Park, this long, gray, volcanic beach on the Caribbean's calm waters has restrooms, a few beach shacks offering cold drinks and snacks, and a huge parking lot. There might be some litter, but the beach is cleaned regularly. Don't come here for solitude, as the beach is a launch point for many dive boats. The snorkeling here is good. Le Rocher de Malendure, a fine seafood restaurant, is perched on a cliff over the bay. ⊠ *Rte. N6, Bouillante, Basse-Terre.*

WHERE TO EAT

$$ ✕ **Caraïbes Café.** This sidewalk café straight out of Paris is the "in" place
CAFÉ for lunch and also a spot for a quick breakfast, a fresh juice cocktail—
try *corossel* (a tropical fruit) and mango juices, a cappuccino, *un coupe* (a sundae), or a *pastis* while you people-watch and listen to French crooners. The *formule* (fixed-price menu) is always the best deal. Service is fast and friendly and can even be in English. Ⓢ *Average main: €15* ⊠ *Pl. de la Victoire, Pointe-à-Pitre, Grande-Terre* ☎ *0590/82–92–23* ⊘ *Closed Sun. No dinner.*

$$$ ✕ **Le Rocher de Malendure.** Guests first climb the worn yellow stairs for
FRENCH the panoramic sea views, but return again and again for the food. If
★ you arrive before noon, when the divers pull in, you might snag one of the primo tables in a gazebo that literally hangs over the Caribbean. Begin with a perfectly executed mojito. With fish just off the boat, don't hesitate to try the sushi *antillaise* or grilled crayfish and lobster from the pool. Ⓢ *Average main: €25* ⊠ *Bord de Mer, Malendure de Pigeon, Bouillante, Basse-Terre* ☎ *0590/98–70–84* ⊘ *Closed Wed. and Sept.–early Oct.*

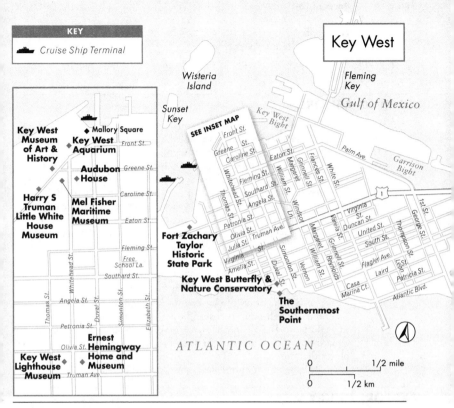

Key West

Wisteria
Island

Fleming
Key

Gulf of Mexico

Sunset
Key

Key West
Bight

SEE INSET MAP

Front St.

Greene St.

Caroline St.

Eaton St.

Palm Ave.

Garrison
Bight

Key West
Museum
of Art &
History

Mallory Square

Key West
Aquarium

Front St.

Greene St.

Caroline St.

Audubon
House

Harry S
Truman
Little White
House
Museum

Mel Fisher
Maritime
Museum

Eaton St.

Fleming St.

Free
School La.

Southard St.

Whitehead St.

Thomas St.

Angela St.

Duval St.

Simonton St.

Elizabeth St.

Petronia St.

Olivia St.

Ernest
Hemingway
Home and
Museum

Key West
Lighthouse
Museum

Truman Ave.

Fort Zachary
Taylor
Historic
State Park

Key West Butterfly &
Nature Conservatory

Whitehead St.

Thomas St.

Fleming St.

Southard St.

Angela St.

Petronia St.

Olivia St.

Julia St.

Virginia St.

Amelia St.

Caroline St.

Greene St.

Eaton St.

Margaret St.

Grinnell St.

Frances St.

William St.

White St.

Truman Ave.

Windsor Ln.

Simonton St.

Duval St.

Vernon St.

William St.

Margaret St.

Grinnell St.

Reynolds St.

Varela St.

Duncan St.

United St.

South St.

Virginia St.

Casa
Marina Ct.

The
Southernmost
Point

Flagler Ave.

Laird St.

Thompson St.

George St.

1st St.

Leo St.

Patricia St.

Atlantic Blvd.

ATLANTIC OCEAN

0   1/2 mile

0   1/2 km

KEY WEST, FLORIDA

Chelle Koster
Walton

Along with the rest of Florida, Key West—the southernmost city in the continental United States—became part of American territory in 1821. In the late 19th century it was Florida's wealthiest city per capita. The locals made their fortunes from "wrecking"—rescuing people and salvaging cargo from ships that foundered on nearby reefs. Cigar making, fishing, shrimping, and sponge gathering also became important industries. Locally dubbed the "Conch Republic," Key West today makes for a unique port of call. A genuinely American town, it nevertheless exudes the relaxed atmosphere and pace of a typical Caribbean island. Major attractions include the home of the Conch Republic's most famous residents, Ernest Hemingway and Harry Truman; the imposing Key West Museum of Art and History, a former U.S. Customs House and site of the military inquest of the USS *Maine*; and the island's renowned sunset celebrations.

ESSENTIALS

CURRENCY The U.S. dollar.

INTERNET **Coffee Plantation.** Get your morning (or afternoon) buzz, and hook up to the Internet in the comfort of a homelike setting in a circa-1890 Conch house. Munch on sandwiches, wraps, and pastries, and sip a hot or cold espresso beverage. ⊠ *713 Caroline St.* ☎ *305/295–9808* ⊕ *www. coffeeplantationkeywest.com.*

You'll be able to find plenty of public phones around Mallory Square. They're also along the major tourist thoroughfares.

COMING ASHORE

Cruise ships dock at three different locations in Key West. Mallory Square and Pier B are within walking distance of Duval and Whitehead streets, the two main tourist thoroughfares. Passengers on ships that dock at Outer Mole Pier (aka Navy Mole) are shuttled via Conch Train or Old Town Trolley to Mallory Square. Because Key West is so easily explored on foot, there is rarely a need to hire a taxi. If you plan to venture beyond the main tourist district, a fun way to get around is by bicycle or scooter (bike rentals begin at about $12 per day). Key West is a cycling town. In fact, there are so many bikes around that cyclists must watch out for one another as much as for cars. You can get tourist information from the Greater Key West Chamber of Commerce, which is located one block off Duval Street, at 510 Greene Street, in the old "city hall."

The Conch Tour Train can be boarded at Mallory Square or Flagler Station every half-hour; it costs $29 per adult for the 90-minute tour. The Old Town Trolley operates trolley-style buses starting from Mallory Square every 30 minutes for the same price, but the smaller trolleys go places the train won't fit. The Old Town Trolley also has pick up and drop off locations at numerous points around the island.

EXPLORING KEY WEST

Audubon House and Tropical Gardens. If you've ever seen an engraving by ornithologist John James Audubon, you'll understand why his name is synonymous with birds. See his works in this three-story house, which was built in the 1840s for Captain John Geiger and filled with period furniture. It now commemorates Audubon's 1832 stop in Key West while he was traveling through Florida to study birds. After an introduction by a docent, you can do a self-guided tour of the house and gardens (or just the gardens). An art gallery sells lithographs of the artist's famed portraits. ⊠ *205 Whitehead St.* ☎ *305/294–2116, 877/294–2470* ⊕ *www.audubonhouse.com* ☜ *$7.50 gardens only; $12 house and gardens* ⊙ *Daily 9:30–5, last tour starts at 4:30.*

★ **Ernest Hemingway Home and Museum.** Amusing anecdotes spice up the guided tours of Ernest Hemingway's home, built in 1801 by the town's most successful wrecker. While living here between 1931 and 1942, Hemingway wrote about 70% of his life's work, including classics like *For Whom the Bell Tolls*. Few of his belongings remain aside from some books, and there's little about his actual work, but photographs help you visualize his day-to-day life. The supposed six-toed descendants of Hemingway's cats—many named for actors, artists, authors, and even a hurricane—have free rein of the property. Tours begin every 10 minutes and take 30 minutes; then you're free to explore on your own.

✉ *907 Whitehead St.* ☎ *305/294–1136* ⊕ *www.hemingwayhome.com* 🖙 *$12.50* ☉ *Daily 9–5.*

★ **Fort Zachary Taylor Historic State Park.** Construction of the fort began in 1845 but was halted during the Civil War. Even though Florida seceded from the Union, Yankee forces used the fort as a base to block Confederate shipping. More than 1,500 Confederate vessels were detained in Key West's harbor. The fort, finally completed in 1866, was also used in the Spanish-American War. Take a 30-minute guided walking tour of the redbrick fort, a National Historic Landmark, at noon and 2, or self-tour anytime between 8 and 5. One of its most popular features is its man-made beach, a rest stop for migrating birds in the spring and fall; there are also hiking and biking trails and a kayak launch. ✉ *Box 6565, end of Southard St., through Truman Annex* ☎ *305/292–6713* ⊕ *www.floridastateparks.org/forttaylor* 🖙 *$4.50 for 1 person, $7 for 2 people, 50¢ per additional person* ☉ *Daily 8–sunset.*

KEY WEST BEST BETS

■ **Boat Cruise.** Being out on the water is what Key West is all about.

■ **Conch Train.** Hop aboard for a narrated tour of the town's tawdry past and rare architectural treasures.

■ **Hemingway.** Visit Ernest Hemingway's historic home for a literary treat.

■ **Duval Crawl.** Shop, eat, drink, repeat.

■ **Sunset in Mallory Square.** The nightly street party is the quintessential Key West experience.

Harry S Truman Little White House Museum. Renovations to this circa-1890 landmark have restored the home and gardens to the Truman era, down to the wallpaper pattern. A free photographic review of visiting dignitaries and presidents—John F. Kennedy, Jimmy Carter, and Bill Clinton are among the chief executives who passed through here—is on display in the back of the gift shop. Engaging 45-minute tours begin every 20 minutes until 4:30. They start with an excellent 10-minute video on the history of the property and Truman's visits. On the grounds of **Truman Annex,** a 103-acre former military parade grounds and barracks, the home served as a winter White House for presidents Truman, Eisenhower, and Kennedy. ■**TIP→ The house tour does require climbing steps. Visitors can do a free self-guided botanical tour of the grounds with a brochure from the museum store.** ✉ *111 Front St.* ☎ *305/294–9911* ⊕ *www.trumanlittlewhitehouse.com* 🖙 *$16* ☉ *Daily 9–5, grounds 7–6.*

☾ ★ **Key West Butterfly & Nature Conservatory.** This air-conditioned refuge for butterflies, birds, and the human spirit gladdens the soul with hundreds of colorful wings—more than 45 species of butterflies alone—in a lovely glass-encased bubble. Waterfalls, artistic benches, paved pathways, birds, and lush, flowering vegetation elevate this above most butterfly attractions. The gift shop and gallery are worth a visit on their own. ✉ *1316 Duval St.* ☎ *305/296–2988, 800/839–4647* ⊕ *www.keywestbutterfly.com* 🖙 *$12* ☉ *Daily 9–5, gallery and shop open until 5:30.*

Key West Lighthouse Museum & Keeper's Quarters Museum. For the best view in town, climb the 88 steps to the top of this 1847 lighthouse. The 92-foot structure has a Fresnel lens, which was installed in the 1860s at a cost of $1 million. The keeper lived in the adjacent 1887 clapboard house, which now exhibits vintage photographs, ship models, nautical charts, and lighthouse artifacts from all along the Key reefs. A kids' room is stocked with books and toys. ⊠ *938 Whitehead St.* ☎ *305/295– 6616* ⊕ *www.kwahs.com* ☞ *$10* ☽ *Daily 9:30–5.*

Fodor's Choice
★ **Key West Museum of Art & History in the Custom House.** When Key West was designated a U.S. port of entry in the early 1820s, a customhouse was established. Salvaged cargoes from ships wrecked on the reefs were brought here, setting the stage for Key West to become—for a time—the richest city in Florida. The imposing redbrick-and-terra-cotta Richard-sonian Romanesque–style building reopened as a museum and art gal-lery in 1999. Smaller galleries have long-term and changing exhibits about the history of Key West, including a Hemingway room and a fine collection of folk artist Mario Sanchez's wood paintings. In 2011, to commemorate the 100th anniversary of the railroad's arrival to Key West in 1912, a new permanent Flagler exhibit opened. ⊠ *281 Front St.* ☎ *305/295–6616* ⊕ *www.kwahs.com* ☞ *$7* ☽ *Daily 9:30–5.*

Mel Fisher Maritime Museum. In 1622 two Spanish galleons laden with riches from South America foundered in a hurricane 40 miles west of the Keys. In 1985 diver Mel Fisher recovered the treasures from the lost ships, the *Nuestra Señora de Atocha* and the *Santa Margarita*. Fisher's incredible adventure tracking these fabled hoards and battling the state of Florida for rights is as amazing as the loot you'll see, touch, and learn about in this museum. Artifacts include a 77.76-carat natural emerald crystal worth almost $250,000. Exhibits on the second floor rotate and might cover slave ships, including the excavated 17th-century *Henrietta Marie,* or the evolution of Florida maritime history. ⊠ *200 Greene St.* ☎ *305/294–2633* ⊕ *www.melfisher.org* ☞ *$12.50* ☽ *Weekdays 8:30–5, weekends 9:30–6.*

The Southernmost Point. Possibly the most photographed site in Key West (even though the actual geographic southernmost point in the continen-tal United States lies across the bay on a naval base, where you see a satellite dish), this is a must-see. Who wouldn't want his picture taken next to the big striped buoy that marks the southernmost point in the continental United States? A plaque next to it honors Cubans who lost their lives trying to escape to America and other signs tell Key West history. ⊠ *Whitehead and South Sts.*

SHOPPING

On these streets you'll find colorful local art of widely varying quality, key limes made into everything imaginable, and the raunchiest T-shirts in the civilized world. Browsing the boutiques—with frequent pub stops along the way—makes for an entertaining stroll down Duval Street. Key West is filled with art galleries, and the variety is truly amazing. Much is locally produced by the town's large artist community, but many galleries carry international artists from as close as Haiti and as far away as France. Local artists do a great job of preserving the island's architecture and spirit.

Bahama Village. Where to start your shopping adventure? This cluster of spruced-up shops, restaurants, and vendors is responsible for the restoration of the colorful historic district where Bahamians settled in the 19th century. The village lies roughly between Whitehead and Fort streets and Angela and Catherine streets. Hemingway frequented the bars, restaurants, and boxing rings in this part of town. ⊠ *Between Whitehead and Fort Sts. and Angela and Catherine Sts.*

> **USED BOOKS**
>
> Leave any paperback novels you have finished for the crew library. You will have more room in your suitcase, and crewmembers will have fresh reading material.

ACTIVITIES

BOAT TOURS

Lazy Dog Kayak Guides. Take a two- or four-hour guided sea kayak–snorkel tour around the mangrove islands just east of Key West. The $35 or $60 charge, respectively, covers transportation, bottled water, a snack, and supplies, including snorkeling gear. Paddleboard tours are $40. Rentals for self-touring are also available. ⊠ *5114 Overseas Hwy.* ☎ *305/295–9898* ⊕ *www.lazydog.com.*

White Knuckle Thrill Boat Ride. For something with an adrenaline boost, book with this speedboat. It holds up to 10 people and does 360s, fishtails, and other water stunts in the gulf. Cost is $69 each, and includes pickup shuttle. ⊠ *Sunset Marina, 555 College Rd.* ☎ *305/797–0459* ⊕ *www.whiteknucklethrillboatride.com.*

DIVING AND SNORKELING

The Florida Keys National Marine Sanctuary extends along Key West and beyond to the Dry Tortugas. Key West National Wildlife Refuge further protects the pristine waters. Most divers don't make it this far out in the Keys, but if you're looking for a day of diving as a break from the nonstop party in Old Town, expect to pay about $65 and upward for a two-tank dive. Serious divers can book dive trips to the Dry Tortugas.

Captain's Corner. This PADI–certified dive shop has classes in several languages and twice-daily snorkel and dive trips ($40–$65) to reefs and wrecks aboard the 60-foot dive boat *Sea Eagle.* Use of weights, belts, masks, and fins is included. ⊠ *125 Ann St.* ☎ *305/296–8865* ⊕ *www.captainscorner.com.*

Snuba of Key West. Safely dive the coral reefs without getting a scuba certification. Ride out to the reef on a catamaran, then follow your guide underwater for a one-hour tour of the coral reefs. You wear a regulator with a breathing hose that is attached to a floating air tank on the surface. No prior diving or snorkeling experience is necessary, but you must know how to swim. The $99 price includes beverages. ⊠ *Garrison Bight Marina, Palm Ave., between Eaton St. and N. Roosevelt Blvd.* ☎ *305/292–4616* ⊕ *www.snubakeywest.com.*

FISHING

Any number of local fishing guides can take you to where the big ones are biting, either in the backcountry for snapper and snook or to the deep water for the marlins and shark that brought Hemingway here in the first place.

Key West Bait & Tackle. Prepare to catch a big one with the live bait, frozen bait, and fishing equipment provided here. This outfitter also has the Live Bait Lounge, where you can sip ice-cold beer while telling fish tales. ⊠ *241 Margaret St.* ☎ *305/292–1961* ⊕ *www.keywestbaitandtackle.com.*

Key West Pro Guides. Trips include flats and backcountry fishing ($400–$450 for a half day) and reef and offshore fishing (starting at $550 for a half day). ⊠ *G-31 Miriam St.* ☎ *866/259–4205* ⊕ *www.keywestproguides.com.*

BEACHES

ℭ **Fort Zachary Taylor Historic State Park.** The park's beach is the best and
★ safest place to swim in Key West. There's an adjoining picnic area with barbecue grills and shade trees, a snack bar, and rental equipment, including snorkeling gear. A café serves sandwiches and other munchies. **Best for:** history-lovers and families. ⊠ *Box 6565; end of Southard St., through Truman Annex* ☎ *305/292–6713* ⊕ *www.floridastateparks.org/forttaylor* ☜ *$4.50 for 1 person, $7 for 2 people, 50¢ per additional person* ☉ *Daily 8–sunset, tours noon and 2.*

WHERE TO EAT

$$ ✕ **El Meson de Pepe.** If you want to get a taste of the island's Cuban
CUBAN heritage, this is the place. Perfect for after watching a Mallory Square sunset, you can dine alfresco or in the dining room on refined versions of Cuban classics. Begin with a megasized mojito while you enjoy the basket of bread and savory sauces. The expansive menu offers *tostones rellenos* (green plantains with different traditional fillings), ceviche (raw fish "cooked" in lemon juice), and more. Choose from Cuban specialties such as roasted pork in a cumin mojo sauce and *ropa vieja* (shredded beef stew). At lunch, the local Cuban population and cruise-ship passengers enjoy Cuban sandwiches and smaller versions of dinner's most popular entrées. A Latin band performs outside at the bar during sunset celebration. $ *Average main: $19* ⊠ *Mallory Sq., 410 Wall St.* ☎ *305/295–2620* ⊕ *www.elmesondepepe.com.*

$ ✕ **Lobo's Mixed Grill.** Famous for its selection of wrap sandwiches, Lobo's
AMERICAN has a reputation among locals for its 8-ounce, charcoal-grilled ground
ℭ chuck burger—thick and juicy and served with lettuce, tomato, and pickle on a toasted bun. Mix it up with toppings like Brie, blue cheese, or portobello mushroom. The menu of 30 wraps includes rib eye, oyster, grouper, Cuban, and chicken Caesar. The menu includes salads and quesadillas, as well as a fried-shrimp-and-oyster combo. Beer and wine are served. This courtyard food stand closes around 5, so eat early. Most of Lobo's business is takeout (it has a half-dozen outdoor

picnic tables), and it offers free delivery within Old Town. $ *Average main: $9* ⊠ *5 Key Lime Sq., east of intersection of Southard and Duval Sts.* ☎ *305/296–5303* ⊕ *www.lobosmixedgrill.com* ⚒ *Reservations not accepted* ⊘ *Closed Sun. Apr.–early Dec.*

NIGHTLIFE

Three spots stand out for first-timers among the saloons frequented by Key West denizens. All are within easy walking distance of the cruise-ship piers.

Capt. Tony's Saloon. When it was the original Sloppy Joe's in the mid-1930s Hemingway was a regular. Later, a young Jimmy Buffett sang here and made this watering hole famous in his song "Last Mango in Paris." Bands play nightly while regulars play pool. ⊠ *428 Greene St.* ☎ *305/294–1838.*

Schooner Wharf Bar. An open-air waterfront bar and grill in the historic seaport district retains its funky Key West charm and hosts live entertainment daily. Its margarita ranks among Key West's best. ⊠ *202 William St.* ☎ *305/292–3302* ⊕ *www.schoonerwharf.com.*

Sloppy Joe's. There's history and good times at the successor to a famous 1937 speakeasy named for its founder, Captain Joe Russell. Decorated with Hemingway memorabilia and marine flags, the bar is popular with travelers and is full and noisy all the time. A Sloppy Joe's T-shirt is a de rigueur Key West souvenir, and the gift shop sells them like crazy. ⊠ *201 Duval St.* ☎ *305/294–5717* ⊕ *www.sloppyjoes.com.*

LA ROMANA, DOMINICAN REPUBLIC

Eileen Robinson Smith

The Dominican Republic is a beautiful island bathed by the Atlantic Ocean to the north and the Caribbean Sea to the south, and some of its most beautiful beaches are in the area surrounding La Romana, notably Bayahibe Bay. The famed Casa de Campo resort and Marina will be the destination for most cruise passengers who land at La Romana's International Tourist Pier. A port call here will allow you to explore the immediate region—even take a day-trip into Santo Domingo—or simply stay and enjoy some nice (but expensive) restaurants and shops. There is also a host of activities cruise passengers can take part in on organized shore excursions.

ESSENTIALS

CURRENCY The coin of the realm is the Dominican peso. The exchange rate fluctuates continuously, but one thing is certain, the Dominican Republic, although still a good value, is not the cheap date it was up until a couple of years ago.

TELEPHONE Telephones are available at the dock, as soon as passengers disembark, and telephone cards can be purchased there as well. Tele-cards can also be bought at the supermarket at Casa de Campo Marina. To call the United States or Canada from the D.R., just punch in 1 plus the area code and number. To make calls on the island, you must tap in the area code (809), plus the seven-digit number; if you are calling a Dominican

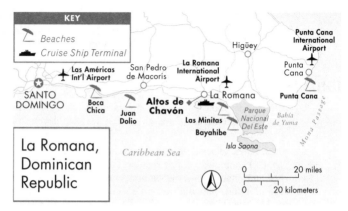

KEY

⌁ Beaches
⛴ Cruise Ship Terminal

**La Romana,
Dominican
Republic**

Las Américas Int'l Airport

SANTO DOMINGO

Boca Chica

Juan Dolio

San Pedro de Macorís

Higüey

La Romana International Airport

Altos de Chavón

Las Minitas

Bayahibe

Caribbean Sea

Parque Nacional Del Este

Isla Saona

Punta Cana International Airport

Punta Cana

La Romana

Bahía de Yuma

Mona Passage

0   20 miles
0   20 kilometers

cell phone, you must first punch in 1 then 809 or 829. Unfortunately, there is no Internet café where cruise-ship passengers can access their email, either at the dock or at Casa de Campo.

COMING ASHORE

Ships enter the Casa de Campo International Tourist Port (Muelle Turïstico Internacional Casa de Campo). A group of folkloric dancers and local musicians, playing merengue, greets passengers as they come down the gangway. An information booth with English-speaking staffers is there to assist cruise-ship passengers; the desk is open the entire time the ship is in port.

It is a 15-minute walk into the town of La Romana, or you can jump into a waiting taxi. It's safe to stroll around town, but it's not particularly beautiful, quaint, or even historic; however, it is a real slice of Dominican life. Most people just board the complimentary shuttle and head for the Casa de Campo Marina and/or Altos de Chavón, both of which are at the Casa de Campo resort. Shuttles run all day long.

Taxis line up at the port's docks, and some, but not all, drivers speak English. Staff members from the information kiosk will help to make taxi arrangements. Most rates are fixed and spelled out on a board: $15 to Casa de Campo Marina, $20 to Altos de Chavón. You may be able to negotiate a somewhat lower rate if a group books a taxi for a tour. You can also rent a car at Casa de Campo from National Car Rental; rates are expensive, usually more than $70 a day. Driving into Santo Domingo can be a hair-raising experience, and isn't for the faint of heart, so we don't recommend it.

EXPLORING LA ROMANA

★ **Altos de Chavón.** This re-creation of a 16th-century Mediterranean village sits on a bluff overlooking the Río Chavón, about 3 miles (5 km) east of the main facilities of Casa de Campo. There are cobblestone streets lined with lanterns, wrought-iron balconies, wooden shutters, courtyards swathed with bougainvillea, and **Iglesia St. Stanislaus,** the romantic setting for many a Casa de Campo wedding. More than a museum piece, this village is a place where artists live, work, and play. Dominican and international painters, sculptors, and artisans come here to teach sculpture, pottery, silkscreen printing, weaving, dance, and music at the school, which is affiliated with New York's Parsons School of Design. The artists work in their studios and crafts shops selling their finished wares. The village also has an amber museum, an archaeological museum, five restaurants, and a number of unique shops. ✉ *La Romana*.

Isla Saona. Off the east coast of Hispaniola lies this island, inhabited by sea turtles, pigeons, and other wildlife, but also not nearly as pristine as it should be for a national park (it's part of Parque Nacional Del Este). Indians once used caves here. The beaches are beautiful, and legend has it that Columbus once strayed here. Getting here, on catamarans and other excursion boats, is half the fun, but it can be a crowd scene. Vendors are allowed to sell to visitors, and there are a number of beach shacks serving lunch and drinks. Most boats traveling here leave out of the beach at Bayahibe Village. ✉ *Bayahibe*.

Santo Domingo. Spanish civilization in the New World began in the 12-block Zona Colonial of Santo Domingo. Strolling its narrow streets, it's easy to imagine this old city as it was when the likes of Columbus, Cortés, and Ponce de León walked the cobblestones, pirates sailed in and out, and colonists were settling themselves. Tourist brochures tout that "history comes alive here"—a surprisingly truthful statement. A fun horse-and-carriage ride throughout the Zone costs $25 for an hour. The steeds are no thoroughbreds, but they clip right along, though any commentary will be in Spanish. The drivers usually hang out in front of the Hostal Nicolas de Ovando. History buffs will want to spend a day exploring the many "firsts" of our continent, which will be included in any cruise-ship excursion. Do wear comfortable shoes.

> ### LA ROMANA BEST BETS
>
> ■ **Altos de Chavón.** You'll find shopping and dining as well as great views.
>
> ■ **Golf.** The Teeth of the Dog is one of the Caribbean's best courses despite the cost.
>
> ■ **Horseback Riding.** Casa de Campo has an excellent equestrian center.
>
> ■ **Isla Saona.** The powder-soft beach and beautiful water are excellent.
>
> ■ **Kandela.** The tropical, Las Vegas–style review is a highlight if your ship stays late in port on a night it is performed.

SHOPPING

Altos de Chavón. Altos de Chavón is a re-creation of a 16th-century Mediterranean village on the grounds of the Casa de Campo resort, where you can find art galleries, boutiques, and souvenir shops grouped around a cobbled square. At the Altos de Chavón Art Studios you can find ceramics, weaving, and screen prints made by local artists. Extra special is Casa Montecristo, a chic cigar lounge, which also offers a tour with cigar history and trivia. The mini-market sells sundries and some food items. ⊠ *Casa de Campo, La Romana.*

The Casa de Campo Marina. Casa de Campo's top-ranked marina is home to shops and international boutiques, galleries, and jewelers scattered amid restaurants, an ice-cream parlor, bars, banks, beauty salons, and a yacht club. It's a great place to spend some time shopping, sightseeing, and staring at the extravagant yachts. The chic shopping scene at the marina includes Bleu Marine, Fiori Coleccion (leather), Mediterraneo (women's fashions from designers like Gucci and Versace), Everett Designs (high-end larimar and amber jewelry, even authentic Spanish coins). Art Arena sells local artisan jewelry and gifts. Dominican designer Jenny Polanco sells clothes, purses, and jewelry in the Bibi Leon boutique, which is known for its tropical-themed home accessories. There's also a marvelous Italian antiques shop, Nuovo Rinascimento, and the Club de Cigarro (Fumo). By the way, the supermercado Nacional at the marina has not only groceries but sundries, postcards, and snacks. ⊠ *Casa de Campo Marina, Calle Barlovento, La Romana.*

ACTIVITIES

Most activities available at Casa de Campo are open to cruise-ship passengers. You'll need to make reservations on the ship, particularly for golf.

FISHING

Blue and white marlin, wahoo, sailfish, dorado, and mahimahi are among the most common catches in these waters.

Casa de Campo Marina. Casa de Campo Marina is the best charter option in the La Romana area. Yachts (22 to 60 footers) are available for deep-sea fishing charters for half or full days. Prices go from $708 to $1,591. They can come equipped with rods, bait, dinghies, drinks, and experienced guides. Going out for the big billfish that swim the depths of the Caribbean is a major adrenaline rush.

Boat excursions for river fishing are available as well. A three-hour excursion takes you down the Chavón River and past the lush vegetation of the bordering tropical forest, and you can go light-tackle angling for championship-size snook (a freshwater fish) as you do so. The price of $110 (minimum two people) includes boat, river guide, tackle, bait, water, and sodas. ⊠ *Casa de Campo, Calle Barlovento 3, La Romana* ☎ *809/523–3333 ext. 3165, 809/523–3333 ext. 3166.*

GOLF

Fodor's Choice ★ **Casa de Campo.** The famed 18-hole Teeth of the Dog course at Casa de Campo, with seven holes on the sea, is ranked as the number-one course in the Caribbean and is among the top courses in the world (coming in 47th in the Top 100 Courses of the World rankings released in late 2011). Green fees in high season for nonhotel guests are $325 per round per golfer; $185 per round per player for guests. The Teeth of the Dog also requires a caddy for each round, an additional $25 (plus tip). Pete Dye has designed this and two other globally acclaimed courses here.

Dye Fore, now with a total of 27 holes, is close to Altos de Chavón, hugging a cliff that looks over the sea, a river, Dominican mountains, and the marina (in high season: $250 for nonguests, $185 for guests). The Links—at this writing scheduled to reopen April 2012—is an 18-hole inland course (in high season: $175 for nonguests; $155 for hotel guests). ⊠ *La Romana* ☎ *809/523–3333, 809/523–8115 golf director* ⊕ *www.casadecampo. com.do.*

> ### CABIN OUTLETS
>
> Most ships' cabins have only one or two electrical outlets located near the desk/vanity table (not counting the shaver-only outlet in the bathroom). A short extension cord allows you to use more than one electrical appliance at once, and gives you a bit more flexibility to move around, particularly if you bring a laptop computer.

4

HORSEBACK RIDING

Equestrian Center at Casa de Campo. The 250-acre Equestrian Center at Casa de Campo has something for both Western and English riders—a dude ranch, a rodeo arena (where Casa's trademark "Donkey Polo" is played), guided trail rides, and jumping and riding lessons. Guided rides run about $56 an hour, $88 for two hours; lessons cost $65 an hour, and jumping lessons are $88 an hour or $55 a half-hour. There are early morning and sunset trail rides, too. Handsome, old-fashioned carriages are available for hire as well. Unlimited horseback riding is included if you are a hotel guest staying on the inclusive supplement. ⊠ *La Romana* ☎ *809/523–3333* ⊕ *www.casadecampo.com.do.*

BEACHES

Cruise passengers can buy a day-pass to use the beach and facilities at Casa de Campo ($75 for adults, $45 for children 4–12 years); with that, you get a place in the sun at **Minitas Beach**, towels, non-motorized water sports, lunch in the Beach Club, and entrance to Altos de Chavón. Otherwise, excursions (sometimes cheaper) are available to several area beaches.

Catalina Island is a diminutive, picture-postcard Caribbean island off the coast of the mainland. Catalina is about a half-hour away by catamaran, and most excursions offer the use of snorkeling equipment as well as a beach barbecue. **Playa Bayahibe** is a beautiful stretch of beach. Shore excursions are organized by the cruise lines to the beach, which is about 30 minutes away from the cruise port by bus. You can also book your own taxi here, and the trip may be cheaper than the cost of a shore excursion if you come with a group. **Saona Island** was once a pristine, idyllic isle. Now, on a busy cruise-ship day there may be as many as 1,000 swimmers there. However, the beach is beautiful. Excursions here usually include a powerboat ride from Casa de Campo Marina; otherwise, you are bused to Bayahibe and board a boat there.

WHERE TO EAT

$$$
ECLECTIC
Fodor's Choice
★

✗ Peperoni. Although the name sounds as Italian as *amore,* this restaurant's menu is much more eclectic than Italian. It has a classy, contemporary, white-dominated decor; waiters are also dressed in white with long aprons. The marina setting is dreamy—you drink quietly, pretending that you just disembarked from one of the gazillion-dollar yachts, like the handsome people at the next table. Strolling musicians perpetuate the mood. Astounding appetizers are found under the Asian section, like the sweet plantain roll or the Peperoni roll. Classic Italian pasta dishes and risottos with rock shrimp or porcinis are authentic, and the more inventive items such as house-made pear-and-goat-cheese ravioli with pine nuts and a key-lime emulsion are delectable. *Pulpo* (octopus) with fava beans stewed in limoncello vinaigrette is now a main rather than an appetizer (by popular demand). You can also opt for stylishly simple charcoal-grilled steaks (or with pepper-mustard-truffle demiglace), burgers, gourmet wood-oven pizzas, sandwiches, or even sushi and sashimi. Desserts are worthy here, including the tart key-lime tart paired with house-made mango sorbet. ⑤ *Average main: $21* ⊠ *Casa de Campo, Plaza Portafino 16, Casa de Campo Marina, La Romana* ☎ *809/523–2228.*

MARTINIQUE (FORT-DE-FRANCE)

Eileen Robinson Smith

The largest of the Windward Islands, Martinique is 4,261 miles (6,817 km) from Paris, but its spirit and language are decidedly French, with more than a soupçon of West Indian spice. Tangible, edible evidence of the fact is the island's cuisine, a superb blend of French and Creole. Martinique is lushly landscaped with tropical flowers. Trees bend under the weight of fruits such as mangoes, papayas, lemons, limes, and bright-red West Indian cherries. Acres of banana plantations, pineapple fields, and waving sugarcane stretch to the horizon. The towering mountains and verdant rain forest in the north lure hikers, while underwater sights and sunken treasures attract snorkelers and scuba divers. Martinique is also wonderful if your idea of exercise is turning over every 10 minutes to get an even tan and your taste in adventure runs to duty-free shopping. A popular excursion goes to St-Pierre, which was buried by ash when Mount Pelée erupted in 1902.

ESSENTIALS

CURRENCY
The euro. You will not be able to use dollars, so plan on getting some euros. You cannot cash traveler's checks or dollars at the bank, only at a bureau de change, so ATMs are your best bet if you need euros. There is a change office at the beginning of Ernest Deproge Street next to the Banque Francaise. Change Caraïbes—is at 14 rue Victor Hugo and Le Bord de Mer. They will still exchange both dollars and traveler's checks and usually offer fair rates.

TELEPHONE
There are no coin-operated phone booths. Public phones now use a télécarte, which you can buy at post offices, café-tabacs, hotels, and *bureaux de change.* To call the United States from Martinique, dial 00 + 1, the area code, and the local seven-digit number. To call locally, you

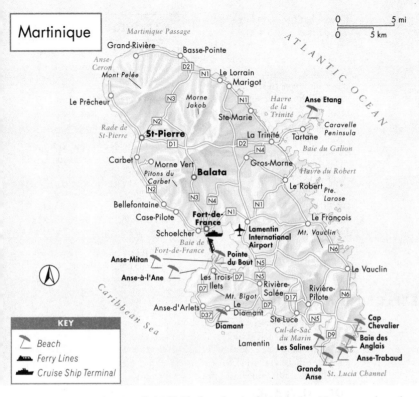

Martinique

KEY

⌇ Beach
⛴ Ferry Lines
🚢 Cruise Ship Terminal

now have to dial 0596 before the six-digit number. You can make collect calls to Canada through the Bell operator; you can get the AT&T or MCI operators from blue, special-service phones at the cruise ports and in town (try Super Sumo snack bar, on rue de la Liberté, near the library).

COMING ASHORE

Most cruise ships call either at Tourelles (in the old port, about 1½ miles [2 km] from Fort-de-France) or at Pointe Simon, right in downtown Fort-de-France. (It is rare to have a ship anchor in the Baie des Flamands and tender passengers ashore.) Tourist information offices are at each cruise terminal. Uniformed dispatchers assist passengers in finding English-speaking taxi drivers. Passengers who do not wish to walk 20 minutes into Fort-de-France from Tourelles can take a taxi (set rate of €8 for up to four passengers in a van, or €2 for each additional passenger). Expect to pay about €40 per hour for touring; in larger vans the price is usually €10 per person per hour. Independent cruisers can explore the capital and the nearby open-air market on their own. Beaming and knowledgeable hostesses in Creole dress greet cruise passengers. Civilian auxiliary police (in blue-and-orange uniforms) supplement the regular police.

Know that traffic in Fort-de-France can be nightmarish. If you want to go to the beach, a much cheaper option is to take a ferry from Fort-de-France. *Vedettes* (ferries) operate daily between the waterfront pier next to the public land-transport terminal and the marina in Pointe du Bout, Anse-Mitan, and Anse-à-l'Ane. Any of the three trips takes about 15 minutes, and the ferries operate about every 30 minutes on weekdays. Renting a car in Fort-de-France is possible, but the heavy traffic can be forbidding. Rates are about €70 per day (high season) for a car with manual transmission; automatics are substantially more expensive and seldom available without reservations.

MARTINIQUE BEST BETS

■ **Beaches.** If you want to relax, the most beautiful beach is Les Salines.

■ **French culture.** Excellent French food and music make this a *paradis* for Francophiles.

■ **La Route des Rhums.** Visit a distillery and become a rum connoisseur.

■ **Shopping.** Browse Fort-de-France's many upscale boutiques and department stores for French wares.

■ **St-Pierre.** Wander the narrow, winding streets of this hill town.

EXPLORING MARTINIQUE

If you want to see the lush island interior and St-Pierre on your own, take the N3, which snakes through dense rain forests, north through the mountains to Le Morne Rouge, then take the coastal N2 back to Fort-de-France via St-Pierre. You can do the 40-mile (64-km) round-trip in half a day, but your best option is to hire an English-speaking driver.

FORT DE FRANCE

With its historic fort and superb location beneath the towering Pitons du Carbet on the Baie des Flamands, Martinique's capital—home to about one-quarter of the island's 400,000 inhabitants—should be a grand place. It hasn't been for decades but it's now coming up fast. An ambitious redevelopment project, still under way, hopes to make it one of the most attractive cities in the Caribbean. The most pleasant districts, such as Didier, Bellevue, and Schoelcher, are on the hillside, reachable only by car or taxi; there are some good shops with Parisian wares and lively street markets. Near the harbor is a marketplace where local crafts and souvenirs are sold. The urban beach between the waterfront and the fort, La Française, has been cleaned up; white sand was brought in, and many cruise-ship passengers frequent it. The new Stewards Urbaine, easily recognized by their red caps and uniforms, are able to answer most visitor questions and give directions.

Bibliothèque Schoelcher. This wildly elaborate Romanesque public library was named after Victor Schoelcher, who led the fight to free the slaves in the French West Indies in the 19th century. The eye-popping structure was built for the 1889 Paris Exposition, after which it was dismantled, shipped to Martinique, and reassembled piece by ornate piece. ⊠ *At rue de la Liberté, which runs along west side of La Savane, Fort-de-France* ☎ *0596/70–26–67* ✉ *Free* ☉ *Mon.–Thurs. 8:30–5:30, Fri.–Sat. 8:30–noon.*

La Savane. The heart of Fort-de-France, La Savane is a 12½-acre park filled with trees, fountains, and benches. It was a popular gathering place and the scene of promenades, parades, and impromptu soccer matches; and it has now been beautifully renovated to its former glory. A massive revitalization was completed in late 2010, and it is a focal point of the city again, with entertainment, shopping, and a pedestrian mall. Attractive wooden stands have been constructed along the edge of the park that house a tourism information office, public restrooms, arts and crafts vendors, a crepe stand, an ice-cream stand, and numerous other eateries (⇨ see Fort-de-France above). Diagonally across from La Savane, you can catch the ferries for the 20-minute run across the bay to Pointe du Bout and the beaches at Anse-Mitan and Anse-à-l'Ane. It's relatively cheap as well as stress-free—much safer, more pleasant, and faster than by car.

> **PRE-PACK**
>
> Set aside a few moments every day to pack up your dirty clothes, then spend the last afternoon of your cruise doing fun things instead of packing.

The most imposing historic site in Fort-de-France is **Ft. St-Louis**, which runs along the east side of La Savane. It is no longer open to the public, as it is now functioning as a military installation. ⊠ Fort-de-France.

★ **Le Musée Régional d'Histoire et d'Ethnographie.** This museum is a learning experience that is best undertaken at the beginning of your vacation, so you can better understand the history, background, and people of the island. Housed in an elaborate former residence (circa 1888) with balconies and fretwork, it has everything from displays of the garish gold jewelry that prostitutes wore after emancipation to reconstructed rooms of a home of proper, middle-class Martinicans. There's even a display of Creole headdresses with details of how they were tied to indicate if a woman was single, married, or otherwise occupied. ⊠ 10 bd. Général de Gaulle, Fort-de-France ☎ 0596/72–81–87 ☑ €3 ⊗ Mon. and Wed.–Fri. 8:30–5, Tues. 2–5, Sat. 8:30–noon.

Rue Victor Schoelcher. Stores sell Paris fashions and French perfume, china, crystal, and liqueurs, as well as local handicrafts along this street running through the center of the capital's primary shopping district, a six-block area bounded by rue de la République, rue de la Liberté, rue Victor Severe, and rue Victor Hugo. ⊠ Fort-de-France.

St-Louis Cathedral. The Romanesque cathedral with its lovely stained-glass windows was built in 1878, the sixth church on this site (the others were destroyed by fires, hurricanes, and earthquakes). ⊠ Rue Victor Schoelcher, Schoelcher ⊗ Dawn to dusk.

ELSEWHERE ON MARTINIQUE

Balata. This quiet little town has two sights worth visiting. Built in 1923 to commemorate those Martinicans who fought and died in World War I, **Balata Church** is an exact replica of Paris's Sacré-Coeur Basilica. The gardens, **Jardin de Balata,** are lovely. ⊠ Balata.

Jardin de Balata (Balata Gardens). The Jardin de Balata has thousands of varieties of tropical flowers and plants. There are shaded benches from which to take in the mountain views and a plantation-style house furnished with period furniture. An aerial path gives visitors an astounding, bird's-eye view of the gardens and surrounding hills, from wooden walkways suspended 50 feet in the air. There is no restaurant, though beverages are available for purchase. You can order anthuriums and other tropical flowers to be delivered to the airport from the habitation's mesmerizing flower boutique. Just 15 minutes from Fort-de-France, in the direction of St-Pierre, this worthy site explains why Martinique is called the Island of Flowers. ■ TIP➡ **The gardens close at 6, but the ticket office will not admit anyone after 4:30.** ⊠ *Km 10, Rte. de Balata, Balata* ☎ *0596/64–48–73* ⊕ *www.jardindebalata.fr* ⊡ *€12.50* ⊙ *Daily 9–6.*

St-Pierre. The rise and fall of St-Pierre is one of the most remarkable stories in the Caribbean. Martinique's modern history began here in 1635. By the turn of the 20th century St-Pierre was a flourishing city of 30,000, known as the Paris of the West Indies. As many as 30 ships at a time stood at anchor. By 1902 it was the most modern town in the Caribbean, with electricity, phones, and a tram. On May 8, 1902, two thunderous explosions rent the air. As the nearby volcano erupted, Mont Pelée split in half, belching forth a cloud of burning ash, poisonous gas, and lava that raced down the mountain at 250 mph. At 3,600°F, it instantly vaporized everything in its path; 30,000 people were killed in two minutes.

The **Cyparis Express,** a small tourist train, will take you around to the main sights with running narrative (in French) for a half hour on Saturday, an hour on weekdays, for €10 (€5 for children).

An Office du Tourisme is on the *moderne* seafront promenade. Stroll the main streets and check the blackboards at the sidewalk cafés before deciding where to lunch. At night some places have live music. Like stage sets for a dramatic opera, there are the ruins of the island's first church (built in 1640), the imposing theater, and the toppled statues. This city, situated on its naturally beautiful harbor and with its narrow, winding streets, has the feel of a European seaside hill town. With every footstep you touch a page of history. Although many of the historic buildings need work, stark modernism has not invaded this burg. There is now a recommendable small hotel on the Bay as well as new ferry service between the town and Guadeloupe. As much potential as it has, this is one place in Martinique where real estate is cheap—for obvious reasons.

Musée Vulcanologique Frank Perret. For those interested in the eruption of 1902, the Musée Vulcanologique Frank Perret is a must. Established in 1933 by Frank Perret, a noted American volcanologist, who came down to study the volcano. The museum houses photographs of the old town, documents, and a number of relics—some gruesome—excavated from the ruins, including molten glass, melted iron, and contorted clocks stopped at 8 am. An English-speaking guide is often available. ⊠ *Rue Victor Hugo* ☎ *0596/78–15–16* ⊡ *€3* ⊙ *Daily 9–5.*

Le Centre de Découverte des Sciences de la Terre. If you want to know more about volcanoes, earthquakes, and hurricanes, check out Le Centre de Découverte des Sciences de la Terre. Housed in a sleek building that looks like a dramatic white box, this earth-science museum has high-tech exhibits and interesting films. Watch the documentary on the volcanoes in the Antilles, highlighting the eruption of the nearby Mont Pelée. This site has fascinating summer programs on Wednesday on dance, cuisine, and ecotourism. ■TIP→ **The Depaz Distillery is nearby, and it's easy to visit both on the same day.** ✉ *Habitation Perinelle* ☎ *0596/52–82–42* 🎫 *€5* 🕐 *Sept.–May, Tues.–Sun. 9–4:30; July–Aug., Tues.–Sun. 9–5:30.*

Depaz Distillery. An excursion to Depaz Distillery is one of the island's nicest treats. Established in 1651, it has sat at the foot of the volcano for four centuries. After a devastating eruption in 1902, the fields of blue cane were replanted, and in time, the rum making began all over again. A self-guided tour includes the workers' gingerbread cottages, and sometimes there will be an exhibit of art and sculpture made from wooden casks and parts of distillery machinery. The tasting room sells its rums, including golden and aged rum, and distinctive liqueurs made from orange, ginger, and basil, among other flavors, that can add creativity to your cooking. Unfortunately, the plantation's great house, or château, which had opened for public tours for the first time, is once again closed. Apparently more renovations were needed, and there is no projected date for completion. A recommendable restaurant, **Le Moulin a Canne,** has both Creole specialties and some French classics on the menu, plus—you guessed it—Depaz rum to wash it down. The restaurant is now a separate entity from the distillery and is open only for lunch (☎ *0596/69–80–44*). ■TIP→ **Shutters are drawn at the tasting room and the staff leaves at exactly 5 pm, so plan to be there by at least 4.** ✉ *Mont Pelée Plantation* ☎ *0596/78–13–14* ⊕ *www.depazrhum.com* 🎫 *Distillery: free* 🕐 *Weekdays 10–5, Sat. 9–4.*

SHOPPING

French fragrances, designer scarves and sunglasses, fine china and crystal, leather goods, wine (amazingly inexpensive at supermarkets), and liquor are all good buys in Fort-de-France. Purchases are further sweetened by the 20% discount on luxury items when paid for with certain credit cards. Among the items produced on the island, look for *bijoux creole* (local jewelry, such as hoop earrings and heavy bead necklaces), white and dark rum, and handcrafted straw goods, pottery, and tapestries.

The area around the cathedral in Fort-de-France has a number of small shops that carry luxury goods. Of particular note are the shops on rue Victor Hugo, rue Moreau de Jones, rue Antoine Siger, and rue Lamartine. The **Galleries Lafayette** department store on rue Schoelcher in downtown Fort-de-France sells everything from perfume to pâté.

ACTIVITIES

FISHING

Deep-sea fishing expeditions in these waters hunt down tuna, barracuda, dolphin fish, kingfish, and bonito, and the big ones—white and blue marlins. You can hire boats from the bigger marinas, particularly in Pointe du Bout, Le Marin, and Le François; most hotels arrange these Hemingway-esque trysts, but will often charge a premium. If you call several days in advance, companies can also put you together with other anglers to keep costs down.

Centre de Peche. The *Centre de Peche*, a fully loaded Davis 47-foot fishing boat, is a sportfisherman's dream. It goes out with a minimum of five anglers for €195 per person for a half day, or €390 per person for a full day, including lunch. Nonanglers can come for the ride for €95 and €190, respectively. Captain Yves speaks English fluently and is a fun guy. ⊠ *Port de Plaisance, bd. Allègre, Le Marin* ☎ *0596/76–24–20, 0696/28–80–58* ⊕ *www.sailfish-marlin.com.*

GOLF

Golf de l'Impératrice Josephine. The 18-hole Le Golf de l'Impératrice Josephine has been renamed in honor of Empress Joséphine Napoléon, whose birthplace, La Pagerie, adjoins this 150-acre track of rolling hills. However, the course is 100% American in design. It is a par-71 Robert Trent Jones course with an English-speaking pro, pro shop, bar, and restaurant. The club offers special green fees to cruise-ship passengers. Normal green fees are €23 for 9 holes (after 3 pm) and €43 for 18; a cart costs another €25 for 9, €40 for 18. Inquire about weekly rates. For those who don't mind walking while admiring the Caribbean view between the palm trees, club trolleys are €6. There are no caddies. ⊠ *Les Trois-Ilets* ☎ *0596/52–04–13.*

HIKING

Parc Naturel Régional de la Martinique. Two-thirds of Martinique is designated as protected land. Trails, all 31 of them, are well marked and maintained. At the beginning of each, a notice is posted advising on the level of difficulty, the duration of a hike, and any interesting facts. The Parc Naturel Régional de la Martinique organizes inexpensive guided excursions year-round. If there have been heavy rains, though, give it up. The tangle of ferns, bamboo trees, and vines is dramatic, but during rainy season, the wet, muddy trails will temper your enthusiasm. ⊠ *9 bd. Général de Gaulle, Fort-de-France* ☎ *0596/64–42–59 Secretary, 0596/64–45–64 Communication Department.*

HORSEBACK RIDING

Horseback-riding excursions can traverse scenic beaches, palm-shaded forests, sugarcane fields, and a variety of other tropical landscapes. Trained guides often include running commentaries on the history, flora, and fauna of the island.

Ranch de Caps. Some guides are English-speaking at Ranch de Caps, where you can take a half-day ride (Western saddle) on the wild southern beaches and across the countryside for €45. These beautiful, deserted beaches are not accessible to cars. Guides will allow those who are capable to gallop. Rides go out in the morning (8:30 to noon) and afternoon (1:30 to 5) every day but Monday. If you can manage a full day in the saddle, it costs €75 and includes lunch. Seasoned riders may even want to attempt the two-day trip (€160).

A real treat is the full-moon ride, but it needs to accrue a group of 10. Most of the 20 mounts are Anglo-Arabs. Riders are encouraged to help cool and wash their horses at day's end. Reserve in advance. Riders of all levels are welcomed. ⊠ *Cap Macré, Le Marin* ☎ *0596/74–70–65, 0696/23–18–18* ⊕ *www.ranchdescaps.com.*

Ranch Jack. Ranch Jack has trail rides (English-style) across some beautiful country for €36 for two hours; half-day excursions for €54 (€62 with transfers from nearby hotels) go through the fields and forests to the beach. Short rides can range from €16 to €25. The lessons for kids are recommendable. ⊠ *Morne habitué, Trois-Ilets* ☎ *0596/68–37–69, 0696/92–26–58* ✎ *ranch.jack@wanadoo.fr.*

BEACHES

Anse-Mitan. This is not the French Riviera, though there are often yachts moored offshore. This long stretch of beach can be particularly fun on Sunday. Small, family-owned seaside restaurants are half-hidden among palm trees and are footsteps from the lapping waves. Nearly all offer grilled lobster and some form of music, perhaps a zouk band. Inexpensive waterfront hotels line the clean, golden beach, which has excellent snorkeling just offshore. Chaise longues are available for rent from hotels for about €7. When you get to Pointe du Bout, take a left at the yellow office of Budget Rent-A-Car, then the next left up a hill, and park near the little white church. ⊠ *Pointe du Bout, Les Trois-Ilets.*

Les Salines. A short drive south of Ste-Anne brings you to a mile-long (1.5-km-long) cove lined with soft white sand and coconut palms. The beach is awash with families and children during holidays and on weekends but quiet during the week. The far end—away from the makeshift souvenir shops—is most appealing. The calm waters are safe for swimming, even for the kids. You can't rent chaise longues, but there are showers. Food vendors roam the sand. From Le Marin, take the coastal road toward Ste-Anne. You will see signs for Les Salines. If you see the sign for Pointe du Marin, you have gone too far. ⊠ *Ste-Anne.*

ⓒ **Pointe du Bout.** The beaches here are small, man-made, and lined with resorts, including the Hotel Bakoua. Each little strip is associated with its resident hotel, and security guards and closed gates make access difficult. However, if you take a left across from the main pedestrian entrance to the marina—after the taxi stand—then go left again, you will reach the beach for Hotel Bakoua, which has especially nice facilities and several options for lunch and drinks. If things are quiet—particularly during the week—one of the beach boys may rent you a chaise; otherwise, just plop your beach towel down, face forward, and enjoy the delightful view of the Fort-de-France skyline. The water is dead calm and quite shallow, but it eventually drops off if you swim out a bit. ⊠ *Pointe du Bout, Les Trois-Ilets.*

WHERE TO EAT

$$ ✕ **Mille & Une Brindilles.** At this trendy salon you can order anything from
CAFÉ a glass of wine to an aromatic pot of tea in flavors like vanilla or mango.
★ You'll find a litany of tapenades, olive cakes, and flans on the prix-fixe menu. Fred, the bubbly Parisian who is both chef and proprietress, is the queen of terrines, and she makes a delicious tart (like Roquefort and

pear) or pâté out of any vegetable or fish. The Saturday brunch (€22) is a very social occasion. The best-ever desserts, such as the Amadéus—as appealing as the classical music that plays—and *moelleux au chocolat*, are what you would want served at your last meal on Earth. Look for the sign on the left side, for the place is easy to miss. $ *Average main: €18* ⊠ *27 rte. de Didier, Didier, Fort-de-France* ☎ *0596/71–75–61* ▭ *No credit cards* ☉ *Closed Sun. and Wed. No dinner.*

MONTEGO BAY, JAMAICA

Catherine
MacGillivray

Today many explorations of MoBay are conducted from a reclining chair—frothy drink in hand—on Doctor's Cave Beach. As home of Jamaica's busiest cruise pier and the north-shore airport, Montego Bay—or MoBay—is the first taste most visitors have of the island. Travelers from around the world come and go in this bustling community, which ranks as Jamaica's second-largest city. The name Montego is derived from *manteca* (lard in Spanish). The Spanish first named this Bahía de Manteca, or Lard Bay. Why? The Spanish once shipped hogs from this port city. Jamaican tourism began here in 1924, when the first resort opened at Doctor's Cave Beach so that health-seekers could "take the waters." If you can pull yourself away from the water's edge and brush the sand off your toes, you can find some very interesting colonial sights in the surrounding area.

ESSENTIALS

CURRENCY   The Jamaican dollar. Currency-exchange booths are set up on the docks at Montego Bay whenever a ship is in port; however, the U.S. dollar is accepted virtually everywhere, though the change you receive back may be made in Jamaican dollars.

INTERNET   A growing number of Internet cafés have sprung up in recent years in Montego Bay hotels and cafés.

TELEPHONE   Public telephones (and faxes) are located at the communications center at the Montego Bay Cruise Terminal. Travelers also find public phones in major Montego Bay malls, such as the City Centre Shopping Mall. Some U.S. phone companies won't permit credit-card calls to be placed from Jamaica because they've been victims of fraud, so collect calls are often the top option. GSM cell phones equipped with tri-band or world-roaming service will find coverage throughout the Montego Bay region.

COMING ASHORE

Ships dock at the Montego Cruise Terminal, operated by the Port Authority of Jamaica. West of Montego Bay, the cruise terminal has five berths and accommodates both cruise and cargo shipping. The terminal has shops, a communications center, a visitor information booth, and a taxi stand supervised by the Port Authority of Jamaica. The cruise port in Montego Bay is not within walking distance of the heart of town; however, there's one shopping center (the Freeport Shopping Centre) within walking distance of the docks. If you just want to visit a beach, then Doctor's Cave or the Cornwall Bathing Beach, both public beaches, are very good nearby alternatives, and they are right in town.

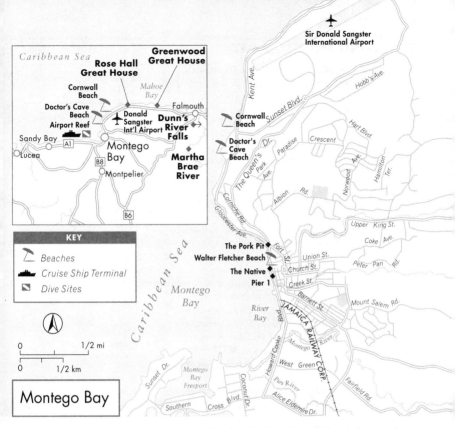

From the Montego Cruise Terminal both taxis and shuttle buses take passengers downtown. Taxi service is about US$5 each way to downtown. Expect to pay US$5 per person each way by shuttle bus to the two crafts markets, the City Centre Shopping Mall, Margaritaville, or Doctor's Cave Beach. A day pass for the shuttle bus is US$15 and allows passengers to get on and off as they wish. Jamaica is one place in the Caribbean where it's usually to your advantage to take an organized shore excursion offered by your ship unless you just want to do a bit of shopping in town. Private taxis and other transportation providers aren't particularly cheap, and a full-day tour for a small group will run $150 to $180; however, road conditions and travel time have improved significantly with the completion of the North Coast Highway.

If you take a private taxi, you should know that rates are per car, not per passenger. You can flag cabs on the street. All licensed and properly insured taxis display red Public Passenger Vehicle (PPV) license plates. Licensed minivans also bear the red PPV plates. If you hire a taxi driver as a tour guide, be sure to agree on a price before the vehicle is put into gear. Car-rental fees in Jamaica include the cost of insurance. It is not difficult to rent a car, but driving in Jamaica is done on the left side of the road, and it can take a little getting used to.

EXPLORING MONTEGO BAY

Fodor's Choice **Dunn's River Falls.** One of Jamaica's
★ most popular attractions is an eye-
catching sight: 600 feet of cold,
clear mountain water splashing
over a series of stone steps to the
warm Caribbean. The best way to
enjoy the falls is to climb the slippery steps: don a swimsuit, take the
hand of the person ahead of you,
and trust that the chain of hands
and bodies leads to an experienced
guide. The leaders of the climbs
are personable fellows who reel off
bits of local lore while telling you
where to step; you can hire a guide's
service for a tip of a few dollars.
After the climb, you exit through a
crowded market, another reminder
that this is one of Jamaica's top
tourist attractions. If you can, try
to schedule a visit on a day when no
cruise ships are in port. ■ TIP→ Always climb with a licensed guide at
Dunn's River Falls. Freelance guides might be a little cheaper, but the experienced guides can tell you just where to plant each footstep—helping you
prevent a fall. ⊠ Off Rte. A1, between St. Ann's Bay and Ocho Rios,
Ocho Rios 📞 876/974–4767 ⊕ www.dunnsriverfallsja.com 💵 $20
⊙ Daily 8:30–4 (last entry 3 pm).

> ## MONTEGO BAY BEST BETS
>
> ■ **Doctor's Cave Beach.** This
> public beach club is right in the
> heart of Montego Bay.
>
> ■ **Dunn's River Falls.** A visit
> to the falls is touristy but still
> exhilarating.
>
> ■ **Martha Brae Rafting.** A slow
> rafting trip down the river is relax-
> ing and very enjoyable.
>
> ■ **Shopping.** MoBay has several
> good shopping centers, as well as
> bustling craft markets.
>
> ■ **Rose Hall Greathouse.** The
> island's most visited greathouse
> offers a peek back into the days
> of the plantations.

★ **Greenwood Great House.** Unlike Rose Hall, Greenwood has no spooky
legend to titillate, but it's much better than Rose Hall at evoking life
on a sugar plantation. The Barrett family, from whom the English poet
Elizabeth Barrett Browning descended, once owned all the land from
Rose Hall to Falmouth; on their vast holdings they built this and several other great houses. (The poet's father, Edward Moulton Barrett,
"the Tyrant of Wimpole Street," was born at nearby Cinnamon Hill,
later the estate of country singer Johnny Cash.) Highlights of Greenwood include oil paintings of the Barretts, china made for the family
by Wedgwood, a library filled with rare books from as early as 1697,
fine antique furniture, and a collection of exotic musical instruments.
There's a pub on-site as well. It's 15 miles (24 km) east of Montego
Bay. ⊠ Greenwood 📞 876/953–1077 ⊕ www.greenwoodgreathouse.
com 💵 $20 ⊙ Daily 9–6 (last tour at 5).

Martha Brae River. This gentle waterway about 25 miles (40 km) southeast of Montego Bay takes its name from an Arawak woman who killed
herself because she refused to reveal the whereabouts of a local gold
mine. According to legend, she agreed to take her Spanish inquisitors
there and, on reaching the river, used magic to change its course, drown-
ing herself and the greedy Spaniards with her. Her *duppy* (ghost) is said

to guard the mine's entrance. Rafting on this river is a very popular activity. ⊠ *Montego Bay.*

Fodor's Choice ★ **Rose Hall.** In the 1700s it may well have been the greatest of great houses in the West Indies. Today it's popular less for its architecture than for the legend surrounding its second mistress, Annie Palmer. As the story goes, Annie was born in 1802 in England to an English mother and Irish father. When she was 10, her family moved to Haiti,

> **BINOCULARS**
>
> Binoculars are as useful indoors as they are outside. You might think they are only for bringing far-off wildlife and sights within view, but take them into museums, churches, and other buildings to examine the details of artwork, sculptures, and architectural elements.

and soon her parents died of yellow fever. Annie was adopted by a Haitian voodoo priestess and soon became skilled in the practice of voodoo. Annie moved to Jamaica, married, and built Rose Hall, an enormous plantation spanning 6,600 acres with more than 2,000 slaves. You can take a spooky nighttime tour of the property, and there's a pub on-site. ⊠ *North Coast Hwy., St. James* ✛ *15 miles (24 km) east of Montego Bay* ☎ *876/953–2323* ⊕ *www.rosehall.com* ⊡ *$20* ☉ *Daily 9:15–5:15 and 6:30–9:15.*

SHOPPING

Jamaican artisans express themselves in silk-screening, wood carvings, resort wear, hand-loomed fabrics, and paintings. Jamaican rum makes a great gift, as do Tia Maria (the famous coffee liqueur) and Blue Mountain coffee. Wood carvings are one of the top purchases; the finest carvings are made from the Jamaican national tree, lignum vitae, or tree of life, a dense wood that talented carvers transform into dolphins, heads, or fish. Bargaining is expected with crafts vendors.

ACTIVITIES

DIVING AND SNORKELING

Jamaica isn't a major dive destination, but you can find a few rich underwater regions, especially off the north coast. MoBay, known for its wall dives, has **Airport Reef** at its southwestern edge. The site is known for its coral caves, tunnels, and canyons. The first marine park in Jamaica, the **Montego Bay Marine Park,** was established to protect the natural resources of the bay; a quick look at the area lets you see the treasures that lie beneath the surface. The north coast is on the edge of the Cayman Trench, so it boasts a wide array of marine life.

Scuba Jamaica. This company offers serious scuba facilities for dedicated divers. The PADI and NAUI operation also offers Nitrox diving and instruction as well as instruction in underwater photography, night diving, and open-water diving. There's a pickup service for the Montego Bay, Runaway Bay, Discovery Bay, and Ocho Rios areas. Along with the Falmouth location, Scuba Jamaica is also found at the Franklyn D Resort in Runaway Bay and at Travellers Resort in Negril. ⊠ *N-Resort,*

North Coast Hwy., Falmouth ☎ *876/617–2500, 876/973–4591 in Run-away Bay, 876/957–3039 in Negril* ⊕ *www.scuba-jamaica.com.*

GOLF

Golfers appreciate both the beauty and the challenges offered by Jamaica's courses. Caddies are almost always mandatory throughout the island, and rates are $15 to $45 per round of golf. Cart rentals are available at most courses; costs are $20 to $40. Some of the best courses in the country are found near MoBay.

★ **Golf at Half Moon.** This Robert Trent Jones–designed 18-hole course is the home of the Red Stripe Pro Am. Green fees are $105 for guests, $150 for nonguests with twilight packages ranging from $75 to $90. In 2005 the course received an upgrade from Jones protégé Roger Rulewich and draws international attention. The course is also home of the Half Moon Golf Academy, which offers one-day sessions, multi-day retreats, and hour-long private sessions. ⊠ *Half Moon Resort, North Coast Hwy., 7 miles (11 km) east of Montego Bay, Montego Bay* ☎ *876/953–2560* ⊕ *halfmoon.rockresorts.com/activities/golf.asp.*

Hilton Rose Hall Resort and Spa. This course 4 miles (6 km) east of the airport hosts several invitational tournaments. Green fees run $149 7–10 am, $119 10 am–1:30 pm, and $99 for a twilight round at the 18-hole championship **Cinnamon Hill Ocean Course.** The course was designed by Robert von Hagge and Rick Baril and is adjacent to historic Cinnamon Hill estate. Rates include green fees, cart, caddie, and tax, and apply to both guests and nonguests. ⊠ *North Coast Hwy., St. James* ✧ *15 miles (24 km) east of Montego Bay* ☎ *876/953–2650.*

★ **Ritz-Carlton Golf and Spa Resort, Rose Hall.** One of the nicest courses in Montego Bay, if not Jamaica, is the **White Witch** course at the Ritz-Carlton. The green fees at this 18-hole championship course are $175 for resort guests, $185 for nonguests, and $109 for a twilight round. Designed by Robert von Hagge and Rick Baril, it is close to the grounds of historic Rose Hall Great House. ⊠ *1 Ritz Carlton Dr., Rose Hall, St. James* ☎ *876/684–0174* ⊕ *www.whitewitchgolf.com.*

RIVER RAFTING

Jamaica's many rivers mean a multitude of freshwater experiences, from mild to wild. Jamaica's first tourist activity off the beaches was relaxing rafting trips aboard bamboo rafts poled by local boatmen. Recently, soft-adventure enthusiasts have also been able to opt for white-water action as well with guided tours through several operators.

Fodor's Choice
★
Bamboo rafting in Jamaica originated on the **Rio Grande,** a river in the Port Antonio area. Jamaicans had long used the bamboo rafts to transport bananas downriver; decades ago actor and Port Antonio resident Errol Flynn saw the rafts and thought they'd make a good tourist attraction, and local entrepreneurs quickly rose to the occasion. Today the slow rides are a favorite with romantic travelers and anyone looking to get off the beach for a few hours. The popularity of the Rio Grande's trips spawned similar trips down the **Martha Brae River,** about 25 miles (40 km) from MoBay. Near Ocho Rios, the **Great River** has lazy river rafting as well as energetic kayaking.

Jamaica Tours Limited. This big tour company conducts raft trips down the River Lethe, approximately 12 miles (19 km) southwest of Mo'Bay (a 50-minute trip); the four-hour excursion can include lunch if requested and takes you through unspoiled hill country. Bookings can be made through hotel tour desks. Price depends on the number of people on the trip. ⊠ *Providence Dr., Montego Bay* ☎ *876/953–3700* ⊕ *www.jamaicatoursltd.com.*

River Raft Ltd. This company leads trips down the Martha Brae River, about 25 miles (40 km) from most hotels in Mo'Bay. The cost is $60 per person for the 1½-hour river run. ⊠ *Martha Brae* ☎ *876/940–6398* ⊕ *www.jamaicarafting.com.*

BEACHES

4

Doctor's Cave Bathing Club. Montego Bay's tourist scene has its roots right on the Hip Strip, the bustling entertainment district along Gloucester Avenue. Here a sea cave whose waters were said to have healing powers drew travelers from around the world. Although the cave was destroyed by a hurricane generations ago, the beach is always busy and has a perpetual spring-break feel. It has some of the best facilities in Jamaica, thanks to the plantation-style clubhouse with changing rooms, showers, a gift shop, a restaurant, and complimentary Wi-Fi. You can rent beach chairs and umbrellas. **Amenities:** food and drink; showers; water sports; toilets; lifeguards; parking (fee). **Best for:** partyers; snorkeling; swimming; sunsets. ⊠ *Gloucester Ave., Montego Bay* ☎ *876/952–2566* ⊕ *www.doctorscavebathingclub.com* ⊠ *$5.*

Walter Fletcher Beach. Although it's not as pretty as Doctor's Cave Beach, Walter Fletcher Beach is home to Aquasol Theme Park, which offers a large beach (with lifeguards and security personnel), glass-bottom boats, snorkeling, go-kart racing, a disco at night, and a bar and restaurant. There is à la carte pricing for most activities. Several times a week Aquasol throws a beach bash with live reggae and mento performances. Near the center of town, the beach has unusually fine swimming; the calm waters make it a good bet for children. **Amenities:** food and drink; water sports; snorkeling; swimming; lifeguard; showers; toilets; parking. **Best for:** partyers; snorkeling; swimming; sunsets. ⊠ *Gloucester Ave., Montego Bay* ☎ *876/979–9447* ⊠ *$5* ☉ *Daily 9–7.*

WHERE TO EAT

§ ✕ **Pork Pit.** A favorite with many Mo'Bay locals, this no-frills eatery serves Jamaican specialties including some fiery jerk—note that it's spiced to local tastes, not watered down for tourist palates. Many get their food to go, but you can also find picnic tables just outside. ⑤ *Average main: $10* ⊠ *27 Gloucester Ave., Montego Bay* ☎ *876/940–3008.*

JAMAICAN

Fodor'sChoice

★

NASSAU, BAHAMAS

Ramona Settle   Nassau, the capital of the Bahamas, has witnessed Spanish invasions and hosted pirates, who made it their headquarters for raids along the Spanish Main. The heritage of old Nassau blends the Southern charm of British loyalists from the Carolinas, the African tribal traditions of freed slaves, and a bawdy history of blockade-running during the Civil War and rum-running in the Roaring 1920s. The sheltered harbor bustles with cruise-ship hubbub, while a block away, broad, shop-lined Bay Street is alive with commercial activity. Over it all is a subtle layer of civility and sophistication, derived from three centuries of British rule. Nassau's charm, however, is often lost in its commercialism. There's excellent shopping, but if you look past the duty-free shops you'll also find sights of historical significance that are worth seeing.

ESSENTIALS

CURRENCY   The Bahamian dollar, which trades one-to-one with the U.S. dollar, which is universally accepted. There's no need to acquire any Bahamian currency.

INTERNET   You'll find Internet kiosks at Prince George Wharf.

TELEPHONE   Calling locally or internationally is easy in the Bahamas. To place a local call, dial the seven-digit phone number. To call the United States, dial 1 plus the area code. Pay phones cost 25¢ per call; Bahamian and U.S. quarters are accepted, as are BATELCO and Indigo phone cards. To place a call using a calling card, use your long-distance carrier's access code or dial 0 for the operator. Be aware that when placing a toll-free call from your hotel you are charged as if for a regular long-distance call.

COMING ASHORE

Cruise ships dock at one of three piers on Prince George Wharf. Taxi drivers who meet the ships may offer you a $2 "ride into town," but the historic government buildings and duty-free shops lie just steps from the dock area. As you leave the pier, look for a tall pink tower—diagonally across from here is the tourist information office. Stop in for maps of the island and downtown Nassau. On most days you can join a one-hour walking tour ($10 per person) conducted by a well-trained guide. Tours generally start every hour on the hour from 10 am to 4 pm; confirm the day's schedule in the office. Just outside, an ATM dispenses U.S. dollars.

As you disembark from your ship, you will find a row of taxis and air-conditioned limousines. Fares are fixed by the government by zones. Unless you plan to jump all over the island, taxis are the most convenient way to get around. The fare is $9 plus $1 bridge toll between downtown Nassau and Paradise Island, $20 from Cable Beach to Paradise Island (plus $1 toll), and $18 from Cable Beach to Nassau. Fares are for two passengers; each additional passenger is $3. It's customary to tip taxi drivers 15%.

Water taxis travel between Prince George Wharf and Paradise Island during daylight hours at half-hour intervals. The one-way cost is $3 per person, and the trip takes 12 minutes.

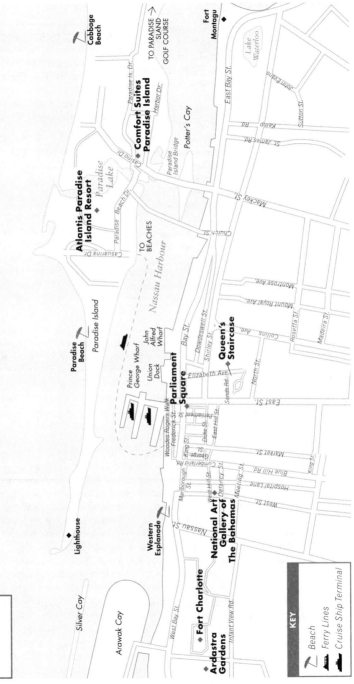

Nassau, Bahamas

300 yards
300 meters

Silver Cay

Arawak Cay

Lighthouse

Paradise Beach

Paradise Island

Cabbage Beach

Comfort Suites Paradise Island

TO PARADISE ISLAND GOLF COURSE

Fort Montagu

Paradise Is.-Dr.

Harbor Dr.

Atlantis Paradise Island Resort

Casino Dr.

Paradise Lake

Paradise Beach Dr.

Casuarina Dr.

Potter's Cay

Paradise Island Bridge

TO BEACHES

Nassau Harbour

Lake Waterloo

John Evans

East Bay St.

Kemp Rd.

St. James Rd.

Sutton St.

Mackey St.

Church St.

Montrose Ave.

Mount Royal Ave.

Collins Ave.

Rosetta St.

Madeira St.

Prince George Wharf

John Alfred Wharf

Union Dock

Woodes Rogers Walk

Bay St.

Dowdeswell St.

Shirley St.

Queen's Staircase

Parliament Square

Frederick St.

Elizabeth Ave.

Sands Rd.

North St.

East St.

East Hill St.

Parliament St.

King St.

Duke St.

George St.

Cumberland Rd.

Market St.

Blue Hill Rd.

Hospital Lane

Meeting St.

West St.

King St.

Marlborough St.

West Hill St.

Delancy St.

Nassau St.

National Art Gallery of The Bahamas

Fort Charlotte

Western Esplanade

West Bay St.

Infant View Rd.

Ardastra Gardens

KEY

Beach

Ferry Lines

Cruise Ship Terminal

EXPLORING NASSAU

Shops angle for tourist dollars with fine imported goods at duty-free prices, yet you will find a handful of stores overflowing with authentic Bahamian crafts, foods, and other delights. Most of Nassau's historic sites are centered around downtown.

With its thoroughly revitalized downtown—the revamped British Colonial Hilton lead the way—Nassau is recapturing some of its glamour. Nevertheless, modern influence is apparent: fancy restaurants, suave clubs, and trendy coffeehouses have popped up everywhere. This trend comes partly in response to the burgeoning uppercrust crowds that now supplement the spring-breakers and cruise passengers who have traditionally flocked to Nassau.

NASSAU BEST BETS

■ **Ardastra Gardens.** Flocks of flamingos, the country's national bird, "march" in three daily shows (you can mingle with the flamboyant pink stars afterward).

■ **Atlantis.** Though very costly, the water park here is a must for families.

■ **Shopping.** To many, shopping is one of Nassau's great delights.

■ **Junkanoo Beach.** Head to this beach (aka Long Wharf Beach) and sit in the shade of a coconut palm (it's a 10-minute walk from the duty-free shops on Bay Street).

Today the seedy air of the town's not-so-distant past is almost unrecognizable. Petty crime is no greater than in other towns of this size, and the streets not only look cleaner but feel safer. You can still find a wild club or a rowdy bar, but you can also sip cappuccino while viewing contemporary Bahamian art or dine by candlelight beneath prints of old Nassau, serenaded by soft, island-inspired calypso music.

Arawak Cay. Known to Nassau residents as "The Fish Fry," Arawak Cay is one of the best places to knock back a Kalik beer, chat with locals, watch or join in a fast-paced game of dominoes, or sample traditional Bahamian fare. You can get small dishes such as conch fritters or full meals at one of the pastel-color waterside shacks. Order a fried snapper served up with a sweet homemade roll, or fresh conch salad (a spicy mixture of chopped conch—just watching the expert chopping is a show as good as any in town—mixed with diced onions, cucumbers, tomatoes, and hot peppers in a lime marinade). The two-story Twin Brothers and Goldie's Enterprises are two of the most popular places. Try their fried "cracked conch" and Goldie's famous Sky Juice (a sweet but potent gin, coconut-water, and sweet-milk concoction sprinkled with nutmeg). There's usually a live band on the outdoor stage Friday and Saturday nights. ⊠ *W. Bay St. and Chippingham Rd.*

Ⓒ **Ardastra Gardens, Zoo, and Conservation Centre.** Marching flamingos? These national birds give a parading performance at Ardastra daily at 10:30, 2:10, and 4:10. The brilliant pink birds are a delight—especially for children, who can walk among the flamingos after the show. The zoo, with more than 5 acres of tropical greenery and ponds, also has an aviary of rare tropical birds including the bright green Bahama parrot,

CLOSE UP

Saving on Atlantis

Frugal cruisers have long known about **Comfort Suites Paradise Island** (⊕ www.comfortsuites.com), which is right across the street from the Atlantis Resort. They use it to avoid paying for expensive and limited ship-sponsored day-passes to the resort, which cost well over $150 per person. Book a room here, and everyone in the room (up to four people, regardless of age) is entitled to a free day-pass to the Atlantis Resort's water park. In addition to the base rate (often more than $300 for two adults and two children depending on the season), you will also have to pay (at check-in) an additional energy surcharge of $13.95 per *adult* and a housekeeper gratuity of $5 per *adult* (over 16 years) on top of the quoted rate, even if you prepay for the room; the third and fourth person cost $40 each *plus* all the service charges. Frankly, this isn't as good a deal as it used to be, but families or groups of four can still save a money by going this route, and then you will have a room in which to shower and change before returning to the ship. Of course, it's a better deal if you can get a discounted rate. (Be aware that you may not have more than four people on a single reservation regardless of their age, and you may not get access to the room in the morning, but it will be ready when you get back from your day of fun at the water park, and the room rate includes free Wi-Fi.) When it's time for lunch, you'll find cheaper restaurants within walking distance of Atlantis. You can also book your room and daypass through the Barbados-based travel agency that operates ⊕ CaribbeanDaypass.com.

native Bahamian creatures such as rock iguanas and the little (and harmless) Bahamian boa constrictors, and a global collection of small animals. ✉ *Chippingham Rd. south of W. Bay St.* ☎ *242/323–5806* ⊕ *www.ardastra.com* 🎟 *$15 adults, $7.50 children* ⊙ *Daily 9–5 except Christmas Day, Boxing Day, and New Year's Day.*

🕐 **Fort Charlotte.** Built in 1788, this imposing fort comes complete with a waterless moat, drawbridge, ramparts, and a dungeon, where children love to see the torture device where prisoners were "stretched." Young local guides bring the fort to life. (Tips are expected.) Lord Dunmore, who built it, named the massive structure in honor of George III's wife. At the time, some called it Dunmore's Folly because of the staggering expense of its construction. It cost eight times more than was originally planned. (Dunmore's superiors in London were less than ecstatic with the high costs, but he managed to survive unscathed.) Ironically, no shots were ever fired in battle from the fort. The fort and its surrounding 100 acres offer a wonderful view of the cricket grounds, the beach, and the ocean beyond. Inquire about Segway tours. ✉ *W. Bay St. at Chippingham Rd.* 🎟 *$5* ⊙ *Tours daily 8–4.*

Fodor's Choice ★ **National Art Gallery of the Bahamas.** Opened in July 2003, the museum houses the works of esteemed Bahamian artists such as Max Taylor, Amos Ferguson, Brent Malone, John Cox, and Antonius Roberts. The glorious Italianate-colonial mansion, built in 1860 and restored in the 1990s, has double-tiered verandas with elegant columns. It was the residence of Sir William Doyle, the first chief justice of the Bahamas. Join locals on the lawn for movie night under the stars; call for schedule. Don't miss the museum's gift shop, where you'll find books about the Bahamas and Bahamian quilts, prints, ceramics, jewelry, and crafts. ⊠ *West and W. Hill Sts., across from St. Francis Xavier Cathedral* ☎ *242/328–5800* ⊕ *www.nagb.org.bs* 🖃 *$5* ☉ *Tues.–Sat. 10–4.*

Parliament Square. Nassau is the seat of the national government. The Bahamian Parliament comprises two houses—a 16-member Senate (Upper House) and a 41-member House of Assembly (Lower House)—and a ministerial cabinet headed by a prime minister. If the House is in session, sit in to watch lawmakers debate. Parliament Square's pink, colonnaded government buildings were constructed in the late 1700s and early 1800s by Loyalists who came to the Bahamas from North Carolina. The square is dominated by a statue of a slim young Queen Victoria that was erected on her birthday, May 24, in 1905. ⊠ *Bay St.* ☎ *242/322–2041* 🖃 *Free* ☉ *Weekdays 10–4.*

Queen's Staircase. A popular early-morning exercise regime for locals, the "66 Steps" (as Bahamians call them) are thought to have been carved out of a solid limestone cliff by slaves in the 1790s. The staircase was later named to honor Queen Victoria's reign. Pick up some souvenirs at the ad hoc straw market along the narrow road that leads to the site. ⊠ *Top of Elizabeth Ave. hill, south of Shirley St.*

SHOPPING

Most of Nassau's shops are on Bay Street between Rawson Square and the British Colonial Hotel, and on the side streets leading off Bay Street. Some stores are popping up on the main shopping thoroughfare's eastern end and just west of the Cable Beach strip. Bargains abound between Bay Street and the waterfront. Upscale stores can also be found in Marina Village and the Crystal Court at Atlantis and in the arcade joining the Sheraton Nassau Beach and the Wyndham on Cable Beach. You'll find duty-free prices—generally 25%–50% less than U.S. prices—on imported items such as crystal, linens, watches, cameras, jewelry, leather goods, and perfumes.

ACTIVITIES

FISHING

The waters here are generally smooth and alive with many species of game fish, which is one of the reasons why the Bahamas has more than 20 fishing tournaments open to visitors every year. A favorite spot just west of Nassau is the Tongue of the Ocean, so called because it looks like that part of the body when viewed from the air. The channel stretches for 100 miles. For boat rental, parties of two to six will pay $600 or so for a half-day, $1,600 for a full day.

Born Free Charters. This charter company has three boats and guarantees a catch on full-day charters—if you don't get a fish, you don't pay. ☎ *242/393–4144* ⊕ *www.bornfreefishing.com.*

Charter Boat Association. The Charter Boat Association has 15 boats available for fishing charters. ☎ 242/393–3739.

GOLF

Cable Beach Golf Club. The oldest golf course in the Bahamas, Cable Beach Golf Club (7,040 yards, par 72), will be completely overhauled

CAUTION

Mail overflowing your mailbox is a neon sign to thieves that you aren't home. Have someone pick it up, or better yet, have the post office hold all your mail for you.

when Baha Mar gets on with its Cable Beach transformation. In 2011 the course was reduced to 9 holes as construction got underway, and at some point the existing course will be closed entirely. Best to inquire when booking your vacation if nearby golf is a must. ⊠ *W. Bay St., SE end of Cable Beach strip* ☎ *242/327–6000* 🖥 *18 holes $95, 9 holes $70; carts included. Clubs $25* ☉ *Daily 7–5:30; last tee off at 5:15.*

One & Only Ocean Club Golf Course. Designed by Tom Weiskopf, One & Only Ocean Club Golf Course (6,805 yards, par 72) is a championship course surrounded by the ocean on three sides, which means that winds can get stiff. Call to check on current availability and up-to-date prices (those not staying at Atlantis or the One & Only Ocean Club may find themselves shut out completely). ⊠ *Paradise Island Dr. next to airport* ☎ *242/363–3925, 800/321–3000 in U.S.* 🖥 *18 holes $260. Clubs $70* ☉ *Daily 6 am–sundown.*

BEACHES

New Providence is blessed with stretches of white sand studded with palm and sea grape trees. Some of the beaches are small and crescent-shaped; others stretch for miles.

Cabbage Beach. Cabbage Beach is 3 miles of white sand lined with shady casuarina trees, sand dunes, and sun worshippers. This is the place to go to rent Jet Skis or get a bird's-eye view of Paradise Island while parasailing. Hair braiders and T-shirt vendors stroll the beach, and hotel guests crowd the areas surrounding the resorts, including Atlantis. For peace and quiet, stroll east.

Cable Beach. Hotels dot the length of this 3-mile beach, so don't expect isolation. Music from the hotel pool decks wafts out onto the sand, Jet Skis race up and down the waves, and vendors sell everything from shell jewelry to coconut drinks right from the shell. If you get tired of lounging around, join a game of beach volleyball.

Junkanoo Beach. Right in downtown Nassau, this beach is spring-break central from late February through April. The man-made beach isn't the prettiest on the island, but it's conveniently located if you only have a few quick hours to catch a tan. Music is provided by bands and DJs to guys with boom boxes; a few bars keep the drinks flowing.

WHERE TO EAT

$ ✗ **Double D's.** Don't let the dark-tinted windows and green lighting over
BAHAMIAN the doorway put you off. Inside you'll find a simply decorated bar offering friendly service and good native food. This is a popular spot with
locals for its Bahamian cuisine and 23-hour service in a town where
most kitchens are closed at 10 pm. Try boil' fish—a peppery lime-based
broth filled with chunks of boiled potatoes, onions, and grouper—or
be adventurous and order a bowl of pig-feet or sheep-tongue souse.
Although souplike, these Bahamian delicacies are typically served only
for breakfast. All come with a chunk of johnnycake or a bowl of steaming white grits. $ *Average main: $15* ✉ *E. Bay St. at the foot of the
bridges from Paradise Island* ☎ *242/393–2771.*

$ ✗ **Green Parrot.** Sip a green-color Parrot Crush while tackling the large
AMERICAN Works Burger as you sit and enjoy the cool breeze and lovely Nassau
Harbour scenery. This casual, all-outdoor restaurant and bar is popular
with locals. The menu includes burgers, wraps, quesadillas, and other
simple but tasty dishes. The conch po'boy is a new favorite. Happy hour
from 5 to 9 and a DJ on Friday nights mean that the huge bar is lively
and packed. $ *Average main: $15* ✉ *E. Bay St. west of the bridges to
Paradise Island* ☎ *242/322–9248* ⊕ *www.greenparrotbar.com.*

NEVIS (CHARLESTOWN)

Jordan Simon In 1493, when Columbus spied a cloud-crowned volcanic isle during
his second voyage to the New World, he named it Nieves—the Spanish
word for "snows"—because it reminded him of the peaks of the Pyr-
enees. Nevis rises from the water in an almost perfect cone, the tip of
its 3,232-foot central mountain hidden by clouds. Even less developed
than sister island St. Kitts—just 2 miles (3 km) away at their closest
point, Nevis is known for its long beaches with white and black sand,
its lush greenery, the charming if slightly dilapidated Georgian capital
of Charlestown, mountain hikes, and its restored sugar plantations
that now house charming inns. Even on a day trip Nevis feels relaxed
and quietly upscale. You might run into celebrities at the Four Seasons
or lunching at the beach bars on Pinney's, the showcase strand. Yet
Nevisians (not to mention the significant expat American and British
presence) never put on airs, offering warm hospitality to all visitors.

ESSENTIALS

CURRENCY The Eastern Caribbean dollar (EC$2.67 to US$1). U.S. dollars, major
credit cards, and traveler's checks are readily accepted, although large
U.S. bills may be difficult to change in small shops—and you'll receive
change in the local currency.

INTERNET Charlestown usually has an operational Internet café, but they rarely
last in one location. The tourist office will have the latest information.

TELEPHONE Phone cards, which you can buy in denominations of $5, $10, and
$20, are handy for making local phone calls, calling other islands, and
accessing U.S. direct lines. To make a local call, dial the seven-digit
number. To call Nevis from the United States, dial the area code 869,
then access code 465, 466, 468, or 469 and the local four-digit number.

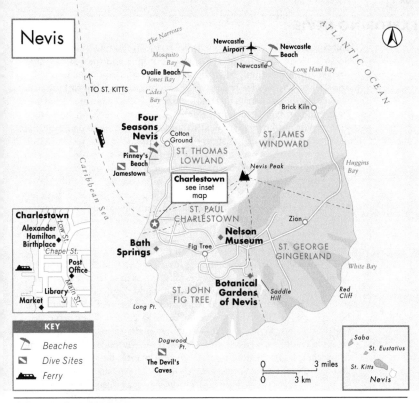

Nevis

Charlestown

- Alexander Hamilton Birthplace
- Chapel St.
- Low St.
- Post Office
- Library
- Market
- Main St.

KEY

- Beaches
- Dive Sites
- Ferry

TO ST. KITTS

The Narrows

Mosquito Bay

Oualie Beach
Jones Bay

Cades Bay

Four Seasons Nevis

Cotton Ground

Pinney's Beach

Jamestown

ST. THOMAS LOWLAND

Charlestown
see inset map

ST. PAUL CHARLESTOWN

Bath Springs

Fig Tree

Nelson Museum

ST. JOHN FIG TREE

Botanical Gardens of Nevis

Long Pt.

Dogwood Pt.

The Devil's Caves

Newcastle Airport

Newcastle Beach

Newcastle

Long Haul Bay

Brick Kiln

ST. JAMES WINDWARD

Nevis Peak

Huggins Bay

Zion

ST. GEORGE GINGERLAND

White Bay

Saddle Hill

Red Cliff

Caribbean Sea

ATLANTIC OCEAN

0   3 miles
0   3 km

Saba

St. Eustatius

St. Kitts

Nevis

COMING ASHORE

Cruise ships dock in Charlestown harbor; all but the smallest ships bring passengers in by tender to the central downtown ferry dock. The pier leads smack onto Main Street, with shops and restaurants steps away. Taxi drivers often greet tenders, and there's also a stand a block away. Fares are fairly expensive, but a three-hour driving tour of Nevis costs about $80 for up to four people. Several restored greathouse plantation inns are known for their lunches; your driver can provide information and arrange drop-off and pickup. Before setting off in a taxi, be sure to clarify whether the rate quoted is in E.C. or U.S. dollars.

If your ship docks in St. Kitts, Nevis is a 30- to 45-minute ferry ride from Basseterre. You can tour Charlestown, the capital, in a half hour or so, but you'll need three to four hours to explore the entire island. Most cruise ships arrive in port around 8 am, and the ferry schedule (figure $18 round-trip) can be irregular, so many passengers sign up for a cruise-line-run shore excursion. If you travel independently, confirm departure times with the tourist office to be sure you'll make it back to your ship on time.

EXPLORING NEVIS

Bath Springs. The Caribbean's first hotel, the Bath Hotel, built by businessman John Huggins in 1778, was so popular in the 19th century that visitors, including such dignitaries as Samuel Taylor Coleridge and Prince William Henry, traveled two months by ship to "take the waters" in the property's hot thermal springs. It suffered extensive hurricane and probably earthquake damage over the years and languished in disrepair until recently. Local volunteers have cleaned up the spring and built a stone pool and steps to enter the waters; now residents and visitors enjoy the springs, which range from 104°F to 108°F, though signs still caution that you bathe at your own risk, especially if you have heart problems. The development houses the Nevis Island Administration offices; there's still talk of adding massage huts, changing rooms, a restaurant, and a cultural center and historic exhibit on the original hotel property. Follow Main Street south from Charlestown. ⊠ *Charlestown outskirts.*

★ **Botanical Gardens of Nevis.** In addition to terraced gardens and arbors, this remarkable 7.8-acre site in the glowering shadow of Mt. Nevis has natural lagoons, streams, and waterfalls, superlative bronze mermaids, egrets and herons, and extravagant fountains. You can find a proper rose garden, sections devoted to orchids and bromeliads, cacti, and flowering trees and shrubs—even a bamboo garden. The entrance to the Rain Forest Conservatory—which attempts to include every conceivable Caribbean ecosystem and then some—duplicates an imposing Maya temple. A splendid re-creation of a plantation-style greathouse contains a café with sweeping sea views, and the upscale Galleria shop selling art, textiles, jewelry, and Indonesian teak furnishings sourced during the owners' world travels. ⊠ *Montpelier Estate* ☎ *869/469–3509* ⊕ *www.botanicalgardennevis.com* ✉ *$13* ⊘ *Mon.–Sat. 9–4.*

★ **Charlestown.** About 1,200 of Nevis's 10,000 inhabitants live in the capital. If you arrive by ferry, as most people do, you'll walk smack onto Main Street from the pier. It's easy to imagine how tiny Charlestown, founded in 1660, must have looked in its heyday. The weathered buildings still have fanciful galleries, elaborate gingerbread fretwork, wooden shutters, and hanging plants. The stone building with the clock tower (1825, but mostly rebuilt after a devastating 1873 fire) houses the courthouse and second-floor **library** (a cool respite on sultry days). The little park next to the library is Memorial Square, dedicated to the fallen of World Wars I and II. Down the street from the square, archaeologists have discovered the remains of a Jewish cemetery and synagogue (Nevis reputedly had the Caribbean's second-oldest congregation), but there's little to see. ⊠ *Nevis.*

Alexander Hamilton Birthplace. The Alexander Hamilton Birthplace, which contains the Hamilton **Museum**, sits on the waterfront. This bougainvillea-draped Georgian-style house is a reconstruction of what is believed to have been the American patriot's original home, built in 1680 and likely destroyed during a mid-19th earthquake. Born here in 1755, Hamilton moved to St. Croix when he was about 12. He moved to the American colonies to continue his education at 17; he became George Washington's Secretary of the Treasury and died in a duel with political rival Aaron Burr in 1804. The Nevis House of Assembly occupies the second floor; the museum downstairs contains Hamilton memorabilia, documents pertaining to the island's history, and displays on island geology, politics, architecture, culture, and cuisine. The gift shop is a wonderful source for historic maps, crafts, and books on Nevis. ⊠ *Low St., Charlestown* ☎ *869/469–5786* ⊕ *www.nevis-nhcs.org* ⊡ *$5, with admission to Nelson Museum of Nevis History $7* ⊗ *Weekdays 9–4, Sat. 9–noon.*

Nelson Museum of Nevis History. Purportedly this is the Western Hemisphere's largest collection of Lord Horatio Nelson memorabilia, including letters, documents, paintings, and even furniture from his flagship. Nelson was based in Antigua but came on military patrol to Nevis, where he met and eventually married Frances Nisbet, who lived on a 64-acre plantation here. Half the space is devoted to often-provocative displays on island life, from leading families to vernacular architecture to the adaptation of traditional African customs, from cuisine to Carnival. The shop is an excellent source for gifts, from homemade soaps to historical guides. ⊠ *Bath Rd. outside Charlestown* ☎ *869/469–0408* ⊕ *www.nevis-nhcs.org* ⊡ *$5, with Hamilton Museum $7* ⊗ *Weekdays 9–4, Sat. 9–noon.*

> ## NEVIS BEST BETS
>
> ■ **Charlestown.** The well-preserved little capital is worth a quick stroll.
>
> ■ **Golf.** The stunner at the Four Seasons provides challenge aplenty.
>
> ■ **Hiking.** Getting out in the countryside on foot is one of the best ways to experience Nevis.
>
> ■ **Pinney's Beach**. This long sensuous strand has several beach bars where you can "lime" with locals.

SHOPPING

Nevis is certainly not the place for a shopping spree, but there are some wonderful surprises, notably the island's stamps, fragrant honey, ceramics, and batik and hand-embroidered clothing. Other than a few hotel boutiques and isolated galleries, virtually all shopping is concentrated on or just off Main Street in Charlestown. The lovely old stonework and wood floors of the waterfront Cotton Ginnery Complex make an appropriate setting for shops of local artisans.

CraftHouse. This marvelous source for local specialties, from vetiver mats to leather moccasins, also has a smaller branch in the Cotton Ginnery. ⊠ *Pinney's Rd., Charlestown* ☎ *869/469–5505.*

Nevis Handicraft Co-op Society. This shop next to the tourist office offers works by local artisans (clothing, ceramic ware, woven goods) and locally produced honey, hot sauces, and jellies (try the guava and soursop). ⊠ *Main St., Charlestown* ☎ *869/469–1746.*

 Philatelic Bureau. Opposite the tourist office, this is the place to go for stamp collectors. St. Kitts and Nevis are famous for their decorative, and sometimes valuable, stamps. Real beauties include the butterfly, hummingbird, and marine-life series. ⊠ *Cotton Ginnery, Charlestown* ☎ *869/469–0617.*

ACTIVITIES

GOLF

Fodor's Choice **Four Seasons Golf Course.** Duffers doff their hats to the beautiful, impec-
★ cably maintained Robert Trent Jones Jr.–designed Four Seasons Golf
Course: the virtual botanical gardens surrounding the fairways almost
qualify as a hazard in themselves. The front 9 holes are fairly flat until
Hole 8, which climbs uphill after your tee shot. Most of the truly stunning views are along the back 9. The signature hole is the 15th, a
660-yard monster that encompasses a deep ravine; other holes include
bridges, steep drops, rolling pitches, extremely tight and unforgiving
fairways, sugar-mill ruins, and fierce doglegs. Attentive attendants can-
vas the course with beverage buggies, handing out chilled, peppermint-
scented towels and preordered Cubanos that help test the wind. Green
fees per 18 holes are $190 for hotel guests, $290 for nonguests. ⊠ *Four
Seasons Resort Nevis, Pinney's Beach* ☎ *869/469–1111* ☞ *18 holes,
par 72, 6,766 yd.*

HIKING

The center of the island is Nevis Peak—also known as Mt. Nevis—
which soars 3,232 feet and is flanked by Hurricane Hill on the north
and Saddle Hill on the south. If you plan to scale Nevis Peak, a daylong
affair, it's highly recommended that you go with a guide. The **Upper
Round Road Trail** is a 9-mile (14.5-km) road constructed in the late 1600s
that was cleared and restored by the Nevis Historical and Conservation
Society. It connects the Golden Rock Plantation Inn, on the east side
of the island, with Nisbet Plantation Beach Club, on the northern tip.
The trail encompasses numerous vegetation zones, including pristine
rain forest, and impressive plantation ruins. The original cobblestones,
walls, and ruins are still evident in many places.

★ **Peak Heaven at Herbert Heights.** This tour company is run by the Herbert family, who lead four-hour nature hikes up to panoramic Herbert
Heights, where you drink in fresh local juices and the views of Montserrat; the powerful telescope, donated by Greenpeace, makes you feel as
if you're staring right into that island's simmering volcano (or staring
down whales during their migratory season). The Herberts painstak-
ingly reconstructed thatched cottages that offer a glimpse of village
life a century ago, dubbed Peak Heaven, at Nelson's Lookout. These
include a small, poignant, history museum; shop selling local crafts; gallery; and massage room. The solar-powered Coal Pot restaurant offers
heaping helpings of affordable island fare (try any soup, the thyme-
seared snapper, and scrumptious homemade ice creams) alongside the
splendid vistas. There's even a small playground at the entrance. Hike
prices start at $25. ⊠ *Nevis* ☎ *869/469–2856, 869/665–6926* ⊕ *www.
peakheavennevis.com.*

Sunrise Tours. Run by Lynell and Earla Liburd, Sunrise Tours offers a
range of hiking trips, but their most popular is Devil's Copper, a rock
configuration full of ghostly legends. Local people gave it its name
because at one time the water was hot—a volcanic thermal stream.
The area features pristine waterfalls and splendid bird-watching. They
also do a Nevis village walk, a Hamilton Estate Walk, a Charlestown

tour, an Amerindian walk along the wild southeast Atlantic coast, and trips to the rain forest and Nevis Peak. They love highlighting Nevisian heritage, explaining time-honored cooking techniques, the many uses of dried grasses, and medicinal plants. Hikes range from $20 to $40 per person, and you receive a certificate of achievement. ⊠ *Nevis* ☎ *869/469–2758* ⊕ *www.nevisnaturetours.com.*

WINDSURFING

★ **Windsurfing Nevis.** Waters are generally calm and northeasterly winds steady yet gentle, making Nevis an excellent spot for beginners and intermediates. Windsurfing Nevis offers top-notch instructors (Winston Crooke is one of the best in the islands) and equipment for $30 per hour. Beginners get equipment and two-hour instruction for $60. Groups are kept small (eight maximum), and the equipment is state-of-the-art from Mistral, North, and Tushingham. It also offers kayak rentals and tours along the coast, stopping at otherwise inaccessible beaches. ⊠ *Oualie Beach* ☎ *869/469–9682.*

BEACHES

All beaches are free to the public (the plantation inns cordon off "private" areas on Pinney's Beach for guests), but there are no changing facilities, so wear a swimsuit under your clothes.

Oualie Beach. South of Mosquito Bay and north of Cades and Jones bays, this beige-sand beach lined with palms and sea grapes is where the folks at Oualie Beach Hotel can mix you a drink and fix you up with water-sports equipment. There's excellent snorkeling amid calm water and fantastic sunset views with St. Kitts silhouetted in the background. Several beach chairs and hammocks (free with lunch, $3 rental without) line the sand and the grassy "lawn" behind it. Oualie is at the island's northwest tip, approximately 3 miles (5 km) west of the airport. ⊠ *Oualie Beach.*

Pinney's Beach. The island's showpiece has soft, golden sand on the calm Caribbean, lined with a magnificent grove of palm trees. The Four Seasons Resort is here, as are the plantation inns' beach clubs and casual beach bars such as Sunshine's, Chevy's, and the Double Deuce. Regrettably, the waters can be murky and filled with kelp if the weather has been inclement anywhere within a hundred miles, depending on the currents. ⊠ *Pinney's Beach.*

WHERE TO EAT

$$ ✕ **Double Deuce.** Mark Roberts, the former chef at Montpelier, decided
SEAFOOD to chuck the "five-star lifestyle" and now co-owns this jammed, jam-
★ ming beach bar, which lures locals with fine, fairly priced fare, creative cocktails, and a Hemingway-esque feel (the shack is plastered with sailing and fishing pictures, as well as Balinese masks, steer horns, license plates, and wind chimes). Peer behind the ramshackle bar and you'll find a gleaming modern kitchen where Mark (and fun-loving firebrand partner Lyndeta) prepare sublime seafood he often catches himself, as well as organic beef burgers, velvety pumpkin soup, creative pastas, and

lip-smacking ribs. The "DD" is as cool and mellow as it gets. Stop by for free Wi-Fi and proper espresso, a game of pool, riotous Thursday-night karaoke, or just to hang out with a Double Deuce Stinger (Lyndy's answer to Sunshine's Killer Bee punch). You'll find more than 5,000 songs on the "jukebox"—Akon to ZZ Top, Sarah Vaughan to Van Morrison; if you can't find your favorite, the "DJ" will download it for you while you take a quick dip. Dinner can be arranged for parties of 6 to 10. $ *Average main: US$20* ⊠ *Pinney's Beach* ☎ *869/469–2222* ⊕ *www.doubledeucenevis.com* ⊴ *Reservations essential* ⊟ *No credit cards* ☾ *Closed Mon.*

$$
CARIBBEAN

✗ **Sunshine's.** Everything about this shack overlooking (and spilling onto) the beach is larger than life, including the Rasta man Llewelyn "Sunshine" Caines himself. Flags and license plates from around the world complement the international patrons (including an occasional movie or sports star wandering down from the Four Seasons). Picnic tables are splashed with bright sunrise-to-sunset colors; even the palm trees are painted, though "it gone upscaled," as locals say, with VIP cabanas. Fishermen cruise up with their catch—you might savor lobster rolls or snapper creole. Don't miss the lethal house specialty, Killer Bee rum punch. As Sunshine boasts, "One and you're stung, two, you're stunned, three, it's a knockout." $ *Average main: US$20* ⊠ *Pinney's Beach* ☎ *869/469–5817.*

OCHO RIOS, JAMAICA

Catherine
MacGillivray

About two hours east of Montego Bay lies Ocho Rios (often just "Ochi"), a lush destination that's favored by honeymooners for its tropical beauty. Often called the garden center of Jamaica, this community is perfumed by flowering hibiscus, bird of paradise, bougainvillea, and other tropical blooms year-round. Ocho Rios is a popular cruise port and the destination where you'll find one of the island's most recognizable attractions: the stairstep Dunn's River Falls, which invites travelers to climb in daisy-chain fashion, hand-in-hand behind a sure-footed guide. This spectacular waterfall is actually a series of falls that cascades from the mountains to the sea. That combination of hills, rivers, and sea also means many activities in the area, from seaside horseback rides to mountain biking and lazy river rafting.

ESSENTIALS

CURRENCY   The Jamaican dollar. Currency-exchange booths are set up on the docks at Ocho Rios whenever a ship is in port. The U.S. dollar is accepted virtually everywhere; at some places change is made in Jamaican dollars. Prices given are in U.S. dollars unless otherwise indicated.

INTERNET   A growing number of facilities offer Internet service; expect to pay about US$2 for 20 minutes.

TELEPHONE   Public telephones are found at the communications center at the Ocho Rios Cruise Pier. Travelers also find public phones in major Ocho Rios malls. Some U.S. phone companies won't permit credit-card calls to be placed from Jamaica because they've been victims of fraud, so collect calls are often the top option. GSM cell phones equipped with

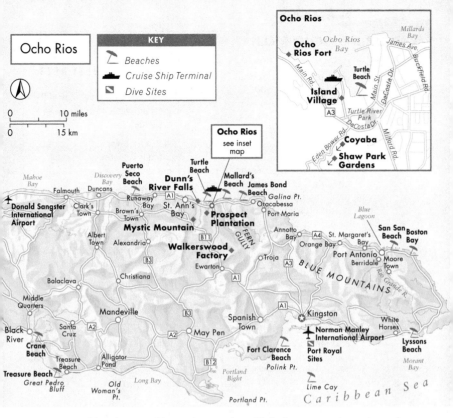

tri-band or world-roaming service will find coverage throughout the Ocho Rios region.

COMING ASHORE

Most cruise ships are able to dock at this port on Jamaica's North Coast, near Dunn's River Falls (a US$10 taxi ride from the pier). Also less than 1 mile (2 km) from the Ocho Rios pier are Island Village (within walking distance), Taj Mahal Duty-Free Shopping Center, and the Ocean Village Shopping Center. If you're going anywhere else beyond Island Village, a taxi is recommended; expect to pay US$8 for a taxi ride downtown. The pier, which includes a cruise terminal with the basic services and transportation, is also within easy walking distance of Turtle Beach.

Licensed taxis are available at the pier; expect to pay about US$35 per hour for a guided taxi tour. Jamaica is one place in the Caribbean where it's usually to your advantage to take an organized shore excursion offered by your ship unless you just want to go to the beach or do a bit of shopping in town. Car rental isn't recommended in Jamaica because of high prices, bad roads, and aggressive drivers.

EXPLORING OCHO RIOS

Fodor's Choice ★ **Dunn's River Falls.** One of Jamaica's most popular attractions is an eye-catching sight: 600 feet of cold, clear mountain water splashing over a series of stone steps to the warm Caribbean. The best way to enjoy the falls is to climb the slippery steps: don a swimsuit, take the hand of the person ahead of you, and trust that the chain of hands and bodies leads to an experienced guide. The leaders of the climbs are personable fellows who reel off bits of local lore while telling you where to step; you can hire a guide's service for a tip of a few dollars. After the climb, you exit through a crowded market, another reminder that this is one of Jamaica's top tourist attractions. ⚠ Always climb with a licensed guide at Dunn's River Falls. Freelance guides might be a little cheaper, but the experienced guides can tell you just where to plant each footstep—helping you prevent a fall. ⊠ *Off Rte. A1, between St. Ann's Bay and Ocho Rios* ☎ *876/974–4767* ⊕ *www.dunnsriverfallsja.com* ⌨ *$15* ⊙ *Daily 8:30–5 (last entry 4 pm).*

> ### OCHO RIOS BEST BETS
>
> ■ **Chukka Caribbean.** Any of the great adventure tours here is sure to please.
>
> ■ **Dunn's River Falls.** A visit to the falls is touristy, yet it's still exhilarating.
>
> ■ **Mystic Mountain.** Live out your *Cool Runnings* fantasies on the bobsled ride.
>
> ■ **Dolphin Cove at Treasure Reef.** Swim with a dolphin, stingray, or shark at this popular stop.
>
> ■ **Firefly.** The former home of playwright Noël Coward can be seen on a guided tour.

Mystic Mountain. This is Ocho Rios' newest attraction, covering 100 acres of mountainside rain forest near Dunn's River Falls. Visitors board the Rainforest Sky Explorer, a chairlift that soars through and over the pristine rain forest to the apex of Mystic Mountain. On top, there is a restaurant with spectacular views of Ocho Rios, arts-and-crafts shops, and the attraction's signature tours, the Rainforest Bobsled Jamaica ride and the Rainforest Zipline Canopy ride. Custom-designed bobsleds, inspired by Jamaica's Olympic bobsled team, run downhill on steel rails with speed controlled by the driver, using simple push-pull levers. Couples can run their bobsleds in tandem. The zipline tours streak through lush rain forest under the care of an expert guide who points out items of interest. The entire facility was built using environmentally friendly techniques and materials so as to leave the native rain forest undisturbed. ⊠ *North Coast Hwy., Ocho Rios* ☎ *876/974–3990* ⊕ *www.rainforestbobsledjamaica.com* ⌨ *$47–$137* ⊙ *9–5 (adventures from 10–3:30).*

Prospect Plantation. To learn about Jamaica's agricultural heritage, a trip to this working plantation, just east of town, is a must. It's not just a place for history lovers, however. Everyone enjoys the views over the White River Gorge and the tour in a tractor-pulled cart. The grounds are full of exotic flowers and tropical trees, some planted over the years by such celebrities as Winston Churchill and Charlie Chaplin. The estate includes a small aviary with free-flying butterflies. You can also saddle up for horseback rides and camel safaris on the plantation's 900 acres, but the actual tour times are usually geared toward the cruise-ship schedule, so call ahead. ⊠ *Rte. A1, 4 miles (3.2 km) east of Ocho Rios* ☎ *876/994–1058* ⊕ *www.prospectplantationtours.com* ⊒ *$32* ◷ *Daily tours at 10:30 am, 2 pm, and 3:30 pm.*

SHOPPING

Ocho Rios has several malls, and they are less hectic than the one in MoBay. Shopping centers include **Pineapple Place, Ocean Village, Taj Mahal,** and **Coconut Grove.** A fun mall that also serves as an entertainment center is **Island Village,** the place nearest to the cruise port. This open-air mall includes shops selling Jamaican handicrafts, duty-free goods and clothing, a Margaritaville restaurant, and a small beach area with a water trampoline and water sports.

ACTIVITIES

DOLPHIN-SWIM PROGRAMS

Dolphin Cove Ocho Rios. This company offers dolphin swims as well as lower-price dolphin encounters for ages 8 and up; dolphin touch programs for ages 6 and over; or simple admission to the grounds, which also includes a short nature walk. Programs cost between $45 and $195, depending on your involvement with the dolphins. Advance reservations are advised. ⊠ *North Coast Hwy., adjacent to Dunn's River Falls, Box 21, Ocho Rios* ☎ *876/974–5335* ⊕ *www. dolphincovejamaica.com.*

GOLF

Ocho Rios courses don't have the prestige of those around Montego Bay, but duffers will find challenges at a few lesser-known courses.

Sandals Golf and Country Club. The golf course in Ocho Rios is 700 feet above sea level (green fees are $100 for 18 holes or $70 for 9 holes for nonguests; free for guests). ⊠ *5 miles (8 km) southeast of Ocho Rios, turn south at White River and continue 4 miles (6 km)* ☎ *876/975–0119.*

HORSEBACK RIDING

With its combination of hills and beaches, Ocho Rios is a natural for horseback excursions. Most are guided tours taken at a slow pace and perfect for those with no previous equestrian experience. Many travelers opt to pack long pants for horseback rides, especially those away from the beach.

Fodor's Choice ★ **Chukka Caribbean Adventures.** Ocho Rios has excellent horseback riding, but the best of the operations is Chukka Caribbean's Ocho Rios stable. You don't have to be an experienced rider to enjoy its tours; horses are well trained and Chukka provides attentive guides to assist all riders along the way. The company's 2½-hour beach ride ($74, $52 for children) is a highlight of many trips to Jamaica. ⊠ *Llandovery, St. Ann's Bay* ☎ *876/972–2506* ⊕ *www.chukkacaribbean.com.*

Prospect Plantation. The plantation offers a horseback rides for ages eight and older. The price ($58) includes use of helmets; advance reservations are required. For the adventurous, Prospect Plantation also offers guided camel rides. ⊠ *Rte. A1, about 3 miles (5 km) east of Ocho Rios* ☎ *876/974–5335* ⊕ *www.prospectplantationtours.com.*

WHITE-WATER RAFTING
White-water rafting is increasingly popular in the Ocho Rios area.

Chukka Caribbean Adventures. The big activity outfitter offers the Chukka River Tubing Safari on the White River, an easy trip that doesn't require any previous tubing experience. This tour allows you to travel in your very own tube through gentle rapids. This tour lasts for three hours and costs $64 for adults and $45 for children. ⊠ *Llandovery, St. Ann's Bay* ☎ *876/972–2506* ⊕ *www.chukkacaribbean.com.*

BEACHES

Dunn's River Falls Beach. You'll find a crowd (especially if there's a cruise ship in town) at the small beach at the foot of the falls. Although tiny—especially considering the crowds that pack the falls—it's got a great view, as well as a beach bar and grill. Look up from the sands for a spectacular view of the cascading water, the roar from which drowns out the sea as you approach. To go to the beach you have to pay the entrance fee to Dunn's River Falls. **Amenities:** food and drink; lifeguards; parking; lifeguards; toilets. **Best for:** swimming. ⊠ *Rte. A1, between St. Ann's Bay and Ocho Rios* ☜ *$20.*

☻ **Turtle Beach.** One of the busiest beaches in Ocho Rios is usually lively and has a mix of both residents and visitors. It's next to the Sunset Jamaica Grande hotel and looks out over the cruise port. **Amenities:** food and drink; lifeguards; parking; toilets, water sports. **Best for:** swimming. ⊠ *Main St., Ocho Rios* ☜ *J$200.*

WHERE TO EAT

$ ✕ **Island Grill.** With 16 locations across the island, this eat-in or take-
JAMAICAN   out restaurant about a block from the main tourist area is Jamaica's version of fast food. Jerk chicken, rice and peas, and Jamaican stew combo meals (called "Yabbas," an African-Jamaican term for bowl) are all on the menu. Many meals are served with festival (Jamaican fried cornbread) and are spiced for the local palate. ⑤ *Average main: $7* ⊠ *59 Main St., Ocho Rios* ☎ *876/974–3160.*

$ ✕ **Ocho Rios Jerk Centre.** This blue-canopied, open-air eatery is a good
JAMAICAN   place to park yourself for frosty Red Stripe beer and fiery jerk pork, chicken, or seafood. Milder barbecued meats, also sold by weight (typically, a quarter or half pound makes a good serving), turn up on the fresh-daily chalkboard menu posted on the wall. It's lively at lunch, especially when passengers from cruise ships swamp the place. ⑤ *Average main: $10* ⊠ *Da Costa Dr., Ocho Rios* ☎ *876/974–2549.*

PROGRESO, MEXICO

Marilst Kast The waterfront town closest to Mérida, Progreso, is not particularly historic. It's also not terribly picturesque; still, it provokes a certain sentimental fondness for those who know it well. On weekdays during most of the year the beaches are deserted, but when school is out (Easter week, July, and August) and on summer weekends it's bustling with families from Mérida. Progreso's charm—or lack of charm—seems to hinge on the weather. When the sun is shining, the water looks translucent green and feels bathtub-warm, and the fine sand makes for lovely long walks. When the wind blows during one of Yucatán's winter *nortes,* the water churns with whitecaps and looks gray and unappealing. Whether the weather is good or bad, however, everyone ends up eventually at one of the restaurants lining the main street, Calle 19. Across the street from the oceanfront malecón, restaurants serve cold beer, seafood cocktails, and freshly grilled fish. Most cruise passengers head immediately for Mérida or for one of the nearby archaeological sites.

ESSENTIALS

CURRENCY The Mexican peso. U.S. dollars and credit cards are accepted by everyone at the port. There is no advantage to paying in dollars, but there may be an advantage to paying in cash.

INTERNET The cruise terminal isn't terribly close to Progreso's downtown area, but if you take a bus or taxi into town, you'll easily find an Internet café with pretty cheap service. If you take an excursion to Mérida, you'll find that Internet cafés there are ubiquitous, particularly on the main square and calles 61 and 63; most charge $1 to $3 per hour.

TELEPHONE In most parts of the country, pay phones (predominantly operated by Telmex) accept only prepaid cards (*tarjetas Lada*), sold in 30-, 50-, 100-, or 200-peso denominations at newsstands, pharmacies, minimarkets, or grocery stores. Coin-only pay phones are few and far between.

COMING ASHORE

The pier in Progreso is long, and cruise ships dock at its end, so passengers are shuttled to the foot of the pier, where the Progreso Cruise Terminal offers visitors their first stop. The terminal houses small restaurants and shops selling locally produced crafts. These are some of the best shops in sleepy Progreso (a much wider selection is available in nearby Mérida). The beach lies just east of the pier and can easily be reached on foot. If you want to enjoy the sun and a peaceful afternoon, a drink at one of the small palapa-roof restaurants that line the beach is a good option.

If you are looking to explore, there are plenty of taxis around the pier. A trip around town should not cost more than $5, but ask the taxi driver to quote you a price. If you want to see more of Progresso, a cab can also take you to the local sightseeing tour bus (which departs about every 10 minutes from the Casa de Cultura), a bright blue, open-air, double-decker bus that travels through town and only costs $2. A taxi ride from Progreso to Mérida runs about $30, and most drivers charge

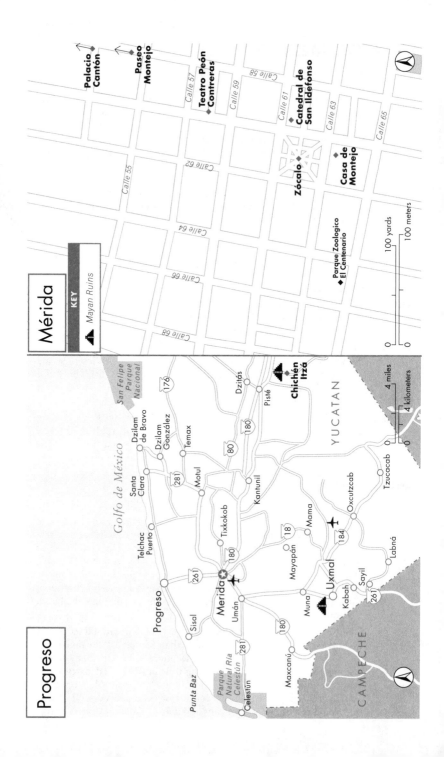

Mérida

KEY

▲ Mayan Ruins

Palacio Cantón

Paseo Montejo

Teatro Peón Contreras

Calle 57

Calle 59

Calle 58

Catedral de San Ildefonso

Calle 61

Calle 63

Calle 65

Calle 55

Calle 62

Zócalo

Casa de Montejo

Calle 64

Calle 66

Parque Zoológico El Centenario

Calle 68

100 yards

100 meters

Progreso

Golfo de México

San Felipe Parque Nacional

176

Dzitás

Pisté

Chichén Itzá

YUCATAN

Dzilam de Bravo

Dzilam González

Temax

180

80

Santa Clara

281

Motul

Kantunil

Telchac Puerto

Tixkokob

180

Mama

18

Oxcutzcab

Tzucacab

4 miles

4 kilometers

Progreso

Mérida

261

Umán

Mayapán

Muna

184

Uxmal

Kabah

Sayil

Labná

261

Sisal

180

Maxcanú

CAMPECHE

Parque Natural Ría Celestún

281

Punta Baz

Celestún

around $15 per hour to show you around. If you plan on renting the cab for a good part of the day, talk about the number of hours and the cost with the driver before you take off. It's difficult to rent a car, so most people just band together in a taxi.

EXPLORING MÉRIDA

Just south of Progreso (about 20 or 30 minutes by taxi), Mérida, the cultural and intellectual hub of the Yucatán, offers a great deal to explore. Mérida is rich in art, history, and tradition. Most streets are numbered, not named, and most run one-way. North–south streets have even numbers, which descend from west to east; east–west streets have odd numbers, which ascend from north to south. One of the best ways to see the city is to hire a *calesa*, a horse-drawn carriage. They congregate on the main square or at the Palacio Cantón, near the anthropology museum. Drivers charge about $20 for an hour-long circuit around downtown and up Paseo de Montejo, and $30 for an extended tour.

Casa de Montejo. Two Franciscos de Montejo—father and son—conquered the peninsula and founded Mérida in January of 1542, and they built their stately "casa" 10 years later. In the late 1970s it was restored by banker Agustín Legorreta, converted to a branch of Banamex bank, and now sits on the south side of the plaza. It's the city's finest—and oldest—example of colonial plateresque architecture, a Spanish architectural style popular in the 16th century and typified by the kind of elaborate ornamentation you'll see here. A bas-relief on the doorway—the facade is all that remains of the original house—depicts Francisco de Montejo the younger, his wife, and daughter, as well as Spanish soldiers standing on the heads of the vanquished Maya. ⊠ *Calle 63, Centro, Mérida* ☎ *999/923–0633* ⊕ *www.museocasamontejo.com* ⊗ *Tues.–Sat. 10–7, Sun. 10–2.*

Catedral de San Ildefonso. Begun in 1561 and completed 38 years later, St. Ildefonso is the oldest cathedral on the American continent (though an older one can be found in the Dominican Republic). It took several hundred Maya laborers, working with stones from the pyramids of the ravaged Mayan city, 36 years to complete it. Designed in the somber Renaissance style by an architect who had worked on the Escorial in Madrid, its facade is stark and unadorned, with gunnery slits instead of windows, and faintly Moorish spires. Inside, the black *Cristo de las Ampollas* (Christ of the Blisters) occupies a side chapel to the left of the main altar. At 23 feet tall, it's the tallest Christ in Mexico inside a church. The statue is a replica of the original, which was destroyed during the revolution in 1910, which is also when the gold that typically decorated Mexican cathedrals was carried off. According to one of many legends, the Christ figure burned all night yet appeared the next morning unscathed—except that it was covered with the blisters for which it's named. You can hear the pipe organ play at the 11 am Sunday Mass. ⊠ *Calles 60 and 61, Centro, Mérida* ⊗ *Daily 7–11:30 and 4:30–8.*

Palacio Cantón. The most compelling of the mansions on **Paseo Montejo**, this stately palacio was built as the residence for a general between 1909 and 1911. Designed by Enrique Deserti, who also did the blueprints for the Teatro Peón Contreras, the building has a grandiose air that seems more characteristic of a mausoleum than a home: there's marble everywhere, as well as Doric and Ionic columns and other Italianate beaux arts flourishes. The building also houses the air-conditioned **Museo Regional de Antropología,** which introduces visitors to ancient Mayan culture. Temporary exhibits sometimes brighten the standard collection. ⊠ *Paseo Montejo 485, at Calle 43, Paseo Montejo, Mérida* ☏ *999/928–6719, 999/923–0557* ⊕ *www.inah.gob.mx* ☜ *$3.50* ⊙ *Tues.–Sun. 8–5.*

> ## PROGRESO BEST BETS
>
> ■ **Chichén Itzá.** The famous Maya city is an easy day trip from Progreso and is home to the enormous and oft-photographed El Castillo pyramid.
>
> ■ **Mérida.** This delightful, though busy, town is full of life as people take to the streets for music, dance, food, and culture.
>
> ■ **Uxmal.** One of the most beautiful Mayan cities is reachable on a day trip from Progreso. If you've seen Chichén Itzá already, go here.

Paseo Montejo. North of downtown, this 10-block-long street was *the* place to reside in the late 19th century, when wealthy plantation owners sought to outdo each other with the opulence of their elegant mansions. Mansion owners typically opted for the decorative styles popular in New Orleans, Cuba, and Paris—imported Carrara marble, European antiques—rather than any style from Mexico. The broad boulevard, lined with tamarind and laurel trees, has lost much of its former panache; some of the mansions have fallen into disrepair. Many are now used as office buildings, while others have been or are being restored as part of a citywide, privately funded beautification program. The street is a lovely place to explore on foot or in a horse-drawn carriage. ⊠ *Mérida.*

Teatro Peón Contreras. This 1908 Italianate theater was built along the same lines as grand turn-of-the-20th-century European theaters and opera houses. In the early 1980s, the marble staircase, dome, and frescoes were restored. Today, in addition to performing arts, the theater houses the **Centro de Información Turística** (Tourist Information Center), which provides maps, brochures, and details about attractions in the city and state. The theater's most popular attraction, however, is the café-bar spilling out into the street facing Parque de la Madre. It's crowded every night with people enjoying the balladeers singing romantic and politically inspired songs. ⊠ *Calle 60, between Calles 57 and 59, Centro, Mérida* ☏ *999/923–7354 Tourist Information Center, 999/924–9290, 999/923–7354 theater* ⊕ *www.culturayucatan.com* ⊙ *Tourist Information Center daily 9–9.*

Zócalo. Méridians traditionally refer to this main square as the Plaza de la Independencia, or the Plaza Principal. Whichever name you prefer, it's a good spot to start a tour of the city, watch dance performances, listen to music, or chill in the shade of a laurel tree when the day gets too hot. The plaza was laid out in 1542 on the ruins of T'hó, the Mayan city demolished to make way for Mérida, and is still the focal point around which the most important public buildings cluster. *Confidenciales* (S-shaped benches) invite intimate tête-à-têtes, and lampposts keep the park beautifully illuminated at night. ⊠ *Bordered by Calles 60, 62, 61, and 63, Centro, Mérida.*

FARTHER AFIELD

Chichén Itzá. One of the most dramatically beautiful of the ancient Maya cities, Chichén Itzá draws some 3,000 visitors a day from all over the world. Since the remains of this once-thriving kingdom were discovered by Europeans in the mid-1800s, many of the travelers who make the pilgrimage here have been archaeologists and scholars, who study the structures and glyphs and try to piece together the mysteries surrounding them. While the artifacts here give fascinating insight into Mayan civilization, they also raise many, many unanswered questions.

The sight of the immense **El Castillo pyramid,** rising imposingly yet gracefully from the surrounding plain, has been known to produce goose pimples on sight. El Castillo (The Castle) dominates the site both in size and in the symmetry of its perfect proportions. Openjawed serpent statues adorn the corners of each of the pyramid's four stairways, honoring the legendary priest-king Kukulcán (also known as Quetzalcóatl), an incarnation of the feathered serpent god. More serpents appear at the top of the building as sculpted columns. At the spring and fall equinoxes, the afternoon light strikes the trapezoidal structure so that the shadow of the snake-god appears to undulate down the side of the pyramid to bless the fertile earth. Thousands of people travel to the site each year to see this phenomenon.

On the other side of El Castillo, just before a small temple dedicated to the planet Venus, a ruined sacbé, or white road, leads to the **Cenote Sagrado** (Holy Well, or Sinkhole), also probably used for ritualistic purposes. Jacques Cousteau and his companions recovered about 80 skeletons from this deep, straight-sided, subsurface pond, as well as thousands of pieces of jewelry and figures of jade, obsidian, wood, bone, and turquoise. In direct alignment with Cenote Sagrado, on the other side of El Castillo, the **Xtaloc Sinkhole** was kept pristine, undoubtedly for bathing and drinking. Adjacent to this water source is a steam bath, its interior lined with benches along the wall like those you'd see in any steam room today. Outside, a tiny pool was used for cooling down during the ritual. ⊠ *Off Hwy. 180, Chichén Itzá* ⊠ *$10; Guides $45* ☉ *Daily 8–4:30.*

Uxmal Ruins. Although much of Uxmal hasn't been restored, the following buildings in particular merit attention:

At 125 feet high, the **Pirámide del Adivino** is the tallest and most prominent structure at the site. Unlike most other Mayan pyramids, which are stepped and angular, the Temple of the Magician has a softer and more-refined round-corner design. This structure was rebuilt five times over hundreds of years, each time on the same foundation, so artifacts found here represent several different kingdoms. The pyramid has a stairway on its western side that leads through a giant open-mouthed mask to two temples at the summit. During restoration work in 2002 the grave of a high-ranking Maya official, a ceramic mask, and a jade necklace were discovered within the pyramid. Continuing excavations have revealed exciting new finds that are still being studied.

West of the pyramid lies the **Cuadrángulo de las Monjas**, considered by some to be the finest part of Uxmal. The name was given to it by the conquistadores, because it reminded them of a convent building in Old Spain (*monjas* means nuns). You may enter the four buildings, each comprising a series of low, gracefully repetitive chambers that look onto a central patio. Elaborate and symbolic decorations—masks, geometric patterns, coiling snakes, and some phallic figures—blanket the upper facades.

Heading south, you'll pass a small ball court before reaching the **Palacio del Gobernador**, which archaeologist Victor von Hagen considered the most magnificent building ever erected in the Americas. Interestingly, the palace faces east, while the rest of Uxmal faces west. Archaeologists believe this is because the palace was built to allow observation of the planet Venus. Covering 5 acres and rising over an immense acropolis, it lies at the heart of what may have been Uxmal's administrative center. ■**TIP**➡ In the summer months, tarantulas are a common sight at the ruins and around the hotels that surround the ruins. *Site, museum, and sound-and-light show $19.50; show only $5; parking $2; use of video camera $4.50 (keep this receipt if visiting other archaeological sites along the Ruta Puuc on the same day); official English-language tour guide $40 Daily 8–5; sound-and-light show 7 pm in winter, 8 pm in summer.*

SHOPPING

In Progreso between Calle 80 and Calle 81, there is also a small downtown area that is a better place to walk than to shop. There you will find banks, supermarkets, and shops with everyday goods for locals as well as several restaurants that serve simple Mexican fare like *tortas* and tacos.

Mérida offers more places to shop, including colorful Mexican markets selling local goods.

Mercado Municipal. The Mercado Municipal has lots of things you won't need, but which are fascinating to look at: songbirds in cane cages, mountains of mysterious fruits and vegetables, ladles made of hollow gourds (the same way they've been made here for a thousand years). There are also lots of crafts for sale, including hammocks, sturdy leather huaraches, and piñatas in every imaginable shape and color. ■**TIP**➡ Guides often approach tourists near this market. They expect a tip and won't necessarily bring you to the best deals. You're better off visiting some specialty stores first to learn about the quality and types of hammocks, hats, and other crafts. Then you'll have an idea of what you're buying—and what it's worth—if you want to bargain in the market. Also be wary of pickpockets within the markets. *Calles 56 and 67, Centro, Mérida.*

WHERE TO EAT

$ ✕**Café La Habana.** A gleaming wood bar and white-jacketed waiters
MEXICAN   contribute to the old European feel at this overwhelmingly popular spot, a branch of a Mexico City café that has been around since the 1950s. Overhead, brass-studded ceiling fans swirl the air-conditioned

air. Sixteen specialty coffees are offered (some spiked with spirits like Kahlúa or cognac), and the menu has light snacks as well as some entrées, including tamales, fajitas, and enchiladas. The waiters are friendly, and there are plenty of them, although service is not always brisk. Both the café and upstairs Internet section are open 24 hours a day; free Wi-Fi is available downstairs for laptop-toting customers, and there is a designated patio for smokers. $ *Average main: $7* ⊠ *Calle 59 No. 511A, at Calle 62, Centro, Mérida* ☎ *999/928–6502.*

PUERTO LIMÓN, COSTA RICA

Jeffrey Van Fleet

Christopher Columbus became Costa Rica's first tourist when he landed on this stretch of coast in 1502 during his fourth and final voyage to the New World. Expecting to find vast mineral wealth, he named the region "Costa Rica" (rich coast). Imagine the Spaniards' surprise eventually to find there was none. Save for a brief skirmish some six decades ago, the country *did* prove itself rich in a long tradition of peace and democracy. No other country in Latin America can make that claim. Costa Rica is also abundantly rich in natural beauty, managing to pack beaches, volcanoes, rain forests, and diverse animal life into an area the size of Vermont and New Hampshire combined. It has successfully parlayed those qualities into its role as one the world's great ecotourism destinations. A day visit is short, but time enough for a quick sample.

ESSENTIALS

CURRENCY   The colón. Most businesses in port gladly accept U.S. dollars.

INTERNET   A bank of Internet computers, operated by International Telecommunication Center, is yours to use at the cruise terminal.

TELEPHONE   Telephone numbers have eight digits. Merely dial the number. There are no area codes. You'll find ample phones for use in the cruise terminal. Public phones accept locally purchased calling cards.

COMING ASHORE

Ships dock at Limón's spacious, spiffy Terminal de Cruceros (cruise terminal), one block south of the city's downtown. You'll find telephones, Internet computers, a craft market, tourist information, and tour operators' desks inside the terminal, as well as a small army of manicurists who do a brisk business. Step outside and walk straight ahead one block to reach Limón's downtown.

A fleet of red taxis waits on the street in front of the terminal. Drivers are happy to help you put together a do-it-yourself tour. Most charge $100 to $150 per carload for a day of touring. There is no place to rent a car here, but you're better off leaving the driving to someone else. Cruise lines offer dozens of shore excursions in Costa Rica, and if you want to go any farther afield than Limón or the coast south, we suggest you take an organized tour. The country looks disarmingly small on a map—it is—but hills give rise to mountains the farther inland you go, and road conditions range from "okay" to "abysmal." Distances are short as the toucan flies, but travel times are longer than you'd expect.

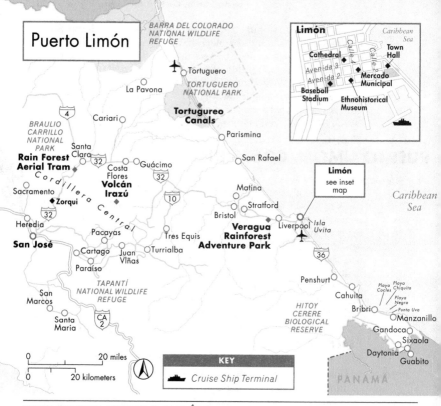

Puerto Limón

BARRA DEL COLORADO
NATIONAL WILDLIFE
REFUGE

✈ Tortuguero

TORTUGUERO
NATIONAL PARK

La Pavona

**Tortugureo
Canals**

Cariari○

Parismina

BRAULIO
CARRILLO
NATIONAL
PARK

Santa
Clara

**Rain Forest
Aerial Tram**

Cordillera

Costa
Flores

Guácimo

San Rafael

**Volcán
Irazú**

Sacramento

◆Zorqui

San Rafael

Matina

Stratford

Bristol

**Veragua
Rainforest
Adventure Park**

Liverpool *Isla
Uvita*

Heredia

Pacayas

San José

Cartago

Juan
Vlñas

Paraíso

Tres Equis

Turrialba

Central

Penshurt

Cahuita

Playa
Cocles

Playa
Chiquita

Playa
Negra

Punta Uva

○Manzanillo

Bribri

TAPANTÍ
NATIONAL WILDLIFE
REFUGE

San
Marcos

Santa
Maria

CA
2

HITOY
CERERE
BIOLOGICAL
RESERVE

Gandoca○

Daytonia

Sixaola

Guabito

Caribbean
Sea

PANAMÁ

Limón
see inset
map

Caribbean
Sea

KEY
⛴ Cruise Ship Terminal

0 ____ 20 miles
0 ____ 20 kilometers

Limón

Caribbean
Sea

Cathedral

Town
Hall

Avenida 3
Avenida 2

Mercado
Municipal

Baseball
Stadium

Ethnohistorical
Museum

EXPLORING PUERTO LIMÓN

LIMÓN

"Sultry and sweltering" describes this port community of 105,000. The country's most ethnically diverse city mixes the Latino flavor of the rest of Costa Rica with Afro-Caribbean and Asian populations, descendants of laborers brought to do construction and farming in the 19th century.

Parque Vargas. The aquamarine wooden port building faces the cruise terminal, and just to the east lies the city's palm-lined central park, Parque Vargas. From the promenade facing the ocean you can see the raised dead coral left stranded by the 1991 earthquake. Nine or so Hoffman's two-toed sloths live in the trees of Parque Vargas; ask a passerby to point them out, as spotting them requires a trained eye.

Rain Forest Aerial Tram. This 2½-square-mile (6-square-km) preserve houses a privately owned and operated engineering marvel: a series of gondolas strung together in a modified ski-lift pulley system. (To lessen the impact on the jungle, the support pylons were lowered into place by helicopter.) The tram gives you a way of seeing the rain-forest canopy and its spectacular array of epiphyte plant life and birds from just above, a feat you could otherwise accomplish only by climbing the trees yourself. If you book online in advance directly with the company, you save

10% off published rates and can get a full refund if your plans change (say your ship can't dock at Limon for some reason). ⊠ *76 miles (120 km) west of Limón, Braulio Carrillo National Park* ☎ *506/2257–5961, 866/759–8726 in North America* ⊕ *www.rainforestadventure.com* ⊠ *$55 tram only; $82.50 tram, lunch, and hike* ⊗ *Daily 7–4.*

SAN JOSÉ

Costa Rica's sprawling, congested capital sits in the middle of the country about three hours inland from the coast. Despite the distance, San José figures as a shore excursion—a long one to be sure—on most ships' itineraries. (The vertical distance is substantial, too; the capital sits on a plateau just under a mile above sea

level. You'll appreciate a jacket here after so many days at sea level.) Although the city dates from the mid-18th century, little from the colonial era remains. The northeastern San José suburb of **Moravia** is chock-full of souvenir stores lining a couple of blocks behind the city's church.

★ **Teatro Nacional.** The National Theater is Costa Rica at its most enchanting. Chagrined that touring prima donna Adelina Patti bypassed San José in 1890 for lack of a suitable venue, wealthy coffee merchants raised import taxes and hired Belgian architects to design this building, lavish with cast iron and Italian marble. The theater was inaugurated in 1897 with a performance of Gounod's *Faust,* featuring an international cast. The sandstone exterior is marked by Italianate arched windows, marble columns with bronze capitals, and statues of strange bedfellows Ludwig van Beethoven (1770–1827) and 17th-century Spanish Golden Age playwright Pedro Calderón de la Barca (1600–81). The Muses of Dance, Music, and Fame are silhouetted in front of an iron cupola. For a nominal admission fee you can move beyond the lobby for a self-guided visit during the day. (The theater is sometimes closed for rehearsals, so call before you go.) If you're downtown on a Tuesday between February and Christmas, take in one of the Teatro al Mediodía (Theater at Midday) performances that begin at noon. It might be a chamber-music recital or a one-act play (in Spanish). Admission is $2. A similar program with similar admission called Música al Atardecer (Music at Dusk) takes place each Thursday at 5 pm. Both take place in the second-floor floyer. ⊠ *Plaza de la Cultura, Barrio La Soledad, San José* ☎ *2221–5341* ⊕ *www.teatronacional.go.cr* ⊠ *$7* ⊗ *Mon.–Sat. 9–4.*

Museo Nacional. In the mango-color Bellavista Fortress, which dates from 1870, the National Museum gives you a quick and insightful lesson in English and Spanish on Costa Rican culture from pre-Columbian times to the present. Cases display pre-Columbian artifacts, period dress, colonial furniture, religious art, and photographs. Some of the country's foremost ethnographers and anthropologists are on the museum's staff. Outside are a veranda and a pleasant, manicured courtyard garden. A former army headquarters, this now-tranquil building saw fierce fighting during a 1931 army mutiny and the 1948 revolution, as the bullet holes pocking its turrets attest. But it was also here that three-time president José "Don Pepe" Figueres abolished the country's military in 1949.

The museum and Costa Rica are abuzz with the repatriation of nearly 1,000 pre-Columbian stone and ceramic artifacts from the Brooklyn Museum. The objects date from about AD 1000 and were taken from the country in the late 19th century by businessman Minor Keith during the construction of the Atlantic Railroad. The museum is arranging display space at this writing. ⊠ *C. 17, Avda. Central–2, Barrio La Soledad, San José* ☎ *2257–1433* ⊕ *www.museocostarica.go.cr* ⊠ *$8* ⊙ *Tues.–Sat. 8:30–4:30, Sun. 9–4:30.*

☾ **Tortuguero National Park.** The name Tortuguero means "turtle region,"
Fodor's Choice and what better place to see sea turtles and observe the age-old cycle of
★ these magnificent animals nesting, hatching, and scurrying to the ocean? ⊠ *Tortuguero* ☎ *2710–2929* ⊠ *$10* ⊙ *Daily 6–6.*

☾ **Veragua Rainforest Adventure Park.** Limon's newest attraction, Veragua Rainforest Adventure Park, is a 4,000-acre nature theme park, about 30 minutes west of the city. It's popular with cruise-ship passengers in port for the day, but if you're in the area, it's well worth a stop. Veragua's great strength is its small army of enthusiastic, superinformed guides who take you through a network of nature trails and exhibits of hummingbirds, snakes, frogs, and butterflies and other insects. A gondola ride overlooks the complex and transports you through the rain-forest canopy. A branch of the Original Canopy Tour, with nine platforms rising 46 meters (150 feet) above the forest floor, is here. The tour is not included in the basic admission to the park but is priced as an add-on. ⊠ *Veragua de Liverpool, 9 miles (15 km) west of Limón* ☎ *2296–5056 in San José* ⊕ *www.veraguarainforest.com* ⊠ *Full-day tour $55; full-day tour with canopy $89; full-day tour with transportation (does not include canopy tour) from San José, $119* ⊙ *Tues.–Sun. 8–4.*

Volcán Irazú. Costa Rica's highest volcano, at 3,422 meters (11,260 feet), is one of the most popular with visitors since you can walk right down into the crater. Its presence is a mixed blessing: The ash fertilizes the Central Valley soil, but the volcano has caused considerable destruction through the centuries. ⚠ **Do not leave anything of value in your car. There have been a lot of thefts in the parking lot here, even though it is supposed to be guarded.** ⊠ *Volcán Irazú National Park* ☎ *2200–5025 for ranger station* ⊠ *$10* ⊙ *Daily 8–3:30.*

SHOPPING

The cruise-ship terminal contains an orderly maze of souvenir stands. Vendors are friendly; there's no pressure to buy. Many shops populate the restored port building across the street as well.

ACTIVITIES

WHITE-WATER RAFTING

You can experience some of the world's premier white-water rafting in Costa Rica.

Ríos Tropicales. Old standby Ríos Tropicales has tours on a Class III to IV section of the Pacuare River between Siquirres and San Martín, as well as the equally difficult section between Tres Equis and Siquirres. Not quite so wild, but still with Class III rapids, is the nearby Florida section of the Reventazón. Day excursions normally begin in San José, but if you're out in this part of the country, you can kick off your excursion here at the company's operations center in Siquirres. ⊠ *On the hwy. in Siquirres, Siquirres* ☎ *2233–6455, 866/722–8273 in North America* ⊕ *www.riostropicales.com.*

ZIP-LINE TOURS

Costa Rica gave birth to the so-called canopy tour, a system of zip lines that transports you from platform to platform in the rain-forest treetops courtesy of a very secure harness. Though billed as a way to get up close with nature, your Tarzan-like yells will probably scare any wildlife away. Think of it more as an outdoor amusement-park ride. The nearest zip-line tour is at **Veragua Rainforest Adventure Park** (*see the listing, above*).

BEACHES

The dark-sand beaches on this sector of the coast are pleasant enough, but won't dazzle you if you've made previous stops at Caribbean islands with their white-sand strands. Nicer beaches than Limón's Playa Bonita lie farther south along the coast and can be reached by taxi or organized shore excursion. Strong undertows make for ideal surfing conditions on these shores, but risky swimming. Exercise caution.

Playa Bonita. Playa Bonita, the name of Limón's own strand, translates as "pretty beach," but it's your typical urban beach, a bit on the cluttered side. ⊠ *1 mile (2 km) north of Limón.*

Playa Blanca. Playa Blanca, one of the coast's few white-sand beaches, lies within the boundaries of Cahuita National Park, right at the southern entrance of the pleasant little town of Cahuita. The park's rain forest extends right to the edge of the beach, and the waters here offer good snorkeling. ⊠ *26 miles (44 km) southeast of Limón, Cahuita.*

Playa Cocles. Playa Cocles, the region's most popular strand of sand, lies just outside Puerto Viejo de Talamanca, one of Costa Rica's archetypal beach towns, with its attendant cafés and bars and all-around good times to be had. ⊠ *38 miles (63 km) southeast of Limón, Puerto Viejo de Talamanca.*

WHERE TO EAT

If you are looking for a bite to eat while off the ship, your best bet is one of the simple "sodas," small restaurants serving local food. There are several in the vicinity of the Mercado Municipal, but Limón isn't a particular pleasant place to stroll around, so if you aren't on a more far-flung tour you may be happier returning to your ship for lunch. Most tours will include lunch.

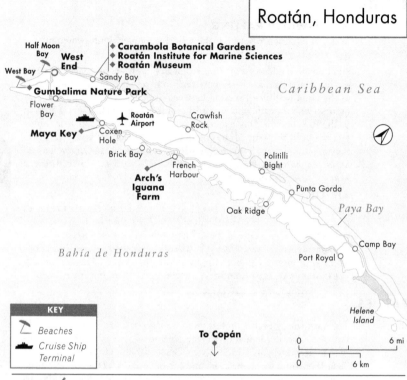

To Copán

0 ──────────── 6 mi

0 ──────────── 6 km

ROATÁN, HONDURAS

Marlise Kast

You'll swear you hear Jimmy Buffett singing as you step off the ship onto Roatán. The flavor is decidedly Margaritaville, but with all there is to do on this island off the north coast of Honduras, you'll never waste away here. Roatán is the largest and most important of the Bay Islands, though at a mere 40 miles (65 km) from tip to tip, and no more than 3 miles (5 km) at its widest; "large" is relative here. As happened elsewhere on Central America's Caribbean coast, the British got here first—the Bay Islands didn't become part of Honduras until the mid-1800s—and left an indelible imprint in the form of place names such as Coxen Hole, French Harbour, and West End, and of course their language, albeit a Caribbean-accented English. The eyes of underwater enthusiasts mist over at the mention of Roatán, one of the world's premier diving destinations, but plenty of topside activity will keep you busy, too.

ESSENTIALS

CURRENCY The Honduran leimpira (L19 to US$1). You'll find an ATM at Banco BAC in the town of Coxen Hole, where cruise ships arrive. There are also ATMs at the HSBC bank just past Warrens Grocery Store in town, at West End at the Dolphin Resort, and in West Bay at the

Mayan Princess Resort. Credit cards are widely accepted, although merchants frequently add a surcharge to offset the high processing fees they are charged by card companies.

INTERNET **Paradise Computers.** Check your email and make international phone calls at Paradise Computers, in their main location inside the new Megaplaza Mall, or at their satellite location on the main drag in West End Village. ⊠ *Megaplaza Mall, French Harbour.*

TELEPHONE Land lines in Honduras have seven digits, while cell phones have eight. There are no area codes, so just dial the number. Public phones are hard to find, but some hotels and businesses will offer phone services to walk-up users for a small fee.

ROATÁN BEST BETS

■ **Diving and Snorkeling.** Roatán is one of the world's great diving destinations. There's snorkeling, too, most of it easily accessible from shore.

■ **Explore Garífuna Culture.** You'd never know it wandering West End, but the island has an original culture that predated the arrival of tourism, and which still dominates Roatán's eastern side.

■ **Hands-on animal adventures.** At the Iguana Farm you can feed and touch hundreds of the famous reptiles; dolphin encounters are available at Anthony's Key Resort.

4

COMING ASHORE

Some ships dock at the Terminal de Cruceros (cruise terminal) in the village of Coxen Hole, the island's administrative center. You'll find telephones, Internet computers, and stands with tour information inside the terminal, as well as a flea market of crafts just outside the gate. Carnival completed a new cruise-ship dock in 2010, and its ships now dock at this new $80-million installation in Mahogany Bay. The new dock is not near any major towns, but it is just a few miles from the new Megaplaza Mall and the town of French Harbour.

Taxis are readily available outside the cruise-ship docks, but be prepared to pay a premium for services there. Trips to the major tourism centers like West End and West Bay beach will cost around $20 per person, round-trip. Negotiate the price before you go, and be sure to clarify if the fare is per person and round-trip. If you would like to save money on your taxi fares, you can walk to the main highway (or into the town of Coxen Hole if you dock near there) and look for taxis marked "Colectivo." These taxis charge a flat rate of L25–L30, depending on the distance. They also pick up as many passengers as they can hold, so plan on riding with other locals or tourists. The local public-transport system consists of blue minivans that leave from Main Street in Coxen Hole to various points on the island until 6 pm. Simply wave if you want a minivan to stop, and expect to pay a flat L22 each time you exit the van.

Look for the cadre of tourist police if you need help with anything. They wear tan shirts and dark-green trousers and are evident on cruise days. You certainly can rent a car here, but the island's compact size makes it unnecessary. Taxis will happily take you anywhere; expect to pay $60 to $120 for a day's private tour, depending on how far you wish to travel.

EXPLORING ROATÁN

Arch's Iguana Farm. West of French Harbour you'll find Arch's Iguana Farm, a strange attraction that has been around for 30 years. Drop in around noon to see the stern-faced lizards have lunch on Arch's driveway. An estimated 3,500 sleepy creatures roam around the reserve, which also has turtles, monkeys, and a fish hatchery. Arch's is open all day, every day. ☒ *French Harbour* ☎ *2445–1498* ✉ *$8* ☉ *Daily 8–5.*

Carambola Botanical Gardens. With one of the country's most extensive orchid collections, the Carambola Botanical Gardens is home to many different varieties of tropical plants. It is also a breeding area for iguanas. There are several trails to follow, and many of the trees and plants are identified by small signs. The longest trail leads up to the top of the hill, where you find an amazing view of the West End of the island and Anthony's Key Resort. Guides can be hired at the visitor center. ☒ *Across from Anthony's Key Resort, Sandy Bay* ☎ *2445–3117* ⊕ *www.carambolagardens.com* ✉ *$10, guided tour $15* ☉ *Daily 8–5.*

Gumbalima Nature Park. This park is part nature reserve, part tacky tourism fun. Macaws, parrots, and monkeys will land on your shoulders as iguanas scuttle around more than 200 tropical tree and plant species. Paved paths lined with boulders lead to sandy beaches and a 91-meter-high (300-ft-high) hanging bridge that crosses a lagoon. The park's Canopy Tour is its main attraction, with 13 ziplines traversing the jungle, and there are also snorkeling, diving, horseback riding, and kayaking. Coxen's Cave is reminiscent of a theme park ride: recreated cave drawings line the walls, and dotting the interior are life-size pirate statues and replicas of maps, weapons, and treasure. Grab a bite at the poolside grill and take a refreshing shower in the outdoor stalls. The park is especially busy on cruise ship days, so head in early to avoid large crowds. Park admission includes the pirate cave, animal preserve, botanical gardens and pool access. All other activities cost extra. ☒ *West Bay* ⊕ *www.gumbalimbapark.com* ✉ *$20* ☉ *Daily 8–5.*

Maya Key. One of the premier day excursions for cruisers visiting Roatán is this small, private island near Coxen Hole. The park offers a wide variety of amenities and activities, including sandy beaches, tropical gardens, a museum with cultural displays, and an animal rescue center, where you can meet the animals. The 10-acre island also offers spectacular snorkeling. Carnival and Norwegian cruise lines offer this option as a shore excursion, or you can book independently on the park's website. This is a great place for families with children. Maya Key is operated by Anthony's Key Resort, which is one of the oldest and most famous resorts in Honduras. It's a 3-minute water shuttle ride from the shuttle pier 50 years east of the Terminal de Cruceros in Coxen Hole. ☒ *Maya Key, Coxen Hole* ☎ *9995–9589* ⊕ *www.mayakeyroatan.com* ✉ *$70 (includes boat shuttle and lunch, advance reservations required)* ☉ *Mon.–Sat. 7 am–4 pm.*

☾ **Roatán Institute for Marine Sciences.** One of the attractions at Anthony's Key Resort, the Roatán Institute for Marine Sciences is an educational center that researches bottlenose dolphins and other marine animals. There is a dolphin show every day at 4, which is free to the public. For an additional fee you can participate in a "dolphin encounter," which allows you to interact with the dolphins either swimming or snorkeling. There are also programs for children ages 5 to 14, including snorkeling experiences, and the "Dolphin Trainer for a Day" program. Cruise-ship passengers must make reservations for dolphin encounters through their ship's shore excursion desk. ⊠ *Anthony's Key Resort, Coxen Hole* ☎ *2445–1327* ⊕ *www.anthonyskey.com* 🖃 *L95* ⊙ *Daily 8:30–5.*

Roatán Museum. Well worth a visit is the tiny Roatán Museum, named one of the best small museums in Central America. The facility, at Anthony's Key Resort, displays archaeological discoveries from Roatán and the rest of the Bay Islands. ⊠ *Anthony's Key Resort, Coxen Hole* ☎ *2445–1327* ⊕ *www.anthonyskey.com* 🖃 *$5* ⊙ *Daily 8:30–5.*

SHOPPING

At the cruise ship dock in Coxen Hole you can find craft vendors, who set up shop outside the cruise-terminal gates; a small number of souvenir shops are scattered around the center of Coxen Hole, a short walk from the docks. Few of the souvenirs for sale here—or anywhere else on the island for that matter—were actually made in Roatán; most come from mainland Honduras. The new cruise-ship dock in Mahogany Bay has a shopping area as well. If you get as far as West End, there are a variety of souvenir and craft sellers in small shops lining the main sand road that runs parallel to the beach.

ACTIVITIES

DIVING AND SNORKELING

Most of the activity on Roatán centers on scuba diving and snorkeling, as well as the newest sensation, snuba, a cross between the two, whereby your mask is connected by a hose to an air source that remains above the water, allowing you to dive for several feet without carrying an air tank on your back. Warm water, great visibility, and thousands of colorful fish make the island a popular destination. Add to this a good chance of seeing a whale shark, and you'll realize why so many people head here each year. Dive sites cluster off the island's western and southern coasts.

One of the most popular destinations—particularly for budget travelers—is West End, offering idyllic beaches stretching as far as the eye can see. One of the loveliest spots is Half Moon Bay, a crescent of brilliant white sand. A huge number of dive shops offer incredibly low-price diving courses.

Competition among the dive shops is fierce in West End, so check out a few. West Bay has great dive sites, but few actual centers. When shopping around, ask about class size (eight is the maximum), the condition of the diving equipment, and the safety equipment on the dive boat.

RECOMMENDED DIVE OPERATORS

Coconut Tree Divers. Just at the entrance to West End, this PADI development center offers a wide range of dives and dive courses. They also have cabins with air-conditioning and fridges, with a discount for divers. ⊠ *West End* ☎ *2445–4081* ⊕ *www.coconuttreedivers.com.*

🌑 **Mayan Divers.** Mayan Divers is run inside the Mayan Princess resort. The five-star PADI dive center has a Bubblemaker program for children 8 and up, plus discovery and open-water courses for all fanatics. The company also offers courses in underwater photography. ⊠ *Mayan Princess Resort, West End* ☎ *2445–5050, 786/299–5929 from the U.S.* ⊕ *www.mayandivers.com.*

Native Sons. Native Sons is one of the most popular dive shops in town. It's run by a native of Roatán who really knows the area. ⊠ *West End* ☎ *2445–4003* ⊕ *www.nativesonsroatan.com.*

Ocean Connections. The popular Ocean Connections is a well-established dive shop. ⊠ *West End* ⊕ *www.ocean-connections.com.*

West End Divers. In business since 1991, this company has a pair of dive boats and is committed to protecting the fragile marine ecology. They offer trips to over 40 dive sites in the area, and have special packages for cruise-ship passengers. ⊠ *West End* ☎ *2445–4289* ⊕ *www.westendivers.com.*

FISHING

Early Bird Fishing Charters. Early Bird Fishing Charters is a great charter fishing company operated by a Roatán native. In addition to deep-sea and flats fishing, you'll have a great opportunity to see the island. Roatán has traditionally had a sea-based economy, and many of the small towns and villages look better from the vantage point of a boat. ⊠ *Sandy Bay* ☎ *2445–3019* ⊕ *www.earlybirdfishingcharters.com.*

BEACHES

You almost can't go wrong with any of Roatán's white-sand beaches. Even those adjacent to populated areas manage to stay clean and uncluttered, thanks to efforts of residents. Water is rougher for swimming on the less-protected north side of the island.

Half Moon Bay. Half Moon Bay, Roatán's most popular beach, is also one of its prettiest. Coconut palms and foliage come up to the crescent shoreline. The beach lies just outside the tourist-friendly West End. Crystal-clear waters offer abundant visibility for snorkeling. ⊠ *Half Moon Bay.*

West Bay Beach. Roatán is famous for the picturesque West Bay Beach. It's a de rigueur listing on every shore-excursions list. Once there, you can lounge on the beach or snorkel. ⊠ *West Bay.*

WHERE TO EAT

$$

SEAFOOD

✕ **Bite on the Beach.** On a beautiful deck overlooking the beach, the restaurant serves up a wide selection of seafood, including conch, crab, and lobster. The menu changes often, but you'll almost always find favorites like Thai shrimp with peanut sauce and yellow coconut curry dishes. The restaurant is easily accessible by water taxi from West End, and the restaurant has Wi-Fi for guests. $⑤$ *Average main: L228* ⌧ *West Bay* ☎ *9663–6317* ⊕ *www.biteonthebeach.net* ⊘ *Closed Sun.*

$$ ✕**Blue Bahia Beach Grill.** Tucked back off the road, just west of Anthony's Key in Sandy Bay, the Blue Bahia Beach Grill is a popular lunch
AMERICAN and dinner destination. Specialties include barbecue from their smoker and delicious seafood. Everything is made from scratch, including the dressings and sauces. The best part is that every table has an ocean view. $⑤$ *Average main: L229* ⌧ *Blue Bahia Resort, KM 9, Sandy Bay* ☎ *2445–3385* ⊕ *www.bluebahiaresort.com* ⊘ *Closed Tues.*

SAMANÁ (CAYO LEVANTADO), DOMINICAN REPUBLIC

Eileen Robin-son Smith

Samaná, the name of both a peninsula in the Dominican Republic as well as the largest town on Samaná Bay, is one of the least-known regions of the country, but the international airport that opened in nearby El Catey in 2006, and the new highway from Santo Domingo that has cut drive-time to two hours, are changing that perception quickly. (Still, only charters fly into El Catey.) Much development is planned, so a visit now will be to a place that is not yet geared to a great deal of mainstream, mass tourism. But with the use of the port by some mega-ships, that, too, is changing rapidly. Samaná is one of the Dominican Republic's newest cruise-ship destinations, with one of the island's greatest varieties of shore excursions. You can explore caves and see an amazing waterfall. And since many humpback whales come here each year to mate and give birth, it's a top whale-watching destination from January through March. While some cruise lines still use Cayo Levantado as a private-island type of experience, for other lines it is just one of several options.

ESSENTIALS

CURRENCY The Dominican peso. Get local currency if you are touring on your own, but most places accept U.S. dollars, though any change will be in pesos. Banks and *cambios* (currency exchange offices) are plentiful.

INTERNET You'll find several convenient Internet cafés in town. The price of going online ranges between RD$40 and RD$80 per hour, inexpensive to be sure. This is still a developing destination, and electrical blackouts are not uncommon. Although most hotels and restaurants have generators, usually these shops do not.

TELEPHONE You can call U.S. or Canadian numbers easily; just dial 1 plus the area code and number.

COMING ASHORE

Cruise ships anchor at a point equidistant between the town of Samaná and Cayo Levantado, an island at the mouth of Samaná Bay with a great beach and facilities to receive 1,500 cruise-ship passengers. Tenders will take you to one of three docks, on the Malecón, referred to

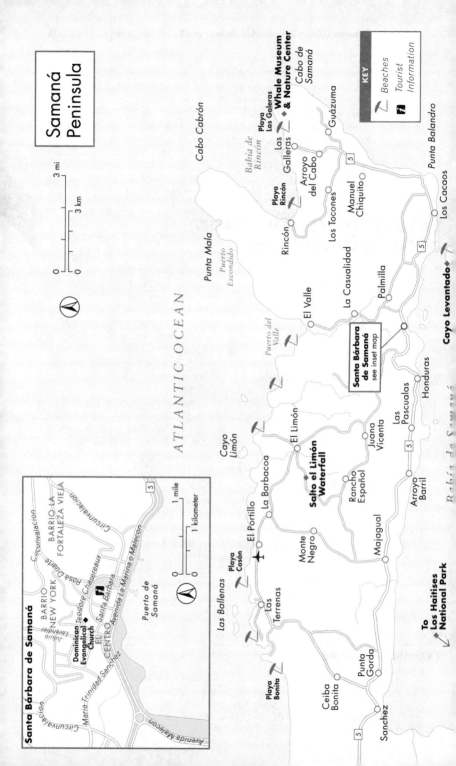

Samaná Peninsula

Santa Bárbara de Samaná

ATLANTIC OCEAN

Cabo Cabrón

Punta Mala

Puerto Escondido

Cayo Limón

Puerto del Valle

Bahía de Rincón

Cabo de Samaná

Whale Museum & Nature Center

Playa Las Galeras

Las Galleras

Arroyo del Cabo

Guázuma

Playa Rincón

Rincón

Los Tocones

Manuel Chiquito

Punta Balandro

El Valle

La Casualidad

Palmilla

Los Cacaos

Las Ballenas

Playa Cosón

El Portillo

La Barbacoa

El Limón

Salto el Limón Waterfall

Santa Bárbara de Samaná see inset map

Las Terrenas

Monte Negro

Majagual

Rancho Español

Juana Vicenta

Las Pascualas

Honduras

Cayo Levantado

To Los Haitises National Park

Punta Gorda

Ceiba Bonita

Playa Bonita

Sanchez

Arroyo Barril

Bahía de Samaná

KEY

Beaches

Tourist Information

Circunvalación

BARRIO LA FORTALEZA VIEJA

BARRIO NEW YORK

Rosa Duarte

Teodoro Chasséreaux

Julia Lavandier

Dominican Evangelical Church

EL CENTRO

Santa Bárbara

Avenida La Marina o Malecón

Matria Trinidad Sanchez

Puerto de Samaná

Avenida Malecón

as the Samaná Bay Piers. The farthest is a five-minute walk from the town center.

Renting a car, although possible, isn't a good option. Driving in the D.R. can be a hectic and even harrowing experience; if you are in port one only day, don't risk it. You'll do better if you combine your resources with friends from the ship and share a taxi to do some independent exploring. Negotiate prices, and settle before getting in the taxi. To give you an idea of what to expect, a minivan that can take eight people will normally charge $90 for the round-trip to Las Terranas, including a two-hour wait while you explore or enjoy the beach. Similarly, you'll pay $80 to travel to Las Galleras or Playa Rincón. Many of the drivers speak some English. Within Samaná, rickshaws are far less costly and are also fun. Called *motoconchos de carretas,* they are not unlike larger versions of the Thai tuk-tuk, but can hold up to six people. The least you will pay is RD$10. They're fine for getting around town, but don't even think about going the distance with them.

> ### SAMANÁ BEST BETS
>
> ■ **Cayo Levantado.** This resort island puts on an excellent show for day-trippers.
>
> ■ **El Limón Waterfall.** A horseback ride into the forest culminates in dazzling falls cascading into a natural pool.
>
> ■ **Los Haitises National Park.** The caves are filled with Taíno drawings; the mangroves are magnificent.
>
> ■ **Playa Rincón.** This rarely accessed beach offers a river, unspoiled mountainside, perfect beach, and privacy.
>
> ■ **Whale-watching.** In season, this is the top activity on the Samaná Peninsula.

EXPLORING SAMANÁ

SANTA BARBARA DE SAMANÁ

The official name of the city is Santa Barbara de Samaná; alas, that saint's name is falling into disuse, and you'll more often hear simply "Samaná" these days. An authentic port town, not just a touristic zone, it has a typical *malecón* (seaside promenade) with gazebos and park benches, ideal for strolling and watching the boats in the harbor. The main avenue that borders this zone is lined with restaurants, shops, and small businesses. A small but bustling town, Samaná is filled with friendly residents, skilled local craftsmen selling their wares, and many outdoor cafés.

Dominican Evangelical Church. Back in 1824, a sailing vessel called the *Turtle Dove,* carrying several hundred slaves that had escaped from Philadelphia, was blown ashore in Samaná. The historic Dominican Evangelical Church is the oldest original building left in Samaná. The structure actually came across the ocean from England in 1881 in a hundred pieces and was reassembled here, serving the spiritual needs of the African-American freedman here. In 1946 a city-wide fire wiped out most of Samaná's wooden buildings and Victorian architecture; this church was miraculously saved. ⊠ *Calle Chaseurox, in front of Catholic church* ☎ *809/538–2579* 🎟 *Donations appreciated* ☉ *Daily dawn–dusk.*

Whale Museum & Nature Center (Centro de Naturaleza). Turn left from the main section of the Malecón, en route to the Hotel Cayacoa, to find the tiny Whale Museum & Nature Center (Centro de Naturaleza), dedicated to the mighty mammals of the sea. Samaná Bay is part of one of the largest marine mammal sanctuaries in the world and is a center for whale-watching during the winter migration of humpback whales. The C.E.B.S.E. (Center for Conservation and Ecodevelopment of Samaná Bay and Its Environment) manages this facility, which features a 40-foot female humpback skeleton. Allow 15 to 45 minutes for a visit, depending on your fascination with the subject and your ability to read Spanish. Information in English is available at the entrance. ✉ *Av. La Marina, Tiro al Blanco* ☎ *809/538–2042* ⊕ *www.Samana. org.do* 💰 *RD$75* ☉ *Mid-Jan.–mid-Mar., daily 8–5; mid-Mar.–mid-Jan., weekdays 8–3.*

ELSEWHERE IN THE SAMANÁ PENINSULA

Cayo Levantado. There are no public beaches in Samaná town, but you can hire a boat to take you to Cayo Levantado, which has a wonderful white-sand beach on an island in Samaná Bay. Today the small island has largely been turned into a commercial enterprise to accommodate the 1,500 cruise-ship passengers who dock here each day; it has dining facilities, bars, restrooms, and lounge chairs on the beautiful beach. The Bahía Príncipe Cayo Levantado, an upscale, all-inclusive resort, claims the eastern two-thirds of the island for its private use and sells one-day passes for $125. Day trips to Los Haitises often stop here for some beach time before returning to Santa Bárbara de Samaná. ✉ *Samaná Bay* 💰 *Public beach free* ☉ *Daily dawn–dusk.*

Fodor's Choice ★ **Los Haitises National Park.** One of the highlights of a trip to the Dominican Republic—and probably the most extraordinary part of a visit to the Samaná Peninsula—is a chance to explore Los Haitises National Park. Los Haitises (pronounced High-*tee*-sis), which is across Samaná Bay from the peninsula, is famous for its karst limestone formations, caves, and grottoes filled with pictographs and petroglyphs left by indigenous Taíno Indians who inhabited this area before Columbus's arrival.

The park is accessible only by boat, and a professionally guided tour is highly recommended—especially so you can kayak along the shoreline (there's no place to rent a kayak without a guide). Another option is to hire a fisherman to take you over on a small boat, but then you'll miss the guidance that an experienced operator can provide.

On a trip you'll sail around dozens of the dramatic rock islands and spectacular cliff faces. Swirling around are hundreds of beautiful coastal birds that represent 121 different species, including Magnificent Frigatebirds, brown pelicans, brown booby, and varieties of egrets and herons. The sight of dozens of different birds continually gliding past the boat at any time is enough to make a bird-watcher out of anyone.

A good tour will let you visit the many caverns. Your flashlight will illuminate Taíno and pre-Taíno petroglyphs. You'll also find out how the forest slowly consumes the caves. But the best experience is being able to kayak here. Unlike mangrove kayaking trips in, say, the Florida Everglades, the mangroves here are dramatically flanked by the karst formations. It's a continual sensory delight. The islands rise dramatically and have wild growths of plant life and birds swooping around. You'll feel tiny, like a human speck surrounded by geological grandeur. ⊠ *Samaná Bay* 🎫 *Admission included with guided tour (recommended)* 🕙 *Daily dawn–dusk.*

★ **Salto el Limón Waterfall.** Provided that you're fit and willing to deal with a long and slippery path on horseback, an adventurous guided trip to the spectacular Salto el Limón Waterfall is a delight. The journey is done mostly on horseback, but includes some walking down rocky, sometimes muddy trails. You'll have to cross two rivers en route. Horse paths are slippery, and the trek is strenuous. The well-mannered horses take you across rivers and up mountains to El Limón, where you can find the 165-foot waterfall amid luxuriant vegetation. Some snacks and drinks are usually included in the guided trip, but a grilled chicken lunch is only a few more pesos. The outpost for the trek, a local guide service called Santi Rancho, is relatively difficult to find; it's best to ask your hotel for detailed directions or arrange a tour from an operator like Flora Tours in Las Terrenas. The trip to the waterfall by horseback takes 40 minutes each way; the entire excursion lasts about three hours. ⊠ *Santi Rancho, El Limón.*

SHOPPING

Rum, coffee, and cigars are popular local products. You may also find good coconut handicrafts, including coconut-shell candles. Whale-oriented gift items are particularly popular. Most of the souvenir shops are on Samaná's malecón or in the market plaza; you will find more on the major downtown streets in town, all within easy walking distance of the tender piers.

ACTIVITIES

DIVING AND SNORKELING

In 1979 three atolls disappeared after a seaquake off Las Terrenas, providing an opportunity for truly memorable dives. Also just offshore from Las Terrenas are the Islas Las Ballenas (The Whale Islands), a cluster of four little islands with good snorkeling. A coral reef is off Playa Jackson, a beach accessible only by boat.

Las Terrenas Divers. Las Terrenas Divers rents surf and Boogie boards and gives surfing lessons. ⊠ *Playa Bonita, Las Terrenas* ☎ *809/889–2422.*

WHALE-WATCHING

Humpback whales come to Samaná Bay to mate and give birth each year, from approximately January 15 through March 30. Samaná Bay is considered one of the top destinations in the world for watching whales. If you're here in season, this can be the experience of a lifetime.

Whale Samaná. Whale Samaná is owned by Kim Beddall, a Canadian who is incredibly knowledgeable about whales and Samaná at large, having lived here for decades. Her operation is far and away the region's best, most professional, and environmentally sensitive. On board a 55-foot motor vessel, a marine mammal specialist narrates and answers questions in several languages. Kim herself conducts almost all the English-speaking trips. The $50 price does not include the RD$100 Marine Mammal Sanctuary entrance fee (price is subject to change). Kim also welcomes cruise passengers, but requires advance reservations. Normal departure times are 9 am for the morning trip and 1:30 pm for the afternoon trip, but she is flexible whenever possible for cruisers. Kim also conducts trips to Los Haitises National Park on Tuesday, Thursday, and Saturday on the *Mistral,* a 45-foot catamaran. These tours, which cost $55 per person, include a terrific lunch and the $3 park entrance fee and last four to five hours. The boat has a dozen kayaks in which teams of two can explore the shoreline. ⊠ *Across street from town dock, beside park, Calle Sra. Morellia Kelly* ☎ *809/538–2042* ✍ *kim. beddall@whalesamana.com* ⊕ *www.whaleSamana.com.*

BEACHES

There are no recommendable beaches in Samaná de Santa Barbara itself. You will have to travel to one of the beautiful ones elsewhere on the peninsula, another reason why the Cayo Levantado excursion is very popular on most ships.

Playa Bonita. On Playa Bonita you can bounce between the golden beach (BYO towel—no chaises) and one of the hotels and restaurants directly across the rough road, where you can have lunch. The beach can disappear during flooding and high tides. It's a quiet stretch of gold sand with leaning coconut trees. ⊠ *Las Terrenas.*

Fodor's Choice ★ **Playa Cosón.** This is a long, wonderful stretch of white sand and the best beach close to the town of Las Terrenas. Previously undeveloped, it's now reachable by a new highway, Carretera Cosón, and there are a dozen condo developments under construction (so the current sense of solitude probably won't last). One excellent restaurant, The Beach, serves the entire 15-mile shore, and there's a new boutique hotel, Casa Cosón. ⊠ *Las Terrenas.*

Playa Las Galeras. Playa Las Galeras is within this tiny coastal town, a 30-minute drive northeast from Samaná town. It's a lovely, long, and uncluttered beach (except for the wild dogs, some local litter, and the boat hawkers and shell vendors around El Kiosko). The sand is nearly white, the Atlantic waters generally calm. It has been designated a "Blue Flag" beach, which means that it's crystal-clean with no pollution, though there are several small hotels here. This is a good snorkeling spot, too. That said, this is really just a departure point for the nearby virgin beaches closer to the cape to the west. Hire a boat and get to them! ⊠ *Las Galeras.*

WHERE TO EAT

$ ✗ **La Mata Rosada.** The French chef/owner of La Mata, Yvonne Bastian, has been luring local expats and foodies since the late 1990s. She sets tables with white linens in an all-white interior that includes an array of ceiling fans to keep you cool; breezes sneak in from the bay across the street. There are plenty of excellent choices, like mahimahi

SEAFOOD

★

in coconut sauce with a mango chutney or a mix of grilled lobster and other shellfish; the red snapper comes to the table wrapped in a banana leaf. Begin with the ceviche, a specialty of this port town, made with *dorado* (mahimahi) and conch. Whether you go local or international, order the creole shrimp or a substantial salad, and you should leave satisfied. The desserts, like the chocolate terrine, are also presented with pride. ⑤ *Average main: $11* ⊠ *Av. Malecón 5B* ☎ *809/538–2388* ⓧ *Closed Wed. June–Nov.*

SAN JUAN, PUERTO RICO

Heather
Rodino

4

Although Puerto Rico is a commonwealth of the United States, few cities in the Caribbean are as steeped in Spanish tradition as San Juan. Within a seven-square-block area in Old San Juan are restored 16th-century buildings, museums, art galleries, bookstores, and 200-year-old houses with balustraded balconies overlooking narrow, cobblestone streets. In contrast, San Juan's sophisticated Condado and Isla Verde areas have glittering hotels, fancy boutiques, casinos, and discos. Out in the countryside is 28,000-acre El Yunque National Forest, a rain forest with more than 240 species of trees growing at least 100 feet high. You can stretch your sea legs on dramatic mountain ranges, numerous trails, in vast caves, at coffee plantations, old sugar mills, and hundreds of beaches. No wonder San Juan is one of the busiest ports of call in the Caribbean. Like any other big city, San Juan has its share of petty crime, so guard your wallet or purse, especially in crowded markets and squares.

ESSENTIALS

CURRENCY The U.S. dollar is the official currency of Puerto Rico.

INTERNET Wi-Fi is available in many chain restaurants, including Burger King and Starbucks, as well as some local cafés.

TELEPHONE Calling the United States from Puerto Rico is the same as calling within the United States, and all U.S. cell phone plans work here just as they do at home. You can use the long-distance telephone service office in the cruise-ship terminal, or you can use your calling card by dialing the toll-free access number of your long-distance provider from any pay phone. You'll find a phone center by the Paseo de la Princesa.

COMING ASHORE

Most cruise ships dock within a couple of blocks of Old San Juan; however, there is a second cruise pier across the bay, and if your ship docks there you'll need to take a taxi to get anywhere on the island. The Paseo de la Princesa, a tree-lined promenade beneath the city wall, is a nice place for a stroll—you can admire the local crafts and stop at the refreshment kiosks. Major sights in the Old San Juan area are mere blocks from the piers, but be aware that the streets are narrow and steeply inclined in places.

It's particularly easy to get to Cataño and the Bacardí Rum Plant on your own; take the ferry (50¢) that leaves from the cruise piers every

Old San Juan

0   1/4 mile

0   400 meters

ATLANTIC OCEAN

Castillo San Felipe del Morro (El Morro)

El Campo Del Morro

Calle del Morro

Galería Nacional

Bajada Matadero

San Miguel

City Wall

San Juan Blvd

Norzagaray

Museo de las Américas

City Wall

San Sebastián

Cristo

Las Monjas

El Convento

Catedral de San Juan Bautista

La Fortaleza

Bahía de San Juan

San José

Calle San Justo

La Fonda del Jíbarito

Sol

Luna

Recinto Sur

O'Donnell

Castillo San Cristóbal

Alcaldia

San Francisco

Fortaleza

Tetuán

Plaza de Armas

Cruz

Comercio

Paseo de Covadonga

Sheraton

Old San Juan

Concepción de Gracia

Paseo Gilberto

Paseo de La Princesa

La Casita (Tourist Information Center)

Pier 1

Pier 2

Pier 3

Pier 4

Cruise Ship Piers

Museo de Arte de Puerto Rico

Presidio

Puntilla

Casa Bacardí Visitor Center

KEY

⚓ *Cruise Ship Terminal*

⛴ *Ferry*

🛈 *Tourist Information*

half hour and then a taxi from the other side. Taxis, which line up to meet ships, are the best option if you want to explore beyond Old San Juan. White taxis labeled "Taxi Turistico" charge set fares of $10 to $20. Less common are metered cabs authorized by the Public Service Commission that charge an initial $1; after that, it's about 10¢ for each additional 1/13 mi. If you take a metered taxi, insist that the meter be turned on, and pay only what is shown, plus a tip of 15% to 20%. You can negotiate with taxi drivers for specific trips, and you can hire a taxi for as little as $36 per hour for sightseeing tours. If you want to see more of the island but don't want to drive, you may want to consider a shore excursion, though almost all trips can be booked more cheaply with local tour operators.

EXPLORING SAN JUAN

Old San Juan, the original city founded in 1521, contains carefully preserved examples of 16th- and 17th-century Spanish-colonial architecture. More than 400 buildings have been beautifully restored. Graceful wrought-iron balconies with lush hanging plants extend over narrow streets paved with *adoquines* (blue-gray stones originally used as ballast on Spanish ships). The Old City is partially enclosed by walls that date from 1633 and once completely surrounded it. Designated a U.S.

National Historic Zone in 1950, Old San Juan is chockablock with shops, open-air cafés, homes, tree-shaded squares, monuments, and people. You can get an overview on a morning's stroll (bear in mind that this "stroll" includes some steep climbs). However, if you plan to immerse yourself in history or to shop, you'll need a couple of days.

OLD SAN JUAN

Alcaldía. San Juan's city hall was built between 1602 and 1789. In 1841, extensive alterations were made so that it would resemble the city hall in Madrid, with arcades, towers, balconies, and an inner courtyard. Renovations have refreshed the facade of the building and some interior rooms, but the architecture remains true to its colonial style. Only the patios are open to public viewings. A municipal tourist information center and an art gallery with rotating exhibits are in the lobby. ⌧ *153 Calle San Francisco, Plaza de Armas, Old San Juan* ☎ *787/480–2548* ⌧ *Free* ☾ *Weekdays 8–4.*

SAN JUAN BEST BETS

■ **El Morro.** Explore the giant labyrinthine fort.

■ **El Yunque National Forest.** This rain forest east of San Juan is a great half-day excursion.

■ **Casa Bacardí.** Rum lovers can jump on the public ferry and then taxi over to the factory.

■ **Old San Juan.** Walk the cobblestone streets of Old San Juan.

■ **Shopping.** Within a few blocks of the port there are plenty of factory outlets and boutiques.

☾ **Castillo San Cristóbal.** This huge stone fortress, built between 1634 and
Fodor's Choice 1790, guarded the city from land attacks from the east. The largest
★ Spanish fortification in the New World, San Cristóbal was known in the 17th and 18th centuries as the Gibraltar of the West Indies. Five freestanding structures divided by dry moats are connected by tunnels. You're free to explore the gun turrets (with cannon in situ), officers' quarters, re-created 18th-century barracks, and gloomy passageways. Along with El Morro, San Cristóbal is a National Historic Site administered by the U.S. Park Service; it's a World Heritage Site as well. Rangers conduct tours in Spanish and English. ⌧ *Calle Norzagaray at Av. Muñoz Rivera, Old San Juan* ☎ *787/729–6777* ⊕ *www.nps.gov/saju* ⌧ *$3; $5 includes admission to El Morro* ☾ *Daily 9–6.*

☾ **Castillo San Felipe del Morro** (*El Morro*). At the northwestern tip of the
Fodor's Choice Old City is El Morro ("the promontory"), a fortress built by the Span-
★ iards between 1539 and 1786. Rising 140 feet above the sea, the massive six-level fortress was built to protect the harbor entrance. It is a labyrinth of cannon batteries, ramps, barracks, turrets, towers, and tunnels. Built to protect the port, El Morro has a commanding view of the harbor. You're free to wander throughout. The cannon emplacement walls and the dank secret passageways are a wonder of engineering. The fort's small but enlightening museum displays ancient Spanish guns and other armaments, military uniforms, and blueprints for Spanish forts in the Americas, although Castillo San Cristóbal has more extensive and impressive exhibits. There's also a gift shop. The fort is a National Historic Site administered by the U.S. Park Service; it's a World Heritage Site as well. Various tours and a video are available in English. ⌧ *Calle*

del Morro, Old San Juan ☎ *787/729–6960* ⊕ *www.nps.gov/saju* 🖃 *$3; $5 includes admission to Castillo San Cristóbal* ⊙ *Daily 9–6.*

Catedral de San Juan Bautista. The Catholic shrine of Puerto Rico had humble beginnings in the early 1520s as a thatch-roofed, wooden structure. After a hurricane destroyed the church, it was rebuilt in 1540, when it was given a graceful circular staircase and vaulted Gothic ceilings. Most of the work on the present cathedral, however, was done in the 19th century. The remains of Ponce de León are behind a marble tomb in the wall near the transept, on the north side. The trompe l'oeil work on the inside of the dome is breathtaking. Unfortunately, many of the other frescoes suffer from water damage. ⊠ *151 Calle Cristo, Old San Juan* ☎ *787/722–0861* ⊕ *www.catedralsanjuan.com* 🖃 *$1 donation suggested* ⊙ *Mon.–Sat. 8–5, Sun. 8–2:30.*

Galería Nacional. Built by Dominican friars in 1523, this convent—the oldest in Puerto Rico—once served as a shelter during Carib Indian attacks and, more recently, as headquarters for the Antilles command of the U.S. Army. The beautifully restored building contains the Galería Nacional, which showcases the collection of the Institute of Puerto Rican Culture. Arranged chronologically, the museum traces the development of Puerto Rican art over the centuries, from José Campeche and Francisco Oller to Rafael Tufiño and Myrna Báez. You'll also find a good collection of *santos*, traditional wood carvings of saints. ⊠ *98 Calle Norzagaray, Old San Juan* ☎ *787/725–2670* ⊕ *www.icp.gobierno. pr* 🖃 *$3* ⊙ *Mon.–Sat. 9:30–5.*

La Fortaleza. Sitting atop the fortified city walls overlooking the harbor, the Fortaleza was built between 1533 and 1540 as a fortress, but it wasn't a very good one. It was attacked numerous times and was occupied twice, by the British in 1598 and the Dutch in 1625. When El Morro and the city's other fortifications were finished, the Fortaleza became the governor's palace. Numerous changes have been made to the original primitive structure over the past four centuries, resulting in the current eclectic yet eye-pleasing collection of marble and mahogany, medieval towers, and stained-glass galleries. It is still the official residence of the island's governor, and is the Western Hemisphere's oldest executive mansion in continual use. Guided tours are conducted several times a day in English and Spanish; both include a short video presentation. Call ahead to verify the day's schedule, as tours are often canceled because of official functions. Proper attire is required: no sleeveless shirts or very short shorts. The tours begin near the main gate in a yellow building called the Real Audiencia, housing the Oficina Estatal de Preservación Histórica. ⊠ *Western end of Calle Fortaleza, Old San Juan* ☎ *787/721–7000* ⊕ *www.fortaleza.gobierno.pr* 🖃 *$3 suggested donanation* ⊙ *Weekdays 9–3:45.*

Museo de las Américas. On the second floor of the imposing former military barracks, Cuartel de Ballajá, this museum houses four permanent exhibits covering the native people of the Americas, African heritage in Puerto Rico, conquest and colonization, and popular arts in the Americas. You'll also find a number of temporary exhibitions. ⊠ *Calle Norza-*

garay and Calle del Morro, Old San Juan ☎ *787/724–5052* ⊕ *www. museolasamericas.org* ▣ *$3* ⊙ *Tues.–Sat. 9–noon, 1–4; Sun. 11–4.*

ELSEWHERE IN SAN JUAN

Casa Bacardí Visitor Center. Exiled from Cuba, the Bacardí family built a small rum distillery here in the 1950s. Today it's the world's largest, with the capacity to produce 100,000 gallons of spirits a day and 21 million cases a year. You can hop on a little tram to take an approximately 45-minute tour of the visitor center, though you don't visit the distillery itself. Yes, you'll be offered a sample. If you don't want to drive, you can reach the factory by taking the ferry from Pier 2 for 50¢ each way and then a *público* (public van service) from the ferry pier to the factory for about $2 or $3 per person. ⊠ *Road 165, Rte. 888, Km 2.6, Cataño* ☎ *787/788–1500* ⊕ *www.casabacardi.org* ▣ *Free* ⊙ *Mon.–Sat. 9–6, last tour at 4:30; Sun. 10–5, last tour at 3:45.*

Fodor's Choice ★ **Museo de Arte de Puerto Rico.** At 130,000 square feet one of the biggest museums in the Caribbean, this beautiful neoclassical building was once the San Juan Municipal Hospital. The collection of Puerto Rican art starts with works from the colonial era, most of them commissioned for churches. Here you'll find works by José Campeche, the island's first great painter. His *Immaculate Conception,* finished in 1794, is a masterpiece. Also well represented is Francisco Oller y Cestero, who was the first to move beyond religious subjects to paint local scenes. His influence is still felt today: another gallery room is filled with works by artists inspired by Oller. The original building, built in the 1920s, proved to be too small to house the museum's collection of Puerto Rican art by itself: the newer east wing here is dominated by a five-story-tall stained-glass window, the work of local artist Eric Tabales.

There's much more to the museum, including a beautiful garden filled with a variety of native flora and a 400-seat theater that's worth seeing for its remarkable hand-crocheted lace curtain. ⊠ *299 Av. José de Diego, Santurce* ☎ *787/977–6277* ⊕ *www.mapr.org* ▣ *$6; free admission Wed. 2–8* ⊙ *Tues.–Sat. 10–5, Sun. 11–6.*

SHOPPING

San Juan is not a duty-free port, so you won't find bargains on electronics and perfumes. However, shopping for native crafts can be fun. Popular souvenirs and gifts include *santos* (small, hand-carved figures of saints or religious scenes), hand-rolled cigars, local coffee, handmade lace, and carnival masks.

In Old San Juan, especially on Calles Fortaleza and Cristo, you can find everything from T-shirt emporiums to selective crafts stores, bookshops, art galleries, jewelry boutiques, and even shops that specialize in made-to-order Panama hats. Calle Cristo is lined with factory-outlet stores, including Coach and Ralph Lauren.

ACTIVITIES

GOLF

★ **Río Mar Country Club.** The Río Mar Country Club has a clubhouse with a pro shop and two restaurants between two 18-hole courses, to grab a sit-down lunch or a quick beverage and a bite. The River Course, designed by Greg Norman, has challenging fairways that skirt the Mameyes River. The Ocean Course, designed by Tom and George Fazio, has slightly wider fairways than its sister; iguanas can usually be spotted sunning themselves near its 4th hole. ■TIP→ **If you're not a resort guest, be sure to reserve tee times at least 24 hours in advance.** ⊠ *Rio Mar Beach Resort & Spa, a Wyndham Grand Resort, 6000 Río Mar Blvd., Río Grande* ☎ *787/888–7060* ⊕ *www.wyndhamriomar.com* ⅄. *Green fees for hotel guests range from $50 (for 9 holes) to $165 (for 18 holes). Fees for walk-ins range from $60–$180.*

BEACHES

San Juan does not have the island's best beaches, but anyone can rent a chair for the day at one of the public entry points.

☾ **Balneario de Carolina.** When people talk of a "beautiful Isla Verde beach," this is the one they're talking about. A government-maintained beach, this balneario east of Isla Verde is so close to the airport that the leaves rustle when planes take off. The long stretch of sand, which runs parallel to Avenida Los Gobernadores, is shaded by palms and almond trees. Thanks to an offshore reef, the surf is not as strong as other nearby beaches, so it's especially good for children and families. There's plenty of room to spread out and lots of amenities: lifeguards, restrooms, changing facilities, picnic tables, and barbecue grills. Although there's a charge for parking, there's not always anyone there to take the money. **Best for:** swimming. ⊠ *Carolina* ⧈ *Parking $3* ☺ *Daily 8–5.*

☾ **Playa del Condado.** East of Old San Juan and west of Ocean Park, this long, wide beach is overshadowed by an unbroken string of hotels and apartment buildings. Beach bars, water-sports outfitters, and chair-rental places abound. You can access the beach from several roads off Avenida Ashford, including Calles Cervantes, Condado, and Candina. The protected water at the small stretch of beach west of the Conrad San Juan Condado Plaza hotel is particularly calm and popular with families; surf elsewhere in Condado can be a bit strong. The stretch of sand near Calle Vendig (behind the Atlantic Beach Hotel) is especially popular with the gay community. If you're driving, on-street parking is your only option. **Best for:** partiers. ⊠ *Condado* ☺ *Daily dawn–dusk.*

NIGHTLIFE

Almost every ship stays in San Juan late or even overnight to give passengers an opportunity to revel in the nightlife - the most sophisticated in the Caribbean.

CASINOS

By law, all casinos are in hotels. The atmosphere is refined, and many patrons dress to the nines, but informal attire (no shorts or tank tops) is usually fine. Casinos set their own hours, which change seasonally, but generally operate from noon to 4 am, although the casino in the Conrad Condado Plaza Hotel and Casino is open 24 hours. Other hotels with casinos include the InterContinental San Juan Resort and Casino, the Ritz-Carlton San Juan Hotel, Spa and Casino, and the Sheraton Old San Juan Hotel and Casino.

BARS AND DANCE CLUBS

El Batey. This legendary hole-in-the-wall bar won't win any prizes for decor, but even still, it has an irresistibly artsy and welcoming vibe. Add your own message to the graffiti-covered walls (they have a B.Y.O.S, or Bring Your Own Sharpie policy), or put your business card alongside the hundreds that cover the lighting fixtures. The ceiling may leak, but the jukebox has the best selection of oldies in town. Join locals in a game of pool. ⊠ *101 Calle Cristo, Old San Juan* ☎ *No phone.*

Krash. A balcony bar overlooks all the drama on the dance floor at this popular club. Most of the time DJs spin house, hip-hop, salsa, and *reggaetón*, but occasionally disco nights send you back to the music of the 1970s and '80s. It's open Wednesday through Saturday. ⊠ *1257 Av. Ponce de León, Santurce* ☎ *787/722–1131* ⊕ *www.krashklubpr.com.*

WHERE TO EAT

$$$

SPANISH

✕ **El Picoteo.** You could make a meal of the small dishes that dominate the menu at this tapas restaurant on a mezzanine balcony at the Hotel El Convento. You won't go wrong ordering the grilled cuttlefish or the pistachio-crusted salmon with a Manchego-cheese sauce and passing them around the table. If you're not into sharing, there are several kinds of paella that arrive on huge plates. There's a long, lively bar inside; one dining area overlooks a pleasant courtyard, and the other looks out onto Calle Cristo. Even if you have dinner plans elsewhere, consider stopping here for a nightcap or a midday pick-me-up. $ *Average main: $30* ⊠ *Hotel El Convento, 100 Calle Cristo, Old San Juan* ☎ *787/723–9202* ⊕ *www.elconvento.com.*

$$

PUERTO RICAN

Fodor's Choice

★

✕ **La Fonda del Jibarito.** The menus are handwritten and the tables wobble, but *sanjuaneros* have favored this casual, no-frills, family-run restaurant—tucked away on a quiet cobbled street—for years. The conch ceviche, goat fricassee, and shredded beef stew are among the specialties on the menu of typical Puerto Rican *comida criolla* dishes. The tiny back porch is filled with plants, and the dining room is filled with fanciful depictions of life on the street outside. Troubadors serenade patrons, including plenty of cruise-ship passengers when ships are in dock. $ *Average main: $15* ⊠ *280 Calle Sol, Old San Juan* ☎ *787/725–8375* ⊕ *www.eljibaritopr.com.*

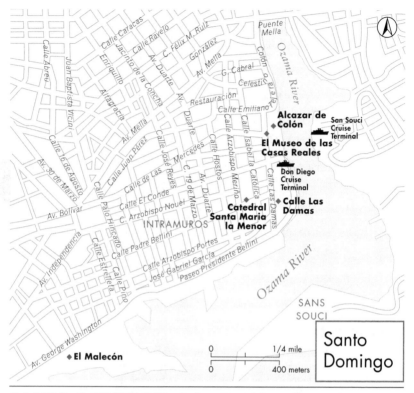

Santo
Domingo

SANTO DOMINGO, DOMINICAN REPUBLIC

Eileen Robin-
son Smith

Spanish civilization in the New World began in Santo Domingo's
12-block Zona Colonial (Colonial Zone). As you stroll its narrow
streets, it's easy to imagine this old city as it was when the likes of
Columbus, Cortés, and Ponce de León walked the cobblestones, when
pirates sailed in and out of the harbor, and when colonists first started
building the New World's largest city. Tourist brochures tout that "history comes alive here"—a surprisingly truthful statement. However,
many tourists bypass the large, sprawling, and noisy city; it's their loss.
The Dominican Republic's seaside capital—despite such detractions as
poverty and sprawl, not to mention a population of some 2 million
people—has some of the country's best hotels, restaurants, and nightlife
(not to mention great casinos). Many of these are right on or near the
Malecón and within the historic Zona Colonial area, which is separated
from the rest of the city by Parque Independencia. If your ship calls or
even embarks here, you'll be treated to a vibrant Latin cultural center
unlike any other in the Caribbean.

ESSENTIALS

CURRENCY The Dominican peso. Independent merchants willingly accept U.S. dollars, but you may need to change some money. Cambios (money exchange offices) are abundant, but you'll get the best rates at either a bank or a casino. Banco Popular has ATMS in the Zona Colonial, but you will be able to get only pesos.

INTERNET Look up, and you will see many Internet shops on the Conde, usually with second-floor locations.

TELEPHONE From the D.R. you need only dial 1 plus the area code and number to call the United States. To make a local call, you must now dial 809 plus the seven-digit number. Phone cards, which are sold at gift shops and grocery stores, can give you considerable savings on your calls home. If you have a tri-band GSM phone, it should work on the island.

COMING ASHORE

Santo Domingo has two stellar cruise-ship terminals, and has become a growing port for cruise passengers. Despite the sluggish economy, the final tally of cruise-ship passengers for 2010 throughout the country was close to 600,000.

The **Port of Don Diego** is on the Ozuma River, facing the Avenida del Puerto, and across the street are steps that lead up to the main pedestrian shopping street of the Zona Colonial, Calle El Conde. A lovely yellow-and-white building, with stained-glass windows and faux gaslights, it has a small cafeteria, and potted palms soften the cordoned-off lines where passengers wait to have their tickets checked and go through immigration. The reception area has telephones, Internet access, and a currency exchange. Just down the dock is an ATM; in front of that is a counter where you can get cold drinks and snacks.

The **Sans Souci Terminal** complex, diagonally across the Ozama River from Don Diego Terminal, on Avenida España, has been operational since early 2010, but this long-term redevelopment project is still a work in progress. Its mezzanine level accommodates immigration and customs, duty-free shops, and both Internet and information centers. Like the Port of Don Diego, it has stunning lighting systems that cover the exterior and perimeter areas for greater security and visibility for visitors. When completed, the complex will have finished its marina, and have a full complement of stores, a 122-acre real-estate development, a new sports arena, and more. This major project is aimed at integrating the port area and the Zona Colonial to create an appealing destination for cruisers, yachtsmen, and high-end tourists.

AIRPORT TRANSFERS

If you are embarking in Santo Domingo, you should fly into Las Américas International Airport (SDQ), about 15 miles (24 km) east of downtown. Upon arrival you will have to pay $10 for a tourist tax. Transportation into the city is usually by taxi; figure on $40 to or from hotels on the Malecón or in the Zona Colonial. You'll be greeted by a melee of hawking taxi drivers and sometimes their English-speaking solicitors (who expect to be tipped, as do the freelance porters who will undoubtedly scoop up your luggage). If you are spending a night or two in Santo Domingo before a cruise, you can probably arrange a driver through your hotel, so you'll be met with someone holding a sign with your name (it's worth the extra $10 or so to avoid the hassle). If you're going straight to your cruise ship, consider taking the cruise line's prearranged transfer. When you disembark from your ship, expect long lines at check-in, and be sure to give yourself a full two hours for check-in and security. The government departure tax should be included in your airline ticket.

EXPLORING SANTO DOMINGO

History buffs will want to spend a day exploring the many "firsts" of our continent. A horse-and-carriage ride throughout the Colonial Zone costs $25 an hour. The steeds are no thoroughbreds, but they clip right along, though any commentary will be in Spanish. You can also negotiate to use them as a taxi, say, down to the Malecón. The drivers hang out in front of the Hostal Nicolas de Ovando hotel.

Alcazar de Colón. The castle of Don Diego Colón, built in 1517, has 40-inch-thick coral-limestone walls. The Renaissance-style structure, with its balustrade and double row of arches, has strong Moorish, Gothic, and Isabelline influences. The 22 rooms are furnished in a style to which the viceroy of the island would have been accustomed—right down to the dishes and the viceregal shaving mug. Costumed "docents" appear on Saturday morning. ⊠ *Plaza de España, off Calle Emiliano Tejera, Zona Colonial* ☎ *809/682–4750* ⬗ *RD$100* ☉ *Mon.–Sat. 9–5, Sun. 9–4. Closed if no cruise ship in port.*

★ **Calle Las Damas.** "Ladies Street" was named after the elegant ladies of the court: in the Spanish tradition, they promenaded in the evening. Here you can see a sundial dating from 1753 and the Casa de los Jesuitas, which houses a fine research library for colonial history as well as the **Institute for Hispanic Culture**; admission is free, and it's open weekdays from 8 to 4:30. If you follow the street going toward the Malecón, you will pass a picturesque alley, fronted by a wrought-iron gate, where there are perfectly maintained colonial structures owned by the Catholic Church. ⊠ *Santo Domingo.*

★ **El Museo de las Casas Reales.** This is a remarkable museum that will help you comprehend the discovery of the New World by Christopher Columbus and the entire 16th-century epic. Housing Taíno finds, colonial artifacts, coins salvaged from wrecks of Spanish galleons, authentic colonial furnishings, as well as a collection of weapons, the museum also has one of the handsomest colonial edifices in the Zone. Built in the Renaissance style, it was the seat of Spanish government, housing the governor's office and the Royal Court. It has beautiful windows, for example, done in the Plateresque style. A frequent wedding venue, it also functions as an art gallery, with rotating shows. When candlelit at night, it's truly magical. ⊠ *Calle Las Damas, Zona Colonial* ☎ *809/688–8298* ⬗ *RD$75* ☉ *Tues.–Sun. 9–5.*

BEACHES

If you are just in port for a day, you'll have a better time if you skip the beach and spend some time in the Zona Colonial and on the Malecón.

Playa Boca Chica. You can walk far out into warm, calm, clear waters protected by coral reefs here. The strip with the rest of the midrise resorts is busy, particularly on weekends, drawing mainly Dominican families and some Europeans. But midweek is better, when the beaches are less crowded. One bad thing: if you choose to go to the public beach, you will be pestered and hounded by a parade of roving sellers of cheap jewelry and sunglasses, hair braiders, seafood cookers, ice-cream men, and masseuses (who are usually peddling more than a simple beach massage).

Young male prostitutes also roam the beach and often hook up with older European and Cuban men. The best section of the public beach is in front of Don Emilio's (the blue hotel), which has a restaurant, bar, decent bathrooms, and parking. Rather than subject yourself to all of that craziness (and danger), go to one of the three waterfront restaurants—Neptuno's Club, Puerco Rosado, and Gusto Tropical—and skip the public beach altogether. ⊠ *Autopista Las Américas, 21 miles (34 km) east of Santo Domingo, Boca Chica.*

> ## SANTO DOMINGO BEST BETS
>
> ■ **Zona Colonial.** Santo Domingo's Colonial Zone is a World Heritage Site and a great place to stroll. It is a trip to the Old World; it is Spain in the 16th century.
>
> ■ **Dining.** Some of the D.R.'s best restaurants can be found in the capital. Take advantage of them if you have any extra time to spend here.
>
> ■ **Shopping.** The country's best shopping can be found in Santo Domingo. You can go souvenir shopping right on Calle Conde, a pedestrian street that is the main drag of the Zona Colonial.

SHOPPING

Exquisitely hand-wrapped cigars continue to be the hottest commodity coming out of the D.R. Only reputable cigar shops sell the real thing. Dominican rum and coffee are also good buys. *Mamajuana,* an herbal liqueur, is said to be the Dominican answer to Viagra. Look also for the delicate, faceless ceramic figurines that symbolize Dominican culture. Though locally crafted products are often very affordable, expect to pay for designer jewelry made of amber and larimar, an indigenous semiprecious stone the color of the Caribbean. Amber, a fossilization of resin from a prehistoric pine tree, often encasing ancient animal and plant life, from leaves to spiders to tiny lizards, is mined extensively. (Beware of fakes, which are especially prevalent in street stalls.)

One of the main shopping streets in the Zone is **Calle El Conde,** a pedestrian thoroughfare. With the advent of so many restorations, the dull and dusty stores with dated merchandise are giving way to some hip new shops. However, many of the offerings, including local designer shops, are still of a caliber and cost that the Dominicans can afford.

Some of the best shops are on **Calle Duarte**, north of the Colonial Zone, between Calle Mella and Avenida de Las Américas. **El Mercado Modelo**, a covered market, borders Calle Mella in the Colonial Zone; vendors here sell a dizzying selection of Dominican crafts.

The **Malecón Center**, the latest complex, adjacent to the classy Hilton Santo Domingo, will eventually house 170 shops, boutiques, and services plus several movie theaters. In the tower above are luxury apartments and Sammy Sosa, in one of the penthouses.

NIGHTLIFE

Santo Domingo's nightlife is vast and ever changing. Check with the concierges and hip *capitaleños*. Get a copy of the free newspapers *Touring, Flow,* and *Aqui o Guía de Bares Restaurantes*—available at the tourist office and at hotels—to find out what's happening. At this writing, there is still a curfew for clubs and bars; they must close at midnight during the week, and 2 am on Friday and Saturday nights. There are some exceptions to the latter, primarily those clubs and casinos located in hotels. Sadly, the curfew has put some clubs out of business, but it has cut down on crime and late-night noise, particularly in the Zone.

WHERE TO EAT

$$
ITALIAN
★
✕ Caffe Bellini. This café has always had a panache far and above its counterparts, for the Italian owners also have the adjacent furniture design center. The modern wicker-weave barrel chairs and the contemporary art and light fixtures are conspicuously hip. The democratic pricing usually offers pasta dishes, such as the trio of raviolis (spinach, beet, and pumpkin) for about $10. (Pricing is the same at lunch and dinner.) Also know that an amuse-bouche, perhaps a tomato bruschetta, can usually suffice for an appetizer. The addition of grilled portabellas to a classic arugula-and-shaved-Parmesan salad is brilliant. Main courses of meat or seafood are accompanied by pasta or grilled vegetables and potato. You can enjoy Italian liquors here such as grappa; dessert might be dark-chocolate mousse and fresh mango sorbet. Service is laudable, the manager, Franco, both professional and charming—and the music like nothing you will hear on the street! ⑤ *Average main: $14* ✉ *Plazaoleta Park, Arzobispo Merino, corner of Padre Bellini, Zona Colonial* ☎ *809/686–0424, 809/686–3387* ☺ *Closed Sun. Closed Mon. 3–6.*

$$$
FRENCH
Fodor's Choice
★
✕ La Residence. This fine-dining enclave has always had the setting—Spanish-colonial architecture, with pillars and archways overlooking a courtyard—but an esoteric lunch-dinner menu with high prices that did not always deliver offset it. Now it has a French Certified Master Chef, Denis Schetrit (there are only 300 such designated chefs), who serves classically grounded yet innovative cuisine. He also cleverly utilizes local produce and offers many moderately priced choices. An amuse-bouche arrives before your meal, and there is an excellent bread service. The three-course daily *menu de chef* is less than $28, including tax. It could be brochettes of spit-roasted duck, chicken au

poivre, or vegetable risotto. You could start with a salad of pan-fried young squid and leave room for a luscious French pastry. Veer from the daily specials menu, and prices can go higher, but they remain fair; even the grilled Angus fillet and braised oxtail with foie-gras sauce and wild mushrooms is reasonable. Often, musicians romantically serenade diners. $ *Average main: $21* ⊠ *Hostal Nicolas de Ovando, Calle Las Damas, Zona Colonial* ☎ *809/685–9955.*

WHERE TO STAY

Since Santo Domingo is a port of embarkation for some ships, we list these hotel recommendations for those who want or need to stay overnight.

For expanded reviews, facilities, and current deals, visit Fodors.com.

$ **Coco Boutique Hotel.** Behind the pale, Caribbean turquoise facade
B&B/INN you'll find a very untypical bed-and-breakfast, not to mention earth tones with white—almost everywhere: the reception and lounge, the stark, wooden staircase, the grillwork on the French doors; it's breathtaking, actually, with the zebra-skin rug and dark green plants offering contrast. **Pros:** amazingly quiet for the Zona Colonial; opposite the picturesque Plaza Pellerano Castro; rooftop terrace with Balinese sun beds from which you can wave to the cruise ships. **Cons:** bathrooms are small; heels on the wooden staircase are noisy. $ *Rooms from: $105* ⊠ *Arzobispo Porte 7, corner of Las Damas, Zona Colonial* ☎ *809/685–8467* ⊕ *www.cocoboutiquehotel.com* ⌨ *5 rooms* ⦿ *Breakfast.*

$$ **Hilton Santo Domingo.** This has become *the* address on the Malecón
HOTEL for businesspeople, convention attendees, and leisure travelers. **Pros:**
★ Sunday brunch is one of the city's top tickets; luxe bedding; totally soundproof rooms; the executive-level lounge. **Cons:** little about the property is authentically Dominican; Vista Bar in lobby is closed on weekends. $ *Rooms from: $189* ⊠ *Av. George Washington 500, Gazcue* ☎ *809/685–0000* ⊕ *hiltoncaribbean.com/santodomingo* ⌨ *228 rooms, 32 suites* ⦿ *No meals.*

$$ **Hostal Nicolas de Ovando.** This branch of the M Gallery, a chain of his-
HOTEL toric boutique hotels, was sculpted from the residence of the first gover-
Fodor's Choice nor of the Americas, and it just might be the best thing to happen in the
★ Zone since Diego Columbus's palace was finished in 1517. **Pros:** lavish breakfast buffet; beautifully restored historic section. **Cons:** breakfast is no longer included; pricey; rooms could be larger. $ *Rooms from: $220* ⊠ *Calle Las Damas, Zona Colonial* ☎ *809/685–9955, 800/763–4835* ⊕ *www.mgallery.com* ⌨ *100 rooms, 4 suites.*

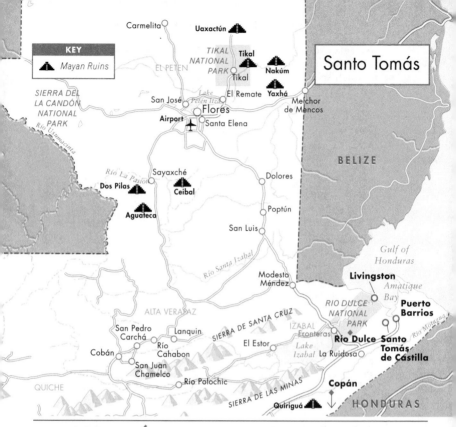

SANTO TOMÁS DE CASTILLA, GUATEMALA

Marlise Kast

Guatemala's short Caribbean shoreline doesn't generate the buzz of those of neighboring Belize and Mexico. The coast weighs in at a scant 74 miles (123 km), and this mostly highland country wears its indigenous culture on its sleeve and has historically looked inland rather than to the sea. You'll be drawn inland, too, with a variety of shore excursions. This is the land of the Maya, after all. But there's plenty to keep you occupied here in the lowlands. Tourist brochures tout the Caribbean coast as "The Other Guatemala." The predominantly indigenous and Spanish cultures of the highlands give way to an Afro-Caribbean tradition that listens more closely to the rhythms of far-off Jamaica rather than taking its cue from Guatemala City. Think of it as mixing a little reggae with your salsa.

ESSENTIALS

CURRENCY The Guatemalan quetzal is named for the brightly plumed bird that is the symbol of the country (Q7.80 to US$1). Take care of any banking matters in the cruise terminal in Santo Tomás de Castilla. You'll find ATMs in Puerto Barrios and Livingston but nowhere else in this region.

INTERNET The Terminal de Cruceros in Santo Tomás de Castilla has Internet computers for your use, the easiest option if you're a day visitor.

TELEPHONE   Guatemalan phone numbers have eight digits. There are no city or area codes. Simply dial the number for any in-country call. Most towns have offices of Telgua, the national telephone company, where you can place both national and international calls. Avoid the ubiquitous public phones with signs promising "Free calls to the USA." The number back home being called gets socked with a hefty bill.

COMING ASHORE

Cruise ships dock at the modern, spacious Terminal de Cruceros, where you'll find a bank, post office, money exchange, telephones, Internet access, a lively craft market, and an office of INGUAT, Guatemala's national tourist office. A marimba band serenades you with its clinking xylophone-like music; a Caribbean ensemble dances for you (and may even pull you in to take part).

Taxis, both vehicular and water, take you to various destinations in the area. Plan on paying $3 to Santo Tomás de Castilla proper, and $5 to Puerto Barrios. Boats transport cruise visitors to Livingston, charging about $6 for the 20-minute trip. The Amatique Bay Resort provides water taxis from port to resort of $10 per person. Vehicular taxis charge $35 per head to travel by land to the resort.

EXPLORING SANTO TOMÁS DE CASTILLA

SANTO TOMÁS DE CASTILLA

Belgian immigrants settled Santo Tomás in the 19th century, but little remains of their heritage today, save for the preponderance of French and Flemish names in the local cemetery. Most visitors move on. Santo Tomás has experienced a small renaissance as the country's most important port, receiving growing numbers of cruise and cargo ships, and serving as the headquarters of the Guatemalan navy.

PUERTO BARRIOS

3 miles (5 km) north of Santo Tomás de Castilla.

Puerto Barrios maintains the atmosphere of an old banana town, humid and a tad down at the heels, perhaps longing for better days. Santo Tomás has replaced it as the country's largest port, and you'll likely zip through the Caribbean coast's biggest city on your way to somewhere else, but the cathedral and municipal market are worth a look if you find yourself here. Water taxis depart from the municipal docks for Livingston, across the bay, where you start your trip up the Río Dulce.

"Bahía de Amatique" denotes the large bay that washes the Caribbean coast of Guatemala and southern Belize just north of Puerto Barrios, but for most travelers the name is inexorably linked with the **Amatique Bay Resort and Marina**, the region's only five-star hotel. The 61-room resort opens itself up for day visitors, and many cruise passengers stop by for a drink, a meal, or an entire day of swimming, watersliding, kayaking, horseback riding, or bicycling. ⊠ *6 miles (10 km) north of Santo Tomás; 14 Calle Final, Finca Pichilingo, Puerto Barrios* ☎ *7931–0000.*

LIVINGSTON

15 miles (25 km) by water northwest of Santo Tomás.

Visitors compare Livingston with Puerto Barrios across the bay, and the former wins hands down, for its sultry, seductive Caribbean flavor. Wooden houses, some on stilts, congregate in this old fishing town, once an important railroad hub, but today inaccessible by land from the outside world. Livingston proudly trumpets its Garífuna heritage, a culture unique to Central America's eastern coast and descended from the intermarriage of African slaves with Caribbean indigenous people. Music and dance traditions and a Caribbean-accented English remain, even if old-timers lament the creeping outside influences, namely Spanish rap and reggae.

> ### SANTO TOMÁS BEST BETS
>
> ■ **Quiriguá.** If you want to see Mayan ruins but don't want to spend an entire day on the bus, nearby Quiriguá can be impressive.
>
> ■ **Copán.** In neighboring Honduras, this Mayan site is a worthwhile day trip from Santo Tomás.
>
> ■ **Riding on the Río Dulce.** The ride on this river is one of Guatemala's most beautiful boat trips.

RÍO DULCE

30 miles (48 km) southwest of Santo Tomás.

The natural crown jewel of this region is the 13,000-hectare (32,000-acre) national park that protects the river leading inland from Livingston to Lago de Izabal, Guatemala's largest lake. Pelicans, herons, egrets, and terns nest and fly along the Río Dulce, which cuts through a heavily forested limestone canyon. Excursions often approach the park by land, but we recommend making the trip upriver from Livingston to immerse yourself in the entire Indiana Jones experience.

Castillo de San Felipe de Lara. Once an important Mayan trade route, the Río Dulce later became the route over which the conquistadors sent the gold and silver they plundered back to Spain. All this wealth attracted Dutch and English pirates, who attacked both the ships and the warehouses on shore. In hopes of curtailing these buccaneers, colonists built a series of fortresses on the river's northern banks. In 1955 the Guatemalan government reconstructed the ruined fortress of Castillo de San Felipe de Lara. Spanish colonists constructed the fortress in 1595 to guard the inland waterway from pirate incursions. It was used as a prison between 1655 and 1660. You can reach it by the road leading west from Río Dulce or by a short boat ride. A 1999 earthquake in this region destroyed the river pier, as well as damaging portions of the fort. If you wish to visit, rather than simply see the structure from the water, you'll need to approach the park overland rather than upriver. ⊠ *Southwest of Fronteras, Río Dulce* 🎫 *$3* ⏱ *Daily 8–5.*

$ 🏨 **Hacienda Tijax.** There is only very basic accommodation here, but people come for the eco-activities, not the rooms. **Pros:** many activities; ecologically minded staff. **Cons:** rustic rooms. Ⓢ *Rooms from: $220* ⊠ *Northeast of Fronteras, Río Dulce* ☎ *7930–5505* ⊕ *www.tijax.com* 🛏 *27 cabins, 20 with bath.*

QUIRIGUÁ
60 miles (96 km) southwest of Puerto Barrios.

Quiriguá. Unlike the hazy remnants of chiseled images you see at most other archaeological sites in Central America, Quiriguá has some that are seemingly untouched by winds and rain. They emerge from the rock faces in breathtaking detail. Quiriguá, a Mayan city that dates from the Classic period, is famous for the amazingly well-preserved stelae, or carved pillars, which are the largest yet discovered, and dwarf those of Copán, Honduras, some 30 miles (50 km) south. Construction began on the Guatemalan lowlands' most important Mayan ruins about AD 500. Its hieroglyphics tell its story: Quiriguá served at the time as a satellite state under the control of Copán. By the height of its power in the 7th century, Quiriguá had overpowered Copán, but just as quickly fell back into submissive status.

The stelae depict Quiriguá's ruling dynasty, especially the powerful Cauac Chan (Jade Sky), whose visage appears on nine of the structures circling the Great Plaza. Stela E, the largest of these, towers 10 meters (33 feet) high and weighs 65 tons. Several monuments, covered with interesting zoomorphic figures, still stand. The most interesting of these depicts Cauac Chan's conquest of Copán and the subsequent beheading of its then-ruler, 18 Rabbit. The remains of an acropolis and other structures have been partially restored.

In ancient times Quiriguá was an important Mayan trading center that stood on the banks of the Río Motagua (the river has since changed its course). The ruins are surrounded by a stand of rain forest—an untouched wilderness in the heart of banana country. Quiriguá still lives in the shadow of its better-known neighbor across the border, and of Tikal in the Petén in northern Guatemala, but it is one of Guatemala's most accessible Mayan sites. A small museum on-site gives insight into the history of Cauac Chan and his contemporaries. ⊠ *54 miles (90 km) southwest of Santo Tomás, El Estor* 🖾 *$10* ☉ *Daily 7:30–5.*

COPÁN
122 miles (203 km) southeast of Santo Tomás.

Copán. You'll approach the ruins via a short stone path, about a 20-minute walk, that leads just outside town. Before you reach the ruins you'll reach some carved Mayan statues, and eventually a gate and admissions building. There is a small house in the parking area where the guides gather to lead tours for the day. Their services are well worth the money. They have a wealth of knowledge regarding the life and activities of the ancient Mayan people, and can interpret the hieroglyphs' literal as well as folkloric meaning.

The area open to the public covers only a small part of the city's ceremonial center. Copán once extended for nearly 1¼ miles (2 km) along the river, making it as large as many Mayan archaeological sites in Guatemala. It's also just as old—more than 3,000 years ago there was an Olmec settlement on this site. Because new structures were usually built on top of existing ones, the great temples that are visible today were built during the reigns of the city's last few rulers.

As you stroll past towering cieba trees on your way to the archaeological site, you'll find the **Great Plaza** to your left. The stelae standing about the plaza were monuments erected to glorify rulers. Some stelae on the periphery are dedicated to King Smoke Jaguar, but the most impressive, located in the middle of the plaza, depict King 18 Rabbit. Besides stroking the egos of the kings, these monuments had religious significance as well. Vaults for ritual offerings have been found beneath most of them.

The city's most important **ball court** lies south of the Great Plaza. One of the largest of its kind in Central America, it was used for more than simple entertainment. Players had to keep a hard rubber ball from touching the ground, perhaps symbolizing the sun's battle to stay aloft. Stylized carvings of macaw heads that line either side of the court may have been used as markers for keeping score, although the game was more spiritual than sportslike in nature. Competitions were incredibly physical and players were likely using hallucinogenic substances. The losers—or the winners in some cases—were killed as a sacrifice to Mayan gods.

Near the ball court is one of the highlights of Copán, the **Hieroglyphic Stairway.** This amazing structure, covered with a canopy to protect it from the weather, contains the single largest collection of hieroglyphs in the world. The 63 steps immortalize the battles won by Copán's kings, especially those of the much revered King Smoke Jaguar. Once placed chronologically, the history can no longer be read because an earthquake knocked many steps free, and archaeologists replaced them in a random order. All may not be lost, however, as experts have located an early photograph of the stairway that helps unlock the proper sequence.

The **Western Court** is thought to have represented the underworld. The structures, with doors that lead to blank walls, appear symbolic. On the east side of the plaza is a reproduction of Altar Q, a key to understanding the history of Copán. The squat platform shows a long line of Copán's rulers passing power down to their heirs. It ends with the last great king, Dawning Sun, facing the first king, Yax Kuk Mo.

The **Acropolis** was partly washed away by the Río Copán, which has since been routed away from the ruins. King Dawning Sun was credited with the construction of many of the buildings surrounding this grand plaza. Below the Acropolis are tunnels that lead to what archaeologists agree are some of the most fascinating discoveries at Copán. Underneath Structure 16 are the near-perfect remains of an older building, called the **Rosalila Temple.** This structure, dating from 571, was subsequently buried below taller structures. Uncovered in 1989, the Rosalila was notable in part because of the paint remains on its surface—rose and lilac—for which it was named. Another tunnel called **Los Jaguares** takes you past tombs, a system of aqueducts, and even an ancient bathroom.

Two other parts of Copán that served as residential and administrative areas are open to the public. Although the architecture is not nearly as impressive as that of the larger buildings, they offer a glimpse into the daily lives of ordinary people. **El Bosque** (the Forest) lies in the woods off the trail to the west of the Principal Group. **Las Sepulturas** (the Graves), which lies 1 mile (2 km) down the main road, is a revealing look into Mayan society. Excavations have shown that the Maya had a highly stratified social system, where the elite owned houses with many rooms.

East of the main entrance to Copán, the marvelous **Museo de Escultura Maya** provides a closeup look at the best of Mayan artistry. All the sculptures and replicas are accompanied by informative signs in English as well as Spanish. Here you'll find a full-scale replica of the Rosalila Temple. The structure, in eye-popping shades of red and green, offers an educated guess at what the ceremonial and political structures of Copán must have looked like at the time they were in use.

The complex employs a bit of à la carte pricing. The $15 entrance fee covers admission to the ruins, and covers admission to nearby sites like El Bosque and Las Sepulturas. Admission to the tunnels to Rosalila and Los Jaguares is $12 extra. Admission to the Museo de Escultura Maya is $5. You can pay in U.S. dollars or lempiras.

It's a good idea to hire a guide, as they are very knowledgeable about the site. English-speaking ones charge about L400 for a two-hour tour, while Spanish-speaking guides charge about half that. A small cafeteria and gift shop are near the entrance.

A visit to the ruins can last anywhere from one to four hours. If your schedule permits, an early-morning visit is ideal. If you can be here when the gate opens at 8 am, the weather will be better, both in terms of cooler temperatures and clearer skies during the rainy season. Sunlight is lower, and that makes for better photography. You're also more likely to catch a glimpse of the animal life that calls the park home, especially the white-tailed deer. On your own, you can easily walk through the ruins and admire the structures and carvings. If you have a guide along, you likely will spend more time getting up close to the carvings, and learning about Mayan hieroglyphics and the history that they record. ⊠ *½ mile (1 km) east of Copán Ruinas, Copán Ruinas, Honduras* ☎ *504/651–4018* 🖾 *Ruins $15 or L300; museum $5 or L100; tunnels $12 or L240* ⊙ *Daily 8–4.*

TIKAL

1 hour by air northwest of Santo Tomás

Some cruise lines offer excursions to Tikal, but it's not cheap getting there, since you'll travel by plane from the airstrip outside Santo Tomás to the small airport in Santa Elena, near the ruins.

Fodor's Choice
★ **Tikal.** The high point of any trip to Guatemala is a visit to Central America's most impressive ruins. There's nothing quite like the sight of the towering temples, ringed on all sides by miles of virgin forest, but you need a lot of quetzales to get here. Although this region was home to Mayan communities as early as 600 BC, Tikal wasn't established until around 200 BC. By AD 500 it's estimated that the city covered more than 18 square miles (47 square km) and had a population of close to 100,000. For almost 1,000 years Tikal remained engulfed by the jungle. Excavation began in earnest in the mid-1800s. Today, after more than

150 years of digging, researchers say that Tikal includes some 3,000 buildings. Countless more are still covered by the jungle. Temple IV, the tallest-known structure built by the Maya, offers an unforgettable view from the top. ⊠ *Parque Nacional Tikal* ☎ *No phone* 🖂 *$20* ⊘ *Daily 6–6.*

SHOPPING

The rest of Guatemala overflows with indigenous crafts and art, but the famous market towns of the highlands are nowhere to be found in Caribbean region. Quite honestly, your best bet for shopping is the Terminal de Cruceros at Santo Tomás de Castilla, and you'll have plenty of opportunity to buy before you board your ship. What you'll find here comes from Guatemala's highlands—the Caribbean has never developed a strong artisan tradition—with a good selection of fabrics, weavings, woodwork, and basketry. Markets in Puerto Barrios and Livingston, the only real urban areas you'll encounter in this region, are more geared toward the workaday needs of residents rather than visitors.

ACTIVITIES

BEACHES AND WATER SPORTS

A beach culture has just never developed in this region of Guatemala the way it has in neighboring Belize and Mexico. The only real beach in the region is found within the confines of the **Amatique Bay Resort & Marina** (⊠ *6 miles [10 km] north of Santo Tomás* ☎ *502/7913–0000* ⊕ *www.amatiquebay.net*), which is the only place here that has a resort atmosphere to it. Day visitors partake in swimming, waterslides, and kayaking. The resort's launch will bring you over from the cruise-ship terminal in Santo Tomás.

HIKING AND KAYAKING

Hacienda Tijax (⊠ *Northeast of Fronteras, near the bridge that crosses over the Río Dulce* ☎ *502/7930–5505* ⊕ *www. tijax.com*), which is pronounced tee-*hahsh*, is inland, near the point where the Río Dulce meets Lake Izabal. The staff oversee kayaking and hiking for day visitors.

ST. BARTHÉLEMY (GUSTAVIA)

Elise Meyer   Hilly St. Barthélemy, popularly known as St. Barth (or St. Barts) is just 8 square miles (21 square km), but the island has at least 20 good beaches. What draws visitors is its sophisticated but unstudied approach to relaxation: the finest food, excellent wine, high-end shopping, and lack of large-scale commercial development. A favorite among upscale cruise-ship passengers, who also appreciate the shopping opportunities and fine dining, St. Barth isn't really equipped for mega-ship visits, which is why most ships calling here are from smaller premium lines. This is one place where you don't need to take the ship's shore excursions to have a good time. Just hail a cab or rent a car and go to one of the many wonderful beaches, where you will find some of the best lunchtime restaurants, or wander around Gustavia, shopping and eating. It's the best way to relax on this most relaxing of islands.

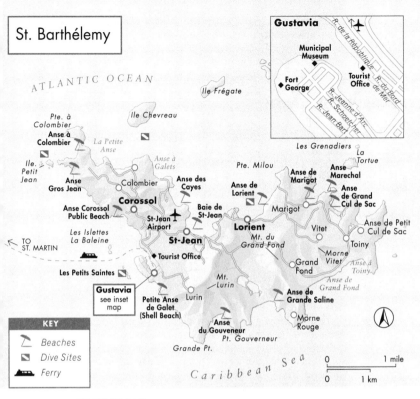

St. Barthélemy

ATLANTIC OCEAN

Gustavia

Municipal Museum

Fort George

Tourist Office

Ile Frégate

Pte. à Colombier
Anse à Colombier
Ile Chevreau
La Petite Anse
Anse à Galets
Pte. Milou
Les Grenadiers
La Tortue
Anse de Marigot
Anse Marechal
Ile. Petit Jean
Anse Gros Jean
Colombier
Corossol
Anse des Cayes
Anse de Lorient
Marigot
Anse de Grand Cul de Sac
Anse Corossol Public Beach
St-Jean Airport
Baie de St-Jean
Lorient
Vitet
Anse de Petit Cul de Sac
Les Islettes
La Baleine
St-Jean
Mt. du Grand Fond
Toiny
TO ST. MARTIN
Tourist Office
Morne Vitet
Anse à Toiny
Les Petits Saintes
Grand Fond
Gustavia
see inset map
Petite Anse de Galet (Shell Beach)
Mt. Lurin
Lurin
Anse de Grande Saline
Anse de Grand Fond
Morne Rouge
Anse du Gouverneur
Pt. Gouverneur
Grande Pt.

Caribbean Sea

KEY
Beaches
Dive Sites
Ferry

0   1 mile
0   1 km

ESSENTIALS

CURRENCY   The euro; however, U.S. dollars are accepted in almost all shops and in many restaurants. Credit cards are widely accepted.

INTERNET   Most restaurants on the island now offer free Wi-Fi for customers, and there is also a free hotspot at the port area.

TELEPHONE   Public telephones accept télécartes, prepaid calling cards that you can buy at the gas station next to the airport and at post offices in Lorient, St-Jean, and Gustavia. Making an international call using a télécarte is the best way to go.

COMING ASHORE

Even medium-size ships must anchor in Gustavia Harbor and bring passengers ashore on tenders. The tiny harbor area is right in Gustavia, which is easily explored on foot. Taxis, which meet all cruise ships, can be expensive. Technically, there's a flat rate for rides up to five minutes long. Each additional three minutes is an additional amount. In reality, however, cabbies usually name a fixed rate—and will not budge. Fares are 50% higher on Sunday and holidays. St. Barth is one port where it's really worth it to arrange a car rental for a full-day exploration of the island, including the island's out-of-the-way beaches. But be aware that during high season there is often a three-day minimum, so this may not be possible except through your ship (and then you'll pay premium rates indeed). Most car-rental firms operate at the airport; however, renting on your own is usually cheaper than what you'll get if you go with one of the ship's car rentals (you may be able to find a car for €50 per day).

EXPLORING ST. BARTH

With a little practice, negotiating St. Barth's narrow, steep roads soon becomes fun. Free maps are everywhere, roads are well marked, and painted signs will point you where you want to be. Take along a towel, sandals, and a bottle of water, and you will surely find a beach upon which to linger.

Corossol. Traces of the island's French provincial origins are evident in this two-street fishing village with a little rocky beach. ☒ *Corossol.*

Inter Oceans Museum/Museum of Shells. Ingenu Magras's Inter Oceans Museum has more than 9,000 seashells and an intriguing collection of sand samples from around the world. You can buy souvenir shells. ☒ *Corossol* ☎ *0590/27–62–97* ▩ *€3* ☉ *Tues.–Sun. 9–12:30 and 2–5.*

Gustavia. You can easily explore all of Gustavia during a two-hour stroll. Most shops close from noon to 3 or 4, so plan lunch accordingly, but stores stay open past 7 in the evening. ☒ *Gustavia.*

Tourist Office. A good spot to park your car is rue de la République, alongside the catamarans, yachts, and sailboats. The tourist office on the pier can provide maps and a wealth of information. During busier holiday periods, the office may be open all day. ☒ *Rue de la République, Gustavia* ☎ *0590/27–87–27* ⊕ *www.saintbarth-tourisme.com* ☉ *Mon. 8:30–12:30, Tues.–Fri. 8–noon and 2–5, Sat. 9–noon.*

Le musée territorial de Saint Barthélemy. On the far side of the harbor known as La Pointe is the charming Municipal Museum, where you can find watercolors, portraits, photographs, and historic documents detailing the island's history, as well as displays of the island's flowers, plants, and marine life. ☒ *La Pointe, Gustavia* ☎ *590/29–71–55* ▩ *€2* ☉ *Mon., Tues., Thurs., and Fri. 8:30–12:30 and 2:30–6, Sat. 9–12:30* ☉ *Closed July 26–August 31.*

Lorient. Site of the first French settlement, Lorient is one of the island's two parishes; a restored church, a school, and a post office mark the spot. Note the gaily decorated graves in the cemetery. ☒ *Lorient.*

St-Jean. There is a monument at the crest of the hill that divides St-Jean from Gustavia. Called *The Arawak,* it symbolizes the soul of St. Barth. A warrior, one of the earliest inhabitants of the area (AD 800–2,500), holds a lance in his right hand and stands on a rock shaped like the island; in his left hand he holds a conch shell, which sounds the cry of nature; perched beside him are a pelican (which symbolizes the air and survival by fishing) and an iguana (which represents the earth). The half-mile-long crescent of sand at St-Jean is the island's most popular beach. A popular activity is watching and photographing the hair-raising airplane landings, but be sure to not stand in the area at the beach end of the runway, where someone was seriously injured. You'll also find some of the best shopping on the island here, as well as several restaurants. ☒ *St-Jean.*

SHOPPING

St. Barth is a duty-free port, and with its sophisticated crowd of visitors, shopping in the island's 200-plus boutiques is a definite delight. In Gustavia boutiques line the three major shopping streets. Quai de la République, which is right on the harbor, rivals New York's Madison Avenue or Paris's avenue Montaigne for high-end designer retail, including shops for **Louis Vuitton, Bulgari, Cartier, Chopard,** and **Hermès.** These shops often carry items that are not available in the United States. The Carré d'Or plaza is great fun to explore. Shops are also clustered in **La Savane Commercial Center** (across from the airport), **La Villa Créole** (in St-Jean), and **Espace Neptune** (on the road to Lorient). It's worth working your way from one end to the other at these shopping complexes—just to see or, perhaps, be seen. Boutiques in all three areas carry the latest in French and Italian sportswear and some haute couture. Bargains may be tough to come by, but you might be able to snag that *pochette* that is sold out stateside, and in any case, you'll have a lot of fun hunting around.

> ## ST. BARTHÉLEMY BEST BETS
>
> ■ **Soaking up the Atmosphere.** It's the French Riviera transported to the Caribbean.
>
> ■ **Beautiful Beaches.** Pick any of the lovely, uncrowded beaches.
>
> ■ **French Food.** St. Barth has some of the best restaurants in the Caribbean.
>
> ■ **Shopping.** There is no better fashion shopping in the Caribbean, especially if you are young and slim.

ACTIVITIES

BOATING AND SAILING

St. Barth is a popular yachting and sailing center, thanks to its location midway between Antigua and St. Thomas. Gustavia's harbor, 13 to 16 feet deep, has mooring and docking facilities for 40 yachts. There are also good anchorages available at Public, Corossol, and Colombier. You can charter sailing and motorboats in Gustavia Harbor for as little as a half day. Stop at the tourist office in Gustavia for an up-to-the minute list of recommended charter companies.

Jicky Marine Service. Jicky Marine Service offers full-day outings, either on a variety of motorboats, or 42- or 46-foot catamaran, to the uninhabited Île Fourchue for swimming, snorkeling, cocktails, and lunch. The cost starts at about $100 per person; an unskippered motor rental runs about $260 a day. ⊠ *Ferry dock, Gustavia* ☎ *0590/27–70–34* ⊕ *www.jickymarine.com.*

DIVING AND SNORKELING

Several dive shops arrange scuba excursions to local sites. Depending on weather conditions, you may dive at **Pain de Sucre, Coco Island,** or toward nearby **Saba.** There's also an underwater shipwreck to explore, plus sharks, rays, sea tortoises, coral, and the usual varieties of colorful fish. The waters on the island's leeward side are the calmest. For the uncertified who still want to see what the island's waters hold, there's an accessible shallow reef right off the beach at Anse de Cayes that you can explore if you have your own mask and fins.

☾ **Plongée Caraïbe.** Plongée Caraïbe is recommended for its up-to-the-minute equipment and dive boat. They also run two-hour group snorkeling trips on the *Blue Cat Catamaran*; a half-day is €40. ⊠ *St. Barthélemy* 🖀🖶 *0590/27–55–94* ⊕ *www.plongee-caraibes.com.*

BEACHES

There are many *anses* (coves) and nearly 20 *plages* (beaches) scattered around the island, each with a distinctive personality and each open to the general public. Even in season you can find a nearly empty beach. Topless sunbathing is common, but nudism is forbidden—although both Grande Saline and Gouverneur are de facto nude beaches.

Anse de Grand Cul de Sac. The shallow, reef-protected beach is nice for small children, fly-fishermen, kayakers, and windsurfers—and for the amusing pelicanlike frigate birds that dive-bomb the water fishing for their lunch. There is a good dive shop. You needn't do your own fishing; you can have a wonderful lunch at one of the excellent restaurants, and use their lounge chairs for the afternoon. ⊠ *Grand Cul de Sac.*

☾ **Anse de Grande Saline.** Anse de Grande Saline. Secluded, with its sandy
Fodor's Choice ocean bottom, this is just about everyone's favorite beach and is great
★ for swimmers, too. Without any major development (although there is some talk of developing a resort here) it's an ideal Caribbean strand. However, there can be a bit of wind here, so you can enjoy yourself more if you go on a calm day. In spite of the prohibition, young and old alike go nude. The beach is a 10-minute walk up a rocky dune trail, so be sure to wear sneakers or water shoes, and bring a blanket, umbrella, and beach towels. Although there are several good restaurants for lunch near the parking area, once you get here, the beach is just sand, sea, and sky. The big salt ponds here are no longer in use, and the place looks a little desolate when you approach, but don't despair. ⊠ *Grande Saline.*

☾ **Anse du Gouverneur.** Because it's so secluded, this beach is a popular
★ place for nude sunbathing. It is truly beautiful, with blissful swimming and views of St. Kitts, Saba, and St. Eustatius. Venture here at the end of the day and watch the sun set behind the hills. The road here from Gustavia also offers spectacular vistas. Legend has it that pirates' treasure is buried in the vicinity. There are no restaurants or other services here, so plan accordingly. ⊠ *Anse du Gouverneur.*

☾ **Baie de St-Jean.** Like a mini–Côte d'Azur—beachside bistros, terrific shopping, bungalow hotels, bronzed bodies, windsurfing, and day-trippers who tend to arrive on BIG yachts—the reef-protected strip is divided by Eden Rock promontory. Except when the hotels are filled to capacity you can rent chaises and umbrellas at La Plage restaurant or at Eden Rock, where you can lounge for hours over lunch. ⊠ *Baie de St-Jean.*

WHERE TO EAT

A service charge is always added by law, but you should leave the server 5% to 10% extra in cash. It is generally advisable to charge restaurant meals on a credit card, as the issuer will offer a better exchange rate than the restaurant.

$$$ ✕ **Le Tamarin.** A leisurely lunch here en route to Grande Saline beach is a
FRENCH St. Barth *must*. But new management makes it tops for dinner, too. Sit
★ on one of the licorice-colored Javanese couches in the lounge area and nibble excellent sushi, or settle at a table under the wondrous tamarind tree for which the restaurant is named. A unique cocktail each day, ultrafresh fish provided by the restaurant's designated fisherman, and gentle prices accommodate local residents as well as the holiday crowd. The restaurant is open year-round. $ *Average main: €21* ⊠ *Grande Saline* ☎ *0590/27–72–12* ⊙ *Closed Tues.*

$$$$ ✕ **Wall House.** The food is excellent—and the service is always friendly—
ECLECTIC at this restaurant on the far side of Gustavia Harbor. The light-as-air
Fodor's Choice gnocci with pesto are legendary, and the rotisserie duck marinated in
★ honey from the rotisserie is a universal favorite. Local businesspeople crowd the restaurant for the bargain €11 prix-fixe lunch menu, with classic dishes like duck-leg confit. For €18 the menu includes the main dish or salad of the day, coffee and petits fours, and a glass of wine or beer. An old-fashioned dessert trolley showcases some really yummy sweets—the sugar topping for your crème brûlée is blazed with a mini-torch tableside. $ *Average main: €33* ⊠ *La Pointe, Gustavia* ☎ *0590/27–71–83* ⊕ *www.wallhouserestaurant.com* ⊰ *Reservations essential* ⊙ *No lunch Sun.*

ST. CROIX (FREDERIKSTED)

Lynda Lohr St. Croix is the largest of the three U.S. Virgin Islands (USVI) that form the northern hook of the Lesser Antilles; it's 40 miles (64 km) south of its sister islands, St. Thomas and St. John. Christopher Columbus landed here in 1493, skirmishing briefly with the native Carib Indians. Since then, the USVI have played a colorful, if painful, role as pawns in the game of European colonialism. Theirs is a history of pirates and privateers, sugar plantations, slave trading, and slave revolt and liberation. Through it all, Denmark had staying power. From the 17th to the 19th century, Danes oversaw a plantation slave economy that produced molasses, rum, cotton, and tobacco. Many of the stones you tread on in the streets were once used as ballast on sailing ships, and the yellow fort of Christiansted is a reminder of the value once placed on this island treasure. Never a major cruise destination, it is still a stop for several ships each year.

ESSENTIALS

CURRENCY The U.S. dollar is the official currency of St. Croix.

INTERNET There's a convenient Internet café in Christiansted if you make it there during your day ashore.

A Better Copy ⊠ *2128 Company St., Christiansted* ☎ *340/692–5303.*

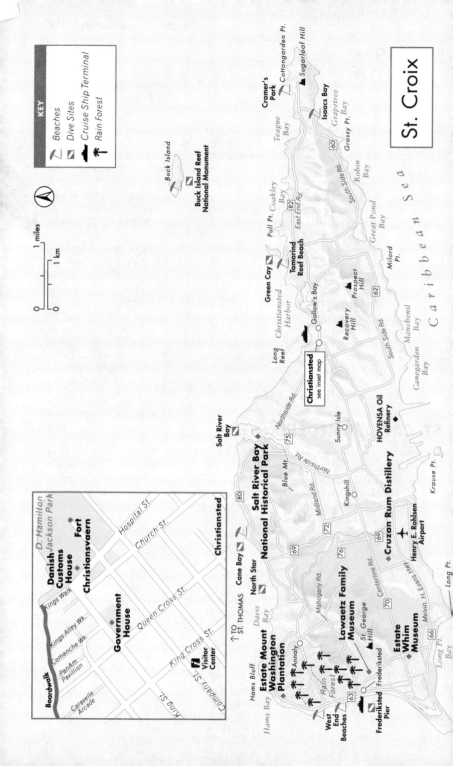

St. Croix

KEY
- Beaches
- Dive Sites
- Cruise Ship Terminal
- Rain Forest

1 miles
1 km

Caribbean Sea

Buck Island
Buck Island Reef
National Monument

Christiansted

Boardwalk
D. Hamilton Jackson Park
Danish Customs House
Fort Christiansvaern
Hospital St.
Church St.
Kings Walk
Kings Alley Wk.
Comanche Wk.
PanAm Pavillion
Caravelle Arcade
Visitor Center
Government House
Queen Cross St.
King Cross St.
Company St.
King St.

Christiansted

↑ TO ST. THOMAS

Cane Bay
North Star
Salt River Bay
National Historical Park
Salt River Bay

Davis Bay

Long Reef
Christiansted Harbor
Gallow's Bay
Green Cay
Tamarind Reef Beach
Pull Pt. Coakley Bay
East End Rd.
Teague Bay
Cramer's Park
Cottongarden Pt.
Sugarloaf Hill
Isaacs Bay
Grapetree Bay
Grassy Pt. Bay

Christiansted
see inset map

Recovery Hill
Prospect Hill
Robin Bay
South Side Rd.
Great Pond Bay
Milord Pt.
Manchenil Bay
Canegarden Bay
Krause Pt.

Northside Rd.
Blue Mt.
Sunny Isle
HOVENSA Oil Refinery
Midland Rd.
Kingshill
South Side Rd.

Hams Bluff
Hams Bay
Estate Mount Washington Plantation
Annaly
Rain Forest
West End Beaches
Frederiksted Pier
Frederiksted
Lawaetz Family Museum
St. George Hill
Mahogany Rd.
Centerline Rd.
Cruzan Rum Distillery
Henry E. Rohlsen Airport
Estate Whim Museum
Melvin H. Evans Hwy.
Long Pt.
Long Pt. Bay

TELEPHONE   Calling the United States from St. Croix works the same way as calling within the United States. Local calls from a public phone cost up to 35¢ for every five minutes. You can use your regular toll-free connections for long-distance services. Most U.S. cell phone plans include the Virgin Islands for no additional cost.

COMING ASHORE

Cruise ships dock in Frederiksted, on the island's west end. You'll find an information center at the pier, and the town is easy to explore on foot. Beaches are nearby. The only difficulty is that you are far from the island's main town, Christiansted. Some cruise lines offer bus transportation there; otherwise, you are probably better off renting a car to explore the island, since both car-rental rates and gasoline prices are reasonable; just remember to drive on the left.

Taxis of all shapes and sizes are available at the cruise-ship pier and at various shopping and resort areas. Remember, too, that you can hail a taxi that's already occupied. Drivers take multiple fares and sometimes even trade passengers at midpoints. Taxis don't have meters, so you should check the list of official rates (available at the visitor centers or from drivers) and agree on a fare before you start, but there are standard rates for most trips. A taxi to Christiansted will cost about $25 for two people for transportation only; an island tour including Christiansted will cost $110 for four people.

Car Rentals

Midwest. This company is outside Frederiksted, but will pick you up at the pier. ☎ *340/772–0438, 877/772–0438* ⊕ *www.midwestautorental.com.*

EXPLORING ST. CROIX

Frederiksted speaks to history buffs with its quaint Victorian architecture and historic fort. There's very little traffic, so this is the perfect place for strolling and shopping. Christiansted is a historic Danish-style town that served as St. Croix's commercial center. Your best bet is to see the historic sights in the morning, when it's still cool. This two-hour endeavor won't tax your walking shoes and leave you with energy to poke around the town's eclectic shops.

CHRISTIANSTED

In the 1700s and 1800s Christiansted was a trading center for sugar, rum, and molasses. Today there are law offices, tourist shops, and restaurants, but many of the buildings, which start at the harbor and go up the gently sloped hillsides, still date from the 18th century. You can't get lost. All streets lead back downhill to the water.

Danish Customs House. Built in 1830 on foundations that date from a century earlier, the historic building, which is near Ft. Christiansvaern, originally served as both a customshouse and a post office. In 1926 it became the Christiansted Library, and it's been a national park facility since 1972. It's closed to the public, but the sweeping front steps make a nice place to take a break. ⊠ *King St., Christiansted* ☎ *340/773–1460* ⊕ *www.nps.gov/chri.*

☺ **Ft. Christiansvaern.** The large yel-
Fodor'sChoice low fortress dominates the water-
★ front. Because it's so easy to spot, it makes a good place to begin a walking tour. In 1749 the Danish built the fort to protect the harbor, but the structure was repeatedly damaged by hurricane-force winds and had to be partially rebuilt in 1771. It's now a national historic site, the best preserved of the few remaining Danish-built forts in the Virgin Islands. The park's visitor center is here. Rangers are on hand to answer questions. ⊠ *Hospital St., Christiansted* ☎ *340/773–1460* ⊕ *www.nps.gov/chri* ✆ *$3 (includes Steeple Bldg.* ☺ *Weekdays 8–4:30, weekends 9–4:30.*

Government House. One of the town's most elegant structures was built as a home for a Danish merchant in 1747. Today it houses offices. If you're here weekdays from 8 to 4:30, slip into the peaceful inner courtyard to admire the still pools and gardens. A sweeping staircase leads you to a second-story ballroom, still used for official government functions. ⊠ *King St., Christiansted* ☎ *340/773–1404.*

MID ISLAND

Cruzan Rum Distillery. A tour of the company's factory, which was established in 1760, culminates in a tasting of its products, all sold here at good prices. It's worth a stop to look at the distillery's charming old buildings even if you're not a rum connoisseur. ⊠ *West Airport Rd., Estate Diamond* ☎ *340/692–2280* ⊕ *www.cruzanrum.com* ✆ *$5* ☺ *Weekdays 9–4.*

☺ **Estate Whim Museum.** The lovingly restored estate, with a windmill, cook
Fodor'sChoice house, and other buildings, gives a sense of what life was like on St.
★ Croix's sugar plantations in the 1800s. The oval-shaped great house has high ceilings and antique furniture and utensils. Notice its fresh, airy atmosphere—the waterless stone moat around the great house was used not for defense but for gathering cooling air. If you have kids, the grounds are the perfect place for them to run around, perhaps while you browse in the museum gift shop. It's just outside of Frederiksted. ⊠ *Rte. 70, Estate Whim* ☎ *340/772–0598* ⊕ *www.stcroixlandmarks. com* ✆ *$10* ☺ *Wed.–Sat. 10–4 and cruise ship days.*

FREDERIKSTED AND ENVIRONS

This town is noted less for its Danish than for its Victorian architecture, which dates from after the slave rebellion and great fire of July 1848.

Caribbean Museum Center for the Arts. Sitting across from the waterfront in a historic building, this small museum hosts an always-changing roster

---

ST. CROIX BEST BETS

■ **Buck Island.** The snorkeling trail here is fun, but go by catamaran.

■ **Christiansted.** The best shopping on the island as well as interesting historical sights are here.

■ **Cruzan Rum Distillery.** This West End rum distillery gives you a tour and samples.

■ **Kayaking.** The Salt River, with few currents, is a great place to take a guided kayak trip.

■ **West End Beaches.** The island's best beaches are on the west end, and are just a short hop from the cruise pier.

of exhibits. Many are cutting-edge multimedia efforts that you might be surprised to find in such an out-of-the way location. The openings are popular events. ⊠ *10 Strand St., Frederiksted* ☎ *340/772–2622* ⊕ *www. cmcarts.org* 🖼 *Free* ⊗ *Tues.–Thurs. and weekends (and any cruise-ship day) 10–4; Fri. 10–7.*

Frederiksted Visitor Center. Head here for brochures from numerous St. Croix businesses, as well as a few exhibits about the island. ⊠ *Pier, Frederiksted* ☎ *340/773–0495* ⊗ *Weekdays 8–5.*

⟳ **Fort Frederik.** On July 3, 1848, 8,000 slaves marched on this fort to demand their freedom. Danish governor Peter von Scholten, fearing they would burn the town to the ground, stood up in his carriage parked in front of the fort and granted their wish. The fort, completed in 1760, houses an art gallery and a number of interesting historical exhibits, including some focusing on the 1848 Emancipation and the 1917 transfer of the Virgin Islands from Denmark to the United States. It's within earshot of the Frederiksted Visitor Center. ⊠ *Waterfront, Frederiksted* ☎ *340/772–2021* 🖼 *$3* ⊗ *Weekdays (and any cruise-ship day) 8:30–4.*

Fodor's Choice ★ **Lawaetz Family Museum.** For a trip back in time, tour this circa-1750 farm, in a valley at La Grange. It's been owned by the prominent Lawaetz family since 1896, which is just after Carl Lawaetz arrived from Denmark. A Lawaetz family member shows you around the lovely two-story house and the farm, noting the four-poster mahogany bed Carl shared with his wife, Marie, the china Marie painted, the family portraits, and the fruit trees that fed the family for several generations. Initially a sugar plantation, the farm was subsequently used to raise cattle and grow produce. ⊠ *Rte. 76, Mahogany Rd., Estate Little La Grange* ☎ *340/772–1539* ⊕ *www.stcroixlandmarks.com* 🖼 *$10* ⊗ *Wed., Thurs., and Sat. 10–4.*

NORTH SHORE

Salt River Bay National Historical Park and Ecological Preserve. This joint national and local park commemorates the area where Christopher Columbus's men skirmished with the Carib Indians in 1493 on his second visit to the New World. The peninsula on the bay's east side is named for the event: Cabo de las Flechas (Cape of the Arrows). Although the park is still developing, it has several sights with cultural significance. A ball court, used by the Caribs in religious ceremonies, was discovered at the spot where the taxis park. Take a short hike up the dirt road to the ruins of an old earthen fort for great views of Salt River Bay. The area also encompasses a coastal estuary with the region's largest remaining mangrove forest, a submarine canyon, and several endangered species, including the hawksbill turtle and the roseate tern. A visitor center, open winter only, sits just uphill to the west. The water at the beach can be on the rough side, but it's a nice place for sunning. ⊠ *Rte. 75 to Rte. 80, Salt River* ☎ *340/773–1460* ⊕ *www.nps.gov/sari* ⊗ *Nov.–June, Tues.–Thurs. 9–4.*

SHOPPING

The selection of duty-free goods on St. Croix is fairly good. The best shopping is in Christiansted, where most stores are in the historic district near the harbor. King Street, Strand Street, and the arcades that lead off them compose the main shopping district and where you'll find **Sonya's,** the jewelry store that first sold the locally popular hook bracelet. The longest arcade is **Caravelle Arcade,** adjacent to the hotel of the same name. In Frederiksted a handful of shops face the cruise-ship pier.

Sonya's. This store is owned and operated by Sonya Hough, who invented the popular hook bracelet. She has added an interesting decoration to these bracelets: the swirling symbol used in weather forecasts to indicate hurricanes. ⊠ *1 Company St., Christiansted* ☎ *340/778–8605* ⊕ *www.sonyaltd.com.*

ACTIVITIES

BOAT TOURS

Many people take a day trip to Buck Island aboard a charter boat. Most leave from the Christiansted waterfront or from Green Cay Marina and stop for a snorkel at the island's eastern end before dropping anchor off a gorgeous sandy beach for a swim, a hike, and lunch. Sailboats can often stop right at the beach; a larger boat might have to anchor a bit farther offshore. A full-day sail runs about $100, with lunch included on most trips. A half-day sail costs about $68.

Big Beard's Adventure Tours. From catamarans that depart from the Christiansted waterfront you'll head to Buck Island for snorkeling before dropping anchor at a private beach for a barbecue lunch. ⊠ *Christiansted* ☎ *340/773–4482* ⊕ *www.bigbeards.com.*

DIVING AND SNORKELING

N2 the Blue. N2 takes divers right off the beach near Coconuts restaurant, on night dives off the Frederiksted Pier, or on boat trips to wrecks and reefs. ⊠ *Frederiksted Pier, Rte. 631, Frederiksted* ☎ *340/772–3483, 877/579–0572* ⊕ *www.n2theblue.com.*

GOLF

★ **Carambola Golf Club.** This spectacular 18-hole course in the northwest valley was designed by Robert Trent Jones Sr. The green fees, $135 for 18 holes, include the use of a golf cart. ⊠ *Remaissance St. Croix Carambola Resort, Rte. 18, Davis Bay* ☎ *340/778–5638* ⊕ *www. golfcarambola.com.*

HORSEBACK RIDING

Paul and Jill's Equestrian Stables. From Sprat Hall, just north of Frederiksted, co-owner Jill Hurd will take you through the rain forest, across the pastures, along the beaches, and through valleys—explaining the flora, fauna, and ruins on the way. A 1½-hour ride costs $90. ⊠ *Rte. 58, Frederiksted* ☎ *340/772–2880, 340/772–2627* ⊕ *www. paulandjills.com.*

KAYAKING

Caribbean Adventure Tours. These kayak tours take you on trips through Salt River Bay National Historical Park and Ecological Preserve, one of the island's most pristine areas. All tours run $45. ⊠ *Salt River Marina, Rte. 80, Salt River* ☎ *340/778–1522* ⊕ *www.stcroixkayak.com.*

BEACHES

West End beaches. There are several unnamed beaches along the coast road north of Frederiksted, but it's best if you don't stray too far from civilization. For safety's sake, most vacationers plop down their towel near one of the casual restaurants spread out along Route 63. The beach at the Rainbow Beach Club, a five-minute drive outside Frederiksted, has a bar, a casual restaurant, water sports, and volleyball. If you want to be close to the cruise-ship pier, just stroll on over to the adjacent sandy beach in front of Ft. Frederik. On the way south out of Frederiksted, the stretch near Sandcastle on the Beach hotel is also lovely. **Amenities:** food and drink; water sports. **Best for:** snorkeling, swimming, walking. ⊠ *Rte. 63, north and south of Frederiksted.*

WHERE TO EAT

$$$
AMERICAN
Fodor'sChoice
★

✕**Blue Moon.** This terrific little bistro, which has a loyal local following, offers a changing menu that draws on Cajun and Caribbean flavors. Try the spicy gumbo with andouille sausage or crab cakes with a spicy aioli for your appetizer. A grilled chicken breast served with spinach and artichoke hearts and topped with Parmesan and cheddar cheeses makes a good entrée. The Almond Joy sundae should be your choice for dessert. There's live jazz on Wednesday and Friday. ⑤ *Average main: $29* ⊠ *7 Strand St., Frederiksted* ☎ *340/772–2222* ⊘ *Closed Mon.*

$$$
ECLECTIC
☾
Fodor'sChoice
★

✕**Rum Runners.** The view is as stellar as the food at this highly popular local standby. Sitting right on the Christiansted boardwalk, Rum Runners serves a little bit of everything, including a to-die-for salad of crispy romaine lettuce and tender grilled lobster drizzled with lemongrass vinaigrette. More hearty fare includes baby-back ribs cooked with the restaurant's special spice blend and Guinness stout. ⑤ *Average main: $23* ⊠ *Hotel Caravelle, 44A Queen Cross St., Christiansted* ☎ *340/773–6585* ⊕ *www.rumrunnersstcroix.com.*

ST. JOHN (CRUZ BAY)

Lynda Lohr

St. John's heart is Virgin Islands National Park, a treasure that takes up a full two-thirds of St. John's 20 square miles (53 square km). The park helps keep the island's interior in its pristine and undisturbed state, but if you go at midday you'll probably have to share your stretch of beach with others, particularly at Trunk Bay. The island is booming, and although it can get a tad crowded at the ever-popular Trunk Bay Beach during the busy winter season, you won't find traffic jams or pollution. It's easy to escape from the fray, however: just head off on a hike. St. John doesn't have a grand agrarian past like her sister island, St. Croix, but if you're hiking in the dry season, you can probably stumble upon

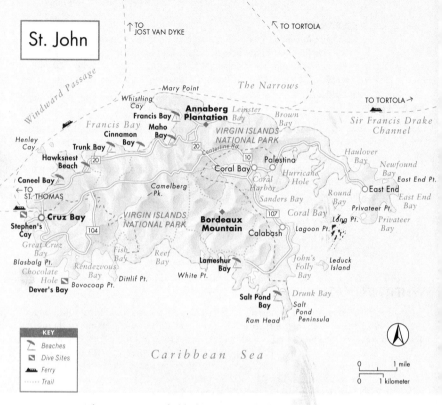

St. John

TO JOST VAN DYKE

TO TORTOLA

Windward Passage

Mary Point

The Narrows

Whistling Cay

Annaberg Leinster
Plantation Bay

Brown Bay

TO TORTOLA →

Francis Bay

Francis Bay

Maho Bay

VIRGIN ISLANDS NATIONAL PARK

Sir Francis Drake Channel

Henley Cay

Cinnamon Bay

Trunk Bay *Bay*

20

Centerline Rd.

10

Palestina

Haulover Bay

Newfound Bay

Hawksnest Beach

20

Coral Bay

Hurricane Hole

East End Pt.

Caneel Bay

Coral Harbor

Round Bay

East End

East End Bay

← TO ST. THOMAS

Camelberg Pk.

Sanders Bay

107

Coral Bay

Long Pt.

Privateer Pt.

Privateer Bay

Cruz Bay

VIRGIN ISLANDS NATIONAL PARK

Bordeaux Mountain

Lagoon Pt.

Stephen's Cay

104

Calabash

John's Folly Bay

Leduck Island

Great Cruz Bay

Fish Bay

Reef Bay

Lameshur Bay

Blasbalg Pt.

Rendezvous Bay

White Pt.

Chocolate Hole

Dittlif Pt.

Dever's Bay

Bovocoap Pt.

Drunk Bay

Salt Pond Bay

Salt Pond Peninsula

Ram Head

Caribbean Sea

0   1 mile
0   1 kilometer

KEY
- Beaches
- Dive Sites
- Ferry
- Trail

the stone ruins of old plantations. The less adventuresome can visit the repaired ruins at the park's Annaberg Plantation and Caneel Bay resort. Of the three U.S. Virgin Islands, St. John, which has 5,000 residents, has the strongest sense of community, which is primarily rooted in a desire to protect the island's natural beauty.

ESSENTIALS

CURRENCY   The U.S. dollar is the official currency of U.S. Virgin Islands; you'll find a few ATMs in Cruz Bay.

TELEPHONE   Both Sprint and AT&T phones work in most of St. John (take care that you're not roaming on the Tortola cell network on the island's north coast, though). It's as easy to call home from St. John as from any city in the United States. On St. John, public phones are near telephone poles midway along the Cruz Bay waterfront.

COMING ASHORE

Although a few smaller ships drop anchor at St. John, most people taking a cruise aboard a larger ship visit St. Thomas's sister island on a shore excursion or on an independent day trip from St. Thomas. If you prefer to not take a tour, ferries leave St. Thomas from the Charlotte

Amalie waterfront and Red Hook. You'll have to take a taxi to reach the ferry dock.

If you're aboard a smaller ship that calls in St. John, your ship may simply pause outside Cruz Bay Harbor to drop you off or drop anchor if it's spending the day. You'll be tendered to shore at the main town of Cruz Bay. The shopping district starts just across the street from the tender landing. You'll find an eclectic collection of shops, cozy restaurants, and places where you can just sit and take it all in. The island has few sights to see. Your best bet is to take a tour of the Virgin Islands National Park. (If your ship doesn't offer such a tour, arrange one with one of the taxi drivers who will meet your tender.) The drive takes you past luscious beaches to a restored sugar plantation. With only a single day in port, you're better off just using the island's shared taxi vans rather than renting a car, but if you want to do some independent exploring, you can rent a car in Cruz Bay.

> ## ST. JOHN BEST BETS
>
> ■ **Hiking in the National Park.** Hiking trails that crisscross the terrain are easy enough for beginners and offer breathtaking scenery.
>
> ■ **Snorkeling Cruises.** The best snorkeling sites are reachable only by boat.
>
> ■ **Trunk Bay Beach.** St. John's national park beach is beautiful and has an underwater snorkeling trail.

4

EXPLORING ST. JOHN

CRUZ BAY

St. John's main town may be compact (it consists of only several blocks), but it's definitely a hub: the ferries from St. Thomas and the British Virgin Islands pull in here, and it's where you can get a taxi or rent a car to travel around the island. There are plenty of shops in which to browse, a number of watering holes where you can stop for a breather, many restaurants, and a grassy square with benches where you can sit back and take everything in. Look for the current edition of the handy, amusing "*Road Map: St. Thomas–St. John*" featuring Max the Mongoose.

V.I. National Park Visitors Center. To pick up a useful guide to St. John's hiking trails, see various large maps of the island, and find out about current Park Service programs, including guided walks and cultural demonstrations, stop by the park visitor center. ⊠ *Near baseball field, Cruz Bay* ☏ *340/776–6201* ⊕ *www.nps.gov/viis* ⊙ *Daily 8–4:30.*

ELSEWHERE ON THE ISLAND

Fodor's Choice
★ **Annaberg Plantation.** In the 18th century, sugar plantations dotted the steep hills of this island. Slaves and free Danes and Dutchmen toiled to harvest the cane that was used to create sugar, molasses, and rum for export. Built in the 1780s, the partially restored plantation at Leinster Bay was once an important sugar mill. Although there are no official visiting hours, the National Park Service has regular tours, and some well-informed taxi drivers will show you around. Occasionally you may see a living-history demonstration—someone making johnnycake or weaving baskets. For information on tours and cultural events, contact

the V.I. National Park Visitors Center. ⊠ *Leinster Bay Rd., Annaberg* ☎ *340/776–6201* ⊕ *www.nps.gov/viis* ✉ *Free* ☉ *Daily dawn–dusk.*

★ **Bordeaux Mountain.** St. John's highest peak rises to 1,277 feet. Route 10 passes near enough to the top to offer breathtaking vistas. Don't stray into the road here—cars whiz by at a good clip along this section. Instead, drive nearly to the end of the dirt road that heads off next to the restaurant and gift shop for spectacular views at Picture Point and the trailhead of the hike downhill to Lameshur. Get a trail map from the park service before you start. ⊠ *Rte. 10, Bordeaux.*

SHOPPING

Luxury goods and handicrafts can be found on St. John. Most shops carry a little of this and a bit of that, so it pays to poke around. The Cruz Bay shopping district runs from **Wharfside Village,** just around the corner from the ferry dock, to **Mongoose Junction,** an inviting shopping center on North Shore Road. (The name of this upscale shopping mall, by the way, is a holdover from a time when those furry island creatures gathered at a nearby garbage bin.) Out on Route 104 stop in at the **Marketplace** to explore its gift and crafts shops. At the island's other end, there are a few stores—selling clothes, jewelry, and artwork—here and there from the village of **Coral Bay** to the small complex at **Shipwreck Landing.**

On St. John, store hours run from 9 or 10 to 5 or 6. Wharfside Village and Mongoose Junction shops in Cruz Bay are often open into the evening.

ACTIVITIES

DIVING AND SNORKELING

Cruz Bay Watersports. The owners of Cruz Bay, Marcus and Patty Johnston, offer regular reef, wreck, and night dives and USVI and BVI snorkel tours. The company holds both PADI Five Star and NAUI-Dream-Resort status. ⊠ *Lumberyard Shopping Complex, Cruz Bay* ☎ *340/776–6234* ⊕ *www.divestjohn.com.*

Low Key Watersports. Low Key Watersports offers two-tank dives and specialty courses. It's certified as a PADI Five Star training facility. ⊠ *1 Bay St., Cruz Bay* ☎ *340/693–8999, 800/835–7718* ⊕ *www.divelowkey.com.*

FISHING

Well-kept charter boats—approved by the U.S. Coast Guard—head out to the north and south drops or troll along the inshore reefs, depending on the season and what's biting. The captains usually provide bait, drinks, and lunch, but you need to bring your own hat and sunscreen. Half-day fishing charters run between about $750 for the boat.

Captain Byron Oliver. Captain Oliver takes you out to the north and south drops. ⊠ *St. John* ☎ *340/693–8339.*

HIKING

Although it's fun to go hiking with a Virgin Islands National Park guide, don't be afraid to head out on your own. To find a hike that suits your ability, stop by the park's visitor center in Cruz Bay and pick up the free trail guide; it details points of interest, trail lengths, and estimated hiking times, as well as any dangers you might encounter. Although the park staff recommends long pants to protect against thorns and insects, most people hike in shorts because it can get very hot. Wear sturdy shoes or hiking boots even if you're hiking to the beach. Don't forget to bring water and insect repellent.

Fodor's Choice ★ **Virgin Islands National Park.** Head to the park for more than 20 trails on the north and south shores, with guided hikes along the most popular routes. A full-day trip to Reef Bay is a must; it's an easy hike through lush and dry forest, past the ruins of an old plantation, and to a sugar factory adjacent to the beach. It can be a bit arduous for young kids, however. The park runs a $30 guided tour to Reef Bay that includes a safari bus ride to the trailhead and a boat ride back to the Visitors Center. The schedule changes from season to season; call for times and to make reservations, which are essential. ⊠ *1300 Cruz Bay Creek, St. John* ☎ *340/776–6201* ⊕ *www.nps.gov/viis.*

BEACHES

Cinnamon Bay Beach. This long, sandy beach faces beautiful cays and abuts the national park campground. You can rent water-sports equipment here—a good thing, because there's excellent snorkeling off the point to the right; look for the big angelfish and large schools of purple triggerfish. Afternoons on Cinnamon Bay can be windy—a boon for windsurfers but an annoyance for sunbathers—so arrive early to beat the gusts. The Cinnamon Bay hiking trail begins across the road from the beach parking lot; ruins mark the trailhead. There are actually two paths here: a level nature trail (signs along it identify the flora) that loops through the woods and passes an old Danish cemetery, and a steep trail that starts where the road bends past the ruins and heads straight up to Route 10. Restrooms are on the main path from the commissary to the beach and scattered around the campground. **Amenities:** food and drink; parking; showers; toilets; water sports. **Best for:** snorkeling; swimming, walking; windsurfing. ⊠ *North Shore Rd., Rte. 20, about 4 miles (6 km) east of Cruz Bay, Cinnamon Bay* ⊕ *www.nps.gov/viis.*

★ **Hawksnest Beach.** Sea grape and waving palm trees line this narrow beach, and there are restrooms, cooking grills, and a covered shed for picnicking. A patchy reef just offshore means snorkeling is an easy swim away, but the best underwater views are reserved for ambitious snorkelers who head farther to the east along the bay's fringes. Watch out for boat traffic—a channel guides dinghies to the beach, but the occasional boater strays into the swim area. It's the closest drivable beach to Cruz Bay, so it's often crowded with locals and visitors. **Amenities:** parking; toilets. **Best for:** snorkeling, swimming. ⊠ *North Shore Rd., Rte. 20, about 2 miles (3 km) east of Cruz Bay, Hawksnest Bay* ⊕ *www.nps.gov/viis.*

Fodor's Choice ★ **Trunk Bay Beach.** St. John's most-photographed beach is also the preferred spot for beginning snorkelers because of its underwater trail. (Cruise-ship passengers interested in snorkeling for a day flock here, so if you're looking for seclusion, arrive early or later in the day.) Crowded or not, this stunning beach is one of the island's most beautiful. There are changing rooms with showers, bathrooms, a snack bar, picnic tables, a gift shop, phones, lockers, and snorkeling-equipment rentals. The parking lot often overflows, but you can park along the road as long as the tires are off the pavement. **Amenities:** food and drink; lifeguards; parking; toilets; water sports. **Best for:** snorkeling; swimming; windsurfing. ⊠ *North Shore Rd., Rte. 20, about 2½ miles (4 km) east of Cruz Bay, Trunk Bay* ⊕ *www.nps.gov/viis* 🖭 *$4.*

WHERE TO EAT

$ ✕ **Deli Grotto.** At this air-conditioned (but no-frills) sandwich shop you
ECLECTIC   place your order at the counter and wait for it to be delivered to your table or for takeout. The portobello panino with savory sautéed onions is a favorite, but the other sandwiches, such as the smoked turkey and artichoke, also get rave reviews. Order a brownie or cookie for dessert. ⑤ *Average main: $9* ⊠ *Mongoose Junction Shopping Center, North Shore Rd., Cruz Bay* ☎ *340/777–3061* ▭ *No credit cards* ☉ *No dinner.*

ST. KITTS (BASSETERRE)

Jordan Simon   Mountainous St. Kitts, the first English settlement in the Leeward Islands, crams some stunning scenery into its 65 square miles (168 square km). Vast, brilliant green fields of sugarcane (the former cash crop, now slowly being replanted) run to the shore. The fertile, lush island has some fascinating natural and historical attractions: a rain forest replete with waterfalls, thick vines, and secret trails; a central mountain range dominated by the 3,792-foot Mt. Liamuiga, whose crater has long been dormant; and Brimstone Hill, known in the 18th century as the Gibraltar of the West Indies. St. Kitts and Nevis, along with Anguilla, achieved self-government as an associated state of Great Britain in 1967. In 1983 St. Kitts and Nevis became an independent nation. English with a strong West Indian lilt is spoken here. People are friendly but shy; always ask before you take photographs. Also, be sure to wear wraps or shorts over beach attire when you're in public places.

ESSENTIALS

CURRENCY   Eastern Caribbean (E.C.) dollar (EC$2.67 to US$1). U.S. dollars are accepted practically everywhere, but you'll usually get change in E.C. currency.

INTERNET   Basseterre usually has an operational Internet café, but it rarely lasts in one location. The tourist office in Pelican Mall will have the latest information.

TELEPHONE   Phone cards, which you can buy in denominations of $5, $10, and $20, are handy for making local phone calls, calling other islands, and accessing U.S. direct lines. To make a local call, dial the seven-digit number. To call St. Kitts from the United States, dial the area code 869, then access code 465, 466, 468, or 469 and the local four-digit number.

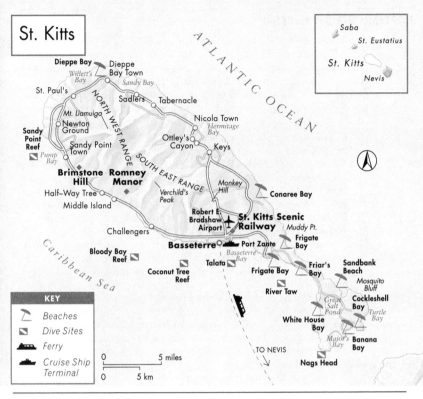

St. Kitts

ATLANTIC OCEAN

Saba

St. Eustatius

St. Kitts

Nevis

Dieppe Bay
Willett's Bay
Dieppe Bay Town
Sandy Bay
St. Paul's
Sadlers
Tabernacle
NORTH WEST RANGE
Mt. Liamuiga
Newton Ground
Nicola Town
Hermitage Bay
Sandy Point Reef
Pump Bay
Sandy Point Town
Ottley's
Cayon
Keys
Brimstone Hill
Romney Manor
SOUTH EAST RANGE
Verchild's Peak
Monkey Hill
Conaree Bay
Half-Way Tree
Middle Island
Robert E. Bradshaw Airport
St. Kitts Scenic Railway
Muddy Pt.
Challengers
Basseterre
Port Zante
Frigate Bay
Bloody Bay Reef
Basseterre Bay
Talata
Frigate Bay
Friar's Bay
Sandbank Beach
Coconut Tree Reef
River Taw
Great Salt Pond
Cockleshell Bay
Mosquito Bluff
Turtle Bay
Caribbean Sea
White House Bay
Major's Bay
Banana Bay
TO NEVIS
Nags Head

KEY
Beaches
Dive Sites
Ferry
Cruise Ship Terminal

0   5 miles
0   5 km

COMING ASHORE

Cruise ships calling at St. Kitts dock at Port Zante, which is a deepwater port directly in Basseterre, the capital of St. Kitts. The cruise-ship terminal is right in the downtown area, two minutes' walk from sights and shops. Taxi rates on St. Kitts are fixed, and should be posted right at the dock. If you'd like to go to Nevis, several daily ferries (30 to 45 minutes, $8–$10 one-way) can take you to Charlestown in Nevis; the Byzantine schedule is subject to change, so double-check times.

Taxi rates on St. Kitts are fairly expensive, and you may have to pay $32 for a ride to Brimstone Hill (for one to four passengers). A four-hour tour of St. Kitts runs about $80. It's often cheaper to arrange an island tour with one of the local companies than to hire a taxi driver to take your group around. Several restored plantation greathouses are known for their lunches; your driver can provide information and arrange drop-off and pickup. Before setting off in a cab, be sure to clarify whether the rate quoted is in E.C. or U.S. dollars.

EXPLORING ST. KITTS

Basseterre. On the south coast, St. Kitts's walkable capital is graced with tall palms and flagstone sidewalks; although many of the buildings appear run-down, there are interesting shops, excellent art galleries, and some beautifully maintained houses. Duty-free shops and boutiques line the streets and courtyards radiating from the octagonal **Circus,** built in the style of London's famous Piccadilly Circus. ⊠ *Basseterre.*

Independence Square. There are lovely gardens on the site of a former slave market at Independence Square. The square is surrounded on three sides by 18th-century Georgian buildings. ⊠ *Off Bank St.*

St. George's Anglican Church. St. George's Anglican Church is a handsome stone building with a crenellated tower originally built by the French in 1670 and called Nôtre-Dame. The British burned it down in 1706 and rebuilt it four years later, naming it after the patron saint of England. Since then it has suffered a fire, an earthquake, and hurricanes and was once again rebuilt in 1869. ⊠ *Cayon St.*

Port Zante. Port Zante is an ambitious, ever-growing 27-acre cruise-ship pier and marina in an area that has been reclaimed from the sea. The domed welcome center is an imposing neoclassical hodgepodge, with columns and stone arches, shops, walkways, fountains, and West Indian–style buildings housing luxury shops, galleries, restaurants, and a small casino. A second pier, 1,434 feet long, has a draft that accommodates even leviathan cruise ships. The selection of shops and restaurants (Tiffany Bar and Deli is a find for fantastic local fare, Twist for global fusion cuisine) is expanding as well. ⊠ *Waterfront, behind Circus.*

National Museum. In the restored former Treasury Building, the National Museum presents an eclectic collection reflecting the history and culture of the island. ⊠ *Bay Rd.* ☏ *869/465–5584* 💳 *EC$1 residents, US$1 nonresidents* ⊗ *Weekdays 9–5, Sat. 9–1.*

★ **Brimstone Hill.** This 38-acre fortress, a UNESCO World Heritage Site, is part of a national park dedicated by Queen Elizabeth in 1985. After routing the French in 1690, the English erected a battery here; by 1736 the fortress held 49 guns, earning it the moniker Gibraltar of the West Indies. In 1782, 8,000 French troops laid siege to the stronghold, which was defended by 350 militia and 600 regular troops of the Royal Scots and East Yorkshires. When the English finally surrendered, they were allowed to march from the fort in full formation out of respect for their bravery (the English afforded the French the same honor when they surrendered the fort a mere year later). A hurricane severely damaged the fortress in 1834, and in 1852 it was evacuated and dismantled. The beautiful stones were carted away to build houses. The citadel has been partially reconstructed and its guns remounted. It's a steep walk up the hill from the parking lot. A seven-minute orientation film recounts the fort's history and restoration. The spectacular view includes Montserrat and Nevis to the southeast; Saba and St. Eustatius to the northwest; and St. Barth and St. Maarten to the north. Nature trails snake through the tangle of surrounding hardwood forest and savanna (a fine spot to catch the green vervet monkeys—inexplicably brought by the French and now outnumbering the residents—skittering about). ✉ *Main Rd., Brimstone Hill* ☎ *869/465-2609* ⊕ *www.brimstonehillfortress.org* ᴤ *$8* ⏱ *Daily 9:30–5:30.*

★ **Romney Manor.** The ruins of this somewhat restored house (reputedly once the property of Thomas Jefferson) and surrounding replicas of chattel-house cottages are set in 6 acres of glorious gardens, with exotic flowers, an old bell tower, and an enormous, gnarled 350-year-old saman tree (sometimes called a rain tree). Inside, at **Caribelle Batik,** you can watch artisans hand-printing fabrics by the 2,500-year-old Indonesian wax-and-dye process known as batik. Look for signs indicating a turnoff for Romney Manor near Old Road. ✉ *Old Road* ☎ *869/465-6253* ⊕ *www.caribellebatikstkitts.com* ᴤ *Free* ⏱ *Daily 9–5.*

ST. KITTS BEST BETS

■ **Brimstone Hill Fortress.** Stop here for some of the best views on St. Kitts and historic ambience.

■ **Nevis.** A trip to Nevis is a worthwhile way to spend the day.

■ **Plantation Greathouses.** Stop for a lunch at Ottley's or Rawlins Plantation.

■ **Rain-forest Hikes.** Several operators on the island lead day-long hikes through the rain forest.

■ **Romney Manor.** This partially restored manor house is enhanced by the chance to shop at Caribelle Batik and watch the elaborate wax-and-dye process.

St. Kitts Scenic Railway. The old narrow-gauge train that had transported sugarcane to the central sugar factory since 1912 is all that remains of the island's once-thriving sugar industry. Two-story cars bedecked in bright Kittitian colors circle the island in just under four hours. Each passenger gets a comfortable, downstairs air-conditioned seat fronting vaulted picture windows and an upstairs open-air observation spot. The conductor's running discourse embraces not only the history of sugar cultivation but also the railway's construction, local folklore, island geography, even other agricultural mainstays from papayas to pigs. You can drink in complimentary tropical beverages (including luscious guava daiquiris) along with the sweeping rain-forest and ocean vistas, accompanied by an a cappella choir's renditions of hymns, spirituals, and predictable standards like "I've Been Workin' on the Railroad." ✉ *Needsmust* ☎ *869/465-7263* ⊕ *www.stkittsscenicrailway.com* ᴤ *$89, children 4–12 $44.50* ⏱ *Departures vary according to cruise-ship schedules (call ahead, but at least once daily Dec.–Apr., usually 8:30 am).*

SHOPPING

St. Kitts has limited shopping, but there are several small duty-free shops with good deals on jewelry, perfume, china, and crystal. Numerous galleries sell excellent paintings and sculptures. The batik fabrics, scarves, caftans, and wall hangings of Caribelle Batik are well known. British expat Kate Spencer is an artist who has lived on the island for years, reproducing its vibrant colors on everything from silk pareus (beach wraps) to note cards to place mats. Other good island buys include crafts, jams, and herbal teas. Don't forget to pick up some CSR (Cane Spirit Rothschild), which is distilled from fresh wild sugarcane right on St. Kitts. The Brinley Gold company has made a splash among spirits connoisseurs for its coffee, mango, coconut, lime, and vanilla rums (there is a tasting room at Port Zante). Most shopping plazas are in downtown Basseterre, on the streets radiating from the Circus.

> ### STORAGE
>
> Take along a hanging shoe organizer for the closet to extend storage space for small items and to keep shoes off the floor. An over-the-door, pocket-style shoe organizer can be hung on the bathroom door. Slip bathroom necessities in the pockets so they are handy and out of the way.

ACTIVITIES

DIVING AND SNORKELING

Though unheralded as a dive destination, St. Kitts has more than a dozen excellent sites, protected by several new marine parks. The surrounding waters feature shoals, hot vents, shallows, canyons, steep walls, and caverns at depths from 40 to nearly 200 feet.

Dive St. Kitts. This PADI–NAUI facility, offers competitive prices, computers to maximize time below, wide range of courses from refresher to technical, and friendly, laid-back dive masters. The Bird Rock location features superb shore diving (unlimited when you book packages): common sightings 20 to 30 feet out include octopuses, nurse sharks, manta and spotted eagle rays, sea horses, even barracudas George and Georgianna. It also offers kayak and snorkeling tours. ⊠ *2 miles (3 km) east of Basseterre, Frigate Bay* ☎ *869/465–1189, 869/465–8914* ⊕ *www. divestkitts.com.*

GOLF

Royal St. Kitts Golf Club. This 18-hole, par-71 links-style championship course underwent a complete redesign by Thomas McBroom to maximize Caribbean and Atlantic views and increase the challenge (there are 12 lakes and 83 bunkers). Holes 15 through 17 (the latter patterned after Pebble Beach No. 18) skirt the Atlantic in their entirety, lending new meaning to the term sand trap. The sudden gusts, wide but twisting fairways, and extremely hilly terrain demand pinpoint accuracy and finesse, yet holes such as 18 require pure power. Green fees are $150 for Marriott guests in high season, $180 for nonguests, with twilight and super-twilight discounts. The development includes practice bunkers, a putting green, a short-game chipping area, and the fairly high-tech Royal Golf Academy. ⊠ *St. Kitts Marriott Resort, Frigate Bay* ☎ *869/466–2700, 866/785–4653* ⊕ *www.royalstkittsgolfclub.com.*

HIKING

Trails in the central mountains vary from easy to don't-try-it-by-yourself. Monkey Hill and Verchild's Peak aren't difficult, although the Verchild's climb will take the better part of a day. Don't attempt Mt. Liamuiga without a guide. You'll start at Belmont Estate—at the west end of the island—on horseback, then proceed on foot to the lip of the crater, at 2,600 feet. You can go down into the crater—1,000 feet deep and 1 mile (1.5 km) wide, with a small freshwater lake—clinging to vines and roots and scaling rocks, even trees. Expect to get muddy. There are several fine operators (each hotel recommends its favorite); tour rates range from $50 for

> **CAUTION**
>
> Pack a small flashlight just in case there's an emergency. You don't want to be stumbling around in the dark.

a rain-forest walk to $95 for a volcano expedition, and usually include round-trip transportation from your hotel and picnic lunch.

★ **Duke of Earl's Adventures.** Owner Earl of Duke is as entertaining as his nickname suggests—and his prices are slightly cheaper ($45 for a rain-forest tour includes refreshments, $70 volcano expeditions add lunch; hotel pickup and drop-off is complimentary). He genuinely loves his island and conveys that enthusiasm, encouraging hikers to swing on vines or sample unusual-looking fruits during his rain-forest trip. He also conducts a thorough volcano tour to the crater's rim and a drive-through ecosafari tour ($50 with lunch). ⊠ *St. Kitts* ☎ *869/465–1899, 869/663–0994.*

Greg's Safaris. Greg Pereira of Greg's Safaris, whose family has lived on St. Kitts since the early 19th century, takes groups on half-day trips into the rain forest and on full-day hikes up the volcano and through the grounds of a private 18th-century greathouse. The rain-forest trips include visits to sacred Carib sites, abandoned sugar mills, and an excursion down a 100-foot coastal canyon containing a wealth of Amerindian petroglyphs. The Off the Beaten Track 4x4 Plantation Tour provides a thorough explanation of the role sugar and rum played in the Caribbean economy and colonial wars. He and his staff relate fascinating historical, folkloric, and botanical information. ⊠ *St. Kitts* ☎ *869/465–4121* ⊕ *www.gregsafaris.com.*

HORSEBACK RIDING

Trinity Stables. Guides from Trinity Stables offer beach rides ($50) and trips into the rain forest ($60), both including hotel pickup. The latter is intriguing, as guides discuss plants' medicinal properties along the way (such as sugarcane to stanch bleeding) and pick oranges right off a tree to squeeze fresh juice. Otherwise, the staffers are cordial but shy; this isn't a place for beginners' instruction. ⊠ *St. Kitts* ☎ *869/465–3226.*

ZIP-LINING

Sky Safari Tours. On these popular tours, would-be Tarzans and Janes whisk through the "Valley of the Giants" (so dubbed for the towering trees) at speeds up to 50 mph (80 kph along five cable lines); the longest (nicknamed "The Boss") stretches 1,350 feet through towering turpentine and mahogany trees draped thickly with bromeliads, suspended 250 feet above the ground. Following the Canadian-based company's mantra of "faster, higher, safer," it uses a specially designed trolley with secure harnesses attached. Many of the routes afford unobstructed views of Brimstone Hill and the sea beyond. Admission is usually $65–$75, depending on the tour chosen. It's open daily 9–6, with the first and last tours departing at 10 and 3. ⊠ *Wingfield Estate* ☎ *869/466–4259, 869/465–4347* ⊕ *www.skysafaristkitts.com.*

BEACHES

The powdery white-sand beaches of St. Kitts, free and open to the public (even those occupied by hotels), are in the Frigate Bay area or on the lower peninsula. Chair rentals cost around $3, though if you order lunch you can negotiate a freebie. Caution: the Atlantic waters are rougher than those on the Caribbean side of the island.

Banana/Cockleshell Bays. These twin connected eyebrows of glittering champagne-color sand—stretching nearly 2 miles (3 km) total at the southeastern tip of the island—feature majestic views of Nevis and are backed by lush vegetation and coconut palms. The first-rate restaurant–bar Spice Mill (next to Rasta-hue Lion Rock Beach Bar—order the knockout Lion Punch) and Reggae Beach Bar & Grill bracket either end of Cockleshell. As of this writing, plans for a 125-room mixed-use Park Hyatt (with additional residential condos and villas), originally slated for development by late 2013, are on hold. The water is generally placid, ideal for swimming. The downside is irregular maintenance, with seaweed (particularly after rough weather) and occasional litter, especially on Banana Bay. Follow Simmonds Highway to the end and bear right, ignoring the turnoff for Turtle Beach. ⊠ *Banana Bay.*

Friar's Bay. Locals consider Friar's Bay, on the Caribbean (southern) side, the island's finest beach. It's a long, tawny scimitar where the water always seems warmer and clearer. Unfortunately, the shelved Marine World development has co-opted nearly half the strand. Still, several happening bars, including Shipwreck, Mongoose, and Sunset Grill, serve terrific, inexpensive local food and cheap, frosty drinks. Chair rentals cost around $3, though if you order lunch, you can negotiate a freebie. Friar's is the first major beach along Southeast Peninsula Drive (aka Simmonds Highway), approximately a mile (1½ km) southeast of Frigate Bay. ⊠ *Friar's Bay.*

Frigate Bay. The Caribbean side offers talcum-powder-fine beige sand framed by coconut palms and sea grapes, and the Atlantic side (a 15-minute stroll)—sometimes called North Frigate Bay—is a favorite with horseback riders. South Frigate Bay is bookended by Sunset Café and the popular, pulsating Buddies Beach Hut. In between are several other lively beach spots, including Cathy's (fabulous jerk ribs), the Monkey Bar, Elvis Love Shack, and Mr. X Shiggidy Shack. Most charge $3 to $5 to rent a chair, though they'll often waive the fee if you ask politely and buy lunch. Locals barhop late into Friday and Saturday nights. Waters are generally calm for swimming; the rockier eastern end offers fine snorkeling. The incomparably scenic Atlantic side is—regrettably—dominated by the Marriott (plentiful dining options), attracting occasional pesky vendors. The surf is choppier and the undertow stronger here. On cruise-ship days, groups stampede both sides. Frigate Bay is easy to find, just less than 3 miles (5 km) from downtown Basseterre. ⊠ *Frigate Bay.*

WHERE TO EAT

$$ ✕ **Reggae Beach Bar & Grill.** Treats at this popular daytime watering hole
ECLECTIC include honey-mustard ribs, coconut shrimp, grilled lobster, decadent
banana bread pudding with rum sauce, and an array of tempting tropi-
cal libations. Business cards and pennants from around the world plas-
ter the bar, and the open-air space is decorated with a variety of nautical
accoutrements, from fishnets and turtle shells to painted wooden crus-
taceans. You can snorkel here, spot hawksbill turtles and the occasional
monkey, visit the enormous house pig Wilbur (who once "ate" beer cans
whole, then moved to "lite" beers—but feeding is no longer encour-
aged), laze in a palm-shaded hammock, or rent a kayak, Hobie Cat or
snorkeling gear. Beach chairs are free. Locals come Sunday afternoons
for dancing to live bands. $ *Average main: US$21* ✉ *S.E. Peninsula
Rd., Cockleshell Beach* ☎ *869/762–5050* ⊕ *www.reggaebeachbar.com*
⊗ *No dinner.*

ST. LUCIA (CASTRIES)

Jane E. Zarem   Magnificent St. Lucia—with its towering mountains, dense rain forest,
fertile green valleys, and acres of banana plantations—lies in the mid-
dle of the Windward Islands. Nicknamed "Helen of the West Indies"
because of its natural beauty, St. Lucia is distinguished from its neigh-
bors by its unusual geological landmarks, the Pitons—the twin peaks
on the southwest coast that soar nearly ½ mile (1 km) above the ocean
floor. Named a World Heritage Site by UNESCO in 2004, the Pitons are
the symbol of this island. Nearby, in the former French colonial capital
of Soufrière, are a "drive-in" volcano, its neighboring sulfur springs that
have rejuvenated bathers for nearly three centuries, and one of the most
beautiful botanical gardens in the Caribbean. A century and a half of
battles between the French and English resulted in St. Lucia's changing
hands 14 times before 1814, when England established possession. In
1979 the island became an independent state within the British Com-
monwealth of Nations. The official language is English, although most
people also speak a French Creole patois.

ESSENTIALS

CURRENCY   Eastern Caribbean (E.C.) dollar (EC$2.67 to US$1). U.S. dollars (but
not coins) are generally accepted, but change is given in E.C. currency.

INTERNET   Internet cafés can be found in Castries, Soufrière, and Rodney Bay.

TELEPHONE   You can make direct-dial overseas and inter-island calls from St. Lucia,
and the connections are excellent. You can charge an overseas call to
a major credit card with no surcharge by dialing 811. Phone cards can
be purchased at many retail outlets.

COMING ASHORE

Most cruise ships dock at the capital city of Castries, on the island's
northwest coast, at either of two docking areas: Pointe Seraphine, a port
of entry and duty-free shopping complex, or Port Castries (Place Care-
nage), a commercial wharf across the harbor. Ferry service connects the

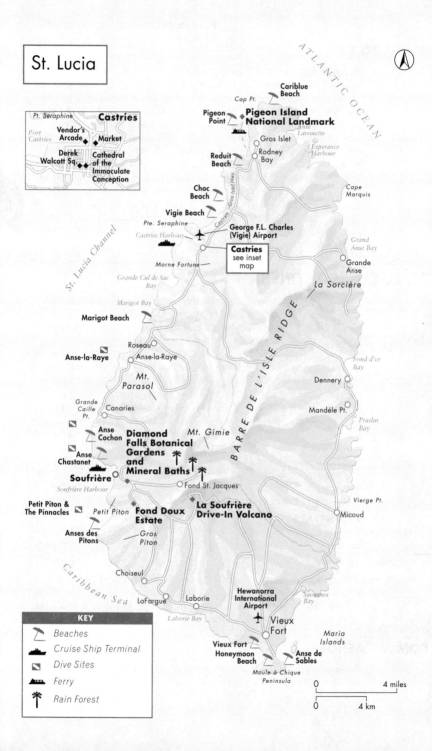

St. Lucia

Castries

Pt. Seraphine
Port Castries
Vendor's Arcade ◆
Derek Walcott Sq. ◆
◆ **Market**
◆ **Cathedral of the Immaculate Conception**

ATLANTIC OCEAN

Cap Pt.
Cariblue Beach
Pigeon Point
Pigeon Island National Landmark
Anse Lavouette
Gros Islet
Reduit Beach
Rodney Bay
Esperance Harbour
Cape Marquis

Choc Beach

Vigie Beach
Pte. Seraphine
Castries Harbour
George F.L. Charles (Vigie) Airport
Castries see inset map
Morne Fortune
Grand Anse Bay
Grande Anse

La Sorcière

St. Lucia Channel

Grande Cul de Sac Bay

Marigot Bay
Marigot Beach

Anse-la-Raye
Roseau
Anse-la-Raye

Fond d'or Bay

Mt. Parasol
Dennery

Grande Caille Pt.
Canaries

BARRE DE L'ISLE RIDGE

Mandéle Pt.
Praslin Bay

Anse Cochon
Diamond Falls Botanical Gardens and Mineral Baths
Mt. Gimie
Anse Chastanet
Soufrière
Soufrière Harbour
Fond St. Jacques

Vierge Pt.

Petit Piton & The Pinnacles
Petit Piton
Fond Doux Estate
La Soufrière Drive-In Volcano
Micoud

Anses des Pitons
Gros Piton

Choiseul

Caribbean Sea

LaFargue
Laborie
Hewanorra International Airport
Laborie Bay
Vieux Fort
Savannes Bay
Maria Islands

Vieux Fort Honeymoon Beach
Anse de Sables
Moule à Chique Peninsula

KEY	
⚓	Beaches
⛴	Cruise Ship Terminal
◹	Dive Sites
⛴	Ferry
✳	Rain Forest

0 — 4 miles
0 — 4 km

two piers. Smaller vessels occasionally call at Soufrière, on the island's southwest coast. Ships calling at Soufrière must anchor offshore and bring passengers ashore via tender. Tourist information booths are at Pointe Seraphine, at Place Carenage, and along the waterfront on Bay Street in Soufrière. Downtown Castries is within walking distance of the pier, and the produce market and adjacent crafts and vendors' markets are the main attractions. Soufrière is a sleepy West Indian town, but it's worth a short walk around the central square to view the French colonial architecture; many of the island's interesting natural sights are in or near Soufrière.

Taxis are available at the docks in Castries. Although they are unmetered, the standard fares are posted at the entrance to Pointe Seraphine. Taxi drivers are well informed and can give you a full tour—often an excellent one—thanks to government-sponsored training programs. From the Castries area, full-day island tours for up to four people cost $40 to $75 per person, depending on the route and whether entrance fees and lunch are included; sightseeing trips to Soufrière cost around $175. If you plan your own day, expect to pay the driver at least $40 per hour plus a 10% tip. Whatever your destination, negotiate the price with the driver before you depart—and be sure that you both understand whether the rate is quoted in EC or U.S. dollars.

ST. LUCIA BEST BETS

■ **The Pitons.** You must see the Pitons, St. Lucia's unique twin peaks.

■ **The Rain Forest.** St. Lucia's lush rain forest is striking.

■ **Diamond Botanical Garden.** Stroll through this tropical paradise to Diamond Waterfall.

■ **Reduit Beach.** St. Lucia's nicest white-sand beach is north of Castries.

■ **Pigeon Island.** This national park is both a historic site and a natural playground.

EXPLORING ST. LUCIA

CASTRIES AND THE NORTH

Castries. The capital, a busy commercial city of about 65,000 people, wraps around a sheltered bay. Morne Fortune rises sharply to the south of town, creating a dramatic green backdrop. The charm of Castries lies in its liveliness rather than its architecture, since four fires that occurred between 1796 and 1948 destroyed most of the colonial buildings. Freighters (exporting bananas, coconut, cocoa, mace, nutmeg, and citrus fruits) and cruise ships come and go frequently, making Castries Harbour one of the Caribbean's busiest ports. **Pointe Seraphine** is a duty-free shopping complex on the north side of the harbor, about a 20-minute walk or two-minute cab ride from the city center; a launch ferries passengers across the harbor when cruise ships are in port. Pointe Seraphine's attractive Spanish-style architecture houses more than 20 upscale duty-free shops, a tourist information kiosk, a taxi stand, and car-rental agencies. **La Place Carenage,** on the south side of the harbor near the pier and markets, is another duty-free shopping complex with a dozen or more shops and a café. **Derek Walcott Square** (formerly Columbus Square), a green oasis bordered by Brazil, Laborie, Micoud, and Bourbon streets, was renamed to honor the hometown poet who won the 1992 Nobel Prize in Literature—one of two Nobel laureates from St. Lucia (the late Sir W. Arthur Lewis won the 1979 Nobel in economic science). Some of the few 19th-century buildings that survived fire, wind, and rain can be seen on Brazil Street, the square's southern border. On the Laborie Street side, there's a huge, 400-year-old samaan (monkeypod) tree with leafy branches that shade a good portion of the square. Directly across Laborie Street from Derek Walcott Square is the Roman Catholic **Cathedral of the Immaculate Conception,** which was built in 1897. Though it's rather somber on the outside, its interior walls are decorated with colorful murals reworked in 1985, just before Pope John Paul II's visit, by St. Lucian artist Dunstan St. Omer. This church has an active parish and is open daily for both public viewing and religious services.

⟳ **Pigeon Island National Landmark.** Jutting out from the northwest coast,
★ Pigeon Island is connected to the mainland by a causeway. Tales are told of the pirate Jambe de Bois (Wooden Leg), who once hid out on this 44-acre hilltop islet—a strategic point during the French and British struggles for control of St. Lucia. Now it's a national park and a venue for concerts, festivals, and family gatherings. There are two small beaches with calm waters for swimming and snorkeling, a restaurant, and picnic areas. Scattered around the grounds are ruins of barracks, batteries, and garrisons that date from 18th-century French and English battles. In the Museum and Interpretative Centre, housed in the restored British officers' mess, a multimedia display explains the island's ecological and historical significance. Pigeon Island National Landmark is administered by the St. Lucia National Trust. ✉ *Pigeon Island, Rodney Bay* ☎ *758/452–5005* ⊕ *www.slunatrust.org* ✉ *$5* ⊗ *Daily 9–5.*

Rodney Bay. This natural bay and an 80-acre man-made lagoon is now surrounded by a huge complex of hotels, popular restaurants, a big mall, and the island's only casino. It's named for Admiral George Rodney, who sailed the British Navy out of Gros Islet Bay in 1780 to attack and ultimately destroy the French fleet. With 232 slips, Rodney Bay Marina is one of the Caribbean's premier yachting centers and the destination of the Atlantic Rally for Cruisers (a transatlantic yacht crossing) each December. Yacht charters and sightseeing day trips can be arranged at the marina. Rodney Bay is about 15 minutes north of Castries; the Rodney Bay Ferry makes hourly crossings between the marina and the mall, as well as daily excursions to Pigeon Island. ✉ *Rodney Bay.*

SOUFRIERE AND THE SOUTH

Fodor's Choice **Diamond Falls Botanical Gardens and Mineral Baths.** These splendid gardens
★ are part of Soufrière Estate, a 2,000-acre land grant presented by King Louis XIV in 1713 to three Devaux brothers from Normandy in recognition of their services to France. The estate is still owned by their descendants; Joan DuBouley Devaux maintains the gardens. Water bubbling to the surface from underground sulfur springs streams downhill in rivulets to become Diamond Waterfall, deep within the botanical

gardens. Near the falls, mineral baths are fed by the underground springs. King Louis XVI of France provided funds in 1784 for the construction of a building with a dozen large stone baths to fortify his troops against the St. Lucian climate. It's claimed that Joséphine Bonaparte bathed here as a young girl while visiting her father's plantation nearby. During the Brigand's War, just after the French Revolution, the bathhouse was destroyed. In 1930 André DuBoulay had the site excavated, and two of the original stone baths were restored for his use. Outside baths were added later. For a small fee, you can slip into your swimsuit and soak for 30 minutes in one of the outside pools; a private bath costs slightly more. ⊠ *Soufrière Estate, Diamond Rd., Soufrière* ☎ *758/459–7155* ⊕ *www.diamondstlucia.com* ✉ *$5, public bath $4, private bath $6* ☉ *Mon.–Sat. 10–5, Sun. 10–3.*

☾ **Fond Doux Estate.** One of the earliest French estates established by land
★ grants (1745 and 1763), this plantation still produces cocoa, citrus, bananas, coconut, and vegetables on 135 hilly acres; the restored 1864 plantation house is still in use, as well. A 30-minute walking tour begins at the cocoa fermentary, where you can see the drying process under way. You then follow a trail through the lush cultivated area, where a guide points out various fruit- or spice-bearing trees and tropical flowers. Additional trails lead to old military ruins, a religious shrine, and another vantage point for viewing the spectacular Pitons. Cool drinks and a Creole buffet lunch are served at the Jardin Cacao restaurant. Souvenirs, including just-made chocolate sticks, are sold at the boutique. ⊠ *Chateaubelair, Soufrière* ☎ *758/459–7545* ⊕ *www. fonddouxestate.com* ✉ *$10; $25 includes buffet lunch* ☉ *Daily 8–4.*

☾ **La Soufrière Drive-In Volcano.** As you approach, your nose will pick up the strong scent of the sulfur springs—more than 20 belching pools of muddy water, multicolor sulfur deposits, and other assorted minerals baking and steaming on the surface. Despite the name, you don't actually drive all the way in—you drive up within a few hundred feet of the gurgling, steaming mass and then walk behind your guide—whose service is included in the admission price—around a fault in the substratum rock. It's a fascinating, educational half hour, though it can also be pretty stinky on a hot day. ⊠ *Soufrière* ☎ *758/459–5500* ✉ *$2* ☉ *Daily 9–5.*

Fodor'sChoice **The Pitons.** Rising precipitously from the cobalt-blue Caribbean Sea just
★ south of Soufrière Bay, these two unusual mountains are a symbol of St. Lucia and also a UNESCO World Heritage Site. Covered with thick tropical vegetation, the massive outcroppings were formed by lava from a volcanic eruption 30 to 40 million years ago. They are not identical twins since—confusingly—2,619-foot Petit Piton is taller than 2,461-foot Gros Piton, though Gros Piton is, as the word translates, broader. It's possible to climb the Pitons, but it's a strenuous trip. Gros Piton is the easier climb, though the trail up even this shorter Piton is still very tough. Either climb requires the permission of the Forest & Lands Department and the use of a knowledgeable guide. ⊠ *Soufrière* ☎ *758/450–2231, 758/450–2078 for St. Lucia Forest & Lands Department* ✉ *Guide services $45* ☉ *Daily by appointment only.*

Soufrière. The oldest town in St. Lucia and the former French colonial capital, Soufrière was founded by the French in 1746 and named for its proximity to the volcano of the same name. The wharf is the center of activity in this sleepy town (which currently has a population of about 9,000), particularly when a cruise ship anchors in pretty Soufrière Bay. French colonial influences are evident in the second-story verandas, gingerbread trim, and other appointments of the wooden buildings that surround the market square. The market building itself is decorated with colorful murals. ⊠ *Soufrière.*

Soufrière Tourist Information Centre. Head here for information about area attractions. Note that souvenir vendors station themselves outside some of the popular attractions in and around Soufrière, and they can be persistent. Be polite but firm if you're not interested. ⊠ *Bay St., Soufrière* ☎ *758/459–7200.*

SHOPPING

The island's best-known products are artwork and woodcarvings; clothing and household articles made from batik and silk-screen fabrics, designed and printed in island workshops; and clay pottery. You can also take home straw hats and baskets and locally grown cocoa, coffee, and spices. Duty-free shopping is at **Pointe Seraphine** or **La Place Carenage**, on opposite sides of the harbor. You must show your passport and cabin key card to get duty-free prices. You'll want to experience the **Castries Market** and scour the adjacent **Vendor's Arcade** and **Craft Market** for handicrafts and souvenirs at bargain prices.

ACTIVITIES

DIVING AND SNORKELING

Fodor'sChoice ★ The coral reefs at Anse Cochon and Anse Chastanet, on the southwest coast, are popular beach-entry dive sites. In the north, Pigeon Island is the most convenient site.

Dive Fair Helen. This PADI center offers half- and full-day excursions to wreck, wall, and marine reserve areas, as well as night dives. ⊠ *Marigot Bay Marina, Marigot Bay* ☎ *758/451–7716, 888/855–2206 in U.S. and Canada* ⊕ *www.divefairhelen.com.*

Scuba St. Lucia. Daily beach and boat dives and resort and certification courses are available from this PADI Five Star facility, and so is underwater photography and snorkeling equipment. Day trips from the north of the island include round-trip speedboat transportation. ⊠ *Anse Chastanet Resort, Anse Chastanet Rd., Soufrière* ☎ *758/459–7755, 888/465–8242 in the U.S.* ⊕ *www.scubastlucia.com.*

FISHING

Sportfishing is generally done on a catch-and-release basis. Neither spearfishing nor collecting live fish in coastal waters is permitted. Half- and full-day deep-sea fishing excursions can be arranged at either Vigie Marina or Rodney Bay Marina. A half day of fishing on a scheduled trip runs about $85 per person to join a scheduled party for a half day or $500 to $1,000 for a private charter for up to six or eight people, depending on the size of the boat and the length of time. Beginners are welcome.

Captain Mike's. The captain's fleet of Bertram powerboats (31 to 38 feet) accommodate as many as eight passengers for half-day or full-day sport-fishing charters; tackle and cold drinks are supplied. ⊠ *Vigie Marina, Castries* ☎ *758/452–7044* ⊕ *www.captmikes.com.*

HORSEBACK RIDING

Creole horses, a breed indigenous to South America and popular on the island, are fairly small, fast, sturdy, and even-tempered animals suitable for beginners. Established stables can accommodate all skill levels and offer countryside trail rides, beach rides with picnic lunches, plantation tours, carriage rides, and lengthy treks. Prices run about $60 for one hour, $70 for two hours, and $85 for a three-hour beach ride and barbecue.

International Pony Club. The beach-picnic ride from the International Pony Club includes time for a swim—with or without your horse. Both English- and Western-style riding are available. ⊠ *Beauséjour Estate, Gros Islet* ☎ *758/452–8139, 758/450–8665.*

Trim's National Riding Stable. At the island's oldest riding stable, there are four sessions per day, plus beach tours, trail rides, and carriage tours to Pigeon Island. ⊠ *Cas-en-Bas, Gros Islet* ☎ *758/450–8273.*

> **BAG IT**
>
> A mesh laundry bag or a "pop-up" mesh clothes hamper are two fairly light items that pack flat in your suitcase. The bag can hang from the closet, but either will keep your closet neat, allow damp clothing to dry out, and help you tote dirty clothes to the self-service laundry room so you can avoid high cleaning charges.

BEACHES

All of St. Lucia's beaches are open to the public, but beaches in the north are particularly accessible to cruise-ship passengers.

Pigeon Point. At this small beach within the Pigeon Island National Landmark, on the northwestern tip of St. Lucia, there's a restaurant serving snacks and drinks; it's also a perfect spot for picnicking. **Amenities:** food and drink; toilets. **Best for:** snorkeling; swimming. ⊠ *Pigeon Island, Gros Islet* ⊠ *$5 park admission.*

Fodor'sChoice
★
Reduit Beach. The long stretch of golden sand that frames Rodney Bay is within walking distance of many hotels and restaurants in Rodney Bay Village. The Rex St. Lucian hotel, which faces the beach, has a water-sports center, where you can rent sports equipment and beach chairs and take windsurfing or waterskiing lessons. Many feel that Reduit (pronounced red-wee) is the island's finest beach. **Amenities:** food and drink; toilets; water sports. **Best for:** snorkeling; swimming; walking; windsurfing. ⊠ *Rodney Bay.*

Vigie Beach (*Malabar Beach*). This 2-mile (3-km) strand runs parallel to the George F.L. Charles Airport runway in Castries and continues on past the Rendezvous resort, where it becomes Malabar Beach. **Amenities:** none. **Best for:** swimming. ⊠ *Adjacent to Vigie airport, Castries.*

WHERE TO EAT

$$$
CARIBBEAN
Fodor's Choice
★

✕ **Dasheene Restaurant and Bar.** The terrace restaurant at Ladera resort has breathtakingly close-up views of the Pitons and the sea between them, especially beautiful at sunset. The ambience is casual by day and magical at night. Executive chef Orlando Satchell describes his creative West Indian menu as "sexy Caribbean." Appetizers may include grilled crab claws with a choice of dips or silky pumpkin soup with ginger. Typical entrées are "fisherman's catch" with a choice of flavored butters or sauces, shrimp Dasheene (panfried with local herbs), grilled rack of lamb with coconut risotto and curry sauce, or pan-seared fillet of beef marinated in lime-and-pepper seasoning. Light dishes, pasta dishes, and fresh salads are also served at lunch—along with the view. Ⓢ *Average main: US$30* ✉ *Ladera, 2 miles (3 km) south of Soufrière, Soufrière* ☎ *758/459–7323* ⊕ *www.ladera.com.*

$$$
SEAFOOD

✕ **Jacques Waterfront Dining.** Chef–owner Jacky Rioux creates magical dishes in his waterfront restaurant overlooking Rodney Bay Marina. (A mainstay of the Vigie Cove scene for many years, the restaurant relocated in fall 2011 after a devastating fire.) The cooking style is decidedly French, as is Rioux, but fresh produce and local spices create a fusion cuisine that's memorable at either lunch or dinner. You might start with a bowl of creamy tomato-basil or pumpkin soup, a grilled portobello mushroom, or octopus and conch in curried coconut sauce. Main courses include fresh seafood, such as oven-baked kingfish with a white wine–and–sweet pepper sauce, or breast of chicken stuffed with smoked salmon in a citrus-butter sauce. The wine list is also impressive. Ⓢ *Average main: US$28* ✉ *Reduit Beach Ave., Rodney Bay, Gros Islet* ☎ *758/458–1900* ⊕ *www.jacquesrestaurant.com* ⚓ *Reservations essential* ⊘ *Closed Sun.*

ST. MAARTEN (PHILIPSBURG)

Elise Meyer

St. Martin/St. Maarten: one tiny island, just 37 square miles (96 square km), with two different accents and ruled by two sovereign nations. Here French and Dutch have lived side by side for hundreds of years, and when you cross from one country to the next there are no border patrols, no customs agents. In fact, the only indication that you have crossed a border at all is a small sign and a change in road surface. St. Martin/St. Maarten epitomizes tourist islands in the sun, where services are well developed but there's still some Caribbean flavor. The Dutch side is ideal for people who like plenty to do. The French side has a more genteel ambience, more fashionable shopping, and a Continental flair. The combination makes an almost ideal port. On the negative side, the island has been completely developed. It can be fun to shop, and you'll find an occasional bargain, but many goods are cheaper in the United States.

ESSENTIALS

CURRENCY

At this writing on the Dutch side, the NAf guilder. On the French side, the currency is the euro. U.S. currency is accepted almost everywhere on the island, and ATMs are plentiful, but you will occasionally find a

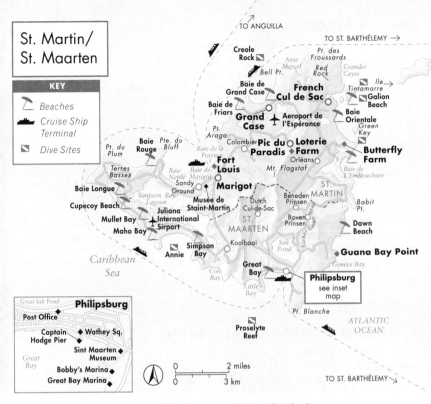

St. Martin/
St. Maarten

KEY

⌐ Beaches
⛴ Cruise Ship
   Terminal
◼ Dive Sites

TO ANGUILLA

TO ST. BARTHÉLEMY →

Creole Rock ◼
Bell Pt. ◼
Anse Marcel
Pt. des Froussards
Red Rock
Grandes Cayes
Ile Tintamarre
Galion Beach
Baie de Grand Case
French Cul de Sac
Baie de Friars
Pt. Arago
Grand Case
Aeroport de l'Espérance
Baie Orientale
Green Key
Colombier
Pic du Paradis
Loterie Farm
Butterfly Farm
Pt. du Plum
Baie Rouge
Pte. du Bluff
Baie de la Potence
Fort Louis
Orléans
Mt. Flagstaf
Baie de L'Embouchure
Terres Basses
Baie Nettlé
Baie de Marigot
Sandy Ground
Marigot
Beneden Prinsen
ST. MARTIN
Babit Pt.
Baie Longue
Simpson Bay Lagoon
Musée de Staint-Martin
Dutch Cul-de-Sac
Boven Prinsen
Cupecoy Beach
Juliana International Sirport
ST. MAARTEN
Dawn Beach
Mullet Bay
Maho Bay
Annie
Simpson Bay
Koolbaai
Salt Pond
Suckes Gut Road
Caribbean Sea
Cole Bay
Great Bay
Guana Bay Point
Geneve Bay
Philipsburg see inset map
Little Bay
Pt. Blanche
ATLANTIC OCEAN
Proselyte Reef ◼
TO ST. BARTHÉLEMY ↘

Great Salt Pond
Philipsburg
Post Office ◆
Captain Hodge Pier
◆ Wathey Sq.
Great Bay
Sint Maarten Museum ◆
Bobby's Marina ◆
Great Bay Marina ◆

0   2 miles
0   3 km

restaurant or small business on the French side that accepts euros on a 1 to 1 basis. The currency on the Dutch side is expected to be changed to the Caribbean guilder in 2012.

INTERNET   There is Wi-Fi service on the boardwalk behind Front Street if you have your own laptop.

TELEPHONE   To phone from the Dutch side to the French, you first must dial 00–590–590 for local numbers, or 00–590–690 for cell phones, then the six-digit local number. To call from the French side to the Dutch, dial 00–599 then the seven-digit local number. Remember that a call from one side to the other is an international call.

At the Landsradio in Philipsburg there are facilities for overseas calls and a USADirect phone, where you're directly in touch with an operator who will accept collect or credit-card calls. To call direct with an AT&T credit card or operator, dial 001–800/872–2881. On the French side, AT&T can be accessed by calling 080–099–00–11. If you need to use public phones, go to the special desk at Marigot's post office and buy a télécarte. There's a public phone at the tourist office in Marigot where you can make credit-card calls: the operator takes your card number (any major card) and assigns you a PIN, which you then use to charge calls to your card.

COMING ASHORE

Most cruise ships drop anchor off the Dutch capital of Philipsburg or dock in the marina at the southern tip of the Philipsburg harbor; a very few small or medium-size ships drop anchor in Marigot Bay and tender passengers ashore in the French capital. If your ship anchors, tenders will ferry you to the town pier in the middle of town, where taxis await passengers. If your ship docks at the marina, downtown is a 15-minute taxi ride away. The walk is not recommended. The island is small, and most spots aren't more than a 30-minute drive from Marigot or Philipsburg.

Doing your own thing will be much less expensive here than a ship-sponsored tour, and since rental cars are cheap (starting at $30 per day for a local car rental), you can easily strike out as soon as your ship docks. This is the best thing to do if you just want to see the island and spend a little time at a beach. Taxis are government-regulated and fairly costly, so they aren't really an option if you want to do much exploring. Authorized taxis display stickers of the St. Maarten Taxi Association. Taxis are also available at Marigot. You may be able to negotiate a favorable deal with a taxi driver for a two- to three-hour island tour for as little as $70 for two passengers or $30 per person for more than two.

EXPLORING ST. MAARTEN/ST-MARTIN

Butterfly Farm. If you arrive early in the morning when the butterflies first break out of their chrysalis, you'll be able to marvel at the absolute wonder of dozens of butterflies and moths from around the world and the particular host plants with which each evolved. At any given time, some 40 species of butterflies—numbering as many as 600 individual insects—flutter inside the lush screened garden and hatch on the plants housed there. Butterfly art and knickknacks are for sale in the gift shop. In case you want to come back, your ticket, which includes a guided tour, is good for your entire stay. ⊠ *Le Galion Beach Rd., Quartier d'Orléans* ☎ *590/87–31–21* ⊕ *www.thebutterflyfarm.com* ⊡ *$12* ⊘ *Daily 9–3:30.*

Fodor'sChoice ★

Fort Louis. Though not much remains of the structure itself, Fort Louis, which was completed by the French in 1789, is great fun if you want to climb the 92 steps to the top for the wonderful views of the island and neighboring Anguilla. On Wednesday and Saturday there is a market in the square at the bottom. ⊠ *Marigot.*

French Cul de Sac. North of Orient Bay Beach, the French colonial mansion of St. Martin's mayor is nestled in the hills. Little, red-roof houses look like open umbrellas tumbling down the green hillside. The area is peaceful and good for hiking. From the beach here, shuttle boats make the five-minute trip to **Ilet Pinel,** an uninhabited island that's fine for picnicking, sunning, and swimming. There are full-service beach clubs there, so just pack the sunscreen and head over. ⊠ *St. Martin.*

Grand Case. The Caribbean's own Restaurant Row is the heart of this French side town, a 10-minute drive from either Orient Bay or

Marigot, stretching along a narrow beach overlooking Anguilla. You'll find a first-rate restaurant for every palate, mood, and wallet. At lunchtime, or with kids, head to the casual lolos (open-air barbecue stands) and feet-in-the-sand beach bars. Twilight drinks and tapas are fun. At night, stroll the strip and

> **CAUTION**
>
> Liquid hand sanitizer is a must-have for adventure excursions or where water might be at a premium. Bring a small bottle you can carry along with you.

preview the sophisticated offerings on the menus posted outside before you settle in for a long and sumptuous meal. If you still have the energy, there are lounges with music (usually a DJ) that get going after 11 pm.

Marigot. It is great fun to spend a few hours exploring the bustling harbor, shopping stalls, open-air cafés, and boutiques of St. Martin's biggest town, especially on Wednesday and Saturday, when the daily open-air craft markets expand to include fresh fruits and veggies, spices, and all manner of seafood. The market might remind you of Provence, especially when aromas of delicious cooking waft by. Be sure to climb up to the fort for the panoramic view, stopping at the museum for an overview of the island. Marina Port La Royale is the shopping–lunch-spot central to the port, but rue de la République and rue de la Liberté, which border the bay, have duty-free shops, boutiques, and bistros. The West Indies Mall offers a deluxe (and air-conditioned) shopping experience, with such shops as Lacoste. There's less bustle here than in Philipsburg, but the open-air cafés are still tempting places to sit and people-watch. Marigot is fun into the night, so you might wish to linger through dinnertime. From the harborfront you can catch ferries for Anguilla and St. Barth. Parking can be a real challenge during the business day, and even at night during the high season.

Philipsburg. The capital of Dutch St. Maarten stretches about a mile (1½ km) along an isthmus between Great Bay and the Salt Pond and has five parallel streets. Most of the village's dozens of shops and restaurants are on Front Street, narrow and cobblestone, closest to Great Bay. It's generally congested when cruise ships are in port, because of its many duty-free shops and several casinos. Little lanes called *steegjes* connect Front Street with Back Street, which has fewer shops and considerably less congestion. Along the beach is a ½-mile-long (1-km-long) board-walk with restaurants and several Wi-Fi hot spots.

Wathey Square (pronounced watty) is in the heart of the village. Directly across from the square are the town hall and the courthouse, in the striking white building with the cupola. The structure was built in 1793 and has served as the commander's home, a fire station, a jail, and a post office. The streets surrounding the square are lined with hotels, duty-free shops, fine restaurants, and cafés. The **Captain Hodge Pier,** just off the square, is a good spot to view Great Bay and the beach that stretches alongside.

Sint Maarten Museum. The Sint Maarten Museum hosts rotating cultural exhibits and a permanent historical display called Forts of St. Maarten–St. Martin. Artifacts range from Arawak pottery shards to objects salvaged from the wreck of the HMS *Proselyte.* ✉ *7 Front St., Philipsburg, St. Maarten* ☎ *721/542–4917* ⊕ *www.speetjens. com/museum* 🎫 *$1* ⏲ *Weekdays 10–4, Sat. 10–2.*

Fodor's Choice ★ **Pic du Paradis.** Between Marigot and Grand Case, "Paradise Peak," at 1,492 feet, is the island's highest point. There are two observation areas. From them, the tropical forest unfolds below, and the vistas are breathtaking. The road is quite isolated and steep, best suited to a four-wheel-drive vehicle, so don't head up here unless you are prepared for the climb. There have also been some problems with crime in this area, so it might be best to go with an experienced local guide. ✉ *Rte. de Pic du Paradis, Pic du Paradis.*

Loterie Farm. Halfway up the road to Pic du Paradis is Loterie Farm, a peaceful 150-acre private nature preserve opened to the public in 1999 by American expat B. J. Welch. There are hiking trails and maps, so you can go on your own (€5) or arrange a guide for a group (€25 for six people). Along the marked trails you will see native forest with tamarind, gum, mango, and mahogany trees, and wildlife including greenback monkeys if you are lucky. In 2011 Loterie opened a lovely spring-fed pool and Jacuzzi area with lounge chairs, great music, and chic tented cabanas called L'Eau Lounge; if you're with a group, consider the VIP package there. Don't miss a treetop lunch or dinner at **Hidden Forest Café** (⇨ *Where to Eat, below*), Loterie Farm's restaurant, where Julie Perkis cooks delicious, healthy meals and snacks. If you are brave—and over 4 feet 5 inches tall—try soaring over trees on one of the longest zip lines in the Western Hemisphere. ✉ *Rte. de Pic du Paradis 103, Rambaud* ☎ *590/87–86–16, 590/57–28–55* ⊕ *www.loteriefarm. com* 🎫 *€35–€55* ⏲ *Tues.–Sun. 9–4*

SHOPPING

It's true that the island sparkles with its myriad outdoor activities—diving, snorkeling, sailing, swimming, and sunning—but shopaholics are drawn to the sparkle within the jewelry stores. The huge array of such stores is almost unrivaled in the Caribbean. In addition, duty-free shops offer substantial savings—about 15% to 30% below U.S. and Canadian prices—on cameras, watches, liquor, cigars, and designer clothing. It's no wonder that each year 500 cruise ships make Philipsburg a port of call. On both sides of the island, be alert for idlers. They can snatch unwatched purses. Prices are in dollars on the Dutch side, in euros on the French side. As for bargains, there are more to be had on the Dutch side.

Philipsburg's **Front Street** has reinvented itself. Now it's mall-like, with a redbrick walk and streets, palm trees lining the sleek boutiques, jewelry stores, souvenir shops, outdoor restaurants, and the old reliables, like McDonald's and Burger King. Here and there a school or a church appears to remind visitors there's more to the island than shopping. Back Street is where you'll find the **Philipsburg Market Place,** a daily open-air market where you can haggle for bargains on such goods as handicrafts, souvenirs, and beachwear. **Old Street,** near the end of Front Street, has stores, boutiques, and open-air cafés offering French crepes, rich chocolates, and island mementos.

On the French side, wrought-iron balconies, colorful awnings, and gingerbread trim decorate Marigot's smart shops, tiny boutiques, and bistros in the **Marina Royale** complex and on the main streets, **rue de la Liberté** and **rue de la République.** Also in Marigot are the pricey **West Indies Mall** and the **Plaza Caraïbes,** which house designer shops, although some shops are closing in the economic downturn.

ACTIVITIES

For a wide range of water sports, including parasailing and waterskiing, head to Orient Beach, where a variety of operators have their headquarters.

DIVING AND SNORKELING

Although St. Maarten is not generally known as a dive destination, the water temperature here is rarely below 70°F (21°C). Visibility is often excellent, averaging about 100 feet to 120 feet. The island has more than 40 good dive sites, from wrecks to rocky labyrinths. For snorkelers, the area around Orient Bay, Caye Verte (Green Key), Ilêt Pinel, and Flat Island is especially lovely, and is officially classified, and protected, as a regional underwater nature reserve. On average, one-tank dives start at $55; two-tank dives are about $100. The average cost of an afternoon snorkeling trip is about $45 to $55 per person.

Dive Safaris. Dive Safaris has a shark-awareness dive on Friday where participants can watch professional feeders give reef sharks a little nosh. The company also offers a full PADI training program and can tailor dive excursions to any level. ⊠ *La Palapa Marina, Simpson Bay* 🕾 *721/545–3213* ⊕ *www.divestmaarten.com.*

Ocean Explorers Dive Shop. Ocean Explorers Dive Shop is St. Maarten's oldest dive shop, and offers different types of certification courses. ⊠ *113 Welfare Rd., Simpson Bay* 🕾 *721/544–5252* ⊕ *www.stmaartendiving.com.*

FISHING

You can angle for yellowtail snapper, grouper, marlin, tuna, and wahoo on deep-sea excursions. Costs range from $150 per person for a half day to $250 for a full day. Prices usually include bait and tackle, instruction for novices, and refreshments. Ask about licensing and insurance.

Lee's Deepsea Fishing. Lee's Deepsea Fishing organizes excursions, and when you return, Lee's Roadside Grill will cook your tuna, wahoo, or whatever else you catch and keep. Rates start at $200 per person for a half-day. ✉ *82 Welfare Rd., Cole Bay* ☎ *721/544–4233* ⊕ *www.leesfish.com.*

Rudy's Deep Sea Fishing. Rudy's Deep Sea Fishing has been around for years, and is one of the more experienced sport-angling outfits. A private charter trip for four people starts at $525 for a half-day excursion. ✉ *14 Airport Rd., Simpson Bay* ☎ *721/545–2177* ⊕ *www. rudysdeepseafishing.com.*

BEACHES

The island's 10 miles (16 km) of beaches are all open to cruise-ship passengers. You can rent chairs and umbrellas at most of the beaches, primarily from beachside restaurants. The best beaches are on the French side. Topless bathing is common on the French side. If you take a cab to a remote beach, be sure to arrange a specific time for the driver to return for you. Don't leave valuables unattended on the beach or in a rental car, even in the trunk.

Baie des Péres (*Friars Bay*). This quiet cove close to Marigot has beach grills and bars, with chaises and umbrellas, calm waters, and a lovely view of Anguilla. Kali's Beach Bar, open daily for lunch and (weather permitting) dinner, has a Rasta vibe and color scheme—it's the best place to be on the full moon, with music, dancing, and a huge bonfire, but you can get lunch, beach chairs, and umbrellas there in any moon phase. Friar´s Bay Beach Café is a French Bistro on the sand. Its open from breakfast to sunset. To get to the beach, take National Road 7 from Marigot, go toward Grand Case to the Morne Valois hill, and turn left on the dead-end road at the sign. **Amenities:** food and drink, toilets. **Best for:** partiers, swimming, walking. ✉ *Friar's Bay.*

Fodor's Choice   **Baie Orientale** (*Orient Bay*). Many consider this the island's most beau-
★   tiful beach, but its 2 miles (3 km) of satiny white sand, underwater marine reserve, variety of water sports, beach clubs, and hotels also make it one of the most crowded. Lots of "naturists" take advantage of the clothing-optional policy, so don't be shocked. Early-morning nude beach walking is de rigueur for the guests at Club Orient, at the southeastern end of the beach. Plan to spend the day at one of the clubs; each bar has different color umbrellas, and all boast terrific restaurants and lively bars. You can have an open-air massage, try any sea toy you fancy, and stay until dark. To get to Baie Orientale from Marigot, take National Road 7 past Grand Case, past the Aéroport de L'Espérance, and watch for the left turn. **Amenities:** food and drink, parking, toilets, water sports. **Best for:** partiers, nudists, swimming, walking, windsurfing. ✉ *Baie Orientale.*

Ilet Pinel. A protected nature reserve, this kid-friendly island is a five-minute ferry ride from French Cul de Sac ($7 per person round-trip). The ferry runs every half hour from midmorning until dusk. The water is clear and shallow, and the shore is sheltered. If you like snorkeling, don your gear and paddle along both coasts of this pencil-shaped speck in the ocean. You can rent equipment on the island or in the parking lot before you board the ferry for about $10. Plan for lunch any day of the week at the water's edge at a palm-shaded beach hut at Karibuni (except in September, when it's closed) for the freshest fish, great salads, tapas, and drinks—try the frozen mojito for a treat. **Amenities:** food and drink. **Best for:** swimming, snorkeling. ⊠ *Ilet Pinel.*

WHERE TO EAT

$$ ✕ **Enoch's Place.** The blue-and-white-striped awning on a corner of the
CARIBBEAN Marigot Market makes this place hard to miss. But Enoch's cooking is what draws the crowds. Specialties include garlic shrimp, fresh lobster, and rice and beans (like your St. Martin mother used to make). Try the saltfish and fried johnnycake—a great breakfast option. The food more than makes up for the lack of decor, and chances are you'll be counting the days until you can return. ⑤ *Average main: €13* ⊠ *Marigot Market, Front de Mer, Marigot* ☎ *590/29–29–88* ⊕ *www.enochsplace. com* ⌛ *Reservations not accepted* ▭ *No credit cards* ⊗ *Closed Sun. No dinner.*

$$ ✕ **Taloula Mango's.** Ribs are the specialty at this casual beachfront res-
ECLECTIC taurant, but the jerk chicken and thin-crust pizza, not to mention a few vegetarian options like the tasty falafel, are not to be ignored. On week-days lunch is accompanied by live music; every Friday during happy hour a DJ spins tunes. In case you're wondering, the restaurant got its name from the owner's golden retriever. ⑤ *Average main: $17* ⊠ *Sint Rose Shopping Mall, off Front St. on beach boardwalk, Philipsburg* ☎ *721/542–1645* ⊕ *www.taloulamango.com.*

ST. THOMAS (CHARLOTTE AMALIE)

Carol
Bareuther
St. Thomas is the busiest cruise port of call in the world. Up to eight mega ships may visit in a single day. Don't expect an exotic island expe-rience: one of the three U.S. Virgin Islands (with St. Croix and St. John), St. Thomas is as American as any place on the mainland, complete with McDonald's and HBO. The positive side of all this development is that there are more tours here than anywhere else in the Caribbean, and every year the excursions get better. Of course, shopping is the big draw in Charlotte Amalie, but experienced travelers remember the days of "real" bargains. Today so many passengers fill the stores that it's a seller's mar-ket. On some days there are so many cruise passengers on St. Thomas that you must book a ship-sponsored shore excursion if you want to do more than just take a taxi to the beach or stroll around Charlotte Amalie.

ESSENTIALS

CURRENCY The U.S. dollar is the official currency of U.S. Virgin Islands, and ATMs are plentiful.

TELEPHONE Both GSM and Sprint phones work in St. Thomas (and the USVI are normally included in most U.S. cell phone plans). It's as easy to call home from St. Thomas and St. John as from any city in the United States. On St. Thomas, public phones are easily found, and AT&T has a telecommunications center across from the Havensight Mall.

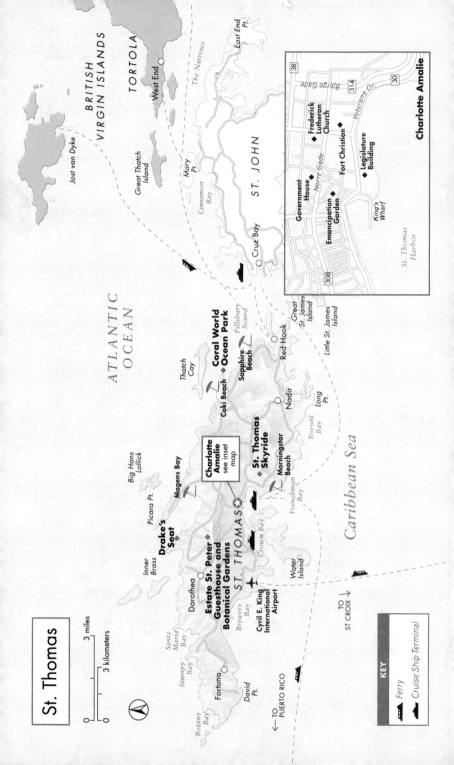

COMING ASHORE

Depending on how many ships are in port, cruise ships drop anchor in the harbor at Charlotte Amalie and tender passengers directly to the waterfront duty-free shops, dock at the Havensight Mall at the eastern end of the crescent bay, or dock at the less convenient Crown Bay Marina a few miles west of town (Holland America almost always docks at Crown Bay).

The distance from Havensight to the duty-free shops is 1½ miles (3 km), which can be walked in less than half an hour; a taxi ride there costs $6 per person ($5 for each additional person). Tourist information offices are at the Havensight Mall (across from Building No. 1) for docking passengers and downtown near Fort Christian (at the eastern end of the waterfront shopping area) for those coming ashore by tender. Both offices distribute free maps. From Crown Bay it's also a half-hour walk or a $5-per-person cab ride ($4 for each additional person). V.I. Taxi Association drivers offer a basic two-hour island tour for $25 per person for two or more people. You can rent a car in St. Thomas, but with all the tour options it's often easier and cheaper to take an organized excursion or just hop in a cab.

EXPLORING ST. THOMAS

CHARLOTTE AMALIE

St. Thomas's major burg is a hilly shopping town. There are also plenty of interesting historic sights—so take the time to see at least a few.

Emancipation Garden. A bronze bust of a freed slave blowing a conch shell commemorates slavery's end, in 1848—the garden was built to mark emancipation's 150th anniversary, in 1998. The gazebo here is used for official ceremonies. Two other monuments show the island's Danish-American connection—a bust of Denmark's King Christian and a scaled-down model of the U.S. Liberty Bell. ⊠ *Between Tolbod Gade and Ft. Christian, Charlotte Amalie.*

Ft. Christian. St. Thomas's oldest standing structure, this remarkable building was built between 1672 and 1680 and now has U.S. National Landmark status. Over the years, it was used as a jail, governor's residence, town hall, courthouse, and church. In 2005, a multimillion-dollar renovation was started to stabilize the structure and halt centuries of deterioration. Delays—including the discovery of human skeletal remains buried in the walls from when the structure was used as a Lutheran church—have plagued the project, and the fort remains closed to the public. You can see from the outside the four renovated faces of its famous 19th-century clock tower. ⊠ *Waterfront Hwy. east of shopping district, Charlotte Amalie* ☎ *340/776–8605.*

Frederick Lutheran Church. This historic church has a massive mahogany altar, and its pews—each with its own door—were once rented to families of the congregation. Lutheranism is the state religion of Denmark, and when the territory was without a minister, the governor—who had his own elevated pew—filled in. ⊠ *7 Norre Gade, Charlotte Amalie* ☎ *340/776–1315* ☉ *Mon.–Sat. 9–4.*

Government House. Built in 1867, this neoclassical white brick-and-wood structure houses the offices of the governor of the Virgin Islands. Inside, the staircases are of native mahogany, as are the plaques, hand-lettered in gold with the names of the governors appointed and, since 1970, elected. Brochures detailing the history of the building are available, but you may have to ask for them. ⊠ *Government Hill, 21–22 Kongens Gade, Charlotte Amalie* ☎ *340/774–0001* ✉ *Free* ⊘ *Weekdays 8–5.*

Legislature Building. Its pastoral-looking lime-green exterior conceals the vociferous political wrangling of the Virgin Islands Senate. Constructed originally by the Danish as a police barracks, the building was later used to billet U.S. Marines, and much later it housed a public school. You're welcome to sit in on sessions in the upstairs chambers. ⊠ *Waterfront Hwy. across from Ft. Christian, Route 30, Charlotte Amalie* ☎ *340/774–0880* ⊘ *Daily 8–5.*

ST. THOMAS BEST BETS

■ **Coral World Ocean Park.** This aquarium attraction is a great bet for families, and it's on one of best snorkeling beaches.

■ **Magen's Bay Beach.** St. Thomas has one of the most picture-postcard perfect beaches you'll ever see. It's great for swimming.

■ **St. John.** It's easy to hop on the ferry to St. John for a day of hiking, then relax for an hour or two on the beach afterward.

■ **Shopping.** Charlotte Amalie is one of the best places in the Caribbean to shop.

ELSEWHERE ON ST. THOMAS

☾ **Coral World Ocean Park.** This interactive aquarium and water-sports cen-
Fodor's Choice ter lets you experience a variety of sea life and other animals. There are
★ several outdoor pools where you can pet baby sharks, feed stingrays, touch starfish, and view endangered sea turtles. During the Sea Trek Helmet Dive, you walk along an underwater trail wearing a helmet that provides a continuous supply of air. You can try "snuba," a cross between snorkeling and scuba diving. Swim with a sea lion and have a chance at playing ball or getting a big, wet, whiskered kiss. You can also buy a cup of nectar and let the cheerful lorikeets perch on your hand and drink. The park also has an offshore underwater observatory, an 80,000-gallon coral reef exhibit (one of the largest in the world), and a nature trail with native ducks and tortoises. Daily feedings take place at most exhibits. ⊠ *Coki Point north of Rte. 38, Estate Fryden-dal* ☎ *340/775–1555* ⊕ *www.coralworldvi.com* ✉ *$19, Sea Lion Swim $105, Sea Lion Encounter $65, Sea Trek $58, Snuba $52, Shark and Turtle Encounters $32, Nautilus $20* ⊘ *Daily 9–4. Off-season (May–Oct.) hrs may vary, so call to confirm.*

Drake's Seat. Sir Francis Drake was supposed to have kept watch over his fleet and looked for enemy ships from this vantage point. The panorama is especially breathtaking (and romantic) at dusk, and if you arrive late in the day, you can miss the hordes of day-trippers on taxi tours who stop here to take a picture. ⊠ *Rte. 40, Estate Zufriedenheit.*

Estate St. Peter Greathouse and Botanical Gardens. This unusual spot is perched on a mountainside 1,000 feet above sea level, with views of more than 20 islands and islets. You can wander through a gallery displaying local art, sip a complimentary rum punch while looking out at the view, or follow a nature trail that leads you past nearly 70 varieties of tropical plants, including 17 varieties of orchids. ⊠ *Rte. 40, 6A St. Peter Mountain Road, Estate St. Peter* ☎ *340/774–4999* ⊠ *$10.*

⊙ **St. Thomas Skyride.** Fly skyward in a gondola to Paradise Point, an
★ overlook with breathtaking views of Charlotte Amalie and the harbor. You'll find several shops, a bar, a restaurant, a wedding gazebo, and a Ferris wheel. A ¼-mile (½-km) hiking trail leads to spectacular views of St. Croix. Wear sturdy shoes, as the trail is steep and rocky. You can also skip the gondola and taxi to the top for $4 per person from the Havensight Dock. ⊠ *Rte. 30, across from Havensight Mall, 9617 Estate Thomas, Havensight* ☎ *340/774–9809* ⊠ *$21* ⊙ *Thurs.–Tues. 9–5, Wed. 9–9.*

SHOPPING

The prime shopping area in **Charlotte Amalie** is between Post Office and Market squares; it consists of two parallel streets that run east–west (Waterfront Highway and Main Street) and the alleyways that connect them. Particularly attractive are the historic **A.H. Riise Alley, Royal Dane Mall, Palm Passage,** and pastel-painted **International Plaza.**

⊙ **Vendors Plaza.** Here merchants sell everything from T-shirts to African attire to leather goods. Look for local art among the ever-changing selections at this busy market. ⊠ *Waterfront, west of Ft. Christian, Charlotte Amalie* ⊙ *Weekdays 8–6, weekends 9–1.*

Havensight Mall, next to the cruise-ship dock, may not be as charming as downtown Charlotte Amalie, but it does have more than 60 shops. It also has an excellent bookstore, a bank, a pharmacy, a gourmet grocery, and smaller branches of many downtown stores. The shops at **Port of Sale,** adjoining Havensight Mall (its buildings are pink instead of brown), sell discount goods. Next door to Port of Sale is the **Yacht Haven Grande** complex, with many upscale shops. At the Crown Bay cruise-ship pier, the **Crown Bay Center,** off the Harwood Highway in Sub Base about ½ mile (¾ km), has quite a few shops.

East of Charlotte Amalie on Route 38, **Tillett Gardens** is an oasis of artistic endeavor across from the Tutu Park Shopping Mall. The late Jim and Rhoda Tillett converted this Danish farm into an artists' retreat in 1959. Today you can watch artisans produce silk-screen fabrics, candles, pottery, and other handicrafts. Something special is often happening in the gardens as well: the Classics in the Gardens program is a classical music series presented under the stars, Arts Alive is an annual arts-and-crafts fair held in November, and the Pistarckle Theater holds its performances here.

ACTIVITIES

DIVING AND SNORKELING

Coki Dive Center. Snorkeling and dive tours in the fish-filled reefs off Coki Beach are available from this PADI Five Star outfit, as are classes, including one on underwater photography. It's run by the avid diver Peter Jackson. ⊠ *Rte. 388, at Coki Point, Estate Frydendal* ☎ *340/775–4220* ⊕ *www.cokidive.com.*

Snuba of St. Thomas. In snuba, a snorkeling and scuba-diving hybrid, a 20-foot air hose connects you to the surface. The cost is $74. Children must be 8 or older to participate. ⊠ *Rte. 388, at Coki Point, Estate Smith Bay* ☎ *340/693–8063* ⊕ *www.visnuba.com.*

FISHING

Charter Boat Center. The Charter Boat Center is a major source for sail and powerboat as well as sportfishing charters. Sportfishing charters offered include full-day trips for marlin as well as full, three-quarter, and half days for offshore and inshore species. ⊠ *6300 Smith Bay 16–3, Red Hook* ☎ *340/775–7990* ⊕ *www.charterboat.vi.*

GOLF

★ **Mahogany Run Golf Course.** The Mahogany Run Golf Course attracts golfers, who are drawn by its spectacular view of the British Virgin Islands and the challenging three-hole Devil's Triangle. At this Tom and George Fazio–designed, par-70, 18-hole course, there's a fully stocked pro shop, snack bar, and open-air clubhouse. Green fees and half-cart fees for 18 holes are $165 in the winter season. The course is open daily, and there are frequently informal weekend tournaments. It's the only course on St. Thomas. ⊠ *Rte. 42, Estate Lovenlund* ☎ *340/777–6006, 800/253–7103* ⊕ *www.mahoganyrungolf.com.*

BEACHES

Coki Beach. Funky beach huts selling local foods such as pâtés (fried turnovers with a spicy ground-beef filling), picnic tables topped with umbrellas sporting beverage logos, quaint vendor kiosks, and a brigade of hair braiders and taxi men make this beach overlooking picturesque Thatch Cay feel like an amusement park. But this is the best place on the island to snorkel and scuba dive. Fish, including grunts, snappers, and wrasses, are like an effervescent cloud you can wave your hand through. Major renovations in late 2011 added a new bathhouse and boardwalk. There are also beefed-up security and regular police patrols in the area after a shooting incident in 2010. **Amenities:** food and drink; lifeguards; watersports. **Best for:** partyers; snorkeling. ⊠ *Rte. 388, next to Coral World Ocean Park.*

Fodor's Choice ★

Magens Bay. Deeded to the island as a public park, this heart-shaped stretch of white sand is considered one of the most beautiful in the world. The bottom of the bay is flat and sandy, so this is a place for sunning and swimming rather than snorkeling. On weekends and holidays the sounds of music from groups partying under the sheds fill the air. There's a bar, snack shack, and beachwear boutique; bathhouses with restrooms, changing rooms, and saltwater showers are close by.

Sunfish and paddleboats are the most popular rentals at the water-sports kiosk. East of the beach is Udder Delight, a one-room shop that serves a Virgin Islands tradition—a milk shake with a splash of Cruzan rum. (Kids can enjoy virgin versions, which have a touch of soursop, mango, or banana flavoring). If you arrive between 8 am and 5 pm, you pay an entrance fee of $4 per person, $2 per vehicle; it's free for children under 12. **Amenities:** food and drink; parking (fee); water sports. **Best for:** partiers; swimming; walking. ⊠ *Rte. 35, at end of road on north side of island* ☎ *340/777–6300.*

★ **Sapphire Beach.** A steady breeze makes this beach a boardsailor's paradise. The swimming is great, as is the snorkeling, especially at the reef near Pettyklip Point. Beach volleyball is big on the weekends. Sapphire Beach Resort and Marina has a snack shop, bar, and water-sports rentals. **Amenities:** food and drink; water sports. **Best for:** snorkeling; swimming; windsurfing. ⊠ *Rte. 38, Sapphire Bay.*

WHERE TO EAT

$$$
CARIBBEAN
✕ **Cuzzin's Caribbean Restaurant and Bar.** In a 19th-century livery stable on Back Street, this restaurant is hard to find but well worth it if you want to sample bona fide Virgin Islands cuisine. For lunch, order tender slivers of conch stewed in a rich onion-and-butter sauce, savory braised oxtail, or curried chicken. At dinner the island-style mutton, served in thick gravy and seasoned with locally grown herbs, offers a tasty treat that's deliciously different. Side dishes include peas and rice, boiled green bananas, fried plantains, and potato stuffing. Ⓢ *Average main: $24* ⊠ *7 Wimmelskafts Gade, also called Back St., Charlotte Amalie* ☎ *340/777–4711.*

$$
CARIBBEAN
Fodor'sChoice
★
✕ **Gladys' Cafe.** Even if the local specialties—conch in butter sauce, salt fish and dumplings, hearty red bean soup—didn't make this a recommended café, it would be worth coming for Gladys's smile. Her cozy alleyway restaurant is rich in atmosphere with its mahogany bar and native stone walls, making dining a double delight. While you're here, pick up a $5 or $10 bottle of her special hot sauce. There are mustard-, oil and vinegar–, and tomato-based versions; the tomato-based sauce is the hottest. Only Amex is accepted. Ⓢ *Average main: $16* ⊠ *Waterfront at Royal Dane Mall, 28A Dronningens Gade, Charlotte Amalie* ☎ *340/774–6604* ◷ *No dinner.*

ST. VINCENT (KINGSTOWN)

Jane E. Zarem

You won't find glitzy resorts or flashy discos in St. Vincent. Rather, you'll be fascinated by its busy capital, mountainous beauty, and fine sailing waters. St. Vincent is the largest and northernmost island in the Grenadines archipelago; Kingstown, the capital city of St. Vincent and the Grenadines, is the government and business center and major port. Except for one barren area on the island's northeast coast—remnants of the 1979 eruption of La Soufrière, one of the last active volcanoes in the Caribbean—the countryside is mountainous, lush, and green. St. Vincent's topography thwarted European settlement for many years.

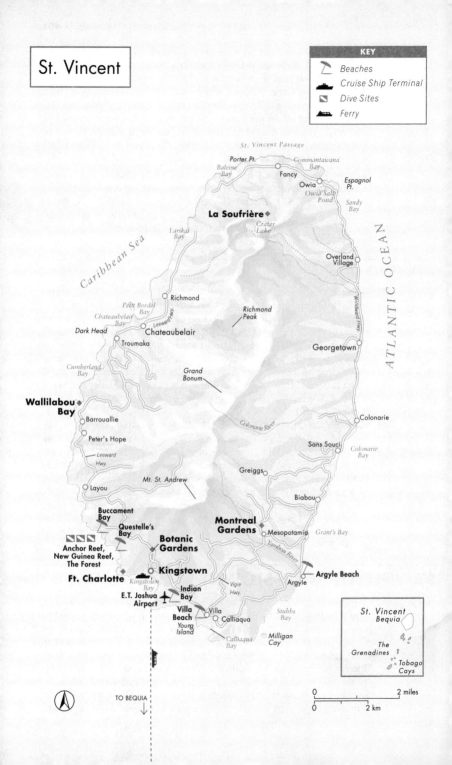

St. Vincent

KEY
- Beaches
- Cruise Ship Terminal
- Dive Sites
- Ferry

St. Vincent Passage

Baleine Bay
Porter Pt.
Commantawana Bay
Fancy
Espagnol Pt.
Owia
Owia Salt Pond
Sandy Bay

La Soufrière
Crater Lake

Larikai Bay

Overland Village

Caribbean Sea

Richmond

Richmond Peak

Petit Bordel Bay
Chateaubelair Bay
Dark Head
Leeward Hwy.
Chateaubelair
Troumaka

Georgetown

Cumberland Bay

Grand Bonum

ATLANTIC OCEAN

Colonarie River

Colonarie

Wallilabou Bay

Barrouallie

Peter's Hope

Sans Souci
Colonarie Bay

Leeward Hwy.

Greiggs

Mt. St. Andrew

Layou

Biabou

Buccament Bay

Questelle's Bay

Botanic Gardens

Montreal Gardens

Mesopotamia
Grant's Bay

Anchor Reef, New Guinea Reef, The Forest

Yambou River

Ft. Charlotte

Kingstown

Kingstown Bay

Argyle Beach

Vigie Hwy.
Argyle

E.T. Joshua Airport

Indian Bay

Villa

Villa Beach

Young Island

Calliaqua

Stubbs Bay

Calliaqua Bay

Milligan Cay

St. Vincent
Bequia

The Grenadines

Tobago Cays

0   2 miles
0   2 km

TO BEQUIA

As colonization advanced elsewhere in the Caribbean, in fact, the island became a refuge for Carib Indians—descendants of whom still live in northeastern St. Vincent. After years of fighting and back-and-forth territorial claims, British troops prevailed by overpowering the French and banishing Carib warriors to Central America. Independent since 1979, St. Vincent and the Grenadines remains a member of the British Commonwealth.

ESSENTIALS

CURRENCY Eastern Caribbean (E.C.) dollar (EC$2.67 to US$1). U.S. dollars (but not coins) are generally accepted, but change is given in E.C. currency.

TELEPHONE Your cell phone should operate in St. Vincent, but roaming charges can be hefty. Pay phones are readily available and best operated with the prepaid phone cards that are sold at many stores. Telephone services are available at the Cruise Ship Complex in Kingstown. For an international operator, dial 115; to charge your call to a credit card, call 117.

COMING ASHORE

The Cruise Ship Complex at Kingstown, St. Vincent's capital city, accommodates two cruise ships; additional vessels anchor offshore and transport passengers to the jetty by launch. The facility has about two-dozen shops that sell duty-free items and handicrafts. There's a communications center, post office, tourist information desk, restaurant, and food court.

Buses and taxis are available at the wharf. Taxi drivers are well equipped to take you on an island tour; expect to pay $30 per hour for up to four passengers. The ferry to Bequia (one hour each way) is at the adjacent pier. Renting a car for just one day isn't advisable, since car rentals are expensive (at least $55 per day) and require a $24 temporary driving permit on top of that. It's almost always a better deal to take a tour, though you don't have to limit yourself to those offered by your ship.

EXPLORING ST. VINCENT

 Botanic Gardens. A few minutes north of downtown by taxi is the oldest
Fodor'sChoice botanical garden in the Western Hemisphere. It was founded in 1765,
★ after Captain Bligh—of *Bounty* fame—brought the first breadfruit tree to this island for landowners to propagate. The prolific bounty of the breadfruit trees was used to feed the slaves. You can see a direct descendant of this original tree among the specimen mahogany, rubber, teak, and other tropical trees and shrubs in the 20 acres of gardens. Two dozen rare St. Vincent parrots, confiscated from illegal collections, live in the small aviary. Guides explain all the medicinal and ornamental trees and shrubs; they also appreciate a tip (about $5 per person) at the end of the tour. ⊠ *Off Leeward Hwy, northeast of town, Montrose, Kingstown* ☎ *784/457–1003* ☎ *Free* ☉ *Daily 6–6.*

★ **Ft. Charlotte.** Started by the French in 1786 and completed by the British in 1806, the fort was named for Queen Charlotte, wife of King George III. It sits on Berkshire Hill, a dramatic promontory 2 miles (3 km) north of Kingstown and 636 feet above sea level, affording a stunning view of the capital city and the Grenadines. Interestingly, cannons face inward—the fear of attack by the French and their Carib allies was far greater than any threat approaching from the sea. In any case, the fort saw no action. Nowadays, the fort serves as a signal station for ships; its ancient cells house historical paintings of the island by Lindsay Prescott. ⊠ *Berkshire Hill, 2 miles north of town, Kingstown.*

Kingstown. The capital city of St. Vincent and the Grenadines is on the island's southwestern coast. The town of 13,500 residents wraps around Kingstown Bay; a ring of green hills and ridges, studded with houses, forms a backdrop for the city. This is very much a working city, with a busy harbor and few concessions to tourists. Kingstown Harbour is the only deepwater port on the island.

ST. VINCENT BEST BETS

■ **Island Tour.** Tour the greater Kingstown area, then travel up the leeward coast to Wallilabou.

■ **Falls of Baleine.** An all-day boat trip to the 60-foot falls is a beautiful way to spend a day.

■ **Ferry to Bequia.** Laid-back Bequia is one hour by ferry from St. Vincent.

■ **Hiking.** Whether you hike in the rain forest or do the more difficult climb of La Soufrière, it's worth exploring some of the island's rugged terrain.

■ **Tobago Cays.** These uninhabited islands in the Grenadines are the top destination for snorkeling.

A few gift shops can be found on and around **Bay Street,** near the harbor. Upper Bay Street, which stretches along the bayfront, bustles with daytime activity—workers going about their business and housewives doing their shopping. Many of Kingstown's downtown buildings are built of stone or brick brought to the island in the holds of 18th-century ships as ballast (and replaced with sugar and spices for the return trip to Europe). The Georgian-style stone arches and second-floor overhangs on former warehouses create shelter from midday sun and the brief, cooling showers common to the tropics.

Grenadines Wharf, at the south end of Bay Street, is busy with schooners loading supplies and ferries loading people bound for the Grenadines. The **Cruise-Ship Complex,** just south of the commercial wharf, has a mall with a dozen or more shops, plus restaurants, a post office, communications facilities, and a taxi-minibus stand.

An almost infinite selection of produce fills the **Kingstown Produce Market,** a three-story building that takes up a whole city block on Upper Bay, Hillsboro, and Bedford streets in the center of town. It's noisy, colorful, and open Monday through Saturday—but the busiest times (and the best times to go) are Friday and Saturday mornings. In the courtyard, vendors sell local arts and crafts. On the upper floors, merchants sell clothing, household items, gifts, and other products.

Little Tokyo, so called because funding for the project was a gift from Japan, is a waterfront shopping area with a bustling indoor fish market and dozens of stalls where you can buy inexpensive homemade meals, drinks, ice cream, bread and cookies, clothing, trinkets, and even get a haircut.

St. George's Cathedral, on Grenville Street, is a pristine, creamy yellow Anglican church built in 1820. The dignified Georgian architecture includes simple wooden pews, an ornate chandelier, and beautiful stained-glass windows; one was a gift from Queen Victoria, who actually commissioned it for London's St. Paul's Cathedral in honor of her first grandson. When the artist created an angel with a red robe, she was horrified by the color and sent it abroad. The markers in the cathedral's graveyard recount the history of the island. Across the street is **St. Mary's Roman Catholic Cathedral of the Assumption,** built in stages beginning in 1823. The strangely appealing design is a blend of Moorish, Georgian, and Romanesque styles applied to black brick. Nearby, freed slaves built the **Kingstown Methodist Church** in 1841. The exterior is brick, simply decorated with quoins (solid blocks that form the corners), and the roof is held together by metal straps, bolts, and wooden pins. **Scots Kirk** was built from 1839 to 1880 by and for Scottish settlers but became a Seventh-Day Adventist church in 1952. ⊠ *Kingstown.*

La Soufrière. This towering volcano, which last erupted in 1979, is 4,048 feet high and so huge in area that its surrounding mountainside covers virtually the entire northern third of the island. The eastern trail to the rim of the crater, a two-hour ascent, begins at Rabacca Dry River. ⊠ *Rabacca Dry River, Rabacca.*

Fodor's Choice ★ **Montreal Gardens.** Welsh-born landscape designer Timothy Vaughn renovated 7½ acres of neglected commercial flower beds and a falling-down plantation house into a stunning yet informal garden spot. Anthurium, ginger lilies, birds-of-paradise, and other tropical flowers are planted in raised beds; tree ferns create a canopy of shade along the walkways. The gardens are in the shadow of majestic Grand Bonhomme Mountain, deep in the Mesopotamia Valley, about 12 miles (19 km) from Kingstown. ⊠ *Montreal St., Mesopotamia* ☎ *784/458–1198* ✉ *$2* ☉ *Dec.–Aug., weekdays 9–5.*

☾ ★ **Wallilabou Bay.** The *Pirates of the Caribbean* movie left its mark at Wallilabou (pronounced wally-la-*boo*), a location used for filming the opening scenes of "The Curse of the Black Pearl" in 2003. Many of the buildings and docks built as stage sets remain, giving the pretty bay (a port of entry for visiting yachts) an intriguingly historic appearance. You can sunbathe, swim, picnic, or buy your lunch at Wallilabou Anchorage. This is a favorite stop for day-trippers returning from the Falls of Baleine and boaters anchoring for the evening. Nearby, at Wallilabou Heritage Park, there's a river with a small waterfall and pool, where you can take a freshwater plunge. ⊠ *Wallilabou.*

SHOPPING

The 12 small blocks that hug the waterfront in **downtown Kingstown** compose St. Vincent's main shopping district. Among the shops that sell goods to fulfill household needs are a few that sell local crafts, gifts, and souvenirs. Bargaining is neither expected nor appreciated. The **cruise-ship complex,** on the waterfront in Kingstown, has a collection of a dozen or so boutiques, shops, and restaurants that cater to cruise-ship passengers.

St. Vincent Craftsmen's Centre. Locally made grass floor mats, place mats, and other straw articles, as well as batik cloth, handmade West Indian dolls, hand-painted calabashes, and framed artwork are all available at this store that's three blocks from the wharf. No credit cards are accepted. ⊠ *Frenches St., Kingstown* ☎ *784/457–2516.*

ACTIVITIES

DIVING AND SNORKELING

Novices and advanced divers alike will be impressed by the marine life in the waters surrounding St. Vincent and the Grenadines—brilliant sponges, huge deepwater coral trees, and shallow reefs teeming with colorful fish. The best dive spots on St. Vincent are in the small bays along the coast between Kingstown and Layou; many are within 20 yards of shore and only 20 feet to 30 feet down.

Anchor Reef has excellent visibility for viewing a deep-black coral garden, schools of squid, seahorses, and maybe a small octopus. The **Forest,** a shallow dive, is still dramatic, with soft corals in pastel colors and schools of small fish. **New Guinea Reef** slopes to 90 feet (28 meters) and can't be matched for its quantity of corals and sponges. The pristine waters surrounding the **Tobago Cays,** in the Southern Grenadines, will give you a world-class diving experience.

Dive Fantasea. On offer are dive and snorkeling trips along the St. Vincent coast and to the Tobago Cays. ⊠ *Villa Beach, Calliaqua* ☎ *784/457–4477.*

Dive St. Vincent. The NAUI- and PADI-certified instructor Bill Tewes and his two certified dive masters offer beginner and certification courses for ages 8 and up, advanced water excursions along the St. Vincent coast and to the southern Grenadines for diving connoisseurs, and an introductory scuba lesson for novices. ⊠ *Young Island Dock, Villa Beach, Calliaqua* ☎ *784/457–4714, 784/457–4928* ⊕ *www.divestvincent.com.*

FISHING

Crystal Blue Sportfishing Charters. These sportfishing charters are on a 34-foot pirogue and are for both casual and serious fishermen. ⊠ *Indian Bay, Calliaqua* ☎ *784/457–4532.*

BEACHES

St. Vincent's origin is volcanic, so its beaches range in color from golden-brown to black. Swimming is recommended only in the lagoons and bays along the leeward coast. By contrast, beaches on Bequia and the rest of the Grenadines have pure white sand, palm trees, and crystal-clear aquamarine water; some are even within walking distance of the jetty.

Indian Bay Beach. South of Kingstown and separated from Villa Beach by a rocky hill, Indian Bay beach has golden sand but is slightly rocky; it's very good for snorkeling. **Amenities:** food and drink. **Best for:** snorkeling; swimming. ⊠ *Villa, Calliaqua.*

Villa Beach. The long stretch of sand in front of the row of hotels and restaurants along the Young Island Channel varies from 20 to 25 feet wide to practically nonexistent. The broadest, sandiest part is in front of Beachcombers Hotel, which is also the perfect spot for sunbathers to get lunch and liquid refreshments. **Amenities:** food and drink; water sports. **Best for:** swimming. ⊠ *Villa, Calliaqua.*

WHERE TO EAT

$$$ ✕ **Basil's Bar and Restaurant.** It's not just the air-conditioning that makes
CARIBBEAN this restaurant cool. Basil's, at street level at the Cobblestone Inn, is owned by Basil Charles, whose Basil's Beach Bar on Mustique is a hangout for the vacationing rich and famous. This is the Kingstown power-lunch venue. Local businesspeople gather for the daily buffet (weekdays) or full menu of salads, sandwiches, barbecued chicken, or fresh seafood platters. Dinner entrées of pasta, local seafood, and chicken are served at candlelit tables. $ *Average main: $20* ⊠ *Cobblestone Inn, Upper Bay St., Kingstown* 🕾 *784/457–2713* ⊘ *Closed Sun.*

$ ✕ **Cobblestone Roof-Top Bar & Restaurant.** To reach what is perhaps the
CARIBBEAN most pleasant, the breeziest, and the most satisfying breakfast and lunch
★ spot in downtown Kingstown, diners must climb the equivalent of three flights of interior stone steps within the historic Cobblestone Inn. But getting to the open-air rooftop restaurant is half the fun, as en route diners get an up-close view of a 19th-century sugar (and later arrowroot) Georgian warehouse that's now a very appealing boutique inn. A full breakfast menu is available to hotel guests and the public alike. The luncheon menu ranges from homemade soups, salads (tuna, chicken, fruit, or tossed), sandwiches, or burgers and fries to full meals of roast beef, stewed chicken, or grilled fish served with rice, plantains, macaroni pie, and fresh local vegetables. $ *Average main: $12* ⊠ *Cobblestone Inn, Upper Bay St., Kingstown* 🕾 *784/456–1937* ⊘ *No dinner.*

TORTOLA (ROAD TOWN)

Lynda Lohr   Once a sleepy backwater, Tortola is definitely busy these days, particularly when several cruise ships tie up at the Road Town dock. Passengers crowd the streets and shops, and open-air jitneys filled with cruise-ship passengers create bottlenecks on the island's byways. That said, most folks visit Tortola to relax on its deserted sands or linger over lunch at one of its many delightful restaurants. Beaches are never more than a few miles away, and the steep green hills that form Tortola's spine are fanned by gentle trade winds. The neighboring islands glimmer like emeralds in a sea of sapphire. Tortola doesn't have many historic sights, but it does have abundant natural beauty. Beware of the roads, which are extraordinarily steep and twisting, making driving demanding. The best beaches are on the north shore.

ESSENTIALS

CURRENCY   The U.S. dollar is the official currency. Some places accept cash only, but major credit cards are widely accepted. You'll find ATMs in Road Town.

TELEPHONE   To call anywhere in the BVI once you've arrived, dial all seven digits. A local call from a pay phone costs 25¢, but such phones are sometimes on the blink. An alternative is a Caribbean phone card, available in

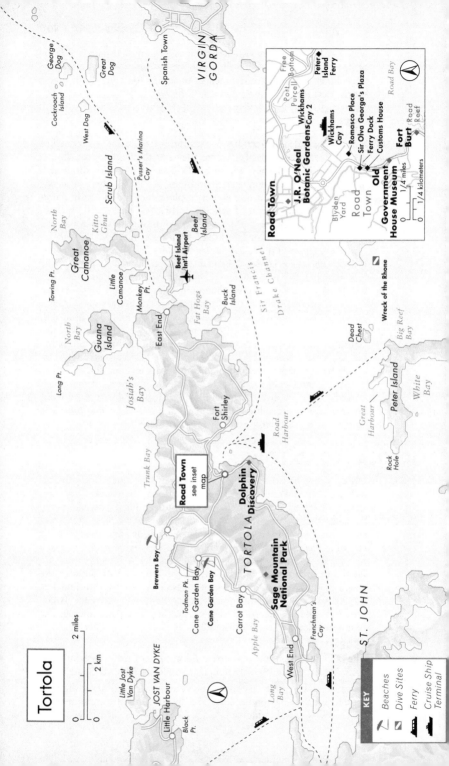

Tortola

Road Town
see inset map

Inset: Road Town

J.R. O'Neal
Botanic Gardens
Peter
Island
Ferry
Wickhams
Cay 1
Wickhams
Cay 2
Romasco Place
Sir Olva George's Plaza
Ferry Dock
Customs House
Fort
Burt
Road
Reef
Road Bay
Free
Bottom
Port
Purcell
Blyden
Yard
Road
Town
Old
Government
House Museum
0   1/4 miles
0   1/4 kilometers

VIRGIN GORDA
Spanish Town

George
Dog
Great
Dog
Cockroach
Island
West Dog
Scrub Island
Purser's Marina
Cay
North
Bay
Kitto
Ghut
Great
Camanoe
Towing Pt.
Little
Camanoe
Monkey
Pt.
Beef Island
Int'l Airport
Beef
Island
Fat Hogs
Bay
Buck
Island
Sir Francis Drake Channel
North
Bay
Guana
Island
Long Pt.
East End
Josiah's
Bay
Fort
Shirley
Wreck of the Rhone
Dead
Chest
Big Reef
Bay
Road
Harbour
Peter Island
Great
Harbour
White
Bay
Rock
Hole
Trunk Bay
Road Town
see inset
map
Dolphin
Discovery
TORTOLA
Sage Mountain
National Park
Brewers Bay
Todman Pk.
Cane Garden Bay
Cane Garden Bay
Carrot Bay
Apple Bay
Frenchman's
Cay
West End
Long Bay
Black
Pt.
Little Harbour
JOST VAN DYKE
Little Jost
Van Dyke
ST. JOHN

0   2 miles
0   2 km

KEY
Beaches
Dive Sites
Ferry
Cruise Ship
Terminal

$5, $10, and $20 denominations. They're sold at most major hotels and many stores, and can be used to call within the BVI as well as all over the Caribbean, and to access USADirect from special phone-card phones. If you're coming ashore at the cruise-ship dock, you'll find pay phones right on the dock. If a tender drops you right in Road Town at the ferry dock, phones are located in the terminal.

AT&T has service in nearby St. John, USVI, so it's possible to get service from there in some spots in Road Town and along the water-front highway that leads to the West End. You may not have to pay international roaming charges on some U.S. cell-phone plans if you can connect with this network.

TORTOLA BEST BETS

■ **The Rhone.** For certified divers, this is one of the best wreck dives in the Caribbean.

■ **Sage Mountain.** The highest peak in the Virgin Islands has breathtaking views and is a great hiking destination.

■ **Sailing Trips.** Because of its proximity to small islets and good snorkeling sights, Tortola is the sailing capital of the Caribbean.

■ **Virgin Gorda.** Ferries link Tortola and Virgin Gorda, making a half-day trip to the Baths quite possible (just be sure to check the ferry schedules before heading out).

COMING ASHORE

Large cruise ships usually anchor in Road Town Harbor and bring passengers ashore by tender. Small ships can sometimes tie up at Wickham's Cay dock. Either way, it's a short stroll to Road Town. If your ship isn't going to Virgin Gorda, you can make the 12-mile (19-km) trip by ferry from the dock in Road Town in about 30 minutes for about $30 round-trip, but you'll still have to take a taxi to get to The Baths for swimming and snorkeling, so it's not necessarily a bad deal to go on your ship's shore excursion.

There are taxi stands at Wickham's Cay and in Road Town. Taxis are unmetered, and there are minimums for travel throughout the island, so it's usually cheaper to travel in groups. Negotiate to get the best fares, as there is no set fee schedule. If you are in the islands for just a day, it's usually more cost-effective to share a taxi with a small group than to rent a car, since you'd have to pay an agency at Wickham's Cay or in Road Town car-rental charges of at least $50 a day. You must be at least age 25 to rent a car.

EXPLORING TORTOLA

The bustling capital of the BVI looks out over Road Harbour. It takes only an hour or so to stroll down Main Street and along the waterfront, checking out the traditional West Indian buildings painted in pastel colors and with corrugated-tin roofs, bright shutters, and delicate fret-work trim. For sightseeing brochures and the latest information on everything from taxi rates to ferry schedules, stop in at the BVI Tourist Board office. Or just choose a seat on one of the benches in Sir Olva

Georges Square, on Waterfront Drive, and watch the people come and go from the ferry dock and customs office across the street.

☺ **Dolphin Discovery.** Get up close and
★ personal with dolphins as they swim in a spacious seaside pen. There are three different programs. In the Royal Swim, dolphins tow participants around the pen. The less expensive Adventure and Discovery programs allow you to touch the dolphins. ⊠ *Prospect Reef Resort, Road Town* ☎ *284/494–7675, 888/393–5158* ⊕ *www.dolphindiscovery.com* ✉ *Royal Swim $149, Adventure $99, Discovery $79* ☉ *Royal Swim daily at 10, noon, 2, and 4. Adventure and Discovery daily at 11 and 1.*

Ft. Burt. The most intact historic ruin on Tortola was built by the Dutch in the early 17th century to safeguard Road Harbour. It sits on a hill at the western edge of Road Town and is now the site of a small hotel and restaurant. The foundations and magazine remain, and the structure offers a commanding view of the harbor. ⊠ *Waterfront Dr., Road Town* ✉ *Free* ☉ *Daily dawn–dusk.*

★ **J.R. O'Neal Botanic Gardens.** Take a walk through this 4-acre showcase of lush plant life. There are sections devoted to prickly cacti and succulents, hothouses for ferns and orchids, gardens of medicinal herbs, and plants and trees indigenous to the seashore. From the tourist office in Road Town, cross Waterfront Drive and walk one block over to Main Street and turn right. Keep walking until you see the high school. The gardens are on your left. ⊠ *Botanic Station, Road Town* ☎ *284/494–3650* ⊕ *www.bvinationalparktrust.org* ✉ *$3* ☉ *Mon.–Sat. 8:30–4:30.*

Fodor's Choice **Old Government House Museum.** The official government residence until
★ 1997, this gracious building now displays a nice collection of artifacts from Tortola's past. The rooms are filled with period furniture, hand-painted china, books signed by Queen Elizabeth II on her 1966 and 1977 visits, and numerous items reflecting Tortola's seafaring legacy. ⊠ *Waterfront Dr., Road Town* ☎ *284/494–4091* ✉ *$3* ☉ *Weekdays 9–3.*

★ **Sage Mountain National Park.** At 1,716 feet, Sage Mountain is the highest peak in the BVI. From the parking area, a trail leads you in a loop not only to the peak itself (and extraordinary views) but also to a small rain forest that is sometimes shrouded in mist. Most of the forest was cut down over the centuries for timber, to create pastureland, or for growing sugarcane, cotton, and other crops. In 1964 this park was established to preserve what remained. Up here you can see mahogany trees, white cedars, mountain guavas, elephant-ear vines, mamey trees, and giant bullet woods, to say nothing of such birds as mountain doves and thrushes. Take a taxi from Road Town or drive up Joe's Hill Road and make a left onto Ridge Road toward Chalwell and Doty villages. The road dead-ends at the park. ⊠ *Ridge Rd., Sage Mountain* ☎ *284/852–3650* ⊕ *www.bvinationalparktrust.org* ✉ *$3* ☉ *Daily dawn–dusk.*

SHOPPING

Many shops and boutiques are clustered along and just off Road Town's **Main Street**. You can shop in Road Town's **Wickham's Cay I** adjacent to the marina. The **Crafts Alive Market** on the Road Town waterfront is a collection of colorful West Indian–style buildings with shops that carry items made in the BVI. You might find pretty baskets or interesting pottery or perhaps a bottle of home-brewed hot sauce. An ever-growing number of art and clothing stores are opening at **Soper's Hole** in West End.

ACTIVITIES

DIVING AND SNORKELING

The *Chikuzen,* sunk northwest of Brewers Bay in 1981, is a 246-foot vessel in 75 feet of water; it's home to thousands of fish, colorful corals, and big rays. In 1867 the **RMS Rhone,** a 310-foot royal mail steamer, split in two when it sank in a devastating hurricane. It's so well preserved that it was used as an underwater prop in the movie *The Deep.* You can see the crow's nest and bowsprit, the cargo hold in the bow, and the engine and enormous propeller shaft in the stern. Its four parts are at various depths from 30 to 80 feet. Get yourself some snorkeling gear and hop aboard a dive boat to this wreck near Salt Island (across the channel from Road Town). Every dive outfit in the BVI runs scuba and snorkel tours to this part of the BVI National Parks Trust; if you have time for only one trip, make it this one. Rates start at around $75 for a one-tank dive and $100 for a two-tank dive.

Blue Waters Divers. If you're chartering a sailboat, Blue Waters Divers' boat will meet yours at Peter, Salt, Norman, or Cooper Island for a rendezvous dive. The company teaches resort, open-water, rescue, and advanced diving courses, and also makes daily dive trips. Rates include all equipment as well as instruction. Reserve two days in advance. ✉ *Nanny Cay* ☎ *284/494–2847* ⊕ *www.bluewaterdiversbvi.com.*

FISHING

Most of the boats that take you deep-sea fishing for bluefish, wahoo, swordfish, and shark leave from nearby St. Thomas, but local anglers like to fish the shallower water for bonefish. A half day runs about $480, a full day around $850.

Caribbean Fly Fishing ✉ *Nanny Cay* ☎ *284/494–4797* ⊕ *www.caribflyfishing. com.*

SAILING

♻ The BVI are among the world's most popular sailing destinations. They're close together and surrounded by calm waters, so it's fairly easy to sail from one anchorage to the next.

Fodor's Choice ★

Aristocat Charters. This company's 48-foot catamaran sets sail daily to Jost Van Dyke, Norman Island, and other small islands. ✉ *West End* ☎ *284/499–1249* ⊕ *www.aristocatcharters.com.*

White Squall II. This 80-foot schooner has regularly scheduled day sails to The Baths at Virgin Gorda, Cooper, the Indians, and the Caves at

Norman Island. ⊠ *Village Cay Marina, Road Town* ☎ *284/494–2564* ⊕ *www.whitesquall2.com.*

BEACHES

Tortola's north side has several perfect palm-fringed white-sand beaches that curl around turquoise bays and coves. Nearly all are accessible by car (preferably one with four-wheel-drive), albeit down bumpy roads that corkscrew precipitously. Facilities run the gamut from absolutely none to a number of beachside bars and restaurants as well as places to rent water-sports equipment.

Brewers Bay. This beach is easy to find, but the steep, twisting paved roads leading down the hill to it can be a bit daunting. An old sugar mill and ruins of a rum distillery are off the beach along the road. You can actually reach the beach from either Brewers Bay Road East or Brewers Bay Road West. **Amenities:** none. **Best for:** snorkeling; swimming. ⊠ *Brewers Bay Rd. E, off Cane Garden Bay Rd.*

Cane Garden Bay. A silky stretch of sand, Cane Garden Bay has exceptionally calm, crystalline waters—except when storms at sea turn the water murky. Snorkeling is good along the edges. Casual guesthouses, restaurants, bars, and shops are steps from the beach in the growing village of the same name. The beach is a laid-back, even somewhat funky place to put down your towel. It's the closest beach to Road Town—one steep uphill and downhill drive—and one of the BVI's best-known anchorages (unfortunately, it can be very crowded). Water-sports shops rent equipment. **Amenities:** food and drink; toilets; water sports. **Best for:** snorkeling; swimming. ⊠ *Cane Garden Bay Rd., off Ridge Rd.*

WHERE TO EAT

$ × **Capriccio di Mare.** Stop by this casual, authentic Italian outdoor café
ITALIAN   for an espresso, a fresh pastry, a bowl of perfectly cooked penne, or
Fodor's Choice   a crispy tomato-and-mozzarella pizza. Drink specialties include a
★   mango Bellini, an adaptation of the famous cocktail served at Harry's Bar in Venice. ⑤ *Average main: $12* ⊠ *Waterfront Dr., Road Town* ☎ *284/494–5369* ⌲ *Reservations not accepted* ☉ *Closed Sun.*

$$$$ × **Village Cay Restaurant.** Docked sailboats stretch nearly as far as the
ECLECTIC   eye can see at this busy Road Town restaurant. Its alfresco dining and convivial atmosphere make it popular with both locals and visitors. For lunch, try the grouper club sandwich with an ancho chili mayonnaise. Dinner offerings run to fish served a variety of ways, including West Indian–style with okra, onions, and peppers, as well as a seafood jambalaya with lobster, crayfish, shrimp, mussels, crab, and fish in a mango-passion-fruit sauce. ⑤ *Average main: $32* ⊠ *Wickhams Cay I, Road Town* ☎ *284/494–2771.*

VIRGIN GORDA (THE VALLEY)

Lynda Lohr

Virgin Gorda, or "Fat Virgin," received its name from Christopher Columbus. The explorer envisioned the island as a pregnant woman in a languid recline with Gorda Peak being her big belly and the boulders of the Baths her toes. Different in topography from Tortola, with its arid landscape covered with scrub brush and cactus, Virgin Gorda has a slower pace of life, too. Goats and cattle own the right-of-way, and the unpretentious friendliness of the people is winning. The top sight (and beach for that matter) is the Baths, which draws scores of cruise-ship passengers and day-trippers to its giant boulders and grottoes that form a perfect snorkeling environment. While ships used to stop only in Tortola, saving Virgin Gorda for shore excursions, smaller ships are coming increasingly to Virgin Gorda directly.

ESSENTIALS

CURRENCY   The U.S. dollar is the official currency here. Some places accept cash only, but major credit cards are widely accepted. First Caribbean International, which has an ATM, isn't far from the ferry dock in Spanish Town.

TELEPHONE   To call anywhere in the BVI once you've arrived, dial all seven digits. There are no longer any pay phones on Virgin Gorda. Instead, get a Caribbean phone card, available in $5, $10, and $20 denominations. They're sold at most major hotels and many stores, and can be used to call within the BVI, as well as all over the Caribbean. Your own cell phone may work in the BVI, but you'll probably pay a hefty roaming fee.

COMING ASHORE

Ships often dock off Spanish Town, Leverick Bay, or in North Sound and tender passengers to the ferry dock. A few taxis will be available at Leverick Bay and at Gun Creek in North Sound—you can set up an island tour for about $45 for two people—but Leverick Bay and North Sound are far away from The Baths, the island's must-see beach, so a shore excursion is often the best choice. If you are tendered to Spanish Town, then it's possible to take a shuttle taxi to The Baths for as little as $4 per person each way. If you are on Virgin Gorda for just a day, it's usually more cost-effective to share a taxi with a small group than to rent a car, since you'd have to pay car-rental charges of at least $50 a day. You must be at least age 25 to rent a car.

EXPLORING VIRGIN GORDA

There are few roads, and most byways don't follow the scalloped shore-line. The main route sticks resolutely to the center of the island, linking the Baths on the southern tip with Gun Creek and Leverick Bay at North Sound. The craggy coast, scissored with grottoes and fringed by palms and boulders, has a primitive beauty. If you drive, you can hit all the sights in one day. Stop to climb Gorda Peak, which is in the island's center. Signage is erratic, so come prepared with a map.

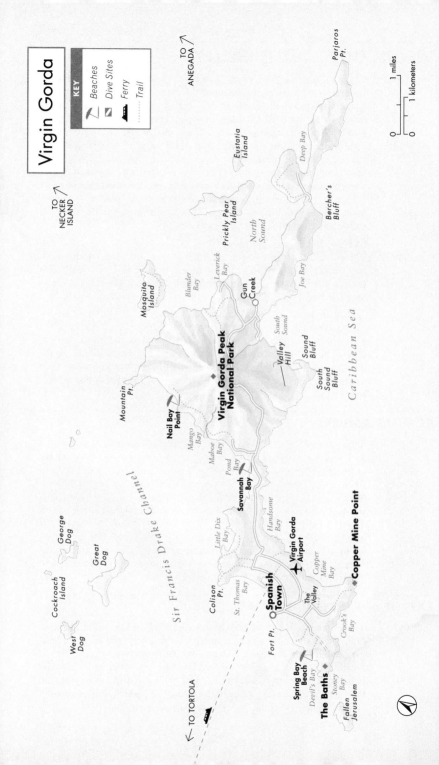

The Baths. At Virgin Gorda's most

celebrated sight, giant boulders are scattered about the beach and in the water. Some are almost as large as houses and form remarkable grottoes. Climb between these rocks to swim in the many placid pools. Early morning and late afternoon are the best times to visit if you want to avoid crowds. If it's privacy you crave, follow the shore northward to quieter bays—Spring Bay, the Crawl, Little Trunk, and Valley Trunk—or head south to Devil's Bay. ⊠ *Off Tower Rd., The Baths* ☎ *284/852–3650* ✉ *$3* ☉ *Daily dawn–dusk.*

> ### VIRGIN GORDA BEST BETS
>
> ■ **The Baths.** This unique beach strewn with giant boulders and grottos is a favorite snorkeling destination.
>
> ■ **Virgin Gorda Peak.** This lofty peak has excellent views and is a great hiking destination.
>
> ■ **Sailing Trips.** Like Tortola, Virgin Gorda is within easy reach of many small islets and good snorkeling sights.

Copper Mine Point. A tall stone shaft silhouetted against the sky and a small stone structure that overlooks the sea are part of what was once a copper mine, now in ruins. Established 400 years ago, it was worked first by the Spanish, then by the English, until the early 20th century. The route is not well marked, so turn inland near LSL Restaurant and look for the hard-to-see sign pointing the way. ⊠ *Copper Mine Rd.* ⊕ *www.bvinationalparkstrust.org* ✉ *Free.*

Spanish Town. Virgin Gorda's peaceful main settlement, on the island's southern wing, is so tiny that it barely qualifies as a town at all. Also known as the Valley, Spanish Town has a marina, some shops, and a couple of car-rental agencies. Just north of town is the ferry slip. At the Virgin Gorda Yacht Harbour you can stroll along the dock and do a little shopping. ⊠ *Virgin Gorda.*

★ **Virgin Gorda Peak National Park.** There are two trails at this 265-acre park, which contains the island's highest point, at 1,359 feet. Small signs on North Sound Road mark both entrances; sometimes, however, the signs are missing, so keep your eyes open for a set of stairs that disappears into the trees. It's about a 15-minute hike from either entrance up to a small clearing, where you can climb a ladder to the platform of a wooden observation tower and a spectacular 360-degree view. ⊠ *North Sound Rd., Gorda Peak* ✉ *Free.*

SHOPPING

Most boutiques are within hotel complexes or at Virgin Gorda Yacht Harbour. Two of the best are at Biras Creek and Little Dix Bay. Other properties—the Bitter End and Leverick Bay—have small but equally select boutiques.

ACTIVITIES

DIVING AND SNORKELING

The dive companies on Virgin Gorda are all certified by PADI. Costs vary, but count on paying about $100 for a one-tank dive and $130 for a two-tank dive. All dive operators offer introductory courses as well as certification and advanced courses. Should you get an attack of the bends, which can happen when you ascend too rapidly, the nearest decompression chamber is at Roy L. Schneider Regional Medical Center in St. Thomas.

Dive BVI. In addition to day trips, Dive BVI also offers expert instruction and certification. ⊠ *Virgin Gorda Yacht Harbour, Spanish Town* 🕾 *284/495–5513, 800/848–7078* ⊕ *www.divebvi.com.*

Sunchaser Scuba. Resort, advanced, and rescue courses are all available here. ⊠ *Bitter End Yacht Club, North Sound* 🕾 *284/495–9638, 800/932–4286* ⊕ *www.sunchaserscuba.com.*

SAILING AND BOATING

The BVI waters are calm, and terrific places to learn to sail. You can also rent sea kayaks, waterskiing equipment, dinghies, and powerboats, or take a parasailing trip.

Double "D" Charters. If you just want to sit back, relax, and let the captain take the helm, choose a sailing or power yacht from Double "D" Charters. Rates are $75 for a half-day trip and $125 for a full-day island-hopping excursion. Private full-day cruises or sails for up to eight people run from $950. ⊠ *Virgin Gorda Yacht Harbour, Spanish Town* 🕾 *284/499–2479* ⊕ *www.doubledbvi.com.*

Leverick Bay Watersports. If you want to rent a Sunfish or a dinghy, check out Leverick Bay Watersports. ⊠ *Leverick Bay, North Sound* 🕾 *284/495–7376* ⊕ *www.watersportsbvi.com.*

BEACHES

The best beaches are easily reached by water, although they're also accessible on foot, usually after a moderately strenuous 10- to 15-minute hike. Anybody going to Virgin Gorda should experience swimming or snorkeling among its unique boulder formations, which can be visited at several beaches along Lee Road. The most popular of these spots is the Baths, but there are several others nearby that are easily reached.

★ **The Baths.** This stunning maze of huge granite boulders extending into the sea is usually crowded midday with day-trippers. The snorkeling is good, and you're likely to see a wide variety of fish, but watch out for dinghies coming ashore from the numerous sailboats anchored offshore. Public bathrooms and a handful of bars and shops are close to the water and at the start of the path that leads to the beach. Lockers are available to keep belongings safe. **Amenities:** food and drink; parking; toilets. **Best for:** snorkeling; swimming. ⊠ *About 1 mile (1½ km) west of Spanish Town ferry dock on Tower Rd., Spring Bay* 🕾 *284/852–3650* ⊕ *www.bvinationalparkstrust.org* 🎟 *$3* ☉ *Daily dawn–dusk.*

★ **Savannah Bay.** This is a wonderfully private beach close to Spanish Town. It may not always be completely deserted, but you can find a spot to yourself on this long stretch of soft, white sand. Bring your own mask, fins, and snorkel, as there are no facilities. The view from above is a photographer's delight. **Amenities:** none. **Best for:** solitude; snorkeling; swimming. ⊠ *Off N. Sound Rd., ¾ mile (1¼ km) east of Spanish Town ferry dock, Savannah Bay* ☎ *Free* ☉ *Daily dawn–dusk.*

> CAUTION:
> OBSTRUCTED VIEWS
>
> If you pick an outside cabin, check to make sure your view of the sea is not obstructed by a lifeboat. The ship's deck plan will help you figure it out.

Spring Bay Beach. This national-park beach that gets much less traffic than the nearby Baths, and has the similarly large, imposing boulders that create interesting grottoes for swimming. It also has no admission fee, unlike the more popular Baths. The snorkeling is excellent, and the grounds include swings and picnic tables. **Amenities:** none. **Best for:** snorkeling; swimming. ⊠ *Off Tower Rd., 1 mile (1½ km) west of Spanish Town ferry dock, Spring Bay* ☎ *284/852–3650* ⊕ *www.bvinationalparkstrust.org* ☎ *Free* ☉ *Daily dawn–dusk.*

WHERE TO EAT

$$ **Bath and Turtle.** You can sit back and relax at this informal tavern
ECLECTIC with a friendly staff—although the noise from the television can sometimes be a bit much. Well-stuffed sandwiches, homemade pizzas, pasta dishes, and daily specials such as conch soup round out the casual menu. Local musicians perform many Wednesday and Sunday nights. ⑤ *Average main: $18* ⊠ *Virgin Gorda Yacht Harbour, Spanish Town* ☎ *284/495–5239* ⊕ *www.bathandturtle.com.*

$$$$ **Top of the Baths.** At the entrance to The Baths, this popular restau-
ECLECTIC rant has tables on an outdoor terrace or in an open-air pavilion; all
☾ have stunning views of the Sir Francis Drake Channel. The restaurant starts serving at starts serving at 8 am; for lunch, hamburgers, coconut chicken sandwiches, and fish-and-chips are among the offerings. For dessert, the key lime pie is excellent. The Sunday barbecue, served from noon until 3 pm, is an island event. ⑤ *Average main: $35* ⊠ *The Valley* ☎ *284/495–5497* ⊕ *www.topofthebaths.com* ☉ *No dinner Mon.*

INDEX

NOTES

NOTES

NOTES

NOTES

NOTES